your Bovée/Thill?

Business Communication Essentials Custom One-Color Option

The Core

Optional Chapters

Contact your local PH Rep for more information on the custom/core option.

Business Communication Essentials

Third Edition

Courtland L. Bovée

Professor of Business Communication
C. Allen Paul Distinguished Chair
Grossmont College

John V. Thill

Chairman and Chief Executive Officer
Global Communication Strategies

PEARSON

Prentice Hall

Upper Saddle River, NJ 07458

Library of Congress Cataloging-in-Publication Data
Bovée, Courtland L.
    Business communication essentials/Courtland L. Bovée, John V. Thill.—3rd ed.
        p. cm.
    Includes bibliographical references and index.
    ISBN 0-13-199536-7 (alk. paper)
    I. Business communication. 2. Business writing. 3. Business presentations. I. Thill,
    John V. II. Title.

HF5718.B659 2008
651.7--dc22   2006021052

Executive Editor: David Parker
VP/Editorial Director: Jeff Shelstad
Product Development Manager: Ashley Santora
Editorial Assistant: Kristen Varina
Marketing Manager: Anne Howard
Marketing Assistant: Susan Osterlitz
Managing Editor, Production: Renata Butera
Production Editor: Marcela Boos
Permissions Coordinator: Charles Morris
Manufacturing Buyer: Diane Peirano
Design/Composition Manager: Christy Mahon
Composition Liaison: Jeanine Furino
Art Director: Janet Slowik
Interior Design: Karen Quigley
Cover Design: Karen Quigley
Cover Photo: Stockbyte/Getty Images
Manager, Visual Research: Beth Brenzel
Image Permission Coordinator: Nancy Seise
Composition: GGS Book Services
Full-Service Project Management: Jeanine Furino, GGS Book Services
Printer/Binder: Donnelley/Willard
Typeface: Minion

Credits and acknowledgments borrowed from other sources and reproduced, with permission, in this textbook appear on page AC-1.

Pearson Education LTD.   Pearson Education Australia PTY, Limited
Pearson Education Singapore, Pte. Ltd   Pearson Education North Asia Ltd
Pearson Education, Canada, Ltd   Pearson Educación de Mexico, S.A. de C.V.
Pearson Education–Japan   Pearson Education Malaysia, Pte. Ltd.

10 9 8 7 6 5 4 3

ISBN: 0-13-199536-7

Contents in Brief

Contents

Unit 2: The Three-Step Writing Process 51

Giving Students Powerful Role Models with the Widest Selection of Contemporary Model Documents

Annotated model documents have long been a hallmark of Bovée/Thill texts, and that tradition continues in *Business Communication Essentials*, Third Edition. From conventional printed documents to e-mail, instant messages, websites, and blogs, the third edition offers the most diverse collection of up-to-date model documents now available. More than half of the model documents are now in electronic media, and a quarter of them are all new in this edition.

The marginal annotations that accompany every document help students understand how to apply the principles discussed in the chapter, and for this edition, both the documents and the annotations have been extensively revised and improved in response to reviewer input.

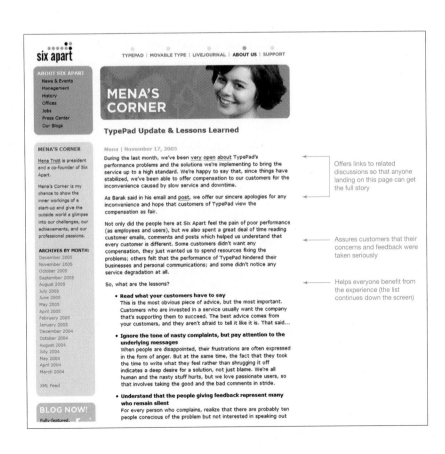

Document Makeover

Improve this E-Mail Message

To practice correcting drafts of actual documents, visit www.prenhall.com/OneKey on the web. Click "Document Makovers," and then click Chapter 7. You will find an e-mail message that contains problems and errors relating to what you've learned in this chapter about routine, good news, and goodwill messages. use the "Final Draft" decision tool to create an improved version of this routine e-mail. Check the message for skilled presentation of the main idea, clarify of detail, proper handling of negative information, appropriate use of resale, and the inclusion of a courteous close.

With the interactive online "Document Makeovers," students also have the opportunity in every chapter to critique and revise a wide selection of documents, including e-mail messages, letters, memos, report sections, and résumés. By experiencing firsthand the elements that make a document successful, students gain the insights they need to analyze and improve their own business messages. Also new in the third edition is a complete set of "Document Makeovers" that automatically feed online gradebooks.

A Total Teaching and Learning Solution

Business Communication Essentials is a fully integrated presentation of communication fundamentals:

- **Text.** The concise, 14-chapter text has numerous contemporary examples for students to follow.
- **Workbook.** The integrated workbook, "Improve Your Grammar, Mechanics, and Usage," appears at the end of every chapter with three levels of assessment and skill building in workplace applications and document critiques.
- **Handbook.** The "Handbook of Grammar, Mechanics, and Usage" (see page H-1) serves as a convenient reference.
- **Online resources.** The "Companion Website" offers interactive grammar, review, and revision activities.

These components work together at four levels to provide seamless coverage of the essentials, from previewing to developing to enhancing to reinforcing.

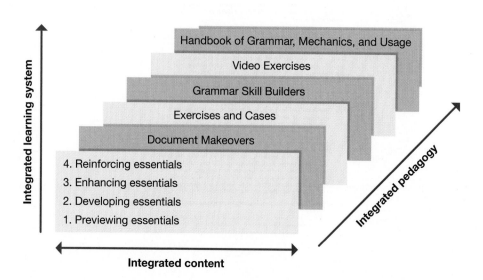

1. Previewing Essentials

Each chapter prepares students with clear learning objectives, an insightful "From the Real World" quotation, and a brief chapter overview.

2. Developing Essentials

Chapter content develops, explains, and elaborates on concepts with a concise, carefully organized presentation of textual and visual material. The three-step process of planning, writing, and completing is clearly explained and reinforced throughout the text in examples ranging from letters to e-mail messages to formal reports. With its heavy emphasis on exercises to improve grammar, punctuation, style, usage, and writing skills, this text offers students—especially those who lack proficiency in business English—the tools they need to succeed in today's workplace.

3. Enhancing Essentials

Contemporary examples, many accompanied by the three-step diagram adapted to each message, show students the specific elements that contribute to successful messages. More than 50 model documents demonstrate effective solutions to a wide variety of real-life communication challenges.

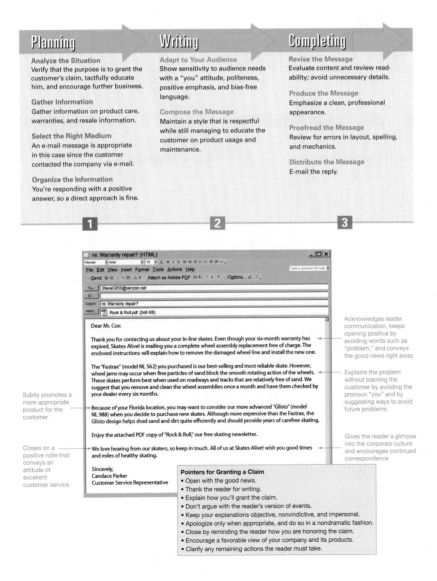

4. Reinforcing Essentials

Student success in any communication course comes down to practice, analysis, and reinforcement. With hundreds of realistic business English exercises and activities, *Business Communication Essentials* offers an unparalleled array of opportunities for students to practice vital skills and put newfound knowledge to immediate use. These resources are logically sorted by category, including "Test Your Knowledge," "Apply Your Knowledge," "Practice Your Knowledge," and "Expand Your Knowledge." Communication cases, most featuring real companies, encourage students to think about contemporary business issues as they put their skills to use in a variety of media, including blogging and podcasting.

The integrated workbook, "Improve Your Grammar, Mechanics, and Usage," further reinforces student skills by helping them assess their current knowledge levels, improve individual sentences, and critique entire documents.

At every stage of the learning experience, *Business Communication Essentials* provides the tools that instructors and students need to succeed.

Features that help students build essential knowledge and skills	Previewing	Developing	Enhancing	Reinforcing
Learning objectives (beginning of chapter)	●			
From the Real World (beginning of chapter)	●			
Chapter overviews (beginning of chapter)	●			
Concise presentations of fundamentals (within chapter)		●		
Three-step writing process diagrams (within chapter)		●		
Real-life examples (within chapter)			●	
Annotated model documents (within chapter)			●	
Handbook of Grammar, Mechanics, and Usage (end of book)			●	
Marginal notes (within chapter)				●
Reviewing Key Points (end of chapter)				●
Test Your Knowledge questions (end of chapter)				●
Apply Your Knowledge questions (end of chapter)				●
Practice Your Knowledge activities and exercises (end of chapter)				●
Expand Your Knowledge web resources (end of chapter/online)				●
Improve Your Grammar, Mechanics, and Usage (end of chapter)				●
Cases (following Chapters 6, 7, 8, 9, 10, 11, 13, and 14)				●
Document Makeovers (online)				●
Interactive Study Guide (online)				●
Peak Performance Grammar and Mechanics (online)				●

Up-to-Date Coverage of Important Topics

The third edition is thoroughly updated, from the learning objectives that launch each chapter to the exercises, activities, and cases that help students apply what they've learned. (A complete list of chapter-by-chapter changes and improvements is available on pp. xxi–xxiii of this Preface.)

Communication Technology

Vital topics in communication technology are interwoven throughout the text, reflecting the expectations and opportunities in today's workplace:

- computer animation
- corporate blogs
- electronic documents
- electronic forms
- electronic presentations
- electronic résumé production
- e-mail
- e-portfolios
- extranets
- graphic design software
- groupware and shared online workspaces
- instant messaging and online chat systems
- intellectual property rights
- interactive media
- Internet telephony (VoIP)
- interview simulators
- intranets
- linked and embedded documents
- multimedia documents
- multimedia presentations

- newsfeeds
- online brainstorming systems
- online research techniques
- online survey tools
- peer-to-peer networking
- podcasting
- résumé scanning systems
- search and metasearch engines
- security and privacy concerns in electronic media (including e-mail hygiene)
- short messaging service (SMS)
- streaming media
- templates and stylesheets
- text messaging
- videoconferencing and telepresence
- virtual agents and bots
- web content management systems
- web directories
- web-based virtual meetings
- webcasts
- wikis
- wireless networks

Teamwork and Listening

Even as technology continues to revolutionize business communication, business leaders are placing renewed emphasis on the human factor—teamwork, listening, etiquette, and ethics. To help students strengthen their communication skills, material on listening and on effectively working in teams has been expanded and updated. Improved coverage provides students with skills they'll need to gain a competitive edge in today's workplace, including recognizing different types of listening and using short-term memorization techniques that boost retention and reduce misinterpretation.

Etiquette

Feedback from employers continues to stress the need for new hires to learn proper business etiquette. *Business Communication Essentials* advises students in such areas as personal appearance, face-to-face interactions, written correspondence (including maintaining etiquette in both negative and persuasive messages), research (such as respecting the privacy of interview subjects), IM and e-mail, telephone interactions (including reducing cell phone disruptions and using voice mail), intercultural interactions, and job searches and interviewing. Moreover, the third edition incorporates the latest thinking on the controversial subject of apologies.

The Three-Step Writing Process

The three-step writing process at the heart of *Business Communication Essentials* has been further refined to present substeps in a more logical order. As before, the process is customized and illustrated throughout the text to show students how to apply it to a wide range of writing tasks.

New to This Edition

■ The primary themes of this revision were responding to recent advances in communication technology and further strengthening BCE's leadership position in the area of model documents—particularly in the use of electronic media for brief messages.

■ Extensive integration of communication-related technologies aligns with the expectations that today's employers have regarding employees' use of these tools.

■ Model documents and accompanying annotations were extensively revised to help students learn from effective and ineffective examples. More than half of the model documents are now in electronic media to accurately reflect practices in today's workplace.

■ The table of contents remains consistent with the proven organization from previous editions, although several improvements to the three-step writing process resulted in some content shifting between Chapters 3 and 4 and between Chapters 10 and 11.

■ Chapter 6 is essentially new, now offering coverage of all key media used for brief messages, including instant messaging, blogging, and podcasting.

■ To accommodate the new material on communication technology without increasing the length of the text, the "Test Your Knowledge" section at the end of each chapter was reduced from 10 questions to 5, and the "Business Communication Notebook" feature was removed.

■ The selection of cases was extensively updated, with 40 new cases on a variety of contemporary business issues—many involving instant messaging, blogging, and podcasting.

Chapter-by-Chapter Changes and Improvements

Feature	Chapter 1	Chapter 2	Chapter 3	Chapter 4	Chapter 5
Learning Objectives	More emphasis on using communication technology effectively	More emphasis on advantages and disadvantages of working in teams and on using meeting and teamwork technologies	More emphasis on why good organization is important (and several objectives were swapped between Chapters 3 and 4 to reflect improvements in the three-step process)	More emphasis on the importance of plain English in business communication and using technology to craft messages efficiently	More emphasis on the value of careful revision and on the factors to consider when distributing messages
From the Real World	**New:** About the importance of listening in business communication, from popular Microsoft blogger Robert Scoble	**New:** About the importance of sharing information with teams, from The Container Store co-founder Kip Tindell	**New:** About the quick adoption of podcasting as a communication medium by employees at IBM	**New:** About the frustration and anger that can result from poor writing that doesnt accommodate audience needs	**New:** About the role played by clear, concise communication in every profe ssional's career success
Chapter Content (subject areas that were added, clarified, expanded, streamlined, or updated for this edition)	• Expanded discussion of ethics, using stealth marketing as an example • Etiquette introduced as critical business skill • Added discussions of xenophobia and cultural pluralism; updated coverage of stereotyping • Added strategies for using communication technology effectively	• Advantages and disadvantages of working in teams (expanded) • Etiquette in team and social settings (expanded) • Three major types of listening • Memorization strategies to improve listening • **New:** Meeting agenda using online meeting system (Fig 2.1)	• Organizing your information is now covered here in Chapter 3; adapting to your audience is now in Chapter 4 • New electronic media, including blogging and podcasting • Expanded discussion of gathering information • Eliminated distinction between channel and medium • Expanded discussion of media options	• Reasons why bias-free language is so important • Advice for building your credibility as a communicator • Using functional and content words correctly • Revised advice on intimacy and humor • Expanded advice on crafting topic sentences and support sentences • New advice on using technology to craft messages	• Evaluating content, organization, style, and tone • Updated and expanded coverage of using technological tools during revision and production • Using lists, bullets, headings, and subheadings were moved here from Chapter 6 • Adding graphics, sound, video, and hypertext • New section on distributing messages
Model Documents and Other Exhibits	• **New:** Blog posting that demonstrates both effective communication and good use of technical tools (Fig 1.3)	• **New:** Meeting minutes as blog posting (Fig 2.2) • **New:** Web-based meetings (Fig 2.3) • **New:** Quick reference guide to telephone skills (Table 2.2)	• **Revised:** Three-step writing process (Fig 3.1). • **New:** Analyzing an audience (Fig 3.2) • **New:** Choosing the best medium (Fig 3.3)	• **New:** Step two of the three-step process (Fig 4.1) • **New:** Fostering a positive relationship with the audience through effective word choices (Fig 4.2)	• **New:** Step three of the three-step process (Fig 5.1) • **Revised:** Revising to improve clarity and using proofreading marks (Fig 5.2) • **New:** Poor and improved document design in an e-mail message (Fig 5.3)
End of Chapter Exercises	• New questions involving the effective use of technology and audience-centered communication • Exploring the Web (one new site)	• New questions involving nonverbal communication in online meetings and leaving effective voicemail messages • Exploring the Web (one new site)	• New questions involving direct vs. indirect approach, media selection, message purpose, and audience analysis • Exploring the Web (two new sites)	• New questions involving the "you" attitude, abstract versus concrete, transitions, and ethics • Exploring the Web (two new sites)	• New questions involving ethics, production tools, and revision skills • Exploring the Web (one new site)
Cases	N/A	N/A	N/A	N/A	N/A

(continued)

Chapter-by-Chapter Changes and Improvements

Feature	Chapter 6	Chapter 7	Chapter 8	Chapter 9	Chapter 10
Learning Objectives	All new in this edition (chapter has been rewritten to include coverage of blogging and podcasting)	More emphasis on creating informative messages	More emphasis on the risks of using the indirect approach, adapting for internal versus external audiences, and crisis communication	More emphasis on building credibility in persuasive messages and avoiding ethical and legal mistakes	More emphasis on adapting the three-step process to reports, conducting research, and evaluating information sources
From the Real World	**New:** About the importance of blogging as a new business communication medium	**New:** Warren Buffett's advice on being an effective communicator	**New:** KPMG's unusual and risky public apology	**New:** On the importance of the "you" attitude in persuasive messages	**New:** On the importance of adapting report information to audience needs
Chapter Content (subject areas that were added, clarified, expanded, streamlined, or updated for this edition)	• Chapter 6 is largely new material in this edition • New sections on blogging and podcasting • Substantially revised coverage of e-mail and IM • Internal versus external communication now in Chapter 1 • Material on improving readability now in Chapter 5	• New section on creating informative messages	• Expanded information on the direct approach • New information on apologies • New information on refusing routine requests • Expanded information on handling bad news about transactions • New advice on negative organizational news • Updated information on rejecting job applications • (Bad-news messages are now called negative messages)	• Persuasive business messages covered separately from marketing and sales messages • Advice on avoiding logical errors • Marketing and sales messages distinguished • In general, more emphasis on persuasive strategies and less on specific message types • Avoiding ethical and legal errors • Fundraising messages no longer addressed	• Selecting the best media for reports • A practical, five-step research process • Planning the research effort • Evaluating sources • Differentiating search engines, metacrawlers, web directories, and online databases • Distinguishing quoting, paraphrasing, and summarizing • Material on organizing and outlining moved here from Chapter 11
Model Documents and Other Exhibits	• **New:** Business e-mail example (Fig 6.3) • **New:** Business IM example (Fig 6.4) • **New:** Elements of an effective business blog (Fig 6.5) • **New:** Tips for effective e-mail (Table 6.1) • **New:** Tips for effective blogging (Table 6.2)	• **New:** Effective IM response to information request (Fig 7.4)	• **New:** Choosing direct or indirect approach (Fig 8.1)	• **New:** Multimedia persuasion with interactive web technology (Fig 9.5) • **New:** Opt-in e-mail for promotions (Fig 9.6)	• **New:** Common business reports and proposals (Fig 10.1) • **New:** Three-step writing process for reports and proposals (Fig 10.2) • **New:** Analytical report focusing on logical arguments (Fig 10.7)
End of Chapter Exercises	• New questions involving blogging, IM, and podcasting • Exploring the Web (three new sites)	• New questions on writing requests, recommendation letters, and ethical choices • Exploring the Web (one new site)	• New questions on crafting negative messages	• New questions on persuasive business and marketing messages • Exploring the Web (one new site)	• New questions on research, evaluating sources, ethics, and report organization • Exploring the Web (three new sites)
Cases	5 new cases	8 new cases	8 new cases	8 new cases	1 new case

(continued)

Chapter-by-Chapter Changes and Improvements

Feature	Chapter 11	Chapter 12	Chapter 13	Chapter 14
Learning Objectives	More emphasis on using software tools to create reports and on choosing effective visuals	More emphasis on the importance of presentation skills, using the three-step process, and giving presentations online	More emphasis on how employers view today's job market and the approach they use to find new employees	More emphasis on what employers look for in an interview and on the subject of preemployment testing
From the Real World	**New:** About the importance of using clear language when communicating about complex topics	**New:** About the role of presentations in HP's successful effort to win a $3 billion contract	**New:** About poorly designed résumés being tossed out without even being read	**New:** About using the job interview to give employers a good idea of who you are and what you offer
Chapter Content (subject areas that were added, clarified, expanded, streamlined, or updated for this edition)	• Using technology to craft reports and proposals • Incorporating maps, drawings, diagrams, and photographs • Using animation and video in reports • Advice on designing effective visuals • Proofreading reports • Distributing reports	• Building your career with oral presentations • More information on audience analysis • Expanded advice on organizing your presentation • Writing readable content for slides • Updated advice on using animation and special effects • Using navigational slides • Giving presentations online	• (Application letters moved to Chapter 14 to balance the length of these two chapters) • Changes in the workplace and in the nature of work • How employers view the job market • What employers look for • Employers' approach to the employment process • Expanded advice on networking • Adapting to your audience	• What employers look for in an interview • Preemployment testing • Writing letters to accept job offers • Writing letters to decline job offers • Writing resignation letters
Model Documents and Other Exhibits	• **New:** The "you" attitude in complex reports (Fig 11.1)	• **New:** Effective outline for 10-minute presentation (Fig 12.2) • **New:** Writing readable content (Fig 12.4) • **New:** Selecting readable fonts and type styles (Fig 12.5) • **New:** PowerPoint slide master (Fig 12.6) • **New:** Blueprint slides (Fig 12.8)	• **New:** How organizations prefer to find new employees (Fig 13.2) • **New:** Online version of a combination résumé (Fig 13.6)	• **New:** Interview simulators (Fig 14.3)
End of Chapter Exercises	• New questions on unsolicited proposals, charts and graphs, ethics, recommendations, using maps, and executive summaries • Exploring the Web (one new site)	• New questions on effective visuals and online presentations • Exploring the Web (three new sites)	• New questions on résumés and job search strategies • Exploring the Web (two new sites)	• New question on ethics • Exploring the Web (one new site)
Cases	8 new cases	N/A	Comparable to BCE2	2 new cases

Versatile Resources for Instructors and Students

The multimedia *Business Communication Essentials* package helps instructors and students take full advantage of the latest advances in instructional technology.

New Instructor Website: www.businesscommunicationblog.com

Stay on top of new technologies, important trends, and hot topics with Business Communication Headline News, which uses the newest Internet technologies to deliver late-breaking news in headlines with concise summaries. You can scan incoming items in a matter of seconds, then simply click through to read the full articles that interest you.

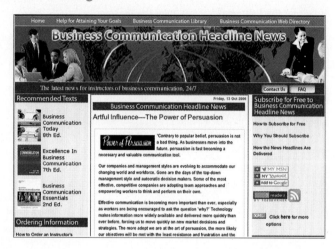

This free service offers numerous ways to enhance lectures and student activities:

- Keep current with the latest information and trends in the field

- Easily update your lecture notes with fresh material

- Create visuals for your classroom presentations

- Supplement your lectures with cutting-edge handouts

- Gather podcasts, online video, and other new media examples to use in the classroom

- Enhance your research projects with the newest data

- Compare best practices from other instructors

- Improve the quality and effectiveness of your teaching by reading about new teaching tips and techniques

- Get free access to the Business Communication Library, available only on this site, where you'll find thousands of articles on a wide variety of topics, plus automated newsfeeds with the latest news about each topic

- Get free access to the Business Communication Web Directory, available only on this site, where you'll find over 240 topics and more than 5,000 links, with a search engine for the site to help you find exactly what you want

Getting started is easy, and you can select from a variety of newsfeed formats to match your Internet usage habits.

Visit today at www.businesscommunicationblog.com.

New Student Website: *www.buscommresources.com*

The new Bovée/Thill student website, www.buscommresources.com, offers a subset of the instructor site features: Business Communication Headline News (headlines oriented toward students), Business Communication Web Directory, Business Communication Library, and Student Resources. Students can use the site for a variety of assignments, special projects, and independent research.

Authors' E-Mail Hotline for Faculty

Integrity, excellence, and responsiveness are the authors' hallmarks. That means providing you with textbooks that are academically sound, creative, timely, and sensitive to instructor and student needs. As an adopter of *Business Communication Essentials*, you are invited to use the authors' E-mail Hotline if you ever have a question or concerns related to the text or its supplements: **hotline@businesscommunicationblog.com**

Instructor's Resource Center

At www.prenhall.com/irc, instructors can access a variety of print, digital, and presentation resources available with this text in downloadable format. Registration is simple and gives you immediate access to new titles and new editions. As a registered faculty member, you can download resource files and receive immediate access and instructions for installing course management content on your campus server.

If you ever need assistance, our dedicated technical support team is ready to help with the media supplements that accompany this text. Visit www.247.prenhall.com for answers to frequently asked questions and toll-free user-support phone numbers.

The following supplements are available to adopting instructors (for detailed descriptions, please visit www.prenhall.com/irc):

- **Instructor's Resource Center (IRC) on CD-ROM**—ISBN: 0-13-240173-8

- **Printed Instructor's Manual**—ISBN: 0-13-240171-1

- **Printed Test Item File**—ISBN: 0-13-232483-0

- **TestGen Test Generating Software**—Available at the IRC (online or on CD-ROM).

- **PowerPoint Slides**—Available at the IRC (online or on CD-ROM).

- **Classroom Response Systems (CRS)**—Available at the IRC (online or on CD-ROM); learn more at www.prenhall.com/crs.

- **Image Bank**—Visit the IRC on CD-ROM for this resource.

- **Custom Videos on DVD**—ISBN: 0-13-225189-2

- **Transparency Package**—ISBN: 0-13-156782-9

OneKey Online Courses: Convenience, Simplicity, and Success

OneKey offers complete teaching and learning online resources all in one place. OneKey is all that instructors need to plan and administer courses, and OneKey is all that students need for anytime, anywhere access to online course material. Conveniently organized by textbook chapter, these resources save time and help students reinforce and apply what they have learned. OneKey is available in three course management platforms: Blackboard, CourseCompass, and WebCT.

OneKey resources include

- **Learning modules** (Each section within each chapter offers a 5-question pretest, a summary for review, an online learning activity, and a 10-question posttest.)

- **Peak Performance Grammar and Mechanics***

- **Two versions of Document Makeovers*** (One version feeds your gradebook, and one provides student practice.)

- **Access to Mydropbox.com**

- **Peer review software**

OneKey requires an access code, which can be shrink-wrapped free of charge with new copies of this text. Please contact your local sales representative for the correct ISBN. Codes may also be purchased separately at www.prenhall.com/management.

*Instructors who wish to use "Peak Performance Grammar and Mechanics" and "Document Makeovers" but not the rest of the OneKey content can access these features in a special section of the Companion Website. This section requires an access code, which you can ask to have shrink-wrapped with new copies of this text. Please contact your local sales representative for the correct ISBN. Codes may also be purchased separately at www.prenhall.com/management.

Companion Website

This text's Companion Website at www.prenhall.com/bovee contains valuable resources for both students and professors, including access to a student version of the PowerPoint package, an online Study Guide, the "English-Spanish Audio Glossary of Business Terms," the "Handbook of Grammar, Mechanics, and Usage," and the "Business Communication Study Hall," which allow students to brush up on several aspects of business communication—grammar, writing skills, critical thinking, report writing, résumés, and PowerPoint development.

SafariX eTextbooks Online

Developed for students looking to save money on required or recommended textbooks, SafariX eTextbooks Online saves students money off the suggested list price of the print text. Students simply select their eText by title or author and purchase immediate access to the content for the duration of the course using any major credit card. With a SafariX eText, students can search for specific keywords or page numbers, make notes online, print out reading assignments that incorporate lecture notes, and bookmark important passages for later review. For more information, or to purchase a SafariX eTextbook, visit www.safarix.com.

Feedback

The authors and the product team would appreciate hearing from you! Let us know what you think about this textbook by writing to college_marketing@prenhall.com. Please include "Feedback about Bovee/Thill 3e" in the subject line.

If you have questions related to this product, please contact our customer service department online at www.247.prenhall.com.

Acknowledgments

The third edition of *Business Communication Essentials* reflects the professional experience of a large team of contributors and advisors. We express our thanks to the many individuals whose valuable suggestions and constructive comments influenced the success of this book.

Reviewers of Previous Editions

Thank you to the following professors: Faridah Awang, Eastern Kentucky University; Yvonne Block, College of Lake County; Mary Bowers, Northern Arizona University; Barbara Cameron, Embry-Riddle Aeronautical University; Darlynn Fink, Clarion University of Pennsylvania; Matthew Gainous, Ogeechee Technical College; Irene Joanette Gallio, Western Nevada Community College; Nancy Goehring, Monterey Peninsula College; Helen Grattan, Des Moines Area Community College; Cynthia Herrera, Orlando Culinary Academy; Pashia Hogan, Northeast State Tech Community College; Rebecca Hsiao, East Los Angeles College; Christy L. Kinnion, Lenior Community College; Deborah Kitchin, City College of San Francisco; Fran Kranz, Oakland University; Ruth Levy, Westchester Community College; Mark Mabrito, Purdue University; Kate Ferguson Marsters, Gannon University; Linda Nitsch, Chadron State College; Diane Paul, TVI Community College; Michele Powell, Holmes Community College; W. Dees Stallings, Park University; Michele Taylor, Ogeechee Technical College; Emily VanDette, Pennsylvania State University; Brian Wilson, College of Marin; Ruth Hopkins Zajdel, Ohio University Chillocothe.

Reviewers of "Document Makeover" Feature

We sincerely thank the following reviewers for their assistance with the Document Makeover feature: Lisa Barley, Eastern Michigan University; Marcia Bordman, Gallaudet University; Jean Bush-Bacelis, Eastern Michigan University; Bobbye Davis, Southern Louisiana University; Cynthia Drexel, Western State College; Kenneth Gibbs, Worcester State College; Ellen Leathers, Bradley University; Diana McKowen, Indiana University; Bobbie Nicholson, Mars Hill College; Andrew Smith, Holyoke Community College; Jay Stubblefield, North Carolina Wesleyan College; Dawn Wallace, South Eastern Louisiana University.

Reviewers of Model Documents

The many model documents in the text and their accompanying annotations received invaluable review from Diane Todd Bucci, Robert Morris University; Dacia Charlesworth, Robert Morris University; Avon Crismore, Indiana University; Estelle Kochis, Suffolk County Community College; Nancy Goehring, Monterey Peninsula College; James Hatfield, Florida Community College at Jacksonville; Sherry Robertson, Arizona State University.

Personal Acknowledgments

We wish to extend a heartfelt thanks to our many friends, acquaintances, and business associates who provided materials or agreed to be interviewed so that we could bring the real world into the classroom.

A very special acknowledgment goes to George Dovel, whose superb editorial skills, distinguished background, and wealth of business experience assured this project of clarity and completeness. Also, recognition and thanks go to Jackie Estrada for her outstanding skills and excellent attention to details. Her creation of the "Peak Performance Grammar and Mechanics" material is especially noteworthy.

We also feel it is important to acknowledge and thank the Association for Business Communication, an organization whose meetings and publications provide a valuable forum for the exchange of ideas and for professional growth.

Additionally, we would like to thank the supplement authors who prepared material for this new edition. They include: Dacia Charlesworth, Robert Morris University; Myles Hassell, University of New Orleans; William Peirce, Prince George's Community College; and Jay Stubblefield, North Carolina Wesleyan College.

We want to extend our warmest appreciation to the devoted professionals at Prentice Hall. They include Jerome Grant, president; Jeff Shelstad, vice-president and editorial director; David Parker, executive editor; Anne Howard, marketing manager; Ashley Santora, product development manager; Kristen Varina, editorial assistant—all of Prentice Hall Business Publishing; and the outstanding Prentice Hall sales representatives. Finally, we thank Renata Butera, managing editor of production, and Marcela Boos, senior production editor, for their dedication; and we are grateful to Jeanine Furino, senior production editor at GGS Book Services, and Janet Slowik, art director, for their superb work.

Courtland L. Bovée
John V. Thill

Business
Communication
Foundations

Unit 1

1

Understanding Business Communication in Today's Workplace

From the Real World

"They know I'm listening, and that alone improves relationships."

—Robert Scoble
Microsoft employee and publisher of the popular *Scobelizer* blog, http://scobleizer.wordpress.com

Learning Objectives

After studying this chapter, you will be able to

1 Explain what effective communication is

2 Discuss five developments in the workplace that are intensifying the need to communicate effectively

3 List and briefly define the six phases of the communication process

4 Identify four ways to improve business communication

5 Differentiate between an ethical dilemma and an ethical lapse

6 Define and briefly discuss four types of cultural differences that can affect communication

Microsoft's Robert Scoble was among the first business professionals to recognize the revolutionary impact that **blogging**, the practice of writing online journals, was going to have on business communication. In sharp contrast to traditional corporate communications, which can come across as impersonal, remote, and even defensive, Scoble's blog is highly personal and quite candid. He even links to blogs that criticize his employer. The online conversation may not always be comfortable from Microsoft's perspective, but that drawback is far outweighed by the value of maintaining effective communication between the company and its customers.[1]

Succeeding Through Effective Communication

Every business organization needs effective communication, both internally and externally.

Professionals such as Robert Scoble understand that achieving success in today's workplace requires the ability to communicate effectively with a wide variety of audiences. **Communication** is the process of sending and receiving messages. During your career, you'll communicate with a wide range of audiences. **Internal communication** refers to the exchange of information and ideas within an organization. You will receive numerous messages from colleagues and supervisors, and you'll be expected to convey information to audiences throughout the company as well. In contrast, **external communication** carries information into and out of the organization. Companies constantly exchange messages with customers, vendors, distributors, competitors, investors, journalists, and community representatives.

For any audience, communication is *effective* only when the message is understood and when it stimulates action or encourages the audience to think in new ways. Effective communication yields a number of important benefits for both you and your company:

Effective communication delivers a variety of important benefits.

- Quicker problem solving
- Stronger decision making
- Increased productivity
- Steadier work flow
- Stronger business relationships
- More compelling promotional messages
- Enhanced professional image
- Improved response from colleagues, employees, supervisors, investors, customers, and other important audiences

People aren't "born" writers or speakers. The more they write and speak, the more their skills improve. This course teaches you how to create effective messages and helps you improve your communication skills through practice in an environment that provides honest, constructive criticism. By working hard in this course to improve your communication skills, you'll gain a distinct advantage in today's job market.

In this course, you will learn how to create effective business messages.

No matter what career you pursue, this course will help you discover how to collaborate in teams, listen well, master nonverbal communication, and participate in productive meetings. You'll learn about communicating across cultural boundaries. You'll learn a three-step process that makes it easier to write effective business messages, and you'll get specific tips for writing a wide variety of messages, from e-mail and instant messages to blogs to online presentations. Plus, you'll learn how to write effective résumés and job application letters and how to handle employment interviews. Throughout this book, you'll see numerous examples with helpful comments to guide you through your own communication efforts.

Preparing for Today's Dynamic Workplace

Good communication skills are more vital today than ever before because people need to adapt to a workplace that is constantly changing. Effective communication will help you meet challenges such as advances in technology, the need to manage vast amounts of information, the growth of globalization and workforce diversity, and the increasing use of teams in the workplace.

Effective communication helps people adapt to change.

- **Communicating amid advancing technology.** From instant messaging (IM) and blogs to wireless networks and video-enabled mobile phones, technology has revolutionized the way businesspeople communicate. Used intelligently, these tools can increase the speed, reach, and effectiveness of your communication efforts and enable you to collaborate with others virtually anywhere on Earth, any time of the day. Figure 1.1 provides an example of effective communication using e-mail. In almost every aspect of business these days, you'll be expected not only to communicate well but to do so using a variety of communication technologies.

- **Communicating in the age of information.** In today's workplace, you must know how to find, evaluate, process, and share information effectively and efficiently. Plus, you must be able to use what information you receive to make strong, speedy decisions. Unfortunately, people are so inundated with information today that they tend to ignore messages they see as less important. Your challenge is to get your audience's attention so that they will read and respond to your messages.

- **Communicating globally and within a culturally diverse workforce.** Chances are good that your business career will require you to communicate across national or

FIGURE 1.1 Technology and Communication: Effective E-Mail
Notice how this message is more formal and "professional sounding" than the e-mail messages you probably send to your friends and family. Except for short messages between close colleagues and team members, most businesses will expect you to communicate with a style that is more formal than the style to which you are currently accustomed.

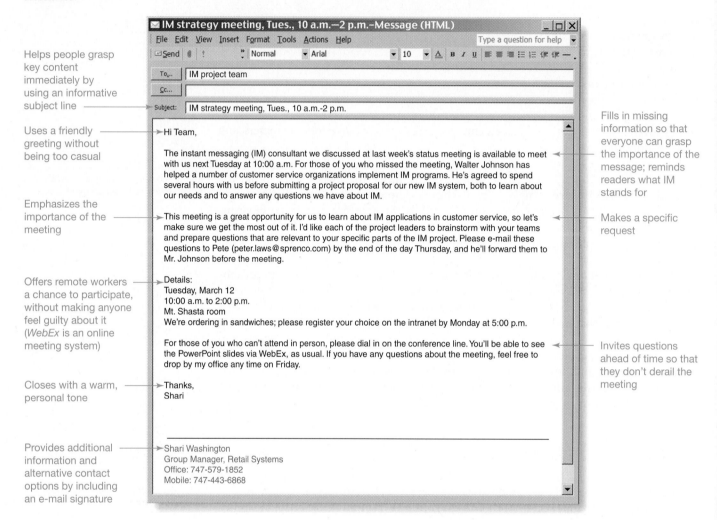

Helps people grasp key content immediately by using an informative subject line

Uses a friendly greeting without being too casual

Emphasizes the importance of the meeting

Offers remote workers a chance to participate, without making anyone feel guilty about it (*WebEx* is an online meeting system)

Closes with a warm, personal tone

Provides additional information and alternative contact options by including an e-mail signature

Fills in missing information so that everyone can grasp the importance of the message; reminds readers what IM stands for

Makes a specific request

Invites questions ahead of time so that they don't derail the meeting

---

cultural borders. For instance, of the top ten export markets for U.S. products, only two (Canada and Great Britain) have English as an official language, and Canada has two official languages, English and French.[2] Within the United States, some companies and brands that you may think of as American (including Ben & Jerry's, Dr. Pepper, Pillsbury, Carnation, and Shell Oil) are in fact owned by organizations based in other countries.[3] Moreover, the workforce in both the United States and other countries is becoming more diverse as countries look worldwide for talent and employees look worldwide for opportunities. To communicate effectively with these varied audiences, you'll have the challenge of understanding other people's backgrounds, personalities, and perceptions.

■ **Communicating in team-based organizations.** Many successful companies today no longer limit decisions to a few managers at the top of a formal hierarchy. These organizations use teams and flexible industry partnerships to collaborate and make fast decisions. As Chapter 2 discusses in detail, before you can function in a team-based organization, you must understand how groups interact. You must be a good listener and correctly interpret the nonverbal cues you receive from others. Such interaction requires a basic understanding of the communication process in organizational settings.

Understanding the Communication Process

Communication is a dynamic, two-way process that can be broken down into six phases (see Figure 1.2):

1. **The sender has an idea.** You conceive an idea and want to share it.
2. **The sender encodes the idea.** You decide on the message's form (words, facial expressions, gestures, illustrations, and so on), length, organization, tone, and style—all of which depend on your idea, your audience, and your personal style or mood.
3. **The sender transmits the message.** To transmit your message to your receiver, you select a **communication channel** such as the telephone, a letter, an e-mail—even a facial gesture. This choice of channel depends on your message, your audience's location, the media available to you, your need for speed, and the formality required.
4. **The receiver gets the message.** Unfortunately, you have no guarantee that your message will actually get through. The receiver may not hear you, or your e-mail might get caught in an antispam filter. In fact, one of the biggest challenges you'll face as a communicator in today's crowded business environment is cutting through clutter and noise.
5. **The receiver decodes the message.** Your receiver tries to extract your idea from the message in a form that he or she can understand, a step known as **decoding**. If all goes well, the receiver interprets your message correctly, assigning the same meaning to your words as you intended.
6. **The receiver sends feedback.** After decoding your message, the receiver has the option of responding in some way. This **feedback** enables you to evaluate the effectiveness of your message: Feedback often initiates another cycle through the process, which can continue until both parties are satisfied with the result. Successful communicators place considerable value on feedback, not only as a way to measure effectiveness but also as a way to learn.

Be aware that this is a simplified model; real-life communication is usually more complicated. For instance, both the sender and receiver might be talking at the same time, or the receiver might be trying to talk on the phone with one person while instant messaging with another.

> The communication process starts with a sender having an idea, then encoding the idea into a message that is transferred to a receiver.

FIGURE 1.2   The Communication Process

This six-step model is a simplified representation of how communication works in real life, but understanding this basic model is vital to improving your communication skills.

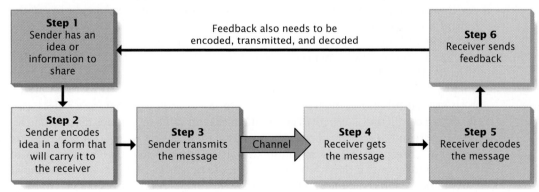

Building Your Business Communication Skills

In the coming chapters, you'll find real-life examples of both effective and ineffective communication, with clear explanations to help you recognize what is good or bad about them. You'll notice that five themes keep surfacing as keys to good communication: (1) committing to ethical communication, (2) adopting an audience-centered approach, (3) improving your intercultural sensitivity, (4) improving your workplace sensitivity, and (5) using communication technology effectively. Close attention to these themes will help you improve your business communication skills.

Committing to Ethical Communication

Ethics are the accepted principles of conduct that govern behavior within a society. Put another way, ethical principles define the boundary between right and wrong. Former Supreme Court Justice Potter Stewart defined ethics as "knowing the difference between what you have a right to do and what is the right thing to do."[4] To make the right choices as a business communicator you have a responsibility to think through not only what you say but also the consequences of saying it.

Of course, people in a society don't always agree on what constitutes ethical behavior. For instance, the emergence of *stealth marketing*, in which customers don't know they're being marketed to, has raised new concerns about ethics. A common stealth marketing technique is paying consumers (or offering them insider information and other benefits) to promote products to their friends without telling them it's a form of advertising. Critics complain that such techniques are deceptive because they don't give their targets the opportunity to raise their instinctive defenses against the persuasive powers of marketing messages.[5]

Ethical communication includes all relevant information, is true in every sense, and is not deceptive in any way. By contrast, unethical communication can include falsehoods and misleading information (or exclude important information). Some examples of unethical communication include:[6]

- **Plagiarism.** Stealing someone else's words or work and claiming it as your own
- **Selective misquoting.** Deliberately omitting damaging or unflattering comments to paint a better (but untruthful) picture of you or your company
- **Misrepresenting numbers.** Increasing or decreasing numbers, exaggerating, altering statistics, or omitting numerical data
- **Distorting visuals.** Making a product look bigger or changing the scale of graphs and charts to exaggerate or conceal differences

On the surface, ethical practices appear fairly easy to recognize, but deciding what is ethical can be a considerable challenge in complex business situations.

Recognizing Ethical Choices

Every company has responsibilities to multiple groups of people inside and outside the firm, and those various groups often have competing interests. For instance, employees generally want higher wages and more benefits, but investors who have risked their money in the company want management to keep costs low so profits are strong enough to drive up the stock price. Both sides have a valid position; neither one is "right" nor "wrong."

An **ethical dilemma** involves choosing among alternatives that aren't clear-cut. Perhaps two conflicting alternatives are both ethical and valid, or perhaps the alternatives lie somewhere in the gray area between clearly right and clearly wrong. Suppose you are president of a company that's losing money. You have a duty to your shareholders to try to reduce your losses and a duty to your employees to be fair and honest. After looking at various options, you conclude that you'll have to lay off 500 people immediately. You suspect you may have to lay off another 100 people later on, but right now you need those

100 workers to finish a project. What do you tell them? If you confess that their jobs are shaky, many of them may quit just when you need them most. However, if you tell them that the future is rosy, you'll be stretching the truth.

Unlike a dilemma, an **ethical lapse** is a clearly unethical (and frequently illegal) choice. For instance, several insurance companies were recently accused of misleading military personnel at Fort Benning in Georgia, Camp Pendleton in California, and other bases around the country. Many of these young men and women thought they were signing up for savings programs when in fact they were buying extremely expensive and frequently unnecessary life insurance policies. The policies were often sold during mandatory financial training sessions for the soldiers, who were given no time to read the documents they signed. After the situation was brought to national attention by the *New York Times* and other news media, at least two of the companies involved, Madison National Life Insurance Company and American Amicable Life Insurance, began issuing full refunds.[7]

> When you choose an alternative that is unethical or illegal, you are committing an ethical lapse.

Making Ethical Choices

Ensuring ethical business communications requires three elements: ethical individuals, ethical company leadership, and the appropriate policies and structures to support ethical decision making.[8] Many companies establish an explicit ethics policy by using a written **code of ethics** to help employees determine what is acceptable. A code is often part of a larger program of employee training and communication channels that allows employees to ask questions and report instances of questionable ethics. For example, United Technologies, a large aerospace and defense company based in Hartford, Connecticut, offers employees, customers, and suppliers a confidential way to report suspected fraud and other ethical concerns. People who share their concerns receive a written response that explains how the situation was resolved.[9]

> Responsible employers establish clear ethical guidelines for their employees to follow.

If you find yourself in a situation in which the law or your employer's code of ethics can't provide sufficient guidance, ask yourself the following questions:[10]

> If company ethics policies don't cover a specific situation, you can ask yourself a number of questions in order to make an ethical choice.

- Have you defined the situation fairly and accurately?
- What is your intention in communicating this message?
- What impact will this message have on the people who receive it, or who might be affected by it?
- Will the message achieve the greatest possible good while doing the least possible harm?
- Will the assumptions you've made change over time? That is, will a decision that seems ethical now seem unethical in the future?
- Are you comfortable with your decision? Would you be embarrassed if it were printed in tomorrow's newspaper or spread across the Internet? Would you be proud to describe your choice to someone you admire and respect?

One helpful way to make sure your messages are ethical is to consider your audience: What does your audience need? What will help your audience the most?

Adopting an Audience-Centered Approach

Adopting an **audience-centered approach** means focusing on and caring about the members of your audience—making every effort to get your message across in a way that is meaningful and respectful to them. In addition to being an excellent demonstration of using technology effectively, the blog posting in Figure 1.3 is a great example of audience-centered communication.

> An effective business message focuses on its audience.

An important element of audience-centered communication is **etiquette**, the expected norms of behavior in a particular situation. In today's hectic, competitive world, the notion of etiquette might seem outdated and unimportant. However, the way you conduct yourself can have a profound influence on your company's success and your career. When executives hire and promote you, they expect your behavior to protect the company's reputation. The more you understand such expectations, the better chance you have of avoiding career-damaging mistakes.

FIGURE 1.3   Audience-Centered Communication

After an upgrade to its TypePad blog-hosting system resulted in a period of poor performance for customers, Six Apart's Mena Trott and her colleagues communicated openly and honestly. They explained what happened, acknowledged customer frustrations, apologized for the inconvenience, offered compensation, and kept their audience up to date. Trott and her colleagues even shared what the experience had taught them as managers and communicators—insights that can help customers handle their own business communication challenges.

TYPEPAD | MOVABLE TYPE | LIVEJOURNAL | **ABOUT US** | SUPPORT

ABOUT SIX APART
News & Events
Management
History
Offices
Jobs
Press Center
Our Blogs

MENA'S CORNER

Mena Trott is president and a co-founder of Six Apart.

Mena's Corner is my chance to show the inner workings of a start-up and give the outside world a glimpse into our challenges, our achievements, and our professional passions.

ARCHIVES BY MONTH:
December 2005
November 2005
October 2005
September 2005
August 2005
July 2005
June 2005
May 2005
April 2005
February 2005
January 2005
December 2004
October 2004
August 2004
July 2004
May 2004
April 2004
March 2004

XML Feed

BLOG NOW!
Fully-featured.

TypePad Update & Lessons Learned

Mena | November 17, 2005

During the last month, we've been <u>very</u> <u>open</u> <u>about</u> TypePad's performance problems and the solutions we're implementing to bring the service up to a high standard. We're happy to say that, since things have stabilized, we've been able to offer compensation to our customers for the inconvenience caused by slow service and downtime.

As Barak said in his email and <u>post</u>, we offer our sincere apologies for any inconvenience and hope that customers of TypePad view the compensation as fair.

Not only did the people here at Six Apart feel the pain of poor performance (as employees and users), but we also spent a great deal of time reading customer emails, comments and posts which helped us understand that every customer is different. Some customers didn't want any compensation, they just wanted us to spend resources fixing the problems; others felt that the performance of TypePad hindered their businesses and personal communications; and some didn't notice any service degradation at all.

So, what are the lessons?

- **Read what your customers have to say**
  This is the most obvious piece of advice, but the most important. Customers who are invested in a service usually want the company that's supporting them to succeed. The best advice comes from your customers, and they aren't afraid to tell it like it is. That said...

- **Ignore the tone of nasty complaints, but pay attention to the underlying messages**
  When people are disappointed, their frustrations are often expressed in the form of anger. But at the same time, the fact that they took the time to write what they feel rather than shrugging it off indicates a deep desire for a solution, not just blame. We're all human and the nasty stuff hurts, but we love passionate users, so that involves taking the good and the bad comments in stride.

- **Understand that the people giving feedback represent many who remain silent**
  For every person who complains, realize that there are probably ten people conscious of the problem but not interested in speaking out

Offers links to related discussions so that anyone landing on this page can get the full story

Assures customers that their concerns and feedback were taken seriously

Helps everyone benefit from the experience (the list continues down the screen)

Improving Your Intercultural Sensitivity

Effective business communicators take cultural differences into account.

To communicate more effectively, be aware of and sensitive to cultural differences. **Culture** is a shared system of symbols, beliefs, attitudes, values, expectations, and norms for behavior. The interaction of culture and communication is so pervasive that separating the two is virtually impossible. The way you communicate—from the language you speak and the nonverbal signals you send to the way you perceive other people—is influenced by the culture in which you were raised. The meaning of words, the significance of gestures, the importance of time and space, the rules of human relationships—these and many other aspects of communication are defined by culture. To a large degree, your culture influences the way you think, which naturally affects the way you communicate as both a sender and a receiver.[11] In other words, achieving intercultural communication is much more complicated than simply matching language between sender and receiver. It goes beyond mere language to beliefs, values, and emotions.

You can improve your ability to communicate effectively across cultures by recognizing such cultural differences, by overcoming your tendency to judge others based on your own standards, by polishing your written intercultural skills, and by polishing your oral intercultural skills.

Improve your cultural sensitivity by
- Recognizing cultural differences
- Overcoming the tendency to stereotype
- Polishing your written intercultural communication skills
- Polishing your oral intercultural communication skills

Recognizing Cultural Differences

Problems often arise when we assume that other people's attitudes and lives are like ours. Start by unlearning the "Golden Rule" you were probably taught as a child, to treat others as you would want them to treat you. Instead, treat others the way *they* want to be treated, not the way *you* want to be treated. More specifically, you can improve intercultural sensitivity by recognizing and accommodating cultural differences in such areas as context, law and ethics, social customs, and nonverbal communication.

Cultural differences exist in areas such as context, ethics, social custom, and nonverbal communication.

Cultural Context   Every attempt at communication occurs within a **cultural context**, the pattern of physical cues, environmental stimuli, and implicit understanding that convey meaning between two members of the same culture. However, cultures around the world vary widely in the role that context plays in communication (see Figure 1.4).

Cultural context includes physical cues, environmental stimuli, and varying degrees of implicit understanding.

In a **high-context culture** such as South Korea or Taiwan, people rely less on verbal communication and more on the context of nonverbal actions and environmental setting to convey meaning. For instance, a Chinese speaker expects the receiver to discover the essence of a message and uses indirectness and metaphor to provide a web of meaning.[12] In high-context cultures, the rules of everyday life are rarely explicit; instead, as individuals grow up, they learn how to recognize situational cues (such as gestures and tone

To communicate in high-context cultures, members rely less on words and more on context.

FIGURE 1.4   How Cultural Context Affects Business Communication
Cultural differences can have a profound effect on business communication. Bear in mind that this is a simplified model; individuals and companies within a given culture can vary widely along the high-context to low-context continuum.

IN LOW-CONTEXT CULTURES	IN HIGH-CONTEXT CULTURES
Executive offices are separate with controlled access.	Executive offices are shared and open to all.
Workers rely on detailed background information.	Workers do not expect or want detailed information.
Information is highly centralized and controlled.	Information is shared with everyone.
Objective data are valued over subjective relationships.	Subjective relationships are valued over objective data.
Business and social relationships are discrete.	Business and social relationships overlap.
Competence is valued as much as position and status.	Position and status are valued much more than competence.
Meetings have fixed agendas and plenty of advance notice.	Meetings are often called on short notice, and key people always accept.

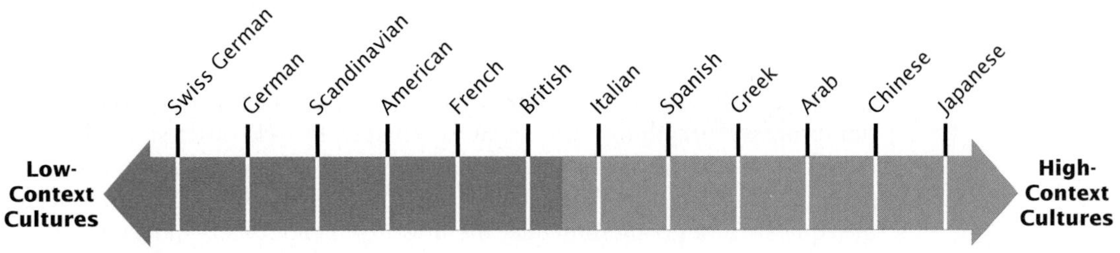

Low-Context Cultures → Swiss German, German, Scandinavian, American, French, British, Italian, Spanish, Greek, Arab, Chinese, Japanese → High-Context Cultures

of voice) and how to respond as expected.[13] Also, in a high-context culture, the primary role of communication is building relationships, not exchanging information.[14]

In a **low-context culture** such as the United States or Germany, people rely more on verbal communication and less on circumstances and cues to convey meaning. An English speaker feels responsible for transmitting the meaning of the message and often places sentences in chronological sequence to establish a cause-and-effect pattern.[15] In a low-context culture, rules and expectations are usually spelled out through explicit statements such as "Please wait until I'm finished" or "You're welcome to browse."[16] Exchanging information is the primary task of communication in low-context cultures.[17]

To communicate in low-context cultures, members rely more on words and less on context.

Legal and Ethical Differences   Legal and ethical behaviors are also affected by cultural context. For example, because members of low-context cultures value the written word, they consider written agreements binding. They also tend to view laws with flexibility. However, members of high-context cultures put less emphasis on the written word and consider personal pledges more important than contracts. Plus, they tend to adhere more strictly to the law.[18]

Members of different cultures sometimes have different views of what is ethical and even legal.

Legal systems differ from culture to culture. In the United Kingdom and the United States, someone is presumed innocent until proved guilty, a principle rooted in English common law. However, in Mexico and Turkey, someone is presumed guilty until proved innocent, a principle rooted in the Napoleonic code.[19] These distinctions are particularly important if your firm must communicate about a legal dispute in another country.

Making ethical choices can be difficult within your own culture. But trying to make these choices across cultures can seem incredibly complicated. When communicating across cultures, keep your messages ethical by applying four basic principles:[20]

Learn the four principles that will help you keep your intercultural messages ethical.

- **Actively seek mutual ground.** Both parties must be flexible and avoid insisting that an interaction take place strictly in terms of one culture or another.
- **Send and receive messages without judgment.** Both parties must recognize that values vary from culture to culture, and they must find a way to trust each other.
- **Send messages that are honest.** Both parties must see a situation as it is—not as they would like it to be. They must be fully aware of their personal and cultural biases.
- **Show respect for cultural differences.** Both parties must understand and acknowledge the other's needs and preserve each other's dignity by communicating without deception.

Social Customs   The nature of social behavior varies among cultures, sometimes dramatically. These behaviors are guided by rules. Some rules are formal and specifically articulated (table manners are a good example), and some are informal, learned over time (such as the comfortable standing distance between two speakers in an office or the acceptability of male and female employees socializing outside of work). The combination of formal and informal rules influences the overall behavior of everyone in a society, or at least most of the people most of the time, in such areas as manners, attitudes toward time, individual versus community values, and attitudes toward status and wealth. For example, the predominant U.S. view is that money solves many problems, that material comfort is a sign of superiority and is earned by individual effort, and that people who work hard are better than those who don't. But other cultures condemn materialism, some prize communal effort above that of the individual, and some value a more carefree lifestyle.

Whether formal or informal, the rules governing social customs differ from culture to culture.

Nonverbal Communication   Nonverbal communication is a vital part of the communication process. Everything from facial expressions to style of dress can influence the way receivers decode messages, and the interpretation of nonverbal signals can vary widely from culture to culture. For instance, a gesture that communicates good luck in Brazil is the equivalent of giving someone "the finger" in Colombia.[21] In fact, the area of gestures in intercultural communication is so complicated that entire books have been written about it. Don't assume that the gestures you grew up with will translate to another culture; doing so could lead to embarrassing mistakes. You'll learn more about nonverbal communication in Chapter 2.

Overcoming Ethnocentrism and Stereotyping

Ethnocentrism is the tendency to judge all other groups according to the standards, behaviors, and customs of one's own group. When making such comparisons, people too often decide that their own group is superior.[22] An even more extreme reaction is **xenophobia**, a fear of strangers and foreigners. Clearly, businesspeople who take these views will not interpret messages from other cultures correctly, nor are they likely to send successful messages.

Distorted views of other cultures or groups also result from **stereotyping**, assigning a wide range of generalized attributes to an individual on the basis of membership in a particular culture or social group, without considering the individual's unique characteristics. For instance, assuming that an older colleague will be out of touch with the youth market or that a younger colleague can't be an inspiring leader is an example of stereotyping age groups.

Those who want to show respect for other people and to communicate effectively in business need to adopt a more positive viewpoint, in the form of **cultural pluralism**—the practice of accepting multiple cultures on their own terms. When crossing cultural boundaries, you'll be even more effective if you move beyond simple acceptance and adapt your own communication style to that of the new cultures you encounter—even integrating aspects of those cultures into your own.[23] A few simple habits can help you avoid both the negativity of ethnocentrism and the oversimplification of stereotyping:

- **Avoid assumptions.** Don't assume that others will act the same way you do, that they will operate from the same values and beliefs, or that they will use language and symbols the same way you do.
- **Avoid judgments.** When people act differently, don't conclude that they are in error, that their way is invalid, or that their customs are inferior to your own.
- **Acknowledge distinctions.** Don't ignore the differences between another person's culture and your own.

Unfortunately, overcoming ethnocentrism and stereotyping is no simple task, even for people who are highly motivated to do so. You may need to change patterns of beliefs that you've had your entire life and even change the way you view yourself and your culture. Moreover, recent research suggests that people often have beliefs and biases that they're not even consciously aware of—and that may even conflict with the beliefs they *think* they have. (To see if you might have some of these *implicit beliefs* visit the Project Implicit website at https:/implicit.harvard.edu/implicit and take some of the simple online tests.[24])

Polishing Your Written Intercultural Skills

The letter in Figure 1.5 communicates across cultures quite effectively. To help you prepare effective written communications for multicultural audiences, remember these tips:[25]

- **Use plain English.** Use short, precise words that say exactly what you mean.
- **Be clear.** Rely on specific terms and concrete examples to explain your points.
- **Address international correspondence properly.** The order and layout of address information vary from country to country, so follow the conventions that appear in the company's letterhead.
- **Cite numbers carefully.** Use figures (27) instead of spelling them out (twenty-seven).
- **Avoid slang, idioms, jargon, and abbreviations.** Words and phrases that you consider to be everyday language may in fact be nonstandard usage and difficult for your audience to translate.
- **Be brief.** Construct sentences that are short and simple.

Ethnocentrism is the tendency to judge all other groups according to the standards, behaviors, and customs of one's own group.

Stereotyping is assigning generalized attributes to an individual on the basis of membership in a particular group.

Cultural pluralism is the acceptance of multiple cultures on their own terms.

Important tips for improving your intercultural writing include using plain English, avoiding slang, and using short sentences and short paragraphs.

FIGURE 1.5 Effective Intercultural Letter

This letter from a U.S. sales representative to an accounting manager in a French company is a good example of successfully adapting to an audience in another culture.

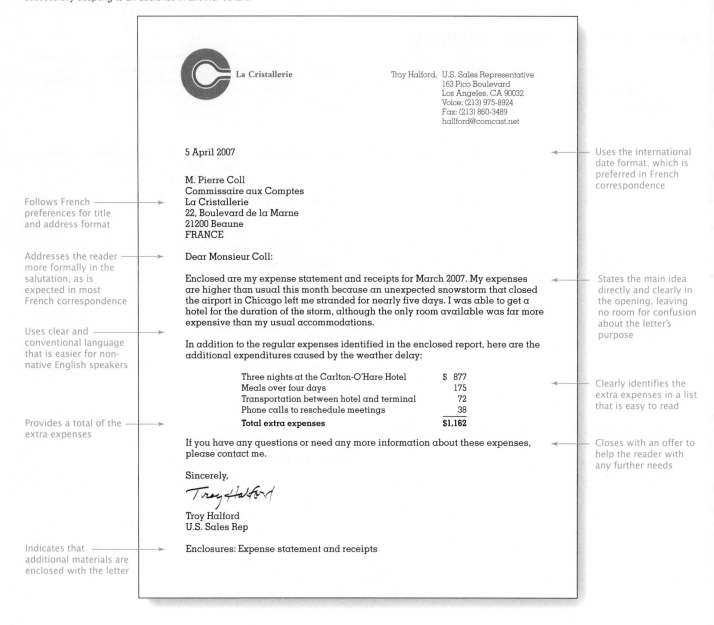

La Cristallerie

Troy Halford, U.S. Sales Representative
163 Pico Boulevard
Los Angeles, CA 90032
Voice: (213) 975-8924
Fax: (213) 860-3489
hallford@comcast.net

5 April 2007

M. Pierre Coll
Commissaire aux Comptes
La Cristallerie
22, Boulevard de la Marne
21200 Beaune
FRANCE

Dear Monsieur Coll:

Enclosed are my expense statement and receipts for March 2007. My expenses are higher than usual this month because an unexpected snowstorm that closed the airport in Chicago left me stranded for nearly five days. I was able to get a hotel for the duration of the storm, although the only room available was far more expensive than my usual accommodations.

In addition to the regular expenses identified in the enclosed report, here are the additional expenditures caused by the weather delay:

Three nights at the Carlton-O'Hare Hotel	$ 877
Meals over four days	175
Transportation between hotel and terminal	72
Phone calls to reschedule meetings	38
Total extra expenses	**$1,162**

If you have any questions or need any more information about these expenses, please contact me.

Sincerely,

Troy Halford

Troy Halford
U.S. Sales Rep

Enclosures: Expense statement and receipts

Callout annotations (left):
- Follows French preferences for title and address format
- Addresses the reader more formally in the salutation, as is expected in most French correspondence
- Uses clear and conventional language that is easier for non-native English speakers
- Provides a total of the extra expenses
- Indicates that additional materials are enclosed with the letter

Callout annotations (right):
- Uses the international date format, which is preferred in French correspondence
- States the main idea directly and clearly in the opening, leaving no room for confusion about the letter's purpose
- Clearly identifies the extra expenses in a list that is easy to read
- Closes with an offer to help the reader with any further needs

- **Use short paragraphs.** Each paragraph should stick to one topic.
- **Use transitional elements.** Help readers follow your train of thought.

Polishing Your Oral Intercultural Skills

When speaking in English to people who speak English as a second language, you may find these tips helpful:

Important tips for improving your oral intercultural skills include speaking clearly and slowly, looking for feedback, and using objective language.

- **Try to eliminate noise.** Pronounce words clearly, stop at distinct punctuation points, and make one point at a time.
- **Look for feedback.** Be alert to signs of confusion in your listener. Realize that nods and smiles don't necessarily mean understanding. If the other person's body language seems at odds with the message, take time to clarify the meaning.
- **Speak slowly and rephrase your sentence when necessary.** If someone doesn't seem to understand you, choose simpler words; don't just repeat the sentence in a louder voice.

- **Clarify your true intent with repetition and examples.** Try to be aware of unintentional meanings that may be read into your message.
- **Don't talk down to the other person.** Try not to overenunciate, and don't "blame" the listener for not understanding. Say, "Am I going too fast?" rather than "Is this too difficult for you?"
- **Use objective, accurate language.** Avoid throwing around adjectives such as *fantastic* and *fabulous,* which people from other cultures might consider unreal and overly dramatic.
- **Learn foreign phrases.** Learn common greetings and a few simple phrases in the other person's native language. Key phrases are usually listed in travel books and in a separate section of most travel dictionaries.
- **Listen carefully and patiently.** Let other people finish what they have to say. If you interrupt, you may miss something important. You'll also show a lack of respect. If you do not understand a comment, ask the person to repeat it.
- **Adapt your conversation style to the other person's.** For instance, if the other person appears to be direct and straightforward, follow suit.
- **Check frequently for comprehension.** Make one point at a time and pause to check on comprehension before moving on.
- **Clarify what will happen next.** At the end of a conversation, be sure that you and the other person agree on what has been said and decided. If appropriate, follow up by writing a letter or a memo summarizing the conversation and thanking the person for meeting with you.
- **Observe body language.** Be alert to roving eyes, glazed looks, and other facial expressions that signal the listener is lost or confused.

In short, take advantage of the other person's presence to make sure that your message is getting across and that you understand his or her message too.

Improving Your Workplace Sensitivity

Today's workforce is composed of people who differ in race, gender, age, culture, family structure, religion, and educational background. Such **cultural diversity** affects how business messages are conceived, planned, sent, received, and interpreted in the workplace. To communicate more effectively with diverse audiences both inside and outside your company, learn all you can about the cultures of these people. In your research, try to learn useful general information while remaining aware of and open to local variations and individual differences. In any cross-cultural situation, you can communicate more effectively if you heed the following tips:[26]

Today's culturally diverse workforce is made up of men and women from various nations, ethnic backgrounds, religions, ages, family structures, and educational backgrounds.

- **Assume differences until similarity is proved.** Don't assume that others are more similar to you than they actually are.

Document Makeover

Improve This Memo

To practice correcting drafts of actual documents, visit your online course or the access-code-protected portion of the Companion Website. Click "Document Makeovers," then click Chapter 1. You will find a memo that contains problems and errors relating to what you've learned in this chapter about improving business communication. Use the Final Draft decision tool to create an improved version of this memo. Check the message for ethical communication, an audience-centered approach, and intercultural sensitivity.

Important tips to communicate effectively in a culturally diverse workforce include withholding judgment, looking beyond superficial differences, and being flexible.

- **Take responsibility for communication.** Don't assume it's the other person's job to communicate with you.
- **Withhold judgment.** Learn to listen to the whole story and accept differences in others without judging them.
- **Show respect.** Learn how respect is communicated in various cultures (through gestures, eye contact, and so on).
- **Empathize.** Before sending a message, put yourself in the receiver's shoes. Imagine the receiver's feelings and point of view.
- **Tolerate ambiguity.** Learn to control your frustration when placed in an unfamiliar or confusing situation.
- **Look beyond the superficial.** Don't be distracted by things such as dress, appearance, or environmental discomforts.
- **Be patient and persistent.** If you want to communicate with someone from another culture, don't give up easily.
- **Recognize your own cultural biases.** Learn to identify when your assumptions are different from the other person's.
- **Be flexible.** Be prepared to change your habits and attitudes when communicating with someone from another culture.
- **Emphasize common ground.** Look for similarities from which to work.
- **Send clear messages.** Make both your verbal and nonverbal signals clear and consistent.
- **Deal with the individual.** Communicate with each person as an individual, not as a stereotypical representative of another group.
- **Learn when to be direct.** Investigate each culture so that you'll know when to send your message in a straightforward manner and when to be indirect.
- **Observe and learn.** Even after you begin to find your way in another culture, continue to assess the feedback provided by recipients of your communication. The more you learn, the more effective you'll be.

Using Communication Technology Effectively

Communicating in today's business environment nearly always requires some level of technical competence as well.

Today's businesses rely heavily on technology to improve the communication process, and you'll be expected to use a variety of these tools on the job. The four-page photo essay "Powerful Tools for Communicating Efficiently" (pp. 16–19) offers an overview of the technologies that connect people in offices, factories, and other business settings. In addition, some aspects of communication technology are undergoing exciting changes almost daily:

- **Voice technologies.** The human voice will always be central to business communication, but today it's being supplemented by a variety of new technologies. *Voice synthesis* regenerates a human speaking voice from computer files that represent words or parts of words. *Voice recognition* converts human speech to computer-compatible data. One of the most exciting new developments is **podcasting** (see chapter 6), the process of recording of audio or video messages that can be distributed via the Internet.
- **Virtual agents.** *Virtual agents*, also known as *bots* (derived from *robot*), are a class of automated tools that perform a variety of communication tasks, such as answering customer service questions and responding to requests for electronic documents.[27]
- **Mobile communication.** If you're accustomed to studying on the go, you'll fit right into today's untethered work environment. In some cases, mobile workers don't even have traditional offices, using temporary cubicles at work, home offices, cars, airports, and even new Internet-equipped airplanes for office space. Geographic data from the **Global Positioning System (GPS)** are also creating new forms of mobile communication, such as location-based advertising (getting an ad on your cell phone from a store you're walking past, for instance) and remote monitoring of medical patients and trucking fleets.
- **Networking advances.** You might already be using some of the new networking technologies that help businesspeople communicate and collaborate. **Peer-to-peer (P2P) computing** lets multiple PCs communicate directly so that they can share files or work

on large problems simultaneously. **Wireless networking**, particularly the commonly used *Wi-Fi* technology, extends the reach of the Internet with wireless access points that connect to PCs and handheld devices via radio signals. **Short messaging service (SMS)** is a text communication feature that has been common on mobile phones in other parts of the world for years and is becoming more popular in North America.

Even as technologies continue to advance, anyone who has used a computer knows that the benefits of technology are not automatic. To communicate effectively, you need to keep technology in perspective, use technological tools productively, and disengage from the computer frequently to communicate in person.

Keeping Technology in Perspective

Technology is an aid to interpersonal communication, not a replacement for it. Technology can't think for you, communicate for you, or make up for a lack of essential skills. The spellchecker in your word processor is a great example. It's happy to run all your words through the dictionary, but it doesn't know whether you're using the correct words or the best words possible.

Don't let technology overwhelm the communication process.

The sheer number of possibilities in many technological tools can also get in the way of successful communication. For example, both senders and receivers may be distracted if they're having trouble configuring their computers to participate in an online meeting. Or the content of a message may be obscured if an electronic presentation is overloaded with amateurish visual effects. By focusing on your message and your audience, you can avoid falling into the trap of letting technology get in the way of successful communication.

Using Technological Tools Productively

You don't have to become an expert to use most communication technologies effectively, but you will need to be familiar with the basic features and functions of the tools your employer expects you to use. For instance, if you don't know the basic functions of your word processor, you could spend hours trying to format a document that a skilled user could format in minutes. Whatever the tool, if you learn the basics, your work will be less frustrating and far more productive.

Employers who are comfortable using communication technologies have a competitive advantage in today's marketplace.

Reconnecting with People Frequently

In spite of technology's efficiency and speed, it may not be the best choice for every communication situation. Even in the best circumstances, technology can't match the rich experience of person-to-person contact. Let's say you IM an employee asking how she did with her sales presentation to an important client, and her answer comes back simply as "Fine." What does *fine* mean? Did she win the sale? Lose it? Oversleep and miss the meeting? If you visit her in person, you can pick up on nonverbal clues and probably engage her in a more meaningful conversation.

No matter how much technology is involved, communication will always be about people connecting with people.

Moreover, even the best communication technologies can't show people who you really are. You can create amazing documents and presentations without ever leaving your desk or meeting anyone in person. You might be funny, bright, and helpful, but you're just a voice on the phone or a name on a screen until people can interact with you in person. Remember to step out from behind the technology frequently to learn more about the people you work with—and to let them learn more about you.

Reviewing Key Points

This chapter highlights the importance of making business communication effective by ensuring that it stimulates action and encourages audiences to think in new ways. The chapter explains how effective communication helps you adapt to today's changing workplace. Amid today's advancing technology, selecting the proper communication tool enables you not only to reach your audiences but also to help them better understand

Powerful Tools for Communicating Efficiently

The tools of business communication evolve with every new generation of digital technology. Selecting the right tool for each situation can enhance your business communication in many ways. In today's flexible office settings, communication technology helps people keep in touch and stay productive. When co-workers in different cities need to collaborate, they can meet and share ideas without costly travel. Manufacturers use communication technology to keep track of parts, orders, and shipments—and to keep customers well-informed. Those same customers can also communicate with companies in many ways at any time of day or night.

Flexible Workstations

Many professionals have abandoned desktop PCs for laptops they can carry home, on travel, and to meetings. Back at their desks, a docking station transforms the laptop into a full-featured PC with network connection. Workers without permanent desks sometimes share PCs that automatically reconfigure themselves to access each user's e-mail and files.

Wireless Networks

Laptop PCs with wireless and handheld capability let workers stay connected to the network from practically anywhere within the office—any desk, any conference room. This technology offers high-speed Internet access within range of a wireless access point. New smart phones will continue this trend of connectivity on the go.

Follow-Me Phone Service

Rather than juggling multiple numbers for home, one or more office locations, and mobile phones, workers can use *follow-me phone service*. Callers dial one number to reach the person anywhere—at the office, a remote site, a home office, or anywhere with cell phone service. The system automatically forwards calls to a list of preprogrammed numbers and transfers unanswered calls to voice mail.

Redefining the Office

Technology makes it easier for people to retrieve information and stay connected with colleagues, suppliers, and customers—wherever they are. To simplify life for employees and reduce office expenses, many companies now enable their staffs to work from home or from special satellite offices that are closer to residential areas than their main office complexes. For example, Sun Microsystems lets staff members choose to work either at the main office or at remote offices called "drop-in centers." Many Sun facilities have specially equipped "iWork" areas that can quickly reconfigure phone and computer connections to meet individual requirements.

Electronic Presentations

Combining a color projector with a laptop or personal digital assistant (PDA) running the right software lets people give informative business presentations that are enhanced with sound, video animation, and live web links. Having everything in electronic form also makes it easy to customize a presentation or to make last-minute changes.

Intranets

Businesses use Internet technologies to create an intranet, a private computer network that simplifies information sharing within the company. Intranets can handle a variety of communication needs and become "virtual office spaces" for geographically dispersed teams. To ensure the security of company communication and information, intranets are shielded from the public Internet.

Communicating in the Office

Wall Displays

Teams commonly solve problems by brainstorming at a whiteboard. Wall displays take this concept one step further, letting participants transmit words and diagrams to distant colleagues via the corporate intranet. Users can even share the virtual pen to make changes and additions from more than one location.

Web-Based Meetings

Workers can actively participate in web-based meetings by logging on from a desktop PC, laptop, or cell phone. Websites such as WebEx help users integrate voice, text, and video, and let them share applications such as Microsoft PowerPoint and Microsoft Word in a single browser window.

Collaborating

Working in teams is essential in almost every business. Teamwork can become complicated, however, when team members work in different parts of the company, in different time zones, or even for different companies. Technology helps bridge the distance by making it possible to brainstorm, attend virtual meetings, and share files from widely separated locations. Communication technology also helps companies save money on costly business travel without losing most of the benefits of face-to-face collaboration.

Shared Workspace

Online workspaces such as eRoom and Groove make it easy for far-flung team members to access shared files anywhere, any time. Accessible through a browser, the workspace contains a collection of folders and has built-in intelligence to control which team members can read, edit, and save specific files.

Internet Videophone

Person-to-person video calling has long been possible through popular instant messaging programs. Internet videophone services do even more, letting multiple users participate in a videoconference without the expense and complexity of a full-fledged videoconferencing system. Some services are flexible enough to include telecommuters who have broadband Internet connections.

Communicating Remotely

Videoconferencing and Telepresence

Less costly than travel, videoconferencing provides many of the same benefits as an in-person meeting. Advanced systems include telepresence and robot surrogates, which use computers to "place" participants in the room virtually, letting them see and hear everyone while being seen and heard themselves. Such realistic interaction makes meetings more productive.

Warehouse RFID

In an effort to reduce the costs and delays associated with manual inventory reports, Wal-Mart requires its top suppliers to put radio-frequency identification (RFID) tags on all their shipping cases and pallets. These tags automatically provide information that was previously collected by hand via barcode scanners.

Extranet

Extranets are s private compu networks that Internet techn to share busine formation with suppliers, venc partners, and customers. Th an extranet as extension of th company intranet that is available to people outside the organization by invitation only.

Wireless Warehouse

Communication technology is a key source of competitive advantage for shipping companies such as FedEx and UPS. Hand-worn scanners use wireless links to help warehouse personnel access instant information that lets them process more packages in less time at transit hubs. Currently, 300 package loaders at four UPS hub facilities are testing the new wireless application called UPScan. A pager-size cordless scanner worn on the loader's hand captures data from a package bar code and transmits the data via Bluetooth® wireless technology to a Symbol Technologies wireless terminal worn on the loader's waist.

Sharing the Latest Information

Companies use a variety of communication technologies to create products and services and deliver them to customers. The ability to easily access and share the latest information improves the flow and timing of supplies, lowers operating costs, and boosts financial performance. Easy information access also helps companies respond to customer needs by providing them timely, accurate information and service and by delivering the right products to them at the right time.

Package Tracking

Senders and receivers often want frequent updates when packages are in transit. Handheld devices such as the FedEx PowerPad enhance customer service by letting delivery personnel instantly upload package data to the FedEx network. The wireless PowerPad also aids drivers by automatically receiving weather advisories.

Supply Chain Management

Advanced software applications let suppliers, manufacturers, and retailers share information—even when they have incompatible computer systems. Improved information flow increases report accuracy and helps each company in the supply chain manage stock levels.

Communicating About Products and Services

Over-the-Shoulder Support

For online shoppers who need instant help, many retail websites make it easy to connect with a live sales rep via phone or instant messaging. The rep can provide quick answers to questions and, with permission, can even control a shopper's browser to help locate particular items.

Help Lines

Some people prefer the personal touch of contact by phone. Moreover, some companies assign preferred customers special ID numbers that let them jump to the front of the calling queue. Many companies are addressing the needs of foreign-language speakers by connecting them with external service providers who offer multilingual support.

Interacting

Maintaining an open dialog with customers is a great way to gain a better understanding of their likes and dislikes. Today's communication technologies make it easier for customers to interact with a company whenever, wherever, and however they wish. A well-coordinated approach to phone, web, and in-store communication helps a company build stronger relationships with its existing customers, which increases the chances of doing more business with each one.

Corporate Blogs

Web-based journals let companies offer advice, answer questions, and promote the benefits of their products and services in a fast, personal style. Elements of a successful blog include frequent updates and the participation of knowledgeable contributors. Adding a subtle mix of useful commentary and marketing messages helps get customers to visit blogs frequently or sign up for automatic updates through really simple syndication (RSS).

Podcasting

With the portability and convenience of downloadable audio and video recordings, podcasts have quickly become a popular means of delivering everything from college lectures to marketing messages. Podcasts are also used for internal communication as well, replacing conference calls, newsletters, and other traditional communication vehicles.

Communicating with Customers

In-Store Kiosks

Staples is among the retailers that let shoppers buy from the web while they're still in the store. Web-connected kiosks were originally used to let shoppers custom-configure their PCs, but the kiosks also give customers access to roughly 8,000 in-store items as well as to the 50,000 products available online.

your messages. In today's age of information, getting your audience's attention prevents people from overlooking vital information that you pass along. With today's global marketplace and diverse workforce, understanding other backgrounds, personalities, and perceptions enables you to communicate clearly with people from other cultures. And since today's companies are committed to working in teams, knowing how to listen to colleagues and to recognize the meaning behind their nonverbal signals helps you collaborate with the others in your work groups.

This chapter also describes the six steps in the communication process. And it cautions you not to pack too much information into each message you send. It explains five ways to improve your business communication: by committing to ethical communication, adopting an audience-centered approach, improving your intercultural sensitivity, improving your workplace sensitivity, and using technology effectively.

The next chapter discusses communicating in teams. It explains how to listen to others by overcoming the common barriers to good listening. It also talks about how to understand nonverbal communication. Finally, it helps you put this new information to work when planning and participating in meetings and when using telephones and voice mail.

Test Your Knowledge

1. What benefits does effective communication give you and your organization?

2. What effects do globalization and workforce diversity have on communication?

3. Define ethics, and explain what ethical communication encompasses.

4. Why should communicators take an audience-centered approach to communication?

5. Why is it important to reconnect in person when using technology to communicate?

Apply Your Knowledge

1. Why do you think communication is vital to the success of every business organization? Explain briefly.

2. How does your understanding of the communication process help you conduct business more effectively?

3. Your company has relocated to a U.S. city where a Vietnamese subculture is strongly established. Many employees will be from this subculture. As a member of the human resources department, what suggestions can you make to improve communication between management and the Vietnamese Americans your company is hiring?

4. When Mena Trott shared with her customers the lessons her company learned after a computer systems failure (refer to the discussion of Figure 1.3 on p. 8), how was she engaging in audience-centered communication?

5. **Ethical Choices**   Because of your excellent communication skills, your boss always asks you to write his reports for him. But when the CEO compliments him on his logical organization and clear writing style, your boss responds as if he'd written all those reports himself. What kind of ethical choice does this represent? What can you do in this situation? Briefly explain your solution and your reasoning.

Practice Your Knowledge

Activities

For active links to all websites discussed in this chapter, visit this text's website at www. prenhall.com/bovee. Locate your book and click on its Companion Website link. Then select Chapter 1, and click on "Featured Websites." Locate the name of the page or the URL related to the material in the text. Please note that links to sites that become inactive after publication of the book will be removed from the Featured Websites section.

1. **Analyze This Document**   Your boss wants to send a brief e-mail message welcoming employees recently transferred to your department from your Hong Kong branch.

They all speak English, but your boss asks you to review her message for clarity. What would you suggest your boss change in the following e-mail message—and why? Would you consider this message to be audience centered? Why or why not?

I wanted to welcome you ASAP to our little family here in the states. It's high time we shook hands in person and not just across the sea. I'm pleased as punch about getting to know you all, and I for one will do my level best to sell you on America.

2. **Ethical Choices**   In less than a page, explain why you think each of the following is or is not ethical:

   a. De-emphasizing negative test results in a report on your product idea

   b. Taking a computer home to finish a work-related assignment

   c. Telling an associate and close friend that she'd better pay more attention to her work responsibilities or management will fire her

   d. Recommending the purchase of excess equipment to use up your allocated funds before the end of the fiscal year so that your budget won't be cut next year

3. **The Changing Workplace: Personal Expression at Work**   Blogging has become a popular way for employees to communicate with customers and other parties outside the company. In some cases, employee blogs have been quite beneficial for both companies and their customers, by providing helpful information and "putting a human face" on otherwise formal and imposing corporations. However, in some other cases, employees have been fired for posting information that their employers said was inappropriate. One particular area of concern is criticism of the company or individual managers. Should employees be allowed to criticize their employers in a public forum such as a blog? In a brief e-mail message, argue for or against company policies that prohibit any critical information in employee blogs.

4. **Internet**   Cisco is a leading manufacturer of equipment for the Internet and corporate networks and has developed a code of ethics that it expects employees to abide by. Visit the company's website at www.cisco.com and find the Code of Conduct. In a brief paragraph, describe three specific examples of things you could do that would violate these provisions; then list at least three opportunities that Cisco provides its employees to report ethics violations or ask questions regarding ethical dilemmas.

5. **Communication Etiquette**   Potential customers often visit your production facility before making purchase decisions. You and the people who report to you in the sales department have received extensive training in etiquette issues because you deal with high-profile clients so frequently. However, the rest of the workforce has not received such training, and you worry that someone might inadvertently say or do something that would offend one of these potential customers. In a two-paragraph e-mail, explain to the general manager why you think anyone who might come in contact with customers should receive basic etiquette training.

6. **Self-Introduction**   Write a paragraph or prepare a two-minute oral presentation introducing yourself to your instructor and your class. Include such things as your background, interests, achievements, and goals.

7. **Teamwork**   Your boss has asked your workgroup to research and report on corporate child-care facilities. Of course, you'll want to know who (besides your boss) will be reading your report. Working with two team members, list four or five other things you'll want to know about the situation and about your audience before starting your research. Briefly explain why each of the items on your list is important.

8. **Communication Process: Analyzing Miscommunication**   Use the six phases of the communication process to analyze a miscommunication you've recently had with a co-worker, supervisor, classmate, teacher, friend, or family member. What idea were

you trying to share? How did you encode and transmit it? Did the receiver get the message? Did the receiver correctly decode the message? How do you know? Based on your analysis, what do you think prevented your successful communication in this instance?

9. **Ethical Choices** Knowing that you have numerous friends throughout the company, your boss relies on you for feedback concerning employee morale and other issues affecting the staff. She recently approached you and asked you to start reporting any behavior that might violate company polices, from taking office supplies home to making personal long-distance calls. List the issues you'd like to discuss with her before you respond to her request.

10. **Intercultural Sensitivity: Recognizing Differences** Your boss represents a Canadian toy company that's negotiating to buy miniature truck wheels from a manufacturer in Osaka, Japan. In the first meeting, he explains that your company expects to control the design of the wheels as well as the materials that are used to make them. The manufacturer's representative looks down and says softly, "Perhaps that will be difficult." Your boss presses for agreement, and to emphasize your company's willingness to buy, he shows the prepared contract he's brought with him. However, the manufacturer seems increasingly vague and uninterested.

    Your task: What cultural differences may be interfering with effective communication in this situation? Explain briefly in an e-mail message to your instructor.

11. **Teamwork** Working with two other students, prepare a list of ten examples of slang (in your own language) that would probably be misinterpreted or misunderstood during a business conversation with someone from another culture. Next to each example, suggest other words you might use to convey the same message. Do the alternatives mean *exactly* the same as the original slang or idiom?

12. **Intercultural Communication: Studying Cultures** Choose a specific country, such as India, Portugal, Bolivia, Thailand, or Nigeria, with which you are not familiar. Research the culture and write a brief summary of what a U.S. businessperson would need to know about concepts of personal space and rules of social behavior in order to conduct business successfully in that country.

13. **Multicultural Workforce: Bridging Differences** Differences in gender, age, and physical abilities contribute to the diversity of today's workforce. Working with a classmate, role-play a conversation in which

    a. A woman is being interviewed for a job by a male personnel manager

    b. An older person is being interviewed for a job by a younger personnel manager

    c. A person using a wheelchair is being interviewed for a job by a person who can walk

    How did differences between the applicant and the interviewer shape the communication? What can you do to improve communication in such situations?

14. **Intercultural Sensitivity: Understanding Attitudes** You are assistant to the director of marketing for a telecommunications firm based in Germany. You're accompanying your boss to negotiate with an official in Guangzhou, China, who's in charge of selecting a new telephone system for the city. Your boss insists that the specifications be spelled out in detail in the contract. However, the Chinese negotiator argues that in developing a long-term business relationship, such minor details are unimportant.

    Your task: What can you suggest that your boss do or say to break this intercultural deadlock and obtain the contract so that both parties are comfortable? Outline your ideas in a brief e-mail message to your instructor.

Expand Your Knowledge

Exploring the Best of the Web

Check Out These Free Resources   The Business Writer's Free Library, www.mapnp.org/library/commskls/cmm_writ.htm, is a terrific resource for business communication material. Categories of information include basic composition skills, basic writing skills, correspondence, reference material, and general resources and advice. Log on and read about the most common errors in English, become a word detective, ask Miss Grammar, review samples of common forms of correspondence, fine-tune your interpersonal skills, join a newsgroup, and more. Follow the links and improve your effectiveness as a business communicator.

Exercises

1. What are some strategies for communicating with an uncooperative audience?
2. What is the value of diversity in the workplace?
3. Why is bad etiquette bad for business?

Exploring the Web on Your Own

Review these chapter-related websites on your own to learn more about achieving communication success in the workplace.

1. Netiquette Home Page, www.albion.com/netiquette/index.html. Learn the do's and don'ts of online communication at this site, then take the Netiquette Quiz.

2. Learn how to improve your cultural savvy and gain an international competitive advantage. Visit Cultural Savvy, www.culturalsavvy.com, and read the country reports and cultural tips. Follow the site's links to interviews, profiles, articles, books, and more.

3. 101 Best Web Sites for Writers, at www.writersdigest.com, points the way to great search engines and general reference sites. While aimed primarily at professional writers, the list has something to offer all business communicators. The site list is updated every year, so be sure to select the current year's list.

Learn Interactively

Interactive Study Guide

Visit www.prenhall.com/bovee, then locate your book and click on its Companion Website link. Select Chapter 1 to take advantage of the interactive "Chapter Quiz" to test your knowledge of chapter concepts. Receive instant feedback on whether you need additional studying. Also, visit the "Study Hall," where you'll find an abundance of valuable resources that will help you succeed in this course.

Peak Performance Grammar and Mechanics

If your instructor has required the use of "Peak Performance Grammar and Mechanics," either in your online course, through the access-code protected portion of the Companion Website, or on CD, you can improve your skill with nouns and pronouns by using the "Peak Performance Grammar and Mechanics" module. Click on "Grammar Basics," and then click "Nouns and Pronouns." Take the Pretest to determine whether you have any weak areas. Then review those areas in the Refresher Course. Take the Follow-Up Test to check your grasp of nouns and pronouns. For an extra challenge or advanced practice, take the Advanced Test. Finally, for additional reinforcement in nouns, go to the "Improve Your Grammar, Mechanics, and Usage" section that follows, and complete the "Level I: Self-Assessment" exercises.

Improve Your Grammar, Mechanics, and Usage

Level 1: Self-Assessment—Nouns

Use the following self-assessment exercises to improve your knowledge of and power over English grammar, mechanics, and usage. Review all of Section 1.1 in the Handbook of

Grammar, Mechanics, and Usage that appears at the end of this book. Answers to these exercises appear on p. AK-1.

In items 1–5, underline the common nouns and circle the proper nouns.

1. Give the balance sheet to Melissa.

2. We'd like to order 50 more satchels for Craigmont Stores, and 3 each for the other stores on our list.

3. Tarnower Corporation donates a portion of its profits to charity every year.

4. Which aluminum bolts are packaged?

5. Please send the Joneses a dozen of the following: stopwatches, canteens, headbands, and wristbands.

In items 6–10, underline the subjects and circle the objects.

6. The technician has already repaired the machine for the client.

7. An attorney will talk to the group about incorporation.

8. After her vacation, the buyer prepared a third-quarter budget.

9. The new flat monitors are serving our department very well.

10. Accuracy overrides speed in importance.

In items 11–15, underline inappropriate noun plurals and possessives, and write the correct form in the space provided.

11. _____ Make sure that all copys include the new addresses.

12. _____ Ask Jennings to collect all employee's donations for the Red Cross drive.

13. _____ Charlie now has two son-in-laws to help him with his two online business's.

14. _____ Avoid using too many parenthesises when writing your reports.

15. _____ Follow President Nesses rules about what constitutes a weeks work.

Level 2: Workplace Applications

The following items contain numerous errors in grammar, capitalization, punctuation, abbreviation, number style, word division, and vocabulary. Rewrite each sentence in the space provided, correcting all errors. Write *C* in the space after any sentence that is already correct.

1. If a broken down unproductive guy like Carl can get a raise; why can't a take charge guy like me get one?

2. Visit our website and sign up for "On Your Toes", our free newsletter that keeps you informed of promotions, discounts and about Internet-only specials.

3. As of March, 2007, the Board of Directors have 9 members including: three women, one African-American, and one American of Hispanic descent.

4. As one of the nearly 3,000,000 New York Life policyholders eligible to vote, we urge you to approve the new investment advisory agreement.

5. Gerrald Higgins, vice president for marketing, told us reporters that Capital One provides financial services to one-fourth of homes in the United States.

6. Our Customer Relations associates work with people everyday to answer questions, provide assistance, and helping solve problems.

7. If anyone breaches the lease, its likely that the landlord will file legal action against them to collect on the remainder of they're lease.

8. A IRA is one of the most common plans for the self-employed because of it's ease of setting up and administering.

9. My advise to you is, to put you're mission statement on your web cite.

10. According to Karen Smiths' report small-business owners do'nt recognize the full effect that layoffs and terminations are liable to have on the motivation of surviving employees'.

11. To exacerbate the processing of your US tax return, use the mailing label and bar coded envelope that comes with your tax package.

12. The NASE have implemented a exciting array of programs that make it more easy for legislative opinions and concerns to be voiced by you.

13. Keep in mind the old saying "When we laugh the world laugh with us, when you cry you cry alone."

14. Albert Edmunds and me are Owners of the real estate firm of Edmunds & Cale, which have recently opened a new office in San Diego co.

15. The memo inferred that the economic downturn will have a greater affect on the company's bottom line then we previously assumed, this was the worse news we could of gotten.

Level 3: Document Critique

The following document contains errors in grammar, capitalization, punctuation, abbreviation, number style, word division, and vocabulary. Correct all errors using standard proofreading marks (see Appendix C).

Memo

TO: All Employees

FROM: R. Smith, Personnel Director

DATE: December 28, 2007

SUBJECT: Time Cards

After reviewing our Current Method of keeping track of employee hours; we have concluded that time cards leave a lot to be desired. So starting Monday, we have a new system, a time clock. You just have to punch in and punch out; whenever you will come and go from your work area's.

The new system may take a little while to get used to, but should be helpful to those of us who are making a new years resolution to be more punctual.

Happy New Year to all!

eg

2

Communicating in Teams and Mastering Listening and Nonverbal Communication Skills

Learning Objectives

After studying this chapter, you will be able to

1 Highlight the advantages and disadvantages of working in teams

2 Discuss the role of etiquette in team settings, both in the workplace and in social settings

3 Identify four planning steps that increase meeting productivity

4 Describe how meeting technologies can help participants communicate more successfully

5 Describe the listening process and explain how good listeners overcome barriers at each stage of the process

6 Explain the importance of nonverbal communication and identify six major categories of nonverbal expression

When Kip Tindell and his partner Garrett Boone set out to create the "best retail store in the United States," they built teamwork and team communication into the very fabric of The Container Store's culture. Tindell and Boone believe so strongly in sharing information that every store location begins and ends the day with a team meeting known as a "huddle." Similar to a huddle in football, it helps to give everyone a common purpose: set goals, share information, boost morale, and bond as a team. The Container Store has rapidly become one of the most respected retail chains in the country, and the commitment to teamwork and open communication is a vital part of this ongoing success.[1]

Improving Your Performance in Teams

No matter where your career takes you, you will surely spend a good deal of your time working in teams and other group situations that will put your communication skills to the test. A **team** is a unit of two or more people who share a mission and the responsibility for working to achieve their goal.[2] Whether the task is to write a report, create a product, or solve a problem, you and your fellow team members must be able to communicate effectively with one another and with people outside your team. The first step toward that goal is understanding the advantages and disadvantages of working in teams.

Advantages and Disadvantages of Teams

Teams are a popular form of organization in business today, and when they are successful, they improve productivity, creativity, employee involvement, and even job security.[3] In fact, many companies now base pay raises and promotions on an employee's effectiveness as a team player.

Good team collaborators are willing to exchange information, examine issues, and work through conflicts that arise. They trust each other, working toward the greater good of the team and organization rather than focusing on personal agendas.[4] The most effective teams have a clear sense of purpose, communicate openly and honestly, reach decisions by consensus, think creatively, and know how to resolve conflict.[5] Learning these team skills takes time and practice, so U.S. companies now teach teamwork more frequently than any other aspect of business.[6]

A successful team can provide a number of advantages:[7]

- **Increased information and knowledge.** By pooling the resources of several individuals, teams have access to more information in the decision-making process.
- **Increased diversity of views.** Team members bring a variety of perspectives to the decision-making process.
- **Increased acceptance of a solution.** Those who participate in making a decision are more likely to support the decision enthusiastically and encourage others to accept it.
- **Higher performance levels.** Working in teams can unleash new amounts of creativity and energy in workers who share a sense of purpose and mutual accountability.

Although teamwork has many advantages, it also has a number of potential disadvantages. Unsuccessful teamwork can waste time and money, generate lower-quality work, and frustrate both managers and employees alike. One of the most common reasons for such failures is poor communication, particularly when teams have to operate across cultures, countries, and time zones.[8] Teams need to be aware of and work to counter the following potential disadvantages:

- **Groupthink.** Like all social structures, business teams can generate tremendous pressures to conform with accepted norms of behavior. **Groupthink** occurs when these peer pressures cause team members to withhold contrary or unpopular opinions. The result can be decisions that are worse than ones the team members might've made individually.
- **Hidden agendas.** Some team members may have a **hidden agenda**—private motives that affect the group's interaction. Each person's hidden agenda can detract from the team's effectiveness.
- **Free riders.** Some team members may be **free riders**—those who don't contribute their fair share to the group's activities.
- **Cost.** Still another drawback to teamwork is the cost of coordinating group activities, such as aligning schedules, arranging meetings, and coordinating individual parts of a project.

Etiquette in Team Settings

As Chapter 1 pointed out, etiquette is now widely considered to be an important business skill, and it is particularly important in team settings because the ability to get along with teammates is vital to everyone's success. Nobody wants to spend weeks or months working with someone who is rude to colleagues or an embarrassment to the company. Here are some key etiquette points to remember when you're in the workplace and out in public. None of the following material is unique to team settings, of course; it's good advice for all your business efforts.

Team members have a shared mission and are collectively responsible for the team's performance.

Effective teams
- Understand their purpose
- Communicate openly and honestly
- Build consensus
- Think creatively
- Stay focused
- Resolve conflict

Teams are unproductive when
- Members feel pressured to conform and agree to unwise decisions
- Group members' personal motives interfere with the group's efforts
- Some team members don't contribute
- The cost of coordinating a team runs high

In the Workplace

Knowing how to behave and how to interact with people in business will help you appear polished, professional, and confident.[9] Understanding business etiquette also helps you put others at ease so that they are comfortable enough to do business with you.[10] Both of these factors—the impression you make on others and your ability to help others feel comfortable—will be major contributors to your career success.

For instance, rightly or wrongly, your personal appearance often has considerable impact on your career success. Pay attention to the style of dress where you work and adjust your style to match, particularly if you work with people from diverse backgrounds and age groups. If you're not sure, dress moderately and simply—earn a reputation for what you can *do*, not for what you can wear. Naturally, you'll need to adapt any wardrobe advice for the specific job, company, and industry because expectations vary widely. The financial industries tend to be more formal than high technology, for instance, and sales and executive positions usually come with more formal expectations than staff positions in engineering or manufacturing. Observe others carefully, and don't be afraid to ask for advice if you're not sure.

In addition to your clothing, *grooming* affects the impression you give others in the workplace. Pay close attention to cleanliness and avoid using products with powerful scents, such as perfumed soaps, colognes, shampoos, and aftershave lotions (many people are bothered by these products, and some are allergic to them). Shampoo frequently, keep hands and nails neatly manicured, use mouthwash and deodorant, and make regular trips to a hair stylist or barber.[11] Some companies have specific policies regarding hairstyles, which you may be expected to follow.[12]

Something as simple as your smile also affects the way people do business with you. When you smile, do so genuinely. A fake smile is obvious because the timing is frequently off and the expression fails to involve all the facial muscles that a genuine smile would.[13] Repeated false smiling may earn you the reputation of being a phony. However, certain occasions require smiling, such as when you're introduced to someone, when you give or receive a compliment, and when you applaud someone's efforts.[14]

Much of your interaction with team members, other colleagues, and customers will take place over the telephone, and phone skills will have a definite impact on your career success. Because phone calls lack the visual richness of face-to-face conversations, you have to rely on your attitude and tone of voice to convey confidence and professionalism. When you place calls, plan them as carefully as you would plan a meeting. Be ready with relevant questions or information, and schedule calls for times that are convenient for the other party. For example, you usually want to avoid calling first thing in the morning, when many people like to answer e-mail and plan the day. Likewise, avoid calling near the end of the day, when most people are trying to wrap up business and leave the office. Table 2.1 summarizes helpful tips for placing and receiving phone calls in a confident, professional manner.

If you're accustomed to using your cell phone anywhere and everywhere, get ready to change your habits; many companies are putting restrictions on their use. Cell phones are causing so much disruption in the workplace that some senior executives now ban their use in meetings, even going so far as to fine employees whose phones ring during meetings. (The fines are typically donated to charity or used to buy team lunches.) As Ian Campbell of Nucleus Research puts it, "A cell phone has gone from a symbol of status to a device of scorn." Moreover, this problem of wireless interruptions is only going to get worse, with the proliferation of personal digital assistants (PDAs), laptop computers, and other devices with wireless access.[15]

In Social Settings

From business lunches to industry conferences, you represent your team and your company when you're out in public, so make sure your appearance and actions are appropriate to the situation. First impressions last a long time, so get to know the customs of the culture when you meet new people. In North America, a firm handshake is expected when two people meet, whereas in Japan a respectful bow of the head is more appropriate. If

Table 2.1	Quick Tips for Improving Your Phone Skills		
General Tips	**Placing Calls**	**Receiving Calls**	**Using Voice Mail**
Use frequent verbal responses that show you're listening ("Oh yes," "I see," "That's right").	Be ready before you call so that you don't waste the other person's time.	Answer promptly and with a smile so that you sound friendly and positive.	When recording your own outgoing message, make it brief and professional.
Increase your volume just slightly to convey your confidence.	Minimize distractions and avoid making noise that could annoy the other party.	Identify yourself and your company (some companies have specific instructions for what to say when you answer).	If you can, record temporary greetings on days when you are unavailable all day so that callers will know you're gone for the day.
Don't speak in a monotone; vary your pitch and inflections so people know you're interested.	Identify yourself and your organization, briefly describe why you're calling, and verify that you've called at a good time.	Establish the needs of your caller by asking. "How may I help you?" If you know the caller's name, use it.	Check your voice-mail messages regularly and return all necessary calls within 24 hours.
Slow down when conversing with people whose native language isn't the same as yours.	Don't take up too much time. Speak quickly and clearly, and get right to the point of the call.	If you can, answer questions promptly and efficiently; If you can't help, tell them what you can do for them.	Leave simple, clear messages with your name, number, purpose for calling, and times when you can be reached.
Stay focused on the call throughout; others can easily tell when you're not paying attention.	Close in a friendly, positive manner and double-check all vital information such as meeting times and dates.	If you must forward a call or put someone on hold, explain what you are doing first.	State your name and telephone number slowly so that the other person can easily write them down; repeat both if the other person doesn't know you.
		If you forward a call to someone else, try to speak with that person first to verify that he or she is available and to introduce the caller.	Be careful what you say; most voice-mail systems allow users to forward messages to anyone else in the system.
		If you take a message for someone else, be complete and accurate, including the caller's name, number, and organization.	Replay your message before leaving the system to make sure it is clear and complete.

you are expected to shake hands, be aware that the passive "dead fish" handshake creates an extremely negative impression. Also, women and men should shake hands on equal terms; the days of a woman offering just her fingertips are long gone in the business world. If you are physically able, always stand when shaking someone's hand.

When introducing yourself, include a brief description of your role in the company. When introducing two other people, speak both their first and last names clearly, then try to offer some information (perhaps a shared professional interest) to help these two people ease into a conversation.[16] Generally speaking, the lower-ranking person is introduced to the senior-ranking person, without regard to gender.[17] When you're introduced to someone, repeat the person's name as soon as possible. Doing so is both a compliment and a good way to remember it.[18]

Business is often conducted over meals, and knowing the basics of dining etiquette will make you more effective in these situations.[19] Choose foods that are easy to eat; you may not want to wrestle with a lobster while trying to carry on a conversation. If a drink is appropriate, save it for the end of the meal so that you can stay clear and composed. Leave business papers under your chair until entrée plates have been removed; the business aspect of the meal doesn't usually begin until then.

Misuse of mobile phones in restaurants and other public places is a common etiquette blunder. When you use your cell phone in public, you send the message that people around you aren't as important as your call and that you don't respect your caller's privacy.[20] Older colleagues who grew up without cell phones may find them particularly offensive in

Poor cell phone etiquette is a common source of complaints in both the workplace and social settings.

social settings. If it's not a matter of life and death—literally—wait until you're back in the office or away from your colleagues.

Business meals are a forum for business, period. Don't get on your soapbox about politics, religion, or any other topic likely to stir up emotions. Some light chatter and questions about personal interests is fine, but don't get too personal. Don't complain about work, avoid profanity, and be careful with humor—a joke that might entertain some people could offend others. In general, learn from coworkers who are respected by customers and colleagues. You'll find that they choose topics carefully, listen with respect, and leave a positive impression with everyone they meet.

Making Your Meetings More Productive

Meetings are a primary communication venue for today's businesses, whether held in formal conference rooms, an informal setting such as The Container Store's daily huddles, or on the Internet as *virtual meetings*. Well-run meetings can help you solve problems, develop ideas, and identify opportunities. Much of your workplace communication will occur in small-group meetings, so to a large degree, your ability to contribute to the company and to be recognized for those contributions will depend on your meeting participation skills.

Unfortunately, many meetings are unproductive. In one study, senior and middle managers reported that only 56 percent of their meetings were actually productive and that 25 percent of them could have been replaced by a phone call or a memo.[21] The three most frequently reported problems with meetings are getting off the subject, not having an agenda, and running too long.[22] Given such demoralizing statistics and the high expense of meetings—which can cost hundreds or thousands of dollars an hour in lost work time and travel expenses—it's no wonder that companies are focusing on making their meetings more productive. You'll help your company make better use of meetings by preparing carefully, conducting meetings efficiently, and using meeting technologies wisely.

Preparing for Meetings

Careful preparation helps you avoid the two biggest meeting mistakes: (1) holding a meeting when a memo or other message would do the job or (2) holding a meeting without a specific goal in mind. Before you even begin preparing for a meeting, make sure it's truly necessary. Once you're sure, proceed with four preparation tasks:

- **Identify your purpose.** Although many meetings combine purposes, most focus on one of two types: *Informational meetings* involve sharing information and perhaps coordinating action. *Decision-making meetings* involve persuasion, analysis, and problem solving. They often include a brainstorming session, followed by a debate on the alternatives. Moreover, decision-making meetings require that each participant be aware of the nature of the problem and the criteria for its solution. Whatever your purpose, make sure it is clear and clearly communicated to all participants.

- **Select participants for the meeting.** With a clear purpose in mind, it's easier to identify the right participants. If the session is purely informational and one person will do most of the talking, you can invite a large group. *Webcasts* (Chapter 12) are an increasingly popular way to reach large or geographically widespread audiences used for such meetings. For problem-solving and decision-making meetings, invite only those people who are in a direct position to help the meeting reach its objective. The more participants, the more comments and confusion you're likely to get, and the longer the meeting will take. However, make sure you invite all the key decision-makers, or your meeting will fail to satisfy its purpose.

- **Choose the time and the facility.** For working sessions, morning meetings are usually more productive than afternoon sessions. Also, consider the seating arrangements: Are

Much of the communication you'll participate in will take place in meetings.

A single poorly run meeting can waste thousands of dollars.

To ensure a successful meeting, decide on your purpose ahead of time, select the right participants, choose the time and facility carefully, and set a clear agenda.

FIGURE 2.1 Typical Meeting Agenda

Agenda formats vary widely, depending on the complexity of the meeting and the presentation technologies that will be used. One good approach is to send out a detailed planning agenda ahead of time, then use a simpler display agenda such as this to guide the meeting.

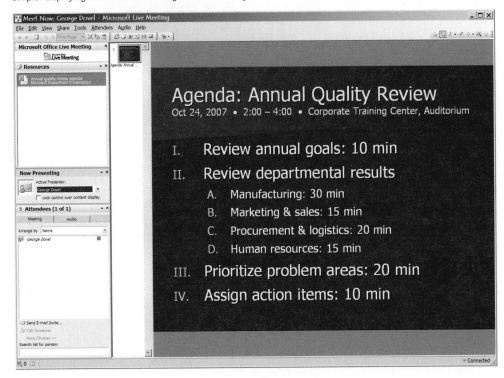

rows of chairs suitable, or do you need a conference table or some other setting? Plus, give some attention to details such as room temperature, lighting, ventilation, acoustics, and refreshments; any of these seemingly minor details can make or break a meeting.

■ **Set the agenda.** The success of any meeting depends on the preparation of the participants. People who will be presenting information need to know what is expected of them, nonpresenters need to know what will be presented so they can prepare questions, and everyone needs to know how long the meeting will last. In addition, the agenda is an important tool for guiding the progress of the meeting (see Figure 2.1). A productive agenda answers three key questions: (1) What do we need to do in this meeting to accomplish our goals? (2) What issues will be of greatest importance to all participants? (3) What information must be available in order to discuss these issues?[23] In addition to improving productivity, this level of agenda detail shows respect for participants and the other demands on their time.

Leading and Participating in Meetings

Everyone in a meeting shares the responsibility for keeping the meeting productive and making it successful. If you're the designated leader of a meeting, however, you have an extra degree of responsibility and accountability. To ensure productive meetings, be sure to do the following:

Everyone shares the responsibility for successful meetings.

■ **Keep the meeting on track.** A good meeting draws out the best ideas and information the group has to offer. Good leaders occasionally guide, mediate, probe, stimulate, and summarize, but mostly they encourage participants to share. Experience will help you recognize when to push the group forward and when to step back and let people talk. If the meeting lags, you'll need to ask questions to encourage participation. Conversely, there will be times when you have no choice but to cut off discussion in order to stay on schedule.

- **Follow agreed-upon rules.** Business meetings run the gamut from informal to extremely formal, complete with detailed rules for speaking, proposing new items to discuss, voting on proposals, and so on. The larger the meeting, the more formal you'll need to be to maintain order. Formal meetings use **parliamentary procedure**, a time-tested method for planning and running effective meetings. The best-known guide to this procedure is *Roberts Rules of Order*. Whatever system of rules you employ, make sure everyone is clear about the expectations.

- **Encourage participation.** As the meeting gets under way, you'll discover that some participants are too quiet and others are too talkative. The quiet participants might be shy, they might be expressing disagreement or resistance, or they might be answering e-mail or instant messages on their laptop computers. Draw them out by asking for their input on issues that particularly pertain to them. For the overly talkative, simply say that time is limited and others need to be heard from.

- **Participate actively.** If you're a meeting participant, try to contribute to both the subject of the meeting and the smooth interaction of the participants. Use your listening skills and powers of observation to size up the interpersonal dynamics of the people, then adapt your behavior to help the group achieve its goals. Speak up if you have something useful to say, but don't monopolize the discussion.

- **Close effectively.** At the conclusion of the meeting, verify that the objectives have been met; if not, arrange for follow-up work as needed. Either summarize the general conclusion of the discussion or list the actions to be taken. Make sure all participants agree on the outcome and give people a chance to clear up any misunderstandings.

For formal meetings, it's good practice to appoint one person to record the *minutes*, a summary of the important information presented and the decisions made during a meeting. In smaller or informal meetings, attendees often make their own notes on their copies of the agenda. In either case, a clear record of the decisions made and the people responsible for follow-up action is essential.

Some companies specify formats for minutes; otherwise you can create whatever format works for the medium you've chosen (see Figure 2.2). Key elements include a list of those present and a list of those who were invited but didn't attend, followed by the times the meeting started and ended, all major decisions reached at the meeting, all assignments of tasks to meeting participants, and all subjects that were deferred to a later meeting. In addition, the minutes objectively summarize important discussions, noting the names of those who contributed major points. Outlines, subheadings, and lists help organize the minutes, and additional documentation (such as tables or charts submitted by meeting participants) are noted in the minutes and attached. Whichever format and medium you use, make sure that responsibilities are clear so that all issues raised at the meeting will be addressed.

Document Makeover

Improve This E-Mail Message

To practice correcting drafts of actual documents, visit your online course or the access-code-protected portion of the Companion Website. Click "Document Makeovers," then click Chapter 2. You will find an e-mail message that contains problems and errors relating to what you've learned in this chapter about communicating in teams. Use the "Final Draft" decision tool to create an improved version of this e-mail message. Check the message for clarity, relevance of topics to meeting participants, and a collaborative tone.

FIGURE 2.2   Typical Meeting Minutes

Intranet and blog postings are a common way to distribute meeting minutes. The specific format of the minutes is less important than making sure you record all the key information, particularly regarding responsibilities that were assigned during the meeting.

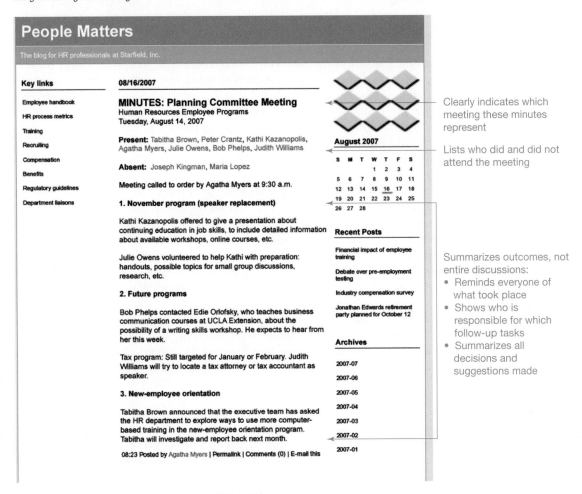

Using Meeting Technologies

In recent years, the high cost of travel, loss of valuable work time, increased security concerns, and growing reliance on global workforces and partnerships have all stimulated a number of advances in meeting technologies. You can expect to use a variety of meeting-related technologies throughout your career. These technologies have spurred the emergence of **virtual teams**, whose members work in different locations and interact electronically through **virtual meetings**. At times, technology replaces meetings entirely, such as when team members use e-mail or instant messaging to interact over the course of several hours or days, rather than meeting online or over the phone at a specific time. One of the newest virtual tools is *online brainstorming*, in which companies conduct "idea campaigns" to generate new ideas from people across the organization. For example, the chemical manufacturing division of W.R. Grace has generated more than 70 new product ideas and more than 60 process improvements through online brainstorming.[24] Another new twist is *wiki* (the Hawaiian word for "quick"), a website technology that allows team members to revise the content of a website as they get new ideas. The community-written online encyclopedia Wikipedia (www.wikipedia.org) is a good example of such collaborative writing on a global scale.

As with most new technologies, electronic meeting tools are evolving rapidly, and the lines separating these tools have become blurred. For example, instant messaging and

Virtual meeting technologies connect people spread around the country or around the world.

videoconferencing are both stand-alone capabilities; both are also common features in **groupware**, an umbrella term for systems that let people communicate, share files, present materials, and work on documents simultaneously.

Shared workspaces are "virtual offices" that give everyone on a team access to the same set of resources and information: databases, calendars, project plans, pertinent IM and e-mail exchanges, shared reference materials, and team-created documents. Workspaces such as Documentum eRoom, Microsoft SharePoint, and IBM Lotus Team Workspace create a seamless environment for collaboration. Such workspaces make it easy for geographically dispersed team members to access shared files anytime, anywhere.

Most systems also have built-in intelligence to control which team members can read, edit, and save specific files. *Revision control* goes one step further: It allows only one person at a time to check out a given file or document and records all the changes that person makes. This feature prevents two people from independently editing the same report at the same time, thus avoiding the messy situation in which a team would end up with two versions of the same document.[25]

Virtual meeting technologies cover a wide range of tools that let team members in different locations interact at the same time without the hassle, risk, and cost of travel.[26] IM chat sessions and telephone conference calls are the simplest forms of virtual meetings. **Videoconferencing** combines audio communication with live video, letting team members see each other, demonstrate products, and transmit other visual information. Videoconferencing is available in both *room systems*, specialized conference room facilities with large-screen displays, and *desktop systems*, which typically use a webcam attached to each participant's computer.

The most sophisticated **web-based meeting systems** combine the best of IM, shared workspaces, and videoconferencing with other tools such as *virtual whiteboards* that let teams collaborate in real time (see Figure 2.3). Attendees can log on from a desktop or laptop PC, a PDA, or even a web-enabled cell phone from almost anywhere in the world.

Shared workspaces give team members instant access to shared resources and information.

Virtual meetings range from videoconferencing to web-based systems.

FIGURE 2.3   Web-Based Meetings

You can expect to participate in many online meetings during your career. Web-based meeting systems offer powerful tools for communication, but you'll need to be proficient at using these tools to be effective during online meetings.

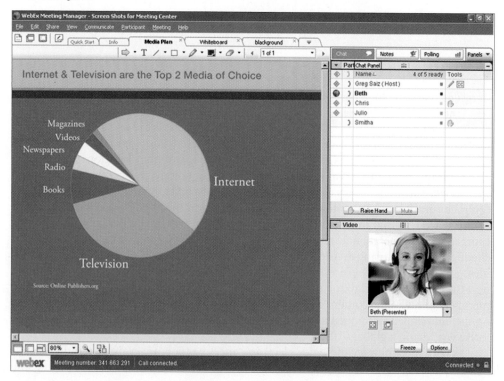

Improving Your Listening Skills

You probably know some people who are good listeners and others who are poor listeners, and the difference is the approach they take to listening. No matter how good you are at other aspects of your job, your career prospects will be limited if you don't have strong listening skills. In fact, some 80 percent of top executives say that listening is the most important skill needed to get things done in the workplace.[27]

Effective listening strengthens organizational relationships, alerts the organization to opportunities for innovation, and allows the organization to manage growing diversity both in the workforce and in the customers it serves.[28] Companies whose employees and managers listen effectively stay informed, up-to-date, and out of trouble. Conversely, poor listening skills can cost companies millions of dollars a year as a result of lost opportunities, legal mistakes, and other errors. Effective listening is also vital to the process of building trust between organizations and between individuals.[29]

If you want to succeed in business, learn how to listen effectively.

Recognizing Various Types of Listening

Effective listeners adapt their listening approaches to different situations. The primary goal of **content listening** is to understand and retain the information in the speaker's message. For instance, Henry Nordhoff, CEO of the San Diego–based pharmaceutical company Gen-Probe, has a business background and relies on content listening to gather technical information from the scientists whose work he oversees.[30] When you're listening for content, ask questions to clarify the material, but don't argue or judge. Try to overlook the speaker's style and any limitations in the presentation; just focus on the information.[31] In contrast, the goal of **critical listening** is to understand and evaluate the meaning of the speaker's message on several levels: the logic of the argument, the strength of the evidence, the validity of the conclusions, the implications of the message for you and your organization, the speaker's intentions and motives, and the omission of any important or relevant points. If you're skeptical, ask questions to explore the speaker's point of view and credibility. Be on the lookout for bias that might color the way the information is presented, and be careful to separate opinions from facts.[32]

The goal of **empathic listening** is to understand the speaker's feelings, needs, and wants so that you can appreciate his or her point of view, regardless of whether you share that perspective. By listening in an empathic way, you help the individual vent emotions that prevent a calm, clear-headed approach to the subject. Avoid the temptation to jump in with advice unless the person specifically asks for it; don't judge the speaker's feelings, and don't try to tell people they shouldn't feel this or that emotion. Instead, let the speaker know that you appreciate his or her feelings and understand the situation. Once you establish that connection, you can then help the speaker move on to search for a solution.[33]

To be a good listener, adapt the way you listen to suit each situation.

Understanding the Listening Process

No matter which mode of listening you use in a given conversation, it's important to recognize that listening is a far more complex process than most people think. As a consequence, most of us aren't very good at it. Given such complexity, it's no wonder most of us listen at or below a 25 percent efficiency rate, remember only about half of what's said during a 10-minute conversation, and forget half of that within 48 hours.[34] Furthermore, when questioned about material we've just heard, we are likely to get the facts mixed up.[35]

Why is such a seemingly simple activity so difficult? The answer lies in the complexity of the process. To listen effectively, you need to successfully complete five separate steps:[36]

Listening involves five steps: receiving, interpreting, remembering, evaluating, and responding.

- **Receiving:** You start by physically hearing the message and acknowledging it.
- **Interpreting:** Your next step is to assign meaning to sounds, which you do according to your own values, beliefs, ideas, expectations, roles, needs, and personal history.

Table 2.2 Distinguishing Effective Listening from Ineffective Listening	
Effective Listeners	**Ineffective Listeners**
• Listen actively	• Listen passively
• Take careful and complete notes	• Take no notes or ineffective notes
• Make frequent eye contact with the speaker (depends on culture to some extent)	• Make little or no eye contact
• Stay focused on the speaker and the content	• Allow their minds to wander, are easily distracted
• Mentally paraphrase key points to maintain attention level and ensure comprehension	• Fail to paraphrase
• Adjust listening style to the situation	• Listen with the same style, regardless of the situation
• Give the speaker nonverbal cues (such as nodding to show agreement or raising eyebrows to show surprise or skepticism)	• Fail to give the speaker nonverbal feedback
• Save questions or points of disagreement until an appropriate time	• Interrupt whenever they disagree or don't understand
• Overlook stylistic differences and focus on the speaker's message	• Are distracted by or unduly influenced by stylistic differences; are judgmental
• Make distinctions between main points and supporting details	• Unable to distinguish main points from details
• Look for opportunities to learn	• Assume they already know everything that's important to know

■ **Remembering:** Before you can act on the information, you need to store it for future processing.

■ **Evaluating:** With the speaker's message captured, you next step is to evaluate it by applying critical thinking skills.

■ **Responding:** After you've evaluated the speaker's message, you then react based on what you've heard and understood.

As you can see in Table 2.2, good listeners take a variety of steps to improve their effectiveness at every stage of the listening process.

Overcoming Barriers to Effective Listening

Good listeners actively try to overcome the barriers to successful listening.

In today's hectic business environment, good listeners look for ways to overcome the many potential barriers to successful listening. Some factors you can't control, such as conference room acoustics, poor cell phone reception, background music, and so on. However, you can certainly control other factors, such as not interrupting speakers and not creating distractions that make it hard for others to pay attention. If you have questions for a speaker, wait until he or she has finished speaking. And don't think that you're not interrupting just because you're not talking. Such actions as rustling papers or checking your watch can interrupt a speaker and lead to communication breakdowns.

Selective listening is one of the most common barriers to effective listening. If your mind wanders, you often stay tuned out until you hear a word or phrase that gets your attention once more. But by that time, you're unable to recall what the speaker *actually* said; instead, you remember what you *think* the speaker probably said.[37]

One reason listeners' minds tend to wander is that people think faster than they speak. Most people speak at about 120 to 150 words per minute. However, humans can process audio information at up to 500 words per minute or more.[38] In other words, your brain has a lot of free time whenever you're listening, and if left unsupervised, it will find a thousand other things to think about. Make a conscious effort to focus on the speaker, and use the extra time to analyze what you hear, prepare questions you might need to ask, and engage in other relevant thinking.

Your mind can process information much faster than most speakers talk, which makes you vulnerable to distractions.

Another common barrier to successful interpretation is prejudgment—making up your mind before truly hearing what another person has to say. Similarly, *selective perception* leads listeners to mold a message to fit what they already believe about a given subject. If you believe you've done an excellent job writing a report but the people reading it try to give you negative feedback, you may not even "hear" what they're saying. Listening with an open mind isn't always easy, but it's the only way to make sure you really hear what people are telling you. Even when your intentions are the best, you can still misinterpret incoming messages if you and the speaker don't share enough language or experience. Lack of common ground is why misinterpretation is so frequent between speakers of different native languages, even when they're trying to speak the same language. When listening to a speaker whose native language or life experience is different from yours, try to paraphrase that person's ideas. Give the speaker a chance to confirm what you think you heard or to correct any misinterpretation.

Selective perception distorts incoming messages by shaping the information to fit what you already believe about the subject.

After you've successfully avoided all these barriers, you then need to retain the information in order to act on it. One simple rule: Don't count on your memory if the information is crucial. Record it, write it down, or capture it in some other physical way. However, if you do need to memorize something, you can capture information in *short-term memory* for a few seconds or a few minutes by repeating it to yourself (silently, if need be), by organizing it into patterns (perhaps in alphabetical order or as steps in a process), and by breaking a long list of items into several shorter lists. To store information in *long-term memory*, four techniques can help:

When information is crucial, don't count on your memory.

- Associate new information with something closely related (such as the restaurant in which you met a new client).
- Categorize the new information into logical groups (such as alphabetizing the names of products you're trying to remember).
- Visualize words and ideas as pictures.
- Create *mnemonics* such as acronyms or rhymes.

Note that all four techniques have an important factor in common, and that's action: You have to *do* something to make the information stick.

Improving Your Nonverbal Communication Skills

Nonverbal communication is the process of sending and receiving information, both intentionally and unintentionally, without using written or spoken language. Nonverbal signals play two important roles in communication. The first is complementing verbal language. Nonverbal signals can strengthen a verbal message (when nonverbal signals match words), weaken a verbal message (when nonverbal signals don't match words), or replace words entirely.

Nonverbal communication supplements spoken language.

The second role for nonverbal signals is revealing truth. People find it much harder to deceive with nonverbal signals. You might tell a client that the project is coming along nicely, but your forced smile and nervous glances send a different message. In fact, nonverbal communication often conveys more to listeners than the words you speak—particularly when they're trying to decide how you really feel about a situation or when they're trying to judge your credibility and aptitude for leadership.[39] However, even the power of nonverbal cues is not infallible when it comes to detecting truth. In one recent study, most people failed to detect dishonest speech roughly half the time; only a tiny fraction of the population are able to consistently detect when people are lying to them.[40]

Nonverbal clues help you ascertain the truth of spoken information.

FIGURE 2.4   Avoiding Nonverbal Mishaps

These few examples demonstrate the complexities of nonverbal communication across cultures. Be sure to learn the basic nonverbal signals of any culture in which you need to communicate.

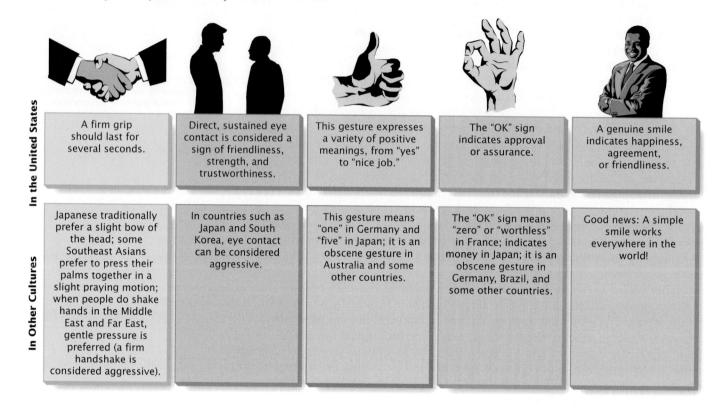

In the United States	A firm grip should last for several seconds.	Direct, sustained eye contact is considered a sign of friendliness, strength, and trustworthiness.	This gesture expresses a variety of positive meanings, from "yes" to "nice job."	The "OK" sign indicates approval or assurance.	A genuine smile indicates happiness, agreement, or friendliness.
In Other Cultures	Japanese traditionally prefer a slight bow of the head; some Southeast Asians prefer to press their palms together in a slight praying motion; when people do shake hands in the Middle East and Far East, gentle pressure is preferred (a firm handshake is considered aggressive).	In countries such as Japan and South Korea, eye contact can be considered aggressive.	This gesture means "one" in Germany and "five" in Japan; it is an obscene gesture in Australia and some other countries.	The "OK" sign means "zero" or "worthless" in France; indicates money in Japan; it is an obscene gesture in Germany, Brazil, and some other countries.	Good news: A simple smile works everywhere in the world!

Although you've been tuned into nonverbal communication since your first contact with other human beings, paying special attention to these signals in the workplace will enhance your ability to communicate successfully. Moreover, as you work with a diverse range of people both inside and outside of your company, you'll also need to grasp the different meaning of common gestures in various cultures (see Figure 2.4).

The range and variety of nonverbal signals is almost endless, but you can grasp the basics by studying six general categories:

Nonverbal signals include facial expression, gesture and posture, vocal characteristics, personal appearance, touch, and time and space.

- **Facial expression.** Your face is the primary site for expressing your emotions; it reveals both the type and the intensity of your feelings.[41] Your eyes are especially effective for indicating attention and interest, influencing others, regulating interaction, and establishing dominance.[42] As with other areas of nonverbal expressions, however, facial signals can vary widely from culture to culture. For instance, maintaining eye contact is usually viewed as a sign of sincerity and openness in the United States, but it can be viewed as rude in Japan.[43]

- **Gesture and posture.** By moving or not moving your body, you express both specific and general messages, some voluntary and some involuntary. Many gestures—a wave of the hand, for example—have a specific and intentional meaning. Other types of body movement are unintentional and express a more general message. Slouching, leaning forward, fidgeting, and walking briskly are all unconscious signals that reveal whether you feel confident or nervous, friendly or hostile, assertive or passive, powerful or powerless.

- **Vocal characteristics.** Your voice also carries both intentional and unintentional messages. Consider the sentence "What have you been up to?" If you repeat that question, changing your tone of voice and stressing various words, you can consciously convey quite different messages. However, your voice can also reveal things of which you are unaware. Your tone and volume, your accent and speaking pace, and all the little *um's* and *ah's* that creep into your speech say a lot about who you are, your relationship with the audience, and the emotions underlying your words.

- **Personal appearance.** People respond to others on the basis of their physical appearance, sometimes fairly and other times unfairly. Although an individual's body type and facial features impose limitations, most people are able to control their appearance to some degree. Grooming, clothing, accessories, style—you can control all of these. If your goal is to make a good impression, adopt the style of the people you want to impress.

- **Touch.** Touch is an important way to convey warmth, comfort, and reassurance. Touch is so powerful, in fact, that it is governed by cultural customs that establish who can touch whom and how in various circumstances. You can learn more about these customs at websites such as www.businessoftouch.com. In general, remember that touch is a complex subject. When in doubt, don't touch.

- **Time and space.** Like touch, time and space can be used to assert authority, imply intimacy, and send other nonverbal messages. For instance, some people try to demonstrate their own importance or disregard for others by making other people wait; others show respect by being on time. Similarly, taking care not to invade private space, such as standing too closely when talking, is a way to show respect for others. Keeping in mind that expectations regarding both time and space vary by culture.

When you listen, be sure to pay attention to the speaker's nonverbal clues. Do they amplify the spoken words or contradict them? Is the speaker intentionally using nonverbal signals to send you a message that he or she can't put into words? Be observant, but don't assume that you can "read someone like a book." Nonverbal signals are powerful, but they aren't infallible. Just because someone doesn't look you square in the eye doesn't mean he or she is lying, contrary to popular belief.[44] If something doesn't feel right, ask the speaker an honest and respectful question—doing so might clear everything up, or it might uncover issues you need to explore further.

Reviewing Key Points

This chapter explains the importance of working in teams. Effective teams are able to accomplish their goals because members collaborate on the necessary tasks.

The chapter points out that for a team to be effective, its members require good listening skills. It discusses the listening process, the barriers to good listening, and effective listening strategies, such as focusing on areas of interest, not interrupting, blocking out competing thoughts, and keeping an open mind. This chapter also describes how understanding nonverbal communication can help you be a more effective team member.

The chapter offers fundamental methods for planning and participating in productive meetings. In addition, it provides an overview of the many meeting-related technologies you can expect to encounter during your career.

The next section introduces the three-step writing process and gives you three full chapters of practice on the fundamentals of planning, writing, and completing messages. You will learn the basic skills required to compose messages that are clear, interesting, concise, diplomatic, and convincing.

Test Your Knowledge

1. In what four ways do organizations benefit from team decision making?

2. What four things must effective teams avoid?

3. What activities make up the listening process?

4. Name the three main barriers to effective listening.

5. In what six ways can an individual communicate nonverbally?

Apply Your Knowledge

1. Whenever your boss asks for feedback, she blasts anyone offering criticism, which causes people to agree with everything she says. You want to talk to her about it, but what should you say? List some of the points you want to make when you discuss this issue with your boss.

2. At your last department meeting, three people monopolized the entire discussion. What might you do at the next meeting to encourage other department members to voluntarily participate?

3. Chester never seems to be paying attention during weekly team meetings. He has never contributed to the discussion, and you've never even seen him take notes. He says he wants to support the team but that he finds it difficult to focus during routine meetings. List some ideas you could give him that might improve his listening skills.

4. Considering what you've learned about nonverbal communication, what are some of the ways in which communication might break down during an online meeting in which the participants can see video images of only the person presenting at any given time—and then only his or her head?

5. **Ethical Choices**   As team leader, you've just received a voice mail message from Tanya Moore, asking to lead next week's meeting. She's been with the company for six weeks and with your team for three. From what you've already observed, she's opinionated (a bit of a know-it-all), and she tends to discourage the more reserved team members from speaking up.

   You can't allow her to run next week's meeting, and without improvement in her attitude toward others, she may never be ready to lead. You consider three options for explaining your view of her position: (1) leaving her a friendly voice mail message, (2) meeting with her, or (3) sending her a friendly e-mail message. What should you do? Explain your choice.

Practice Your Knowledge

Activities

For active links to all websites discussed in this chapter, visit this text's website at www.prenhall.com/bovee. Locate your book and click on its Companion Website link. Then select Chapter 2, and click on "Featured Websites." Locate the name of the page or the URL related to the material in the text. Please note that links to sites that become inactive after publication of the book will be removed from the Featured Websites section.

1. **Analyze This Document**   A project leader has made notes about covering the following items at the quarterly budget meeting. Prepare an agenda by putting these items into a logical order and rewriting them, where necessary, to give phrases a more consistent sound:

   Budget Committee Meeting to be held on December 12, 2007, at 9:30 a.m.

   - I will call the meeting to order.
   - Site director's report: A closer look at cost overruns on Greentree site.
   - The group will review and approve the minutes from last quarter's meeting.
   - I will ask the finance director to report on actual vs. projected quarterly revenues and expenses.
   - I will distribute copies of the overall divisional budget and announce the date of the next budget meeting.
   - Discussion: How can we do a better job of anticipating and preventing cost overruns?
   - Meeting will take place in Conference Room 3.
   - What additional budget issues must be considered during this quarter?

2. **Teamwork**   With a classmate, attend a local community or campus meeting where you can observe group discussion. Take notes individually during the meeting and then work together to answer the following questions:

   a. What is your evaluation of this meeting? In your answer, consider (1) the leader's ability to clearly state the meeting's goals, (2) the leader's ability to engage members in a meaningful discussion, and (3) the group's listening skills.

   b. How well did the individual participants listen? How could you tell?

   c. Compare the notes you took during the meeting with those of your classmate. What differences do you notice? How do you account for these differences?

3. **Team Communication**   Every month, each employee in your department is expected to give a brief oral presentation on the status of his or her project. However, your department has recently hired an employee with a severe speech impediment that prevents people from understanding most of what he has to say.

   Your task: As assistant department manager, how will you resolve this dilemma? Please explain.

4. **Meeting Productivity: Analyzing Agendas**   Obtain a copy of the agenda from a recent campus or work meeting. Does this agenda show a start time or end time? Is it specific enough that you, as an outsider, would be able to understand what was to be discussed? If not, how would you improve the agenda?

5. **Listening Skills: Overcoming Barriers**   Identify some of your bad listening habits and make a list of some ways you could correct them. For the next 30 days, review your list and jot down any improvements you've noticed as a result of your effort.

6. **Listening Skills: Self-Assessment**   How good are your listening skills? Rate yourself on each of the following elements of good listening, then examine your ratings to identify where you are strongest and where you can improve, using the tips in this chapter.

Elements of Listening	Always	Frequently	Occasionally	Never
1. I look for areas of interest when people speak.	_____	_____	_____	_____
2. I focus on content rather than delivery.	_____	_____	_____	_____
3. I wait to respond until I understand the content.	_____	_____	_____	_____
4. I listen for ideas and themes, not isolated facts.	_____	_____	_____	_____
5. I take notes only when needed.	_____	_____	_____	_____
6. I really concentrate on what speakers are saying.	_____	_____	_____	_____
7. I stay focused even when the ideas are complex.	_____	_____	_____	_____
8. I keep an open mind despite emotionally charged language.	_____	_____	_____	_____

7. **Telephones and Voice Mail**   Late on a Friday afternoon, you learn that the facilities department is going to move you—and your computer, your desk, and all your files—to another office first thing Monday morning. However, you have an important client meeting scheduled in your office for Monday afternoon, and you need to

finalize some contract details on Monday morning. You simply can't lose access to your office at this point, and you're more than a little annoyed that your boss didn't ask you before approving the move. He has already left for day, but you know he usually checks his voice mail over the weekend so you decide to leave a voice mail message asking him to cancel the move or at least call you at home as soon as possible. Using the voice mail guidelines listed in Table 2.1, plan your message (use an imaginary phone number as your contact number and make up any other details you need for the call). As directed by your instructor, submit either a written script of the message or a podcast recording of the actual message.

8. **Nonverbal Communication: Analyzing Written Messages**   Select a business letter and envelope that you have received at work or at home. Analyze their appearance. What nonverbal messages do they send? Are these messages consistent with the content of the letter? If not, what could the sender have done to make the nonverbal communication consistent with the verbal communication?

9. **Nonverbal Communication: Analyzing Body Language**   Describe what the following body movements suggest when they are exhibited by someone during a conversation. How do such movements influence your interpretation of spoken words?

   a. Shifting one's body continuously while seated

   b. Twirling and playing with one's hair

   c. Sitting in a sprawled position

   d. Rolling one's eyes

   e. Extending a weak handshake

Expand Your Knowledge

Exploring the Best of the Web

Making Meetings Work   The 3M Meeting Network, www.3m.com/meetingnetwork, contains a wide selection of articles on planning meetings, designing activities to build teamwork, and making better presentations. Click on "Articles and Advice," find the appropriate articles, and then answer the following questions.

Exercises

1. How can you know if a meeting should be held or not?

2. How can good leaders show they trust the group's ability to perform successfully?

3. What are the advantages and disadvantages of "open space" meetings, which take place without formal agendas or facilitation?

Exploring the Web on Your Own

Review these chapter-related websites on your own to learn more about achieving communication success in the workplace.

1. CRInfo, www.crinfo.org, is a website dedicated to providing support for conflict resolution.

2. The Business of Touch website, www.businessoftouch.com, lets you explore cultural standards and expectations for touching, physical distance, and other elements of nonverbal communication between business colleagues in more than 15 countries.

3. Symbols.com, www.symbols.com, offers a graphical search engine that explains the meaning of 2,500 graphical symbols. Find out what that unusual symbol on a foreign-language website means, or verify that the symbols you plan to use don't convey some inappropriate nonverbal meaning. The Word Index feature lets you see the graphical symbols associated with thousands of words and ideas.

Learn Interactively

Interactive Study Guide

Visit www.prenhall.com/bovee, then locate your book and click on its Companion Website link. Select Chapter 2 to take advantage of the interactive "Chapter Quiz" to test your knowledge of chapter concepts. Receive instant feedback on whether you need additional studying. Also, visit the "Study Hall," where you'll find an abundance of valuable resources that will help you succeed in this course.

Peak Performance Grammar and Mechanics

If your instructor has required the use of "Peak Performance Grammar and Mechanics," either in your online course, through the access-code protected portion of the Companion Website, or on CD, you can continue to improve your skill with nouns and pronouns by using the "Peak Performance Grammar and Mechanics" module. Click on "Grammar Basics," and then click "Nouns and Pronouns." Take the Pretest to determine whether you have any weak areas. Then review those areas in the Refresher Course. Take the Follow-Up Test to check your grasp of nouns and pronouns. For an extra challenge or advanced practice, take the Advanced Test. Finally, for additional reinforcement in pronouns, go to the "Improve Your Grammar, Mechanics, and Usage" section that follows, and complete the "Level I: Self-Assessment" exercises.

Improve Your Grammar, Mechanics, and Usage

Level 1: Self-Assessment—Pronouns

Review Section 1.2 in the Handbook of Grammar, Mechanics, and Usage, and then look at the following 15 items.

In items 1–5, replace the underlined nouns with the correct pronouns:

1. _____ To which retailer will you send your merchandise?

2. _____ Have you given John and Nancy a list of parts?

3. _____ The main office sent the invoice to Mr. and Mrs. Litvak on December 5.

4. _____ The company settled the company's accounts before the end of the year.

5. _____ Which person's umbrella is this?

In items 6–15, write the correct pronouns in the spaces provided:

6. The sales staff is preparing guidelines for _____ (*their, its*) clients.

7. Few of the sales representatives turn in _____ (*their, its*) reports on time.

8. The board of directors has chosen _____ (*their, its*) officers.

9. Gomez and Archer have told _____ (*his, their*) clients about the new program.

10. Each manager plans to expand _____ (*his, their, his or her*) sphere of control next year.

11. Has everyone supplied _____ (*his, their, his or her*) Social Security number?

12. After giving every employee _____ (*his, their, a*) raise, George told _____ (*them, they, all*) about the increased workload.

13. Bob and Tim have opposite ideas about how to achieve company goals. _____ (*Who, Whom*) do you think will win the debate?

14. City Securities has just announced _____ (*who, whom*) it will hire as CEO.

15. Either of the new products would readily find _____ (*their, its*) niche in the marketplace.

Level 2: Workplace Applications

The following items contain numerous errors in grammar, capitalization, punctuation, abbreviation, number style, word division, and vocabulary. Rewrite each sentence in the space provided, correcting all errors. Write *C* in the space after any sentence that is already correct.

1. Anita Doig from Data Providers will outline their data interpretations as it relates to industry trends, additionally Miss Doig will be asked to comment on how their data should be ulililized.

2. You're order for 2000 mylar bags has been received by us; please be advised that orders of less than 5000 bags only get a 20 percent discount.

3. Just between you and I, the new 'customer centric' philosophy seems pretty confusing.

4. Podcasting can be an effective way to distribute messages to a widespread audience, but you need to pay close attention to the demands of an audio medium.

5. Among the specialties of Product Marketers International is promotional efforts for clients, including presence on the Internet, radio, and on television.

6. An overview of a typical marketing plan will be covered in the introduction to this report, to give you an idea of what's in it.

7. Subsidiary rights sales can be a discreet source of income and compliment your overall sales.

8. Special events ranging from author breakfasts and luncheons to awards programs and reception's offers a great way to make industry contacts.

9. We will show you how not only to meet the challenges of information rich material but also the challenges of electronic distance learning.

10. To site just one problem, the reason that the market is in such a state of confusion is the appalling lack of standards whether for hardware, software or for metadata.

11. Two leading business consultants Doug Smith and Carla McNeil will share their insights on how specialty stores can effectively compete in a world of Corporate Superstores.

12. One of the big questions we need to address are "How does buying effect inventory levels"?

13. The closing of many industry digital entities have greatly affected the perception of e-books as a viable platform.

14. A competent, motivated, and enthusiastic staff can be a managers' most important asset in a competitive marketplace.

15. Come by the Technology Lounge where you can log on to computers and plug into laptops and check out demos of sponsor's websites.

Level 3: Document Critique

The following document contains errors in grammar, capitalization, punctuation, abbreviation, number style, and vocabulary. Correct all errors using standard proofreading marks (see Appendix C).

Date: Thurs, 14 November 2007 11:07:33 -0800

From: rick glissmeyer <rickg@aol.com>

To: richard herman <rcherman@ddc.com>

CC:

BCC:

Attached:

Subject: Please supply shipping costs

Dear Richard:

As you requested heres the complete order for seed mixes required by Roberta Mcdonald in Vancouver:

* Fifty-lb. 80/20 canary seed mix @ $15.45

* 50 lbs. soak seed @ $20.25

* Total order: $305.70

The seeds are to be shipped to:

Roberta C. McDonald

1725 w. Third Av.

Vancuover, BC, V5M-5R6

We will mail our check, as soon as you reply with the amount of shipping costs. Roberta says "her flock's getting ready for breeding," and she needs the soak seed by the end of this month.

Thanks for your Quick Srevice

Rick Glissmeyer

The Three-Step
Writing Process

Unit 2

3

Planning Business Messages

Learning Objectives

After studying this chapter, you will be able to

1 Describe the three-step writing process

2 List four questions that can help you test the purpose of your message

3 Describe the importance of analyzing your audience and identify the six factors you should consider when developing an audience profile

4 Discuss gathering information for simple messages and identify three attributes of quality information

5 List factors to consider when choosing the most appropriate medium for your message

6 Explain why good organization is important to both you and your audience

7 Summarize the process for organizing business messages effectively

After launching a breakthrough podcasting series called "IBM and the Future of . . ." as a way of letting IBM experts share knowledge on a wide range of topics with customers and investors, the company made podcasting tools available to all its employees, then sat back to see how they might take advantage of this exciting new medium. Not surprisingly for a company full of bright, creative people, IBM staffers began distributing a wide variety of messages via podcast. One gained an instant following by podcasting about the daily challenges and rewards of being a mobile information worker. Another saved hundreds of thousands of dollars a year in telephone charges simply by replacing a massive weekly teleconference with podcasts. No matter what the technology, innovators such as IBM are constantly looking for new ways to reach their audiences with effective messages.[1]

Understanding the Three-Step Writing Process

Choosing the medium is one of the most important steps in planning your business messages, and as IBM demonstrates, the options seem to multiply all the time. Whether you're creating simple e-mails and instant messages or complex reports and presentations that may require weeks of planning and writing, your goal is to create messages that have a clear purpose, meet the needs of your audience, and communicate efficiently. For every

FIGURE 3.1 **The Three-Step Writing Process**

This three-step process will help you create more effective messages in any medium. As you get more practice with the process, it will become easier and more automatic.

Planning

Analyze the Situation
Define your purpose and develop an audience profile.

Gather Information
Determine audience needs and obtain the information necessary to satisfy those needs.

Select the Right Medium
Choose the best medium for delivering your message.

Organize the Information
Define your main idea, limit your scope, select a direct or an indirect approach, and outline your content.

1

Writing

Adapt to Your Audience
Be sensitive to audience needs with a "you" attitude, politeness, positive emphasis, and bias-free language. Build a strong relationship with your audience by establishing your credibility and projecting your company's image. Control your style with a conversational tone, plain English, and appropriate voice.

Compose the Message
Choose strong words that will help you create effective sentences and coherent paragraphs.

2

Completing

Revise the Message
Evaluate content and review readability, then edit and rewrite for conciseness and clarity.

Produce the Message
Use effective design elements and suitable layout for a clean, professional appearance.

Proofread the Message
Review for errors in layout, spelling, and mechanics.

Distribute the Message
Deliver your message using the chosen medium; make sure all documents and all relevant files are distributed successfully.

3

---

message you send, you can reduce the time and energy it takes to achieve this goal by following a clear and proven three-step process (see Figure 3.1):

- **Planning business messages.** To plan any message, first *analyze the situation* by defining your purpose and developing a profile of your audience. With that in mind, you can *gather information* that will meet your audience's needs. Next, *select the right medium* (oral, written, or electronic) to deliver your message. With those three factors in place, you're ready to *organize the information* by defining your main idea, limiting your scope, selecting an approach, and outlining your content. Planning messages is the focus of this chapter.

- **Writing business messages.** Once you've planned your message, *adapt to your audience* with sensitivity, relationship skills, and style. Then you're ready to *compose your message* by choosing strong words, creating effective sentences, and developing coherent paragraphs. Writing business messages is discussed in Chapter 4.

- **Completing business messages.** After writing your first draft, *revise your message* to make sure it is clear, concise, and correct. Next *produce your message*, giving it an attractive, professional appearance. *Proofread* the final product for typos, spelling errors, and other mechanical problems. Finally, *distribute your message* using the best combination of personal and technological tools. Completing business messages is discussed in Chapter 5.

Throughout this book, you'll see the three steps in this process applied to a wide variety of business messages: basic tasks for short messages (Chapters 6 through 9), additional tasks for longer messages (Chapter 10 and 11), special tasks for oral presentations (Chapter 12), and distinct tasks for employment messages (Chapter 14).

The more you use the three-step writing process, the easier and faster it will become. You'll also get better at allotting your time for each step. As a general rule, try using roughly half your time for planning, a quarter of your time for writing, and the remaining quarter for completing the project. Even for small writing projects, resist the temptation to skip the planning step. For instance, spending even just a minute or two to think

> The three-step writing process consists of planning, writing, and completing your messages.

> As a starting point, try to use half your time for planning, one quarter for writing, and one quarter for completing your messages.

53

through the purpose of an e-mail message can help you write much faster because you'll know in advance what you want to say. And leave plenty of time to complete your documents, too; you don't want to compromise the quality of a good message by shortchanging the important steps of revising, producing, proofreading, and distributing.[2]

Analyzing Your Situation

A successful message starts with a clear purpose that connects the sender's needs with the audience's needs. Identifying your purpose and your audience is usually a straightforward task for simple, routine messages; however, this task can be more demanding in more complex situations. For instance, if you need to communicate about a shipping problem between your Beijing and Los Angeles factories, your purpose might be simply to alert upper management to the situation, or it might involve asking the two factory managers to explore and solve the problem. These two scenarios have different purposes and different audiences; therefore, they yield dramatically different messages. If you launch directly into writing without clarifying both your purpose and your audience, you'll waste time and energy, and you'll probably generate a less effective message.

Defining Your Purpose

Business messages have both a general and a specific purpose.

All business messages have a **general purpose**: to inform, to persuade, or to collaborate with your audience. This purpose helps define the overall approach you'll need to take, from gathering information to organizing your message. Within the scope of that general purpose, each message also has a **specific purpose**, which identifies what you hope to accomplish with your message. State your specific purpose as precisely as possible, even identifying which audience members should respond, how they should respond, and when.

After defining your purpose, verify that the message will be worth the time and effort required to create, send, and receive it.

Once you have defined your specific purpose, make sure it merits the time and effort required for you to prepare and send the message. Ask these four questions:

- **Will anything change as a result of your message?** Make sure you don't contribute to information overload by sending messages that won't change anything. Complaining about things that you have no influence over is a good example of a message that probably shouldn't be sent.
- **Is your purpose realistic?** If your purpose involves a radical shift in action or attitude, proceed carefully. Consider proposing a first step so that your message acts as the beginning of a learning process.
- **Is the time right?** People who are busy or distracted when they receive your message are less likely to pay attention to it.
- **Is your purpose acceptable to your organization?** Your company's business objectives and policies, and even laws that apply to your particular industry, may dictate whether a given purpose is acceptable.

Once you are satisfied that you have a clear and meaningful purpose and that now is a smart time to proceed, your next step is to understand the members of your audience and their needs.

Developing an Audience Profile

Before an audience takes the time to read or hear your message, they need to be interested in what you're saying. They need to see what's in it for them—which of their needs will be met or problems will be solved by listening to your advice or doing what you ask. The more

FIGURE 3.2   Using Audience Analysis to Plan a Message

For simple, routine messages, you usually don't need to analyze your audience in depth. However, for complex messages or messages for indifferent or hostile audiences, take the time to study their information needs and potential reactions to your message.

Audience Analysis Notes

Project: A report recommending that we close down the on-site exercise facility and subsidize private memberships at local health clubs.

- **Primary audience:** Nicole Perazzo, vice president of operations, and her supervisory team.

- **Size and geographic distribution:** Nine managers total; Nicole and five of her staff are here on site; three other supervisors are based in Hong Kong.

- **Composition:** All have experience in operations management, but several are new to the company.

- **Level of understanding:** All will no doubt understand the financial considerations, but the newer managers might not understand the importance of the on-site exercise facility to many of our employees.

- **Expectations and preferences.** They're expecting a firm recommendation, backed up with well-thought-out financial rationale and suggestions for communicating the bad news to employees. For a decision of this magnitude, a formal report is appropriate; e-mail distribution is expected.

- **Probable reaction.** From one-on-one discussions, I know that several of the managers receiving this report are active users of the on-site facility and won't welcome the suggestion that we should shut it down. However, some nonexercisers generally think it's a luxury the company can't afford. Audience reactions will range from highly positive to highly negative; the report should focus on overcoming the highly negative reactions since they're the ones I need to convince.

you know about your audience, their needs, and their expectations, the more effectively you'll be able to communicate with them. For an example of the kind of information you need to compile in an audience analysis, see the planning sheet shown in Figure 3.2. To conduct an audience analysis:

- **Identify your primary audience.** For some messages, certain audience members might be more important than others. Don't ignore the needs of less influential members, but make sure you address the concerns of the key decision makers.
- **Determine audience size and geographic distribution.** A message aimed at 10,000 people spread around the globe might require a different approach than one aimed at a dozen people down the hall.
- **Determine audience composition.** Look for both similarities and differences in culture, language, age, education, organizational rank and status, attitudes, experience, motivations, and any other factors that might affect the success of your message.
- **Gauge audience members' level of understanding.** If audience members share your general background, they'll probably understand your material without difficulty. If not, your message will need an element of education, and deciding how much information to include can be a challenge. Try to include only enough information to accomplish the specific purpose of your message. If the members of your audience have various levels of understanding, gear your coverage to your primary audience (the key decision makers).
- **Understand audience expectations and preferences.** Will members of your audience expect complete details or just a summary of the main points? Do they want an e-mail

Ask yourself some key questions about your audience:
- *Who are they?*
- *How many people do you need to reach?*
- *How much do they already know about the subject?*
- *What is their probable reaction to your message?*

If audience members have different levels of understanding of the topic, aim your message at the most influential decision makers.

or will they expect a formal memo? In general, the higher up the organization your message goes, the fewer details people want to see, simply because they have less time to read them.

■ **Forecast probable audience reaction.** As you'll read later in the chapter, audience reaction affects message organization. If you expect a favorable response, you can state conclusions and recommendations up front and offer minimal supporting evidence. If you expect skepticism, you'll probably want to introduce conclusions gradually, with more proof along the way.

A gradual approach and plenty of evidence are required to win over a skeptical audience.

Gathering Information

With a clear picture of your audience, your next step is to assemble the information that you will include in your message. For simple messages, you may already have all the information at hand, but more complex messages can require considerable research and analysis before you're ready to begin writing. Chapter 10 explores formal techniques for finding, evaluating, and processing information, but you can often use a variety of informal techniques to gather insights and focus your research efforts:

■ **Consider other viewpoints.** Putting yourself in someone else's position helps you consider what that person might be thinking, feeling, or planning.

■ **Read reports and other company documents.** Your company's files may be a rich source of the information you need for a particular memo or e-mail message. Seek out annual reports, financial statements, news releases, memos, marketing reports, and customer surveys for helpful information. Find out whether your company has a *knowledge management system*, a centralized database that collects the experiences and insights of employees throughout the organization.

■ **Talk with supervisors, colleagues, or customers.** Fellow workers and customers may have information you need, or they may know what your audience will be interested in.

■ **Ask your audience for input.** If you're unsure of what audience members need from your message, ask them. Admitting you don't know but want to meet their needs will impress an audience more than guessing and getting it wrong.

Uncovering Audience Needs

If you're given a vague request, ask questions to clarify it before you plan a response.

In many situations, your audience's information needs are readily apparent, such as when a consumer sends an e-mail asking a specific question. In other cases, your audience might be unable to articulate exactly what is needed. If someone makes a vague or broad request, ask questions to narrow the focus. If your boss says, "Find out everything you can about Interscope Records," ask which aspect of the company and its business is most important. Asking a question or two often forces the person to think through the request and define more precisely what is required.

Include any additional information that might be helpful, even though the requester didn't specifically ask for it.

Also, try to think of information needs that your audience may not even be aware of. Suppose your company has just hired a new employee from out of town, and you've been assigned to coordinate this person's relocation. At a minimum, you would write a welcoming letter describing your company's procedures for relocating employees. With a little extra thought, however, you might include some information about the city: perhaps a guide to residential areas, a map or two, brochures about cultural activities, or information on schools and transportation. In some cases, you may be able to tell your audience something they consider important but wouldn't have thought to ask. Although adding information of this sort lengthens your message, it can also create goodwill.

Providing Required Information

Test the completeness of your document by making sure it answers all the important questions: who, what, when, where, why, and how.

Once you've defined your audience's information needs, your next step is to satisfy those needs completely. Use the journalistic approach to make sure your information answers *who, what, when, where, why,* and *how.* In addition to delivering the right *quantity* of required information, you are responsible for verifying the *quality* of that information. Ask yourself these three questions:

- **Is the information accurate?** Inaccuracies can cause a host of problems, from embarrassment and lost productivity to serious safety and legal issues. Be sure to review any mathematical or financial calculations. Check all dates and schedules, and examine your own assumptions and conclusions to be certain they are valid.
- **Is the information ethical?** By working hard to ensure the accuracy of the information you gather, you'll also avoid many ethical problems in your messages. However, messages can also be unethical if important information is omitted or obscured.
- **Is the information pertinent?** Remember that some points will be more important to your audience than others. Moreover, by focusing on the information that concerns your audience the most, you increase your chances of sending an effective message.

Selecting the Right Medium

Selecting the best medium for your message can make the difference between effective and ineffective communication.[3] A **medium** is the form through which you choose to communicate your message. You may choose to talk with someone face-to-face, write a letter, send an e-mail message, or record a podcast—with today's ever-expanding technology, you often have a variety of media options from which to choose.

In fact, media categories have become increasingly blurred in recent years with so many options that include multimedia formats. For the sake of discussion, you can think of media as traditionally being either oral or written, and electronic media extend the reach of both. Each type of medium has advantages and disadvantages.

Oral Media

Primary oral media include face-to-face conversations, interviews, speeches, in-person presentations, and meetings. Being able to see, hear, and react to each other can benefit communicators, giving oral media several advantages:

- They provide immediate feedback.
- They allow a certain ease of interaction.
- They involve rich nonverbal cues (both physical gestures and vocal inflections).
- They help you express the emotion behind your message.

Oral communication is best when you need to encourage interaction, express emotions, or monitor emotional responses.

Traditional oral media are useful for getting people to ask questions, make comments, and work together to reach a consensus or decision. However, if you don't want or need all that interaction, then oral media can have several disadvantages:

- They restrict participation to those physically present.
- Unless recorded, they provide no permanent, verifiable record of the communication.
- They can reduce the communicator's control over the message, if people interrupt or ask unanticipated questions.
- They often rule out the chance to revise or edit your spoken words.

Oral media limit participation to those who are present, reduce your control over the message, and make it difficult to revise or edit your message.

Written Media

Written messages take many forms, from traditional memos to glossy reports that rival magazines in production quality. *Memos* are used for the routine, day-to-day exchange of information within an organization. E-mail continues to replace traditional paper memos in many circumstances, although writers who want more formality or permanence can still opt for paper memos. *Letters* are written messages sent to recipients outside the organization, so in addition to conveying a particular message, they perform an important public relations function in fostering good working relationships. *Reports* may be distributed to insiders or outsiders, depending on their purpose and subject. They come in many formats, including preprinted forms, letters, memos, and manuscripts, in lengths from a few pages to several hundred.

Written media have a number of advantages over oral media:

- They allow you to plan and control your message.
- They offer a permanent, verifiable record.
- They help you reach an audience that is geographically dispersed.
- They minimize the distortion that can accompany oral messages.
- They can be used to avoid immediate interactions, including emotional confrontations when communicating controversial messages.

Disadvantages of written media include the following:

- Many are not conducive to speedy feedback.
- They lack the rich nonverbal cues provided by oral media.
- They often take more time and more resources to create and distribute.
- Elaborate printed documents can require special skills in preparation and production.

Electronic Media

Electronic media span a diverse and expanding range of technologies, from e-mail and IM to blogs and podcasts. The growth of electronic communication options is both a blessing and a curse. You have more tools than ever to choose from, but you need to choose the right tools for each message. Although no hard rules dictate which tool to use in each case, here are a few pointers that will help you determine when to select electronic over more traditional forms:[4]

- **Telephone calls** are still the lifeblood of many organizations, for both internal and external communication. But even the humble telephone has joined the Internet age, thanks to the emerging capability to place phone calls over the Internet. Known by the technical term VoIP (which stands for *Voice over IP*, the Internet Protocol), Internet-based phone service promises to offer cheaper long-distance service for businesses worldwide, and companies such as Skype even offer free basic phone service between computers.[5] Through the use of *webcams*, video phone service is now an inexpensive option for one-to-one phone calls, teleconferences, and online meetings.
- **Voice mail** can replace short memos and phone calls when an immediate response isn't crucial. However, voice mail is a poor choice for lengthy, complex messages, since the information is more difficult for receivers to process.
- **Teleconferencing**, **videoconferencing**, and **online meetings** are best for informational meetings and are less effective for highly interactive meetings such as negotiation.
- **DVDs** (and to a declining extent, videotapes) are effective for sending audiovisual messages to a large number of people. With the growing availability of high-speed Internet service, many video messages once delivered on tape or disk are now delivered online.
- **Electronic documents** include both word processor files and Adobe's widely popular Portable Document Format (PDF). Computer users can view PDFs on screen with free reader software, and PDFs are more secure and less vulnerable to viruses than word processor files.
- **Faxes** have been replaced by e-mail and PDF files in many cases, but they still play an important role in many companies. Internet-based fax services, such as eFax (www.efax.com), lower the cost by eliminating the need for a dedicated fax line and fax machine.

- **E-mail** offers speed, low cost, portability, and convenience. It's best for brief, noncomplex information that is time sensitive. With such a quick turnaround time, e-mail tends to be more conversational than traditional media, but not as conversational as instant messaging.

- **Instant messaging (IM)** allows real-time, one-on-one and small-group text conversations via personal computer. At technology giant IBM, for instance, employees send more than 5 million instant messages a month.[6] IM is more versatile than a phone call and quicker than e-mail, and newer IM systems offer file attachments, streaming audio and video, and other enhancements. *Text messaging*, a phone-based medium that has long been popular with consumers in Asia and Europe, is finally catching on in the United States.[7] Although it lacks many of the capabilities of IM, text messaging does give businesses an easy way to transmit simple messages between mobile workers.

- **Websites and blogs** have become vital communication platforms for many businesses. A well-designed website can tailor the same information for numerous readers by steering each audience group to specific sections on a website. Blogs have become common in business in recent years as communicators search for fast, informal ways to reach customers and other audiences. *Video blogs* (*vlogs*) and *mobile blogs* (*moblogs*) extend the blogging concept in intriguing new ways.[8] Blog content is often distributed through RSS (Really Simple Syndication), which automatically sends new content to subscribers.

- **Podcasts** are one of the newest and most exciting media choices for business communicators. Both audio and video podcasts give you a means to reach customers and colleagues with a human touch that isn't always easy to replicate in text-only media.

You'll read more about e-mail, IM, blogs, and podcasting in Chapter 6. As you can see, electronic messages offer considerable advantages:

- They deliver messages with great speed.
- They reach audiences physically separated from you.
- They reach a dispersed audience personally.
- They offer the persuasive power of multimedia formats.
- They can increase accessibility and openness in an organization.

In general, use electronic media to deliver messages quickly, to reach widely dispersed audiences, and to take advantage of rich multimedia formats.

For all their good points, electronic media are not problem-free. Consider some of these disadvantages:

- **They can inadvertently create tension and conflict.** Electronic messages can give the illusion of anonymity, so people sometimes say things online that they would never say in person or in a traditional document. Blogs have been a particularly controversial medium in this respect, with several companies firing employees for their blog postings. Many companies are still wrestling with the phenomenon of employee blogs, as they try to find the appropriate balance between protecting confidential information and corporate reputations and respecting the free-speech rights of their employees.[9]

- **They are easy to overuse.** The ability to send or forward messages to multiple recipients has become a major cause of information overload.

- **They expose companies to data security threats and malicious software.** Connecting computers to the Internet exposes companies to a host of potential security problems, including computer viruses, information theft, and *spyware* (malicious software that sneaks onto personal computers to capture credit card numbers and other confidential information).

- **They often lack privacy.** More than a few businesspeople have discovered to their embarrassment that IMs, e-mails, and voice mails can wind up in places they never envisioned. In addition, employers can legally monitor electronic messages, and these messages can be subpoenaed for court cases.

Electronic media can suffer from a lack of privacy and can reduce productivity when people send too many low-value messages.

■ **They can seriously drain employee productivity.** Employees can be easily distracted by the constant streams of e-mail, IM, voice mail, conference calls, and faxes or the temptation to surf nonbusiness-related websites during working hours.

Factors to Consider When Choosing Media

When choosing a medium for your message, select the medium that balances your needs and your audience's needs (see Figure 3.3). Just as critical, however, is considering how your message is affected by important factors such as the following:

The more complicated the message, the richer the medium required.

■ **Media richness.** Richness is a medium's ability to (1) convey a message through more than one *informational cue* (visual, verbal, vocal), (2) facilitate feedback, and (3) establish personal focus. The richest medium is face-to-face communication; it's personal, it provides immediate feedback (verbal and nonverbal), and it conveys the emotion behind a message.[10] Multimedia presentations and multimedia webpages are also quite rich. At the other extreme are the leanest media—those that communicate in the simplest ways, provide no opportunity for audience feedback, and aren't personalized, such as memos, posters, and podcasts. Generally speaking, use the richest media to send more complex messages and to help communicate emotion. Use leaner media to send simple, routine messages.
■ **Message formality.** Your media choice governs the style and tone of your message. For instance, IM and e-mail can be considered inappropriate for formal messages.
■ **Media limitations.** Every medium has limitations. For example, although face-to-face communication is a rich medium, it's one of the most restrictive because you and your

FIGURE 3.3   Choosing the Most Appropriate Medium
With so many media choices at your disposal today, make sure you choose the most efficient and most effective medium for every message.

Use Written Media When	Use Oral Media When
• You don't need or want immediate feedback • You don't want or need immediate interaction with the audience • Your message is complex • You need a permanent, verifiable record • Your audience is large and geographically dispersed • You need to ensure that the message cannot be altered after you send it • Your message has limited emotional content • The situation calls for more formality	• You want immediate feedback from the audience • Your message is straightforward and easy to accept • You don't need a permanent record • You can gather your audience conveniently and economically • You want to encourage interaction to solve a problem or reach a group decision • You want to read the audience's body language or hear the tone of their response • Your message has an emotional content

Use Electronic Media When

• You need to deliver a message quickly
• You're physically separated from your audience
• You want to give the audience an opportunity to edit the message (such as editing a word processing document)
• Your message can benefit from multiple media, such as audio and video
• You want to take advantage of electronic media

audience must be in the same place at the same time.[11] Similarly, instant messaging is perfect for communicating short, simple messages, but it is ineffective for sending complex ones.

- **Sender intentions.** Your choice of medium also influences audience perceptions of your intentions. For instance, to emphasize formality, use a more formal medium, such as a memo or a letter. Or, to let people know that you welcome feedback, meet face-to-face, make a phone call, or use IM.[12]

  Your intentions heavily influence your choice of medium.

- **Audience preferences.** Make sure to consider which media your audience expects or prefers.[13] For example, the United States, Canada, and Germany emphasize written messages, whereas Japan emphasizes oral messages—perhaps because its high-context culture carries so much of the message in nonverbal cues and "between the lines" interpretation.[14]

  When choosing the appropriate medium, don't forget to consider your audience's expectations.

- **Urgency and cost.** Various media have different costs and time requirements, so you often need to balance urgency and expense. Newer media options such as blogs and podcasting make it easier to deliver messages quickly at low cost.

  Time and cost also affect medium selection.

Once you select the best medium for your purpose, situation, and audience, you are ready to start thinking about the organization of your message.

Organizing Your Message

Misinterpreted messages waste time, lead to poor decision making, and shatter business relationships. So you can see how valuable clear writing and good organization can be.[15] Successful communicators rely on good organization to make their messages meaningful.[16]

What exactly makes a particular organization "good"? Although the definition of good organization varies from country to country, in the United States and Canada it generally means creating a linear message that proceeds point by point (see Figure 3.4).

What does good organization do for you? First and foremost, it saves you time. Your draft goes more quickly because you're not putting ideas in the wrong places or composing material you don't need. In addition, you can use your organizational plan to get some advance input from your audience, making sure you're on the right track before spending hours working on your draft. And, if your project is large and complex, you can even use your organization plan to divide the writing job among coworkers.

Good message organization helps you by reducing the time and energy needed to create messages and by making your messages more effective.

In addition to helping you, good organization helps your audience:

- **Good organization helps your audience understand your message.** By making your main point clear at the outset, and by stating your needs precisely, your well-organized message will satisfy your audience's need for information.

  Good organization helps your audiences by helping them understand and accept your message in less time.

- **Good organization helps your audience accept your message.** Even when your message is logical, you need to select and organize your points in a diplomatic way. Softening refusals and leaving a good impression enhances credibility and adds authority to your messages.

- **Good organization saves your audience time.** Audience members receive only the information they need, and because that information is relevant, brief, and logically placed, your audience can follow your thought pattern without a struggle.

You can achieve good organization by clearly defining your main idea, limiting the scope of your message, grouping supporting points, and establishing their sequence by selecting either a direct or an indirect approach.

To organize a message,
- *Define your main idea*
- *Limit the scope*
- *Choose the direct or indirect approach*
- *Group your points*

Defining Your Main Idea

The broad subject, or **topic**, of every business message is condensed to one idea, whether it's soliciting the executive committee for a larger budget or apologizing to a client for an incident of poor customer service. Your entire message supports, explains, or demonstrates your **main idea**—a specific statement about the topic of your message.

The topic is the broad subject; the main idea makes a statement about the topic.

FIGURE 3.4 Improving the Organization of a Message

The poorly written draft displays weak organization, while the organization is much improved in the revised version.
Before you begin to write, think about what you're going to say and how you're going to say it.

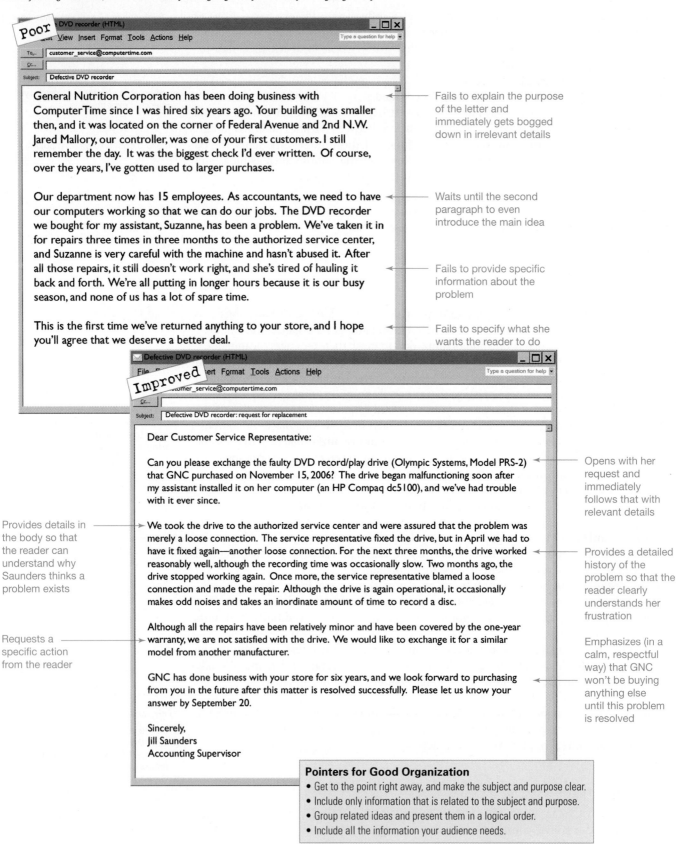

Poor

To...: customer_service@computertime.com
Cc...:
Subject: Defective DVD recorder

General Nutrition Corporation has been doing business with ComputerTime since I was hired six years ago. Your building was smaller then, and it was located on the corner of Federal Avenue and 2nd N.W. Jared Mallory, our controller, was one of your first customers. I still remember the day. It was the biggest check I'd ever written. Of course, over the years, I've gotten used to larger purchases.

Our department now has 15 employees. As accountants, we need to have our computers working so that we can do our jobs. The DVD recorder we bought for my assistant, Suzanne, has been a problem. We've taken it in for repairs three times in three months to the authorized service center, and Suzanne is very careful with the machine and hasn't abused it. After all those repairs, it still doesn't work right, and she's tired of hauling it back and forth. We're all putting in longer hours because it is our busy season, and none of us has a lot of spare time.

This is the first time we've returned anything to your store, and I hope you'll agree that we deserve a better deal.

Fails to explain the purpose of the letter and immediately gets bogged down in irrelevant details

Waits until the second paragraph to even introduce the main idea

Fails to provide specific information about the problem

Fails to specify what she wants the reader to do

Improved

customer_service@computertime.com
Cc...:
Subject: Defective DVD recorder: request for replacement

Dear Customer Service Representative:

Can you please exchange the faulty DVD record/play drive (Olympic Systems, Model PRS-2) that GNC purchased on November 15, 2006? The drive began malfunctioning soon after my assistant installed it on her computer (an HP Compaq dc5100), and we've had trouble with it ever since.

We took the drive to the authorized service center and were assured that the problem was merely a loose connection. The service representative fixed the drive, but in April we had to have it fixed again—another loose connection. For the next three months, the drive worked reasonably well, although the recording time was occasionally slow. Two months ago, the drive stopped working again. Once more, the service representative blamed a loose connection and made the repair. Although the drive is again operational, it occasionally makes odd noises and takes an inordinate amount of time to record a disc.

Although all the repairs have been relatively minor and have been covered by the one-year warranty, we are not satisfied with the drive. We would like to exchange it for a similar model from another manufacturer.

GNC has done business with your store for six years, and we look forward to purchasing from you in the future after this matter is resolved successfully. Please let us know your answer by September 20.

Sincerely,
Jill Saunders
Accounting Supervisor

Provides details in the body so that the reader can understand why Saunders thinks a problem exists

Requests a specific action from the reader

Opens with her request and immediately follows that with relevant details

Provides a detailed history of the problem so that the reader clearly understands her frustration

Emphasizes (in a calm, respectful way) that GNC won't be buying anything else until this problem is resolved

Pointers for Good Organization
- Get to the point right away, and make the subject and purpose clear.
- Include only information that is related to the subject and purpose.
- Group related ideas and present them in a logical order.
- Include all the information your audience needs.

Your main idea may be obvious when you're preparing a brief message with simple facts that have little emotional impact on your audience. If you're responding to a request for information, your main idea may be simply, "Here is what you wanted." However, defining your main idea is more complicated when you're trying to persuade someone or when you have disappointing information to convey. In these situations, try to define a main idea that will establish a good relationship between you and your audience. In longer documents and presentations, you often need to unify a mass of material, so you'll need to define a main idea that encompasses all the individual points you want to make. Sometimes you won't even be sure what your main idea is until you sort through the information. For tough assignments like these, consider a variety of techniques to generate creative ideas:

Defining your main idea is more difficult when you're trying to persuade someone or convey disappointing information.

- **Brainstorming.** Working alone or with others, generate as many ideas and questions as you can, without stopping to criticize or organize. After you capture all these pieces, look for patterns and connections to help identify the main idea and the groups of supporting ideas.
- **Journalistic approach.** The journalistic approach asks *who, what, when, where, why,* and *how* questions to distill major ideas from piles of unorganized information.
- **Question-and-answer chain.** Start with a key question, from the audience's perspective, and work back toward your message. In most cases, you'll find that each answer generates new questions, until you identify the information that needs to be in your message.
- **Storyteller's tour.** Some writers find it easier to talk through a communication challenge before they try to write. Describe what you intend to write and capture it on tape or disk. Then listen to your talk, identify ways to tighten and clarify the message, and repeat the process until you distill the main idea down to a single, concise message.

Limiting Your Scope

The **scope** of your message is the range of information you present, the overall length, and the level of detail—all of which need to correspond to your main idea. Many business documents have a preset length limit, either from a boss's instructions, a technological limit, or a time frame such as individual speaker slots during a seminar. Even if you don't have a preset limit, it's vital to limit yourself to the scope needed to convey your message—and no more.

Whatever the length of your message, limit the number of major support points to half a dozen or so—and if you can get your idea across with fewer points, all the better. Listing 20 or 30 support points might feel as if you're being thorough, but your audience will view such detail as rambling and mind-numbing. Instead, look for ways to group supporting points under major headings, such as finance, customers, competitors, employees, or whatever is appropriate for your subject. You may need to refine your major support points so that you have a smaller number with greater impact.

If your message is brief (say, a 4-minute speech or a 1-page letter), plan on only 1 minute or one paragraph each for the introduction, conclusion, and major points. Because the amount of evidence you can present is limited, your main idea will have to be both easy to understand and easy to accept. However, if your message is long (say, 60 minutes or 20 pages), you can develop the major points in considerable detail. You can spend about 10 minutes or 10 paragraphs (more than 3 pages of double-spaced, typewritten text) on each of your key points, and you'll still have room for your introduction and conclusion.

Choosing Between Direct and Indirect Approaches

After you've defined your ideas, you're ready to decide on the sequence you will use to present your points. You have two basic options:

- **Direct approach (deductive).** When you know your audience will be receptive to your message, start with the main idea (such as a recommendation, a conclusion, or a request), and follow that with your supporting evidence.

FIGURE 3.5   Choosing Between the Direct and Indirect Approaches
Think about the way your audience is likely to respond before choosing your approach.

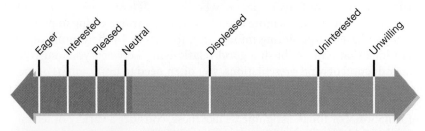

	Direct approach	Indirect approach	
Audience Reaction	Eager/interested/ pleased/neutral	Displeased	Uninterested/unwilling
Message Opening	Start with the main idea, the request, or the good news.	Start with a neutral statement that acts as a transition to the reasons for the bad news.	Start with a statement or question that captures attention.
Message Body	Provide necessary details.	Give reasons to justify a negative answer. State or imply the bad news, and make a positive suggestion.	Arouse the audience's interest in the subject. Build the audience's desire to comply.
Message Close	Close with a cordial comment, a reference to the good news, or a statement about the specific action desired.	Close cordially.	Request action.

■ **Indirect approach (inductive).** When your audience will be skeptical about or even resistant to your message, start with the evidence first and build your case before presenting the main idea.

Use a direct approach if the audience's reaction is likely to be positive and the indirect approach if it is likely to be negative.

To choose between these two alternatives, analyze your audience's likely reaction to your purpose and message. Bear in mind, however, that each message is unique. No simple formula will solve all your communication problems. For example, although an indirect approach may be best when you're sending bad news to outsiders, if you're writing a memo to an associate, you may want to get directly to the point, even if your message is unpleasant. The direct approach might also be a good choice for long messages, regardless of your audience's attitude—because delaying the main idea could cause confusion and frustration. Figure 3.5 summarizes how your approach may differ depending on the likely audience reaction. The type of message also influences the choice of a direct or indirect approach. In the coming chapters, you'll get specific advice on choosing the best approach for a variety of different communication challenges.

Outlining Your Content

Once you have chosen the right approach, it's time to figure out the most logical and effective way to provide your supporting details. Even if you've resisted creating outlines in your school assignments over the years, try to get into the habit when you're preparing business documents and presentations. You'll save time, get better results, and do a better job of navigating through complicated business situations. Whether you use a specialized outlining and idea-mapping software, use the outlining features provided with word-processing software, or simply jot down three or four points on paper, making a plan and sticking to it will help you cover the important details.

You're no doubt familiar with the basic outline formats that identify each point with a number or letter and that indent certain points to show which ones are of equal status.

FIGURE 3.6 Two Common Outline Forms

Your company may have a tradition of using a particular outline form for formal reports and other documents. If not, either of these two approaches will work for most any writing project.

ALPHANUMERIC OUTLINE	DECIMAL OUTLINE
I. First Major Point	1.0 First Major Point
A. First subpoint	1.1 First subpoint
B. Second subpoint	1.2 Second subpoint
1. Evidence	1.2.1 Evidence
2. Evidence	1.2.2 Evidence
a. Detail	1.2.2.1 Detail
b. Detail	1.2.2.2 Detail
3. Evidence	1.2.3 Evidence
C. Third subpoint	1.3 Third subpoint
II. Second Major Point	2.0 Second Major Point
A. First subpoint	2.1 First subpoint
1. Evidence	2.1.1 Evidence
2. Evidence	2.1.2 Evidence
B. Second subpoint	2.2 Second subpoint

A good outline divides a topic into at least two parts, restricts each subdivision to one category, and ensures that each subdivision is separate and distinct (see Figure 3.6).

Whichever outlining or organizing scheme you use, start your message with the main idea, follow that with major supporting points, and then illustrate these points with evidence:

- **Start with the main idea.** The main idea helps you establish the goals and general strategy of the message, and it summarizes two things: (1) what you want your audience to do or think and (2) why they should do so. Everything in your message either supports the main idea or explains its implications.
- **State the major points.** Now it's time to support your main idea with the major points that clarify and explain your ideas in more concrete terms. If your purpose is to inform, your major points might be based on something physical or financial, for instance. When you're describing a process, the major points are almost inevitably steps in the process. When you're describing an object, the major points correspond to the components of the object. When you're giving a historical account, major points represent events in the chronological chain. If your purpose is to persuade or to collaborate, select major points that develop a line of reasoning or a logical argument that proves your central message and motivates your audience to act.
- **Illustrate with evidence.** After you've defined the main idea and identified supporting points, you're ready to illustrate each point with specific evidence that helps audience members understand and remember the more abstract concepts you're presenting.

Up to a point, the more evidence you provide, the more conclusive your case will be. If your subject is complex and unfamiliar, or if your audience is skeptical, you'll need a lot of facts and figures to demonstrate your points. On the other hand, if your subject is routine and your audience is positively inclined, you can be more sparing with the evidence. You want to provide enough support to be convincing but not so much that your message becomes boring or difficult to read.

Provide enough evidence to make your message convincing, but don't overload the audience with too many minor support points.

Reviewing Key Points

This chapter introduces the three-step writing process: planning, writing, and completing business messages. It discusses how the process works and how to schedule your time for each step. The majority of this chapter covers the first step of the three-step writing

Document Makeover

Improve This Letter

To practice correcting drafts of actual documents, visit your online course or the access-code-protected portion of the Companion Website. Click "Document Makeovers," then click Chapter 3. You will find a letter that contains problems and errors relating to what you've learned in this chapter about planning and organizing business messages. Use the Final Draft decision tool to create an improved version of this letter. Check the document for audience focus, the right choice of medium, and the proper choice of direct or indirect approach.

process, which includes four planning tasks. The first of these is analyzing your situation, which includes defining both a general and a specific purpose and developing a profile of your audience by identifying the primary audience, determining audience size, determining audience composition, gauging your audience's level of understanding, projecting your audience's expectations and preferences, and estimating your audience's probable reaction. The second task is gathering necessary information by exploring audience needs then collecting information that will meet those needs. The third task is selecting the right medium; the chapter offered an overview of oral, written, and electronic media. The fourth and final task is how to organize your message by defining the main idea, limiting the scope, grouping your points, choosing the direct or indirect approach, then crafting an outline.

The next chapter focuses on the second step of the writing process: writing business messages. There you'll explore two major tasks, adapting to your audience by being sensitive to their needs and building a strong relationship with them and then composing your messages. You will learn about controlling your style and tone, selecting the best words, creating effective sentences, and developing coherent paragraphs.

Test Your Knowledge

1. What are the three steps in the writing process?

2. What two types of purposes do all business messages have?

3. What do you need to know in order to develop an audience profile?

4. When including information in your message, what three conditions must you satisfy?

5. What are the main advantages of oral media? Of written media?

Apply Your Knowledge

1. Some writers argue that planning messages wastes time because they inevitably change their plans as they go along. How would you respond to this argument? Briefly explain.

2. As a member of the public relations department, which medium (or media) would you recommend using to inform the local community that your toxic-waste cleanup program has been successful? Justify your choice.

3. Would you use a direct or an indirect approach to ask employees to work overtime to meet an important deadline? Please explain.

4. Considering how fast, easy, inexpensive, they are, should e-mail, instant messages, blogs, and podcasts completely replace meetings and other face-to-face communication in your company? Why or why not?

5. **Ethical Choices**   The company president has asked you to draft a memo for her signature to the board of directors, informing them that sales in the new line of gourmet fruit jams have far exceeded anyone's expectations. As a member of the purchasing department, you happen to know that sales of moderately priced jams have declined quite a bit (many customers have switched to the more expensive jams). You were not directed to add that tidbit of information. Should you write the memo and limit your information to the expensive gourmet jams? Or should you include the information about the decline in moderately priced jams? Please explain.

Practice Your Knowledge

Exercises for Perfecting Your Writing

Specific Purpose   For each of the following communication tasks, state a specific purpose (if you have trouble, try beginning with "I want to . . .").

1. A report to your boss, the store manager, about the outdated items in the warehouse

2. A blog posting (on your external website) to customers and the news media about your company's plans to acquire a competitor

3. A letter to a customer who hasn't made a payment for three months

4. An e-mail message to employees about the office's high water bills

5. A phone call to a supplier checking on an overdue parts shipment

6. A podcast to new users of the company's online content management system

Audience Profile   For each communication task below, write brief answers to three questions: (1) Who is my audience? (2) What is my audience's general attitude toward my subject? (3) What does my audience need to know?

7. A final-notice collection letter from an appliance manufacturer to an appliance dealer, sent ten days before initiating legal collection procedures

8. A promotional message on your company's e-retailing website, announcing a temporary price reduction on high-definition television sets

9. An advertisement for peanut butter

10. A letter to the property management company responsible for maintaining your office building, complaining about persistent problems with the heating and air conditioning

11. A cover letter sent along with your résumé to a potential employer

12. A request (to the seller) for a price adjustment on a piano that incurred $150 in damage during delivery to a banquet room in the hotel you manage

Media and Purpose   List three messages you have read, viewed, or listened to lately (such as direct-mail promotions, letters, e-mail or instant messages, phone solicitations, podcasts, and lectures). For each message, determine the general and the specific purpose; then answer the questions listed.

Message #1:

13. General purpose:

14. Specific purpose:

15. Was the message well timed?

16. Did the sender choose an appropriate medium for the message?

17. Was the sender's purpose realistic?

Message #2:

18. General purpose:

19. Specific purpose:

20. Was the message well timed?

21. Did the sender choose an appropriate medium for the message?

22. Was the sender's purpose realistic?

Message #3:

23. General purpose:

24. Specific purpose:

25. Was the message well timed?

26. Did the sender choose an appropriate medium for the message?

27. Was the sender's purpose realistic?

Message Organization: Choosing the Approach   Indicate whether the direct or the indirect approach would be best in each of the following situations. Write *direct* or *indirect* in the space provided.

28. _____ An e-mail message to a car dealer asking about the availability of a specific make and model of car

29. _____ A letter from a recent college graduate requesting a letter of recommendation from a former instructor

30. _____ A letter turning down a job applicant

31. _____ A blog posting explaining that because of high air-conditioning costs, the plant temperature will be held at 78 degrees during the summer

32. _____ A final request to settle a delinquent debt

Message Organization: Drafting Persuasive Messages   If you were trying to persuade people to take the following actions, how would you organize your argument? Write *direct* or *indirect* in the space provided.

33. _____ You want your boss to approve your plan for hiring two new people.

34. _____ You want to be hired for a job.

35. _____ You want to be granted a business loan.

36. _____ You want to collect a small amount from a regular customer whose account is slightly past due.

37. _____ You want to collect a large amount from a customer whose account is seriously past due.

Activities

For active links to all websites discussed in this chapter, visit this text's website at www. prenhall.com/bovee. Locate your book and click on its Companion Website link. Then select Chapter 3, and click on "Featured Websites." Locate the name of the page or the URL related to the material in the text. Please note that links to sites that become inactive after publication of the book will be removed from the Featured Websites section.

1. **Analyze This Document**   A writer is working on an insurance information brochure and is having trouble grouping the ideas logically into an outline. Prepare the outline, paying attention to appropriate subordination of ideas. If necessary, rewrite phrases to give them a more consistent sound.

   Accident Protection Insurance Plan

   - Coverage is only pennies a day
   - Benefit is $100,000 for accidental death on common carrier
   - Benefit is $100 a day for hospitalization as result of motor vehicle or common carrier accident
   - Benefit is $20,000 for accidental death in motor vehicle accident
   - Individual coverage is only $17.85 per quarter; family coverage is just $26.85 per quarter
   - No physical exam or health questions
   - Convenient payment—billed quarterly
   - Guaranteed acceptance for all applicants
   - No individual rate increases
   - Free, no-obligation examination period
   - Cash paid in addition to any other insurance carried
   - Covers accidental death when riding as fare-paying passenger on public transportation, including buses, trains, jets, ships, trolleys, subways, or any other common carrier
   - Covers accidental death in motor vehicle accidents occurring while driving or riding in or on automobile, truck, camper, motor home, or nonmotorized bicycle

2. **Message Planning Skills: Self-Assessment**   How good are you at planning business messages? Use the following chart to rate yourself on each of the following elements of planning an audience-centered business message. Then examine your ratings to identify where you are strongest and where you can improve.

Element of Planning	Always	Frequently	Occasionally	Never
1. I start by defining my purpose.	_____	_____	_____	_____
2. I analyze my audience before writing a message.	_____	_____	_____	_____
3. I investigate what my audience wants to know.	_____	_____	_____	_____
4. I check that my information is accurate, ethical, and pertinent.	_____	_____	_____	_____
5. I consider my audience and purpose when selecting media.	_____	_____	_____	_____
6. I consider the audience's likely reaction to my message before deciding on a direct or indirect approach.	_____	_____	_____	_____
7. I plan carefully, particularly for longer or complex messages, to make sure I use my time wisely.	_____	_____	_____	_____
8. I limit the scope of my messages to the extent of information needed to accomplish my specific purpose.	_____	_____	_____	_____

Expand Your Knowledge

Exploring the Best of the Web

Learn from the Best in the Business See how some of today's brightest entrepreneurs and business managers are using blogging to reach their target markets. *Forbes* magazine regularly highlights business-oriented blogs that its editors believe make effective use of the unique benefits of blogging. At the www.forbes.com/bow page, click on "Blogs" in the "Departments" heading, then check out the Marketing and Small Business blogging sections.

Exercises

1. What are some of the reasons *Forbes* selected these particular blogs as being among the best on the web?
2. What weaknesses does the magazine see in some of these blogs?
3. What can you learn from these blogs that you could apply to your own future as an entrepreneur or business manager?

Exploring the Web on Your Own

Review these chapter-related websites on your own to learn more about achieving communication success in the workplace:

1. Get hundreds of free tips on improving your business writing at Bull's Eye Business Writing Tips, www.businesswritingtips.com.
2. See how to put phone text messaging to work in business applications at Text.It, www.text.it (click on "Text for Business").
3. Discover how e-mail works and how to improve your e-mail communications by following the steps at About Internet for Beginners—Harness E-Mail, www.learnthenet.com/english/section/email.html.

Learn Interactively

Interactive Study Guide

Visit www.prenhall.com/bovee, then locate your book and click on its Companion Website link. Select Chapter 3 to take advantage of the interactive "Chapter Quiz" to test your knowledge of chapter concepts. Receive instant feedback on whether you need additional studying. Also, visit the "Study Hall," where you'll find an abundance of valuable resources that will help you succeed in this course.

Peak Performance Grammar and Mechanics

If your instructor has required the use of "Peak Performance Grammar and Mechanics," either in your online course or on CD, you can improve your skill with verbs by using the "Peak Performance Grammar and Mechanics" module. Click on "Grammar Basics," and then click "Verbs." Take the Pretest to determine whether you have any weak areas. Then review those areas in the Refresher Course. Take the Follow-Up Test to check your grasp of verbs. For an extra challenge or advanced practice, take the Advanced Test. Finally, for additional reinforcement in verbs, go to the "Improve Your Grammar, Mechanics, and Usage" section that follows, and complete the "Level I: Self-Assessment" exercises.

Improve Your Grammar, Mechanics, and Usage

Level 1: Self-Assessment—Verbs

Review Section 1.3 in the Handbook of Grammar, Mechanics, and Usage, and then complete the following 15 items.

In items 1–5, provide the verb form called for in the following exercises:

1. I _____ (present perfect, *become*) the resident expert on repairing the copy machine.

2. She _____ (past, *know*) how to conduct an audit when she came to work for us.

3. Since Joan was promoted, she _____ (past perfect, *move*) all the files to her office.

4. Next week, call John to tell him what you _____ (future, *do*) to help him set up the seminar.

5. By the time you finish the analysis, he _____ (future perfect, *return*) from his vacation.

For items 6–10, rewrite the sentences so that they use active voice instead of passive:

6. The report will be written by Leslie Cartwright.

7. The failure to record the transaction was mine.

8. Have you been notified by the claims department of your rights?

9. We are dependent on their services for our operation.

10. The damaged equipment was returned by the customer before we even located a repair facility.

In items 11–15, circle the correct verb form provided in parentheses:

11. Everyone upstairs (*receive/receives*) mail before we do.

12. Neither the main office nor the branches (*is/are*) blameless.

13. C&B sales (*is/are*) listed in the directory.

14. When measuring shelves, 7 inches (*is/are*) significant.

15. About 90 percent of the employees (*plan/plans*) to come to the company picnic.

Level 2: Workplace Applications

The following items contain numerous errors in grammar, capitalization, punctuation, abbreviation, number style, word division, and vocabulary. Rewrite each sentence in the space provided, correcting all errors. Write *C* in the space after any sentence that is already correct.

1. Cut two inches off trunk and place in a water stand, and fill with water.

2. The newly-elected officers of the Board are: John Rogers, president, Robin Doig, vice-president, and Mary Sturhann, secretary.

3. Employees were stunned when they are notified that the trainee got promoted to Manager only after her 4th week with the company.

4. Seeking reliable data on U.S. publishers, *Literary Marketplace* is by far the best source.

5. Who did you wish to speak to?

6. The keynote address will be delivered by Seth Goodwin, who is the author of six popular books on marketing, has written two novels, and writes a column for "Fortune" magazine.

7. Often the reputation of an entire company depend on one employee that officially represents that company to the public.

8. The executive director, along with his staff, are working quickly to determine who should receive the Award.

9. Him and his co-workers, the top bowling team in the tournament, will represent our Company in the league finals on saturday.

10. Listening on the extension, details of the embezzlement plot were overheard by the Security Chief.

11. The acceptance of visa cards are in response to our customer's demand for a more efficient and convenient way of paying for parking here at San Diego International airport.

12. The human resources dept. interviewed dozens of people, they are seeking the better candidate for the opening.

13. Libraries' can be a challenging; yet lucrative market if you learn how to work the "system" to gain maximum visibility for you're products and services.

14. Either a supermarket or a discount art gallery are scheduled to open in the Mall.

15. I have told my supervisor that whomever shares my office with me cannot wear perfume, use spray deodorant, or other scented products.

Level 3: Document Critique

The following document may contain errors in grammar, capitalization, punctuation, abbreviation, number style, vocabulary, and spelling. You will also find errors relating to topics in this chapter. Concentrate on using the "you" attitude, emphasizing the positive, being polite, and using bias-free language as you improve this memo. Correct all errors using standard proofreading marks (see Appendix C).

Memo

TO: Blockbuster mngrs.

FROM: Tom Dooley, deputy chairmen, Viacom, Inc.

              in care of Blockbuster Entertainment Group

              Corporate headquarters, Renaissance Tower

              1201 Elm street; Dallas TX 75270

DATE: May 8 2007

SUB: Recent Cash Flow and consumer response—Survey

Now that our stores have been re-organized with your hard work and cooperation, we hope revenues will rise to new heights; if we re-emphasize video rentals as Blockbusters core business and reduce the visibility of our sideline retail products. Just in case though, we want to be certain that these changes are having the postive affect on our cash flow that we all except and look forward to.

To help us make that determination, respond to the following survey questions and fax them back. Answer concisely; but use extra paper if necessary—for details and explanations.

When you finish the survey it will help headquarters improve service to you; but also, help us all improve service to our customers. Return your survey before before May 15 to my attention. Then blockbuster hopefully can thrive in a marketplace, that critics say we cannot conquer. Blockbuster must choose wisely and serve it's customers well in a difficult video-rental business environment.

Times are very tough but if we work hard at it its possible we might make Blockbuster 'the man on the streets' favorite 'place to go to rent videos!'

Writing Business Messages

Learning Objectives

After studying this chapter, you will be able to

1 Explain the importance of adapting your messages to the needs and expectations of your audience

2 Define the "you" attitude and its role in successful communication

3 Discuss four ways of achieving a businesslike tone with a style that is clear and concise

4 Explain the meaning of plain English and its value in business communication

5 Briefly describe how to select words that are not only correct but also effective

6 Explain how sentence style affects emphasis within your message

7 List five ways to develop coherent paragraphs

8 Identify the most common software features that help you craft messages more efficiently

The situation described in the quote to the left is all too common in business these days: murky, confusing messages that do more to anger and alienate than to communicate. Your success in business will depend to a large degree on how well you can inform and persuade others—how successful do you think you'll be if your messages cause reactions like this? Fortunately, writing effective, audience-focused messages is within the grasp of every professional who is willing to learn a few basic concepts.

With a solid plan in place (see Chapter 3), you're ready to choose the words and craft the sentences and paragraphs that will carry your ideas to their intended audiences. Figure 4.1 lists the tasks involved in adapting to your audience and composing your message.

Adapting to Your Audience

Audiences want to know how your messages will benefit them.

Whether consciously or not, audiences greet most incoming messages with a question: "What's in this for me?" If your intended audience thinks a message does not apply to them or doesn't meet their needs, they'll be far less inclined to pay attention to it. By adapting your communication to the needs and expectations of your audiences, you'll provide a more compelling answer to the "What's in this for me?" question and improve

FIGURE 4.1 Step Two in the Three-Step Writing Process: Writing Your Messages
The second step in the three-step writing process includes two vital tasks: adapting to your audience and composing your message.

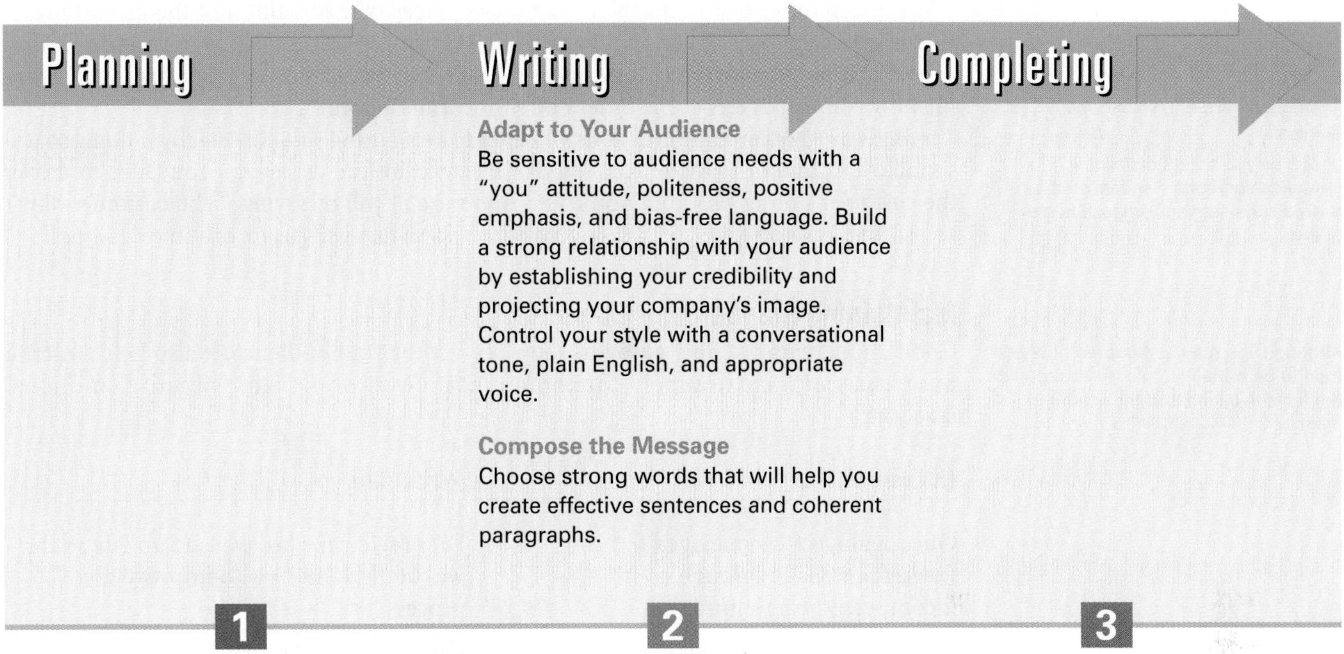

Planning   **Writing**   **Completing**

Adapt to Your Audience
Be sensitive to audience needs with a "you" attitude, politeness, positive emphasis, and bias-free language. Build a strong relationship with your audience by establishing your credibility and projecting your company's image. Control your style with a conversational tone, plain English, and appropriate voice.

Compose the Message
Choose strong words that will help you create effective sentences and coherent paragraphs.

1   **2**   **3**

the chances of your message being successful. To adapt your message to your audience, try to be sensitive to your audience's needs, build a strong relationship with your audience, and control your style to maintain a professional tone.

Being Sensitive to Your Audience's Needs

In any business message, you can use all the right words and still not be sensitive to your audience and their needs. To demonstrate true audience sensitivity, adopt the "you" attitude, maintain good standards of etiquette, emphasize the positive, and use bias-free language.

Using the "You" Attitude

You are already becoming familiar with the audience-centered approach, trying to see a subject through your audience's eyes. Now you want to project this approach in your messages by adopting a **"you" attitude**—that is, by speaking and writing in terms of your audience's wishes, interests, hopes, and preferences.

The "you" attitude is best implemented by expressing your message in terms of the audience's interests and needs.

On the simplest level, you can adopt the "you" attitude by replacing terms that refer to yourself and your company with terms that refer to your audience. In other words, use *you* and *yours* instead of *I, me, mine, we, us,* and *ours*:

Instead of This	Write This
To help us process this order, we must ask for another copy of the requisition.	So that your order can be filled promptly, please send another copy of the requisition.
We offer MP3 players with 50, 75, or 100 gigabytes of storage capacity.	Select your MP3 player from three models with 50, 75, or 100 gigabytes of storage capacity.

You'll find that using "you" and "yours" often requires some finesse to avoid creating awkward sentences or messages that sound like nonstop sales pitches.[2] Keep in mind that the "you" attitude is not intended to be manipulative or insincere. Nor is the "you" attitude simply a matter of using one pronoun rather than another; it's a matter of genuine empathy. You can use *you* 25 times in a single page and still ignore your audience's true concerns. In other words, it's the thought and sincerity that count, not the pronoun *you*. If you're talking to a retailer, try to think like a retailer; if you're dealing with a production supervisor, put yourself in that position; if you're writing to a dissatisfied customer, imagine how you would feel at the other end of the transaction.

Be aware that on some occasions it's better to avoid using *you*, particularly if doing so will sound overly authoritative or accusing. For instance, instead of saying, "You failed to deliver the customer's order on time," you could minimize ill will by saying, "The customer didn't receive the order on time," or "Let's figure out a system that will ensure on-time deliveries."

Avoid using *you* and *yours* when doing so

■ Makes you sound dictatorial
■ Makes someone else feel guilty
■ Goes against your organization's style

Maintaining Standards of Etiquette

Good etiquette is not only a way to show respect for your audience, it also helps foster a more successful environment for communication by minimizing negative emotional reaction:

Although you may be tempted now and then to be brutally frank, try to express the facts in a kind and thoughtful manner.

Instead of This	Write This
Once again, you've managed to bring down the website through your incompetent programming.	Let's review the last website update so that we can find out how to improve the process.
You've been sitting on our order for two weeks, and we need it now!	Our production schedules depend on timely delivery of parts and supplies, but we have not yet received the order you promised to deliver two weeks ago. Please respond today with a firm delivery commitment.

Use extra tact when communicating with people higher up the organization chart or outside the company.

Of course, some situations require more diplomacy than others. If you know your audience well, a less formal approach might be more appropriate. However, when you are communicating with people who outrank you or with people outside your organization, an added measure of courtesy is usually needed.

Written communication and most forms of electronic media generally require more tact than oral communication (Figure 4.2). When you're speaking, your words are softened by your tone of voice and facial expression. Plus, you can adjust your approach according to the feedback you get. If you inadvertently offend someone in writing or in a podcast, for example, you usually won't get the immediate feedback you would need to resolve the situation. In fact, you may never know that you offended your audience.

Emphasizing the Positive

You can communicate negative news without being negative.

Sensitive communicators understand the difference between delivering negative news and being negative. For example, when Alaska Airlines instituted surcharges for heavy luggage in an attempt to reduce injuries to baggage handlers, the company presented the change to passengers in a positive light with the message, "Pack Light & Save."[3] Never try to hide the negative news, but look for positive points that will foster a good relationship with your audience:[4]

Instead of This	Write This
It is impossible to repair your car today.	Your car can be ready by Tuesday. Would you like a loaner until then?
We wasted $300,000 advertising in that magazine.	Our $300,000 advertising investment did not pay off; let's analyze the experience and apply the insights to future campaigns.

FIGURE 4.2 Fostering a Positive Relationship with an Audience

In the "poor" example, notice how the customer service agent's unfortunate word choices immediately derail this instant-messaging exchange. In the "improved" example, a more sensitive approach allows both people to focus on solving the problem.

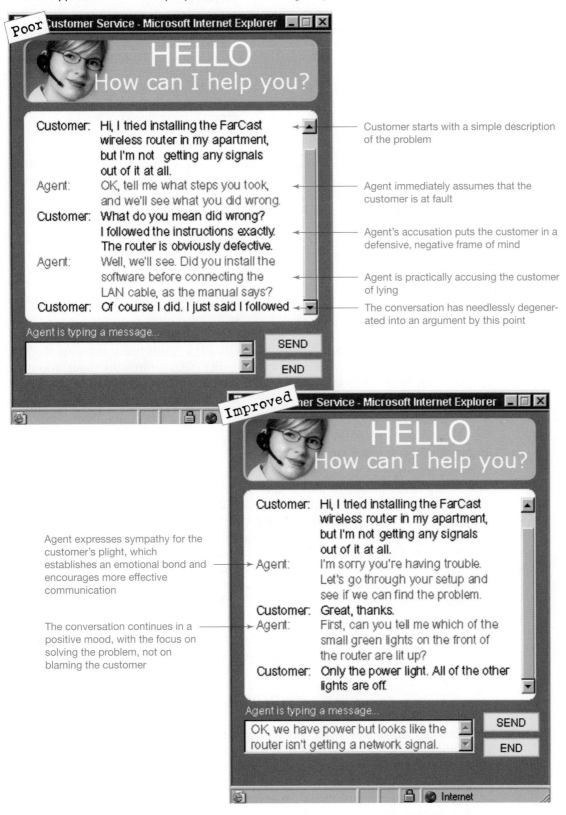

Poor

Customer Service - Microsoft Internet Explorer

HELLO
How can I help you?

Customer: Hi, I tried installing the FarCast wireless router in my apartment, but I'm not getting any signals out of it at all.

Agent: OK, tell me what steps you took, and we'll see what you did wrong.

Customer: What do you mean did wrong? I followed the instructions exactly. The router is obviously defective.

Agent: Well, we'll see. Did you install the software before connecting the LAN cable, as the manual says?

Customer: Of course I did. I just said I followed

Agent is typing a message...

SEND
END

Customer starts with a simple description of the problem

Agent immediately assumes that the customer is at fault

Agent's accusation puts the customer in a defensive, negative frame of mind

Agent is practically accusing the customer of lying

The conversation has needlessly degenerated into an argument by this point

Improved

...mer Service - Microsoft Internet Explorer

HELLO
How can I help you?

Customer: Hi, I tried installing the FarCast wireless router in my apartment, but I'm not getting any signals out of it at all.

Agent: I'm sorry you're having trouble. Let's go through your setup and see if we can find the problem.

Customer: Great, thanks.

Agent: First, can you tell me which of the small green lights on the front of the router are lit up?

Customer: Only the power light. All of the other lights are off.

Agent is typing a message...

OK, we have power but looks like the router isn't getting a network signal.

SEND
END

Internet

Agent expresses sympathy for the customer's plight, which establishes an emotional bond and encourages more effective communication

The conversation continues in a positive mood, with the focus on solving the problem, not on blaming the customer

Show your audience how they will benefit from complying with your message.

If you're trying to persuade the audience to perform a particular action, point out how doing so will benefit them:

Instead of This	Write This
We will notify all three credit reporting agencies if you do not pay your overdue bill within 10 days.	Paying your overdue bill within 10 days will prevent a negative entry on your credit record.
I am tired of seeing so many errors in the customer service blog.	Proofreading your blog postings will help you avoid embarrassing mistakes that generate more customer service complaints.

Try to avoid words with negative connotations; use meaningful euphemisms instead.

In general, try to state your message without using words that might hurt or offend your audience. Substitute *euphemisms* (mild terms) for those that have unpleasant connotations. You can be honest without being harsh. Gentle language won't change the facts, but it will make them more acceptable:

Instead of This	Write This
cheap merchandise	economy merchandise
failing	underperforming
fake	imitation or faux

Be aware that when using euphemisms, you walk a fine line between softening the blow and hiding the facts. It would be unethical to speak to your community about "relocating refuse" when you're really talking about your plans for disposing of toxic waste. People respond better to an honest message delivered with integrity than they do to a sugar-coated message filled with empty talk.

Using Bias-Free Language

Avoid biased language that might offend your audience.

Bias-free language avoids words and phrases that unfairly and even unethically categorize or stigmatize people in ways related to gender, race, ethnicity, age, or disability. Contrary to what some might think, biased language is not simply about "labels." To a significant degree, language reflects the way people think and what they believe, and biased language may well perpetuate the underlying stereotypes and prejudices that it represents.[5] Moreover, since communication is all about perception, being fair and objective isn't enough; to establish a good relationship with your audience, you must also *appear* to be fair.[6] Good communicators make every effort to change biased language (see Table 4.1). Bias can come in a variety of forms:

- **Gender bias.** You can avoid sexist language by using the same label for everyone (don't call a woman *chairperson* and then call a man *chairman*). Reword sentences to use *they* or to use no pronoun at all. Vary traditional patterns by sometimes putting women first (*women and men, she and he, her and his*). Note that the preferred title for women in business is *Ms.,* unless the individual asks to be addressed as *Miss* or *Mrs.* or has some other title, such as *Dr.*
- **Racial and ethnic bias.** Avoid identifying people by race or ethnic origin unless such identification is relevant to the matter at hand—and it rarely is.
- **Age bias.** Mention the age of a person only when it is relevant. Moreover, be careful of the context in which you use words that refer to age; such words carry a variety of positive and negative connotations. For example, *young* can imply youthfulness, inexperience, or even immaturity, depending on how it's used.
- **Disability bias.** No painless label exists for people with a physical, mental, sensory, or emotional impairment. Avoid mentioning a disability unless it is pertinent. However, if

Table 4.1	Overcoming Bias in Language	
Examples	**Unacceptable**	**Preferable**
Gender Bias		
Using words containing "man"	Man-made	Artificial, synthetic, manufactured, constructed
	Mankind	Humanity, human beings, human race, people
	Manpower	Workers, workforce
	Businessman	Executive, manager, businessperson
	Salesman	Sales representative, salesperson, clerk
	Foreman	Supervisor
Using female-gender words	Actress, stewardess	Actor, flight attendant
Using special designations	Woman doctor, male nurse	Doctor, nurse
Using "he" to refer to "everyone"	The average worker . . . he	The average worker . . . he or she
Identifying roles with gender	The typical executive spends four hours of his day in meetings.	Most executives spend four hours a day in meetings.
	the consumer . . . she	consumers . . . they
	the nurse/teacher . . . she	nurses/teachers . . . they
Identifying women by marital status	Norm Lindstrom and Maria	Norm Lindstrom and Maria Drake
	Norm Lindstrom and Ms. Lindstrom	Mr. Lindstrom and Ms. Drake
Racial/Ethnic Bias		
Assigning stereotypes	My African-American assistant speaks more articulately than I do.	My assistant speaks more articulately than I do.
	Jim Wong is an unusually tall Asian.	Jim Wong is tall.
Identifying people by race or ethnicity	Mario M. Cuomo, Italian American politician and ex-governor of New York	Mario M. Cuomo, politician and ex-governor of New York
Age Bias		
Including age when irrelevant	Mary Kirazy, 58, has just joined our trust department.	Mary Kirazy has just joined our trust department.
Disability Bias		
Putting the disability before the person	Crippled workers face many barriers on the job.	Workers with physical disabilities face many barriers on the job.
	An epileptic, Tracy has no trouble doing her job.	Tracy's epilepsy has no effect on her job performance.

you must refer to someone's disability, avoid terms such as *handicapped*, *crippled*, or *retarded*. Put the person first and the disability second.[7]

Building Strong Relationships with Your Audience

Focusing on your audience's needs is vital to effective communication, but you must also attend to your own priorities as a communicator. You can address your own needs while building a positive relationship by establishing your credibility and projecting your company's image.

Establishing Your Credibility

Your audience's response to every message you send depends heavily on their perception of your **credibility**, a measure of your believability based on how reliable you are and how much trust you evoke in others. Whether you're working to build credibility with a new

People are more likely to react positively to your message when they have confidence in you.

audience, to maintain credibility with an existing audience—or to restore credibility after a mistake—emphasize the following:

To enhance your credibility, emphasize such factors as honesty, objectivity, and awareness of audience needs.

- **Honesty.** Demonstrating honesty and integrity will earn you the respect of your audiences, even if they don't always agree with or welcome your messages.
- **Objectivity.** Show that you can distance yourself from emotional situations and look at all sides of an issue.
- **Awareness of audience needs.** Let your audience know that you understand what's important to them.
- **Credentials, knowledge, and expertise.** Audiences need to know that you have whatever it takes to back up your message, whether it's education, professional certification, special training, past successes, or simply the fact that you've done your research.
- **Endorsements.** If your audience doesn't know anything about you, try to get assistance from someone they do know and trust.
- **Performance.** Demonstrating impressive communication skills is not enough; people need to know they can count on you to get the job done.
- **Confidence.** Audiences also need to know that you believe in yourself and your message. If you are convinced that your message is sound, you can state your case confidently, without sounding boastful or arrogant.
- **Communication style.** Support your points with evidence, not empty terms such as *amazing*, *incredible*, or *extraordinary*.
- **Sincerity.** When you offer praise, don't use hyperbole, such as "you are the most fantastic employee I could ever imagine." Instead, point out specific qualities that warrant praise.

Finally, keep in mind that credibility can take days, months, even years to establish—and it can be wiped out in an instant. An occasional mistake or letdown is usually forgiven, but major lapses in honesty or integrity can destroy your reputation. On the other hand, when you do establish credibility, communication becomes much easier because you no longer have to spend time and energy convincing people that you are a trustworthy source of information and ideas.

Projecting the Company's Image

Your company's interests and reputation take precedence over your personal communication style.

When you communicate with outsiders, on even the most routine matter, you serve as the spokesperson for your organization. The impression you make can enhance or damage the reputation of the entire company. Thus, your own views and personality must be subordinated, at least to some extent, to the interests and style of your company.

Many organizations have specific communication guidelines that show everything from the correct use of the company name to preferred abbreviations and other grammatical details. Specifying a desired style of communication is more difficult, however. Observe more experienced colleagues to see how they communicate, and never hesitate to ask for editorial help to make sure you're conveying the appropriate tone. For instance,

Document Makeover

Improve This Letter

To practice correcting drafts of actual documents, visit your online course or the access-code-protected portion of the Companion Website. Click "Document Makeovers," then click Chapter 4. You will find a letter that contains problems and errors relating to what you've learned in this chapter about writing business messages. Use the Final Draft decision tool to create an improved version of this letter. Check the message for appropriate choice of approach, a conversational tone, correct use of active voice, and logical paragraphs.

with clients entrusting thousands or millions of dollars to it, an investment firm communicates in a style quite different from that of a clothing retailer. And a clothing retailer specializing in high-quality business attire communicates in a style different from that of a store catering to the latest trends in casual wear.

Controlling Your Style and Tone

Style is the way you use words to achieve a certain **tone**, or overall impression. You can vary your style—your sentence structure and vocabulary—to sound forceful or objective, personal or formal, colorful or dry. The right choice depends on the nature of your message and your relationship with the reader.

Using a Conversational Tone

The tone of your business messages can range from informal to conversational to formal. If you're in a large organization and you're communicating with your superiors or with customers, your tone would tend to be more formal and respectful.[8] However, that formal tone might sound distant and cold if used with close colleagues.

Compare the three versions of the letter in Table 4.2. The first is too formal and stuffy for today's audiences, whereas the third is too casual for any audience other than close associates or friends. The second message demonstrates the conversational tone used in most business communication—using plain language that sounds businesslike without being stuffy or full of jargon. You can achieve a conversational tone in your messages by following these guidelines:

> Most business messages aim for a conversational style that is warm but still businesslike.

- **Avoid obsolete and pompous language.** Most companies now shy away from such dated phrases as "attached please find" and "please be advised that." Similarly, avoid

Table 4.2	Formal, Conversational, and Informal Tones	
Formal Tone	**Conversational Tone**	**Informal Tone**
Reserved for the most formal occasions	Preferred for most business communication	Reserved for communication with friends and close associates
Dear Ms. Navarro:	Dear Ms. Navarro:	Hi Gabriella:
Enclosed please find the information that was requested during our telephone communication of May 14. As was mentioned at that time, Midville Hospital has significantly more doctors of exceptional quality than any other health facility in the state.	Here's the information you requested during our phone conversation on Friday. As I mentioned, Midville Hospital has the best doctors and more of them than any other hospital in the state.	Hope all is well. Just sending along the information you asked for. As I said on Friday, Midville Hospital has more and better doctors than any other hospital in the state.
As you were also informed, our organization has quite an impressive network of doctors and other health-care professionals with offices located throughout the state. In the event that you should need a specialist, our professionals will be able to make an appropriate recommendation.	In addition, we have a vast network of doctors and other health professionals with offices throughout the state. If you need a specialist, they can refer you to the right one.	We also have a large group of doctors and other health professionals with offices close to you at work or at home. Need a specialist? They'll refer you to the right one.
In the event that you have questions or would like additional information, you may certainly contact me during regular business hours.	If you would like more information, please call any time between 9:00 and 5:00, Monday through Friday.	Just give me a ring if you want to know more. Any time from 9:00 to 5:00 should be fine.
Most sincerely yours,	Sincerely,	Take care,
Samuel G. Berenz	Samuel G. Berenz	Sam

using obscure words, trite expressions, and overly complicated sentences to impress others.

- **Avoid preaching and bragging.** Few things are more irritating than people who think that they know everything and that others know nothing. If you do need to remind your audience of something obvious, try to work in the information casually, perhaps in the middle of a paragraph, where it will sound like a secondary comment rather than a major revelation. Also, avoid bragging about your accomplishments or those of your organization (unless your audience is a part of your organization).
- **Be careful with intimacy.** Business messages should generally avoid intimacy, such as sharing personal details or adopting a casual, unprofessional tone. However, when you do have a close relationship with your audience, such as among the members of a close-knit team, a more intimate tone is sometimes appropriate and even expected.
- **Be careful with humor.** Never use humor in formal messages or when you're communicating across cultural boundaries. Humor can easily backfire and divert attention from your message. If you don't know your audience well or you're not skilled at using humor in a business setting, don't use it at all.

Using Plain English

What do you think this sentence is trying to say?

> We continually exist to synergistically supply value-added deliverables such that we may continue to proactively maintain enterprise-wide data to stay competitive in tomorrow's world.[9]

If you don't have any idea what it means, you're not alone. However, this is a real sentence from a real company. This sort of incomprehensible, buzzword-filled writing is driving a widespread call to use *plain English.*

> **Audiences can understand and act on plain English without reading it over and over.**

Plain English is a way of presenting information in a simple, unadorned style so that your audience can easily grasp your meaning—language "that the intended audience can read, understand and act upon the first time they read it."[10] You can see how this definition supports using the "you" attitude and shows respect for your audience. Murky, pompous, or unnecessarily complex writing is the very antithesis of the "you" attitude.

For all its advantages, be aware that plain English does have some limitations. For instance, it sometimes lacks the precision or subtlety necessary for scientific research, engineering documents, intense feeling, and personal insight.

Selecting Active or Passive Voice

Your choice of active or passive voice also affects the tone of your message. You are using **active voice** when the subject performs the action, and the object receives the action: "John rented the office." You're using **passive voice** when the subject receives the action: "The office was rented by John." As you can see, the passive voice combines the helping verb *to be* with a form of the verb that is usually similar to the past tense.

> **Active sentences are usually stronger than passive ones.**

Using the active voice helps make your writing more direct, livelier, and easier to read (see Table 4.3). Passive voice is not wrong grammatically, but it can be cumbersome, lengthy, and vague. In most cases, the active voice is your best choice.[11] Nevertheless, using the passive voice can help you demonstrate the "you" attitude in some situations:

> **Use passive sentences to soften bad news, to put yourself in the background, or to create an impersonal tone.**

- When you want to be diplomatic about pointing out a problem or error of some kind
- When you want to point out what's being done without taking or attributing either the credit or the blame
- When you want to avoid personal pronouns (*I* and *we*) in order to create an objective tone

The second half of Table 4.3 illustrates several situations in which the passive voice helps you focus your message on your audience.

Table 4.3	Choosing Active or Passive Voice

In general, avoid passive voice in order to make your writing lively and direct

Dull and Indirect in Passive Voice	Lively and Direct in Active Voice
The new procedure was developed by the operations team.	The operations team developed the new procedure.
Legal problems are created by this contract.	This contract creates legal problems.
Reception preparations have been undertaken by our PR people for the new CEO's arrival.	Our PR people have begun planning a reception for the new CEO.

However, passive voice is helpful when you need to be diplomatic or want to focus attention on problems or solutions rather than on people

Accusatory or Self-Congratulatory in Active Voice	More Diplomatic in Passive Voice
You lost the shipment.	The shipment was lost.
I recruited seven engineers last month.	Seven engineers were recruited last month.
We are investigating the high rate of failures on the final assembly line.	The high rate of failures on the final assembly line is being investigated.

Composing Your Message

With these insights into how you can adapt to your audience, you're ready to begin composing your message. As you compose your first draft, try to let your creativity flow. Don't try to draft and edit at the same time or worry about getting everything perfect. Make up words if you can't think of the right word, draw pictures, talk out loud—do whatever it takes to get the ideas out of your head and onto your computer screen or a piece of paper. You'll have time to revise and refine the material later.

The most successful messages have three important elements: strong words, effective sentences, and coherent paragraphs.

Choosing Strong Words

Effective messages depend on carefully chosen words, whether you select them during your first draft or edit them in later.[12] First, pay close attention to correctness. If you make grammatical or usage errors, you lose credibility with your audience—even if your message is otherwise correct. Poor grammar implies that you're uninformed, and audiences put less faith in an uninformed source. Worse still, poor grammar can imply that you don't respect your audience enough to get things right. If you have doubts about what is correct, look up the answer, and use the proper form of expression. Check the "Handbook of Grammar, Mechanics, and Usage" at the end of this book, or consult the many special reference books and resources available in libraries, in bookstores, and on the Internet.

Correctness is the first consideration when choosing words.

Just as important as selecting the correct word is selecting the most suitable word for the job at hand. Naturally, using the right words is important in life-and-death situations. But even when you're dealing with less perilous circumstances, the right words can dramatically affect the success of your communication efforts. Compare these two sentences:

Effectiveness is the second consideration when choosing words.

Talk Energy is a network of homeowners, engineers, architects, and designers [who] are interested in energy efficiency and renewable energy.[13]

Talk Energy is a group of homeowners, engineers, architects, and designers [who] are interested in energy efficiency and renewable energy.

Both sentences are correct, but the word *network* in the first sentence does a much better job of conveying the notion of being connected and mutually supportive than *group* in the second sentence. Moreover, even though "network" is a noun here, it suggests action and energy because the very essence of networking is making connections, whereas "group" is a much more static concept.

Balancing Abstract and Concrete Words

The more abstract a word is, the more it is removed from the tangible, objective world of things that can be perceived with the senses.

Words vary dramatically in the degree of abstraction or concreteness they convey. An **abstract word** expresses a concept, quality, or characteristic. Abstractions are usually broad, encompassing a category of ideas, and they are often intellectual, academic, or philosophical. *Love, honor, progress, tradition,* and *beauty* are abstractions, as are such important business concepts as *productivity, profits, quality,* and *motivation.* In contrast, a **concrete word** stands for something you can touch, see, or visualize. Most concrete terms are anchored in the tangible, material world. *Chair, table, horse, rose, kick, kiss, red, green,* and *two* are concrete words; they are direct, clear, and exact. Incidentally, technology continues to generate new words and new meanings that describe things that don't have a physical presence but are nonetheless concrete: *software, database, signal,* and *code* are all concrete terms as well.

As you can imagine, abstractions tend to cause more trouble for writers and readers than concrete words. Abstractions tend to be "fuzzy" and subject to more than one interpretation. The best way to minimize such problems is to blend abstract terms with concrete ones, the general with the specific. State the concept, then pin it down with details expressed in more concrete terms. Save the abstractions for ideas that cannot be expressed any other way. In addition, abstract words such as *small, numerous, sizable, near, soon, good,* and *fine* are imprecise, so try to replace them with terms that are more accurate. Instead of referring to a *sizable loss,* talk about a *loss of $32 million.*

Finding Words That Communicate

When you compose your business messages, think carefully to find the words that communicate exactly what you want to say (see Table 4.4).

Try to use words that are powerful and familiar.

■ **Choose powerful words.** Choose words that express your thoughts most clearly, specifically, and dynamically. For instance, if find yourself using many adjectives and

Table 4.4	Finding Words That Communicate with Power
Avoid Weak Phrases	**Use Strong Terms**
Wealthy businessperson	Tycoon
Business prosperity	Economic Boom
Hard times	Slump
Avoid Unfamiliar Words	**Use Familiar Words**
Ascertain	Find out, learn
Consummate	Close, bring about
Peruse	Read, study
Circumvent	Avoid
Increment	Growth, increase
Unequivocal	Certain
Avoid Clichés and Buzzwords	**Use Plain Language**
An uphill battle	A challenge
Writing on the wall	Prediction
Call the shots	Be in charge
Take by storm	Attack
Cost an arm and a leg	Expensive
A new ballgame	Fresh start
Fall through the cracks	Be overlooked
Think outside the box	Be creative

adverbs, chances are you're trying to compensate for weak nouns and verbs. Saying that *sales plummeted* is stronger and more efficient than saying *sales dropped dramatically* or *sales experienced a dramatic drop.*

- **Choose familiar words.** You'll communicate best with words that are familiar to both you and your readers.
- **Avoid clichés and buzzwords.** Although familiar words are generally the best choice, beware of *clichés*—terms and phrases so common that they have lost some of their power to communicate—and *buzzwords*—trendy new terms often quickly fall out of style. When people use these terms frequently, it's often a sign that they don't know how to express themselves otherwise and don't invest the energy required for original writing.[14]
- **Use jargon carefully.** Handle technical or professional terms with care. Using them with the wrong audience can confuse and frustrate readers, but *not* using them with audiences that routinely communicate using such terms can label you as inexperienced or unaware.

> Avoid clichés and trendy buzzwords in your writing, and use jargon only when your audience is completely familiar with it.

Creating Effective Sentences

Making every sentence count is a key step in creating effective messages. Start by selecting the optimum type of sentence, then arrange words to emphasize the most important point in each sentence.

Choosing from the Four Types of Sentences

Sentences come in four basic varieties: simple, compound, complex, and compound-complex. A **simple sentence** has one main clause (a single subject and a single predicate), although it may be expanded by nouns and pronouns serving as objects of the action and by modifying phrases. Here's a typical example (with the subject underlined once and the predicate verb underlined twice):

> Profits increased in the past year.

> A simple sentence has one main clause.

A **compound sentence** has two main clauses that express two or more independent but related thoughts of equal importance, usually joined by *and, but,* or *or.* In effect, a compound sentence is a merger of two or more simple sentences (independent clauses) that are related. For example:

> Wages have declined by 5 percent, and employee turnover has been high.

> A compound sentence has two main clauses.

The independent clauses in a compound sentence are always separated by a comma or by a semicolon (in which case the conjunction—*and, but, or*—is dropped).

A **complex sentence** expresses one main thought (the independent clause) and one or more subordinate thoughts (dependent clauses) related to it, often separated by a comma. The subordinate thought, which comes first in the following sentence, could not stand alone:

> Although you may question Gerald's conclusions, you must admit that his research is thorough.

> A complex sentence has one main clause and one subordinate clause.

A **compound-complex sentence** has two main clauses, at least one of which contains a subordinate clause:

> Profits have increased in the past year, and although you may question Gerald's conclusions, you must admit that his research is thorough.

> A compound-complex sentence has two main clauses and at least one dependent clause.

From these examples, you can see the power and variety that the different sentence types can bring to your writing. To make your writing as effective as possible, strive for variety and balance using all four sentence types. If you use too many simple sentences, you won't be able to properly express the relationships among your ideas, and your writing will sound choppy and abrupt. If you use too many long, compound sentences, your writing will sound monotonous. On the other hand, an uninterrupted series of complex or compound-complex sentences is hard to follow.

> Writing is more effective if it balances all four sentence types.

Emphasize parts of a sentence by
- Devoting more words to them
- Putting them at the beginning or at the end of the sentence
- Making them the subject of the sentence

Using Sentence Style to Emphasize Key Thoughts

In every message, some ideas are more important than others. You can emphasize these key ideas through your sentence style. One obvious technique is to give important points the most space. When you want to call attention to a thought, use extra words to describe it. Consider this sentence:

> The chairperson called for a vote of the shareholders.

To emphasize the importance of the chairperson, you might describe her more fully:

> Having considerable experience in corporate takeover battles, the chairperson called for a vote of the shareholders.

You can increase the emphasis even more by adding a separate, short sentence to augment the first:

> The chairperson called for a vote of the shareholders. She has considerable experience in corporate takeover battles.

You can also call attention to a thought by making it the subject of the sentence. In the following example, the emphasis is on the person:

> *I* can write letters much more quickly using a computer.

However, by changing the subject, the computer takes center stage:

> The *computer* enables me to write letters much more quickly.

Another way to emphasize an idea is to place it either at the beginning or at the end of a sentence:

> **Less Emphatic:** We are cutting the *price* to stimulate demand.
> **More Emphatic:** To stimulate demand, we are cutting the *price*.

Placement of dependent clauses can determine emphasis.

In complex sentences, the placement of the dependent clause hinges on the relationship between the ideas expressed. If you want to emphasize the idea expressed in the dependent clause, put that clause at the end of the sentence (the most emphatic position) or at the beginning (the second most emphatic position). If you want to downplay the idea, position the dependent clause within the sentence.

> **Most Emphatic:** The electronic parts are manufactured in Mexico, *which has lower wage rates than the United States*.
> **Emphatic:** *Because wage rates are lower there*, the electronic parts are manufactured in Mexico.
> **Least Emphatic:** Mexico, *which has lower wage rates*, was selected as the production site for the electronic parts.

In every writing project, a clear plan and strong knowledge of your audience will help you make the most effective sentence choices.

Crafting Coherent Paragraphs

Paragraphs organize sentences related to the same general topic. Readers expect each paragraph to focus on a single unit of thought and to be a logical link in an organized sequence of the thoughts that make up a complete message. As with sentences, controlling the elements of each paragraph helps your readers grasp the main idea of your document and understand how the specific pieces of support material back up that idea.

Understanding the Elements of the Paragraph

Paragraphs vary widely in length and form, but most contain three basic elements: a topic sentence, support sentences that develop the topic, and transitional words and phrases.

Topic Sentence   Every properly constructed paragraph is *unified*; it deals with a single topic. The sentence that introduces that topic is called the **topic sentence**. The topic sentence gives readers a summary of the general idea that will be covered in the rest of the paragraph. In business writing, the topic sentence is usually explicit and is often the first sentence in the paragraph. The following examples show how a topic sentence can introduce the subject and suggest the way that subject will be developed:

> The medical products division has been troubled for many years by public relations problems. [In the rest of the paragraph, readers will learn the details of the problems.]

> Relocating the plant in New York has two main disadvantages. [The disadvantages will be explained in subsequent sentences.]

Support Sentences   In most paragraphs, the topic sentence needs to be explained, justified, or extended with one or more support sentences. These related sentences must all have a bearing on the general subject and must provide enough specific details to make the topic clear:

> The medical products division has been troubled for many years by public relations problems. Since 2002 the local newspaper has published 15 articles that portray the division in a negative light. We have been accused of everything from mistreating laboratory animals to polluting the local groundwater. Our facility has been described as a health hazard. Our scientists are referred to as "Frankensteins," and our profits are considered "obscene."

The support sentences are all more specific than the topic sentence. Each one provides another piece of evidence to demonstrate the general truth of the main thought. Also, each sentence is clearly related to the general idea being developed, which gives the paragraph its unity. A paragraph is well developed when (1) it contains enough information to make the topic sentence convincing and interesting and (2) it contains no extraneous, unrelated sentences.

Transitional Elements   In addition to being unified and well supported, effective paragraphs are *coherent*; that is, they are arranged in a logical order so that the audience can understand the train of thought. You achieve coherence by using transitions that show the relationship between paragraphs and among sentences within paragraphs. **Transitions** are words or phrases that tie ideas together by showing how one thought is related to another. They not only help readers understand the connections you're trying to make but also smooth your writing. Ideally, you begin planning these transitions while you're outlining, as you decide how the various ideas and blocks of information will be arranged and connected.[15]

You can establish transitions in a variety of ways:

- **Use connecting words:** *and, but, or, nevertheless, however, in addition,* and so on.
- **Echo a word or phrase from a previous paragraph or sentence:** "A system should be established for monitoring inventory levels. *This system* will provide . . ."
- **Use a pronoun that refers to a noun used previously:** "Ms. Arthur is the leading candidate for the president's position. *She* has excellent qualifications."
- **Use words that are frequently paired:** "The machine has a *minimum* output of . . . Its *maximum* output is . . ."

Some transitional elements serve as mood changers; that is, they alert the reader to a change in mood from the previous paragraph. Some announce a total contrast with what's gone on before, some announce a causal relationship, and some signal a change in

Most paragraphs consist of
- A topic sentence that reveals the subject of the paragraph
- Related sentences that support and expand the topic
- Transitional elements that help readers move between sentences and paragraphs

Transitional elements include
- Connecting words (conjunctions)
- Repeated words or phrases
- Pronouns
- Words that are frequently paired

time. Here is a list of transitions frequently used to move readers smoothly between sentences and paragraphs:

Additional detail:	moreover, furthermore, in addition, besides, first, second, third, finally
Causal relationship:	therefore, because, accordingly, thus, consequently, hence, as a result, so
Comparison:	similarly, here again, likewise, in comparison, still
Contrast:	yet, conversely, whereas, nevertheless, on the other hand, however, but, nonetheless
Condition:	although, if
Illustration:	for example, in particular, in this case, for instance
Time sequence:	formerly, after, when, meanwhile, sometimes
Intensification:	indeed, in fact, in any event
Summary:	in brief, in short, to sum up
Repetition:	that is, in other words, as I mentioned earlier

Consider using a transition whenever it might help the reader understand your ideas and follow you from point to point. You can use transitions inside paragraphs to tie related points together and between paragraphs to ease the shift from one distinct thought to another. In longer reports, transitions that link major sections or chapters are often complete paragraphs that serve as summaries of the ideas presented in the section just ending or as mini-introductions to the next section.

Developing Paragraphs

Five ways to develop paragraphs:

- Illustration
- Comparison or contrast
- Cause and effect
- Classification
- Problem and solution

A paragraph's coherence strongly depends on how you develop it, and the best way to do that is to use a structure that is familiar to your readers, appropriate to the idea you're trying to portray, and suited to your purpose. Five of the most common development techniques are illustration, comparison or contrast, cause and effect, classification, and problem and solution (see Table 4.5).

Using Technology to Compose and Shape Your Messages

Take full advantage of your word processor's formatting capabilities to help you produce effective, professional documents in less time.

As with every phase of business communication, careful use of technology can help you compose and shape better messages in less time. As you probably know, today's software (including both word processors and online publishing systems for websites and blogs) provides a wide range of tools to help writers compose documents:

- **Style sheets** and **templates**. Most word processors offer some form of style sheets, which are master lists of predefined styles (typeface, type size, and so on) for headlines, paragraph text, and so on (here, the word *style* should not be confused with *writing style*, discussed earlier in the chapter). Many organizations provide employees with approved style sheets to ensure a consistent look for all company documents. Moreover, style sheets can eliminate hours of design time by making many of your choices for you. Templates can go beyond style sheets by defining such factors as page design, available fonts, and other features. Templates can include *boilerplate*, or sections of text that are reused from document to document. Like style sheets, templates save time by making choices for you in advance. (Depending on the version of Microsoft Word you're using, style sheets may have been replaced by templates.)
- **Autocompletion.** Software called *autocompletion* (or something similar) inserts a ready-made block of text when you type the first few characters. For example, instead of typing your company's name, address, phone number, fax number, e-mail address,

Table 4.5	Five Techniques for Developing Paragraphs	
Technique	**Description**	**Sample**
Illustration	Giving examples that demonstrate the general idea	Some of our most popular products are available through local distributors. For example, Everett & Lemmings carries our frozen soups and entrees. The J. B. Green Company carries our complete line of seasonings, as well as the frozen soups. Wilmont Foods, also a major distributor, now carries our new line of frozen desserts.
Comparison or Contrast	Using similarities or differences to develop the topic	When the company was small, the recruiting function could be handled informally. The need for new employees was limited, and each manager could comfortably screen and hire her or his own staff. However, our successful bid on the Owens contract means that we will be doubling our labor force over the next six months. To hire that many people without disrupting our ongoing activities, we will create a separate recruiting group within the human resources department.
Cause and Effect	Focusing on the reasons for something	The heavy-duty fabric of your Wanderer tent probably broke down for one of two reasons: (1) a sharp object punctured the fabric, and without reinforcement, the hole was enlarged by the stress of pitching the tent daily for a week or (2) the fibers gradually rotted because the tent was folded and stored while still wet.
Classification	Showing how a general idea is broken into specific categories	Successful candidates for our supervisor trainee program generally come from one of several groups. The largest group, by far, consists of recent graduates of accredited business management programs. The next largest group comes from within our own company, as we try to promote promising staff workers to positions of greater responsibility. Finally, we do occasionally accept candidates with outstanding supervisory experience in related industries.
Problem and Solution	Presenting a problem and then discussing the solution	Selling handmade toys online is a challenge because consumers are accustomed to buying heavily advertised toys from major chain stores or well-known websites such as Amazon.com. However, if we develop an appealing website, we can compete on the basis of product novelty and quality. In addition, we can provide unusual crafts at a competitive price: a rocking horse of birch, with a hand-knit tail and mane; a music box with the child's name painted on the top; a real teepee, made by Native American artisans.

and website URL, you can set the software to enter all this information as soon as you type the first three letters of the company name.

- **Autocorrection**. Another automatic feature in some programs instantly corrects spelling and typing errors and converts text to symbols, such as converting (c) to the © copyright symbol. However, autocorrection may make changes that you *don't* want made, such as converting "nd," "st," or "th" to superscript characters when paired with numbers, as in "21st century." (Although the use of such superscripts is common in word processing, many design professionals consider it poor typesetting.)

- **File merge** and **mail merge**. Today's software makes it easy to combine files—an especially handy feature when several members of a team write different sections of a report. For particularly complex reports, you can set up a master document that merges a number of subdocuments automatically when it's time to print. *Mail merge* lets you personalize form letters by inserting names and addresses from a database.

- **Endnotes, footnotes, indexes,** and **tables of contents.** Your computer can also help you track footnotes and endnotes, renumbering them every time you add or delete references. For a report's indexes and table of contents, you can simply flag the items you want to include, and the software assembles the lists for you.

- **Wizards**. Programs such as Microsoft Word offer *wizards* that guide you through the process of creating letters, résumés, and other common documents.

As with other forms of communication technology, using these tools efficiently and effectively requires some balance. You need to learn enough about the features to be handy with them, without spending so much time that the tools distract the writing process.

Reviewing Key Points

This chapter discusses the second step in the three-step writing process: writing business messages, including the two key tasks of adapting to your audience and composing your message. First, the chapter helps you adapt to your audience by explaining how to be sensitive to your audience's needs: using the "you" attitude, practicing good etiquette, emphasizing the positive, and using bias-free language. Next, it shows you how to build strong relationships with your audience by establishing your credibility and projecting your company's image. The final aspect of adapting to your audience is controlling your style and tone: using a conversational tone, emphasizing plain English, and making effective use of active and passive voice.

The second part of the chapter helps you compose your message. It explains how to select the best words by blending abstract and concrete words, choosing words that are strong and familiar, and avoiding clichés and jargon. The chapter shows you how to create effective sentences by using all four types, selecting active or passive voice, and emphasizing key thoughts. The chapter next explains how to develop coherent paragraphs by adapting paragraph length, using five development techniques, and using transitions to achieve both unity and coherence. The chapter concludes with advice on using communication technology wisely.

The next chapter focuses on the last step of the writing process: completing business messages. It discusses how to revise your messages for conciseness and clarity. It covers how to produce your message by choosing the right design elements, making those design elements effective, and using computers to improve your finished documents. In addition, you will learn how to proofread your business messages—what to look for and how to adapt the process.

Test Your Knowledge

1. Which writing characteristics should you avoid if you want to achieve a conversational tone?

2. How does an abstract word differ from a concrete word?

3. In what three situations should you use passive voice?

4. How can you use sentence style to emphasize key thoughts?

5. What functions do transitions serve?

Apply Your Knowledge

1. How can you apply the "you" approach if you don't know your audience personally?

2. When composing business messages, how can you be yourself and project your company's image at the same time?

3. What steps can you take to make abstract concepts such as *opportunity* feel more concrete in your messages?

4. Should you bother using transitional elements if the logical sequence of your message is already obvious? Why or why not?

5. **Ethical Choices**   Seven million people in the United States are allergic to one or more food ingredients. Every year 30,000 of these people end up in the emergency room after suffering an allergic reaction, and 200 of them die. Many of these tragic events are tied to poorly written food labels that either fail to identify dangerous allergens or use scientific terms that most consumers don't recognize. Do food manufacturers have a responsibility to ensure that consumers read, understand, and follow warnings on food products? Explain your answer.

Practice Your Knowledge

Exercises for Perfecting Your Writing

The "You" Attitude   Rewrite the following sentences to reflect your audience's viewpoint.

1. We request that you use the order form supplied in the back of our catalog.

2. We insist that you always bring your credit card to the store.

3. We want to get rid of all our 15-inch monitors to make room in our warehouse for the 19-inch screens. Thus we are offering a 25 percent discount on all sales this week.

4. I am applying for the position of bookkeeper in your office. I feel that my grades prove that I am bright and capable, and I think I can do a good job for you.

5. As requested, we are sending the refund for $25.

Emphasizing the Positive   Revise these sentences to be positive rather than negative.

6. To avoid the loss of your credit rating, please remit payment within 10 days.

7. We don't make refunds on returned merchandise that is soiled.

8. Because we are temporarily out of Baby Cry dolls, we won't be able to ship your order for 10 days.

9. You failed to specify the color of the blouse that you ordered.

10. You should have realized that waterbeds will freeze in unheated houses during winter. Therefore, our guarantee does not cover the valve damage and you must pay the $9.50 valve-replacement fee (plus postage).

Emphasizing the Positive   Revise the following sentences to replace unflattering terms (in italics) with euphemisms:

11. The new boss is _____ (*stubborn*) when it comes to doing things by the book.

12. When you say we've doubled our profit level, you are _____ (*wrong*).

13. Just be careful not to make any _____ (*stupid*) choices this week.

14. Jim Riley is _____ (*incompetent*) for that kind of promotion.

15. Glen monopolizes every meeting by being _____ (*a loudmouth*).

Courteous Communication   Revise the following sentences to make them more courteous:

16. You claim that you mailed your check last Thursday, but we have not received it.

17. It is not our policy to exchange sale items, especially after they have been worn.

18. You neglected to sign the enclosed contract.

19. I received your letter, in which you assert that our shipment was three days late.

20. You failed to enclose your instructions for your new will.

Bias-Free Language   Rewrite each of the following sentences to eliminate bias:

21. For an Indian, Maggie certainly is outgoing.

22. He needs a wheelchair, but he doesn't let his handicap affect his job performance.

23. A pilot must have the ability to stay calm under pressure, and then he must be trained to cope with any problem that arises.

24. Candidate Renata Parsons, married and the mother of a teenager, will attend the debate.

25. Senior citizen Sam Nugent is still an active salesman.

Message Composition: Selecting Words   In the following sentences, replace vague phrases (underlined) with concrete phrases. Make up any details you might need.

26. We will be opening our new facility <u>sometime this spring</u>.

27. You can now purchase our new Leaf-Away yard and lawn blower <u>at a substantial savings.</u>

28. After the reception, we were surprised that <u>such a large number attended.</u>

29. The new production line has been operating <u>with increased efficiency</u> on every run.

30. Over the holiday, we hired a crew to <u>expand the work area.</u>

Message Composition: Selecting Words   In the following sentences, replace weak terms (in italics) with words that are stronger:

31. The two reporters _____ (*ran after*) every lead enthusiastically.

32. Even large fashion houses have to match staff size to the normal _____ (*seasonal ups and downs*).

33. The _____ (*bright*) colors in that ad are keeping customers from seeing what we have to sell.

34. Health costs _____ (*suddenly rise*) when management forgets to emphasize safety issues.

35. Once we solved the zoning issue, new business construction _____ (*moved forward*), and the district has been flourishing ever since.

Message Composition: Selecting Words   Rewrite these sentences to replace the clichés with fresh, personal expressions:

36. Being a jack-of-all-trades, Dave worked well in his new selling job.

37. Moving Leslie into the accounting department, where she was literally a fish out of water, was like putting a square peg into a round hole, if you get my drift.

38. I knew she was at death's door, but I thought the doctor would pull her through.

39. Movies aren't really my cup of tea; as far as I am concerned, they can't hold a candle to a good book.

40. It's a dog-eat-dog world out there in the rat race of the asphalt jungle.

Message Composition: Selecting Words   In the following sentences, replace long, complicated words with short, simple ones:

41. Management _____ (*inaugurated*) the recycling policy six months ago.

42. You can convey the same meaning without _____ (*utilizing*) the same words.

43. You'll never be promoted unless you _____ (*endeavor*) to be more patient.

44. I have to wait until payday to _____ (*ascertain*) whether I got the raise or not.

45. John will send you a copy, once he's inserted all the _____ (*alterations*) you've requested.

46. Grand Tree _____ (*fabricates*) office furniture that is both durable and attractive.

47. I understand from your letter that you expect a full refund, _____ (*nevertheless*) your warranty expired more than a year ago.

Message Composition: Selecting Words   Rewrite the following sentences, replacing obsolete phrases with up-to-date versions. Write *none* if you think there is no appropriate substitute.

48. I have completed the form and returned it to my insurance company, as per your instructions.

49. Attached herewith is a copy of our new contract for your records.

50. Even though it will increase the price of the fence, we have decided to use the redwood in lieu of the cedar.

51. Saunders & Saunders has received your request for the Greenwood file, and in reply I wish to state that we will send you copies of Mr. Greenwood's documents only after Judge Taylor makes her ruling and orders us to do so.

52. Please be advised that your account with National Bank has been compromised, and we advise you to close it as soon as possible.

Message Composition: Creating Sentences   Rewrite each sentence so that it is active rather than passive:

53. The raw data are submitted to the data processing division by the sales representative each Friday.

54. High profits are publicized by management.

55. The policies announced in the directive were implemented by the staff.

56. Our computers are serviced by the Santee Company.

57. The employees were represented by Janet Hogan.

Message Organization: Transitional Elements   Add transitional elements to the following sentences to improve the flow of ideas. (*Note*: You may need to eliminate or add some words to smooth out your sentences.)

58. Steve Case saw infinite possibilities for the Internet. Steve Case was determined to turn his vision into reality. The techies scoffed at his strategy of building a simple Internet service for ordinary people. Case doggedly pursued his dream. He analyzed other online services. He assessed the needs of his customers. He responded to their desires for an easier way to access information over the Internet. In 1992, Steve Case named his company America Online (AOL). Critics predicted the company's demise. By the end of the century, AOL was a profitable powerhouse. AOL grew so big that it was able to merge with the giant traditional media company Time Warner. The merger was widely criticized. The merger did not live up to Case's expectations. He eventually left the company.

59. Facing some of the toughest competitors in the world, Harley-Davidson had to make some changes. The company introduced new products. Harley's management team set out to rebuild the company's production process. New products were coming to market and the company was turning a profit. Harley's quality standards were not on par with those of its foreign competitors. Harley's costs were still among the highest in the industry. Harley made a U-turn and restructured the company's organizational structure. Harley's efforts have paid off.

60. Whether you're indulging in a doughnut in New York or California, Krispy Kreme wants you to enjoy the same delicious taste with every bite. The company maintains consistent product quality by carefully controlling every step of the production process. Krispy Kreme tests all raw ingredients against established quality standards. Every delivery of wheat flour is sampled and measured for its moisture content and protein levels. Krispy Kreme blends the ingredients. Krispy Kreme tests the doughnut mix for quality. Krispy Kreme delivers the mix to its stores. Krispy Kreme knows that it takes more than a quality mix to produce perfect doughnuts all the time. The company supplies its stores with everything they need to produce premium doughnuts—mix, icings, fillings, equipment—you name it.

Activities

For active links to all websites discussed in this chapter, visit this text's website at www.prenhall.com/bovee. Locate your book and click on its Companion Website link. Then select Chapter 4, and click on "Featured Websites." Locate the name of the page or the URL related to the material in the text. Please note that links to sites that become inactive after publication of the book will be removed from the Featured Websites section.

1. **Analyze This Document**   Read the following document, then (1) analyze the strengths and weaknesses of each sentence, and (2) revise the document so that it follows this chapter's guidelines.

I am a new publisher with some really great books to sell. I saw your announcement in *Publishers Weekly* about the bookseller's show you're having this summer, and I think it's a great idea. Count me in, folks! I would like to get some space to show my books. I thought it would be a neat thing if I could do some airbrushing on T-shirts live to help promote my hot new title, *T-Shirt Art*. Before I got into publishing, I was an airbrush artist, and I could demonstrate my techniques. I've done hundreds of advertising illustrations and have been a sign painter all my life, so I'll also be promoting my other book, hot off the presses, *How to Make Money in the Sign Painting Business*.

I will be starting my PR campaign about May 2005 with ads in *PW* and some art trade papers, so my books should be well known by the time the show comes around in August. In case you would like to use my appearance there as part of your publicity, I have enclosed a biography and photo of myself.

P.S. Please let me know what it costs for booth space as soon as possible so that I can figure out whether I can afford to attend. Being a new publisher is mighty expensive!

2. **Teamwork**   Working with four other students, divide the following five topics and write one paragraph on your selected topic. Be sure one student writes a paragraph using the illustration technique, one using the comparison-or-contrast technique, one using a discussion of cause and effect, one using the classification technique, and one using a discussion of problem and solution. Then exchange paragraphs within the team and pick out the main idea and general purpose of the paragraph one of your teammates wrote. Was everyone able to correctly identify the main idea and purpose? If not, suggest how the paragraph might be rewritten for clarity.

   a. Types of cameras (or dogs or automobiles) available for sale

   b. Advantages and disadvantages of eating at fast-food restaurants

   c. Finding that first full-time job

   d. Good qualities of my car (or house, or apartment, or neighborhood)

   e. How to make a favorite dessert (or barbecue a steak or make coffee)

Expand Your Knowledge

Exploring the Best of the Web

Compose a Better Business Message At Purdue University's Online Writing Lab (OWL), http://owl.english.purdue.edu, you'll find tools to help you improve your business messages. For advice on composing written messages, for help with grammar, and for referrals to other information sources, you'd be wise to visit this site. Purdue's OWL offers online services and an introduction to Internet search tools. You can also download a variety of handouts on writing skills. Check out the resources at the OWL homepage, then answer the following questions.

Exercises

1. Explain why positive wording in a message is more effective than negative wording. Why should you be concerned about the position of good news or bad news in your written message?

2. What six factors of tone should you consider when conveying your message to your audience?
3. What points should you include in the close of your business message? Why?

Exploring the Web on Your Own

Review these chapter-related websites on your own to learn more about writing business messages.

1. Write it right by paying attention to these writing tips, grammar pointers, style suggestions, and reference sources at www.webgrammar.com.
2. Can't find the right word to use when writing about specialized topics? Check out one of the hundreds of subject-area glossaries available at www.glossarist.com.
3. Need some advice about what's legal to write about in your blog? Visit the Electronic Frontier Foundation's Legal Guide for Bloggers at www.eff.org/bloggers/lg.

Learn Interactively

Interactive Study Guide

Visit www.prenhall.com/bovee, then locate your book and click on its Companion Website link. Select Chapter 4 to take advantage of the interactive "Chapter Quiz" to test your knowledge of chapter concepts. Receive instant feedback on whether you need additional studying. Also, visit the "Study Hall," where you'll find an abundance of valuable resources that will help you succeed in this course.

Peak Performance Grammar and Mechanics

If your instructor has required the use of "Peak Performance Grammar and Mechanics," either in your online course, through the access-code protected portion of the Companion Website, or on CD, you can improve your skill with adjectives and adverbs by using the "Peak Performance Grammar and Mechanics" module. Click on "Grammar Basics," and then click "Adjectives and Adverbs." Take the Pretest to determine whether you have any weak areas. Then review those areas in the Refresher Course. Take the Follow-Up Test to check your grasp of adjectives and adverbs. For an extra challenge or advanced practice, take the Advanced Test. Finally, for additional reinforcement in adjectives and adverbs, go to the "Improve Your Grammar, Mechanics, and Usage" section that follows, and complete the "Level I: Self-Assessment" exercises.

Improve Your Grammar, Mechanics, and Usage

Level 1: Self-Assessment—Adjectives

Review Sections 1.4 in the Handbook of Grammar, Mechanics, and Usage, and then look at the following 15 items.

In items 1–5, fill in the appropriate form of the adjective that appears in parentheses:

1. Of the two products, this one has the _____ (*great*) potential.

2. The _____ (*perfect*) solution is *d*.

3. Here is the _____ (*interesting*) of all the ideas I have heard so far.

4. Our service is _____ (*good*) than theirs.

5. The _____ (*hard*) part of my job is firing people.

In items 6–10, insert hyphens wherever required:

6. A highly placed source revealed Dotson's last ditch efforts to cover up the mistake.

7. Please send an extra large dust cover for my photocopier.

8. A top secret document was taken from the president's office last night.

9. A 30 year old person should know better.

10. If I write a large scale report, I want to know that it will be read by upper level management.

In items 11–15, insert required commas between adjectives:

11. The two companies are engaged in an all-out no-holds-barred struggle for dominance.

12. A tiny metal shaving is responsible for the problem.

13. She came to the office with a bruised swollen knee.

14. A chipped cracked sheet of glass is useless to us.

15. You'll receive our usual cheerful prompt service.

Level 2: Workplace Applications

The following items contain numerous errors in grammar, capitalization, punctuation, abbreviation, number style, word division, and vocabulary. Rewrite each sentence in the space provided, correcting all errors. Write *C* in the space after any sentence that is already correct.

1. Its time that you learned the skills one needs to work with suppliers and vendors to get what you want and need.

2. Easy flexible wireless calling plans start for as little as $19 dollars a month.

3. There's several criteria used to select customer's to receive this offer.

4. PetFood Warehouse officially became PETsMART, Jim left the co. due to health reasons.

5. First quarter sales gains are evident in both the grocery store sector (up 1.03%) and the restaurant sector (up 3.17 per cent) according to Food Institute estimates.

6. Whatever your challenge, learning stronger "negotiating" tactics and strategies will improve the way people work and the results that comes from their efforts.

7. To meet the increasing demand for Penta bottled-drinking-water, production capacity is being expanded by Bio-Hydration Research Lab by 80 percent.

8. Seminars begin at 9 A.M. and wrap up at 4:00 P.M.

9. Temple, Texas-based McLane Co. a subsidiary of Wal-Mart has bought a facility in Northfield, Minn that it will use to distribute products to customers such as convenience stores, stores that sell items at a discount, and mass merchants.

10. The British Retail Consortium are releasing the 3rd edition of its Technical Standards on Apr. 22, reported The New York Times.

11. The reason SkillPath is the fastest growing training company in the world is because of our commitment to providing clients with the highest-quality learning experiences possible.

12. According to professor Charles Noussair of the economics department of Purdue University, opinion surveys "Capture the respondent in the role of a voter, not in the role of a consumer".

13. The Study found that people, exposed to Purina banner ads, were almost 50 percent more likely to volunteer Purina as the first Dog Food brand that came to mind.

14. In a consent decree with the food and drug administration, E'Ola International a dietary supplement maker agreed not to sell any more products containing the drug, ephedrine.

15. Dennis Dickson is looking for a company both to make and distribute plaidberries under an exclusive license, plaidberries is blackberries that are mixed with extracts and they are used as a filling.

Level 3: Document Critique

The following document may contain errors in grammar, capitalization, punctuation, abbreviation, number style, vocabulary, and spelling. You will also find errors relating to topics in this chapter. Concentrate on using the "you" attitude, emphasizing the positive, being polite, and using bias-free language as you improve this memo. Correct all errors using standard proofreading marks (see Appendix C).

Burdette's
• Special Sizes •
For Special Ladies and Gentleman

820 10th Avenue South, Seattle, WA 98134 ▪ (206) 777-1234 ▪ Fax: (206) 777-1235 • www.burdetters.com

10/19/07

Mrs. Bruce Crandall

1597 Church Street

Grants Pass, Oreg. 97526

Dear Mrs. Crandall,

Order no. 89-97526-277

We were so happy to recieve your order—We know you'll be enjoying the dress you've selected from our fall catalog. We feel its a popular number because its so versitile and flatters our heavier customers. We think you'll get alot of use out of it on your trip to San Francisco.

Unfortunately, you forgot to indicate what size you need. We can't ship your dress until you tell us your size. Plus, if you don't mail in the postage paid card that we've enclosed for you to use very soon we can't be guaranteeing that your attractive new dress will arrive in time for your trip!

Sincerely,

5

Completing Business Messages

Learning Objectives

After studying this chapter, you will be able to

1 Discuss the value of careful revision and list the main tasks involved in completing a business message

2 List four writing techniques you can use to improve the readability of your messages

3 Describe the steps you can take to improve the clarity of your writing

4 Discuss why it's important to make your message more concise and give four tips on how to do so

5 Explain how design elements help determine the effectiveness of your documents

6 Highlight the types of errors to look for when proofreading

7 Discuss the most important issues to consider when distributing your messages

Robert Hartwell Fiske (quoted at the left) knows the value of effective communication, particularly communication that is clear, concise, and efficient. Conversely, poorly written messages can damage company reputations, hinder sales efforts, and damage careers.[2] Careful revision often means the difference between a rambling, unfocused message and a lively, direct message that gets attention and spurs action.

Revising Your Message

If you have time, put your draft aside for a day or two before you begin the revision process.

Even though you've generally done some revising while writing the first draft, be sure to set aside time for a thorough, top-to-bottom revision after completing the draft. With an important message, the best approach is to put it aside for a day or two before you begin the revision process so that you can approach the material with a fresh eye. Then start with the "big picture," making sure that the document accomplishes your overall goals, before moving to finer points such as readability, clarity, and conciseness. Figure 5.1 lists the tasks in the third step of the three-step writing process: revising your message to achieve optimum quality, then producing, proofreading, and distributing it.

Resist the temptation to cut corners when performing the tasks in the third step of the three-step writing process. You've spent a lot of time and energy planning and writing a strong message, so make sure it is produced and delivered with professional quality.

Planning ➤ Writing ➤ Completing ➤

Revise the Message
Evaluate content and review readability, then edit and rewrite for conciseness and clarity.

Produce the Message
Use effective design elements and suitable layout for a clean, professional appearance.

Proofread the Message
Review for errors in layout, spelling, and mechanics.

Distribute the Message
Deliver your message using the chosen medium; make sure all documents and all relevant files are distributed successfully.

1   **2**   **3**

Evaluating Your Content, Organization, Style, and Tone

When you begin the revision process, focus your attention on content, organization, style, and tone. Today's time-pressed readers want messages that convey important content clearly and quickly.[3] To evaluate the content of your message, ask yourself these questions:

- Is the information accurate?
- Is the information relevant to your audience?
- Is there enough information to satisfy your reader's needs?
- Is there a good balance between the general and the specific?

Once you are satisfied with the content of your message, you can review its organization. Ask yourself another set of questions:

- Are all your points covered in the most logical order?
- Do the most important ideas receive the most space, and are they placed in the most prominent positions?
- Would the message be more convincing if it were arranged in another sequence?
- Are any points repeated unnecessarily?
- Are details grouped together logically, or are some still scattered through the document?

With the content in place and effectively organized, next consider whether you have achieved the right style and tone for your audience. Is your writing formal enough to meet the audience's expectations without being too formal or academic? Is it too casual for a serious subject? Does your message emphasize the audience's needs over your own?

Spend a few extra moments on the beginning and ending of your message; these sections have the greatest impact on the audience. Be sure that the opening of your document is relevant, interesting, and geared to the reader's probable reaction. In longer documents, check to see that the first few paragraphs establish the subject, purpose, and organization of the material. Review the conclusion to be sure that it summarizes the main idea and leaves the audience with a positive impression.

The beginning and end of a message have the greatest impact on your readers.

103

Review for Readability

Once you're satisfied with the content, organization, style, and tone of your message, make a second pass to improve its readability. You can adopt a number of techniques to make your message easier to read: varying sentence length, using shorter paragraphs, using lists and bullets instead of narrative, and adding effective headings and subheadings. Note that these techniques also make your documents easier to skim, which many businesspeople do before deciding whether to read documents in depth.

Vary Your Sentence Length

To keep readers' interest, use a variety of short, medium, and long sentences.

Keep a close eye on sentence length as you revise. Effective documents usually combine a mixture of sentences that are short (up to 15 words or so), medium (15–25 words), and long (more than 25 words). Each sentence length has its advantages. Short sentences can be processed quickly and are easier for nonnative speakers and translators to interpret. Medium-length sentences are useful for showing the relationships among ideas. Long sentences are often the best way to convey complex ideas, list multiple related points, or summarize or preview information.

Of course, each sentence length also has disadvantages. Too many short sentences in a row can make your writing choppy, and they can make it hard for audiences to connect your ideas. Medium sentences lack the punch of short sentences and the informative power of longer sentences. Meanwhile, long sentences are usually harder to understand than short sentences because they are packed with information. They are also harder to skim because readers can absorb only a few words per glance. Consequently, the longer the sentence, the greater the possibility that the reader who skims it will not read enough words to process its full meaning.

Keep Your Paragraphs Short

Short paragraphs are easier to read than long ones.

Unlike the variety needed with sentences, the optimum paragraph length is short to medium in most cases. Large blocks of text can be intimidating, even to the most dedicated reader. Short paragraphs (of 100 words or fewer; this paragraph has 77 words) are easier to read than long ones, and they make your writing look inviting. They also help audiences read more carefully. You can also emphasize an idea by isolating it in a short, forceful paragraph.

However, don't go overboard with short paragraphs. Be careful to use one-sentence paragraphs only occasionally and only for emphasis. Also, if you need to divide a subject into several pieces in order to keep paragraphs short, be sure to help your readers keep the ideas connected by guiding them with plenty of transitional elements.

Use Lists and Bullets to Clarify and Emphasize

Lists are effective tools for highlighting and simplifying material.

An effective alternative to using conventional sentences is to set off important ideas in a **list**—a series of words, names, or other items. Lists can show the sequence of your ideas, heighten their impact visually, and increase the likelihood that readers will find your key points. In addition, lists simplify complex subjects, highlight the main point, ease the skimming process for busy readers, and give them a breather. Consider the difference between the following two approaches to the same information:

Narrative	List
Owning your own business has many advantages. One is the ease of establishment. Another advantage is the satisfaction of working for yourself. As a sole proprietor, you also have the advantage of privacy because you do not have to reveal your information or plans to anyone.	Owning your own business has three advantages: • Ease of establishment • Satisfaction of working for yourself • Privacy of information

When creating a list, you can separate items with numbers, letters, or *bullets* (a general term for any kind of graphical element that precedes each item). Bullets are generally preferred over numbers, unless the list is in some logical sequence or ranking, or specific list items will be referred to later on.

Lists are easier to locate and read if the entire numbered or bulleted section is set off by extra space before and after, as the preceding examples demonstrate. Furthermore, when using lists, make sure to introduce them clearly so that people know what they're about to read.

Add Headings and Subheadings

A **heading** is a brief title that tells readers about the content of the section that follows. Headings are similar to the subject line in memos and e-mail correspondence. However, subject lines merely identify the purpose of the memo or e-mail, whereas headings and subheadings also advise the reader about the material included in the section to follow. **Subheadings** indicate subsections within a major section; complex documents may have several levels of subheadings. Headings and subheadings help in three important ways: They show readers at a glance how the material is organized, they call attention to important points, and they highlight connections and transitions between ideas.

Headings fall into two categories. **Descriptive headings**, such as "Production Costs," identify a topic but do little more. **Informative headings**, such as "A New Way to Cut Costs," put your reader right into the context of your message. They are also helpful in guiding your work as a writer, because they specify the information you need to convey in each section. Well-written informative headings are self-contained, which means that readers can skim just the headings and subheadings and understand them without reading the rest of the document. Whatever types of headings you choose, keep them brief, and use parallel construction as you would for an outline, lists, or a series of words.

Use headings to grab the reader's attention and organize material into short sections.

Informative headings are generally more helpful than descriptive ones.

Editing for Clarity

Once you've reviewed and revised your message for readability, you'll want to make sure that your message is clear. The tips in this section will help.

Clarity is essential to getting your message across accurately and efficiently.

Break Up Overly Long Sentences

If you find yourself stuck in a long sentence, you're probably trying to make the sentence do more than it can reasonably do, such as expressing two dissimilar thoughts or peppering the reader with too many pieces of supporting evidence at once (did you notice how difficult this long sentence was to read?).

Rewrite Hedging Sentences

Sometimes you have to write *may* or *seems* to avoid stating a judgment as a fact, but avoid overqualifying your sentences to the point that you lose all authority:

Don't be afraid to present your opinions without qualification; excessive hedging undermines your authority.

Instead of This	Write This
I believe that Mr. Johnson's employment record seems to show that he may be capable of handling the position.	Mr. Johnson's employment record shows that he is capable of handling the position.

Impose Parallelism

When you have two or more similar ideas to express, repeating the same grammatical construction shows that the ideas are related, are of similar importance, and are on the same level of generality. Repeating the pattern tells readers that the ideas are comparable, and it makes your writing easier to read. Parallelism can be achieved by repeating the pattern in words, phrases, clauses, or entire sentences:

When you use parallel grammatical patterns to express two or more ideas, you show that they are comparable thoughts.

Instead of This	Write This
To waste time and missing deadlines are bad habits.	Wasting time and missing deadlines are bad habits.
Interviews are a matter of acting confident and to stay relaxed.	Interviews are a matter of acting confident and staying relaxed.

Correct Dangling Modifiers

Be careful not to leave modifying phrases "dangling," with no connection to the subject of the sentence. In the first example below, for instance, the poor version seems to say that the *budget* was working as quickly as possible:

Instead of This	Write This
Working as quickly as possible, the budget was soon ready.	Working as quickly as possible, the committee soon had the budget ready.
After a three-week slump, we increased sales.	After a three-week slump, sales increased.

Reword Long Noun Sequences

When too many nouns are strung together as modifiers, the resulting sentence is hard to read. You can often clarify such a sentence by putting some of the nouns in a modifying phrase:

Instead of This	Write This
The aluminum window sash installation company will give us an estimate on Friday.	The company that installs aluminum window sashes will give us an estimate on Friday.

Replace Camouflaged Verbs

Watch for word endings such as *ion, tion, ing, ment, ant, ent, ence, ance,* and *ency*. Most of them "camouflage" a verb by changing it into a noun or an adjective—which requires you to add another verb in order to complete your sentence:

Instead of This	Write This
The manager undertook implementation of the rules.	The manager implemented the rules.
Verification of the shipments occurs weekly.	Shipments are verified weekly.

Clarify Sentence Structure

Keep the subject and predicate of a sentence as close together as possible. When subject and predicate are far apart, readers have to read the sentence twice to figure out who did what:

Subject and predicate should be placed as close together as possible, as should modifiers and the words they modify.

Instead of This	Write This
A 10 percent decline in market share, which resulted from quality problems and an aggressive sales campaign by Armitage, the market leader in the Northeast, was the major problem in 2006.	The major problem in 2006 was a 10 percent loss of market share, which resulted from both quality problems and an aggressive sales campaign by Armitage, the market leader in the Northeast.

Similarly, adjectives, adverbs, and prepositional phrases usually make the most sense when they're placed as close as possible to the words they modify:

Instead of This	Write This
These ergonomic chairs are ideal for professionals who must spend many hours working at their computers with their adjustable sitting, kneeling, and standing positions.	With their adjustable sitting, kneeling, and standing positions, these ergonomic chairs are ideal for professionals who must spend many hours working at their computers.

Clarify Awkward References

Be careful with directional phrases such as *the above-mentioned, as mentioned above, the aforementioned, the former, the latter,* and *respectively.* They often force readers to jump from point to point to figure out what you're saying. You're usually better off using specific references:

Instead of This	Write This
The Law Office and the Accounting Office distribute computer supplies for legal secretaries and beginning accountants, respectively.	The Law Office distributes computer supplies for legal secretaries; the Accounting Office distributes those for beginning accountants.

Moderate Your Enthusiasm

An occasional adjective or adverb intensifies and emphasizes your meaning, but too many can ruin your writing by making you sound insincere:

Showing enthusiasm for ideas is fine, but be careful not to go so far that you sound unprofessional.

Instead of This	Write This
We are extremely pleased to offer you a position on our staff of exceptionally skilled and highly educated employees. The work offers extraordinary challenges and a very large salary.	We are pleased to offer you a position on our staff of skilled and well-educated employees. The work offers challenges and an attractive salary.

Editing for Conciseness

In addition to clarity, readers appreciate conciseness—particularly in new media formats such as blogs and instant messages. The good news is that most first drafts can be cut by as much as 50 percent.[4] Consider the following tips.

Make your documents tighter by removing unnecessary words.

Delete Unnecessary Words and Phrases

To test whether a word or phrase is essential, try the sentence without it. If the meaning doesn't change, leave it out. For instance, *very* is often nothing but clutter. There's no need to call someone "very methodical." The person is either methodical or not. Also, some combinations of words have one-word equivalents that are more efficient:

Instead of This	Write This
for the sum of	for
in the event that	if
on the occasion of	on
prior to the start of	before
in the near future	soon

Instead of This	Write This (*Continued*)
at this point in time	now
due to the fact that	because
in view of the fact that	because
until such time as	when
with reference to	about

In addition, avoid the clutter of too many or poorly placed relative pronouns (*who, that, which*):

Instead of This	Write This
Cars that are sold after January will not have a six-month warranty.	Cars sold after January will not have a six-month warranty.
Employees who are driving to work should park in the spaces that are marked "Staff."	Employees driving to work should park in the spaces marked "Staff."

However, well-placed relative pronouns and articles prevent confusion. Notice how the meaning changes depending on where "that" is placed in these sentences:

Instead of This	Write This
The project manager told the engineers last week the specifications were changed.	The project manager told the engineers last week *that* the specifications were changed.
	The project manager told the engineers *that* last week the specifications were changed.

Shorten Long Words and Phrases

Short words are generally more vivid and easier to read than long ones. The idea is to use short, simple words, *not* simple concepts:[5]

Instead of This	Write This
During the preceding year, the company accelerated productive operations.	Last year the company sped up operations.
The action was predicated on the assumption that the company was operating at a financial deficit.	The action was based on the belief that the company was losing money.

Also, by using infinitives in place of some phrases, you not only shorten your sentences but also make them clearer. Be careful to use infinitives rather than wordy phrases:

Instead of This	Write This
If you want success as a writer, you must work hard.	To be a successful writer, you must work hard.
He went to the library for the purpose of studying.	He went to the library to study.
The employer increased salaries so that she could improve morale.	The employer increased salaries to improve morale.

Eliminate Redundancies

In some word combinations, the words tend to say the same thing. For instance, "visible to the eye" is redundant because *visible* is enough. Eliminate the redundant word(s):

Instead of This	Write This
absolutely complete	complete
basic fundamentals	fundamentals
follows after	follows
reduce down	reduce
free and clear	free
refer back	refer
repeat again	repeat
collect together	collect
future plans	plans
return back	return
end result	result
actual truth	truth
final outcome	outcome
surrounded on all sides	surrounded

In addition, avoid using double modifiers with the same meaning.

Instead of This	Write This
modern, up-to-date equipment	modern equipment

Recast "It Is/There Are" Starters

If you start a sentence with *It is* or *There are*, you might be able to rewrite the sentence to remove this phrase and thereby make the sentence shorter:

Instead of This	Write This
It would be appreciated if you would sign the lease today.	Please sign the lease today.
There are five employees in this division who were late to work today.	Five employees in this division were late to work today.

As you rewrite, concentrate on how each word contributes to an effective sentence and on how that sentence helps to develop a coherent paragraph. Look for opportunities to make the material more interesting through the use of strong, lively words and phrases (as discussed in Chapter 4). Sometimes you'll find that the most difficult problem in a sentence can be solved by simply removing the problem itself. When you come upon a troublesome element, ask yourself, "Do I need it at all?" Possibly not. In fact, you may find that it was giving you so much grief precisely because it was trying to do an unnecessary job.[6]

Figure 5.2 provides an example of revising for clarity and conciseness. Notice how the changes remove unnecessary words, clarify the message, and demonstrate the "you" attitude.

FIGURE 5.2 Improving a Customer Letter Through Careful Revision

Careful revision makes this draft shorter, clearer, and more focused. The proofreading symbols you see here are still widely used whenever printed documents are edited and revised; you can find a complete list of symbols in Appendix C. Note that many business documents are now "marked up" using such technological tools as *revision marks* in Microsoft Word and *comments* in Adobe Acrobat. No matter what the medium, however, careful revision is key to more effective messages. (You can see a finished version of this letter on page 132 in Chapter 6.)

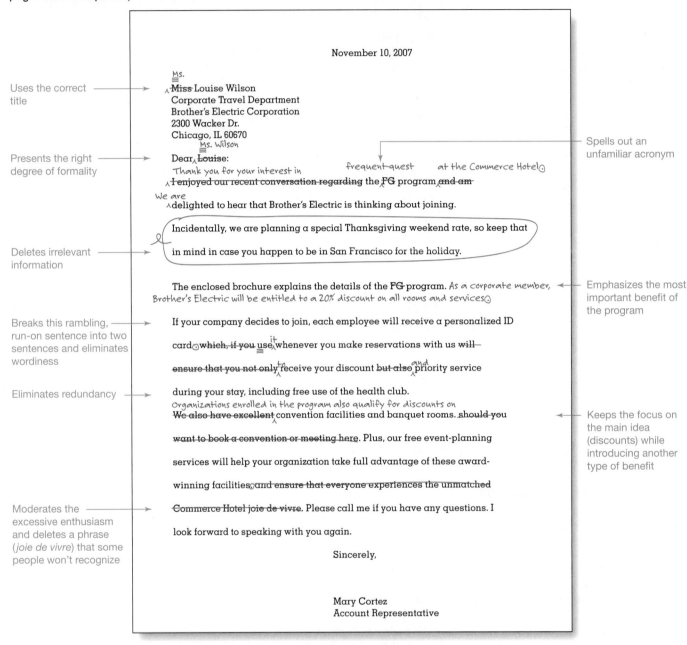

Uses the correct title

Presents the right degree of formality

Deletes irrelevant information

Breaks this rambling, run-on sentence into two sentences and eliminates wordiness

Eliminates redundancy

Moderates the excessive enthusiasm and deletes a phrase (*joie de vivre*) that some people won't recognize

Spells out an unfamiliar acronym

Emphasizes the most important benefit of the program

Keeps the focus on the main idea (discounts) while introducing another type of benefit

November 10, 2007

Ms.
~~Miss~~ Louise Wilson
Corporate Travel Department
Brother's Electric Corporation
2300 Wacker Dr.
Chicago, IL 60670

Ms. Wilson
Dear ~~Louise~~:
Thank you for your interest in
~~I enjoyed our recent conversation regarding~~ the ~~FG~~ frequent-guest program ~~and am~~ at the Commerce Hotel.
We are
delighted to hear that Brother's Electric is thinking about joining.

(Incidentally, we are planning a special Thanksgiving weekend rate, so keep that in mind in case you happen to be in San Francisco for the holiday.)

The enclosed brochure explains the details of the ~~FG~~ program. As a corporate member, Brother's Electric will be entitled to a 20% discount on all rooms and services.

If your company decides to join, each employee will receive a personalized ID card ~~which, if you use~~ it whenever you make reservations with us ~~will ensure that you not only~~ to receive your discount ~~but also~~ and priority service during your stay, including free use of the health club.

Organizations enrolled in the program also qualify for discounts on
~~We also have excellent~~ convention facilities and banquet rooms. ~~should you want to book a convention or meeting here.~~ Plus, our free event-planning services will help your organization take full advantage of these award-winning facilities, ~~and ensure that everyone experiences the unmatched Commerce Hotel joie de vivre.~~ Please call me if you have any questions. I look forward to speaking with you again.

Sincerely,

Mary Cortez
Account Representative

Common Proofreading Symbols (see page A-29 for more)

~~strikethrough~~	Delete text
ℓ	Delete individual character or a circled block of text
∧	Insert text (text to insert is written above)
⊙	Insert period
∧	Insert comma
⌐	Start new line
¶	Start new paragraph
≡	Capitalize

Using Technology to Revise Your Message

When it's time to revise and polish your message, take full advantage of your tools, whether a word processor, a blogging system, or any other technology. Avoid drudgery and minimize errors with functions such as *cut and paste* (taking a block of text out of one section of a document and pasting it in somewhere else) and *search and replace* (tracking down words or phrases and changing them if you need to). Pay close attention to what the tool is doing for you, of course. For example, finding *power* and replacing all occurrences with *strength* will also change the word *powerful* to *strengthful*.

Software tools such as *revision marks* and *commenting* keep track of proposed editing changes electronically and provide a history of a document's revisions. For instance, in Microsoft Word, the revisions appear in a different font color than the original text, giving you a chance to review changes before accepting or rejecting them. Adobe Acrobat lets you attach notes and mark text changes to PDF files. In addition, Word, Acrobat, and other software tools, including groupware systems, now provide a host of features to keep track of editing changes made by multiple members of a team.

In addition to the many revision tools, four software functions can help bring out the best in your documents. First, a *spell checker* compares your document with an electronic dictionary, highlights unrecognized words, and suggests correct spellings. Spell checkers are a wonderful way to weed major typos out of your documents, but they are no substitute for good spelling skills. For example, if you use *their* when you mean to use *there*, your spell checker won't notice, because *their* is spelled correctly. If you're in a hurry and accidentally omit the *p* at the end of *top*, your spell checker will read *to* as correct. Plus, some of the "errors" that the spell checker indicates may actually be proper names, technical words, words that you misspelled on purpose, or simply words that weren't included in the spell checker's dictionary. It's up to you to decide whether each flagged word should be corrected or left alone, and it's up to you to find the errors that your spell checker has overlooked.

Second, a computer *thesaurus* gives you alternative words, just as a printed thesaurus does. A computer thesaurus is much faster and lets you try multiple alternatives in just a few seconds to see which works best. The best uses of any thesaurus, printed or computerized, are to find fresh, interesting words when you've been using the same word too many times and to find the word that most accurately conveys your intended meaning. Don't use them simply to add impressive-sounding words.

Third, the *grammar checker* tries to do for your grammar what a spell checker does for your spelling. Because the program doesn't have a clue about what you're trying to say, it can't tell whether you've said it correctly or clearly. However, grammar checkers can perform some helpful review tasks (such as pointing out noun-verb agreement problems) and highlighting items you should consider changing, such as passive voice, long sentences, and frequently misused words.

Fourth, a *style checker* can also monitor your word and sentence choices and suggest alternatives that might produce more effective writing. For instance, the style checking options in Microsoft Word range from basic issues such as spelling out numbers and using contractions to more subjective matters, such as sentence structure and the use of technical terminology.

By all means, use any software that you find helpful when revising your documents. Just remember that it's unwise to rely on them to do all your revision work, and you're responsible for the final product.

> Spell checkers, computerized thesauruses, grammar checkers, and style checkers can all help with the revision process, but they can't take the place of good writing and editing skills.

Producing Your Message

Now it's time to put your hard work on display. The *production quality* of your message—the total effect of page design, graphical elements, typography, screen presence, and so on—plays an important role in its effectiveness. A polished, inviting design not only makes your document easier to read but also conveys a sense of professionalism and importance.[7]

> The quality of your document design, both on paper and on screen, affects readability and audience perceptions.

Document Makeover

Improve This Letter

To practice correcting drafts of actual documents, visit your online course or the access-code-protected portion of the Companion Website. Click "Document Makeovers," then click Chapter 5. You will find a letter that contains problems and errors relating to what you've learned in this chapter about revising messages. Use the Final Draft decision tool to create an improved version of this routine e-mail. Check the message for organization, readability, clarity, and conciseness.

Adding Graphics, Sound, Video, and Hypertext

Take advantage of your software's ability to incorporate other communication elements.

Fortunately, today's word processors and other software tools make it easy to produce impressive documents that enliven your text with not only full-color graphics but also sound, video, and hypertext links. The software for creating business visuals falls into two basic groups: *presentation software*, which helps you create overhead transparencies and computerized slide shows (electronic presentations are discussed in Chapter 12), and *graphics software*, which ranges from basic tools that help you create simple business diagrams to the comprehensive tools preferred by artists and graphic designers. You can create graphics yourself, use *clip art* (collections of uncopyrighted images), or scan in drawings or photographs.

Adding sound bites or video clips to electronic documents is an exciting new way to get your message across. Several systems let you record brief messages and attach them to particular places in a document. The reader then clicks on a speaker icon to play each comment, such as "Please convert this paragraph to a bulleted list."

You can also use hypertext markup language (HTML) to insert hyperlinks into your message. Readers can easily jump from one document to another by clicking on such a link. They can go directly to a website, jump to another section of your document, or go to a different document altogether. By using hyperlinks, you can customize your documents to meet the individual information needs of your readers—just as you can on a webpage.

Designing for Readability

Good design enhances the readability of your material.

The design of your document affects readability in two important ways. First, good design improves the effectiveness of your message. Conversely, poor design can act as a barrier to communication. Second, the visual design itself sends a nonverbal message to the audience, influencing their perceptions of the communication before they read a single word (Figure 5.3).

To achieve an effective design, pay careful attention to the following design elements:

For effective design, pay attention to
- Consistency
- Balance
- Restraint
- Detail

- **Consistency.** Throughout each message, be consistent in your use of margins, typeface, type size, spacing, color, and position.
- **Balance.** Try to balance the space devoted to text, visuals, and *white space*. For instance, many pages or screens in a row with nothing but text can be intimidating to readers. Conversely, a design can have too many visuals, which breaks the text into disjointed chunks that are more difficult to read.
- **Restraint.** Strive for simplicity. Don't clutter your message with too many design elements, too many colors, or too many decorative touches.
- **Detail.** Pay attention to the details. For instance, headings and subheadings that appear at the bottom of a column or a page can annoy readers when the promised information doesn't appear until the next column or page.

FIGURE 5.3 Poor and Improved Document Design

Compare these two e-mail screens. They contain virtually the same information but send dramatically different messages to the reader. The unprofessional appearance of the "poor" version makes it uninviting and difficult to read. The amateurish use of color is distracting. In contrast, the "improved" version is clear, inviting, and easy to either read entirely or scan quickly.

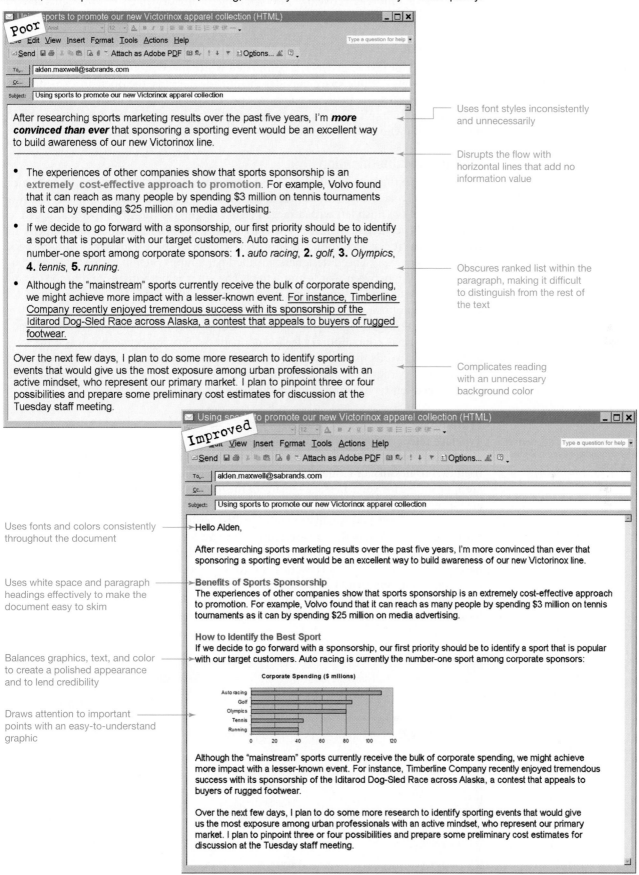

Uses font styles inconsistently and unnecessarily

Disrupts the flow with horizontal lines that add no information value

Obscures ranked list within the paragraph, making it difficult to distinguish from the rest of the text

Complicates reading with an unnecessary background color

Uses fonts and colors consistently throughout the document

Uses white space and paragraph headings effectively to make the document easy to skim

Balances graphics, text, and color to create a polished appearance and to lend credibility

Draws attention to important points with an easy-to-understand graphic

Even without special training in graphic design, you can make your printed and electronic messages more effective by understanding the use of white space, margins and line justification, typefaces, and type styles.

White Space

White space separates elements in a document and helps guide the reader's eye.

Any space free of text or artwork is considered **white space** (note that "white space" isn't necessarily white). White space includes the outside margins, the open area surrounding headings, vertical space between columns, and paragraph indents or extra space between unindented paragraphs. To increase the chance that readers will read your documents, be generous with white space; it makes pages feel less intimidating and easier to read.[8]

Margins and Justification

Most business documents use a flush-left margin and a ragged right margin.

Margins define the space around your text and between text columns. They're influenced by the way you place lines of type, which can be set (1) justified (flush on the left and flush on the right), (2) flush left with a ragged right margin, (3) flush right with a ragged left margin, or (4) centered. Justified type is frequently used in magazines, newspapers, and books because it can accommodate more text in a given space. However, without special attention from experienced designers, justified paragraphs often have awkward gaps and variable spacing between words and letters. The effect is both disrupting to look at and more difficult to read.[9] Writers without the time or skill needed to "tweak" justified text are better off not using it.

Flush-left, ragged-right type "lightens" your message's appearance. It gives a document an informal, contemporary feeling of openness. Spacing between words is the same, and only long words that fall at the ends of lines are hyphenated. Centered type is rarely used for text paragraphs but is commonly used for headings and subheadings. Flush-right, ragged-left type is rarely used in business documents.

Typefaces

Serif typefaces are commonly used for text; sans serif typefaces are commonly used for headings.

Typeface refers to the physical design of letters, numbers, and other text characters (see Table 5.1). Typeface influences the tone of your message, making it look authoritative or friendly, businesslike or casual, classic or modern, and so on. Be sure to choose fonts that are appropriate for your message—many of the fonts on your computer are not appropriate for business use.

Serif typefaces have small crosslines (called serifs) at the ends of each letter stroke. Serif faces such as Times Roman are commonly used for text; they can look busy and cluttered when set in large sizes for headings or other display treatments. **Sans serif typefaces** have no serifs. Faces such as Helvetica and Arial are ideal for display treatments that use larger type, but sans serif faces can be difficult to read in long blocks of text.

Using too many typefaces clutters the document and can produce an amateurish look. For most documents, you shouldn't need more than two typefaces. You can't go too

Table 5.1	Typeface Personalities: Serious to Casual to Playful	
Serif Typefaces (Best for text)	**Sans Serif Typefaces** (Best for headlines; some work well for text)	**Specialty Typefaces** (For decorative purposes only)
Bookman Old Style	Arial	ANNA
Century Schoolbook	**Eras Bold**	Bauhaus
Courier	Franklin Gothic Book	Edwardian
Garamond	Frutiger	Lucida Handwriting
Rockwell	Gill Sans	Old English
Times Roman	Verdana	STENCIL

far wrong with a sans serif typeface (such as Arial) for heads and subheads, and a serif typeface (such as Times New Roman) for text and captions. However, if you want to make captions or other text elements stand out, consider adding a third font.[10]

Type Styles

Type style refers to any modification that lends contrast or emphasis to type, including **boldface**, *italic*, and underlining. In general, boldface is the most emphatic, followed by italics, then by underlining. Use all three styles in moderation and avoid using any style in a way that slows your audience's progress through the message. For instance, underlining or using all-uppercase letters can interfere with your reader's ability to recognize the shapes of words, improperly placed boldface or italicized type can slow down your reader, and shadowed or outlined type can seriously hinder legibility.

> Avoid using any type style that inhibits your audience's ability to read your messages.

Make sure the size of your type is proportionate to the importance of your message and the space allotted. For most business messages, use a type size of 10 to 12 points for regular text, and 12 to 18 points for headings and subheadings (a point is approximately 1/72 of an inch). Resist the temptation to reduce your type size to squeeze in text or to enlarge it to fill up space. Type that is too small is hard to read, whereas extra-large type looks unprofessional.

Using Technology to Produce Your Message

The production tools you'll have at your disposal vary widely, depending on the software and systems you're using. Some IM and e-mail systems offer limited formatting and production capabilities, whereas most word processors now offer some capabilities that rival professional publishing software for many day-to-day business needs. *Desktop publishing software* such as Quark XPress and Adobe InDesign goes beyond word processing with more advanced layout capabilities that are designed to accommodate photos, technical drawings, and other elements. (These programs are used mainly by design professionals.) For online content, web publishing systems make it easy to produce great-looking webpages quickly. Similarly, most blogging systems now simplify the production of blog content, making it easy to rapidly post new content. Multimedia production tools such as Microsoft Producer let you combine slides, audio commentary, video clips, and other features into computer-based presentations that once cost thousands of dollars to create.

No matter what system you're using, become familiar with the basic formatting capabilities. A few hours of exploration on your own or an introductory training course can dramatically improve the production quality of your documents. Depending on the types of messages you're creating, you'll benefit from being proficient with the following features:

> Your word processor will probably be your primary communication tool; learn to use it effectively.

- **Templates and stylesheets.** As Chapter 4 noted, you can save a tremendous amount of time by using templates and stylesheets. Many companies provide these to their employees to ensure a consistent look and feel for all print and online documents.
- **Page setup.** Use page setup to control margins, orientation (*portrait* is vertical; *landscape* is horizontal), and the location of *headers* (text and graphics that repeat at the top of every page) and *footers* (similar to headers but at the bottom of the page).
- **Column formatting.** Most business documents use a single column of text per page, but multiple columns can be an attractive format for documents such as newsletters. Columns are also a handy way to format long lists.
- **Paragraph formatting.** Take advantage of the various paragraph formatting controls to enhance the look of your documents. You can offset quotations by increasing margin width around a single paragraph, subtly compress line spacing to fit a document on a single page, or use hanging indents to offset the first line of a paragraph.

> Paragraph formatting gives you greater control over the look of your documents.

- **Numbered and bulleted lists.** Let your word processor or online publishing system do the busywork of formatting numbered and bulleted lists, too. It can also automatically renumber lists when you add or remove items, saving you the embarrassment of misnumbered lists.

- **Tables.** Tables are a great way to display any information that lends itself to rows and columns: calendars, numerical data, comparisons, and so on. Use paragraph and font formatting thoughtfully within tables for the best look.
- **Pictures, text boxes, and objects.** Your word processor probably lets you insert a wide variety of *pictures* (using one of the industry-standard formats such as JPEG or GIF). *Text boxes* are small blocks of text that stand apart from the main text (great for captions, callouts, margin notes, and so on). *Objects* can be anything from a spreadsheet to a sound clip to an engineering drawing.

By improving the appearance of your documents with these tools, you'll improve your readers' impressions of you and your messages, too.

Proofreading Your Message

Your credibility is affected by your attention to the details of mechanics and form.

Think of proofreading as the quality inspection stage for your documents, as your last chance to make sure that your document is ready to carry your message—and your reputation—to the intended audience. (Strictly speaking, *proofreading* is the process of inspecting a printed piece to make sure that all necessary corrections have been made, but you can benefit by approaching proofreading as an overall quality-assurance review.)

The types of details to look for when proofreading include language errors, missing material, design errors, and typographical errors.

Look for two types of problems: (1) undetected mistakes from the writing, design, and layout stages, and (2) mistakes that crept in during production. For the first category, you can review format and layout guidelines in Appendix A on page A-1 and brush up on writing basics with "Handbook of Grammar, Mechanics, and Usage" on page H-1. The second category can include anything from computer glitches such as incorrect fonts or misaligned page elements to problems with the ink used in printing. Be particularly vigilant with complex documents and complex production processes that involve teams of people and multiple computers. Strange things can happen as files move from computer to computer, especially when lots of graphics and different fonts are involved.

Far from being a casual scan up and down the page or screen, proofreading should be a methodical procedure in which you look for specific problems. Here is some advice from the pros:

- **Make multiple passes.** Go through the document several times, focusing on a different aspect each time. For instance, look for content errors the first time, then layout errors the second time.
- **Use perceptual tricks.** To keep from missing things that are "in plain sight," try reading pages backward, placing your finger under each word and reading it silently, covering everything but the line you're currently reading, and reading the document aloud.
- **Focus on high-priority items.** Double-check the spelling of names and the accuracy of dates, addresses, and any number that could cause grief if incorrect.
- **Get some distance.** If possible, don't proofread immediately after finishing the document; let your brain wander off to new topics, then come back fresh later on.
- **Stay focused and vigilant.** Try to block out distractions, and focus as completely as possible on your proofreading task. Avoid reading large amounts of material in one sitting, and try not to proofread when you're tired.
- **Exercise caution.** Take your time. Quick proofreading is not careful proofreading.

Table 5.2 offers some handy tips to improve your proofreading efforts.

Distributing Your Message

With the production finished, you're ready to distribute the message. As with every other aspect of business communication, your options for distribution multiply with every advance in technology. When planning your distribution, consider the following factors:

Table 5.2	Proofreading Tips

Look for writing and typing errors

Typographical mistakes

Misspelled words

Grammatical errors

Punctuation mistakes

Look for design and layout errors

Adherence to company standards

Page or screen layout errors (such as incorrect margins and column formatting)

Clumsy page breaks

Inconsistent font usage (such as with headings and subheadings)

Alignment (columns, headers, footers, and graphics)

Look for missing elements or extraneous elements (those that shouldn't be there)

Page and section numbers

Page headers or footers

URLs, e-mail addresses, or other contact information

Photos and other graphical elements

Source notes, copyright notices, or other reference items

Look for production errors

Printing problems

Browser compatibility problems

■ **Cost.** Cost won't be a concern for most messages, but for lengthy reports or multimedia production, it might well be. Weigh the cost and the benefits before you decide.

■ **Convenience.** Make sure your audience can conveniently access the material you send. For instance, sending huge files may be fine on the fast local office network, but it can be a major headache for colleagues trying to download them over slow wireless networks or dial-up connections. Similarly, websites that require specialized *plug-ins* can cause trouble for visitors who don't have the latest versions.

■ **Time.** How soon does the message need to reach the audience? Don't waste money on overnight delivery if the recipient won't read the report for a week.

■ **Security and privacy.** The convenience offered by IM, e-mail, blogs, and other technologies needs to be weighed against security and privacy concerns. For the most sensitive documents, your company will probably restrict both the people who can receive the documents as well as the means you can use to distribute them. In addition, most computer users are wary of opening attachments. Instead of sending Word files (which might be vulnerable to macro viruses and other risks), consider using Adobe Acrobat to convert your documents to PDF files.

Consider cost, convenience, time, security, and privacy when choosing a distribution method.

Distribution technologies continue to advance, so be on the lookout for new ways to put your messages in the hands of your audience. For example, newsletters and marketing materials that were once printed and sent through the mail are now routinely sent via e-mail—and many of those e-mails are already being replaced by blogs, podcasts, and other new media.

Reviewing Key Points

This chapter discusses the third step in the three-step writing process: completing business messages by revising, producing, proofreading, and distributing them. The chapter explains a variety of techniques for improving the clarity and conciseness of your messages.

In this chapter, you learn how to produce your message. You learn how to select the right design elements and ensure the effectiveness of those elements. You also learn the value of using technology to improve your documents. The chapter explains what to look for when proofreading and concludes with some advice on distributing your messages using the best media choices at your disposal.

The next section focuses on brief business correspondence. Chapter 6 introduces you to a variety of message forms, including traditional printed memos and letters as well as a variety of electronic media: e-mail, instant messaging, blogs, and podcasting. Chapters 7, 8, and 9 then discuss strategies and tactics for routine messages, negatives messages, and persuasive messages.

Test Your Knowledge

1. What are the three main tasks involved in completing a business message?

2. What is a hedging sentence, and how can you correct one?

3. What is parallel construction, and why is it important?

4. How do readers benefit from white space?

5. Why is proofreading an important part of the writing process?

Apply Your Knowledge

1. Why should you let your draft "age" a day before you begin the revision process?

2. Why is it important that your business messages be clear?

3. Why is it important that your business messages be concise?

4. Which distribution method would you choose for a highly confidential strategic planning report that needs to be sent to top executives at six locations in North America, Asia, and Europe? Explain your choice.

5. Ethical Choices   What are the ethical implications of murky, complex writing in a document explaining how customers can appeal the result of a decision made in the company's favor during a dispute?

Practice Your Knowledge

Exercises for Perfecting Your Writing

Revising Messages: Clarity   Break these sentences into shorter ones by adding more periods:

1. The next time you write something, check your average sentence length in a 100-word passage, and if your sentences average more than 16 to 20 words, see whether you can break up some of the sentences.

2. Don't do what the village blacksmith did when he instructed his apprentice as follows: "When I take the shoe out of the fire, I'll lay it on the anvil, and when I nod my head, you hit it with the hammer." The apprentice did just as he was told, and now he's the village blacksmith.

3. Unfortunately, no gadget will produce excellent writing, but using spell checkers and grammar checkers can help by catching common spelling errors and raising grammatical points that writers might want to reconsider, such as suspect sentence structure and problems with noun-verb agreement.

4. Know the flexibility of the written word and its power to convey an idea, and know how to make your words behave so that your readers will understand.

Revising Messages: Conciseness   Cross out unnecessary words in the following:

5. The board cannot act without a consensus of opinion.

6. To surpass our competitors, we need new innovations both in products and in company operations.

7. George McClannahan has wanted to be head of engineering a long period of time, and now he has finally gotten the promotion.

8. Don't pay more than you have to, you can get our new fragrance for a price of just $50.

Revising Messages: Conciseness   Revise the following sentences, using shorter, simpler words:

9. The antiquated calculator is ineffectual for solving sophisticated problems.

10. It is imperative that the pay increments be terminated before an inordinate deficit is accumulated.

11. There was unanimity among the executives that Ms. Jackson's idiosyncrasies were cause for a mandatory meeting with the company's personnel director.

12. The impending liquidation of the company's assets was cause for jubilation among the company's competitors.

Revising Messages: Conciseness   Use infinitives as substitutes for the overly long phrases in these sentences:

13. For living, I require money.

14. They did not find sufficient evidence for believing in the future.

15. Bringing about the destruction of a dream is tragic.

Revising Messages: Conciseness   Condense these sentences to as few words as possible:

16. We are of the conviction that writing is important.

17. In all probability, we're likely to have a price increase.

18. Our goals include making a determination about that in the near future.

19. When all is said and done at the conclusion of this experiment, I'd like to summarize the final windup.

Revising Messages: Modifiers   Remove all the unnecessary modifiers from these sentences:

20. Tremendously high pay increases were given to the extraordinarily skilled and extremely conscientious employees.

21. The union's proposals were highly inflationary, extremely demanding, and exceptionally bold.

Revising Messages: Hedging   Rewrite these sentences so that they no longer contain any hedging:

22. It would appear that someone apparently entered illegally.

23. It may be possible that sometime in the near future the situation is likely to improve.

24. Your report seems to suggest that we might be losing money.

25. I believe Nancy apparently has somewhat greater influence over employees in the word-processing department.

Revising Messages: Indefinite Starters   Rewrite these sentences to eliminate the indefinite starters:

26. There are several examples here to show that Elaine can't hold a position very long.

27. It would be greatly appreciated if every employee would make a generous contribution to Mildred Cook's retirement party.

28. It has been learned in Washington today from generally reliable sources that an important announcement will be made shortly by the White House.

29. There is a rule that states that we cannot work overtime without permission.

Revising Messages: Parallelism   Present the ideas in these sentences in parallel form:

30. Mr. Hill is expected to lecture three days a week, to counsel two days a week, and must write for publication in his spare time.

31. She knows not only accounting, but she also reads Latin.

32. Both applicants had families, college degrees, and were in their thirties, with considerable accounting experience but few social connections.

33. This book was exciting, well written, and held my interest.

Revising Messages: Awkward Pointers   Revise the following sentences to delete the awkward pointers:

34. The vice president in charge of sales and the production manager are responsible for the keys to 34A and 35A, respectively.

35. The keys to 34A and 35A are in executive hands, with the former belonging to the vice president in charge of sales and the latter belonging to the production manager.

36. The keys to 34A and 35A have been given to the production manager, with the aforementioned keys being gold embossed.

37. A laser printer and an inkjet printer were delivered to John and Megan, respectively.

Revising Messages: Dangling Modifiers   Rewrite these sentences to clarify the dangling modifiers:

38. Running down the railroad tracks in a cloud of smoke, we watched the countryside glide by.

39. Lying on the shelf, Ruby saw the seashell.

40. Based on the information, I think we should buy the property.

41. Being cluttered and filthy, Sandy took the whole afternoon to clean up her desk.

Revising Messages: Noun Sequences   Rewrite the following sentences to eliminate the long strings of nouns:

42. The focus of the meeting was a discussion of the bank interest rate deregulation issue.

43. Following the government task force report recommendations, we are revising our job applicant evaluation procedures.

44. The production department quality assurance program components include employee training, supplier cooperation, and computerized detection equipment.

45. The supermarket warehouse inventory reduction plan will be implemented next month.

Revising Messages: Sentence Structure   Rearrange the following sentences to bring the subjects closer to their verbs:

46. Trudy, when she first saw the bull pawing the ground, ran.

47. It was Terri who, according to Ted, who is probably the worst gossip in the office (Tom excepted), mailed the wrong order.

48. William Oberstreet, in his book *Investment Capital Reconsidered*, writes of the mistakes that bankers through the decades have made.

49. Judy Schimmel, after passing up several sensible investment opportunities, despite the warnings of her friends and family, invested her inheritance in a jojoba plantation.

Revising Messages: Camouflaged Verbs   Rewrite each sentence so that the verbs are no longer camouflaged:

50. Adaptation to the new rules was performed easily by the employees.

51. The assessor will make a determination of the tax due.

52. Verification of the identity of the employees must be made daily.

53. The board of directors made a recommendation that Mr. Ronson be assigned to a new division.

Activities

For active links to all websites discussed in this chapter, visit this text's website at www.prenhall.com/bovee. Locate your book and click on its Companion Website link. Then select Chapter 5, and click on "Featured Websites." Locate the name of the page or the URL related to the material in the text. Please note that links to sites that become inactive after publication of the book will be removed from the Featured Websites section.

1. Analyze This Document   Read the following document, then (1) analyze the strengths and weaknesses of each sentence, and (2) revise it so that it follows the guidelines in Chapters 3 through 5.

I have so many questions I would like to ask you: Did you encounter any unforeseen costs when you were first starting up your franchise? Did you have trouble fitting into the franchise mold? How much say did you have in the location of your store? In its size? How long did it take you to start making a profit? How many hours a week do you work? Do you have any costs that are not covered by the franchise fee? How do you calculate royalty and advertising fees? How much say do you have in choosing suppliers? Do Subway's advertising programs satisfy your needs? How much did Subway help you in the beginning?

As a potential franchisee, I am investigating Subway operations. Can you help me answer some of these questions? With your experience, you can provide the kind of information I need. Can you help me? I would be so grateful. You can reach me at (918) 555-9983, day or evening. My cell phone is (918) 555-8838.

Please let me hear from you soon; I hope to make my franchise decision fairly quickly.

2. Internet   Visit the stock market page of Bloomberg's website at www.bloomberg.com, and evaluate the use of design in presenting the latest news. What design improvements can you suggest to enhance readability of the information posted on this page?

3. Proofreading Messages: E-Mail   Proofread the following e-mail message and revise it to correct any problems you find:

Our final company orrientation of the year will be held on Dec. 20. In preparation for this sesssion, please order 20 copies of the Policy handbook, the confindentiality agreenemt, the employee benefits Manual, please let me know if you anticipate any delays in obtaining these materials.

Expand Your Knowledge

Exploring the Best of the Web

Write it Right: Tips to Help You Rethink and Revise   Are you sure that readers perceive your written message as you intended? If you want help revising a message that you're completing, use the Paradigm Online Writing Assistant (POWA) at www.powa.org. With this interactive writer's guide, you can select topics to get tips on how to edit your work, reshape your thoughts, and rewrite for clarity. Read discussions about perfecting your writing skills, and for practice, complete one of the many online activities provided to reinforce what you've learned. Or select the Forum to talk about writing. Explore POWA's advice then answer the following questions.

Exercises

1. Why is it better to write out ideas in a rough format and later reread your message to revise its content? When revising your message, what questions can you ask about your writing?
2. Name the four elements of the "writing context." Imagine that you're the reader of your message. What questions might you ask?
3. When you revise a written message, what is the purpose of "tightening"? What is one way to tighten your writing as you complete a message?

Exploring the Web on Your Own

Review these chapter-related websites on your own to learn more about writing business messages.

1. Learn the ins and outs of document design at About. com's Desktop Publishing section. Use the great tips on graphic design and typography to produce professional-quality business documents. Visit http://desktoppub. about.com then look in the Essentials menu for "DTP, Graphic Design, Typography Info."
2. Troubled by those tricky word choices that bother every writer? Not sure if "alternate" or "alternative" is the right choice? Visit the Grammar Slammer at http://english plus.com/grammar and click on "Common Mistakes and Choices" for advice on dozens of common word-choice dilemmas.
3. Learn the basics of page layout in Microsoft Word to make sure your documents are designed effectively. Visit http://office.microsoft.com, click on Assistance, find the link to browse assistance for Word, then click through the pages of advice on document formatting.

Learn Interactively

Interactive Study Guide

Visit www.prenhall.com/bovee, then locate your book and click on its Companion Website link. Select Chapter 5 to take advantage of the interactive "Chapter Quiz" to test your knowledge of chapter concepts. Receive instant feedback on whether you need additional studying. Also, visit the "Study Hall," where you'll find an abundance of valuable resources that will help you succeed in this course.

Peak Performance Grammar and Mechanics

If your instructor has required the use of "Peak Performance Grammar and Mechanics," either in your online course, through the access-code protected portion of the Companion Website, or on CD, you can continue to improve your skill with adjectives and adverbs by using the "Peak Performance Grammar and Mechanics" module. Click on "Grammar Basics," and then click "Adjectives and Adverbs." Take the Pretest to determine whether you have any weak areas. Then review those areas in the Refresher Course. Take the Follow-Up Test to check your grasp of adjectives and adverbs. For an extra challenge or advanced practice, take the Advanced Test. Finally, for additional reinforcement in adjectives and adverbs, go to the "Improve Your Grammar, Mechanics, and Usage" section that follows, and complete the "Level I: Self-Assessment" exercises.

Improve Your Grammar, Mechanics, and Usage

Level 1: Self-Assessment—Adverbs

Review Section 1.5 in the Handbook of Grammar, Mechanics, and Usage, and then look at the following 15 items.

In items 1–5, select the correct word (in italics), and write it in the space provided:

1. Their performance has been _____ (*good/well*).

2. I _____ (*sure/surely*) do not know how to help you.

3. He feels _____ (*sick/sickly*) again today.

4. Customs dogs are chosen because they smell _____ (*good/well*).

5. The redecorated offices look _____ (*good/well*).

In items 6–10, provide the correct form of the adverb in parentheses:

6. Which of the two programs computes (*fast*) _____?

7. Kate has held five jobs over 13 years, and she was (*recently*) _____ employed by Graphicon.

8. Could they be (*happily*) _____ employed than they are now?

9. Of the two we have in stock, this model is the (*well*) _____ designed.

10. Of all the arguments I've ever heard, yours is the (*logically*) _____ reasoned.

In items 10–15, rewrite the sentences to correct double negatives.

11. He doesn't seem to have none.

12. That machine is scarcely never used.

13. They can't get no replacement parts until Thursday.

14. It wasn't no different from the first event we promoted.

15. We've looked for it, and it doesn't seem to be nowhere.

Level 2: Workplace Applications

The following items contain numerous errors in grammar, capitalization, punctuation, abbreviation, number style, word division, and vocabulary. Rewrite each sentence in the space provided, correcting all errors. Write *C* in the space after any sentence that is already correct.

1. All too often, whomever leaves the most out of his cost estimate is the one who wins the bid - if you can call it winning.

2. Carol Bartz CEO for fourteen years guided Autodesk; from a small company, to it's preeminent position in the computer aided design (cad) software market.

3. Shoppers were disinterested in the world-wide Web initially because many hyped services, offered no real cost or convenience advantages over offline stores.

4. Different jobs and different customers call for different pricing, estimating, and negotiating strategies.

5. Get to know the customer and their expectations, get the customer to talk about their primary use for you're product.

6. To homeowners, who feel they have found a competent contractor who has they're best interest's at heart, price will not matter nearly as much.

7. If I was you, I would of avoided investing in large conglomerates in light of the collapse of energy trader, Enron Corp., over accounting irregularities.

8. Outdoor goods retailer REI has had significant, success with in-store kiosks that let customers choose between several types of merchandise.

9. To people in some areas of cyberspace "Advertising" is a four letter word but "Marketing" is perfectly acceptable.

10. In any business effort, making money requires planning. Strategic marketing, a good product, good customer service, considerable shrewdness—and much hard work.

11. Investors must decide weather to put their capitol into bonds or CDs.

12. Running at full capacity, millions of Nike shoes are being produced by manufacturing plants every day.

13. Metropolis' stationary has a picture of the Empire state building on it.

14. Starbucks are planning to add fruit drinks to their menu in states throughout the south.

15. Credit ratings ain't what they used to be.

Level 3: Document Critique

The following document may contain errors in grammar, punctuation, capitalization, abbreviation, number style, vocabulary, and spelling. You will also find errors relating to topics in this chapter. For example, look for long words and phrases, redundancies, dangling modifiers, camouflaged verbs, or ways to impose parallelism as you improve this memo. Correct all errors using standard proofreading marks (see Appendix C).

Memorandum

TO: Metro power Employees

FROM: Susannah Beech, Hr Administrator

SUBJECT: Ways to improve your response to technology failures

Date: 22 September 2007

Dear Metro Employees:

THere is always a chance of racing toward a deadline and suddenly having equipment fall. The following includes a few proposed suggestions to help you stave off, and cope with, technical equipment and system failures:

- Stay cool. There are many technical failures so they are commonplace in business; and it is likely that your bosses and co-workers will understand that you're having a prolbem and why.

- Practice preventive maintenance: Use cleaning cloths and sprays regularly, liquids and foods should be kept away from keyboards and printers; and you should make sure systems are shut down when you leave at night.

- It is important for faster repair asistance to promptly report computer failures to Bart Stone assistant director of information services ext. 2238, who will get to your poblem as soon as it is humanly possible for him to do so but you must keep in mind that there are many people demanding his focused attention at any given time;

- If you suspect that a problem may be developing, don't wait until the crucial last moment to call for assistance.

- When a last-minute technical failure of equipment threatens to disrupt your composure you might want to consider taking a walk to calm down.

The last suggestion is perhaps the most important to keep your career on track. Lost tempers; taking out your feelings in violent outbursts, and rude language are threatening to co-workers and could result in a reprimand or other disciplinary action. By calling technical support lines for help, your equipment can stay in good working order and your temper will stay calm.

The timely implemention of repairs is important, so ask your supervisor for a list of support numbers to keep handy. Then, the next time you experience a technology giltch in your equipment or systems, there are going to be quite a few numbers handy for you to call to help you handle it as just another aspect of your business regeem.

Sincerely,

Susannah Beech

Human Resources administrator

Brief Business Messages

6

Choosing and Using Media for Brief Messages

Learning Objectives

After studying this chapter, you will be able to

1 Compare the strengths and weaknesses of the print and electronic media available for short messages

2 Identify the attributes of successful memos and letters and explain the difference between the two formats

3 Describe the steps for creating successful e-mail messages and explain the importance of e-mail hygiene and e-mail etiquette

4 Identify the common business applications of instant messaging (IM) and list guidelines for effective business IM

5 Explain the role of blogging in business communication

6 Describe the process for creating, sending, and receiving podcasts

While some people might be tempted to view blogs and other new media as technological gadgets that have little to do with everyday business communication, Toby Bloomberg's observation (at the left) wisely points out that just the opposite is true. A core principle of the "you" attitude is delivering messages in a form that your audience wants and expects, and with millions of customers, employees, and business partners now turning to blogs as sources of information, successful businesses are responding by blogging. Business communicators now use a wide variety of technologies, as you'll learn in this chapter on choosing and using media for brief messages.

Choosing Media for Brief Messages: Traditional to Leading-Edge

In recent years, the options for sending short business messages have expanded considerably, from traditional printed memos and letters to a variety of electronic formats. Don't be surprised if you continue to encounter new media options on the job, too. Whenever a new communication technology appears, creative businesspeople usually find a way to apply it to business challenges.

Here are the short-message media you are likely to encounter on the job in the next few years:

■ **Memos and letters.** Printed memos (for internal communication) and letters (for external communication) have been primary communication vehicles for hundreds of years. In many companies, however, e-mail and other electronic media have largely replaced traditional printed memos. Letters are still used often for external communication with customers, but electronic media are replacing many letters as well. Both memos and letters can be distributed with fax machines, in addition to hand delivery and postal services.

- **E-mail.** The high speed and low cost of e-mail make it an attractive alternative to printed messages, and in fact e-mail is now a primary medium for most companies. As technologies continue to evolve, however, e-mail is in turn being replaced in many instances by instant messaging, blogging, *wikis* (online resources that allow users to add and edit content collectively), and other tools that provide better support for real-time collaboration.

- **Instant messaging (IM).** After consumers around the world began to adopt IM as a faster and simpler alternative to e-mail, businesses weren't far behind; IM usage now rivals e-mail in many companies.

- **Blogs.** Blogs are another great example of how businesses quickly adopt technologies that promise more efficient and effective communication. From internal communication among small teams to executive blogs with thousands of regular readers, blogs are now a common feature in business communication.

- **Podcasts.** You may be familiar with podcasts as the online equivalent of recorded radio or video broadcasts (video podcasts are often called *vidcasts* or *vodcasts*). Businesses are now using podcasts to replace or supplement conference calls, training courses, and other communication activities.

You now have multiple options for sending short messages:

- Printed memos
- Printed letters
- E-mail messages
- Instant messages
- Blog postings
- Podcasts

Creating Effective Memos and Letters

As noted earlier, printed memos and letters used to be primary communication vehicles for most businesses, but various electronic formats continue to replace printed messages for many types of routine communication. Chances are you won't write many paper memos during your career, but you probably will have reason to write paper letters when communicating with customers, community members, and other external audiences. Here are several good reasons for using a printed message over electronic alternatives:

E-mail and instant messages have replaced printed memos and letters in many instances.

- **When you want to make a formal impression.** For special messages, such as sending congratulations or condolences, the formality of printed documents is a much better choice than an electronic message.

- **When you need to accompany products with other physical materials.** If you're mailing brochures or shipping products, for example, a printed letter is a great way to accompany the delivery with a short message to the recipient.

- **When you want to stand out from the flood of electronic messages.** Ironically, the rapid growth of electronic messages creates an opportunity for printed memos and letters. If your audience's computers are overflowing with e-mail, IM, and newsfeeds, a printed message could stand out enough to get noticed.

- **When you are legally required to provide information in printed form.** Business contracts and government regulations sometimes require information to be provided on paper. The laws that cover such disclosures continue to evolve, so make sure you consult with your firm's legal staff if you're not sure.

Consider printed messages when you want to create a more formal impression, to accompany other physical material, to stand out from electronic messages, or when you are legally or contractually required to do so.

Obviously, if your audience doesn't have access to electronic media or you don't have the necessary e-mail or IM addresses, you'll need to use a printed message.

Regardless of their purpose, business letters usually follow certain design conventions, as the letter in Figure 6.1 illustrates. Most business letters are printed on *letterhead stationery*, which includes the company's name, address, and other contact information. The first thing to appear after the letterhead is the date, followed by the inside address,

Letters typically have the following elements:

- Preprinted letterhead stationery
- Date
- Inside address
- Salutation
- Complimentary close
- Signature block

131

FIGURE 6.1   A Formal Customer Letter

Note the clean, well-organized look of this business letter and the conversational but professional tone of the message. Printed letters have a unique ability to convey external messages with a formal, respectful touch.

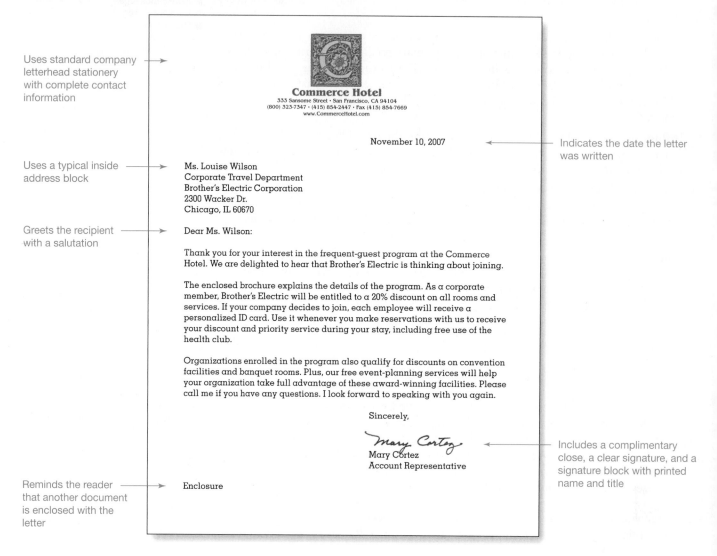

Uses standard company letterhead stationery with complete contact information

Uses a typical inside address block

Greets the recipient with a salutation

Indicates the date the letter was written

Includes a complimentary close, a clear signature, and a signature block with printed name and title

Reminds the reader that another document is enclosed with the letter

which identifies the person receiving the letter. Next is the salutation, usually in the form of *Dear Mr.* or *Ms. Last Name*. The message comes next, followed by the complimentary close, usually *Sincerely* or *Cordially*. And last comes the signature block: space for the signature, followed by the sender's printed name and title. Your company will probably have a standard format to follow for letters, possibly along with a template in Microsoft Word or whatever word processor is standard in the organization. For in-depth format information on letter formats, see Appendix A: "Format and Layout of Business Documents."

Like letters, business memos usually follow a preset design, and your employer will probably have a standard format or template for you to use. Most memos begin with a title such as *Memo, Memorandum,* or *Interoffice Correspondence*. Following that are usually four headings: *Date, To, From,* and *Subject* (*Re:*, short for *Regarding*, is sometimes used instead of *Subject*). Memos usually don't use a salutation, complimentary close, or signature, although in most companies, signing your initials next to your name on the *From* line is standard practice. Bear in mind that memos are often distributed without sealed envelopes, so they are less private than most other message formats. Figure 6.2 shows a typical business memo.

Memos are usually identified by a title such as Memo or Memorandum.

FIGURE 6.2 A Typical Business Memo
This memo shows the elements usually included in a memo. Note that in many instances today, this information would be transmitted via e-mail instead of a printed memo.

Uses standard company memo stationery with title indicating that this is a memo

Uses four standard headings for memos

Does not begin with a salutation

Carnival

INTERNAL MEMORANDUM

DATE: June 11, 2007
TO: Lauren Eastman
FROM: Brad Lymans
SUBJECT: Capacity for Carnival Corporation Cruise Ships

Here is the capacity data you requested along with a brief explanation of the figures:

Cruise Brand	Number of Ships	Passenger Capacity	Primary Market
Carnival	15	30,020	North America
Holland America	10	13,348	North America
Costa	7	9,200	Europe
Cunard	2	2,458	Worldwide
Seabourn	6	1,614	North America
Windstar	4	756	North America
Airtours-Sun	4	4,352	Europe
Total	48	61,748	

All passenger capacities are calculated based on two passengers per cabin, even though some cabins can accommodate three or four passengers.

Cruising capacity has grown in recent years, and management expects it to continue because all the major cruise companies are planning to introduce new ships into service. Carnival Corporation will build 16 additional cruise ships over the next five years, increasing the company's passenger capacity by 36,830, which will bring the total to 98,578.

To utilize this new capacity, we must increase our share of the overall vacation market. Keep in mind that demand for cruises may be affected by (1) the strength of the countries where the ships operate; (2) political instability in areas where the ships travel; and (3) adverse incidents involving cruise ships in general.

Please let me know if you have any further questions or need any additional data.

Does not include a complimentary close or a signature block

Creating Effective E-Mail Messages

Chances are you already have quite a bit of experience using e-mail, but e-mail in the workplace is a more formal medium than you are probably accustomed to for personal communication. To create effective e-mail messages at work, you should take care to treat e-mail as a professional communication medium, follow your company's e-mail policy (if it has one), write effective subject lines, and demonstrate good e-mail etiquette. Figure 6.3 demonstrates the principles of successful business e-mail.

Treat E-Mail as a Professional Communication Medium

Perhaps the most important single point to recognize about e-mail in the workplace is that the nature of business e-mail is dramatically different from that of personal e-mail. Too many people, particularly younger professionals accustomed to using e-mail (and

Business e-mail messages are more formal than the e-mail messages you send to family and friends.

FIGURE 6.3   E-Mail for Business Communication

In this response to an e-mail query from a colleague, Elaine Burgman takes advantage of her e-mail system's features to create an efficient and effective message.

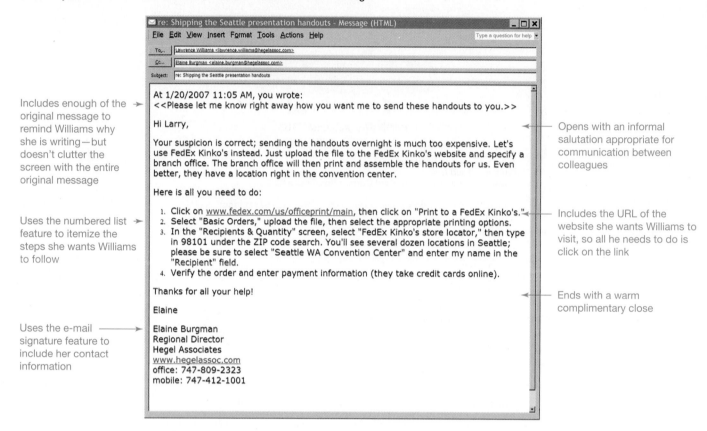

Includes enough of the original message to remind Williams why she is writing—but doesn't clutter the screen with the entire original message

Uses the numbered list feature to itemize the steps she wants Williams to follow

Uses the e-mail signature feature to include her contact information

Opens with an informal salutation appropriate for communication between colleagues

Includes the URL of the website she wants Williams to visit, so all he needs to do is click on the link

Ends with a warm complimentary close

IM, text messaging, and blogging) for personal communication, assume that the usual standards and expectations of business communication don't apply to e-mail. Some seasoned businesspeople even advocate a general disregard for punctuation, grammar, spelling, and other conventions in e-mail writing because paying attention to such details takes too much time.

Granted, you don't need to compose perfect works of literature to inform people that lunch will be served in the conference room, but as a general rule, the time you might save with careless e-mail writing won't make up for the damage it can do to your career.[2] First, sloppy writing may require less time for writers, but it usually demands *more* time from readers who are forced to dig the meaning out of misspelled words and confusing sentences. Second, people who care about effective communication—a group that includes most senior executives—often judge the quality of your *work* by the quality of your *writing.* Third, at the click of somebody else's mouse, e-mail messages can travel to places you never imagined, including the CEO's computer screen, a newspaper, a lawyer's office, or any number of websites and blogs.

Moreover, e-mail and other electronic documents have the same legal weight as printed documents. In numerous instances in recent years, e-mail and other electronic message forms have been used as evidence in lawsuits and criminal investigations involving everything from sexual harassment to financial fraud.[3]

Follow Company E-Mail Policy

E-mail presents considerable legal hazards, and many companies now have formal e-mail policies.

The legal hazards of inappropriate e-mail are only one of the serious risks that e-mail presents. Other concerns include the possibility of disclosing confidential information and exposing company networks to security problems. To minimize the potential for trouble, many companies now have formal e-mail policies that specify how employees can use e-mail, including restrictions against personal use of company e-mail service and sending material that might be deemed objectionable. Moreover, roughly a quarter of employers now monitor internal e-mail, and half of them monitor incoming and outgoing e-mail. This monitoring can involve both automated scans using software programmed to look for sensitive content and manual scans in which selected e-mail messages are actually read by security staff.[4]

Of course, company e-mail policies are effective only if employees are diligent about following them. Every e-mail user has a responsibility to avoid actions that could cause trouble, from downloading virus-infected software to sending objectionable photographs. *E-mail hygiene* refers to all the efforts that companies are making to keep e-mail clean and safe—from spam blocking and virus protection to content filtering.[5] Make sure you understand what your employer expects from you, and follow those guidelines.

Write Effective Subject Lines

The subject line in an e-mail might seem like a minor detail, but it's actually one of the most important parts of every e-mail message because it helps recipients decide which messages to read and when to read them. Missing or poorly written subject lines often result in messages being deleted without even being opened. To capture your audience's attention, make sure your subject line is both informative and compelling. Do more than just describe or classify message content. Use the opportunity to build interest with key words, quotations, directions, or questions:[6]

A poorly written subject line could mean that a message will be deleted or ignored.

Ineffective Subject Line	Effective Subject Line
July sales figures	Send figures for July sales
Tomorrow's meeting	Bring consultant's report to Friday's meeting
Marketing report	Need budget for marketing report
Employee parking	Revised resurfacing schedule for parking lot
Status report	Website redesign is on schedule

If you are exchanging multiple e-mails with someone on the same topic, be sure to periodically modify the subject line of your message to reflect the revised message content. Most e-mail programs will copy the subject line when you click on Reply, so you need only revise it. When numerous messages have identical subject lines, trying to find a particular one can be confusing and frustrating.

Demonstrate Good E-Mail Etiquette

E-mail plays such an important part in the daily lives of most businesspeople that attention to etiquette is essential. Before you even start writing, make sure every e-mail you send is necessary so that you don't contribute to the deluge of messages of dubious importance. Many busy professionals now struggle to keep up with the flow of e-mail messages—some report receiving as many as 50 messages an hour from colleagues and clients.[7] In particular, think twice before sending copies to multiple recipients with the "cc" (courtesy copy) function. Let's say you send a message to your boss and cc five colleagues, simply because you want them to see that you're giving the boss some good information. Each of those five people not only has to read your message but might also feel compelled to reply so that the boss doesn't think they're being negligent. Then everyone will start replying to *those* replies, and on and on. What should have been a single message exchange between you and your boss quickly turns into a flurry of messages that wastes everybody's time.

Attention to etiquette is vital with e-mail communication.

Also, be sure to respect the chain of command. In many companies, any employee can e-mail anyone else, including the president and CEO. However, take care that you don't abuse this freedom. For instance, when corresponding with superiors, don't send an e-mail complaint straight to the top just because it's easy to do so. Your e-mail will usually be more effective if you follow the organizational hierarchy and give each person a chance to address the situation in turn.

Never let your emotions get the best of you when you're composing e-mail. A message that contains insensitive, insulting, or critical comments is called a *flame*. If you're upset about something or angry with someone, compose yourself before composing your e-mail. If you're fuming, cool off before writing your e-mail message. If you do write an emotionally charged message, let it sit for at least a day. Ask yourself, "Would I say this to my audience face to face?" Remember that a live person is on the receiving end of your communication—and that your message can be forwarded easily and stored forever.

Lastly, pause and verify what you're doing before you click "Send." Double-check your addressees to make sure you've included everyone necessary—and no one else. Did you click on "Reply All" when you meant to hit "Reply"? The difference could be embarrassing or even career-threatening. Don't include people in the cc (courtesy copy) or bcc (blind courtesy copy) fields unless you know how these features work (everyone can see who is on the cc line). Also, don't set the message priority to "High" or "Urgent" unless your message is truly urgent.

Table 6.1 lists a number of other helpful tips that will help ensure that your e-mail messages are both effective at their purpose and at establishing you as a knowledgeable professional when it comes to using this vital business tool.

Creating Effective Instant Messages

While e-mail is here to stay as a business medium, its disadvantages—including viruses, spam, and rampant overuse—are driving many people to explore alternatives.[8] One of the most important of those alternatives is instant messaging (IM). For both routine communication and exchanges during online meetings, IM is now widely used throughout the business world. Business-grade IM systems offer a range of capabilities, including basic chat, *presence awareness* (the ability to quickly see which people are at their desks and available to IM), remote display of documents, video capabilities, remote control of other computers, automated newsfeeds from blogs and websites, and the bot capability you read about in Chapter 1.[9]

Business Benefits of Instant Messaging

The benefits of IM include its rapid response to urgent messages, lower cost than both phone calls and e-mail, ability to mimic conversation more closely than e-mail, and availability on a wide range of devices from PCs to mobile phones to PDAs.[10] In addition, because it more closely mimics real conversation, IM doesn't get misused as a broadcast mechanism as often as e-mail does.[11]

Of course, wherever technology goes, trouble seems to follow. The potential drawbacks of IM include security problems (both the risks of computer viruses and the worry that sensitive messages might be intercepted by outsiders), the need for user authentication (making sure that online correspondents are really who they appear to be), the challenge of logging messages for later review and archiving, and incompatibility between competing IM systems. Fortunately, with the growth of *enterprise instant messaging* (EIM), IM systems designed for large-scale corporate use, many of these problems are being overcome.

Guidelines for Successful IM in the Workplace

To use IM effectively, all users need to pay attention to some important behavioral issues: the potential for constant interruptions, the ease of accidentally mixing personal and business messages, the risk of being out of the loop (if a hot discussion or impromptu

---

Keep your emotions in check when you compose e-mail messages; flaming can damage your reputation.

Instant messaging is used as often as e-mail in many companies.

IM offers many benefits:
- Rapid response
- Lower cost
- Ability to mimic conversation
- Wide availability

Table 6.1	Tips for Effective E-mail Messages

Tip	Why It's Important
When you request information or action, make it clear what you're asking for, why it's important, and how soon you need it; don't make your reader write back for details.	People will be tempted to ignore your messages if they're not clear about what you want or how soon you want it.
When responding to a request, either paraphrase the request or include enough of the original message to remind the reader what you're replying to.	Some businesspeople get hundreds of e-mail messages a day and may need reminding what your specific response is about.
If possible, avoid sending long, complex messages via e-mail.	Long messages are easier to read as printed reports or web content.
Adjust the level of formality to the message and the audience.	Overly formal messages to colleagues are perceived as stuffy and distant; overly informal messages to customers or top executives are perceived as disrespectful.
Activate a signature file, which automatically pastes your contact information into every message you create.	Saves you the trouble of retyping vital information and ensures that recipients know how to reach you through other means.
Don't let unread messages pile up in your in-basket.	You'll miss important information and create the impression that you're ignoring other people.
Never type in all caps.	ALL CAPS ARE INTERPRETED AS SCREAMING.
Don't overformat your messages with background colors, colored type, unusual fonts, and so on.	Such messages can be difficult and annoying to read on screen.
Remember that messages can be forwarded anywhere and saved forever.	Don't let a moment of anger or poor judgment haunt you for the rest of your career.
Use the "return receipt requested" feature only for the most critical messages.	This feature triggers a message back to you whenever someone receives or opens your message; many consider this an invasion of privacy.
Make sure your computer has up-to-date virus protection.	One of the worst breaches of "netiquette" is unknowingly infecting other computers because you haven't bothered to protect your own system.
Pay attention to grammar, spelling, and capitalization.	Some people don't think e-mail needs formal rules, but careless messages make you look unprofessional and can annoy readers.
Use acronyms sparingly.	Shorthand such as IMHO (in my humble opinion) and LOL (laughing out loud) can be useful in informal correspondence with colleagues, but don't use them in other messages.

meeting flares up when you're away from your PC or other IM device), and the "vast potential for wasted time" (in the words of MIT labor economist David Autor). On top of all that, you're at the mercy of other people's typing abilities, which can make IM agonizingly slow.[12]

Regardless of the system you're using, you can make IM more efficient and effective by following these tips:[13]

Understand the guidelines for successful business IM before you begin to use it.

- Unless a meeting is scheduled, make yourself unavailable when you need to focus on other work.
- If you're not on a secure system, don't send confidential information.
- Be extremely careful about sending personal messages—they have a tendency to pop up on other people's computers at embarrassing moments.
- Don't use IM for important but impromptu meetings if you can't verify that everyone concerned will be available.
- Unless your system is set up for it, don't use IM for lengthy, complex messages; e-mail is better for those.

FIGURE 6.4   Instant Messaging for Business Communication

Instant messaging is widely used in business, but it does not use the same informal style of communication you probably use to IM your friends and family.

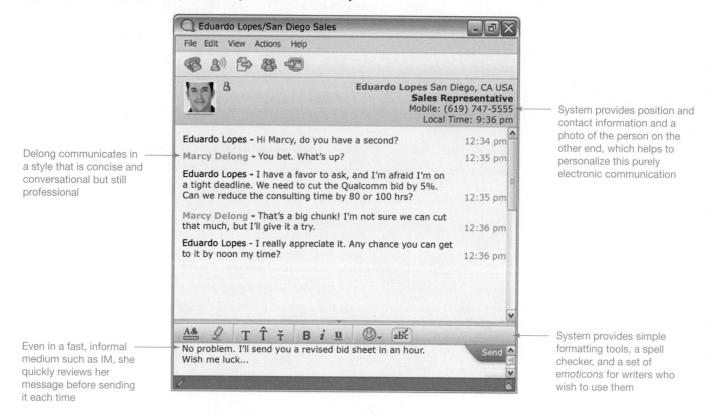

Delong communicates in a style that is concise and conversational but still professional

System provides position and contact information and a photo of the person on the other end, which helps to personalize this purely electronic communication

Even in a fast, informal medium such as IM, she quickly reviews her message before sending it each time

System provides simple formatting tools, a spell checker, and a set of *emoticons* for writers who wish to use them

- Try to avoid carrying on multiple IM conversations at once to minimize the chance of sending messages to the wrong people.
- Don't assume that whatever IM slang you might use in personal communications is appropriate for business messages; your colleagues may not be familiar or comfortable with it.
- If your IM system has filters for *spim*, the IM version of e-mail spam, make sure they're active and up-to-date.[14]

In the IM exchange in Figure 6.4, notice how the participants communicate quickly and rather informally but still maintain good etiquette and a professional tone.

Creating Effective Business Blogs

Blogs have a unique ability to encourage interaction with a large, geographically dispersed audience.

On the surface, blogs might seem like just another new medium, but at their best, blogs redefine the very nature of business communication. To an extent unmatched by any other medium, blogs can engage large, widely distributed audiences. In a sense, a blog combines the global reach and reference value of a website with the conversational exchanges of e-mail or IM. Good business blogs accomplish this by paying close attention to several important elements:

- **Communicating with personal style and an authentic voice.** Most business messages designed for large audiences are carefully scripted and written in a "corporate voice" that is impersonal and objective. In contrast, successful business blogs are written by individuals and exhibit their personal style. Audiences relate to this fresh approach and often build closer emotional bonds with the blogger's organization as a result. For instance, Microsoft's Channel 9 video blog, or *vlog* (http://channel9.msdn.com) features online informal, personable video clips in which several of the company's technical experts answer questions and criticisms from software developers. Channel 9 and other employee blogs are credited with helping to repair Microsoft's reputation among software customers.[15]

- **Delivering new information quickly.** Today's blogging tools let you post new material within seconds of writing it. Not only does this feature allow you to respond quickly when needed—such as during a corporate crisis—but it also lets your audiences know that an active conversation is taking place.

- **Choosing topics of peak interest to audiences.** Successful blogs cover topics that readers care about. For instance, General Motors' popular FastLane blog (http://fastlane.gmblogs.com) features top executives writing about GM cars and responding to questions and criticisms from car enthusiasts. The people who read the blog and write comments obviously care about cars and want the latest information from GM.[16]

- **Encouraging audiences to join the conversation.** Not all blogs invite comments, although most do. These comments are a valuable source of news, information, and insights. In addition, the less-formal nature of blogging seems to make it easier for companies to "let their guards down" and converse with their audiences. For instance, when blogging consultant Paul Chaney wanted to devise a new strategy for his company, Radiant Marketing Group (http://radiantmarketinggroup.com), he asked his blog audience for their input. Readers responded with comments ranging from their impressions of his reputation in the industry to critiques of his proposed company slogans.[17]

Most business blogs invite readers to leave comments.

Given the unique ability of blogs to convey topical information quickly in a conversational format, their rapid adoption by businesses in virtually every industry should come as no surprise. The following sections offer an overview of the business applications of blogging and some guidelines for successful business blogging.

Business Applications of Blogging

Blogs are a potential solution whenever you have a continuing stream of information to share with virtually any online audience—and particularly when you want the audience to have the opportunity to respond to your post. Here are some of the many ways businesses are using blogs:[18]

The business applications of blogs include a wide range of internal and external communication tasks.

- **Project management.** Keeping project teams up-to-date.
- **Intranet replacements.** Blogs are easier to set up and maintain, so many companies now use them in place of conventional intranet sites.
- **Company news.** Informing employees about general business matters.
- **Customer support.** Answering questions and offering tips and advice.

Document Makeover

Improve This Blog

To practice correcting drafts of actual documents, visit your online course or the access-code-protected Prentice Hall Business Communication Website. Click "Document Makeovers," then click Chapter 6. You will find a blog posting that contains problems and errors relating to what you've learned in this chapter about writing for electronic media. Use the Final Draft decision tool to create an improved version of this posting.

- **Public relations and media relations.** Sharing company news with both the general public and journalists.
- **Recruiting.** Telling potential employees about the benefits of working at a firm and responding to their questions.
- **Policy and issue discussions.** Offering a public forum for discussing legislation, regulations, and other broad issues of interest to an organization.
- **Crisis communication.** Providing up-to-the-minute information during emergencies, correcting misinformation, or responding to rumors.
- **Market research.** Soliciting feedback from customers and experts.
- **Brainstorming.** Giving people a forum to toss ideas around and build on each others' contributions.
- **Viral marketing.** Spreading the word about your company and your products; *viral marketing* refers to the transmission of messages in much the same way that biological viruses are transmitted from person to person.

The uses of blogs are limited only by your creativity, so be on the lookout for new ways you can foster positive relationships with colleagues, customers, and other important audiences. For a good example of business blogging, see Figure 6.5.

FIGURE 6.5   Elements of an Effective Business Blog
Blogs exist in many forms and formats, but visitors expect a few basic elements, such as access to archives, links to related information, and a convenient way to subscribe to an automatic newsfeed. Note the style and tone of the writing in this blog; it is far more engaging and conversational than the traditional "corporate voice." Moreover, it is about the *customers*, not the *company*.

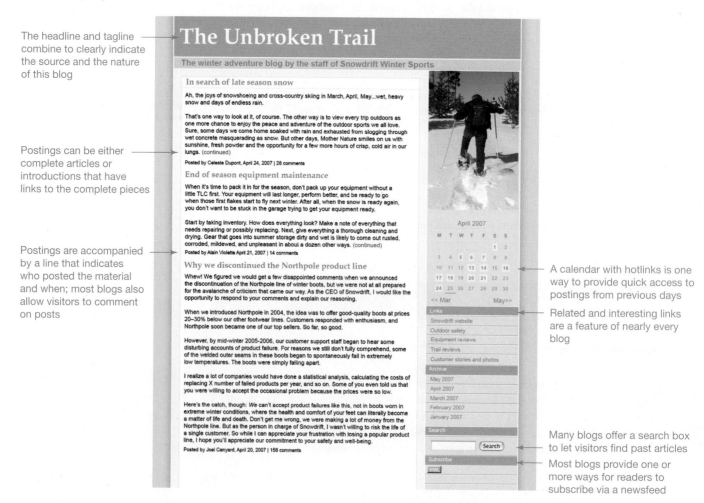

The headline and tagline combine to clearly indicate the source and the nature of this blog

Postings can be either complete articles or introductions that have links to the complete pieces

Postings are accompanied by a line that indicates who posted the material and when; most blogs also allow visitors to comment on posts

A calendar with hotlinks is one way to provide quick access to postings from previous days

Related and interesting links are a feature of nearly every blog

Many blogs offer a search box to let visitors find past articles

Most blogs provide one or more ways for readers to subscribe via a newsfeed

Guidelines for Successful Business Blogging

Although blogs deliver business messages in a unique way, the three-step writing process you've already learned is easy to adapt to blogging tasks. The planning step is particularly important if you're considering starting a blog, because you're planning an entire communication channel, not just a single message. Pay close attention to your audience, your purpose, and your scope:

- **Audience:** Except for team blogs and other efforts with an obvious and well-defined audience, defining your target audience can be a challenge. You want an audience large enough to justify the time you'll be investing, but narrow enough that you can provide an identifiable focus for the blog. For instance, if you work for a firm that develops computer games, would you focus your blog on "hardcore" players, the type who spend thousands of dollars on super-fast PCs optimized for video games, or would you broaden the reach to include all video gamers? The decision often comes down to business strategy.

- **Purpose:** Unlike a personal blog, in which you typically write about whatever interests you, a business blog needs to have a business-related purpose that is important to both your company and your chosen audience. For instance, if you're a technical expert, you might create a blog to give the audience tips and techniques for using your company's products more effectively. This would be the *general purpose* of your blog, then each posting would have a *specific purpose* within the context of that general purpose. Finally, if you are not writing an official company blog but rather blogging as an individual employee, make sure you understand your employer's blogging guidelines. As with e-mail and IM, more and more companies are putting policies in place to prevent employee mistakes with blogging.[19]

- **Scope:** As with your audience, defining the scope of your blog can be a bit tricky. You want to cover a subject area that is broad enough to offer discussion possibilities for months or years, but narrow enough to have an identifiable focus. For instance, GM's FastLane blog is about GM cars only—not GM's stock price, labor negotiations, and so on. Moreover, the scope of your blog needs to remain fairly stable so that you can build an audience over time. If you start out discussing product support but then shift to talking about your company's advertising programs, you'll probably lose readers along the way.

After you begin writing your blog (or posting messages to a multiauthor blog that someone else has created), the careful planning needs to continue with each message. Unless you're posting to a restricted-access blog, such as an internal blog on a company intranet, you can never be sure who might see your posts. Other bloggers might link to them months or years later. Consider the situation before you post to make sure the information you'll be putting online is appropriate for a public audience.

Write in a comfortable, personal style. Blog audiences don't want to hear from your company; they want to hear from *you*. Naturally, they expect you to be knowledgeable in the subject area your blog covers, but you don't need to know everything about a topic. If you don't have all the information yourself, simply provide links to other blogs and websites that supply relevant information. In fact, many blog audiences consider carefully screened links to be an essential part of blogging.

Completing messages for your blog is usually quite easy. Evaluate the content and readability of your message, proofread to correct any errors, then post using your blogging system's tools for doing so. If your blog doesn't already have one, be sure to include one or more *newsfeed* options so that your audience can automatically receive headlines (and summaries, if you choose) of new blog posts. Audiences subscribe to your feed by using a *news aggregator* (sometimes called a *newsreader*) that they can install on their computers or access online. The orange "XML" button in the blog in Figure 6.5 is an example of a newsfeed link; various newsfeed formats exist, including Atom and RSS. Linking and newsfeed technologies continue to evolve, so check with your blog service provider for the most current technique to use.

Before you launch a blog, make sure you have a clear understanding of your target audience, the purpose of your blog, and the scope of subjects you plan to cover.

Write blog postings in a comfortable—but not careless—style.

Table 6.2	Tips for Effective Business Blogging
Tip	**Why It's Important**
Don't blog without a clear plan.	Without a clear plan, your blog is likely to wander from topic to topic without providing compelling information or building a sense of community with your audience.
Post frequently.	The whole point of a blog is fresh material; if you don't have a constant supply of new information or new links, create a traditional website instead.
Make it about your customers and the issues that are important to them.	Readers want to know how your blog will help them, entertain them, or give them a chance to communicate with others who have similar interests.
Write in an authentic voice; never create an artificial character who supposedly writes a blog.	*Flogs*, or fake blogs, violate the spirit of blogging, show disrespect for your audience, and will turn audiences against you as soon as they uncover the truth.
Link generously—but carefully.	Providing interesting links to other blogs and websites is a fundamental aspect of blogging, but think twice before putting these links in your blog. Make sure the links will be of value to your readers, and make sure they don't point to material that could damage your reputation.
Keep it brief.	Most online readers don't have the patience to read lengthy reports.
Don't post anything you wouldn't want the entire world to see.	Future employers, government regulators, competitors, journalists, and community critics are just a few of the people who might eventually see what you've written.
Don't engage in blatant product promotion.	Readers who think they're being advertised to will stop reading.
Take time to write compelling, specific headlines for your postings.	Readers usually decide within a couple of seconds whether to read your postings; boring or vague headlines will turn them away instantly.
Pay attention to spelling, grammar, and mechanics.	No matter how smart or experienced you are, poor-quality writing undermines your credibility with intelligent audiences.
Respond to criticism openly and honestly.	Hiding sends the message that you don't have a valid response to the criticism. If your critics are wrong, patiently explain why you think they're wrong. If they are right, explain how you'll fix the situation.
Listen and learn.	If you don't take the time to analyze the comments people leave on your blog or the comments other bloggers make about you, you're missing out on one of the most valuable aspects of blogging.
Respect intellectual property.	You not only have an ethical obligation to not use material you don't own, doing so can also violate copyright laws.
Be scrupulously honest and careful with facts.	Honesty is an absolute requirement for every ethical business communicator, of course, but you need to be extra careful online because inaccuracies (both intentional and unintentional) are likely to be discovered quickly and shared widely.

Table 6.2 summarizes some of the key points to remember when creating and writing a business blog, and you can always get updated advice from some of the many blogs and websites dedicated to blogging.

Creating Effective Podcasts

Podcasting can be used to deliver a wide range of audio and video messages.

Podcasting offers a number of interesting possibilities for business communication. The most obvious use is to replace existing audio and video messages, such as large teleconferences in which a speaker provides information without expecting to engage in conversation with the listeners. Training is another good use of podcasting. One of the first podcasts recorded by technical experts at IBM gave other employees advice on setting up blogs, for example.[20] Sales representatives who travel to meet with potential customers can listen to podcasts to get the latest information on their companies' products. Podcasts are also an increasingly common feature on blogs, letting audiences listen to or watch recordings of their favorite bloggers. New services can even transcribe blogs into podcasts and vice versa.[21]

In the coming years, podcasts may also begin to replace other media options as well. Real estate agents could record audio podcasts that potential homebuyers could listen to while walking through houses. Marketing departments could replace expensive printed brochures with video podcasts that demonstrate new products in action. Human resource departments could offer video tours of their companies to entice new recruits.

Although not quite as simple as blogging, podcasting is a fairly easy process for any business with basic computer systems. As with blogs, the three-step process also adapts nicely to podcasting. You've already chosen the medium, so focus the planning step on analyzing the situation, gathering the information you'll need, and organizing your material. As you organize and move into the writing step, pay close attention to previews, transitions, and reviews. These steering devices are especially vital in audio and video recordings because these formats lack the "street signs" that audiences rely on in print media. For instance, if readers get lost or confused while reading a printed document, they can easily scan backward through the document to find key phrases or subheadings. Scanning back and forth to find specific parts of the message is much harder with audio and video, so you need to do everything possible to make sure your audience successfully receives and interprets your message on the first try.

Steering devices such as transitions, previews, and reviews are vital in podcasts.

As you'll see in Chapter 12 in the discussion of oral presentations, you'll need to decide whether to (a) script your podcast completely then read it word for word or (b) improvise from a speaking outline and notes. One of the attractions of podcasting is the conversational, person-to-person feel of the recordings, so unless you need to capture exact wording, speaking from an outline and notes is usually the best choice.

In the completing step, keep in mind that making edits is much more difficult in an audio or video medium such as podcasting. Therefore, take extra care to revise your script or think through your speaking notes before you begin to record. You don't want to get halfway through the recording process and realize that you should've said something else in the introduction.

Plan your podcast content carefully; edits are much more difficult to make than in textual messages.

The equipment needed to record podcasts depends on the degree of production quality you want to achieve. For the most basic podcasts, a low-cost microphone (most laptop computers now have built-in microphones) and some recording software (many free versions are available online) are all you need. If you need higher quality, the flexibility to combine several audio tracks, or the addition of video, you'll need to add additional pieces of hardware and software such as filters and mixers. To learn more about the technical requirements of podcasting, pick up one of the many new books on the subject. Some of these even come with free recording software.[22]

Reviewing Key Points

This chapter takes a closer look at the wide variety of media options for short business messages. The chapter starts with a discussion of the two traditional options: printed memos for internal audiences and printed letters for external audiences. While both forms still have their place in business today, particularly in the case of printed letters for customers and other outside audiences, they have been replaced in many instances by electronic media.

This chapter explores the four electronic media used most frequently for brief messages. Most written, internal messages in most companies are now conveyed through e-mail or instant messaging. The chapter describes the advantages and disadvantages of both media as well as guidelines for producing effective messages in both.

The chapter also introduces the business communication applications of two newer electronic media, blogging and podcasting. You learn that blogging is more than simply a new way to deliver written messages—it is a way to engage a large, distributed audience in an ongoing conversation. Podcasting is still entering the mainstream as a business medium, but it should find use wherever audio or video messages are good choices.

In the next three chapters, you'll put these short message media to work in a variety of communication situations: routine messages, routine requests, and positive messages (Chapter 7); negative messages (Chapter 8); and persuasive messages (Chapter 9).

Test Your Knowledge

1. What four electronic media choices are replacing traditional memos and letters in many instances?

2. Why are subject lines important in e-mail messages?

3. Should you use common IM slang terms and abbreviations such as IMHO (in my humble opinion) or TY (thank you) in business IM? Why or why not?

4. Why does a personal style of writing help blogs build stronger relationships with audiences?

5. Could a podcast replace an employee newsletter that is currently printed and mailed to employees' homes? Why or why not?

Apply Your Knowledge

1. Is instant messaging replacing many instances of e-mail for the same reasons that e-mail replaced many instances of printed memos and letters? Explain your answer.

2. If one of the benefits of blogging is the personal, intimate style of writing, is it a good idea to limit your creativity by adhering to conventional rules of grammar, spelling, and mechanics? Why or why not?

3. In your work as a video game designer, you know how eager players search the web for any scrap of information they can find about upcoming releases. In fact, to build interest, your company's own public relations department carefully doles out small bits of information in the months before a new title hits the market. However, you and others in the company are also concerned about competitors getting their hands on all this "prerelease" information. If they learn too much too soon, they can use that information to improve their own products more quickly. You and several other designers and programmers maintain blogs that give players insights into game design techniques and that occasionally share tips and tricks. You have thousands of readers, and you know your blog helps build customer loyalty. The company president wants to ban blogging entirely so that bloggers don't accidentally share too much prerelease information about upcoming games. Would this be a wise move? Why or why not?

4. Should podcasting be considered as a potential replacement for your company's employee newsletter, which is currently sent by e-mail? Why or why not?

5. **Ethical Choices**   Your boss wants you to send a message to the production staff, thanking all six members for their hard work and overtime to get the new manufacturing line set up and running on schedule. Your boss has been working a lot of overtime herself, and she's been under a lot of pressure. She wants to send the thank-you message by e-mail and asks you to work on the wording. You think each member of the production staff should receive a formal letter to keep for future promotions or other jobs. You know your boss won't like being interrupted about an issue that she thinks is off her desk, and you know how valuable her time is.

   a. Should you draft the letter and produce six copies so that you don't have to bother your boss?

   b. Should you simply draft the e-mail message as requested to save everyone time?

   c. Should you discuss the issue with your boss, regardless of taking her away from the tasks she so desperately needs to get done?

Practice Your Knowledge

Exercises for Perfecting Your Writing

Form and Audience   Barbara Marquardt is in charge of public relations for a cruise line that operates out of Miami. She is shocked to read a letter in a local newspaper from a disgruntled passenger, complaining about the service and entertainment on a recent cruise. Marquardt will have to respond to these publicized criticisms in some way.

1. What audiences will she need to consider in her response?

2. For each of these audiences, should Marquardt send her message via letter, memo, or e-mail?

Teamwork   Your team has been studying a new method for testing the durability of your company's electric hand tools. Now your team needs to summarize the findings in three separate reports: (a) one for company managers who will decide whether to purchase the new testing equipment needed for this new method, (b) one for company engineers who design and develop the hand tools, and (c) one for the trainers from the test equipment company, who will be showing your workers how to use the new testing equipment. Working with at least two other students, answer the following questions for each of the three reports:

3. For each audience, should your team send the report by letter, memo, or e-mail?

   a. Managers

   b. Engineers

   c. Trainers

4. Should the language be formal or conversational?

   a. Managers

   b. Engineers

   c. Trainers

Better Blogging   The members of the project team of which you are the leader have enthusiastically embraced blogging as a communication medium. Unfortunately, as emotions heat up during the project, some of the blog postings are getting too casual, too personal, and even sloppy. Because your boss and other managers around the company also read this project blog, you don't want the team to look unprofessional in anyone's eyes. Revise the following blog posting so that it communicates in a more businesslike manner while retaining the informal, conversational tone of a blog (be sure to correct any spelling and punctuation mistakes you find as well).

5. Well, to the profound surprise of absolutely nobody, we are not going to be able meet the June 1 commitment to ship 100 operating tables to Southeast Surgical Supply. (For those of you who have been living in a cave the past six month, we have been

fighting to get our hands on enough high-grade chromium steel to meet our production schedule.) Sure enough, we got news, this morning that we will only get enough for 30 tables. Yes, we look lik fools for not being able to follow through on promises we made to the customer, but no, this didn't have to happpen. Six month's ago, purchasing warned us about shrinking supplies and suggested we advance-buy as much as we would need for the next 12 months, or so. We naturally tried to followed their advice, but just as naturally were shot down by the bean counters at corporate who trotted out the policy about never buying more than three months worth of materials in advance. Of course, it'll be us–not the bean counters who'll take the flak when everybody starts asking why revenues are down next quarter and why Southeast is talking to our friends at Crighton Manuf!!! Maybe, some day this company will get its head out of the sand and realize that we need to have some financial flexibility in order to compete.

Making Subject Lines Informative Use your imagination to make the following e-mail subject lines more informative:

6. New budget figures

7. Your opinion on our current marketing brochure

8. Production schedule

Activities

For active links to all websites discussed in this chapter, visit this text's website at www.prenhall.com/bovee. Locate your book and click on its Companion Website link. Then select Chapter 6, and click on "Featured Websites." Locate the name of the page or the URL related to the material in the text. Please note that links to sites that become inactive after publication of the book will be removed from the Featured Websites section.

1. Analyze This Document Read the following document, then (1) analyze the strengths and weaknesses of each sentence and (2) revise it so that it follows the guidelines in Chapters 3 through 6.

Dear Ms. Giraud:

Enclosed herewith please find the manuscript for your book, *Careers in Woolgathering*. After perusing the first two chapters of your 1,500-page manuscript, I was forced to conclude that the subject matter, handicrafts and artwork using wool fibers, is not coincident with the publishing program of Framingham Press, which to this date has issued only works on business endeavors, avoiding all other topics completely.

Although our firm is unable to consider your impressive work at the present time, I have taken the liberty of recording some comments on some of the pages. I am of the opinion that any feedback that a writer can obtain from those well versed in the publishing realm can only serve to improve the writer's authorial skills.

In view of the fact that your residence is in the Boston area, might I suggest that you secure an appointment with someone of high editorial stature at the Cambridge Heritage Press, which I believe might have something of an interest in works of the nature you have produced.

Wishing you the best of luck in your literary endeavors, I remain

Arthur J. Cogswell
Editor

2. **Analyze This Document**   Read the following product instruction sheet, then (1) analyze the strengths and weaknesses of each sentence and (2) revise it so that it follows the guidelines in Chapters 3 through 6.

For delicious, air-popped popcorn, please read the following instructions: The popper is designed to pop 1/2 cup of popcorn kernels at one time. Never add more than 1/2 cup. A half cup of corn will produce three to four quarts of popcorn. More batches may be made separately after completion of the first batch. Popcorn is popped by hot air. Oil or shortening is not needed for popping corn. Add only popcorn kernels to the popping chamber. Standard grades of popcorn are recommended for use. Premium or gourmet-type popping corns may be used. Ingredients such as oil, shortening, butter, margarine, or salt should never be added to the popping chamber. The popper, with popping chute in position, may be preheated for two minutes before adding the corn. Turn the popper off before adding the corn. Use electricity safely and wisely. Observe safety precautions when using the popper. Do not touch the popper when it is hot. The popper should not be left unattended when it is plugged into an outlet. Do not use the popper if it or its cord has been damaged. Do not use the popper if it is not working properly. Before using the first time, wash the chute and butter/measuring cup in hot soapy water. Use a dishcloth or sponge. Wipe the outside of the popper base. Use a damp cloth. Dry the base. Do not immerse the popper base in water or other liquid. Replace the chute and butter/measuring cup. The popper is ready to use.

3. **Planning a Memo: Learn While You Earn—Memo Announcing Burger King's Educational Benefits**   Herb Schervish, owner of a Burger King store in Detroit's downtown Renaissance Center, is worried about employee turnover. He needs to keep 50 people on the payroll to operate the outlet, but recruiting and retaining those people is tough. The average employee leaves after about seven months, so Schervish has to hire and train 90 people a year just to maintain a 50-person crew. At a cost of $1,500 per hire, the price tag for all that turnover is approximately $60,000 a year.

Schervish knows that a lot of his best employees quit because they think that flipping burgers is a dead-end job. But what if it weren't a dead-end job? What if a person could really get someplace flipping burgers? What if Schervish offered to help pay his employees' way through college if they remained with the store? Would that keep them behind the counter?

He's decided to give educational incentives a try. Employees who choose to participate will continue to earn their usual salary, but they will also get free books and college tuition, keyed to the number of hours they work each week. Those who work from 10 to 15 hours a week can take one free course at nearby Wayne County Community College; those who work 16 to 25 hours can take two courses; and those who work 26 to 40 hours can take three courses. The program is open to all employees, regardless of how long they have worked for Burger King, but no one is obligated to participate.

Your task: If you were Herb Schervish, or if you worked for him, how would you plan and write a memo announcing the new educational incentives? The purpose is clear (to inform employees about the new offer), the audience has already been defined (all Renaissance Center Burger King employees), and the medium has been chosen (a written memo). Now use the following questions to continue your planning, choosing the best answer for each one. Then, creating sentences of your own, draft the memo based on what you've learned from this planning exercise.

a. Which sentence best expresses the memo's main idea?
1. Turnover at the Renaissance Center Burger King costs approximately $60,000 a year.
2. Flipping burgers doesn't have to be a dead-end job.
3. The Renaissance Center Burger King is offering its employees an exciting new educational program.
4. The new educational incentive program is open to all employees, no matter how long they've worked for Burger King.

b. Which of these sentences will help you establish a good relationship with your audience?
1. We are hoping that many of you will take advantage of the new program because it will reduce our turnover.
2. Employees need not attend college to continue working for us.
3. We hope that you will find the program useful.
4. Now you can earn free college tuition while you work at Burger King.

c. What must the body of your message accomplish? (Choose all that apply.)
1. Tell employees how to take advantage of the educational offer.
2. Explain how working hours relate to tuition payments.
3. Describe how Mr. Schervish came up with his idea.
4. Influence employees to attend college.

d. Which of the following methods will be best for conveying the relationship between hours worked and tuition paid?
1. A two-column table with the headings: "Those Who Work" (listing hours per week) and "May Take" (listing number of courses paid for).
2. A paragraph explaining the connection between hours worked and courses paid for.
3. A bulleted list with parallel entries such as, "If you work 10–15 hours, you'll get one free course; If you work 16–25 hours, you'll get two free courses"; etc.
4. A paragraph suggesting that details can be obtained from Mr. Schervish's office for those interested in taking advantage of the program.

e. To close the memo, which of the following sentences is the best choice?
1. We hope you'll take advantage of this offer, since doing so will help us reduce our turnover problem.
2. You don't have to take college courses to continue working for us.
3. I'll be happy to answer any questions you might have about how working for Burger King can help you earn free college tuition; just ask me.
4. If you're thinking of quitting, this may give you second thoughts.

Now imagine that you are Herb Schervish and draft your own memo in your own words.

4. **Revising an E-Mail Message: Break-Time Blues—Message Requesting a New Employee Procedure** The following e-mail message contains numerous errors related to what you've learned about planning and writing business messages. First, list the flaws you find in this version. Then follow the steps below to plan and write a better memo:

TO: Felicia August <fb_august@evertrust.com>
CC:
SUBJECT: Compliance with new break procedure

Some of you may not like the rules about break times; however, we determined that keeping track of employees while they took breaks at times they determined rather than regular breaks at prescribed times was not working as well as we would have liked it to work. The new rules are not going to be an option. If you do not follow the new rules, you could be docked from your pay for hours when you turned up missing, since your direct supervisor will not be able to tell whether you were on a "break" or not and will assume that you have walked away from your job. We cannot be responsible for any errors that result from your inattentiveness to the new rules. I have already heard complaints from some of you and I hope this memo will end this issue once and for all. The decision has already been made.

Starting Monday, January 1, you will all be required to take a regular 15-minute break in the morning and again in the afternoon, and a regular thirty-minute lunch at the times specified by your supervisor, NOT when you think you need a break or when you "get around to it."

There will be no exceptions to this new rule!

Felicia August
Manager
Billing and accounting

    a. Describe the flaws you discovered in this e-mail message:

    b. Develop a plan for rewriting the message. Use the following steps to organize your efforts before you begin writing:
        1. Determine the purpose
        2. Identify and analyze your audience
        3. Define the main idea
        4. Outline the major supporting points
        5. Choose between a direct and an indirect approach

    c. Now rewrite the e-mail message. Don't forget to leave ample time for revision of your own work before you turn it in.

5. Revising a Memo: Moving Day—Blog Posting Informing Employees About an Office Relocation From what you've learned about planning and writing business messages, you should be able to identify numerous errors made by the writer of the following blog posting. List them below, then plan and write a better post, following the guidelines given.

Get Ready!

We are hoping to be back at work soon, with everything running smoothly, same production schedule and no late projects or missed deadlines. So you need to clean out your desk, put your stuff in boxes, and clean off the walls. You can put the items you had up on your walls in boxes, also.

We have provided boxes. The move will happen this weekend. We'll be in our new offices when you arrive on Monday.

We will not be responsible for personal belongings during the move.

Posted by David Burke at 10:42 AM 09-27-07.

    a. Describe the flaws you discovered in this blog post.

    b. Develop a plan for rewriting the post. Use the following steps to organize your efforts before you begin writing:
        1. Determine the purpose
        2. Identify and analyze your audience
        3. Define the main idea
        4. Outline the major supporting points
        5. Choose between direct and indirect approaches

    c. Now rewrite the post. Don't forget to leave ample time for revision of your own work before you turn it in.

Expand Your Knowledge

Exploring the Best of the Web

Ready to Start Blogging? Blogging is easy to do if you have the right information. Start with the helpful tutorials at www.website101.com/RSS-Blogs-Blogging. More than 30 brief articles cover everything from creating a blog to attracting more readers to setting up RSS newsfeeds. Learn the techniques for adding audio and photo files to your blog. Learn how search engines treat blogs and how you can use search engines to help more people find your blog.

Exercises

1. What are five ways to attract more readers to your blog?
2. Why are blogs good for marketing?
3. What is a newsfeed and why is it a vital part of blogging?

Exploring the Web on Your Own

Review these chapter-related websites on your own to learn more about writing business messages.

1. Become fluent in your e-mail usage, from basic setup to advanced techniques, by taking the tutorial at www.webteacher.org/home-windows/index.html. On the homepage, click "Communicating," then select "E-mail."

2. Learn positive IM behavior with Taming the Beast's IM etiquette tutorial at www.tamingthebeast.net/articles6/messaging-chat-etiquette.htm.

3. Learn the ins and outs of successful podcasting from the Voxmedia Wiki, "How to Podcast," at www.voxmedia.org/wiki/How_to_Podcast.

Learn Interactively

Interactive Study Guide

Visit www.prenhall.com/bovee, then locate your book and click on its Companion Website link. Select Chapter 6 to take advantage of the interactive "Chapter Quiz" to test your knowledge of chapter concepts. Receive instant feedback on whether you need additional studying. Also, visit the "Study Hall," where you'll find an abundance of valuable resources that will help you succeed in this course.

Peak Performance Grammar and Mechanics

If your instructor has required the use of "Peak Performance Grammar and Mechanics," either in your online course, through the access-code protected portion of the Companion Website, or on CD, you can improve your skill with prepositions, conjunctions, and articles by using the "Peak Performance Grammar and Mechanics" module. Click "Grammar Basics," and then click "Prepositions, conjunctions, and articles." Take the Pretest to determine whether you have any weak areas. Then review those areas in the Refresher Course. Take the Follow-Up Test to check your grasp of prepositions, conjunctions, and articles. For an extra challenge or advanced practice, take the Advanced Test. Finally, for additional reinforcement in prepositions, conjunctions, and articles, go to the "Improve Your Grammar, Mechanics, and Usage" section that follows the cases, and complete the "Level 1: Self-Assessment" exercises.

CASES

Apply the three-step writing process to the following cases, as assigned by your instructor.

1. Selling without Selling: Blog Posting about a GPS Rescue

Promoting products through customer success stories can be a great marketing tactic, as long as you keep the customer as the "star" of the story and don't promote the product too blatantly. You've recently joined Garmin, a leading manufacturing of electronic navigation equipment, including a popular line of handheld Global Positioning System (GPS) devices used by hikers, kayakers, and others who venture off the beaten path.

Your Task As a communication specialist, your responsibilities include writing blog postings that highlight dramatic stories in which people used Garmin GPS units to rescue themselves or others from potentially dangerous situations. Visit Garmin's website at www.garmin.com, click on What's New, then GPS Adventures (or access the page directly at www.garmin.com/whatsNew/adventures.html). Select a customer story that involves a wilderness rescue in which a Garmin product played an important role. Using the information provided by the customer, rewrite the story in the third person (changing "I" or "we" references to "he," "she," or "they") for an audience that isn't familiar with the product in question. Subtly work in references to the product and the benefits it provided in this scenario, but keep the focus on the customer. Limit yourself to 400 words.

2. Time to Think: E-Mail Requesting a Change in Your Workload

The description of your job as a global marketing manager for New Balance is full of responsibilities that require creative thinking, from predicting consumer and retailing trends to establishing seasonal priorities for the global merchandising effort. You love these challenges—in fact, they're the main reason you took the job at this respected maker of athletic shoes and apparel. Unfortunately, between department meetings, status reports, budgets, and an endless array of other required chores, you hardly have time to think at all, much less engage in the sort of unstructured, "blue sky" thinking that is crucial to creative strategizing. You have virtually no time at work for such thinking, and after 50 or 60 hours a week at the office or on the road, you're too exhausted to brainstorm on your own time.

Your Task Write an e-mail to your boss, Paul Heffernan, the executive vice president of global marketing, persuading him that you need to reshuffle your assignments to free up more time to think. This is a tricky request because you know that Heffernan faces the same challenge. However, you're convinced that by spending less time on tasks that could be done by someone else (or perhaps shouldn't be done at all), you'll be able to do a better job of creating marketing strategies—and maybe even set a good example for other New Balance executives. You have a preliminary list of changes you'd like to make, but you know you need to discuss the entire scope of your job with Heffernan before finalizing the list. Your purpose: Invite him to lunch to begin a discussion of reshaping your responsibilities.[23]

3. Mercedes Merchandise: Letter Announcing Exclusive Online Gift Shop

Mercedes-Benz owners take their accessories seriously, which is why you get angry letters when they buy fake Mercedes merchandise produced by "sweatshop entrepreneurs," as your boss calls them. Too often, these unauthorized imitations fall apart, and it's Mercedes' high-class image that suffers.

That's why Mercedes started producing and promoting its own high-quality accessories, from T-shirts and toddler's jumpers to travel alarm clocks. First the company hired top-of-the-line manufacturers and designers to produce a glossy, full-color catalog of "Mercedes-Benz Personal and Automotive Accessories." Now the catalog has moved online.

At www.mbusi.com/Merchant2/merchant.mvc, the online store for the Mercedes-Benz manufacturing plant in Tuscaloosa, Alabama, shoppers can follow links to the online gift shop. But first they need to know it exists.

Your Task As assistant for Steve Beaty, vice president of accessories marketing, you're to draft an informative letter to

Mercedes owners telling them about the online gift shop. Visit the website to learn more about it, then write the letter using a style you think suits the car manufacturer's image.

4. Measuring Suppliers: E-Mail Message Requesting Reviews at Microsoft

Microsoft evaluates employees regularly to determine their performance—so why not do the same with the independent contractors the company hires to perform key functions? Nearly every department uses outside providers these days—a practice called *outsourcing*. So if there's a gap between what Microsoft expects from contractors and what the contractors actually deliver, shouldn't Microsoft tell them how they can improve their performance?

You've been discussing these questions all morning in a meeting with other members of the Employee Services Group. Your boss is convinced that regular reviews of independent contractors are essential.

"It's all about improving clarity in terms of goals and expectations," he says, adding that if contractors receive constructive feedback, Microsoft can develop good relationships with them instead of having to look for new service suppliers all the time.

Your boss assigns your team the task of informing all Microsoft departments that they'll be required to evaluate subcontractors every six months, beginning immediately. The goal of the review is to determine the performance of independent contractors so that Microsoft can (1) give them constructive feedback and continue a strong relationship or (2) end the relationship if service is substandard. Departments will need to rate each contractor on a scale of 1 (poor) to 5 (excellent) for each of several factors that your group is going to determine. Departments will be sending their reports to Roxanna Frost, group program manager for Microsoft's Executive Management and Development Group.

Your Task Working as a team with your classmates, develop a list of factors that will help you rate the overall service of independent contractors. You'll need to consider "cost," "quality of work," "innovation," "delivery," and other factors similar to those you'd encounter in a job performance review. Then compose an e-mail to all Microsoft department managers: Explain the new review requirements and include your list of factors to be rated on the 1-to-5 scale.[24]

5. Yes, We Do Purple: IM Skills from Lands' End

When clothing retailer Lands' End offered its 2,500 telephone service representatives the chance to train on its new instant messaging system, "Lands' End Live," you jumped at the opportunity. As it turned out, so many volunteered for the new training that the company had to give preference to a few hundred who'd been on the job longest. You were one of the lucky ones.

Now you've had months of practice answering messages like the one you just received from a customer named Alicia. She wants to know if she can have a red Polartec Aircore-200 Scarf custom monogrammed—not in the standard, contrasting, wheat-colored thread, but in radiant purple as a gift for her husband, whose favorite colors are red and purple.

On its website, Lands' End promises to fulfill nonstandard monogram requests "if technical limitations allow." You've done a quick check and yes, her husband can have his initials in bright purple on the red background.

Your Task Write the instant message reply to Alicia, telling her the good news.[25]

6. No Exaggeration: Short E-Mail Describing Internship Duties

You've been laboring all summer at an internship, learning how business is conducted. You've done work nobody else wanted to do, but that's okay. Even the smallest tasks can make a good impression on your future résumé.

This morning, your supervisor asks you to write a description of the job you've been doing. "Include everything, even the filing," she suggests, "and address it to me in an e-mail message."

She says a future boss might assign such a task prior to a performance review. "You can practice describing your work without exaggeration—or too much modesty," she says, smiling.

Your Task Using good techniques for short messages and relying on your real-life work experience, write an e-mail that will impress your supervisor.

7. Satisfaction Guaranteed: Letter from L.L. Bean Granting a Claim

One of the nicest things about working in customer service for sporting goods and clothing retailer L.L. Bean is that company policy guarantees satisfaction, "no questions asked." This means you always get to say yes to angry customers who want a refund.

In your hand is a package from Arvin Bummel (212 North Star, Traverse City, Mich. 49684). You open it to find (a) one pair of wool twill trousers, stiff and shrunken, (b) a Maine guide shirt, also two sizes smaller than it should be, and (c) an angry letter from Mr. Bummel saying the clothes were ruined the first time he washed them.

You're not surprised, since both items clearly say, "Dry Clean Only."

Your Task Write a letter to Mr. Bummel granting him a refund of $127.85, to be credited to his MasterCard. Visit the L.L. Bean website, www.llbean.com, to find suggestions for washable clothing he might want to try. But remember not to blame him in your letter; an L.L. Bean customer is always right.

BLOGGING SKILLS

8. Meet the Parents: Blog Posting Announcing the Acquisition of Golden West

As the human resources director for Golden West Financial, you know how proud your fellow employees are to work for one of the most admired banking companies in the United States. Golden West, which serves retail customers through its World Savings Bank branches across the West, was founded in Oakland, California, in the 1960s by the husband-and-wife team of Herbert and Marion Sandler. For decades, Golden West flourished as an independent company, but in 2006, the Sandlers decided to sell Golden West to Wachovia, a financial giant based in Charlotte, North Carolina.

Over the coming weeks, you'll provide Golden West employees with more information about the impact of the huge deal, but for now you want them to be aware of four key points:

- The deal allows Golden West to expand beyond its core offering of home mortgages to provide other financial services that its customers have requested for some time.
- The Sandlers carefully selected Wachovia because of its compatible values of integrity, customer-first business practices, and teamwork.
- World Savings Bank operations will continue from existing locations under the existing World Savings Bank brand name. New financial services from Wachovia will be added over time.
- The company's commitment to providing excellent career opportunities for women and minorities will not change.[26]

Your Task Write a short posting for Golden West's internal blog, announcing the deal and communicating the four key points listed above (in your own words). Close by telling your colleagues how excited you are by the deal and that you'll be providing more information in the day and weeks ahead.

E-MAIL SKILLS

9. Environmental Planning: E-Mail Announcing a Committee Meeting

You've probably worked as a volunteer on a committee or with team members for class assignments. You know how hard it is to get a diverse group of individuals together for a productive meeting. Maybe you've tried different locations—one member's home or a table at the library. This time you're going to suggest a local restaurant.

The committee you're leading is a volunteer group planning a trash-clearing project at an area park. Your meeting goal is to brainstorm ways to encourage public participation in this environmental event, to be held next Earth Day.

Your Task Develop a short e-mail message telling committee members about the meeting. Include time, date, duration, and location (choose a place you know). Mention the meeting goal to encourage attendance.

PODCASTING SKILLS

10. Why Me? Introducing Yourself to a Potential Employer

While writing the many letters and e-mail messages that are part of the job search process, you find yourself wishing that you could just talk to some of these companies so your personality could shine through. Well, you've just gotten that opportunity. One of the companies that you've applied to has e-mailed you back, asking you to submit a two-minute podcast introducing yourself and explaining why you would be a good person to hire.

Your Task Identify a company that you'd like to work for after graduation and select a job that would be a good match for your skills and interests. Write a script for a two-minute podcast (two minutes represents roughly 250 words for most speakers). Introduce yourself and the position you're applying for, describe your background, and explain why you think you're a good candidate for the job. Make up any details you need. If your instructor indicates, record the podcast and submit the file.

11. Hi, My Name Is: Introducing Yourself on a Business Network

Business networking websites such as www.linkedin.com, www.ryze.com, and www.spoke.com have become popular ways for professionals to make connections that would be difficult or impossible to make without the Internet. (You might be familiar with MySpace.com or Friendster.com, sites that help individuals meet through networks of people they already know and trust.) These business-oriented sites follow the same principle, but instead of using them to find new friends or dates, you use them to find new customers, new suppliers, or other important business connections. For instance, you might find that the ideal contact person in a company you'd like to do business with is the aunt of your boss's tennis partner.

An important aspect of business networking is being able to provide a clear description of your professional background and interests. For example, a manufacturing consultant can list the industries in which she has experience, the types of projects she has worked on, and the nature of work she'd like to pursue in the future (such as a full-time position for a company or additional independent projects).

Your Task Write a brief statement introducing yourself, including your educational background, your job history, and the types of connections you'd like to make. Feel free to "fast forward" to your graduation and list your degree, the business specialty you plan to pursue, and any relevant experience. If you have business experience already, feel free to use that information instead. Make sure your statement is clear, concise (no more than two sentences), and compelling, so that anyone looking for someone like you would want to get in touch with you after reading your introduction.

Improve Your Grammar, Mechanics, and Usage

Level 1: Self-Assessment—Prepositions and Conjunctions

Review Sections 1.6.1 and 1.6.2 in the Handbook of Grammar, Mechanics, and Usage, and then look at the following items.

Rewrite items 1–5, deleting unnecessary words and prepositions, and adding required prepositions:

1. Where was your argument leading to?

2. I wish he would get off of the phone.

3. This is a project into which you can sink your teeth.

4. U.S. Mercantile must become aware and sensitive to its customers' concerns.

5. We are responsible for aircraft safety in the air, the hangars, and the runways.

In items 6–10, write the correct preposition in the blank:

6. Dr. Namaguchi will be talking _____ the marketing class, but she has no time for questions.

7. Matters like this are decided after thorough discussion _____ all seven department managers.

8. We can't wait _____ their decision much longer.

9. Their computer is similar _____ ours.

10. This model is different _____ the one we ordered.

In items 11–15, rewrite the sentences in the space provided to make phrases parallel:

11. She is active in not only a civic group but also in an athletic organization.

12. That is either a mistake or was an intentional omission.

13. The question is whether to set up a booth at the convention or be hosting a hospitality suite.

14. We are doing better in both overall sales and in profits.

15. She had neither the preferred educational background, nor did she have suitable experience.

Level 2: Workplace Applications

The following items contain numerous errors in grammar, capitalization, punctuation, abbreviation, number style, word division, and vocabulary. Rewrite each sentence in the space provided, correcting all errors. Write *C* in the space after any sentence that is already correct.

1. Peabody Energys commitment to environmental excellence is driven by the companies' mission statement which states that when mining is complete, the company will leave the land in a condition equal or better than it was before mining.

2. In 1998, Blockbuster opened a state of the art distribution center in McKinney, Texas, just North of the company's Dallas Headquarters.

3. Miss Tucci was responsible for developing Terraspring's business plan, establishing the brand, and for launching the company.

4. The principle goals of the new venture will be to offer tailored financial products and meeting the needs of the community.

5. Nestle Waters North America are the number one bottled water company in the US. and Canada.

6. The reason egg prices dropped sharply is because of a Post Easter reduction in demand.

7. Joining bank officials during the announcement of the program were U.S. congressman Luis V. Guitierrez, Carlos Manuel Sada Solana, General Consul of Mexico in the Midwest, and "Don Francisco", the leading hispanic entertainment figure in the United States and Latin America.

8. The summer advertising campaign is the most unique in 7-Eleven's history.

9. Upon introducing it's new Quadruple Fudge flavor, consumers are expected to flock to Baskin-Robbins ice cream parlors.

10. The signing of a Trade Pact between the european union and Chile, is being delayed by european negotiators who insist the deal includes an agreement requiring Chile to stop using the names Cognac, Champagne, and Burgundy.

11. Federal Trade commissioner, Mrs. Sheila F. Anthony called on the dietary supplement industry to institute better self regulation, and called on the media to refuse ads containing claims that are obviously false.

12. Founded in 1971, GSD&M has grown to become a nationally-acclaimed advertising agency with more than 500 employees and having billings of over $1 billion dollars.

13. Although marketing may seem to be the easier place to cut costs during a downturn its actually the last place you should look to make strategic cuts.

14. After closing their plant in Mecosta county, Green Mountain will have less than 200 employees.

15. The purchasing needs of professional's differ from blue collar workers.

Level 3: Document Critique

The following document may contain errors in grammar, capitalization, punctuation, abbreviation, number style, vocabulary, and spelling. You may also find errors relating to topics in this chapter, such as the subject line. Correct all errors using standard proofreading marks (see Appendix C).

TO: George Kimball <g.kimball@sprenco.com>

CC:

SUBJECT: My trip back East

Dear George:

I went back to New York for apresentation the 15th of this month and I found it very informative. The sponsor of my visat was Vern Grouper. Vern is the Manager of IS at headquarters; that is, their centralized information systems operation. They've got quite a bit of power out there. And they do encourage us to utilize their capibilities, there services, and experiences to whatever extent will be beneficial to us. However, you could say it would be my observation that although they have a tremendous amount of computing capability that capability is directed toward a business dimension very different than ours and unlike anything we have. However, their are certain services that might be performed in our behalf by headquarters. For example, we could utilize people such as Vern to come and address our IS advisory group since I am planning on convening that group on a monthly basis.

By the way, I need to talk to you about the IS advicory group when you get a chance. I have 1 or 2 thoughts about some new approaches we can take with it I'd like to run by you if you don't mind. Its not too complicated just some simple ideas.

Let me know what you think of this idea about Vern coming here. If you like it than I will go ahead and set things in motion with Vern.

Sincerely,

John

7

Writing Routine and Positive Messages

Learning Objectives

After studying this chapter, you will be able to

1 Apply the three-step writing process to routine and positive messages

2 Outline an effective strategy for writing routine requests

3 Explain how to ask for specific action in a courteous manner

4 Describe a strategy for writing routine replies and positive messages

5 Discuss the importance of knowing who is responsible when granting claims and requests for adjustment

6 Explain how creating informative messages differs from responding to information requests

7 Describe the importance of goodwill messages and explain how to make them effective

Warren Buffett's financial acumen has made him and many of his shareholders wealthy, but he is recognized almost as widely for his communication skills. His letters, essays, and annual reports communicate complex financial topics in simple language that his readers can easily understand. His approach is simple: Even for a document that will be read by thousands of people, he visualizes a single person (often one of his sisters) as his audience. He treats this audience member as an intelligent human being who just doesn't have the same level of experience with the subject matter that he has. From there, he proceeds to organize and write his messages in a way that clarifies all the essential information and doesn't try to impress or obscure with complicated language. Whether you're writing an e-mail message to your boss or a report for an audience of thousands, Buffet's approach is a great example to follow.[1]

Using the Three-Step Writing Process for Routine and Positive Messages

Most business communication is about routine matters: orders, company policies, claims, credit, employees, products, operations, and so on. Such messages are rarely long or complex, but the three-step writing process still gives you a great way to produce effective messages efficiently:

Even simple messages can benefit from thoughtful planning.

■ **Step 1: Plan your message.** Planning routine and positive messages may take only a few minutes, but be sure to analyze the situation and make sure that your purpose is clear, gather the information your audience needs to know, select the most appropriate medium, and organize your information effectively.

- ◼ **Step 2: Write your message.** Adapt to your audience as the situation requires, maintaining a "you" attitude, being polite, emphasizing the positive, and using bias-free language. Compose your message using plain English and writing in the active voice. With some practice, you'll be able to compose most routine messages quickly.

- ◼ **Step 3: Complete your message.** Even though most routine messages are brief, spend a few moments to revise your messages to make sure they are clear and concise. Use templates and style sheets to speed up the production of routine messages. Finally, make sure you know how to take full advantage of whatever medium you're using to distribute your messages, whether it's e-mail, instant messaging, blogging, or any other system.

Making Routine Requests

Making requests—for information, action, products, adjustments, or other matters—is a routine part of business. In most cases, your audience will be prepared to comply, as long as you're not being unreasonable or asking someone to do something they would expect you to do yourself. By applying a clear strategy and tailoring your approach to each situation, you'll be able to generate effective requests quickly.

Strategy for Routine Requests

Like all business messages, routine requests have three parts: an opening, a body, and a close. Using the direct approach, open with your main idea, which is a clear statement of your request. Use the body to give details and justify your request. Then close by requesting specific action.

For routine requests and positive messages,
- ◼ State the request or main idea
- ◼ Give necessary details
- ◼ Close with a cordial request for specific action

State Your Request Up Front

Begin routine requests by placing your request first. Of course, getting right to the point should not be interpreted as a license to be abrupt or tactless:

Take care that your direct approach doesn't come across as abrupt or tactless.

- ◼ **Pay attention to tone.** Even though you expect a favorable response, the tone of your initial request is important. Instead of demanding action ("Send me the latest version of the budget spreadsheet"), soften your request with words such as *please* and *I would appreciate.*
- ◼ **Assume your audience will comply.** An impatient demand for rapid service isn't necessary. You can generally make the assumption that your audience will comply with your request once the reason for it is clearly understood.
- ◼ **Be specific.** State precisely what you want. For example, if you request the latest market data from your research department, be sure to say whether you want a one-page summary or a hundred pages of raw data.

Explain and Justify Your Request

Use the body of your message to explain your initial request. Make the explanation a smooth and logical outgrowth of your opening remarks. If possible, point out how complying with the request could benefit the reader. You can also use the body of your request to list a series of questions, which will help you organize the message and help your audience identify the information you need. Follow these tips:

- ◼ **Ask the most important questions first.** If cost is your main concern, you might begin with a question such as "How much will it cost to have our new website created by an outside firm?" Then you may want to ask more specific but related questions, such as discounts for paying early.

- **Ask only relevant questions.** To help expedite the response to your request, ask only those questions that are central to your main request.
- **Deal with only one topic per question.** If you have an unusual or complex request, break it down into specific, individual questions so that the reader can address each one separately. This consideration not only shows respect for your audience's time but also gets you a more accurate answer in less time.

Request Specific Action in a Courteous Close

Close request messages with
- A request for some specific action
- Information about how you can be reached
- An expression of appreciation

Close your message with three important elements: (1) a specific request that includes any relevant deadlines, (2) information about how you can be reached (if it isn't obvious), and (3) an expression of appreciation or goodwill. When you ask readers to perform a specific action, ask that they respond by a specific time, if appropriate ("Please send the figures by April 5 so that I can return first-quarter results to you before the April 15 board meeting"). Conclude your message by sincerely expressing your goodwill and appreciation. However, don't thank the reader "in advance" for cooperating. If the reader's reply warrants a word of thanks, send it after you've received the reply.

Common Examples of Routine Requests

Most of the routine messages that you'll be writing will likely fall into a few main categories: asking for information and action, asking for recommendations, and making claims and requesting adjustments.

Asking for Information and Action

When you need to know about something, to elicit an opinion from someone, or to request a simple action, you usually need only ask. In essence, simple requests say

- What you want to know or what you want readers to do
- Why you're making the request
- Why it may be in your readers' interest to help you

If your reader is able to do what you want, such a straightforward request gets the job done with a minimum of fuss. In more complex situations, readers might be unwilling to respond unless they understand how the request benefits them, so be sure to include this information in your explanation. Naturally, you'll adapt your request to your audience and the situation. For instance, requests to fellow employees are usually casual and get straight to the point (Figure 7.1).

Asking for Recommendations

The need to inquire about people arises often in business. For example, before awarding credit, contracts, jobs, promotions, scholarships, and so on, some companies ask applicants to supply references who can vouch for their ability, skills, integrity, character, and so on. If you're applying for a job and your potential employer asks for references, you may want to ask a former instructor or professional associate to write a letter of recommendation. Or, if you're an employer considering whether to hire an applicant, you may want to write directly to the person the applicant named as a reference. Before you volunteer someone's name as a reference, make sure you have permission to do so. Some people are not comfortable writing recommendation letters, and some organizations have policies that prohibit employees from endorsing former colleagues or suppliers.

Always ask for permission before using someone as a reference.

Because requests for recommendations and references are routine, you can assume that your reader will honor your request, and you can organize your inquiry using the direct approach. Open your message by clearly stating that you're applying for a position and that you would like your reader to write a letter of recommendation. If you haven't had contact with the person for some time, use the opening to recall the nature of the

Refresh the memory of any potential reference you haven't been in touch with for a while.

FIGURE 7.1 Effective Memo Requesting Action

This memo effectively requests action by explaining why the information is needed and how giving it will benefit the recipients. Notice how the three-step writing process is easily adapted to this message. (In many instances, a memo such as this would be sent via e-mail instead, but this writer needs the recipients to sign and return the reply form, so a printed memo is the best choice.)

Planning

Analyze the Situation
Verify that the purpose is to request feedback from fellow employees.

Gather Information
Gather accurate, complete information on program benefits and local gyms.

Select the Right Medium
Office memo is appropriate for this message; printed format makes it easy for readers to sign and return the form.

Organize the Information
The main idea is saving money while staying healthy. Save time and meet audience expectations by using a direct approach.

Writing

Adapt to Your Audience
Show sensitivity to audience needs with a "you" attitude, politeness, positive emphasis, and bias-free language. Writer already has credibility as manager of the department.

Compose the Message
Maintain a style that is conversational, but businesslike, using plain English and appropriate voice.

Completing

Revise the Message
Evaluate content and review readability; avoid unnecessary details.

Produce the Message
Simple memo format is all the design this message needs.

Proofread the Message
Review for errors in layout, spelling, and mechanics.

Distribute the Message
Deliver the message via the company's interoffice mail delivery system.

ACE _Ace Hardware Corporation_

INTERNAL MEMORANDUM

DATE: October 15, 2007
TO: All Employees
FROM: Tony Ramirez, Human Resources
SUBJ: New Wellness Program Opportunity

The Benefits Package Committee has asked me to contact everyone about an opportunity to save money and stay healthier. As you know, the Benefits Committee has been meeting to decide on changes in our benefits package. Last week, we sent you a memo detailing the Synergy Wellness Program.

In addition to the package as described in last week's memo (life, medical, and dental insurance), Synergy has made the offer even more attractive by offering us a 10% discount. However, to qualify for the discount, we have to show proof that at least 25% of our employees participate in aerobic exercise at least three times a week for at least 20 minutes.

After looking around, we discovered a gymnasium just a few blocks south on Haley Boulevard. Sports Midwest will give our employees unlimited daytime access to their indoor track, gym, and pool for a group fee that comes to approximately $4.50 per month per employee if at least half of us sign up.

In addition to using the track and pools, we can play volleyball, participate in Jazzercise, form our own intramural basketball teams, and much more. Our spouses and children can also participate at a deeply discounted monthly fee. If you have questions, please e-mail or call me (or any member of the committee). Let us know your wishes on the following form.

Please mark your choice(s) on the form below, then sign and return it to your immediate supervisor no later than Friday, October 26.
= =

_____ Yes, I will participate in the Synergy Wellness Program and pay $4.50 a month.
_____ Yes, I am interested in a discounted family membership.
_____ No, I prefer not to participate.

Signature _____

Employee ID Number _____

Routes message efficiently, with all needed information

Presents the situation that makes the inquiry necessary

Gives clear instructions and a deadline for response

Provides an easy-to-use response form

States purpose in opening to avoid wasting busy readers' time

Lists reader benefits and requests action

Pointers for Making a Routine Request
• Be direct, since your readers will respond favorably.
• Use a polite, personal tone and don't demand a response.
• Justify the request or explain its importance.
• Explain the benefits of responding.
• Close courteously with a request for specific action.

relationship you had, the dates of association, and any special events that might bring a clear, favorable picture of you to mind. Consider including an updated résumé if you've had significant career advancement since your last contact.

Close your letter with an expression of appreciation and the full name and address of the person to whom the letter should be sent. When asking for an immediate recommendation, you should also mention the deadline. You'll make a response more likely if you enclose a stamped, preaddressed envelope, which is a considerate step in any event. See Figure 7.2 on page 165 for an example.

Making Claims and Requesting Adjustments

If you're dissatisfied with a company's product or service, you can opt to make a **claim** (a formal complaint) or request an **adjustment** (a claim settlement). In either case, it's important to maintain a professional tone in all your communication, no matter how angry or frustrated you might be. Keeping your cool will help you get the situation resolved sooner. In addition, be sure to document your initial complaint and all correspondence after that.

In most cases, and especially in your first letter, assume that a fair adjustment will be made, and use a direct approach. Open with a straightforward statement of the problem. In the body, give a complete, specific explanation. Provide any information an adjuster would need to verify your complaint. In your close, politely request specific action or convey a sincere desire to find a solution. And if appropriate, suggest that the business relationship will continue if the problem is solved satisfactorily.

Companies usually accept the customer's explanation of what's wrong, so ethically it's important to be entirely honest when filing claims. Also, be prepared to back up your claim with invoices, sales receipts, credit card statements, dated correspondence, and any other relevant documents. Send copies and keep the originals for your files.

If the remedy is obvious, tell your reader exactly what you expect from the company, such as exchanging incorrectly shipped merchandise for the right item or issuing a refund if the item is out of stock. In some cases, you might ask the reader to resolve a problem. However, if you're uncertain about the precise nature of the trouble, you could ask the company to make an assessment, then advise you on how the situation could be fixed. Supply your contact information so that the company can discuss the situation with you if necessary. Compare the poor and improved versions in Figure 7.3 on page 166 for an example of making a claim.

Sending Routine Replies and Positive Messages

Just as you'll make numerous requests for information and action throughout your career, you'll also respond to similar requests from other people. When you are responding positively to a request, sending routine announcements, or sending a positive or goodwill message, you have several goals: to communicate the information or the good news, answer all questions, provide all required details, and leave your reader with a good impression of you and your firm.

Strategy for Routine Replies and Positive Messages

Because readers receiving these messages will generally be interested in what you have to say, you'll usually use the direct approach. Place your main idea (the positive reply or the good news) in the opening. Use the body to explain all the relevant details, and close cordially, perhaps highlighting a benefit to your reader.

Start with the Main Idea

By opening your routine and positive messages with the main idea or good news, you're preparing your audience for the details that follow. Make your opening clear and concise. Although the following introductory statements make the same point, one is cluttered

---

In your claim letter,
- Explain the problem and give details
- Provide backup information
- Request specific action

Be prepared to document your claim. Send copies and keep the original documents.

Use a direct approach for positive messages.

Prepare your audience for the detail that follows by beginning your positive message with the main idea or good news.

FIGURE 7.2 **Effective Request for a Recommendation**

This writer uses a direct approach when asking for a recommendation from a former professor. Note how she takes care to refresh the professor's memory, since the class was taken a year and a half ago. She also indicates the date by which the letter is needed and points to the enclosure of a stamped, preaddressed envelope.

Planning

Analyze the Situation
Verify that the purpose is to request a recommendation letter from a college professor.

Gather Information
Gather information on classes and dates to help the reader recall you and to clarify the position you seek.

Select the Right Medium
The letter format gives this message an appropriate level of formality, although many professors prefer to be contacted by e-mail.

Organize the Information
Messages like this are common and expected, so a direct approach is fine.

Writing

Adapt to Your Audience
Show sensitivity to audience needs with a "you" attitude, politeness, positive emphasis, and bias-free language.

Compose the Message
Style is respectful and businesslike, while still using plain English and appropriate voice.

Completing

Revise the Message
Evaluate content and review readability; avoid unnecessary details.

Produce the Message
Simple memo format is all the design this message needs.

Proofread the Message
Review for errors in layout, spelling, and mechanics.

Distribute the Message
Deliver the message via postal mail or e-mail if you have the professor's e-mail address.

1 **2** **3**

1181 Ashport Drive
Tate Springs, TN 38101
March 14, 2007

Professor Lyndon Kenton
School of Business
University of Tennessee, Knoxville
Knoxville, TN 37916

Dear Professor Kenton:

I recently interviewed with Strategic Investments and have been called for a second interview for their Analyst Training Program (ATP). They have requested at least one recommendation from a professor, and I immediately thought of you. May I have a letter of recommendation from you?

> *Opens by stating the purpose of the letter and making the request, assuming the reader will want to comply with the request*

As you may recall, I took BUS 485, Financial Analysis, from you in the fall of 2005. I enjoyed the class and finished the term with an "A." Professor Kenton, your comments on assertiveness and cold-calling impressed me beyond the scope of the actual course material. In fact, taking your course helped me decide on a future as a financial analyst.

> *Includes information near the opening to refresh the reader's memory about this former student*

My enclosed résumé includes all my relevant work experience and volunteer activities. I would also like to add that I've handled the financial planning for our family since my father passed away several years ago. Although I initially learned by trial and error, I have increasingly applied my business training in deciding what stocks or bonds to trade. This, I believe, has given me a practical edge over others who may be applying for the same job.

> *Refers to résumé in the body and mentions experience that could set applicant apart from other candidates*

If possible, Ms. Blackmon in Human Resources needs to receive your letter by March 30. For your convenience, I've enclosed a preaddressed, stamped envelope.

> *Gives a deadline for response and includes information about the person expecting the recommendation*

> *Mentions the preaddressed, stamped envelope to encourage a timely response*

I appreciate your time and effort in writing this letter of recommendation for me. It will be great to put my education to work, and I'll keep you informed of my progress. Thank you for your consideration in this matter.

Sincerely,

Joanne Tucker

Joanne Tucker

Enclosure

FIGURE 7.3   **Poor and Improved Versions of a Claim**

Note the difference in both tone and information content in these two versions. The poor version is emotional and unprofessional, whereas the improved version communicates calmly and clearly.

with unnecessary information that buries the purpose, whereas the other is brief and to the point:

Instead of This	Write This
I am pleased to inform you that after deliberating the matter carefully, our human resources committee has recommended you for appointment as a financial analyst.	We would like to offer you the position of financial analyst in our Cleveland headquarters.

The best way to write a clear opening is to have a clear idea of what you want to say. Before you put one word on paper, ask yourself, "What is the single most important message I have for the audience?"

Provide Necessary Details and Explanation

Use the body of your message to explain your point completely so that your audience will experience no confusion or lingering doubt. In addition to providing details in the body, maintain the supportive tone established in the opening. This tone is easy to continue when your message is entirely positive, as in this example:

> Your educational background and internship have impressed us, and we believe you would be a valuable addition to Green Valley Properties. As discussed during your interview, your salary will be $4,300 per month, plus benefits. In that regard, you will meet with our benefits manager, Paula Sanchez, at 8 a.m. on Monday, March 21. She will assist you with all the paperwork necessary to tailor our benefit package to your family situation. She will also arrange various orientation activities to help you acclimate to our company.

However, if your routine message is mixed and must convey mildly disappointing information, put the negative portion of your message into as favorable a context as possible:

Try to embed any negative information in a positive context.

Instead of This	Write This
No, we no longer carry the Sportsgirl line of sweaters.	The new Olympic line has replaced the Sportsgirl sweaters that you asked about. Olympic features a wider range of colors and sizes and more contemporary styling.

The more complete description is less negative and emphasizes how the audience can benefit from the change. Be careful, though: You can use negative information in this type of message *only* if you're reasonably sure the audience will respond positively. Otherwise, use an indirect approach (discussed in Chapter 8).

End with a Courteous Close

Your message is most likely to succeed if your readers are left feeling that you have their best interests in mind. You can accomplish this task either by highlighting a benefit to the audience or by expressing appreciation or goodwill. If follow-up action is required, clearly state who will do what next.

Make sure the audience understands what to do next and how that action will benefit them.

Common Examples of Routine Replies and Positive Messages

As with routine requests, you'll encounter the need for a wide variety of routine replies and positive messages. Most routine and positive messages fall into six main categories: answers to requests for information and action, grants of claims and requests for adjustment, recommendations, informative messages, good-news announcements, and goodwill messages.

Document Makeover

Improve This E-Mail Message

To practice correcting drafts of actual documents, visit your online course or the access-code-protected Prentice Hall Business Communication Website. Click "Document Makeovers," then click Chapter 7. You will find an e-mail message that contains problems and errors relating to what you've learned in this chapter about writing routine and positive messages. Use the Final Draft decision tool to create an improved version of this letter.

Answering Requests for Information and Action

Every professional answers requests for information and action from time to time. If the response to a request is a simple yes or some other straightforward information, a direct approach is appropriate. A prompt, gracious, and thorough response will positively influence how people think about you and the organization you represent. Depending on the resources your company offers, you might use letters, memos, e-mail, or instant messaging to answer these requests (see Figure 7.4).

FIGURE 7.4   **Effective IM Response to Information Request**
This quick and courteous exchange is typical of IM communication in such areas as customer service and technical support. The agent (Janice) solves the problem quickly and leaves the customer with a positive impression of the company.

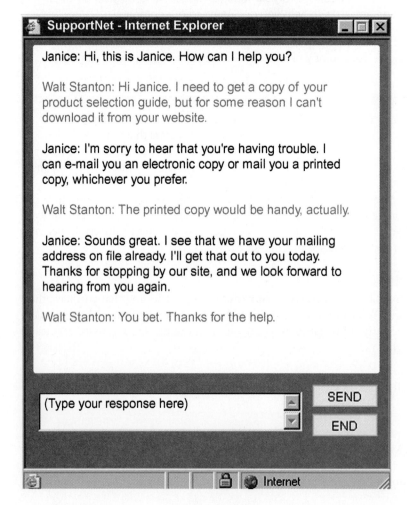

FIGURE 7.5   Personalized Reply to Request for Information
This e-mail message personalizes a standardized response by including the recipient's name in the greeting.

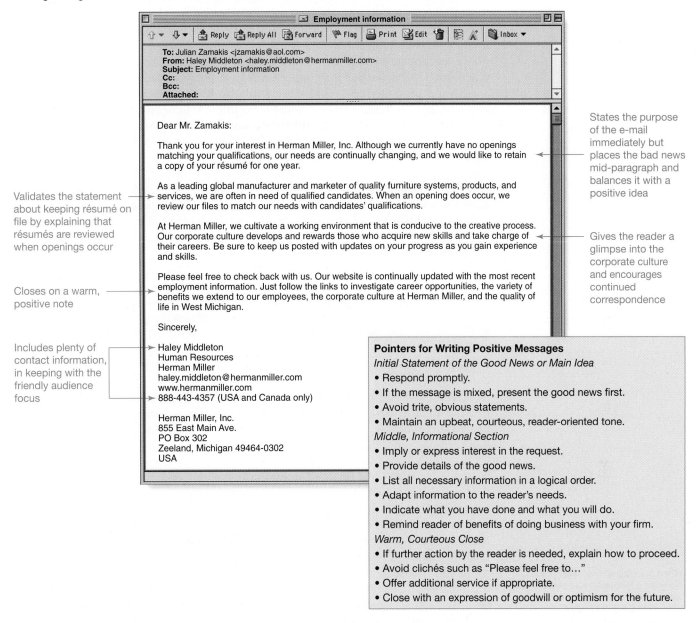

States the purpose of the e-mail immediately but places the bad news mid-paragraph and balances it with a positive idea

Validates the statement about keeping résumé on file by explaining that résumés are reviewed when openings occur

Gives the reader a glimpse into the corporate culture and encourages continued correspondence

Closes on a warm, positive note

Includes plenty of contact information, in keeping with the friendly audience focus

To: Julian Zamakis <jzamakis@aol.com>
From: Haley Middleton <haley.middleton@hermanmiller.com>
Subject: Employment information
Cc:
Bcc:
Attached:

Dear Mr. Zamakis:

Thank you for your interest in Herman Miller, Inc. Although we currently have no openings matching your qualifications, our needs are continually changing, and we would like to retain a copy of your résumé for one year.

As a leading global manufacturer and marketer of quality furniture systems, products, and services, we are often in need of qualified candidates. When an opening does occur, we review our files to match our needs with candidates' qualifications.

At Herman Miller, we cultivate a working environment that is conducive to the creative process. Our corporate culture develops and rewards those who acquire new skills and take charge of their careers. Be sure to keep us posted with updates on your progress as you gain experience and skills.

Please feel free to check back with us. Our website is continually updated with the most recent employment information. Just follow the links to investigate career opportunities, the variety of benefits we extend to our employees, the corporate culture at Herman Miller, and the quality of life in West Michigan.

Sincerely,

Haley Middleton
Human Resources
Herman Miller
haley.middleton@hermanmiller.com
www.hermanmiller.com
888-443-4357 (USA and Canada only)

Herman Miller, Inc.
855 East Main Ave.
PO Box 302
Zeeland, Michigan 49464-0302
USA

Pointers for Writing Positive Messages
Initial Statement of the Good News or Main Idea
• Respond promptly.
• If the message is mixed, present the good news first.
• Avoid trite, obvious statements.
• Maintain an upbeat, courteous, reader-oriented tone.
Middle, Informational Section
• Imply or express interest in the request.
• Provide details of the good news.
• List all necessary information in a logical order.
• Adapt information to the reader's needs.
• Indicate what you have done and what you will do.
• Remind reader of benefits of doing business with your firm.
Warm, Courteous Close
• If further action by the reader is needed, explain how to proceed.
• Avoid clichés such as "Please feel free to…"
• Offer additional service if appropriate.
• Close with an expression of goodwill or optimism for the future.

Most businesses receive many similar requests. For example, a human resources department gets numerous routine inquiries about job openings. To handle repetitive queries like these quickly and consistently, companies usually develop form responses. With a form message as the starting point, you can personalize it for each recipient by using the mail merge capability in your word processor or other document preparation software. For example, instead of addressing a form reply to "Dear Applicant," you can have the computer insert the recipient's name. If you have time and the message is important, go beyond this and revise the content of each letter with unique information about each recipient (Figure 7.5).

Granting Claims and Requests for Adjustment

Even the best-run companies make mistakes, from shipping the wrong order to billing the customer's credit card inaccurately. In other cases, the customer or a third party might be responsible for the mistake, such as misusing a product or damaging it in shipment. Each of these events represents a turning point in your relationship with your customer. If you handle the situation well, your customer will likely be even more loyal than before, because you've proven that you're serious about customer satisfaction. However, if a customer believes that you mishandled a complaint, you'll make the situation even worse. Dissatisfied customers often take their business elsewhere and are likely to tell numerous friends and colleagues about the negative experience. A transaction that might be worth only a few dollars by itself could cost you many times that amount in lost business. In other words, every mistake is an opportunity to improve a relationship.

Few people go to the trouble of requesting an adjustment unless they actually have a problem, so most businesses start from the assumption that the customer is correct. From there, your response to the complaint depends on both your company's policies for resolving such issues and your assessment of whether the company, the customer, or some third party is at fault.

When Your Company Is at Fault   Whenever you communicate about a mistake your company has made, do so carefully. Before you respond, make sure you know your company's policies in such cases, which might even dictate specific legal and financial steps to be taken. Most routine responses should take your company's specific policies into account and address the following points:

- Acknowledge receipt of the customer's claim or complaint.
- Take (or assign) personal responsibility for setting matters straight.
- Sympathize with the customer's inconvenience or frustration.
- Explain precisely how you have resolved, or plan to resolve, the situation.
- Take steps to repair the relationship.
- Follow up to verify your response was correct.

In addition to these positive steps, maintain professional demeanor by avoiding some key negative steps as well: Don't blame anyone in your organization by name, don't make exaggerated apologies that sound insincere, don't imply that the customer is at fault, and don't promise more than you can deliver.

When the Customer Is at Fault   Communication about a claim is a delicate matter when the customer is clearly at fault. You can (1) refuse the claim and attempt to justify your refusal or (2) simply do what the customer asks. If you refuse the claim, you may lose your customer—as well as many of the customer's friends and colleagues, who will hear only one side of the dispute. You must weigh the cost of making the adjustment against the cost of losing future business from one or more customers.

If you choose to grant the claim, you can open with the good news: You're replacing the merchandise or refunding the purchase price. However, the body needs more attention. Your job is to make the customer realize that the merchandise was mistreated, but you want to avoid being condescending ("Perhaps you failed to read the instructions carefully") or preachy ("You should know that wool shrinks in hot water"). The dilemma is this: If the customer fails to realize what went wrong, you may commit your firm to an endless procession of returned merchandise; but if you insult the customer, your cash refund will have been wasted because you'll lose your customer anyway. Close in a courteous manner that expresses your appreciation for the customer's business (see Figure 7.6).

When a Third Party Is at Fault   Sometimes neither your company nor your customer is at fault. For example, ordering a book from Amazon.com involves not only Amazon.com but also a delivery service such as Federal Express or the U.S. Postal Service, the publisher and possibly a distributor of the book, a credit card issuer, and a company that processes credit card transactions. Any one of these other partners might be at fault, but the customer is likely to blame Amazon.com, since that is the entity that receives the customer's payment.

No general scheme applies to every case involving a third party, so evaluate the situation carefully and know your company's policies before responding. For instance, an

When granting an unjustified claim, maintain a respectful and positive tone while informing the customer that the claim was a result of misuse or mistreatment of the product.

FIGURE 7.6   **Responding to a Claim When the Buyer Is at Fault**

In the interest of positive customer relationships, this company agreed to provide replacement parts for a customer's in-line skates, even though the product is outside its warranty period. (For the sake of clarity, the content of the customer's original e-mail message is not reproduced here.)

Planning

Analyze the Situation
Verify that the purpose is to grant the customer's claim, tactfully educate him, and encourage further business.

Gather Information
Gather information on product care, warranties, and resale information.

Select the Right Medium
An e-mail message is appropriate in this case since the customer contacted the company via e-mail.

Organize the Information
You're responding with a positive answer, so a direct approach is fine.

1

Writing

Adapt to Your Audience
Show sensitivity to audience needs with a "you" attitude, politeness, positive emphasis, and bias-free language.

Compose the Message
Maintain a style that is respectful while still managing to educate the customer on product usage and maintenance.

2

Completing

Revise the Message
Evaluate content and review readability; avoid unnecessary details.

Produce the Message
Emphasize a clean, professional appearance.

Proofread the Message
Review for errors in layout, spelling, and mechanics.

Distribute the Message
E-mail the reply.

3

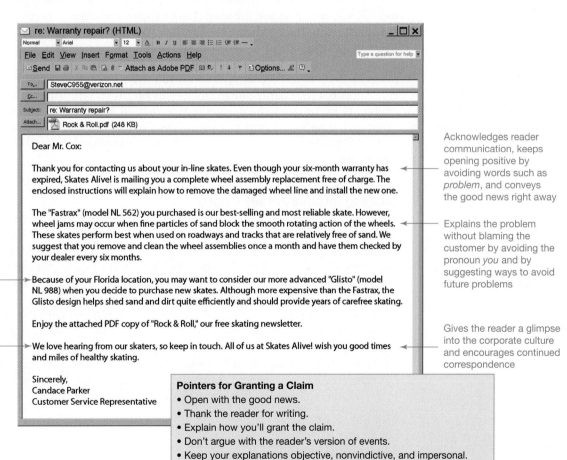

re: Warranty repair? (HTML)

To..: SteveC955@verizon.net
Cc...:
Subject: re: Warranty repair?
Attach...: Rock & Roll.pdf (248 KB)

Dear Mr. Cox:

Thank you for contacting us about your in-line skates. Even though your six-month warranty has expired, Skates Alive! is mailing you a complete wheel assembly replacement free of charge. The enclosed instructions will explain how to remove the damaged wheel line and install the new one.

The "Fastrax" (model NL 562) you purchased is our best-selling and most reliable skate. However, wheel jams may occur when fine particles of sand block the smooth rotating action of the wheels. These skates perform best when used on roadways and tracks that are relatively free of sand. We suggest that you remove and clean the wheel assemblies once a month and have them checked by your dealer every six months.

Because of your Florida location, you may want to consider our more advanced "Glisto" (model NL 988) when you decide to purchase new skates. Although more expensive than the Fastrax, the Glisto design helps shed sand and dirt quite efficiently and should provide years of carefree skating.

Enjoy the attached PDF copy of "Rock & Roll," our free skating newsletter.

We love hearing from our skaters, so keep in touch. All of us at Skates Alive! wish you good times and miles of healthy skating.

Sincerely,
Candace Parker
Customer Service Representative

Acknowledges reader communication, keeps opening positive by avoiding words such as problem, and conveys the good news right away

Explains the problem without blaming the customer by avoiding the pronoun you and by suggesting ways to avoid future problems

Gives the reader a glimpse into the corporate culture and encourages continued correspondence

Subtly promotes a more appropriate product for the customer

Closes on a positive note that conveys an attitude of excellent customer service

Pointers for Granting a Claim
• Open with the good news.
• Thank the reader for writing.
• Explain how you'll grant the claim.
• Don't argue with the reader's version of events.
• Keep your explanations objective, nonvindictive, and impersonal.
• Apologize only when appropriate, and do so in a nondramatic fashion.
• Close by reminding the reader how you are honoring the claim.
• Encourage a favorable view of your company and its products.
• Clarify any remaining actions the reader must take.

online retailer and the companies that manufacture its merchandise might have an agreement specifying that the manufacturers automatically handle all complaints about product quality. However, regardless of who eventually resolves the problem, if customers contact you, you need to respond with messages that explain how the problem will be solved. Pointing fingers is both unproductive and unprofessional; resolving the situation is the only issue customers care about.

Providing Recommendations

When writing a letter of recommendation, your goal is to convince readers that the person being recommended has the characteristics necessary for the job, project assignment, or other objective the person is seeking. A successful recommendation letter contains a number of relevant details:

- The candidate's full name
- The position or other objective the candidate is seeking
- The nature of your relationship with the candidate
- An indication of whether you're answering a request from the person or taking the initiative to write
- Facts and evidence relevant to the candidate and the opportunity
- Your overall evaluation of the candidate's suitability for the opportunity

As surprising as this might sound, the most difficult recommendation letters to write are often those for truly outstanding candidates. Your audience will have trouble believing uninterrupted praise for someone's talents and accomplishments. To enhance your credibility—and the candidate's—illustrate your general points with specific examples that highlight the candidate's abilities and fitness for the job opening.

If the candidate has shortcomings that are relevant to the opportunity, you'll need to decide how to handle the situation. You may opt not to write the letter, in which case you're not necessarily obliged to explain why. If you do write the letter, you have an ethical obligation not to hide negative information. You don't have to present the shortcomings as simple criticisms, however. A good option is to list them as areas for improvement, particularly if the person is already committed to making improvements (see Figure 7.7).

Creating Informative Messages

All companies send routine informative messages, such as reminder notices and policy statements. Use the opening to state the purpose (to inform) and briefly mention the nature of the information you are providing. Unlike the replies discussed earlier, informative messages are not solicited by your reader, so make it clear up front why the reader is receiving this particular message. In the body, provide the necessary details and end your message with a courteous close.

Most informative communications are neutral and straightforward, but some may require additional care. For instance, policy statements or procedural changes may be good news for a company (perhaps by saving money). However, it may not be obvious to employees that such savings may make available additional employee resources or even pay raises. In instances where the reader may not initially view the information positively, use the body of the message to highlight the potential benefits from the reader's perspective.

Fostering Goodwill

All business messages should be written with an eye toward fostering goodwill among business contacts, but some messages are written specifically to build goodwill. You can use these messages to enhance your relationships with customers, colleagues, and other businesspeople by sending friendly, even unexpected notes with no direct business purpose.

Sidebar notes:

When a third party is at fault, your response depends on your company's agreements with that organization.

A serious shortcoming cannot be ignored, but beware of being libelous:
- Include only relevant, factual information
- Avoid value judgments
- Balance criticisms with favorable points

When writing informative messages,
- State the purpose at the beginning and briefly mention the nature of the information you are providing
- Provide the necessary details
- End with a courteous close

Goodwill is the positive feeling that encourages people to maintain a business relationship.

FIGURE 7.7   Effective Recommendation Letter

This letter clearly states the nature of the writer's relationship to the candidate and provides specific examples to support the writer's endorsements.

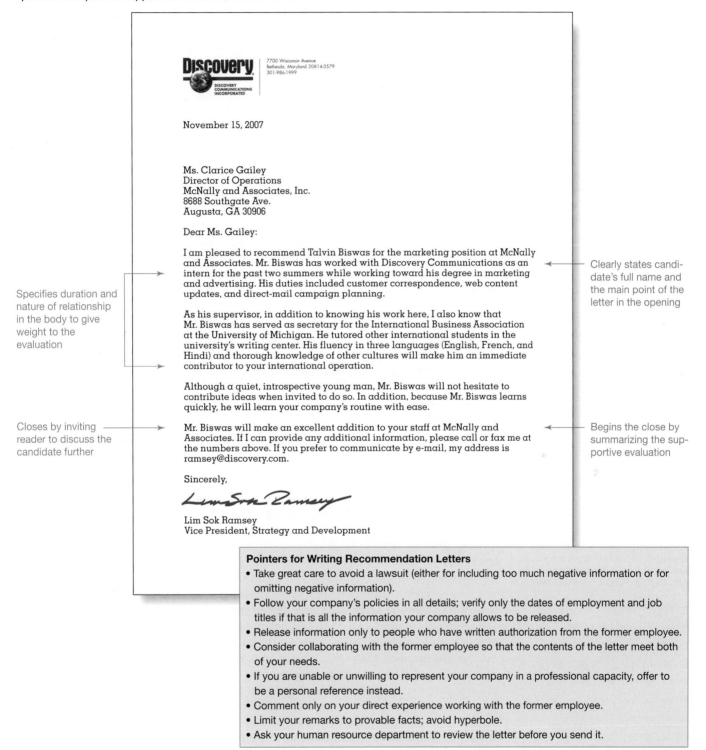

Specifies duration and nature of relationship in the body to give weight to the evaluation

Closes by inviting reader to discuss the candidate further

Clearly states candidate's full name and the main point of the letter in the opening

Begins the close by summarizing the supportive evaluation

November 15, 2007

Ms. Clarice Gailey
Director of Operations
McNally and Associates, Inc.
8688 Southgate Ave.
Augusta, GA 30906

Dear Ms. Gailey:

I am pleased to recommend Talvin Biswas for the marketing position at McNally and Associates. Mr. Biswas has worked with Discovery Communications as an intern for the past two summers while working toward his degree in marketing and advertising. His duties included customer correspondence, web content updates, and direct-mail campaign planning.

As his supervisor, in addition to knowing his work here, I also know that Mr. Biswas has served as secretary for the International Business Association at the University of Michigan. He tutored other international students in the university's writing center. His fluency in three languages (English, French, and Hindi) and thorough knowledge of other cultures will make him an immediate contributor to your international operation.

Although a quiet, introspective young man, Mr. Biswas will not hesitate to contribute ideas when invited to do so. In addition, because Mr. Biswas learns quickly, he will learn your company's routine with ease.

Mr. Biswas will make an excellent addition to your staff at McNally and Associates. If I can provide any additional information, please call or fax me at the numbers above. If you prefer to communicate by e-mail, my address is ramsey@discovery.com.

Sincerely,

Lim Sok Ramsey
Vice President, Strategy and Development

Pointers for Writing Recommendation Letters

- Take great care to avoid a lawsuit (either for including too much negative information or for omitting negative information).
- Follow your company's policies in all details; verify only the dates of employment and job titles if that is all the information your company allows to be released.
- Release information only to people who have written authorization from the former employee.
- Consider collaborating with the former employee so that the contents of the letter meet both of your needs.
- If you are unable or unwilling to represent your company in a professional capacity, offer to be a personal reference instead.
- Comment only on your direct experience working with the former employee.
- Limit your remarks to provable facts; avoid hyperbole.
- Ask your human resource department to review the letter before you send it.

Effective goodwill messages must be sincere and honest. Otherwise, you'll appear to be interested in personal gain rather than in benefiting customers, fellow workers, or your organization. To come across as sincere, avoid exaggerating, and back up any compliments with specific points. In addition, readers often regard more restrained praise as being more sincere:

Make sure your compliments are both sincere and honest.

Instead of This	Write This
Words cannot express my appreciation for the great job you did. Thanks. No one could have done it better. You're terrific! You've made the whole firm sit up and take notice, and we are ecstatic to have you working here.	Thanks again for taking charge of the meeting in my absence and doing such an excellent job. With just an hour's notice, you managed to pull the legal and public relations departments together so that we could present a united front in the negotiations. Your dedication and communication abilities have been noted and are truly appreciated.

Taking note of significant events in someone's personal life helps cement the business relationship.

Sending Congratulations   One prime opportunity for sending goodwill messages is to congratulate someone for a significant business achievement—perhaps for being promoted or for attaining an important civic position. Compare the poor and improved versions of the congratulatory note in Figure 7.8. The poor version sounds vague and insincere, and it doesn't bother to actually offer congratulations until the final sentence. In contrast, the revised version moves swiftly to the subject: the good news. It gives reasons for expecting success and avoids extravagant and essentially meaningless praise such as "Only you can do the job!" Note that a printed letter is often a good media choice for goodwill messages, since it is more formal than electronic media.

An effective message of appreciation documents a person's contributions.

Sending Messages of Appreciation   An important business quality is the ability to recognize the contributions of employees, colleagues, suppliers, and other associates. Your praise does more than just make the person feel good; it encourages further excellence. Moreover, a message of appreciation may become an important part of someone's personnel file. So when you write a message of appreciation, try to specifically mention the person or people you want to praise. The brief message that follows expresses gratitude and reveals the happy result:

> Thank you for sending the air-conditioning components by overnight delivery. You allowed us to satisfy the needs of two tenants who were getting very impatient with the heat.

> Special thanks to Susan Brown, who answered our call for help and never said, "It can't be done." Her initiative on our behalf is greatly appreciated.

The primary purpose of condolence messages is to let the audience know that you and the organization you represent care about the person's loss.

Offering Condolences   In times of serious trouble and deep sadness, well-written condolences and expressions of sympathy can mean a great deal to people who've experienced loss. Granted, this type of message is difficult to write, but don't let the difficulty of the task keep you from responding promptly. Those who have experienced a health problem, the death of a loved one, or a business misfortune appreciate knowing that others care.

Open condolences with a brief statement of sympathy, such as "I was deeply sorry to hear of your loss." In the body, mention the good qualities or the positive contributions made by the deceased. State what the person or business meant to you. In closing, you can offer your condolences and your best wishes. One considerate way to end this type of message is to say something that will give the reader a little lift, such as a reference to a brighter future. Here are a few general suggestions for writing condolence messages:

- **Keep reminiscences brief.** Recount a memory or an anecdote (even a humorous one), but don't dwell on the details of the loss, lest you add to the reader's anguish.
- **Write in your own words.** Write as if you were speaking privately to the person. Don't quote "poetic" passages or use stilted or formal phrases. If the loss is a death, refer to it as such rather than as "passing away" or "departing."
- **Be tactful.** Mention your shock and dismay, but remember that bereaved and distressed loved ones take little comfort in lines such as "Richard was too young to die" or "Starting all over again will be so difficult." Try to strike a balance between superficial

FIGURE 7.8 Poor and Improved Versions of a Letter Congratulating a Business Acquaintance
The improved version of this letter sounds much more sincere and focuses the attention on
the recipient's accomplishments.

Poor

We are so pleased when companies that we admire do well. When we attended
our convention in Atlanta last month, we heard about your firm's recent selection
to design and print media advertisements for the National Association of
Business Suppliers (ABS).

We have long believed that high-visibility projects such as these should be awarded
to only the top-tier companies in the industry, and Lambert, Cutchen & Browt is
clearly the only company for the job.

We wish you the best of luck with your new ad campaign. Congratulations on a
job well done!

Sincerely,

Janice McCarthy.

Jaince McCarthy
Director, Media Relations

Sounds condescending and
self-centered—expressing
the reason but failing to
actually congratulate
the reader

Seems insincere because of
the lack of supporting reasons
and the exaggeration

Congratulating the reader
in the close makes it seem
like an afterthought

Improved

Office DEPOT, Inc.
2200 Old Germantown Road, Delray Beach, FL 33445   407/278-4800

March 2, 2007

Mr. Ralph Lambert, President
Lambert, Cutchen & Browt, Inc.
14355 Pasadena Parkway
Pasadena, TX 74229

Dear Mr. Lambert:

Congratulations on your firm's recent selection to design and print media
advertisements for the National Association of Business Suppliers (ABS). Your
appointment was announced at the national convention in Atlanta last month,
and here at Office Depot we can think of no better firm to help our industry
achieve wide recognition.

Over the course of many years, your firm's work for Office Depot has been
nothing short of excellent. Both our corporate advertising staff here in Florida
and regional promotional managers around the country continue to offer
compliments on the quality of LCB's efforts. The campaign you will design for
ABS is sure to yield similar positive responses.

You can be sure we will follow your media campaign with great interest.

Sincerely,

Janice McCarthy.

Janice McCarthy
Director, Media Relations

tw

Opens by immediately
expressing the reason
for congratulating the
reader

Uses the body to make
compliment more
effective by showing
knowledge of the
reader's work—
without exaggeration

Closes by expressing
interest in following the
future success of the firm

expressions of sympathy and painful references to a happier past or the likelihood of a bleak future.

■ **Take special care.** Be sure to spell names correctly and to be accurate in your review of facts. Try to be prompt.

■ **Write about special qualities of the deceased.** You may have to rely on reputation to do this, but let the grieving person know you valued his or her loved one.

■ **Write about special qualities of the bereaved person.** A pat on the back helps a bereaved family member feel more confident about handling things during such a traumatic time.[2]

Supervisor George Bigalow sent the following condolence letter to his administrative assistant, Janice Case, after learning of the death of Janice's husband:

> My sympathy to you and your children. All your friends at Carter Electric were so very sorry to learn of John's death. Although I never had the opportunity to meet him, I do know how very special he was to you. Your tales of your family's camping trips and his rafting expeditions were always memorable.

Reviewing Key Points

This chapter introduces strategies for routine and positive messages and explains how to apply the three-step writing process to such messages.

The chapter describes how to make routine requests by stating the request up front, explaining and justifying your request, and requesting specific action in a courteous close. It outlines techniques for requesting information and action, requesting recommendations, making claims, and requesting adjustments. The chapter explains how to prepare positive replies to requests and write other types of routine messages. With all, you open with the main idea, provide details and explanations in the body, and close courteously. This chapter explains techniques to use when granting requests for information and action, granting claims, providing recommendations, and sending goodwill messages.

In the next chapter, you'll learn how to apply the three-step writing process to negative messages. The chapter explains the strategies for delivering bad news in a professional manner that remains sensitive to audience needs and discusses various types of negative messages.

Test Your Knowledge

1. What are three guidelines for asking a series of questions in a routine request?

2. Should you use the direct or indirect approach for most routine messages? Why?

3. What six pieces of information must be included in a letter of recommendation?

4. How can you avoid sounding insincere when writing a goodwill message?

5. What are six guidelines for writing condolence messages?

Apply Your Knowledge

1. Why is it good practice to explain that replying to a request could benefit the reader?

2. Your company's error cost an important business customer a new client; you know it and your customer knows it. Do you apologize, or do you refer to the incident in a positive light without admitting any responsibility? Briefly explain.

3. You've been asked to write a letter of recommendation for an employee who worked for you some years ago. You recall that the employee did an admirable job, but you can't remember any specific information at this point. Should you write the letter anyway? Explain.

4. Every time you send a direct-request memo to Ted Jackson, he delays or refuses to comply. You're beginning to get impatient. Should you send Jackson an e-mail message to ask what's wrong? Complain to your supervisor about Jackson's uncooperative attitude? Arrange a face-to-face meeting with Jackson? Bring up the problem at the next staff meeting? Explain.

5. Ethical Choices You have a complaint against one of your suppliers, but you have no documentation to back it up. Should you request an adjustment anyway? Why or why not?

Practice Your Knowledge

Exercises for Perfecting Your Writing

Revising Messages: Direct Approach   Revise the following short e-mail messages so that they are more direct and concise; develop a subject line for each revised message.

1. I'm contacting you about your recent order for a High Country backpack. You didn't tell us which backpack you wanted, and you know we make a lot of different ones. We have the canvas models with the plastic frames and vinyl trim, and we have the canvas models with leather trim, and we have the ones that have more pockets than the other ones. Plus they come in lots of different colors. Also they make the ones that are large for a big-boned person and the smaller versions for little women or kids.

   Subject line: _____

2. Thank you for contacting us about the difficulty you had collecting your luggage at the Denver airport. We are very sorry for the inconvenience this has caused you. As you know, traveling can create problems of this sort regardless of how careful the airline personnel might be. To receive compensation, please send us a detailed list of the items that you lost and complete the following questionnaire. You can e-mail it back to us.

   Subject line: _____

3. Sorry it took us so long to get back to you. We were flooded with résumés. Anyway, your résumé made the final ten, and after meeting three hours yesterday, we've decided we'd like to meet with you. What is your schedule like for next week? Can you come in for an interview on June 15 at 3:00 p.m.? Please get back to us by the end of this work week and let us know if you will be able to attend. As you can imagine, this is our busy season.

   Subject line: _____

Revising Messages: Direct Approach   Rewrite the following sentences so that they are direct and concise.

4. We wanted to invite you to our special 40 percent off by-invitation-only sale. The sale is taking place on November 9.

5. We wanted to let you know that we are giving a tote bag and a free Phish CD with every $50 donation you make to our radio station.

6. The director planned to go to the meeting that will be held on Monday at a little before 11:00 A.M.

7. In today's meeting, we were happy to have the opportunity to welcome Paul Eccelson. He reviewed some of the newest types of order forms. If you have any questions about these new forms, feel free to call him at his office.

Teamwork With another student, conduct an audience analysis of the following message topic: A notice to all employees about the placement of recycling bins by the elevator doors.

8. What is the purpose of this message?

9. What is the most appropriate format for communicating this written message?

10. How is the audience likely to respond to this message?

11. Based on this audience analysis, would you use the direct or the indirect approach for this message? Explain your reasoning.

Revising Messages: Closing Paragraphs How would you rewrite each of the following closing paragraphs to be concise, courteous, and specific?

12. I need your response sometime soon so I can order the parts in time for your service appointment. Otherwise your air-conditioning system may not be in tip-top condition for the start of the summer season.

13. Thank you in advance for sending me as much information as you can about your products. I look forward to receiving your package in the very near future.

14. To schedule an appointment with one of our knowledgeable mortgage specialists in your area, you can always call our hotline at 1-800-555-8765. This is also the number to call if you have more questions about mortgage rates, closing procedures, or any other aspect of the mortgage process. Remember, we're here to make the home-buying experience as painless as possible.

Activities

For active links to all websites discussed in this chapter, visit this text's website at www.prenhall.com/bovee. Locate your book and click on its Companion Website link. Then select Chapter 7, and click on "Featured Websites." Locate the name of the page or the URL related to the material in the text. Please note that links to sites that become inactive after publication of the book will be removed from the Featured Websites section.

1. Analyze This Document   Read the following document, then (1) analyze the strengths and weaknesses of each sentence, and (2) revise the document so that it follows this chapter's guidelines.

> Our college is closing its dining hall for financial reasons, so we want to do something to help the students prepare their own food in their dorm rooms if they so choose. Your colorful ad in *Collegiate Magazine* caught our eye. We need the following information before we make our decision.
>
> 1. Would you be able to ship the microwaves by August 15th? I realize this is short notice, but our board of trustees just made the decision to close the dining hall last week and we're scrambling around trying to figure out what to do.
> 2. Do they have any kind of a warranty? College students can be pretty hard on things, as you know, so we will need a good warranty.
> 3. How much does it cost? Do you give a discount for a big order?
> 4. Do we have to provide a special outlet?
> 5. Will students know how to use them, or will we need to provide instructions?
>
> As I said before, we're on a tight time frame and need good information from you as soon as possible to help us make our decision about ordering. You never know what the board might come up with next. I'm looking at several other companies, also, so please let us know ASAP.

2. Analyze This Document   Read the following document, then (1) analyze the strengths and weaknesses of each sentence and (2) revise the document so that it follows this chapter's guidelines.

> At a local business-supply store, I recently purchased your "Negotiator Pro" for my computer. I bought the CD because I saw your ad for it in *MacWorld* magazine, and it looked as if it might be an effective tool for use in my corporate seminar on negotiation.
>
> Unfortunately, when I inserted it in my office computer, it wouldn't work. I returned it to the store, but since I had already opened it, they refused to exchange it for a CD that would work or give me a refund. They told me to contact you and that you might be able to send me a version that would work with my computer.
>
> You can send the information to me at the letterhead address. If you cannot send me the correct disk, please refund my $79.95. Thanks in advance for any help you can give me in this matter.

3. **Analyze This Document**   Read the following document, then (1) analyze the strengths and weaknesses of each sentence and (2) revise the document so that it follows this chapter's guidelines.

We read your letter requesting your deposit refund. We couldn't figure out why you hadn't received it, so we talked to our maintenance engineer as you suggested. He said you had left one of the doors off the hinges in your apartment in order to get a large sofa through the door. He also confirmed that you had paid him $5.00 to replace the door since you had to turn in the U-Haul trailer and were in a big hurry.

This entire situation really was caused by a lack of communication between our housekeeping inspector and the maintenance engineer. All we knew was that the door was off the hinges when it was inspected by Sally Tarnley. You know that our policy states that if anything is wrong with the apartment, we keep the deposit. We had no way of knowing that George just hadn't gotten around to replacing the door.

But we have good news. We approved the deposit refund, which will be mailed to you from our home office in Teaneck, New Jersey. I'm not sure how long that will take, however. If you don't receive the check by the end of next month, give me a call.

Next time, it's really a good idea to stay with your apartment until it's inspected as stipulated in your lease agreement. That way, you'll be sure to receive your refund when you expect it. Hope you have a good summer.

4. **Analyze This Document**   Read the following document, then (1) analyze the strengths and weaknesses of each sentence and (2) revise the document so that it follows this chapter's guidelines.

Your letter to Kunitake Ando, President of Sony, was forwarded to me because I am the human resources director. In my job as head of HR, I have access to performance reviews for all of the Sony employees in the United States. This means, of course, that I would be the person best qualified to answer your request for information on Nick Oshinski.

In your letter of the 15th, you asked about Nick Oshinski's employment record with us because he has applied to work for your company. Mr. Oshinski was employed with us from January 5, 1997, until March 1, 2007. During that time, Mr. Oshinski received ratings ranging from 2.5 up to 9.6, with 10 being the top score. As you can see, he must have done better reporting to some managers than to others. In addition, he took all vacation days, which is a bit unusual. Although I did not know Mr. Oshinski personally, I know that our best workers seldom use all the vacation time they earn. I do not know if that applies in this case.

In summary, Nick Oshinski performed his tasks well depending on who managed him.

5. **Internet**   Visit the Career eCards section of the Blue Mountain site at www.blue mountain.com and analyze one of the electronic greeting cards bearing a goodwill message of appreciation for good performance. Under what circumstances would you send this electronic message? How could you personalize it for the recipient and the occasion? What would be an appropriate close for this message?

6. **Ethical Choices**   Your company markets a line of automotive accessories for people who like to "tune" their cars for maximum performance. A customer has just written a furious e-mail, claiming that a supercharger he purchased from your website didn't deliver the extra engine power he expected. Your company has a standard refund process to handle situations such as this, and you have the information you need to inform the customer about that. You also have information that could help the customer find a more compatible supercharger from one of your competitors, but the

customer's e-mail message is so abusive that you don't feel obligated to help. Is this an appropriate response? Why or why not?

7. **Planning a Letter: Air Rage Fiasco**   Letter requesting refund from British Airways. You've been administrative assistant to Samantha Alberts, vice president of sales for Richter Office Solutions, for two years. You handle all her travel arrangements and you've never seen her so upset. The "air rage" incident happened on Friday and now it's Monday, but she's still pale and shaky.

"There we were, cruising over the Atlantic, and the guy just erupted! I couldn't believe it!" she says for the third time.

She was flying back from a conference in London to make a presentation at your New York branch. Then she was to catch a plane home to San Francisco on Saturday. With airline security so tight these days, she expected a calm flight and lots of time to prepare her presentation notes as she crossed the ocean. As it turned out, she spent most of that time fearing for her life.

"What made the guy angry?" you ask.

"Apparently some passengers complained about 'offensive images' he was viewing on his laptop. When the steward politely asked him to stop, the guy went nuts and started hitting people, swearing all the while. At first I thought he was a hijacker and I was going to die on that plane! Thank goodness several crew members and passengers were able to subdue him and handcuff him into a back row seat. But we still had hours over the Atlantic before the pilot could land, so we had to listen to him screaming profanity. Finally, a passenger who was a pediatrician injected him with a sedative."

"Did they arrest him?" you want to know.

"As soon as we got on the ground. Police cars were everywhere. He just kept muttering, 'I thought they were going to kill me.'" She shudders. "But the flight attendants and airline officials were wonderful. They told us to write to the airline, explain the details, and ask for a refund."

"Of course, I was late and unprepared for my presentation. When they heard what happened, the folks in our New York office just handed me a cup of herb tea, sat me on a couch with a blanket, and told me to forget about making any presentations that day."

Samantha leaves you her ticket stubs and other documents. She's expecting you to write the refund request to British Airways Ticket Refunds USA, 75-20 Astoria Blvd., Jackson Heights, N.Y 11370. Before you begin, consider these questions:[3]

a. For the purpose of this exercise, what details will you need to make up to write the request?

b. Will you use a direct or indirect approach? Why?

c. What tone should you adopt? What should you avoid?

d. How will you support the claim?

e. What would be an effective closing for this request?

8. **Planning a Letter: Intercultural Condolences**   You've been working two years as administrative assistant to J. T. "Ted" Childs, Jr., vice president of global workforce diversity at IBM's Learning Center in Armonk, New York. After listening to so many of his speeches on maintaining multicultural sensitivity in the workplace, you know you're facing a sensitive situation right now. You need to stop and think before you act.

Your coworker Chana Panichpapiboon's husband was killed in a bus accident yesterday, along with 19 others. The bus skidded on icy pavement into a deep ravine, tipping over and crushing the occupants before rescue workers could get to them.

You met her husband, Surin, last year at a company banquet. You can still picture his warm smile and the easy way he joked with you and others over chicken Florentine, even though you were complete strangers to him. He was only 32 years old, and he left Chana with two children, a 12-year-old boy, Arsa, and a 10-year-old girl, Veera. His death is a terrible tragedy.

Normally, you'd write a condolence letter immediately. But Chana Panichpapiboon is a native of Thailand, and so was Surin. You know you'd better do a little research first. Is Chana Buddhist or Catholic? Is there anything about the typical Western practice of expressing sympathy that might be inappropriate? Offensive?

After making some discreet inquiries among Chana's closest friends at work, you learn that she is Theravada Buddhist, as are most people in Thailand. In a reference book your boss lends you about doing business around the world, you read that in Thailand, "the person takes precedence over rule or law" and "people gain their social position as a result of karma, not personal achievement," which means Chana may believe in reincarnation. But the book also says that Theravada Buddhists are free to choose which precepts of their religion, if any, they will follow. So Chana's beliefs are still a mystery.

You do know that her husband was very important to her and much loved by all their family. That, at least, is universal. And you're considering using a poetic line you remember, "The hand of time lightly lays, softly soothing sorrow's wound." Is it appropriate?

You've decided to handwrite the condolence note on a blank greeting card you've found that bears a peaceful, "Eastern-flavor" image. You know you're risking a cultural gaffe, but you don't want to commit the offense of not writing at all. Use the following questions to help you think through your choices before you begin writing:[4]

a. If you had to choose among these sentences, which one would make the best opening?
 1. I was so sorry to hear the news about your husband.
 2. What a terrible tragedy you have suffered.
 3. If there's anything I can do for you, Chana, please let me know.
 4. You and your children must be so upset, and who could blame you?

b. In the body of the letter, you want to express something meaningful, but you're concerned about Chana's beliefs and you're not sure what's safe. Choose the best idea from the following:
 1. You could quote the poem about "the hand of time" mentioned in the case.
 2. You might say something about the bus driver's terrible carelessness on slippery pavement.

    3. You could express your sorrow for Chana's children.

    4. You could mention something nice about Surin you learned during your brief meeting.

c. For your closing paragraph, which of these ideas is best?

    1. Take a moment to express your thoughts about death and the hereafter.

    2. Say something positive and encouraging about Chana.

    3. Explain that you don't understand her religious beliefs and aren't sure what's appropriate to say at this time.

    4. All of the above.

d. In the following list, circle all of the words you should avoid as you write:

    1. Death

    2. Departure

    3. Karma

    4. Unbearable

Now write the condolence letter in your own words. Remember that sincerity is the most important tool in overcoming differences of custom or tradition.

9. Revising a Letter: Vacation Planning   The following letter requesting information about resorts in Florida contains numerous errors, based on what you've learned in this chapter. Read the letter carefully and analyze its flaws. Then use the steps below to outline and write a better version of the request.

5493 Beechwood Drive
Trenton, N.J. 08608
April 12, 2005

Florida Resort Bureau
1555 Palm Beach Lakes Boulevard
West Palm Beach, FL 33401

Dear Sir:

My wife and I are planning a late September vacation with our two teenage children. We need this information in the next two weeks so I can schedule my time off from work in the fall.

I enjoy the beach and the golf course, but we also want to be near night entertainment suitable for the whole family. I am particularly interested in resort areas that have public transportation available; some family members may want to participate in activities away from the resort.

In addition to the brochures your advertisement promises, will you please also tell me which resorts are near large cities, which are reached by public transportation and have attractions for teenagers and do the off-season rates include all the amenities? Can you tell me additionally about the weather during September in Florida, and who we should call for concert schedules during our vacation?

Your advertisement about Florida resorts in the April 2005 issue of *Smithsonian* magazine caught my eye.

Frank C. Atlas

a. Describe the flaws you discovered in this letter requesting information.

b. Develop a plan for rewriting the letter. Use the following steps to organize your efforts before you begin writing:

    1. Create a clear statement of your request.

    2. Decide what explanation is needed to justify your request.

    3. Determine whether you can use lists effectively in your letter.

    4. Ask for specific action.

    5. Mention a deadline and reason to respond, if appropriate.

c. Now rewrite the letter. Don't forget to leave ample time for revision of your own work before you turn it in.

Expand Your Knowledge

Exploring the Best of the Web

Whether you're continuing to graduate school or entering the workforce with your undergraduate degree, recommendation letters could play an important role in the next few steps of your career. From selecting the people to ask for recommendation letters to knowing what makes an effective letter, About.com extends the advice offered in this chapter with real-life examples and suggestions. Visit About.com's Business Majors website at http://businessmajors.about.com and click on "Recommendation letters." Read the advice you find, then answer the following questions.

Exercises

1. What is a good process for identifying the best people to ask for recommendation letters?
2. What information should you provide to letter writers to help them produce a credible and compelling letter on your behalf?

3. What are the most common mistakes you need to avoid with recommendation letters?

Exploring on Your Own

1. Get answers to just about any grammar question at GrammarStation, www.grammarstation.com. Check your writing using the online grammar checker, review the basic parts of speech, and get intensive practice from the basics up to advanced writing concepts.

2. Need to write a press release but don't have time to become an expert? Learn from any expert at www.stetson.edu/~rhansen/prguide.html.

3. Get advice on writing sensitive condolence letters at www.abusinessresource.com (search for "condolence letter").

Learn Interactively

Interactive Study Guide

Visit www.prenhall.com/bovee, then locate your book and click on its Companion Website link. Select Chapter 7 to take advantage of the interactive "Chapter Quiz" to test your knowledge of chapter concepts. Receive instant feedback on whether you need additional studying. Also, visit the "Study Hall," where you'll find an abundance of valuable resources that will help you succeed in this course.

Peak Performance Grammar and Mechanics

If your instructor has required the use of "Peak Performance Grammar and Mechanics," either in your online course, through the access-code protected portion of the Companion Website, or on CD, you can improve your skill with sentences by using the "Peak Performance Grammar and Mechanics" module. Click "Sentences," then take the Pretest to determine whether you have any weak areas. Then review those areas in the Refresher Course. Take the Follow-Up Test to check your grasp of sentences. For an extra challenge or advanced practice, take the Advanced Test. Finally, for additional reinforcement in sentences, go to the "Improve Your Grammar, Mechanics, and Usage" section that follows the cases, and complete the "Level 1: Self-Assessment" exercises.

CASES

Apply the three-step writing process to the following cases, as assigned by your instructor.

1. Breathing Life Back into Your Biotech Career: E-Mail Requesting a Recommendation

After five years of work in the human resources department at Cell Genesys (a company that is developing cancer treatment drugs), you were laid off in a round of cost-cutting moves that rippled through the biotech industry in recent years. The good news is that you found stable employment in the grocery distribution industry. The bad news is that in the three years since you left Cell Genesys, you truly miss working in the exciting biotechnology field and having the opportunity to be a part of something as important as helping people recover from life-threatening diseases. You know that careers in biotech are uncertain, but you have a few dollars in the bank now, so you're more willing to accept the risk of being laid off at some point in the future.

Your Task Draft an e-mail to Calvin Morris, your old boss at Cell Genesys, reminding him of the time you worked together and asking him to write a letter of recommendation for you.[5]

█ IM
█ SKILLS

2. Trans-Global Exchange: Instant Message Request for Information from Chinese Manufacturer

Thank goodness your company, Diagonal Imports, chose the instant messaging software produced by IBM Lotus, called Sametime. Other products might allow you to carry on real-time exchanges with colleagues on the other side of the planet, but Sametime supports bidirectional machine translation, and you're going to need it.

It seems that production on a popular line of decorative lighting appliances produced at your Chinese manufacturing plant inexplicably came to a halt last month. As the product manager in the United States, you have many resources you could call on to help, such as new sources for faulty parts. But you can't do anything if you don't know the details. You've tried telephoning top managers in China, but they're evasive, telling you only what they think you want to hear.

Finally, your friend Kuei-chen Tsao has returned from a business trip. You met her during your trip to China last year. She doesn't speak English, but she's the line engineer responsible for this particular product: a fiber-optic lighting display, featuring a plastic base with a rotating color-wheel. As the wheel turns, light emitted from the spray of fiber-optic threads changes color in soothing patterns. Product #3347XM is one of Diagonal's most popular items and you've got orders from novelty stores around the United States waiting to be filled. Kuei-chen should be able to explain the problem, determine whether you can help, and tell you how long before regular shipping resumes.

Your Task Write the first of what you hope will be a productive instant message exchange with Kuei-Chen. Remember, your words will be machine-translated.[6]

█ TEXT MESSAGING
█ SKILLS

3. Tracking the New Product Buzz: Text Message to Colleagues at a Trade Show

The vast Consumer Electronics Show (CES) is the premier promotional event in the electronics industry. More than 130,000 industry insiders from all over the world come to see the exciting new products on display from nearly 1,500 companies—everything from video game gadgets to Internet-enabled refrigerators with built-in computer screens. You've just stumbled on a videogame controller that has a built-in webcam to allow networked gamers to see and hear each other while they play. Your company also makes game controllers, and you're worried that your customers will flock to this new controller-cam. You need to know how much "buzz" is circulating around the show: Have people seen it? What are they saying about it? Are they excited about it?

Your Task Compose a text message to your colleagues at the show, alerting them to the new controller-cam and asking them to listen for any "buzz" that it might be generating among the attendees at the Las Vegas Convention Center and the several surrounding hotels where the show takes place. Here's the catch: Your text messaging service limits messages to 160 characters, including spaces and punctuation, so your message can't be any longer than this.[7]

4. Temper, Temper: E-Mail to Metro Power Employees About Technology Failures

This is the third time in two months that your company, Metro Power, has had to escort an employee from the building after a violent episode. Frankly, everyone is a little frightened by this development, and as a human resources administrator, you have the unhappy task of trying to quell the storm.

Metro Power rarely fires employees, preferring to transfer them to new responsibilities, which may either draw out their finer points (and prove better for everyone in the long run) or help them decide to seek greener pastures. But in three cases, you had no choice. In one incident, a man punched out his computer screen after the system failed. In another, a man threw his keyboard across the room when he couldn't get access to the company's intranet. And in a third incident, a woman kicked a printer while screaming obscenities.

In all three cases, coworkers were terrified by these sudden outbursts. Too many disgruntled workers have committed too many violent acts against others in recent years, and whenever workers lose their temper on the job these days, it causes great fear—not to mention financial losses from the destruction of property and the disruption of work flow.

Employees are on edge at Metro Power right now. Rising energy costs, public and government scrutiny, and cries of price gouging are causing additional work and stress for everyone. Plus, too much overtime, unrealistic expectations for overworked departments, and high demands on sensitive equipment are contributing to the problem. Tempers are high and nerves are strained. You're concerned that these three incidents are just the tip of the iceberg.

Your department head suggests that you write a reminder to all employees about controlling tempers in the workplace. "Tell them that technology glitches are commonplace and not some unholy disaster. And remind them to report routine computer failures to Bart Stone. He'll get to them in due course."

You say nothing to contradict her idea, but you wonder how to do what she asks without sounding trite or condescending. You don't want to sound like some nagging parent—no one will pay attention to your message. You sigh deeply as your boss strolls calmly back to her office. You're fairly certain that every employee already knows about reporting computer failures to Bart Stone, assistant director of information services.

Even so, you can think of a few suggestions that might be helpful, such as taking a walk to cool down or recognizing that machines, like humans, are not infallible. You want cooler heads to prevail, and that's just the sort of cliché you'd like to avoid in your message.

Your Task Write the e-mail message to all employees. Instead of uttering platitudes or wagging your finger, include preventive maintenance tips for office equipment, such as turning systems off at night, keeping food and liquids away from keyboards, making use of dusting sprays and special cloths, and so on. Your boss also asked you to make it clear that abusive behavior will be reprimanded, so include that point in a tactful way.[8]

5. Listening to Business: Using the iPod to Train Employees

As a training specialist in Winnebago Industries human resources department, you're always on the lookout for new ways to help employees learn vital job skills. While watching a production worker page through a training manual while learning how to assemble a new recreational vehicle, you get what seems to be a great idea: record the assembly instructions as audio files that workers can listen to while performing the necessary steps. With audio instructions, they wouldn't need to keep shifting their eyes between the product and the manual—and constantly losing their place. They could focus on the product and listen for each instruction. Plus, the new system wouldn't cost much at all; any computer can record the audio files, and you'd simply make them available on an intranet site for download into iPods or other digital music players.

Your Task You immediately run your new idea past your boss, who has heard about podcasting but doesn't think it has any place in business. He asks you to prove the viability of the idea by recording a demonstration. Choose a process that you engage in yourself—anything from replacing the strings on a guitar to sewing a quilt to changing the oil in a car—and write a brief (one page or less) description of the process that could be recorded as an audio file. Think carefully about the limitations of the audio format as a replacement for printed text (for instance, do you need to tell people to pause the audio while they perform a time-consuming task?).

6. Auto-Talk: E-Mail Messages for Highway Bytes Computers to Be Sent Automatically

You are director of customer services at Highway Bytes, which markets a series of small, handlebar-mounted computers for bicyclists. These Cycle Computers do everything, from computing speed and distance traveled to displaying street maps. Serious cyclists love them, but your company is growing so fast that you can't keep up with all the customer service requests you receive every day. Your boss wants not only to speed up response time but also to reduce staffing costs and allow your technical experts the time they need to focus on the most difficult and important questions.

You've just been reading about automated response systems, and you quickly review a few articles before discussing the options with your boss. Artificial intelligence researchers have been working for decades to design systems that can actually converse with customers, ask questions, and respond to requests. Some of today's systems have vocabularies of thousands of words and the ability to understand simple sentences. For example, *chatterbots* are automated bots that can actually mimic human conversation. (You can see what it's like to carry on a conversation with some of these bots by visiting www.botspot.com, clicking on "Artificial Life Bots," and then selecting "Chatterbots.")

Unfortunately, even though chatterbots hold a lot of promise, human communication is so complex that a truly automated customer service agent could take years to perfect (and may even prove to be impossible). However, the simplest automated systems, called *autoresponders* or *e-mail-on-demand*, are fast and extremely inexpensive. They have no built-in intelligence, so they do nothing more than send back the same reply to every message they receive.

You explain to your boss that although some of the messages you receive require the attention of your product specialists, many are simply requests for straightforward information. In fact, the customer service staff already answers some 70 percent of e-mail queries with three ready-made attachments:

- **Installing Your Cycle Computer.** Gives customers advice on installing the cycle computer the first time or reinstalling it on a new bike. In most cases, the computer and wheel sensor bolt directly to the bike without modification, but certain bikes do require extra work.
- **Troubleshooting Your Cycle Computer.** Provides a step-by-step guide to figuring out what might be wrong with a malfunctioning cycle computer. Most problems are simple, such as dead batteries or loose wires, but others are beyond the capabilities of your typical customer.
- **Upgrading the Software in Your Cycle Computer.** Tells customers how to attach the cycle computer to their home or office PC and download new software from Highway Bytes.

Your boss is enthusiastic when you explain that you can program your current e-mail system to look for specific words in incoming messages and then respond, based on what it finds. For example, if a customer message contains the word "installation," you can program the system to reply with the "Installing Your Cycle Computer" attachment. This reconfigured system should be able to handle a sizeable portion of the hundreds of e-mails your customer service group gets every week.

Your Task First, draft a list of key words that you'll want your e-mail system to look for. You'll need to be creative and spend some time with a thesaurus. Identify all the words and word combinations that could identify a message as pertaining to one of the three subject areas. For instance, the word *attach* would probably indicate a need for the installation material, whereas *new software* would most likely suggest a need for the upgrade attachment.

Second, draft three short e-mail messages to accompany each ready-made attachment, explaining that the attached document answers the most common questions on a particular subject (installation, troubleshooting, or upgrading). Your messages should invite recipients to write back if the attached document doesn't solve the problem, and don't forget to provide the e-mail address: support2@highwaybytes.com.

Third, draft a fourth message to be sent out whenever your new system is unable to figure out what the customer is asking for. Simply thank the customer for writing and explain that the query will be passed on to a customer service specialist who will respond shortly.

7. The Special Courier: Letter of Recommendation for an Old Friend

In today's mail you get a letter from Non-Stop Messenger Service, 899 Sparks St., Ottawa, Ontario K1A 0G9, Canada. It concerns a friend of yours who has applied for a job. Here is the letter:

Kathryn Norquist has applied for the position of special courier with our firm, and she has given us your name as a reference. Our special couriers convey materials of considerable value or confidentiality to their recipients. It is not an easy job. Special couriers must sometimes remain alert for periods of up to 20 hours, and they cannot expect to follow the usual "three square meals and eight hours' sleep" routine because they often travel long distances on short notice. On occasion, a special courier must react quickly and decisively to threatening situations.

For this type of work, we hire only people of unquestioned integrity, as demonstrated both by their public records and by references from people, like you, who have known them personally or professionally.

We would appreciate a letter from you, supplying detailed answers to the following questions: (1) How long and in what circumstances have you have known the applicant? (2) What qualities does she possess that would qualify her for the position of special courier? (3) What qualities might be improved before she is put on permanent assignment in this job?

As vice president of human resources at DHL, you know how much weight a strong personal reference can carry, and you don't really mind that Kathryn never contacted you for permission to list your name—that's Kathryn. You met her during your sophomore year at San Diego State University—that would have been 1994—and you two were roommates for several years after. Her undergraduate degree was in journalism, and her investigative reporting was relentless. You have never known anyone who could match Kathryn's stamina when she was on a story. Of course, when she was between stories, she could sleep longer and do less than anyone else you have ever known.

After a few years of reporting, Kathryn went back to school and earned her MBA from the University of San Diego, and after that you lost track of her for awhile. Somebody said that she had joined the FBI—or was it the CIA?—you never really knew. You received a couple of postcards from Paris and one from Madrid.

Two years ago, you met Kathryn for dinner. Only in town for the evening, she was on her way to Borneo to "do the text" for a photographer friend of hers who worked for *National Geographic*. You read the article last year on the shrinking habitat for orangutans. It was powerful.

Although you're in no position to say much about Kathryn's career accomplishments, you can certainly recommend her energy and enthusiasm, her ability to focus on a task or assignment, her devotion to ethics, and her style. She always seems unshakable—organized, thorough, and honorable, whether digging into political corruption or trudging the jungles of Borneo. You're not sure that her free spirit would flourish in a courier's position, and you wonder if she wouldn't be a bit overqualified for the job. But knowing Kathryn, you're confident she wouldn't apply for a position unless she truly wanted it.

Your Task Supplying any details you can think of, write as supportive a letter as possible about your friend Kathryn to Roscoe de la Penda, Human Resources Specialist, Non-Stop Messenger.

■ **E-MAIL SKILLS**

8. Lighten Up: E-Mail Reply to a Website Designer at Organizers Unlimited

When Kendra Williams, owner of Organizers Unlimited, wanted to create a website to sell her Superclean Organizer, she asked you, her assistant, to find a designer. After some research, you found three promising individuals. Williams chose Pete Womack, whose résumé impressed both of you. Now he's e-mailed his first design proposal and Williams is not happy.

"I detest cluttered websites!" she explodes. "This homepage has too many graphics and animations, too much 'dancing baloney.' He must have included at least a megabyte of bouncing cotton balls and jogging soap bars! Clever, maybe, but we don't want it! If the homepage takes too long to load, our customers won't wait for it and we'll lose sales."

Williams's dislike of clutter is what inspired her to invent the Superclean Organizer in the first place, a neat device for organizing bathroom items.

Your Task "You found him," says Williams, "now you can answer and tell him what's wrong with this design." Before you write the e-mail reply to Womack explaining the need for a simpler homepage, read some of the articles offering

tips at www.sitepoint.com. On the homepage, under "Before You Code," select "Site Planning" and under "Design and Layout" select "Design Principles." Use these ideas to support your message.[9]

■ **E-MAIL SKILLS**

9. Leveraging the Good News: Blog Announcement of a Prestigious Professional Award

You and your staff in the public relations (PR) department at Epson of America were delighted when the communication campaign you created for the new PictureMate Personal Photo Lab (www.epson.com/picturemate) was awarded the prestigious Silver Anvil award by the Public Relations Society of America. Now you'd like to give your team a pat on the back by sharing the news with the rest of the company.

Your Task Write a one-paragraph message for the PR department blog (which is read by people throughout the company but is not accessible outside the company), announcing the award. Take care not to "toot your own horn" as the manager of the PR department and use the opportunity to compliment the rest of the company for designing and producing such an innovative product.[10]

10. Our Sympathy: Condolence Letter to an Aetna Underwriter

As chief administrator for the underwriting department of Aetna Health Plans in Walnut Creek, California, you're facing a difficult task. One of your best underwriters, Hector Almeida, recently lost his wife in an automobile accident (he and his teenaged daughter weren't with her at the time). Since you're the boss, everyone in the close-knit department is looking to you to communicate the group's sympathy and concern.

Someone suggested a simple greeting card that everyone could sign, but that seems so impersonal for someone you've worked with every day for nearly five years. So you decided to write a personal note on behalf of the whole department. You met Hector's wife, Rosalia, at a few company functions although you knew her mostly through Hector's frequent references to her. Although you didn't know her well, you do know important things about her life, which you can celebrate in the letter.

Right now he's devastated by the loss. But if anyone can overcome this tragedy, Hector can. He's always determined to get a job done no matter what obstacles present themselves, and he does it with an upbeat attitude. That's why everyone in the office likes him so much.

You also plan to suggest that when he returns to work, he might like to move his schedule up an hour so that he'll have more time to spend with his daughter, Lisa, after school. It's your way of helping make things a little easier for them during this period of adjustment.

Your Task Write the letter to Hector Almeida, who lives at 47 West Ave., #10, Walnut Creek, CA 94596. (Feel free to make up any details you need.)[11]

11. Unhappy Customer: Claim Letter from You Requesting an Adjustment

As a consumer, you've probably bought something that didn't work right or paid for a service that did not turn out the way you expected. Maybe it was a pair of jeans with a rip in a seam that you didn't find until you got home or a watch that broke a week after you bought it. Or maybe your family hired a lawn service to do some yard work—and no one from the company showed up on the day promised. When a man finally appeared, he did not do what he'd been hired for, but did other things that wound up damaging valuable plants.

In either case, you'd be wise to write a claim letter asking for a refund, repair, replacement, or other adjustment. You'll need to include all the details of the transaction, plus your contact address and phone number.

Your Task To practice writing claim letters, choose an experience like this from your own background or make up details for these imaginary situations. If your experience is real, you might want to mail the letter. The reply you receive will provide a good test of your claim-writing skills.

Improve Your Grammar, Mechanics, and Usage

Level 1: Self-Assessment—Periods, Question Marks, and Exclamation Points

Review Sections 2.1, 2.2, and 2.3 in the Handbook of Grammar, Mechanics, and Usage, and then look at the following 15 items.

In items 1–15, add periods, question marks, and exclamation points wherever they are appropriate.

1. Dr Eleanor H Hutton has requested information on TaskMasters, Inc

2. That qualifies us as a rapidly growing new company, don't you think

3. Our president, Daniel Gruber, is a CPA On your behalf, I asked him why he started the company

4. In the past three years, we have experienced phenomenal growth of 800 percent

5. Contact me at 1358 N Parsons Avenue, Tulsa, OK 74204

6. Jack asked, "Why does he want to know Maybe he plans to become a competitor"

7. The debt load fluctuates with the movement of the US prime rate

8. I can't believe we could have missed such a promising opportunity

9. Is consumer loyalty extinct Yes and No.

10. Johnson and Kane, Inc, has gone out of business What a surprise

11. Will you please send us a check today so that we can settle your account

12. Mr James R Capp will be our new CEO, beginning January 20, 2008

13. The rag doll originally sold for $1098, but we have lowered the price to a mere $599

14. Will you be able to make the presentation at the conference, or should we find someone else

15. So I ask you, "When will we admit defeat" Never

Level 2: Workplace Applications

The following items contain numerous errors in grammar, capitalization, punctuation, abbreviation, number style, word division, and vocabulary. Rewrite each sentence in the space provided, correcting all errors. Write *C* in the space after any sentence that is already correct.

1. Attached to both the Train Station and the Marriott hotel, one doesnt even need to step outside the convention center to go from train to meeting room.

2. According to Federal statistics, 61 percent of the nations employers have less than 5 workers.

3. "The problem", said Business Owner Mike Millorn, "Was getting vendor's of raw materials to take my endeavor serious."

4. After pouring over trade journals, quizzing industry experts, and talks with other snack makers, the Harpers' decided to go in the pita chip business.

5. Some argue that a Mac with half as much RAM and a slower processor is as fast or faster than a PC.

6. The couple has done relatively little advertising, instead they give away samples in person at trade shows, cooking demonstrations, and in grocery stores.

7. CME Information Services started by videotaping doctor's conventions, and selling the recorded presentations to nonattending physicians that wanted to keep track of the latest developments.

8. For many companies, the two biggest challenges to using intranets are: getting people to use it and content freshness.

9. Company meetings including 'lunch and learn' sessions are held online often.

10. Most Children's Orchard franchisees, are men and women between the ages of 30–50; first time business owners with a wide range of computer skills.

11. Joining the company in 1993, she had watched it expand and grow from a single small office to a entire floor of a skyscraper.

12. One issue that effected practically everyone was that they needed to train interns.

13. The website includes information on subjects as mundane as the filling out of a federal express form, and as complex as researching a policy issue.

14. "Some management theories are good, but how many people actually implement them the right way?", says Jack Hartnett President of D. L. Rogers Corp.

15. Taking orders through car windows, customers are served by roller-skating carhops at Sonic restaurants.

Level 3: Document Critique

The following document may contain errors in grammar, punctuation, capitalization, abbreviation, number style, vocabulary, and spelling. You will also find errors relating to topics in this chapter. For example, consider the organization and relevance of material as you improve this routine request for information. Correct all errors using standard proof-reading marks (see Appendix C).

Risa Zenaili

883 Middleton Aven.

Bartlesville OK 74005

918-555-9983

rzenaili@ppri.com

March 13 2007

Tharita Jones Owner

Subway Restaurant

120 W Greenfield Str.

Tulsa, Oklahoma, 74133

Dear Ms. Jones,

I am investigatting careers in vareous fast-food enviroments, since I expect to complete my degreee in business administration within the next 3 years and that should leave me enough time to grow into a management position. Subway gave me your name when I asked for a franchise owner who might be willing to answer some questions about managment careers with the company. You may be able to provide the kind of informaton I'll never get from coporate brochures.

For example I'd like to know how long I can expect to work at an entry level before promotions are considered. How many levels must I rise before reaching assistant manager. And how many before I would be considered as manager, assuming I've performed well. Sometimes a person is promoted because they are qualified and sometimes it just because they willing to work long hours, so I want to know this before I commit myself!

I'm looking for a company that will offer me the best future in the most promising environment and since there are so many to choose from I am trying to be very careful in making this choice. I'd be really gratefull if you could take a moment to share any advice or encouragment you might have for me because as you know this kind of decision is one we all must make one day and it will effect us for a long, long time to come

I also like to know: How many hour a week can I expect to work to be on management career track? Once I reach management level: will those hours increase?

What qualifications do you look for in your managers and assitant managers? Plus: Benefits the company offers, special training—availibility and qualifications; how to improve my chances for promation if I choose Subway?

Please let me hear from you before the end of the month.

If you prefer to call than write; you reach me at 918 555-9983 day or evening. My cell phone number is (918) 555-8838. Or you can send a reply to me at the address above or to my e-mail address rzeinali@earthlink.net.

Sincerely:

Risa Zeinali

8

Writing Negative Messages

Learning Objectives

After studying this chapter, you will be able to

1 Apply the three-step writing process to negative messages

2 Explain the differences between the direct and the indirect approaches to negative messages, including when it's appropriate to use each one

3 Identify the risks of using the indirect approach, and explain how to avoid such problems

4 Adapt negative messages for internal and external audiences

5 Define defamation and explain how to avoid it in negative messages

6 Explain the role of communication in crisis management

7 List three guidelines for delivering negative news to job applicants, and give a brief explanation of each one

The statement on the left from the large accounting firm KPMG seems fairly simple on the surface, but it is anything but simple. After the U.S. Internal Revenue Service ruled that certain investments the company had advised for some of its clients were illegal, KPMG had a serious communication dilemma. It faced both a criminal investigation from the Justice Department and multiple lawsuits from clients, accusing the company of encouraging them to break the law. If it publicly apologized in an effort to avoid criminal prosecution, that admission of guilt could be used against it in all those civil suits. Apparently deciding that a criminal charge would be more dangerous, KPMG issued the apology. The statement seemed to help, as the firm avoided a criminal indictment, but the admission of guilt was welcomed by lawyers representing clients. With those lawsuits likely to drag on for years, only time will tell how well that admission served the company.[1]

Using the Three-Step Writing Process for Negative Messages

Chances are slim that you'll ever need to issue statements as serious as KPMG's, but you will need to deliver negative messages many times in your career. When you need to deliver bad news, you have five goals: (1) to convey the bad news, (2) to gain acceptance for it, (3) to maintain as much goodwill as possible with your audience, (4) to maintain a good image for your organization, and (5) if appropriate, to reduce or eliminate the need for future correspondence on the matter. Five goals are clearly a lot to accomplish in one message, so careful attention to planning, writing, and completing your message is vital.

Step 1: Plan Your Message

When planning negative messages, you can't avoid the fact that your audience does not want to hear what you have to say. To minimize the damage to business relationships and to encourage the acceptance of your message, plan carefully. With a clear purpose and your audience's needs in mind, identify and gather the information your audience will need in order to understand and accept your message.

Careful planning is necessary to avoid alienating your readers.

Selecting the right medium is critical. For instance, experts advise that bad news for employees always be delivered in person whenever possible, both to show respect for the employees and to give them an opportunity to ask questions. Of course, delivering bad news is never easy, and an increasing number of managers appear to be using e-mail and other electronic media to convey negative messages to employees.[2] However, employees are more likely to accept messages and maintain respect for the sender if bad news is delivered in person.

Choose the medium with care when preparing negative messages.

Finally, because you are delivering bad news, the organization of your message requires particular care. This chapter presents in-depth advice on using both direct and indirect approaches to organization.

The appropriate organization helps readers accept your negative news.

Step 2: Write Your Message

By writing clearly and sensitively, you can take some of the sting out of bad news and help your reader accept the decision and move on. If your credibility hasn't already been established with an audience, lay out your qualifications for making the decision in question. Recipients of negative messages who don't think you are credible are more likely to challenge your decision.

When you use language that conveys respect and avoids an accusing tone, you protect your audience's pride. This kind of communication etiquette is always important, but it demands special care with negative messages. Moreover, you can ease the sense of disappointment by using positive words rather than negative, counterproductive ones (see Table 8.1).

Table 8.1	Choosing Positive Words
Examples of Negative Phrasings	**Positive Alternatives**
Your request doesn't make any sense.	Please clarify your request.
The damage won't be fixed for a week.	The item will be repaired next week.
Although it wasn't our fault, there will be an unavoidable delay in your order.	We will process your order as soon as we receive an aluminum shipment from our supplier, which we expect to happen within 10 days.
You are clearly dissatisfied.	We are doing what we can to make things right.
I regret the misunderstanding.	I'll try my best to be more clear from now on.
I was shocked to learn that you're unhappy.	Thank you for sharing your concerns about the service you received while shopping with us.
Unfortunately, we haven't received it.	It hasn't arrived yet.
The enclosed statement is wrong.	Please recheck the enclosed statement.

Step 3: Complete Your Message

The need for careful attention to detail continues as you complete your message. Revise your content to make sure everything is clear, complete, and concise—even small flaws can be magnified as readers react to your negative news. Produce clean, professional documents, and proofread carefully to eliminate mistakes. Finally, be especially sure that your negative messages are delivered promptly; waiting for bad news is never easy.

Developing Negative Messages

As you apply the three-step writing process to develop negative messages, one of the most critical decisions is whether to use a direct or an indirect approach. To help decide in any situation you encounter, ask yourself the following questions:

- **Will the bad news come as a shock?** In some instances, such as when an entrepreneur requests investment funds for a new company, negative news is disappointing but not necessarily surprising, so a direct approach would be fine. However, if the bad news might come as a shock, use an indirect approach to help your reader prepare.
- **Does the reader prefer short messages that get right to the point?** For example, if you know that your boss always wants brief messages that get right to the point, even when they deliver bad news, the direct approach is your best choice.
- **How important is this news to the reader?** For minor or routine scenarios, the direct approach is nearly always best. However, if the reader has an emotional investment in the situation or the consequences to the reader are considerable, the indirect approach is often better.
- **Do you need to maintain a close working relationship with the reader?** The indirect approach makes it easier to soften the blow of bad news and can therefore help you preserve a good relationship.
- **Do you need to get the reader's attention?** If someone has ignored repeated messages, the direct approach can help you get his or her attention.
- **What is your organization's preferred style?** Some companies have a distinct communication style, ranging from blunt and direct to gentle and indirect. In most cases, people in the organization expect everyone to follow that general style.

Using the Direct Approach Effectively

Use the direct approach when your negative answer or information will have minimal personal impact.

A negative message using the direct approach opens with the bad news, proceeds to the reasons for the situation or the decision, and ends with a positive statement aimed at maintaining a good relationship with the audience (see Figure 8.1). The message may also offer alternatives or a plan of action to fix the situation under discussion. Stating the bad news at the beginning can have two advantages: (1) It makes a shorter message possible, and (2) it requires less time for the audience to reach the main idea of the message.

Open with a Clear Statement of the Bad News

If you've chosen a direct approach to convey bad news, come right out and say it. Even if the news is devastating, maintain a calm, professional tone that keeps the focus on the news and not on individual failures. Also, if necessary, remind the reader why you're writing:

Reminds the reader that he or she applied for life insurance with your firm, and announces your decision

> Transnation Life is unable to grant your application for SafetyNet term life insurance.

Eases into the bad news with a personal acknowledgment to the staff, even though it delivers the news directly and immediately

> In spite of everyone's best efforts to close more sales this past quarter, revenue fell 14 percent compared to the third quarter last year.

FIGURE 8.1   Choosing the Indirect or Direct Approach for Negative Messages
Analyze the situation carefully before choosing your approach to organizing negative messages.

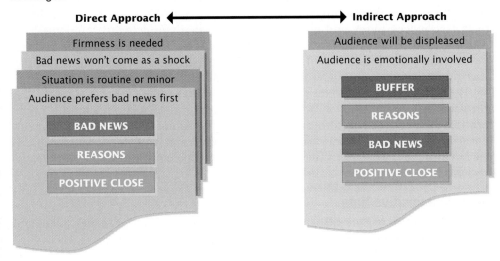

Notice how the second example still manages to ease into the bad news, even though it delivers the bad news directly and quickly. In both instances, the recipient gets the news immediately.

Provide Reasons and Additional Information

In most cases, you'll follow the direct opening with an explanation of why the news is negative:

> Transnation Life is unable to grant your application for SafetyNet term life insurance. **The SafetyNet program has specific health history requirements that your application does not meet.**

Offers a general explanation as the reason the application was denied and discourages further communication on the matter

> In spite of everyone's best efforts to close more sales this past quarter, revenue fell 14 percent compared to the third quarter last year. **Reports from the field offices indicate that the economic downturn in Asia has reduced demand for our products.**

Lets readers know why the news is negative and reassures them that job performance is not the reason

The extent of your explanation depends on the nature of your news and your relationship with the reader. In the first example, the insurance company provides a general reason for the denial because listing a specific health issue might encourage additional communication from the reader to negotiate or to explain the situation. The company's decision is final, and any further communication on the issue would be counterproductive for both parties. In some situations, it's a good idea to follow the explanation with a statement of how you plan to correct or respond to the negative news. In the case of the sales decline, you might follow by telling the staff you plan to increase advertising to help stimulate sales.

The amount of detail you provide depends on your relationship with the audience.

You will encounter some situations in which explaining negative news is neither appropriate nor helpful, such as when the reasons are confidential, excessively complicated, or irrelevant to the reader. To maintain a cordial working relationship with the reader, you might want to explain why you can't provide the information.

Sometimes detailed reasons should not be provided.

When a company has made a serious mistake, those who communicate the negative news need to address the question of apologies. As the KPMG example at the beginning of the chapter illustrates, this question does not have a simple answer. To some people, an *apology* simply means an expression of sympathy that something negative has happened to another person. Others think it means admitting fault and taking responsibility for specific compensations or corrections to atone for the mistake.

The decision whether to apologize depends on a number of factors.

Some experts have advised that a company should never apologize, even when it knows it has made a mistake, as the apology might be taken as a confession of guilt that could be used against the company in a lawsuit. However, several states have laws that specifically prevent expressions of sympathy from being used as evidence of legal liability. In fact, judges, juries, and plaintiffs tend to be more forgiving of companies that express sympathy for wronged parties. Recently, some prosecutors have begun pressing executives to publicly admit guilt and apologize as part of the settlement of criminal cases—unlike the common tactic of paying fines but refusing to admit any wrongdoing.[3]

The best general advice in the event of a serious mistake or accident is to immediately and sincerely express sympathy and offer help if appropriate, without admitting guilt; then seek the advice of your company's lawyers before elaborating. A straightforward, sincere apology can go a long way toward healing wounds and rebuilding relationships. As one recent survey concluded, "The risks of making an apology are low, and the potential reward is high."[4]

Close on a Positive Note

Close your message in a positive but respectful tone.

After you've explained the negative news, close the message in a positive, but still honest and respectful, manner:

Ends on a respectful note, knowing that life insurance is an important subject for the reader, but also makes it clear that the company's decision is final

Transnation Life is unable to grant your application for SafetyNet term life insurance. The SafetyNet program has specific health history requirements that your application does not meet. **We wish you success in finding coverage through another provider.**

Helps readers respond to the news by letting them know that the company plans to fix the situation, even if the plan for doing so isn't clear yet

In spite of everyone's best efforts to close more sales this past quarter, revenue fell 14 percent compared to the third quarter last year. Reports from the field offices indicate that the economic downturn in Asia has reduced demand for our products. **However, I continue to believe that we have the best product for these customers, and we'll continue to explore ways to boost sales in these key markets.**

Notice how both examples deliver bad news quickly and efficiently, then move on. Consider offering your readers an alternative solution, if you can. For instance, if you know that another insurance company has a program for higher-risk policies, you can alert your reader to that opportunity.

Using the Indirect Approach Effectively

Use the indirect approach when some preparation will help your audience accept your bad news.

The indirect approach helps readers prepare for the bad news by presenting the reasons for it first. However, the indirect approach is not meant to obscure bad news, delay it, or limit your responsibility. The purpose of this approach is to ease the blow and help readers accept the situation. When done poorly, the indirect approach can be disrespectful and even unethical. But when done well, it is a good example of "you"-oriented communication crafted with attention to both ethics and etiquette.

Open with a Buffer

A buffer establishes common ground with the reader.

The first step in using the indirect approach is to write a **buffer**, a neutral, noncontroversial statement that is closely related to the point of the message. A buffer establishes common ground with your reader, and if you're responding to a request, a buffer validates that request. Some critics believe that using a buffer is manipulative and unethical, even dishonest. However, buffers are unethical only if they're insincere or deceptive. Showing consideration for the feelings of others is never dishonest.

Poorly written buffers mislead or insult the reader.

A poorly written buffer might trivialize the reader's concerns, divert attention from the problem with insincere flattery or irrelevant material, or mislead the reader into thinking your message actually contains good news. A good buffer, on the other hand, can express your appreciation for being considered (if you're responding to a request), assure your reader of your attention to the request, or indicate your understanding of the reader's needs.

The following examples were all written in response to a manager of the order fulfillment department, who requested some temporary staffing help from your department (a request you won't be able to fulfill):

Our department shares your goal of processing orders quickly and efficiently. → Establishes common ground with the reader and validates the concerns that prompted the original request—without promising a positive answer

As a result of the last downsizing, every department in the company is running shorthanded. → Establishes common ground, but in a negative way that downplays the recipient's concerns

You folks are doing a great job over there, and I'd love to be able to help out. → Potentially misleads the reader into concluding that you will comply with the request

Those new state labor regulations are driving me crazy over here; how about in your department? → Trivializes the reader's concerns by opening with an irrelevant issue

Only the first of these buffers can be considered effective; the other three are likely to damage your relationship with the other manager—and to lower his or her opinion of you. Table 8.2 shows several types of effective buffers you could use to tactfully open a negative message. Whichever approach you choose, make sure your buffer is respectful, relevant, and neutral. Moreover, make sure it provides a smooth transition to the reasons that follow.

Provide Reasons and Additional Information

An effective buffer serves as a stepping-stone to the next part of your message, in which you build up the explanations and information that will culminate in your negative news. As with the direct approach, the nature of the information depends on the audience and the situation. However, the way you portray this information differs from any portrayal in a direct message because your reader doesn't know your conclusion yet.

Table 8.2	Types of Buffers	
Buffer Type	**Strategy**	**Example**
Agreement	Find a point on which you and the reader share similar views.	We both know how hard it is to make a profit in this industry.
Appreciation	Express sincere thanks for receiving something.	Your check for $127.17 arrived yesterday. Thank you.
Cooperation	Convey your willingness to help in any way you realistically can.	Employee Services is here to smooth the way for all of you who work to achieve company goals.
Fairness	Assure the reader that you've closely examined and carefully considered the problem, or mention an appropriate action that has already been taken.	For the past week, we have carefully monitored those using the photocopying machine to see whether we can detect any pattern of use that might explain its frequent breakdowns.
Good news	Start with the part of your message that is favorable.	A replacement knob for your range is on its way, shipped February 10 via UPS.
Praise	Find an attribute or an achievement to compliment.	The Stratford Group clearly has an impressive record of accomplishment in helping clients resolve financial reporting problems.
Resale	Favorably discuss the product or company related to the subject of the letter.	With their heavy-duty, full-suspension hardware and fine veneers, the desks and file cabinets in our Montclair line have become a hit with value-conscious professionals.
Understanding	Demonstrate that you understand the reader's goals and needs.	So that you can more easily find the printer with the features you need, we are enclosing a brochure that describes all the Panasonic printers currently available.

Phrase your reasons to signal the negative news ahead.

An ideal explanation section leads readers to your conclusion before you come right out and say it. The reader has followed your line of reasoning and is ready for the answer. By giving your reasons effectively, you help maintain focus on the issues at hand and defuse the emotions that always accompany significantly bad news.

As you lay out your reasons, guide your readers' responses by starting with the most positive points first and moving forward to increasingly negative ones. Provide enough detail for the audience to understand your reasons, but be concise. Your reasons need to convince your audience that your decision is justified, fair, and logical.

Don't hide behind "company policy" when you deliver bad news.

Avoid hiding behind company policy to cushion your bad news. If you say, "Company policy forbids our hiring anyone who does not have two years' supervisory experience," you imply that you won't consider anyone on his or her individual merits. Skilled and sympathetic communicators explain company policy (without referring to it as "policy") so that the audience can try to meet the requirements at a later time. Consider this response to a job applicant:

Shows that the decision is based on a methodical analysis and not on some arbitrary guidline

Establishes the criteria behind the decision and lets the reader know what to expect

Because these management positions are quite challenging, the human relations department has researched the qualifications needed to succeed in them. The findings show that the two most important qualifications are a bachelor's degree in business administration and two years' supervisory experience.

The paragraph does a good job of stating reasons for the refusal:

Well-written reasons are
- Detailed
- Tactful
- Individualized
- Unapologetic
- Positive

- It provides enough detail to logically support the refusal.
- It implies that the applicant is better off avoiding a program in which he or she might fail.
- It explains the company's policy as logical rather than arbitrary.
- It offers no apology for the decision because no one is at fault.
- It avoids negative personal expressions (such as "You do not meet our requirements").

Even valid, well-thought-out reasons won't convince every reader in every situation, but if you've done a good job of laying out your reasoning, then you've done everything you can to prepare the reader for the main idea, which is the negative news itself.

Continue with a Clear Statement of the Bad News

Now that you've laid out your reasons thoughtfully and logically, and now that readers are prepared to receive the bad news, your audience may still reject your message if the bad news is handled carelessly. Three techniques are especially useful for saying no as clearly and as kindly as possible. First, deemphasize the bad news:

To handle bad news carefully,
- Deemphasize the bad news visually and grammatically
- Use a conditional statement if appropriate
- Tell what you did do, not what you didn't do

- Minimize the space or time devoted to the bad news—without trivializing it or withholding any important information.
- Subordinate bad news within a complex or compound sentence ("My department is already shorthanded, so I'll need all my staff for at least the next two months").
- Embed bad news in the middle of a paragraph or use parenthetical expressions ("Our profits, which are down, are only part of the picture").

However, keep in mind that it's possible to abuse this notion of deemphasis. For instance, if the primary point of your message is that profits are down, it would be inappropriate to marginalize that news by burying it in the middle of a sentence. State the negative news clearly, then make a smooth transition to any positive news that might balance the story.

Second, use a conditional (*if* or *when*) statement to imply that the audience could have received, or might someday receive, a favorable answer ("When you have more managerial experience, you are welcome to reapply"). Such a statement could motivate applicants to improve their qualifications.

Don't disguise bad news when you emphasize the positive.

Third, emphasize what you can do or have done, rather than what you cannot do. Also, by implying the bad news, you may not need to actually state it, thereby making the bad news less personal ("The five positions currently open have been filled with people whose qualifications match those uncovered in our research"). However, make sure your audience understands the entire message—including the bad news. If an implied message might lead to uncertainty, state your decision in direct terms. Just be sure to avoid overly blunt statements that are likely to cause pain and anger:

Instead of This	Write This
I *must refuse* your request.	I will be out of town on the day you need me.
We *must deny* your application.	The position has been filled.
I *am unable* to grant your request.	Contact us again when you have established . . .
We *cannot afford* to continue the program.	The program will conclude on May 1.
Much as I would like to attend . . .	Our budget meeting ends too late for me to attend.
We *must reject* your proposal.	We've accepted the proposal from AAA Builders.
We *must turn down* your extension request.	Please send in your payment by June 14.

Close on a Positive Note

The conclusion is your opportunity to emphasize your respect for your audience, even though you've just delivered unpleasant news. If you can find a positive angle that's meaningful to your audience, by all means consider adding it to your conclusion. However, don't try to pretend that the negative news didn't happen or that it won't affect the reader. Suggest alternative solutions if such information is available. In a message to a customer or potential customer, the ending can include **resale information** (favorable comments about a product or service that the customer has already purchased) or **sales promotion** (favorable comments that encourage interest in goods or services the reader has not yet committed to purchase). If you've asked readers to decide between alternatives or to take some action, make sure that they know what to do, when to do it, and how to do it. Whatever type of conclusion you use, follow these guidelines:

- Don't refer to, repeat, or apologize for the bad news, and refrain from expressing any doubt that your reasons will be accepted.
- Encourage additional communication *only* if you're willing to discuss your decision further.
- Don't anticipate problems (avoid statements such as "Should you have further problems, please let us know").
- Steer clear of clichés that are insincere in view of the bad news (if you can't help, don't say, "If we can be of any help, please contact us").

Finally, keep in mind that the closing is the last thing the audience has to remember you by. Try to make the memory a positive one.

A positive close
- Builds goodwill
- Offers a suggestion for action
- Provides a look toward the future

Exploring Common Examples of Negative Messages

In the course of your business career, you might write a wide variety of negative messages, from announcing declines in revenue to giving negative performance reviews. The following sections offer examples of the most common negative messages, dealing with topics such as routine business matters, organizational news, and employment messages.

Document Makeover

Improve This Memo

To practice correcting drafts of actual documents, visit your online course or the access-code-protected Prentice Hall Business Communication Website. Click "Document Makeovers," then click Chapter 8. You will find a memo that contains problems and errors relating to what you've learned in this chapter about writing negative business messages. Use the Final Draft decision tool to create an improved version of this memo. Check the message for the use of buffers, apologies, explanations, subordination, embedding, positive action, conditional phrases, and upbeat perspectives.

Sending Negative Messages on Routine Business Matters

Most companies receive numerous requests for information and donations or invitations to join community or industry organizations. As you progress in your career and become more visible in your industry and community, you will probably receive a wide variety of personal invitations to speak at private or public functions or to volunteer your time for a variety of organizations. In addition, routine business matters such as credit applications and requests for adjustment will often require negative responses. Neither you nor your company will be able to say yes to every request. Crafting negative responses quickly and graciously is an important skill for many professionals.

Refusing Routine Requests

Routine requests may come both from groups and from individuals outside the company, as well as from colleagues inside the organization. When you aren't able to meet the request, your primary communication challenge is to give a clear negative response without generating negative feelings or damaging either your personal reputation or the company's. As simple as these messages may appear to be, they can test your skills as a communicator because you often need to deliver negative information while maintaining a positive relationship with the other party.

When turning down an invitation or a request for a favor, consider your relationship with the reader.

Saying no is a routine part of business and shouldn't reflect negatively on you. If you said yes to every request that crossed your desk, you'd never get any work done. The direct approach will work best for most routine negative responses. It not only helps your audience get your answer quickly and move on to other possibilities but also helps you save time, since the direct approach is often easier to write. The indirect approach works best when the stakes are high for you or for the receiver, when you or your company has an established relationship with the person making the request, or when you're forced to decline a request that you might have said yes to in the past (see Figure 8.2).

Consider the following points as you develop your routine negative messages:

- **Manage your time carefully.** Focus your limited time on the most important relationships and requests; craft quick, standard responses for less important situations.
- **If the matter is closed, don't imply that it's still open.** If your answer is truly no, don't use phrases such as "Let me think about it and get back to you" as a way to delay saying no.
- **Offer alternative ideas if you can.** However, remember to use your time wisely in such matters. Unless the relationship is vital to your company, you probably shouldn't spend time researching alternatives for the other person.

If you aren't in a position to offer additional information or assistance, don't imply that you are.

- **Don't imply that other assistance or information might be available if it isn't.** Don't close your negative message with a cheery but insincere "Please contact us if we can offer any additional assistance." An empty attempt to mollify hostile feelings could simply lead to another request you'll have to refuse.

FIGURE 8.2 Effective Letter Declining a Routine Request

In declining a request to use her company's facilities, May Yee Kwan took note of the fact that her company has a long-standing relationship with the college and wants to maintain that positive relationship. Because the news is unexpected based on past experience, she chose an indirect approach to build up to her announcement.

Planning

Analyze the Situation
Verify that the purpose is to decline a request and offer alternatives; audience is likely to be surprised by the refusal.

Gather Information
Determine audience needs and obtain the necessary information.

Select the Right Medium
For formal messages, printed letters on company letterhead are best.

Organize the Information
Main idea is to refuse the request so limit your scope to that; select an indirect approach based on the audience and the situation.

1

Writing

Adapt to Your Audience
Adjust the level of formality based on degree of familiarity with the audience; maintain a positive relationship by using the "you" attitude, politeness, positive emphasis, and bias-free language.

Compose the Message
Use a conversational but professional style and keep the message brief, clear, and as helpful as possible.

2

Completing

Revise the Message
Evaluate content and review readability to make sure the negative information won't be misinterpreted; make sure your tone stays positive without being artificial.

Produce the Message
Emphasize a clean, professional appearance on company letterhead.

Proofread the Message
Review for errors in layout, spelling, and mechanics.

Distribute the Message
Deliver your message using the chosen medium.

3

InfoTech

927 Dawson Valley Road, Tulsa, Oklahoma 74151
Voice: (918) 669-4428   Fax: (918) 669-4429
www.infotech.com

March 6, 2007

Dr. Sandra Wofford, President
Whittier Community College
333 Whittier Avenue
Tulsa, OK 74150

Dear Dr. Wofford:

Buffers negative response by demonstrating respect and recapping the request →

Infotech has been happy to support Whittier Community College in many ways over the years, and we appreciate the opportunities you and your organization provide to so many deserving students. Thank you for considering our grounds for your graduation ceremony on June 3.

We would certainly like to accommodate Whittier as we have in years past, but our company-wide sales meetings will be held this year during the weeks of May 29 and June 5. With over 200 sales representatives and their families from around the world joining us, activities will be taking place throughout our facility.

← *States a meaningful reason for the negative response, without apologizing (since the company is not at fault)*

Suggests an alternative, showing that Kwan cares about the college and has given the matter some thought →

My assistant, Robert Seagers, suggests you contact the Municipal Botanical Gardens as a possible graduation site. He recommends calling Jerry Kane, director of public relations.

We remain firm in our commitment to you, President Wofford, and to the fine students you represent. Through our internship program, academic research grants, and other initiatives, we will continue to be a strong corporate partner to Whittier College and will support your efforts as you move forward.

← *Closes by emphasizing the importance of the relationship and the company's continuing commitment*

Sincerely,

May Yee Kwan

May Yee Kwan
Public Relations Director

Pointers for Writing Negative Messages
- Carefully chose a direct or indirect approach.
- If using an indirect approach, establish rapport without implying that a positive response is coming.
- Smoothly transition from the buffer to the reasons for the negative response or news; help the reader anticipate the bad news before reaching it.
- Explain how the decision or news might benefit your audience—but only if it really does benefit them.
- Apologize only if appropriate and only if allowed by company policy.
- State the negative news as positively as possible, but without misleading your audience.
- Maintain a calm, objective tone throughout.
- Carefully consider the amount of detail to include.
- Don't invite questions or discussion if the decision is final.
- Close with a positive—but honest—outlook on the future.

Handling Bad News About Transactions

For any number of reasons, businesses must sometimes convey bad news concerning the sale and delivery of products and services. Bad news about transactions is always unwelcome and usually unexpected. These messages have three goals: to modify the customer's expectations regarding the transaction, to explain how you plan to resolve the situation, and to repair whatever damage might've been done to the business relationship.

Some negative messages regarding transactions carry significant business ramifications.

The specific content and tone of each message can vary widely, depending on the nature of the transaction and your relationship with the customer. Telling an individual consumer that his new sweater will be arriving a week later than you promised is a much simpler task than telling General Motors that 30,000 transmission parts will be a week late, especially since you know the company will be forced to idle a multimillion-dollar production facility as a result.

Negative messages about transactions come in two basic flavors. If you haven't done anything specific to set the customer's expectations—such as promising delivery within 24 hours—the message simply needs to inform the customer, with little or no emphasis on apologies (Figure 8.3).

Your approach to bad news about business transactions depends on the customer's expectations.

If you did set the customer's expectations and now find you can't meet them, your task is more complicated. In addition to resetting the customer's expectations and explaining how you'll resolve the problem, you may need to include an element of apology. The scope of the apology depends on the magnitude of the mistake. For the customer who ordered a sweater, a simple apology, followed by a clear statement of when the sweater will arrive, would probably be sufficient. For larger business-to-business transactions, the customer may want an explanation of what went wrong in order to determine whether you'll be able to perform as you promise in the future.

If you've failed to meet expectations that you set for the customer, an element of apology should be considered.

To help repair the damage to the relationship and encourage repeat business, many companies offer discounts on future purchases, free merchandise, or other considerations. Even modest efforts can go a long way to rebuilding the customer's confidence in your company. However, you don't always have a choice. Business-to-business purchasing contracts often include performance clauses that legally entitle the customer to discounts or other restitution in the event of late delivery. In such cases, a simple apology is clearly inadequate.

Refusing Claims and Requests for Adjustment

Almost every customer who makes a claim or requests an adjustment is emotionally involved; therefore, the indirect method is usually the best approach for a refusal. Your job as a writer is to avoid accepting responsibility for the unfortunate situation and yet avoid blaming or accusing the customer. To steer clear of these pitfalls, pay special attention to the tone of your letter. Demonstrate that you understand and have considered the complaint carefully, then rationally explain why you are refusing the request. End the letter on a respectful and action-oriented note (see Figure 8.4).

Use the indirect approach in most cases of refusing a claim.

If you deal with enough customers over a long-enough period, chances are you'll get a request that is particularly outrageous. You may even be positive that the person is being dishonest. You must resist the temptation to call the person dishonest or incompetent. If you don't, you could be sued for **defamation**, a false statement that tends to damage someone's character or reputation. (Written defamation is called *libel*; spoken defamation is called *slander*.) Someone suing for defamation must prove (1) that the statement is false, (2) that the language is injurious to the person's reputation, and (3) that the statement has been published.

If you can prove that your accusations are true, you haven't defamed the person. The courts are likely to give you the benefit of the doubt because our society believes that ordinary business communication should not be hampered by fear of lawsuits. However, if the message has no necessary business purpose and is expressed in abusive language that hints of malice, you'll lose the case. To avoid being accused of defamation, follow these guidelines:

You can help avoid defamation by not responding emotionally.

■ Avoid using any kind of abusive language or terms that could be considered defamatory. If you wish to express your own personal opinions about a sensitive matter, use your own stationery (not company letterhead), and don't include your job title or position. Just be aware that by doing so, you take responsibility for your own opinions, you

FIGURE 8.3 Effective E-Mail Advising of a Back Order

This message, which is a combination of good and bad news, uses the indirect approach—with the good news serving as a buffer for the bad news. In this case, the customer wasn't promised delivery by a certain date, so the writer simply informs the customer when to expect the rest of the order. The writer also takes steps to repair the relationship and encourage future business with her firm.

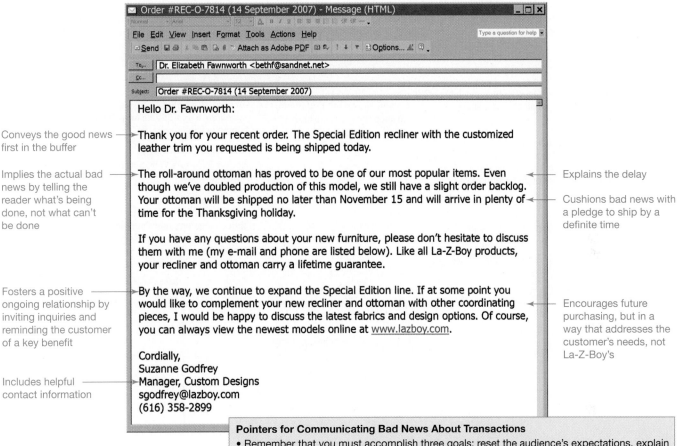

Conveys the good news first in the buffer

Implies the actual bad news by telling the reader what's being done, not what can't be done

Fosters a positive ongoing relationship by inviting inquiries and reminding the customer of a key benefit

Includes helpful contact information

Explains the delay

Cushions bad news with a pledge to ship by a definite time

Encourages future purchasing, but in a way that addresses the customer's needs, not La-Z-Boy's

Pointers for Communicating Bad News About Transactions

- Remember that you must accomplish three goals: reset the audience's expectations, explain how you are resolving the problem, and repair the relationship.
- Establish rapport with a buffer, such as thanking a customer for ordering from you.
- If the news is mixed, use the good news as a buffer.
- Explain the reasons without laying the blame or making excuses.
- Describe exactly what will happen and when; focus on solutions, not problems.
- Reinforce the customer's confidence in your firm by emphasizing the advantages of doing business with you.
- Express the negative news succinctly and clearly.
- Offer alternatives if appropriate.
- Consider including resale information to encourage future business; however, this must be done tactfully because the customer already has reasons to question your ability to meet his or her needs.
- Close on a positive note that shows continued attention to the customer's needs.

are no longer acting within the scope of your duties with the company, and you are personally liable for any resulting legal action.

- Provide accurate information and stick to the facts.
- Never let anger or malice motivate your messages.
- Consult your company's legal department or an attorney whenever you think a message might have legal consequences.
- Communicate honestly, and make sure that what you're saying is what you believe to be true.
- Emphasize a desire for a good relationship in the future.

FIGURE 8.4 **Effectively Refusing a Claim**

Daniel Lindmeier, who purchased a digital video camera from Village Electronics a year ago, wrote to say that the unit doesn't work properly and to inquire about the warranty. He incorrectly believed that the warranty covers one year, when it actually covers only three months. In this response, Walter Brodie uses an indirect approach to convey the bad news and to offer additional helpful information.

Planning ➤ Writing ➤ Completing

Analyze the Situation
Verify that the purpose is to refuse a warranty claim and offer repairs; audience's likely reaction will be disappointment and surprise.

Gather Information
Gather information on warranty policies and procedures, repair services, and resale information.

Select the Right Medium
Choose the best medium for delivering your message; for formal messages, printed letters on company letterhead are best.

Organize the Information
Your main idea is to refuse the claim and promote an alternative solution; select an indirect approach based on the audience and the situation.

Adapt to Your Audience
Adjust the level of formality based on degree of familiarity with the audience; maintain a positive relationship by using the "you" attitude, politeness, positive emphasis, and bias-free language.

Compose the Message
Use a conversational but professional style and keep the message brief, clear, and as helpful as possible.

Revise the Message
Evaluate content and review readability to make sure the negative information won't be misinterpreted; make sure your tone stays positive without being artificial.

Produce the Message
Emphasize a clean, professional appearance appropriate for a letter on company stationery.

Proofread the Message
Review for errors in layout, spelling, and mechanics.

Distribute the Message
Deliver your message using the chosen medium; make sure the reader receives any necessary support documents as well.

1 **2** **3**

NUMBER ONE IN ENTERTAINMENT

Village Electronics

68 Lake Itasca Boulevard • Hannover, MN 55341
Voice: (612) 878-1312 • Fax: (612) 878-1316

May 3, 2007

Mr. Daniel Lindmeier
849 Cedar St.
Lake Elmo, MN 55042

Dear Mr. Lindmeier:

[Buffers the bad news by emphasizing a point the reader and writer both agree on] Thank you for your letter about the battery release switch on your JVC digital camera. Village Electronics believes, as you do, that electronic equipment should be built to last. That's why we stand behind our products with a 90-day warranty.

[Puts company's policy in a favorable light] *[States bad news indirectly, tactfully leaving the repair decision to the customer]* Even though your JVC camera is a year old and therefore out of warranty, we can still help. Please package your camera carefully and ship it to our store in Hannover. Include your complete name, address, phone number, and a brief description of the malfunction, along with a check for $35 for an initial examination. After assessing the unit, we will give you a written estimate of the needed parts and labor. Then just let us know whether you want us to make the repairs—either by phone or by filling out the prepaid card we'll send you with the estimate.

[Helps soothe the reader with a positive alternative] If you choose to repair the unit, the $35 will be applied toward your bill, the balance of which is payable by check or credit card. JVC also has service centers available in your area. If you would prefer to take the unit to one of them, please see the enclosed list.

[Closes by blending sales promotion with an acknowledgment of the customer's interests] Thanks again for inquiring about our service. I've also enclosed a catalog of our latest cameras and accessories, in which you'll find information about JVC's "Trade-Up Special." If you're ready to move up to one of the newest cameras, JVC will offer a generous trade-in allowance on your current model.

Sincerely,

Walter Brodie

Walter Brodie
Customer Service Manager

Enclosures: List of service centers
Catalog

Pointers for Refusing Claims
- Use the buffer to indicate that you received and understand the request or complaint.
- In the body, provide an accurate, objective account of the transaction.
- Make the refusal clear without being abrupt, insulting, or accusatory.
- Maintain an impersonal tone that doesn't offend the reader.
- Don't apologize for refusing, since your company hasn't done anything wrong (otherwise, you would be granting the claim).
- Offer an alternative solution on fair terms.
- Emphasize your continued desire for a positive relationship with the customer.
- Close with resale information if appropriate.
- Make any suggested actions easy for the reader to follow.

Remember that nothing positive can come out of antagonizing a customer, even a customer who has verbally abused you or your colleagues. Reject the claim or request for adjustment and move on to the next challenge.

Sending Negative Organizational News

In addition to routine matters involving individual customers and other parties, you may encounter special cases that require you to issue negative announcements regarding some aspect of your products, services, or operations. Some of these messages include changes that negatively affect one or more groups (such as losing a major contract or canceling a popular product), announcements of workforce reductions, and crisis communication regarding environmental incidents or workplace accidents. In some instances, you have plenty of time to plan the message. In others, a crisis hits without warning, and you must respond instantly.

Negative organizational messages to external audiences often require extensive planning.

When making negative announcements about operations, follow these guidelines:

- **Match your approach to the situation.** For example, in an emergency such as product tampering or a toxic spill, get to the point immediately.
- **Consider the unique needs of each group.** When a facility closes, for instance, employees need time to find new jobs, and community leaders may need to be prepared to help people who've lost their jobs.
- **Minimize the element of surprise whenever possible.** Don't delay bad news just because you're not ready to face your audience; the more time they have to repair, the more grateful they'll be.

Give people as much time as possible to react to negative news.

- **If possible, give yourself enough time to plan and manage a response.** Make sure you're ready with answers to expected questions.
- **Look for positive angles, but don't exude false optimism.** Laying off 10,000 people does not give them "an opportunity to explore new horizons." It's a traumatic event that can affect employees, their families, and their communities for years. Phony optimism would only make a bad situation worse. The best you may be able to do is to thank people for their past support and to wish them well in the future.
- **Seek expert advice.** Many significant negative announcements have important technical, financial, or legal elements that require the expertise of lawyers, accountants, or other specialists.

Ask for legal help and other assistance if you're not sure how to handle a significant negative announcement.

Negative situations will test your skills both as a communicator and as a leader. Inspirational leaders try to seize such opportunities as a chance to reshape or reinvigorate the organization, and they offer encouragement to those around them (see Figure 8.5).

Sending Negative Employment Messages

All managers must convey bad news about individual employees from time to time. You can use the direct approach when writing to job applicants or when communicating with other companies to send a negative reference to a prospective employer. But it's best to use the indirect approach when giving negative performance reviews to employees; they will most certainly be emotionally involved. In addition, choose the media you use for these messages with care. E-mail and other written forms let you control the message and avoid personal confrontation, but one-on-one conversations are more sensitive and facilitate questions and answers.

Refusing Requests for Recommendation Letters

Many states have passed laws to protect employers who provide open and honest job references for former employees, but legal hazards persist.[5] That's why many employers still refuse to write recommendation letters—especially for former employees whose job

FIGURE 8.5   Effective E-Mail Providing Bad News About Company Operations

In this message to employees at Sybervantage, Frank Leslie shares the unpleasant news that a hoped-for licensing agreement with Warner Brothers has been rejected. Rather than dwell on the bad news, he focuses on options for the future. The upbeat close diminishes the effect of the bad news without hiding or downplaying the news itself.

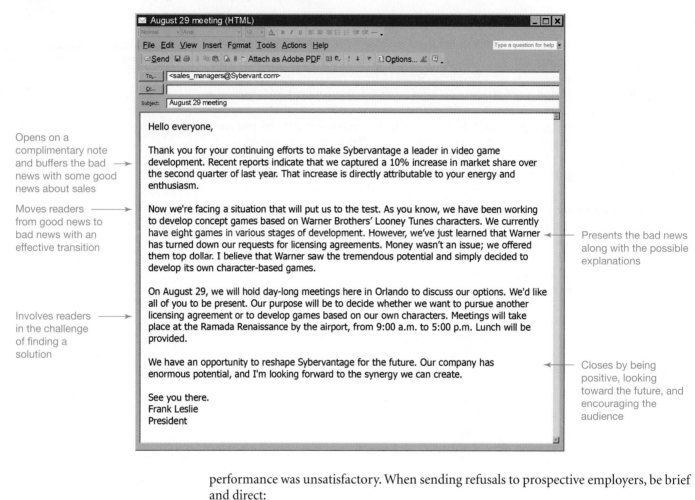

Opens on a complimentary note and buffers the bad news with some good news about sales

Moves readers from good news to bad news with an effective transition

Involves readers in the challenge of finding a solution

Presents the bad news along with the possible explanations

Closes by being positive, looking toward the future, and encouraging the audience

---

performance was unsatisfactory. When sending refusals to prospective employers, be brief and direct:

Implies that company policy prohibits the release of any more information but does provide what information is available

Ends on a positive note

> Our human resources department has authorized me to confirm that Yolanda Johnson worked for Tandy, Inc., for three years, from June 1999 to July 2001. Best of luck as you interview administrative applicants.

In letters informing prospective employers that you will not provide a recommendation, be direct, brief, and factual (to avoid legal pitfalls).

This message doesn't need to say, "We cannot comply with your request." It simply gets down to the business of giving readers the information that is allowable.

Refusing an applicant's direct request for a recommendation letter is another matter. Any refusal to cooperate may seem a personal slight and a threat to the applicant's future. Diplomacy and preparation help readers accept your refusal:

Uses the indirect approach since the other party is probably expecting a positive response

> Thank you for letting me know about your job opportunity with Coca-Cola. Your internship there and the MBA you've worked so hard to earn should place you in an excellent position to land the marketing job.

Announces that the writer cannot comply with the request, without explicitly blaming it on "policy"

Offers to fulfill as much of the request as possible, then offers an alternative

Ends on a positive note

> Although we do not send out formal recommendations here at PepsiCo, I can certainly send Coca-Cola a confirmation of your employment dates. And if you haven't considered this already, be sure to ask several of your professors to write evaluations of your marketing skills. Best of luck to you in your career.

This letter deftly and tactfully avoids hurting the reader's feelings, because it makes positive comments about the reader's recent activities, implies the refusal, suggests an alternative, and uses a polite close.

Rejecting Job Applications

Telling job applicants that you won't be offering them employment is another frequent communication challenge. Traditionally, businesses always made a point of responding to applications, but the rapid growth of e-mailed résumés and online job sites such as Monster.com have flooded some companies with so many applicants that they say they can no longer reply to them all.[6] However, you should make every effort to respond; failing to do so builds ill will and can harm your company's reputation.

As you write, bear in mind that poorly written rejection letters have negative consequences, ranging from the loss of qualified candidates for future openings to the loss of potential customers (not only the rejected applicants but also their friends and family).[7] Poorly phrased rejection letters can even invite legal troubles. When delivering bad news to job applicants, follow three guidelines:[8]

- **Choose your approach carefully.** Experts disagree on whether a direct or an indirect approach is best for rejection letters. On the one hand, job applicants know they won't get many of the positions they apply for, so negative news during a job search is not generally a shock. On the other hand, people put their hopes and dreams on the line when they apply for work, so job applicants have a deep emotional investment in the process, which is one of the factors to consider in using an indirect approach. If you opt for an indirect approach, be careful not to mislead the reader with effusive praise or delay the bad news for more than a sentence or two. A simple "Thank you for considering ABC as the place to start your career" is a quick, courteous buffer that shows your company is flattered to be considered.

- **Clearly state why the applicant was not selected.** Make your rejection less personal by stating that you hired someone with more experience or whose qualifications match the position requirements more closely.

- **Close by suggesting alternatives.** If you believe the applicant is qualified, mention other openings within your company. You might suggest professional organizations that could help the applicant find employment. Such suggestions may help the applicant be less disappointed and view your company more positively.

> Experts disagree on whether a direct or indirect approach is better for rejecting job applications.

A rejection letter need not be long. After all, the applicant wants to know only one thing: Did I land the job? Your brief message conveys the information clearly and with tactful consideration for the applicant's feelings (Figure 8.6).

Giving Negative Performance Reviews

Few other communication tasks require such a broad range of skills and strategy as those needed for employee performance reviews. The main purpose of these reviews is to improve employee performance by (1) emphasizing and clarifying job requirements, (2) giving employees feedback on their efforts toward fulfilling those requirements, and (3) guiding continued efforts by developing a plan of action, which includes rewards and opportunities. In addition to improving employee performance, performance reviews help companies set organizational standards and communicate organizational values.[9] Whether the review is generally positive or generally negative, the tone should be objective and unbiased, the language nonjudgmental, and the focus on problem resolution.[10]

> An important goal of any performance evaluation is giving the employee a plan of action for improving his or her performance.

It's difficult to criticize employees face-to-face, and it's just as hard to include criticism in written performance evaluations. Nevertheless, if you fire an employee for incompetence and the performance evaluations are all positive, the employee can sue your company, maintaining you had no cause to terminate employment.[11] Also, your company could be sued for negligence if an injury is caused by an employee who received a negative

FIGURE 8.6

Poor and Improved E-Mails Rejecting a Job Application

This e-mail response was drafted by Marvin Fichter to communicate the bad news to Carol DeCicco following her interview with Bradley Jackson. After reviewing the first draft, Fichter made several changes to improve the communication. The revised e-mail helps DeCicco understand that (1) she would have been hired if she'd had more tax experience and (2) she shouldn't be discouraged.

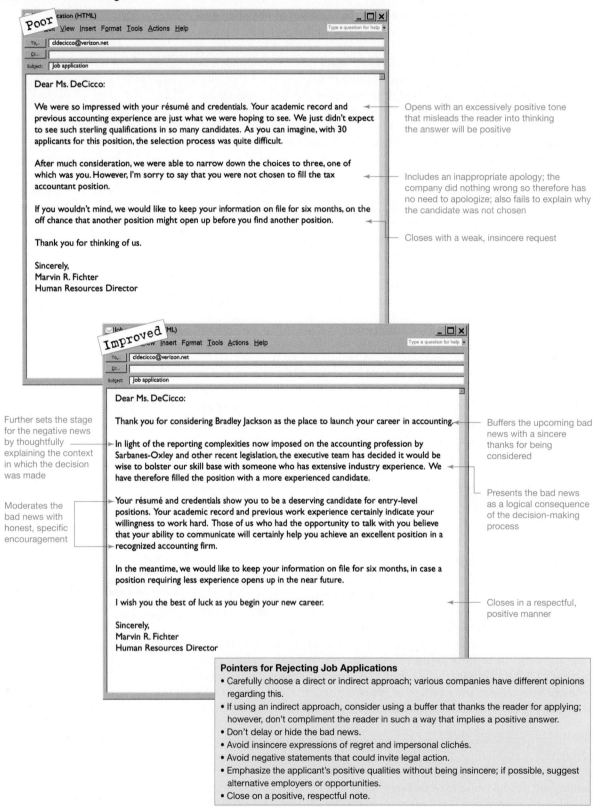

Poor

cation (HTML)

View Insert Format Tools Actions Help   Type a question for help

To...: cldecicco@verizon.net
Cc...:
Subject: Job application

Dear Ms. DeCicco:

We were so impressed with your résumé and credentials. Your academic record and previous accounting experience are just what we were hoping to see. We just didn't expect to see such sterling qualifications in so many candidates. As you can imagine, with 30 applicants for this position, the selection process was quite difficult.

After much consideration, we were able to narrow down the choices to three, one of which was you. However, I'm sorry to say that you were not chosen to fill the tax accountant position.

If you wouldn't mind, we would like to keep your information on file for six months, on the off chance that another position might open up before you find another position.

Thank you for thinking of us.

Sincerely,
Marvin R. Fichter
Human Resources Director

— Opens with an excessively positive tone that misleads the reader into thinking the answer will be positive

— Includes an inappropriate apology; the company did nothing wrong so therefore has no need to apologize; also fails to explain why the candidate was not chosen

— Closes with a weak, insincere request

Improved

Job   ML)

ew Insert Format Tools Actions Help   Type a question for help

To...: cldecicco@verizon.net
Cc...:
Subject: Job application

Dear Ms. DeCicco:

Thank you for considering Bradley Jackson as the place to launch your career in accounting.

In light of the reporting complexities now imposed on the accounting profession by Sarbanes-Oxley and other recent legislation, the executive team has decided it would be wise to bolster our skill base with someone who has extensive industry experience. We have therefore filled the position with a more experienced candidate.

Your résumé and credentials show you to be a deserving candidate for entry-level positions. Your academic record and previous work experience certainly indicate your willingness to work hard. Those of us who had the opportunity to talk with you believe that your ability to communicate will certainly help you achieve an excellent position in a recognized accounting firm.

In the meantime, we would like to keep your information on file for six months, in case a position requiring less experience opens up in the near future.

I wish you the best of luck as you begin your new career.

Sincerely,
Marvin R. Fichter
Human Resources Director

Further sets the stage for the negative news by thoughtfully explaining the context in which the decision was made

Moderates the bad news with honest, specific encouragement

Buffers the upcoming bad news with a sincere thanks for being considered

Presents the bad news as a logical consequence of the decision-making process

Closes in a respectful, positive manner

Pointers for Rejecting Job Applications
- Carefully choose a direct or indirect approach; various companies have different opinions regarding this.
- If using an indirect approach, consider using a buffer that thanks the reader for applying; however, don't compliment the reader in such a way that implies a positive answer.
- Don't delay or hide the bad news.
- Avoid insincere expressions of regret and impersonal clichés.
- Avoid negative statements that could invite legal action.
- Emphasize the applicant's positive qualities without being insincere; if possible, suggest alternative employers or opportunities.
- Close on a positive, respectful note.

evaluation but received no corrective action (such as retraining).[12] So as difficult as it may be, make sure your performance evaluations are well balanced and honest.

When you need to give a negative performance review, follow these guidelines:[13]

- **Confront the problem right away.** Avoiding performance problems only makes them worse. Moreover, if you don't document problems when they occur, you may make it more difficult to terminate employment later on, if the situation comes to that.[14]
- **Plan your message.** Be clear about your concerns, and include examples of the employee's specific actions. Think about any possible biases you may have, and get feedback from others. Collect and verify all relevant facts (both strengths and weaknesses).
- **Deliver the message in private.** Whether in writing or in person, be sure to address the performance problem privately.

  Address performance problems in private.

- **Focus on the problem.** Discuss the problems caused by the employee's behavior, comparing the employee's performance with what's expected, with company goals, or with job requirements. Identify the consequences of continuing poor performance, and show that you're committed to helping solve the problem.
- **Ask for a commitment from the employee.** Help the employee understand that planning for and making improvements are the employee's responsibility. However, finalize decisions jointly so that you can be sure any action to be taken is achievable. Set a schedule for improvement and for following up with evaluations of that improvement.

Even if your employee's performance has been disappointing, you would do well to begin by mentioning some good points in your performance review. Then clearly and tactfully state how the employee can better meet the responsibilities of the job. If the performance review is to be effective, be sure to suggest ways that the employee can improve.[15] For example, instead of only telling an employee that he damaged some expensive machinery, suggest that he take a refresher course in the correct operation of that machinery. The goal is to help the employee succeed.

Terminating Employment

When writing a termination letter, you have three goals: (1) present the reasons for this difficult action, (2) avoid statements that might expose the company to a wrongful termination lawsuit, and (3) leave the relationship between the terminated employee and the firm as favorable as possible. For both legal and personal reasons, present specific justification for asking the employee to leave.[16] If the employee is working under contract, your company's lawyers will be able to tell you whether the employee's performance is legal grounds for termination.

Carefully word a termination letter to avoid creating undue ill will and grounds for legal action.

Make sure that all your reasons are accurate and verifiable. Avoid words that are open to interpretation, such as *untidy* and *difficult*. Make sure the employee leaves with feelings that are as positive as the circumstances allow. You can do so by telling the truth about the termination and by helping as much as you can to make the employee's transition as smooth as possible.[17]

Reviewing Key Points

This chapter introduces strategies for negative messages and discusses some specific types. It describes how to send sensitive but effective negative messages by creating an audience-centered tone and choosing between direct and indirect approaches. The chapter presents techniques for beginning indirect messages with a buffer, following with reasons, stating the bad news, and ending with a positive close. The chapter also covers how to prepare negative answers to routine requests, including refusing requests for information, refusing invitations and requests for favors, handling bad news about orders, and refusing claims. This chapter shows you how to send negative news about products and about company operations. It also introduces techniques for sending negative employment messages such as refusing requests for recommendations, rejecting job applicants, and sending negative performance reviews.

In the next chapter, you will learn how to apply the three-step writing process to persuasive messages, both persuasive business messages and marketing and sales messages.

Test Your Knowledge

1. What are the five main goals in delivering bad news?

2. Why is it particularly important to adapt your medium and tone to your audience's needs and preferences when writing a negative message?

3. What is the sequence of elements in a negative message organized using an indirect approach?

4. What is a buffer, and why do some critics consider it unethical?

5. When using an indirect approach to announce a negative decision, what is the purpose of presenting your reasons before explaining the decision itself?

Apply Your Knowledge

1. Why is it important to end your negative message on a positive note? Explain.

2. If company policy changes, should you explain those changes to employees and customers at about the same time, or should you explain them to employees first? Why?

3. If the purpose of your letter is to convey bad news, should you take the time to suggest alternatives to your reader? Why or why not?

4. When a company suffers a setback, should you soften the impact by letting out the bad news a little at a time? Why or why not?

5. **Ethical Choices**   Is intentionally deemphasizing bad news the same as distorting graphs and charts to deemphasize unfavorable data? Why or why not?

Practice Your Knowledge

Exercises for Perfecting Your Writing

Teamwork   Working alone, revise the following statements to deemphasize the bad news without hiding it or distorting it. (*Hint*: Minimize the space devoted to the bad news, subordinate it, embed it, or use the passive voice.) Then team up with a classmate and read each other's revisions. Did you both use the same approach in every case? Which approach seems to be most effective for each of the revised statements?

1. The airline can't refund your money. The "Conditions" segment on the back of your ticket states that there are no refunds for missed flights. Sometimes the airline makes exceptions, but only when life and death are involved. Of course, your ticket is still valid and can be used on a flight to the same destination.

2. I'm sorry to tell you, we can't supply the custom decorations you requested. We called every supplier and none of them can do what you want on such short notice. You can, however, get a standard decorative package on the same theme in time. I found a supplier that stocks these. Of course, it won't have quite the flair you originally requested.

3. We can't refund your money for the malfunctioning MP3 player. You shouldn't have immersed the unit in water while swimming; the users manual clearly states the unit is not designed to be used in adverse environments.

Indirect Approach: Buffers Answer the following pertaining to buffers.

4. You have to tell a local restaurant owner that your plans have changed and you have to cancel the 90-person banquet scheduled for next month. Do you need to use a buffer? Why or why not?

5. Write a buffer for a letter declining an invitation to speak at the association's annual fund-raising event. Show your appreciation for being asked.

6. Write a buffer for a letter rejecting a job applicant who speaks three foreign languages fluently. Include praise for the applicant's accomplishments.

Indirect or Direct Approach Select which approach you would use (direct or indirect) for the following negative messages.

7. An e-mail message to your boss informing her that one of your key clients is taking its business to a different accounting firm

8. An e-mail message to a customer informing her that one of the books she ordered from your website is temporarily out of stock

9. A letter to a customer explaining that the DVD burner he ordered for his new custom computer is on back order and that, as a consequence, the shipping of the entire order will be delayed

Activities

For active links to all websites discussed in this chapter, visit this text's website at www.prenhall.com/bovee. Locate your book and click on its Companion Website link. Then select Chapter 8, and click on "Featured Websites." Locate the name of the page or the URL related to the material in the text. Please note that links to sites that become inactive after publication of the book will be removed from the Featured Websites section.

1. **Analyze This Document** Read the following document, then (1) analyze the strengths and weaknesses of each sentence, and (2) revise each document so that it follows this chapter's guidelines.

   Your spring fraternity party sounds like fun. We're glad you've again chosen us as your caterer. Unfortunately, we have changed a few of our policies, and I wanted you to know about these changes in advance so that we won't have any misunderstandings on the day of the party.

   We will arrange the delivery of tables and chairs as usual the evening before the party. However, if you want us to set up, there is now a $100 charge for that service. Of course, you might want to get some of the brothers and pledges to do it, which would save you money. We've also added a small charge for cleanup. This is only $3 per person (you can estimate because I know a lot of people come and go later in the evening).

   Other than that, all the arrangements will be the same. We'll provide the skirt for the band stage, tablecloths, bar setup, and of course, the barbecue. Will you have the tubs of ice with soft drinks again? We can do that for you as well, but there will be a fee.

   Please let me know if you have any problems with these changes and we'll try to work them out. I know it's going to be a great party.

2. **Analyze This Document** Read the following document, then (1) analyze the strengths and weaknesses of each sentence, and (2) revise the message so that it follows this chapter's guidelines.

   I am responding to your letter of about six weeks ago asking for an adjustment on your wireless, model WM39Z. We test all our products before they leave the factory; therefore, it could not have been our fault that your hub didn't work.

   If you or someone in your office dropped the unit, it might have caused the damage. Or the damage could have been caused by the shipper if he dropped it. If so, you should file a claim with the shipper. At any rate, it wasn't our fault. The parts are already covered by warranty. However, we will provide labor for the repairs for $50, which is less than our cost, since you are a valued customer.

   We will have a booth at the upcoming trade fair there and hope to see you or someone from your office. We have many new models of computing and networking accessories that we're sure you'll want to see. I've enclosed our latest catalog. Hope to see you there.

3. **Analyze This Document** Read the following document, then (1) analyze the strengths and weaknesses of each sentence, and (2) revise the message so that it follows this chapter's guidelines.

I regret to inform you that you were not selected for our summer intern program at Equifax. We had over a thousand résumés and cover letters to go through and simply could not get to them all. We have been asked to notify everyone that we have already selected students for the 25 positions based on those who applied early and were qualified.

We're sure you will be able to find a suitable position for summer work in your field and wish you the best of luck. We deeply regret any inconvenience associated with our reply.

4. **Ethical Choices**   The insurance company where you work is planning to raise all premiums for health-care coverage. Your boss has asked you to read a draft of her letter to customers announcing the new, higher rates. The first two paragraphs discuss some exciting medical advances and the expanded coverage offered by your company. Only in the final paragraph do customers learn that they will have to pay more for coverage starting next year. What are the ethical implications of this draft? What changes would you suggest?

5. **Revising an E-Mail Message: Budgetary Cutbacks at Black & Decker**   The following bad-news e-mail about travel budget cutbacks contains numerous blunders. Using what you've learned in the chapter, read the message carefully and analyze its faults. Then use the questions below to outline and write an improved message.

Date: Wed, 28 May 2007 4:20:15 -0800
From: M. Juhasz, Travel & Meeting Services <mjuhasz@blackanddecker.com>
To: [mailing list]
CC:
BCC:
Attached:
Subject: Travel Budget Cuts Effective Immediately

Dear Traveling Executives:

We need you to start using some of the budget suggestions we are going to issue as a separate memorandum. These include using videoconference equipment instead of traveling to meetings, staying in cheaper hotels, arranging flights for cheaper times, and flying from less-convenient but also less-expensive suburban airports.

The company needs to cut travel expenses by fifty percent, just as we've cut costs in all departments of Black & Decker. This means you'll no longer be able to stay in fancy hotels and make last-minute, costly changes to your travel plans.

You'll also be expected to avoid hotel phone surcharges. Compose your e-mail offline when you're in the hotel. And never return a rental car with an empty tank! That causes the rental agency to charge us a premium price for the gas they sell when they fill it up upon your return.

You'll be expected to make these changes in your travel habits immediately.

Sincerely,
M. Juhasz

Travel & Meeting Services

a. Describe the flaws you discovered in this bad-news e-mail about company operations.

b. Develop a plan for rewriting the e-mail, using the direct approach for company insiders. The following steps will help you organize your efforts before you begin writing:
   1. Create an opening statement of the bad news, using the "you" attitude.
   2. Decide what explanation is needed to justify the news.

3. Determine whether you can use lists effectively.
4. Choose some positive suggestions you can include to soften the news.
5. Develop an upbeat closing.

c. Now rewrite the e-mail. Don't forget to leave ample time for revision of your own work before you turn it in.

6. **Teamwork: Revising a Letter—Refusal from Home Depot to New Faucet Manufacturer** The following letter rejecting a faucet manufacturer's product presentation contains many errors in judgment. Working with your classmates in a team effort, you should be able to improve its effectiveness as a negative message. First, analyze and discuss the letter's flaws. How can it be improved? Use the questions below to help guide your discussion and development of an improved version.

July 15, 2007
Pamela Wilson, Operations Manager
Sterling Manufacturing
133 Industrial Avenue
Gary, IN 46403

Dear Ms. Wilson:

We regret to inform you that your presentation at Home Depot's recent product review sessions in St. Petersburg did not meet our expert panelists' expectations. We require new products that will satisfy our customers' high standards. Yours did not match this goal.

Our primary concern is to continue our commitment to product excellence, customer knowledge, and price competitiveness, which has helped make Home Depot a Fortune 500 company with more than a thousand stores nationwide. The panel found flaws in your design and materials. Also, your cost per unit was too high.

The product review sessions occur annually. You are allowed to try again; just apply as you did this year. Again, I'm sorry things didn't work out for you this time.

Sincerely,
Hilary Buchman, Assistant to the Vice President, Sales
HB:kl

a. Describe the problems you found with this letter rejecting a product presentation.

b. Develop a plan for rewriting the letter, using the indirect approach. First, organize your thinking before you begin writing:
1. Select a buffer for the opening, using the "you" attitude.
2. Choose the reasons you'll use to explain the rejection.
3. Develop a way to soften or embed the bad news.
4. Create a conditional (if/then) statement to encourage the recipient to try again.
5. Find a way to close on a positive, encouraging note.

c. Now rewrite the letter. Don't forget to leave ample time for revision of your own work before you turn it in.

Expand Your Knowledge

Exploring the Best of the Web

Protect Yourself When Sending Negative Employment Messages   A visit to CCH's Business Owner's Toolkit, www.toolkit.cch.com, can help you reduce your legal liability, whether you are laying off an employee, firing an employee, or contemplating a company-wide reduction in your workforce. Find out the safest way to fire someone from a legal standpoint before it's too late. Learn why it's important to document disciplinary actions. Discover why some bad news should be given face-to-face and never by a letter or over the phone. Read CCH's advice, then answer these questions.

Exercises

1. What should a manager communicate to an employee during a termination meeting?
2. Why is it important to document employee disciplinary actions?
3. What steps should you take before firing an employee for misconduct or poor work?

Exploring the Web on Your Own

Review these chapter-related websites on your own to learn more about the negative issues human resources departments are facing today.

1. Workforce magazine online, www.workforce.com, has the basics and the latest on human resource issues such as recruiting, laws, managing the workforce, incentives, strategies, and more. Read the current edition online.

2. HR.com, www.hr.com, is the place to go to read about workplace trends, legislation affecting employers, recruiting, compensation, benefits, staffing, and more. Log on and learn.

3. BusinessTown.com, www.businesstown.com, offers information on a wide range of business topics, including advice on conducting successful employee performance reviews.

Learn Interactively

Interactive Study Guide

Visit www.prenhall.com/bovee, then locate your book and click on its Companion Website link. Select Chapter 8 to take advantage of the interactive "Chapter Quiz" to test your knowledge of chapter concepts. Receive instant feedback on whether you need additional studying. Also, visit the "Study Hall," where you'll find an abundance of valuable resources that will help you succeed in this course.

Peak Performance Grammar and Mechanics

If your instructor has required the use of "Peak Performance Grammar and Mechanics," either in your online course, through the access-code protected portion of the Companion Website, or on CD, you can improve your skill with commas, semicolons, and colons by using the "Peak Performance Grammar and Mechanics" module. Click "Punctuation," and then click "Punctuation I." Take the Pretest to determine whether you have any weak areas. Then review those areas in the Refresher Course. Take the Follow-Up Test to check your grasp of commas, semicolons, and colons. For an extra challenge or advanced practice, take the Advanced Test. Finally, for additional reinforcement in commas, go to the "Improve Your Grammar, Mechanics, and Usage" section that follows the cases, and complete the "Level 1: Self-Assessment" exercises.

CASES

Apply the three-step writing process to the following cases, as assigned by your instructor.

██ **BLOGGING**
██ **SKILLS**

1. Removing the Obstacles on the On-Ramp: Blog Posting to Ernst & Young Employees

Like many companies these days, the accounting firm Ernst & Young is fighting a brain drain as experienced executives and professionals leave in midcareer to pursue charitable interests, devote more time to family matters, or pursue a variety of other dreams or obligations. The problem is particularly acute among women, since on average they step off the career track more often than men do. As general manager of the largest division in the company, you've been tapped to draft a set of guidelines to make it easier for employees who've taken some time off to move back into the company.

However, as soon as word gets out about what you're planning, several of your top performers, people who've never left the company for personal time off—or "taken the off ramp," in current buzzword-speak—march into your office to complain. They fear that encouraging the "off-rampers" to return isn't fair to the employees who've remained loyal to the firm, as they put it. One goes as far to say that anyone who leaves the company doesn't deserve to be asked back. Two others claim that the additional experience and skills they've gained as they continued to work should guarantee them higher pay and more responsibilities than employees who took time off for themselves.[18]

Your Task As unhappy as these several employees are, the program needs to be implemented if Ernst & Young hopes to bring off-rampers back into the company—thereby making sure they don't go work for competitors instead. However, you also can't afford to antagonize the existing workforce, and if the people who've already complained are any indication, you have a sizable morale problem on your hands. You decide that your first step is to clearly explain why the program is necessary, including how it will benefit everyone in the company by making Ernst & Young more competitive. Write a short posting for the company's internal blog, explaining that in spite of the objections some employees have raised, the firm is going ahead with the program as planned. Balance this news (which some employees will obviously view as negative) with positive reassurances that all current employees will be treated fairly in terms of both compensation and promotion opportunities. Close with a call for continued communication on this issue,

inviting people to meet with you in person or to post their thoughts on the blog.

2. Listen to the Music, Partner: Delivering an Ultimatum to a Business Associate

You're a marketing manager for Stanton, one of the premier suppliers of DJ equipment (turntables, amplifiers, speakers, mixers, and related accessories). Your company's latest creation, the FinalScratch system, has been flying off retailers' shelves. Both professional and amateur DJs love the way that FinalScratch gives them the feel of working with vinyl records by letting them control digital music files from any analog turntable or CD player, while giving them access to the endless possibilities of digital music technology. (For more information about the product, go to www.stantondj.com.) Sales are strong everywhere except in Music99 stores, a retail chain in the Mid-Atlantic region. You suspect the cause: The owners of this chain refused to let their salespeople attend the free product training you offered when FinalScratch was introduced, claiming their people were smart enough to train themselves.

To explore the situation, you head out from Stanton headquarters in Hollywood, Florida, on an undercover shopping mission. After visiting a few Music99 locations, you're appalled by what you see. The salespeople in these stores clearly don't understand the FinalScratch concept, so they either give potential customers bad information about it or steer them to products from your competitors. No wonder sales are so bad at this chain.[19]

Your Task You're tempted to pull your products out of this chain immediately, but based on your experience in this market, you know how difficult and expensive it is to recruit new retailers. However, this situation can't go on; you're losing thousands of dollars of potential business every week. Write a letter to Jackson Fletcher, the CEO of Music99 (14014 Preston Pike, Dover, Delaware, 19901), expressing your disappointment in what you observed and explaining that the Music99 sales staff will need to agree to attend product training or else your company's management team will consider terminating the business relationship. You've met Mr. Fletcher in person once and talked on the phone several times, and you know him well enough to know that he will not be pleased by this ultimatum. Music99 does a good job selling other Stanton products—and he'll probably be furious to learn that you were "spying" on his sales staff.

3. Message to the Boss: Refusing a Project on Ethical Grounds

A not-so-secret secret is getting more attention than you'd really like after an article in *BusinessWeek* gave the world an inside look at how much money you and other electronics retailers make from extended warranties (sometimes called service contracts). The article explained that typically half of the warranty price goes to the salesperson as a commission and that only 20 percent of the total amount customers pay for warranties eventually goes to product repair.

You also know why extended warranties are such a profitable business. Many electronics products follow a predictable pattern of failure: a high failure rate early in their lives, then a "midlife" period during which failures go way down, and finally an "old age" period when failure rates ramp back up again (engineers refer to the phenomenon as the *bathtub curve* because it looks like a bathtub from the side—high at both ends and low in the middle). Those early failures are usually covered by manufacturers' warranties, and the extended warranties you sell are designed to cover that middle part of the life span. In other words, many extended warranties cover the period of time during which consumers are *least* likely to need them and offer no coverage when consumers need them *most*. (Consumers can actually benefit from extended warranties in a few product categories, including laptop computers and plasma TVs. Of course, the more sense the warranty makes for the consumer, the less financial sense it makes for your company.)[20]

Your Task Worried that consumers will start buying fewer extended warranties, your boss has directed you to put together a sales training program that will help cashiers sell the extended warranties even more aggressively. The more you ponder this challenge, though, the more you're convinced that your company should change its strategy so it doesn't rely so much on profits from these warranties. In addition to offering questionable value to the consumer, they risk creating a consumer backlash that could lead to lower sales of all your products. You would prefer to voice your concerns to your boss in person, but both of you are traveling on hectic schedules for the next week. You'll have to write an e-mail instead. Draft a brief message explaining why you think the sales training specifically and the warranties in general are both bad ideas.

4. When a Recall Isn't Really a Recall: Voice Recording Informing Customers That an Unsafe Product Won't Be Replaced

Vail Products of Toledo, Ohio, manufactured a line of beds for use in hospitals and other institutions where there is a need to protect patients who might otherwise fall out of bed and injure themselves (including patients with cognitive impairments or patterns of spasms or seizures). These "enclosed bed systems" use a netted canopy to keep patients in bed, rather than the traditional method of using physical restraints such as straps or tranquilizing drugs. The intent is humane, but the design is flawed: At least 30 patients have become trapped in the various parts of the mattress and canopy structure, and 8 of them have suffocated.

Working with the U.S. Food and Drug Administration (FDA), Vail issued a recall on the beds, as manufacturers often do in the case of unsafe products. However, the recall is not really a recall. Vail will not be replacing or modifying the beds, nor will it accept returns. Instead, the company is urging institutions to move patients to other beds if possible. Vail has also sent out revised manuals and warning labels to be placed on the beds. The company also announced that it is ceasing production of enclosed beds.

Your Task A flurry of phone calls from concerned patients, family members, and institutional staff is overwhelming the support staff. As a writer in Vail's corporate communications office, you've been asked to draft a short script to be recorded on the company's phone system. When people call the main number, they'll hear "Press 1 for information regarding the recall of Model 500, Model 1000, and Model 2000 enclosed beds." After they press 1, they'll hear the message you're about to write, explaining that although the action is classified as a recall, Vail will not be accepting returned beds, nor will it replace any of the affected beds. The message should also assure customers that Vail has already sent revised operating manuals and warning labels to every registered owner of the beds in question. The phone system has limited memory, and you've been directed to keep the message to 75 words or less.[21]

5. Sorry, But We Don't Have a Choice: E-Mail About Monitoring Employee Blogs

You can certainly sympathize with employees when they complain about having their e-mail and instant messages monitored, but you're only implementing a company policy that all employees agree to abide by when they join the company. Your firm, Webcor Builders of San Mateo, California, is one of the estimated 60 percent of U.S. companies with such monitoring systems in place. More and more companies use these systems (which typically operate by scanning messages for key words that suggest confidential, illegal, or otherwise inappropriate content) in an attempt to avoid instances of sexual harassment and other problems.

As the chief information officer, the manager in charge of computer systems in the company, you're often the target when employees complain about being monitored. Consequently, you know you're really going to hear it when employees learn that the monitoring program will be expanded to personal blogs as well.[22]

Your Task Write an e-mail to be distributed to the entire workforce, explaining that the automated monitoring program is about to be expanded to include employees' personal blogs. Explain that while you sympathize with employee concerns regarding privacy and freedom of speech, the management team's responsibility is to protect the company's intellectual property and the value of the company name. Therefore, employees' personal blogs will be added to the monitoring system to ensure that employees don't intentionally or accidentally expose company secrets or criticize management in a way that could harm the company.

▌PHONE
▌SKILLS

6. Reacting to a Lost Contract: Phone Call Rescinding a Job Offer

As the human resources manager at Alion Science and Technology, a military research firm in McLean, Virginia, you were thrilled when one of the nation's top computer visualization specialists accepted your job offer. Claus Gunnstein's skills would've made a major contribution to Alion's work in designing flight simulators and other systems. Unfortunately, the day after he accepted the offer, Alion received news that a major Pentagon contract had been canceled. In addition to letting several dozen current employees know that the company will be forced to lay them off, you need to tell Gunnstein that Alion has no choice but to rescind the job offer.[23]

Your Task Outline the points you'll need to make in a telephone call to Gunnstein. Pay special attention to your opening and closing statements. (You'll review your plans for the phone call with Alion's legal staff to make sure everything you say follows employment law guidelines; for now, just focus on the way you'll present the negative news to Gunnstein. Feel free to make up any details you need.)

▌IM
▌SKILLS

7. Midair Let-Down: Instant Message About Flight Cancellations at United Airlines

It used to be that airline passengers didn't learn about cancelled connecting flights until after they'd landed. Sometimes a captain would announce cancellations just before touching down at a major hub, but how were passengers to notify waiting relatives or business associates on the ground?

As a customer service supervisor for United Airlines, you've just received information that all United flights from Chicago's O'Hare International Airport to Boston's Logan International have been cancelled until further notice. A late winter storm has already blanketed Boston with snow and they're expecting freezing rain overnight. The way the weather report looks, United will probably be lodging Boston-bound connecting passengers in Chicago-area hotels tonight. Meanwhile, you'll be using some of United's newest communication tools to notify travelers of the bad news.

United Airlines now partners with Verizon Airfone to provide JetConnect information services, giving travelers access to instant messaging and other resources while they're airborne. For a small fee, they can plug their laptop computers into the Airfone jack, activating their own instant messaging software to send and receive messages. If they've signed up for United's EasyUpdate flight status notification service, they'll also receive instant message alerts for flight cancellations, delays, seating upgrades, and so on.

Your Task Write the cancellation alert, staying within the 65-word limit of many instant messaging programs. You might want to mention the airline's policy of providing overnight lodging for passengers who planned to use the Boston route as a connecting flight to complete journeys in progress.[24]

▌E-MAIL
▌SKILLS

8. Career Moves: E-Mail Refusing to Write a Recommendation

Tom Weiss worked in the office at Opal Pools and Patios for four months, under your supervision (you're office manager). On the basis of what he told you he could do, you started him off as a file clerk. However, his organizational skills proved inadequate for the job, so you transferred him to logging in accounts receivable, where he performed almost adequately. Then he assured you that his "real strength" was customer relations, so you moved him to the complaint department. After he spent three weeks making angry customers even angrier, you were convinced that no place in your office was appropriate for the talents of Mr. Weiss. Five weeks ago, you encouraged him to resign before being formally fired.

Today's e-mail brings a request from Weiss asking you to write a letter recommending him for a sales position with a florist shop. You can't assess Weiss's sales abilities, but you do know him to be an incompetent file clerk, a careless bookkeeper, and an insensitive customer service representative. Someone else is more likely to deserve the sales job, so you decide that you have done enough favors for Tom Weiss for one lifetime and plan to refuse his request.

Your Task Write an e-mail reply to Mr. Weiss (tomweiss@aol.com) indicating that you have chosen not to write a letter of recommendation for him.

9. Juggling Diversity and Performance: Memo Giving a Negative Performance Review at SBC Pacific Bell

As billing adjustments department manager at SBC Pacific Bell, you've been trained to handle a culturally diverse workforce. One of your best recent hires is 22-year-old Jorge Gutierrez. In record time, he was entering and testing complex price changes, mastering the challenges of your monumental computerized billing software. He was a real find—except for one problem: His close family ties often distract him from work duties.

His parents immigrated from Central America when Jorge and his sisters were young children, and you understand and deeply respect the importance that family plays in the lives of many Hispanic Americans. However, every morning Gutierrez's mother calls to be sure he got to work safely. Then his father calls. And three times this month, his younger sister has called him away from work with three separate emergencies. Friends and extended family members seem to call at all hours of the day.

Gutierrez says he's asked friends and family not to call his office number. Now they dial his cell phone instead. He's reluctant to shut off his cell phone during work hours, in case someone in his family needs him.

At this point, you have given Gutierrez several verbal warnings. You really can't afford to lose him, so you're hoping that a written, negative review will give him greater incentive to persuade friends and relatives. You'll deliver the letter in a meeting and help him find ways to resolve the issue within a mutually agreed-upon time frame.

Your Task Write the memo using suggestions in this chapter to help you put the bad news in a constructive light. Avoid culturally biased remarks or innuendo.

▌E-MAIL
▌SKILLS

10. Cell Phone Violations: E-Mail Message to Associates at Wilkes Artis Law Firm

"Company policy states that personnel are not to conduct business using cell phones while driving," David Finch reminds you. He's a partner at the law firm of Wilkes Artis in Washington, D.C., where you work as his administrative assistant.

You nod, waiting for him to explain. He already issued a memo about this rule last year, after that 15-year-old girl was hit and killed by an attorney from another firm. Driving back from a client meeting, the attorney was distracted while talking on her cell phone. The girl's family sued the firm and won $30 million, but that's not the point. The point is that cell phones can cause people to be hurt, even killed.

Finch explains, "Yesterday one of our associates called his secretary while driving his car. We can't allow this. According to the National Highway Transportation Safety Administration, 20 to 30 percent of all driving accidents are related to cell phone usage. From now on, any violation of our cell phone policy will result in suspension without pay, unless the call is a genuine health or traffic emergency."[25]

Your Task Finch asks you to write an e-mail message to all employees, announcing the new penalty for violating company policy.

▌TEAM
▌SKILLS

11. Safe Selling: Memo About Dangerous Scooters at The Sports Authority

You're not surprised that the Consumer Product Safety Commission (CPSC) has issued a consumer advisory on the dangers of motorized scooters. Unlike a motorcycle or bicycle, a scooter can be mastered by first-timers almost immediately. So both children and adults are hopping on, riding off—without helmets or other safety gear—and turning up with broken arms and legs, scraped faces, and bumped heads.

The popular electric or gas-powered scooters feature two wheels similar to in-line skates and travel 9 to 14 miles per hour. Over a six-month period, says the CPSC, emergency rooms around the country reported 2,250 motorized scooter injuries and 3 deaths. The riders who were killed (ages 6, 11, and 46), might all have lived if they'd been wearing helmets. As a result, some states have already enacted laws restricting scooter operations.

You are a merchandising assistant at The Sports Authority, which sells a wide selection of both the foot-powered ($25 to $150) and motorized scooters ($350 to $1,000). Your company is as concerned about the rise in injuries as they are about the CPSC advisory's potential negative effect on sales and legality. Thus, you've been assigned to a team that will brainstorm ideas for improving the situation. For example, one team member has suggested developing a safety brochure to give to customers; another wants to train salespeople to discuss safety issues with customers before they buy.

"We'd like to see increased sales of reflective gear ($6 to $15), helmets ($24), and elbow and knee pads ($19)," a store executive tells your team, "not to improve on our $1.5 billion annual revenue, but to save lives."

Your Task Working with classmates, discuss how The Sports Authority can use positive actions (including those mentioned in the case) to soften the effect of the CPSC advisory. Choose the best ideas and decide how to use them in a bad-news memo notifying the chain's 198 store managers about the consumer advisory. Then write the memo your team has outlined.[26]

▌IM
▌SKILLS

12. Quick Answer: Instant Message Turning Down Employee Request at Hewlett-Packard

If she'd asked you a week ago, Lewinda Johnson might have been granted her request to attend a conference on the use of blogging for business, which is being held in New York City next month. Instead, Johnson waited until you were stuck in this meeting, and she needs your response within the hour. She'll have to take no for an answer: With travel budgets under tight restrictions, you would need at least three days to send her request up the chain of command. Furthermore, Johnson hasn't given you sufficient justification for her attendance, since she's already familiar with blogging.

Your Task Write a 60- to 75-word instant message to Lewinda Johnson, declining her request. Decide whether the direct or indirect approach is appropriate.[27]

Improve Your Grammar, Mechanics, and Usage

Level 1: Self-Assessment—Semicolons and Colons

Review Sections 2.4 and 2.5 in the Handbook of Grammar, Mechanics, and Usage, and then look at the following 15 items.

In items 1–15, insert all required semicolons, colons, and commas.

1. This letter looks good that one doesn't.

2. I want to make one thing perfectly clear neither of you will be promoted if sales figures don't improve.

3. The Zurich airport has been snowed in therefore I won't be able to meet with you before January 4.

4. His motivation was obvious to get Meg fired.

5. Only two firms have responded to our survey J. J. Perkins and Tucker & Tucker.

6. Send a copy to Mary Kent Marketing Director Robert Bache Comptroller and Dennis Mann Sales Director.

7. Please be sure to inverview these employees next week Henry Gold, Doris Hatch, and George Iosupovich.

8. We have observed your hard work because of it we are promoting you to manager of your department.

9. You shipped three items on June 7 however we received only one of them.

10. The convention kit includes the following response cards, giveaways, brochures, and a display rack.

11. The workers wanted an immediate wage increase they had not had a raise in nearly two years.

12. This, then, is our goal for 2007 to increase sales 35 percent.

13. His writing skills are excellent however he still needs to polish his management style.

14. We would like to address three issues efficiency, profitability, and market penetration.

15. Remember this rule When in doubt, leave it out.

Level 2: Workplace Applications

The following items contain numerous errors in grammar, capitalization, punctuation, abbreviation, number style, word division, and vocabulary. Rewrite each sentence in the space provided, correcting all errors. Write *C* in the space after any sentence that is already correct.

1. Hector's, Julie's, and Tim's report was well-received by the Committee.

2. Everyone who are interested in signing up for the training seminar must do so by 3:00 o'clock PM on friday.

3. David Stern is a management and training expert that has spent a major part of his career coaching, counseling, and giving advise both to managers and workers.

4. Be aware and comply with local "zoning ordnances" and building codes.

5. Garrett didn't seem phased when her supervisor didn't except her excuse for being late, she forgot to set her alarm.

6. Copyright laws on the Internet is not always clearly defined, be sure your research doesn't extend to "borrowing" a competitors' keywords or copy.

7. Sauder Woodworking, in Archibald, Ohio sell a line of ready to assemble computer carts, desks, file cabinets, and furniture that is modular that can be mixed and matched to meet each business owners' personal taste.

8. Spamming is the most certain way to loose you're e-mail account, Web site, and you're reputation.

9. Us programmers have always tried to help others learn the tricks of the trade, especially Roger and myself.

10. The person whom was handling Miss Martinez' account told her that an error had been made by the bank in her favor.

11. "The trouble with focus groups" says Marketing Expert Frances Knight, "Is that consumers rarely act in real life they way they do in a "laboratory" setting."

12. In a industry in which design firms tend to come and go Skyline has licensed seventy products and grown to 8 employees.

13. If youv'e ever wondered why fast food restaurants are on the left and gift shops are on the right as you walk toward the gate into a newly-constructed airport you should read Malcolm Gladwells article, 'The Science of Shopping,' in the *New Yorker*.

14. Anyone whose starting a business should consider using their life story, as a way to generate customer's interest.

15. Having been in business since 1993, over 1000s of sales calls has been made by Mr. Jurzang, on prospects for his minority owned company.

Level 3: Document Critique

The following e-mail message may contain errors in grammar, capitalization, punctuation, abbreviation, number style, vocabulary, and spelling. You may also discover problems with wordiness, usage, and appropriateness of tone for negative messages. Correct all errors using standard proofreading marks (see Appendix C).

To: <all.employees>

Subject: Health insurance—Changes

Unlike many companies, Bright Manufacturing has always paid a hundred % of medical car insurance for it's employees, absorbing the recent 10–20 percent annual cost increases in order to provide this important benefit. This year; Blue Cross gave us some terrible news: the cost increase for our employee's medical coverage would be a staggering fourty percent per month next year

To mange the increase and continue to offer you and your family highquality medical coverage we have negotiated several changes with Blue Cross; a new cost saving alternative is also being offered by us:

1. Under the Blue Cross Plus plan, copay amounts for office visits will be ten dollars next year/ $50 for emergency room visits.

2. 80 % of employees' insurance coverage (including 10 percent of the cost increase) will be paid by Bright next year and 100 % of the prescription drug costs (including a 23 percent cost increase). The

remaining twenty percent of medical coverage will be deducted by us monthly from your salary, if you choose to remain on a Blue Cross Plus plan. We realize this is alot, but its still less than many companies charge their employees.

3. A fully paid alternative health plan, Blue Cross HMO, will now be provided by Bright at no cost to employees. But be warned that there is a deadline. If you want to switch to this new plan you must do so during our open enrollment period, Nov. 20 to December 1, and we will not consder applications for the change after that time so don't get your forms in late.

There are forms available in the Human Resources office for changing your coverage. They must be returned between November 20 and December 1. If you wish to remain on a Blue Cross Plus policy, you do not need to notify us; payroll deductions for company employees on the plan will occur automatic beginning January first.

If you have questions, please call our new Medical Benefits Information line at ext. 3392. Our Intranet sight will also provide you easy with information about health care coverage online if you click the "Medical Benefits" icon. Since our founding in 1946, we have provided our company employees with the best medical coverage available. We all hate rising costs and although things are looking bleak for the future but we're doing all we can do to hold on to this helpful benefit for you.

Lucinda Goodman, Benefits Mangr., Human resources

9

Writing Persuasive Messages

Learning Objectives

After studying this chapter, you will be able to

1 Apply the three-step writing process to persuasive messages

2 Identify seven ways to establish credibility in persuasive messages

3 Describe the AIDA model for persuasive messages

4 Distinguish between emotional and logical appeals and discuss how to balance them

5 Identify four common mistakes in writing persuasive messages

6 Discuss an effective approach to identifying selling points and audience benefits

7 Identify steps you can take to avoid ethical lapses in marketing and sales messages

The "you" attitude is important in any business message, but it's absolutely vital in persuasive writing. If your audience doesn't believe that you have their best interests at heart, they won't be easily persuaded by anything you write. Follow the advice of successful persuasive writers such as Brian Clark (quoted at the left) and make sure your messages are about your readers, not about you.

Using the Three-Step Writing Process for Persuasive Messages

Persuasion is the attempt to change someone's attitudes, beliefs, or actions.

Every business depends on persuasive messages in both internal and external communication. Whether you're convincing your boss to open a new office in Europe or encouraging potential customers to try your products, you'll use many of the same techniques of **persuasion**—the attempt to change an audience's attitudes, beliefs, or actions.[2] Successful professionals understand that persuasion is not about trickery or getting people to make choices that aren't in their best interest; rather, it lets your audience know they have a choice and helps them choose to agree with you.[3]

Step 1: Plan Your Message

Unlike the routine positive messages discussed in Chapter 7, persuasive messages aim to influence audiences who may be inclined to resist at first. Even if they agree that your idea or product is attractive, they face so many options in today's crowded markets that you'll often need to use persuasive techniques to convince them that your choice is the best of all the attractive alternatives.

In today's information-saturated business environment, having a great idea or a great product is no longer enough. Every day, untold numbers of good ideas go unnoticed and good products go unsold simply because the messages meant to promote them aren't compelling enough to rise above the competitive noise. Creating successful persuasive messages in these challenging situations demands careful attention to all four tasks in the planning step, starting with an insightful analysis of your purpose and your audience.

Analyzing Your Situation

In defining your purpose, make sure you're clear about what you really hope to achieve. Suppose you want to persuade top management to support a particular research project. But what does "support" mean? Do you want them to pat you on the back and wish you well? Or do you want them to give you a staff of five researchers and a $1 million annual budget? All of the aspects of creating an audience profile that you learned in Chapter 4 apply to persuasive messages. If your message is aimed at a single large organization, you can direct it specifically toward a few top managers who make the kinds of decisions you're asking for. In contrast, for a message aimed at a million consumers, you'll never know each one individually; the best you can do is sample a small number who represent the entire audience.

The best persuasive messages are closely connected to your audience's desires and interests.[4] Consider these important questions: Who is my audience? What are their needs? What do I want them to do? How might they resist? Are there alternative positions I need to examine? What does the decision-maker consider the most important issue? How might the organization's culture influence my strategy?

To understand and categorize audience needs, you can refer to specific information such as **demographics** (the age, gender, occupation, income, education, and other quantifiable characteristics of the people you're trying to persuade) and **psychographics** (personality, attitudes, lifestyle, and other psychological characteristics). Both types of information are strongly influenced by culture. When analyzing your audience, take into account their cultural expectations and practices so that you don't undermine your persuasive message by using an inappropriate appeal or by organizing your message in a way that seems unfamiliar or uncomfortable to your audience.

Gathering Information

Once your situation analysis is complete, you need to gather the information necessary to close the gap between what your audience knows, believes, or feels right now and what you want them to know, believe, or feel as a result of receiving your message. Most persuasive messages are a combination of logical and emotional factors, but the ratio varies dramatically from message to message. You can get a sense of this variation by comparing the websites of American Fastener Technology (industrial goods, www.americanfastener.com), Chrysler (automobiles, www.chrysler.com), and Lancôme (beauty products, www.lancome.com).

American Fasteners relies primarily on straightforward product information to convince buyers, whereas Lancôme tries to evoke a more emotional response through its visual and verbal imagery. Chrysler is somewhere in the middle, providing plenty of facts and figures about its cars but also including strong emotional messages about the joy of driving. By identifying the mix of factors that will most likely persuade your audience, you'll know what sort of information you need to gather. You'll learn more about the types of information to offer when you read "Developing Persuasive Business Messages" later in the chapter. Chapter 10 presents advice on how to find the information you need.

Selecting the Right Medium

Persuasive messages can be found in virtually every communication medium ever devised, from instant messages and computer animations to radio ads and skywriting. For persuasive business messages, your choice of medium will closely follow the guidelines presented in Chapter 4. However, for marketing and sales messages, your options are far more numerous. In fact, advertising agencies employ media specialists whose only job is to analyze the media options available and select the most cost-effective combination for each client and each ad campaign.

To further complicate matters, various members of your audience might prefer different media for the same message. Some consumers like to do all their car shopping in person, whereas others do most of their research online. Some people don't mind promotional e-mail messages for products they're interested in; others resent every piece of commercial e-mail they receive. If you can't be sure you can reach most or all of your audience with a single medium, you'll need to use two or more, such as following up an e-mail campaign with printed letters.

> You may need to use multiple media to reach your entire audience.

Organizing Your Information

The most effective main ideas for persuasive messages have one thing in common: They are about the receiver, not the sender. For instance, if you're trying to convince others to join you in a business venture, explain how it will help them, not how it will help you.

Limiting your scope is vital: In many cases your message is not entirely welcome, so you need to make your point quickly. Include only the information needed to encourage your audience to take the next step toward the ultimate decision or ultimate action you want.

> Limit your scope to include only the information needed to help your audience take the next step toward making a favorable decision.

As with routine and negative messages, the best organizational approach is based on your audience's likely reaction to your message. However, because the nature of persuasion is to convince your audience to change their attitudes, beliefs, or actions, most persuasive messages use an indirect approach. That means you'll want to explain your reasons and build interest before asking for a decision or for action—or perhaps even before revealing your purpose. In contrast, when you have a close relationship with your audience, and the message is welcome or at least neutral, a direct approach can be effective (Figure 9.1).

> Use the direct approach if your audience is ready to hear your proposal.

If you use the direct approach, keep in mind that even though your audience may be easy to convince, you'll still want to include at least a brief justification or explanation. Don't expect your reader to accept your idea on blind faith. For example, consider the following two openers:

Instead of This	Write This
I recommend building our new retail outlet on the West Main Street site.	After comparing the four possible sites for our new retail outlet, I recommend West Main Street as the only site that fulfills our criteria for visibility, proximity to mass transportation, and square footage.

> Choice of approach is also influenced by your position (or authority within the organization) relative to your audience's.

Your choice between the direct and indirect approaches is also influenced by the extent of your authority, expertise, or power in an organization. As a first-line manager writing a persuasive message to top management, you may try to be diplomatic and use an indirect approach. On the other hand, you may try to save your supervisors time by using a direct approach, which might be perceived as brash and presumptuous. Similarly, when writing a persuasive message to employees, you may use the indirect approach to ease into a major change, but your audience might see your message as weak, even wishy-washy. Think carefully about your corporate culture and what your audience expects before selecting your approach.

FIGURE 9.1   Proposal E-Mail Using a Direct Approach
In this e-mail message, Bette McGiboney, an administrative assistant to the athletic director of Auburn University, presents a solution to the problem of high phone bills during the month of August. She already has a close relationship with her boss, who is likely to welcome the money-saving idea, so the direct approach is a fast, efficient way to communicate her proposal.

Uses the subject line to announce the nature of the message (a proposal) and a compelling benefit to the reader (saving money)

Describes the solution in enough detail to help the reader imagine how it will work

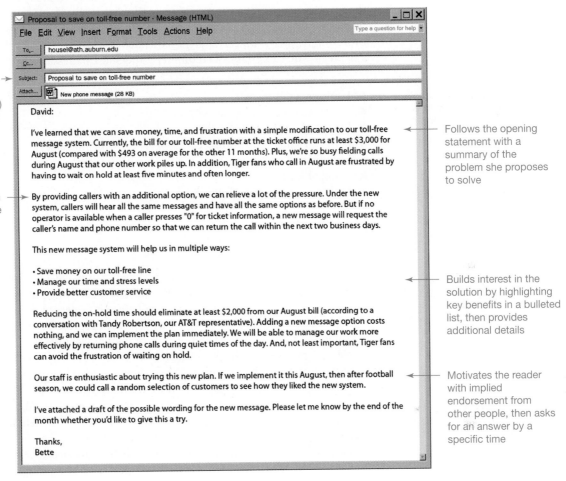

Follows the opening statement with a summary of the problem she proposes to solve

Builds interest in the solution by highlighting key benefits in a bulleted list, then provides additional details

Motivates the reader with implied endorsement from other people, then asks for an answer by a specific time

Step 2: Write Your Message

The generally uninvited and occasionally even unwelcome nature of persuasive messages means the "you" attitude is more critical than ever when it comes to writing them. You can encourage a more welcome reception by (1) using positive and polite language, (2) understanding and respecting cultural differences, (3) being sensitive to organizational cultures, and (4) taking steps to establish your credibility.

Positive language usually happens naturally with persuasive messages, since you're promoting an idea or product you believe in. However, polite language isn't as automatic, surprisingly enough. For instance, some writers inadvertently insult their readers by implying that they've been making poor choices in the past.

Your understanding and respect for cultural differences will help you satisfy the needs of your audience and will help your audience respect you. That's because persuasion is different in different cultures. In France, an aggressive, hard-sell technique is likely to antagonize your audience. In Germany, where people tend to focus on technical matters, plan on verifying any figures you use for support, and make sure they are exact. In Sweden, audiences tend to focus on theoretical questions and strategic implications, whereas U.S. audiences are usually concerned with more practical matters.[5]

Just as culture within various social groups affects the success of a persuasive message, so too does the culture within various organizations. For instance, some organizations

Persuasive messages are often unexpected or even unwelcome, so the "you" attitude is crucial.

Cultural differences influence your persuasion attempts.

handle disagreement and conflict in an indirect, behind-the-scenes way, whereas others accept and even encourage open discussion and sharing of differing viewpoints. When you accept and follow these traditions, you show the audience that you understand them and respect their values. Finally, when trying to persuade a skeptical or hostile audience, you must convince people that you know what you're talking about and that you're not trying to mislead them. Your credibility is even more important in persuasive messages than it is in other business messages. Without it, your efforts to persuade will seem ineffective at best and manipulative at worst. Research strongly suggests that most managers overestimate their own credibility—considerably.[6] In addition to the steps you learned in Chapter 4, you can establish credibility in persuasive messages by

> Audiences often respond unfavorably to over-the-top language, so keep your writing simple and straightforward.

- Using clear language
- Supporting your message with facts
- Identifying your sources
- Being an expert (or finding one to support your message)
- Establishing common ground with your audience
- Being objective
- Displaying your good intentions

Step 3: Complete Your Message

The pros know from experience that the details can make or break a persuasive message, so they're careful not to shortchange this part of the writing process. Advertisers may have a dozen or more people review a message before it's released to the public. Ads and commercial websites are often tested extensively with representative recipients to make sure the intended audience gets the information the sender intends.

When you evaluate your content, try to judge your argument objectively and try not to overestimate your credibility. When revising for clarity and conciseness, carefully match the purpose and organization to audience needs. If possible, ask an experienced colleague who knows your audience well to review your draft. Your design elements must complement, not detract from, your argument. In addition, meticulous proofreading will identify any mechanical or spelling errors that would weaken your persuasive potential. Finally, make sure your distribution methods fit your audience's expectations as well as your purpose. Don't start your persuasive efforts on the wrong foot by annoying your audience with an unwelcome delivery method.

With the three-step model in mind, you're ready to begin composing persuasive messages, starting with persuasive business messages (those that try to convince readers to approve new projects, enter into business partnerships, and so on), followed by marketing and sales messages (those that try to convince readers to consider and then purchase products and services).

Developing Persuasive Business Messages

> Your success in business will depend on writing persuasive messages effectively.

Your success as a businessperson is closely tied to your ability to convince others to accept new ideas, change old habits, or act on your recommendations. Even early in your career, you might have the opportunity to convince your manager to let you join an exciting project or to improve an important process. As you move into positions of greater responsibility, your persuasive messages could start to influence multimillion-dollar investments and the careers of hundreds or thousands of employees. Obviously, the increase in your persuasive skills needs to be matched by the care and thoroughness of your analysis and planning so that the ideas you convince others to adopt are sound.

Persuasive messages are a diverse category, with audiences that range from a single person in your own department to government agencies, investors, clients, community leaders, and other external groups. Most of your messages will consist of *persuasive business messages*, which are any persuasive messages designed to elicit a preferred response in a nonsales situation.

Strategies for Persuasive Business Messages

The goal of your persuasive business message is to convince your reader that your request or idea is reasonable and that it will benefit your reader in some way. Within the context of the three-step process, effective persuasion involves four essential strategies: framing your arguments, balancing emotional and logical appeals, reinforcing your position, and anticipating objections.

Framing Your Arguments

Many persuasive messages follow some variation of the indirect approach. In fact, experts in persuasive communication have developed a number of specific models that take an indirect approach. One of the most commonly used is called the **AIDA model**, which organizes your presentation into those four phases: (1) **a**ttention, (2) **i**nterest, (3) **d**esire, and (4) **a**ction (see Table 9.1):

Organize persuasive messages using the AIDA model:
- Attention
- Interest
- Desire
- Action

- **Attention.** Your first objective is to encourage your audience to want to hear about your problem, idea, new product—whatever your main idea is. Write a brief and engaging opening sentence, with no extravagant claims or irrelevant points. And be sure to find some common ground on which to build your case (Figure 9.2).

- **Interest.** Explain the relevance of your message to your audience. Continuing the theme you started with, paint a more detailed picture with words. Get your audience thinking.

- **Desire.** Help audience members embrace your idea by explaining how the change will benefit them. Reduce resistance by identifying and answering in advance any questions the audience might have. Back up your claims in order to increase audience willingness to take the action that you suggest in the next section.

- **Action.** Suggest the specific action you want your audience to take. Making the action as easy as possible reduces the chance that they will delay or forget. Include a deadline when applicable.

The AIDA model is tailor-made for using the indirect approach, allowing you to save your main idea for the action phase. However, this model can also be used for the direct approach, in which case you use your main idea as an attention-getter, build interest with your argument, create desire with your evidence, and emphasize your main idea in the action phase with the specific action you want your audience to take.

The AIDA model is ideal for the indirect approach.

When your AIDA message uses an indirect approach and is delivered by memo or e-mail, keep in mind that your subject line usually catches your reader's eye first. Your challenge is to make it interesting and relevant enough to capture reader attention without

Table 9.1	The AIDA Model
Phase	**Objective**
Attention	Get the reader's attention with the benefit that is of real interest or value.
Interest	Build the reader's interest by further explaining benefits and appealing to her logic or emotions.
Desire	Build desire by providing additional supporting details and answering potential questions.
Action	Motivate the reader to take the next step by closing with a compelling call to action and providing a convenient means for the reader to respond.

FIGURE 9.2   Persuasive Message Using the AIDA Model

Randy Thumwolt uses the AIDA model in a persuasive memo about a program that would try to reduce Host Marriott's annual plastics costs and try to curtail consumer complaints about the company's recycling record. Note how Thumwolt "sells the problem" before attempting to sell the solution. Few people are interested in hearing about solutions to problems they don't know about or don't believe exist. His interest section introduces an additional, unforeseen problem with plastic product containers.

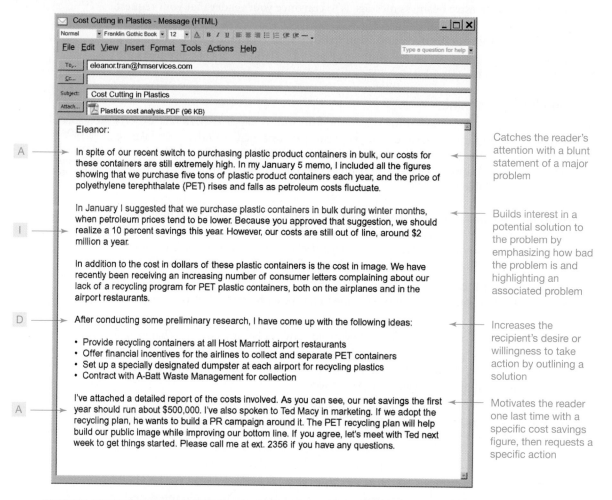

Pointers for Developing Persuasive Messages

- Open with a reader benefit, stimulating question, eye-opening fact, or other attention-getter.
- Balance emotional and logical appeals to help the audience accept your message.
- Indicate that you understand the reader's concerns.
- Elaborate on the principle benefits as you continue to stimulate interest and build desire.
- Support your claims with relevant evidence.
- Confidently ask for a decision, stressing the positive results of the action.
- Include pertinent action details such as deadlines.
- Make the desired response simple to understand and easy to accomplish.
- Close with one last reminder of how the audience can benefit.

---

revealing your main idea. If you put your request in the subject line, you're likely to get a quick "no" before you've had a chance to present your arguments:

Instead of This	Write This
Proposal to install new phone message system	Reducing the cost of our toll-free number

Balancing Emotional and Logical Appeals

Few persuasive appeals are purely logical or purely emotional, and a key skill in persuasive communication is finding the right balance of the two for each message. Take four factors into consideration: (1) the actions you hope to motivate, (2) your reader's expectations, (3) the degree of resistance you need to overcome, and (4) how far you feel empowered to go to sell your point of view.[7]

An **emotional appeal** calls on feelings, basing the argument on audience needs or sympathies; however, such an appeal must be subtle.[8] For instance, you can make use of the emotion surrounding certain words. The word *freedom* evokes strong feelings, as do words such as *success, prestige, compassion, free, value,* and *comfort.* Such words put your audience in a certain frame of mind and help them accept your message. However, emotional appeals aren't necessarily effective by themselves. For most business situations, the best use of emotion is working in tandem with logic. Even if your audience reaches a conclusion based on emotions, they'll look to you to provide logical support as well.

A **logical appeal** calls on reason. When appealing to your audience's logic, you might use three types of reasoning:

- **Analogy.** With analogy, you reason from specific evidence to specific evidence. For instance, to persuade reluctant employees to attend a planning session, you might use a town meeting analogy, comparing your company to a small community and your employees to valued members of that community.

- **Induction.** With inductive reasoning, you work from specific evidence to a general conclusion. To convince your team to change a certain production process, you could point out that every company who has adopted it has increased profits, so it must be a smart idea.

- **Deduction.** With deductive reasoning, you work from a generalization to a specific conclusion. To persuade your boss to hire additional customer support staff, you might point to industry surveys that show how crucial customer satisfaction is to corporate profits.

Every method of reasoning is vulnerable to misuse, both intentional and unintentional, so verify each of your rational arguments before you distribute your message. To avoid faulty logic, practice the following guidelines:[9]

- **Avoid hasty generalizations.** Make sure you have plenty of evidence before drawing conclusions.

- **Avoid circular reasoning.** *Circular reasoning* is a logical fallacy in which you try to support your claim by restating it in different words. The statement "We know temporary workers cannot handle this task because temps are unqualified for it" doesn't prove anything because the claim and the supporting evidence are essentially identical.

- **Avoid attacking an opponent.** Attack the argument your opponent is making, not your opponent's character.

- **Avoid oversimplifying a complex issue.** For instance, don't reduce a complex situation to a simple "either/or" statement if the situation isn't that simple or clear-cut.

- **Avoid mistaken assumptions of cause and effect.** If you can't isolate the impact of a specific factor, you can't assume it's the cause of whatever effect you're discussing. The complexity of many business situations makes cause and effect a particular challenge. You lowered prices and sales went up. Were lower prices the cause? Maybe, but the sales increase might've been caused by a competitor with delivery problems, a better advertising campaign, or any of a host of other factors.

- **Avoid faulty analogies.** Be sure that the two objects or situations being compared are similar enough for the analogy to hold. Even if A resembles B in one respect, this may not hold true in other important respects.

Emotional appeals attempt to connect with the reader's feelings or sympathies.

Logical appeals are based on the reader's notions of reason; these appeals can use analogy, induction, or deduction.

Logical flaws include hasty generalizations, circular reasoning, attacks on opponents, oversimplifications, false assumptions of cause and effect, and faulty analogies.

Reinforcing Your Position

Choose your words carefully and use abstractions to enhance emotional content.

After you've worked out the basic elements of your argument, step back and look for ways to bolster the strength of your position. Can you find more powerful words to convey your message? For example, if your company is in serious financial trouble, talking about *survival* is more powerful than talking about *continued operations*. As with any powerful tool, though, use vivid language and abstractions carefully and honestly.

In addition to individual word choices, consider using *metaphors* and other figures of speech. If you want to describe a quality-control system as being designed to catch every possible product flaw, you might call it a "spider web" to imply that it catches everything that comes its way.

Beyond the specific wording of your message, consider timing and other forces and factors that can reinforce your position. For instance, virtually all organizations operate in cycles of some sort—incoming payments from major customers, outgoing tax payments, seasonal demand for products, and so on. Study these patterns to see whether they might work for or against you. The best time to ask for additional staff might be right after a period of intense activity that prompted multiple customers to complain about poor service, when the experience is still fresh in everyone's mind. If you wait several months for the annual budgeting cycle, the emotional aspect of the experience will have faded, and your request will look like just another cost increase.

Anticipating Objections

Even powerful persuasive messages can encounter resistance from the audience.

Even the most powerful persuasive messages can expect to encounter some resistance. Anticipate as many objections as you can and address them before your audience can even bring them up. You'll not only get this issue out of the way sooner, but you'll demonstrate a broad appreciation of the issue and imply confidence in your message.[10]

Present both sides of an issue when you expect to encounter strong resistance.

If you expect a hostile audience that is biased against your plan from the beginning, be sure to present all sides of the situation. As you cover each option, explain the pros and cons. You'll gain additional credibility if you present these options before presenting your recommendation or decision.[11] If you can, involve your audience in the design of the solution; people are more likely to support ideas they help create.

Avoid the common mistakes of using a hard sell, resisting compromise, relying solely on argumentation, and assuming persuasion is a one-time event.

When putting together persuasive arguments, avoid common mistakes such as these:[12]

- **Using an up-front hard sell.** Don't push. Setting out a strong position at the start of a persuasive message puts potential opponents on guard.
- **Resisting compromise.** Don't dig your heels in. Persuasion is a process of give-and-take.
- **Relying solely on great arguments.** Great arguments are important, but connecting with your audience on the right emotional level and communicating through vivid language are just as vital.
- **Assuming persuasion is a one-shot effort.** Persuasion is often a process, not a one-time event. In many cases, you need to move your audience along one small step at a time, rather than trying to convince them to say "yes" in one huge step.

Common Examples of Persuasive Business Messages

Throughout your career, you'll have numerous opportunities to write persuasive messages within your organization: selling a supervisor on an idea for cutting costs, suggesting more efficient operating procedures, eliciting cooperation from competing departments, winning employee support for a new benefits package, requesting money for new equipment or funding for a special project. Similarly, you may send a variety of persuasive messages to people outside the organization: promoting products, soliciting investment funds, shaping public opinions, or requesting adjustments that go beyond a supplier's contractual obligations. In addition, many of the routine requests you studied in Chapter 7 can become persuasive messages if you want a nonroutine result or believe that you haven't received fair treatment. Most of these messages can be divided into persuasive requests for action, persuasive presentation of ideas, and persuasive claims and requests for adjustment.

Persuasive Requests for Action

The bulk of your persuasive business messages will involve requests for action. In some cases, your request will be anticipated, so the direct approach is fine. In others, you'll need to introduce your intention indirectly, and the AIDA model is ideal for this purpose.

When making a persuasive request for action, be sure to use the AIDA plan to frame your argument.

Open with an attention-getting device and show readers that you know something about their concerns. Use the interest and desire sections of your message to demonstrate that you have good reason for making such a request and to cover what you know about the situation: the facts and figures, the benefits of helping, and any history or experience that will enhance your appeal. Your goals are (1) to gain credibility (for yourself and your request) and (2) to make your readers believe that helping you will indeed help solve a significant problem. Once you've demonstrated that your message is relevant to your reader, you can close with a request for some specific action (Figure 9.3).

Persuasive Presentation of Ideas

Most internal persuasive messages focus on getting the audience to make a specific decision or take some specific action. However, you will encounter situations in which you simply want to change attitudes or beliefs about a particular topic, without asking the audience to decide or do anything—at least not yet. The goal of your first message might be nothing more than convincing your audience to re-examine long-held opinions or admit the possibility of new ways of thinking.

Sometimes the objective of persuasive messages is simply to encourage people to consider a new idea.

For instance, you think your company is spending too much time processing payroll, and you've found an outside firm that can do it for less money than you now spend on internal staff and systems (a practice known as *outsourcing*). However, your company president is philosophically opposed to outsourcing any critical business function. Until and unless you can bring about a change in the president's way of thinking, there is no point is pushing for a decision about outsourcing.

Persuasive Claims and Requests for Adjustments

Most claim letters are routine messages and use the direct approach discussed in Chapter 7. However, you may encounter situations in which you want someone to consider an unusual claim or request. For instance, you might have signed off on a project done by an outside contractor, then discovered problems with the work later. You previously said the work was acceptable, so you'll need to build a persuasive case to ask for additional work or perhaps a refund.

Document Makeover

Improve This E-Mail Message

To practice correcting drafts of actual documents, visit your online course or the access-code-protected Prentice Hall Business Communication Website. Click "Document Makeovers," then click Chapter 9. You will find an e-mail message that contains problems and errors relating to what you've learned in this chapter about writing persuasive business messages. Use the Final Draft decision tool to create an improved version of this e-mail. Check the message for its effectiveness at gaining attention, building interest, stimulating desire, motivating action, focusing on the primary goal, and dealing with resistance.

FIGURE 9.3   Using the AIDA Model to Request Action

Leslie Jorgensen believes the new Airbus A380 could help Qantas meet its growth needs while lowering its operating costs. Here she uses the AIDA model to solicit her boss's approval for a study of the plane's market potential. Note that because she also wants to provide some printed materials to support her argument, she opted for a printed memo rather than an e-mail message.

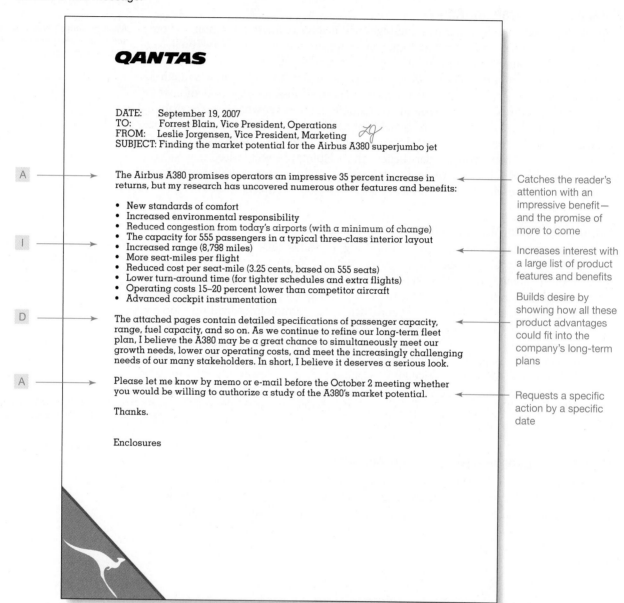

Fortunately, most people in business are open to settling claims fairly. It's to their advantage to maintain customer goodwill by resolving problems quickly. The key ingredients of a good persuasive claim are a complete and specific review of the facts and a confident and positive tone. Assume that the other person is not trying to cheat you but that you also have the right to be satisfied with the transaction. Begin persuasive claims by stating the basic problem or reviewing what has been done about it so far. Include a statement that both you and your audience can agree with or that clarifies what you wish to convince your audience about. Be as specific as possible about what you want to happen.

Next, give your reader a good reason for granting your claim. Show how your audience is responsible for the problem, and appeal to your reader's sense of fair play, goodwill, or moral responsibility. Explain how you feel about the problem, but don't get carried away, don't complain too much, and don't make threats. People generally respond more favorably to requests that are both calm and reasonable.

Developing Marketing and Sales Messages

Marketing and sales messages use the same basic techniques as other persuasive messages, with the added emphasis of encouraging someone to participate in a commercial transaction. Although the terms *marketing message* and *sales message* are often used interchangeably, they are slightly different: Marketing messages usher potential buyers through the purchasing process without asking them to make an immediate decision; that's when sales messages take over. Marketing messages focus on such tasks as introducing new brands to the public, providing competitive comparisons, encouraging customers to visit websites for more information, and reminding buyers that a particular product or service is available. In contrast, a sales message makes a specific request for people to place an order for a particular product or service.

Marketing and sales messages use many of the same techniques as persuasive business messages.

Strategies for Marketing and Sales Messages

Most marketing and sales messages, particularly in larger companies, are created and delivered by professionals with specific training in marketing, advertising, sales, or public relations. However, you may be called on to review the work of these specialists or even to write such messages in smaller companies, so a good understanding of how these messages work will help you be a more effective manager. The basic strategies to consider include assessing customer needs, analyzing your competition, determining key selling points and benefits, anticipating purchase objections, applying the AIDA model, and maintaining high standards of ethics, legal compliance, and etiquette.

Assessing Audience Needs

As with every other business message, successful marketing and sales messages start with an understanding of audience needs. For some products and services, this assessment is a simple matter. For instance, customers compare only a few basic attributes when purchasing copy or printer paper, including weight, brightness, color, and finish. In contrast, they might consider dozens of features when shopping for real estate, cars, professional services, and other complex purchases. In addition, customer needs often extend beyond the basic product or service. For example, clothes do far more than simply keep you warm. What you wear makes a statement about who you are, which social groups you want to be associated with (or not), and how you view your relationship with the people around you.

Purchasing decisions often involve more than just the basic product or service.

Analyzing Your Competition

Marketing and sales messages nearly always compete with messages from other companies trying to reach the same audience. When Chrysler plans a sales letter to introduce a new model to current customers, the company knows that its audience has also been exposed to messages from Ford, Honda, Volkswagen, and numerous other car companies. In crowded markets, writers sometimes have to search for words and phrases that other companies aren't already using. They might also want to avoid themes, writing styles, or creative approaches that are too similar to those of competitive messages.

Most marketing and sales messages have to compete for the audience's attention.

Determining Key Selling Points and Benefits

With some insight into audience needs and existing messages from the competition, you're ready to decide which benefits and features of your product or service to highlight. For all but the simplest products, you'll want to prioritize the items you plan to discuss. You'll also want to distinguish between selling points and benefits. As Table 9.2 shows, **selling points** are the most attractive features of an idea or product, whereas **benefits** are the particular advantages that readers will realize from those features. Selling points focus on the product. Benefits focus on the user. For example, if you say that your snow shovel

Selling points focus on the product; benefits focus on the user.

Table 9.2   Features Versus Benefits

Product Feature	Customer Benefit
Our easy financing plan includes no money down, no interest, and no payments for 24 months.	You can buy what you want right now, even if you have limited cash on hand.
Our marketing communication audit accurately measures the impact of your advertising and public relations efforts.	You can find out whether your message is reaching the target audience and whether you're spending your marketing budget in the best possible manner.
The spools in our fly fishing reels are machined from solid blocks of aircraft-grade aluminium.	Go fishing with confidence: These lightweight reels will stand up to the toughest conditions.

has "an ergonomically designed handle," you've described a good feature. But to persuade someone to buy that shovel, say "the ergonomically designed handle will reduce your risk of back injury." That's a benefit.

Anticipating Purchase Objections

Anticipating objections is crucial to effective marketing and sales messages.

As with persuasive business messages, marketing and sales messages usually encounter objections, and once again, the best way to handle them is to identify them up front and try to address as many as you can. Keep in mind that with marketing and sales messages, you often don't get a second chance to present your case. If your website for fashion jewelry aimed at college-age consumers strikes visitors as too juvenile, for instance, they'll click away to another site within seconds.

Objections can range from high price to low quality to a lack of compatibility with existing products. Perceived risk is another common objection. Consumers might worry that a car won't be safe enough for a family or that a jacket will make them look unattractive. Business buyers might worry about disrupting operations or failing to realize the financial returns on a purchase. Price can be a particularly tricky issue in any promotional message. Whether you highlight or downplay the price of your product, prepare your readers for it with words such as *luxurious* and *economical*.

If price is a major selling point, give it a position of prominence, such as in the headline or as the last item in a paragraph. If price is not a major selling point, you can handle it in several ways. You could leave the price out altogether or de-emphasize it by putting the figure in the middle of a paragraph that comes well after you've presented the benefits and selling points:

Emphasizes the rarity of the edition to signal value and thus prepare the reader for the price that follows

Embeds the actual price in the middle of a sentence and ties it in with another remainder of the exclusivity of the offer

Only 100 prints of this exclusive, limited-edition lithograph will be created. On June 15, they will be made available to the general public, but you can reserve one now for only $3,500, the special advance reservation price. Simply rush the enclosed reservation card back today so that your order is in before the June 15 publication date.

If price is likely to be a major objection, look for persuasive ways to minimize customer resistance. Comparing your price with a comparable product or service is a common tactic: "The cost of owning your own exercise equipment is less than you'd pay for a health club membership." In some cases, you can also compare the costs of *not* buying the product or service: "Ignoring small repairs now increases the risks of major repairs in the future."

Applying the AIDA model

Most marketing and sales messages are prepared according to the AIDA plan or some variation of it. Begin with an attention-getting device, generate interest by describing some of the product or service's unique features, increase desire by highlighting the benefits that are most appealing to your audience, and close by suggesting the action you want the audience to take.

Getting Attention   Professionals use a wide range of techniques to attract their audience's attention:

You can employ a variety of attention-getting devices in marketing and sales messages.

- **Your product's strongest feature or benefit.** "1,000 Songs. Impossibly small. iPod nano."[13]

- **A piece of genuine news.** "Take entertainment to a whole new place" (promoting Verizon's V Cast service, which lets people download a variety of entertainment services to their mobile phones).[14]

- **A point of common ground with the audience.** "An SUV adventurous enough to accommodate your spontaneity and the gear that comes with it."[15]

- **A personal appeal to the reader's emotions and values.** "The only thing worse than paying taxes is paying taxes when you don't have to."

- **The promise of insider information.** "You may be one of those people who dream of working and living in France and don't know how to go about simply doing it. This guide tells how—from the inside out—how others like yourself have managed to work within the French system."[16]

- **The promise of savings.** "Right now, you can get huge savings on a new camera phone."[17]

- **A sample or demonstration of the product.** "Here's your free sample of the new Romalite packing sheet."

- **A solution to a problem.** "This backpack's designed to endure all a kid's dropping and dragging."[18]

Of course, words aren't the only attention-getting device at your disposal. Strong, evocative images are a common attention getter. With online messages, you have even more options, including audio, animation, and video.

Building Interest   Use the interest section of your message to build on the intrigue you created with your opening. This section should also offer support for whatever claims or promises you might've made in the opening. For instance, after opening with the headline that claims "1,000 Songs. Impossibly small. iPod nano," the Apple iPod webpage continues with[19]

To build interest, expand on and support the promises in your attention-getting opening.

> Take everything you love about iPod and shrink it. Now shrink it again. With 2GB (500 songs) and 4GB (1,000 songs) models starting at $199, the pencil-thin iPod nano packs the entire iPod experience into an impossibly small design. So small, it will take your music places you never dreamed of.

Explains the concept of the iPod nano by relating it to what millions of consumers already know about the original iPod

Puts size in a position of emphasis, since size—not price—is the major selling point for the iPod nano

At this point in the message, Apple has offered enough information to help people understand how they might use the product, and it has answered a couple of potential objections as well (compatibility with Windows and the price). Anyone interested in a digital music player is probably intrigued enough to keep reading.

Increasing Desire   To build desire for the product, service, or idea, continue to expand and explain how accepting it will benefit the recipient. Think carefully about the sequence of support points, and use plenty of subheadings, hyperlinks, and other devices to help people find the information they need quickly. For example, after reading this much about the iPod, some users might want to know more about the iTunes Music Store, whereas others will want technical specifications. The iPod product page continues with detailed discussions of various product features and benefits, but it also offers numerous links to pages with other kinds of support information. The ability to provide flexible access to information is just one of the reasons the web is such a powerful medium for marketing and sales.

Add details and audience benefits to increase desire for the product or service.

Throughout the body of your message, remember to keep the focus on the audience, not on your company or your product. When you talk about product features, remember to stress the benefits and talk in terms that make sense to users. Listing the capacity of the iPod as 10,000 songs is a lot more meaningful for most readers than saying it has 40 gigabytes of memory.

To keep readers interested, use colorful verbs and adjectives that convey a dynamic image. Be careful, however, not to overdo it: If you say "Your factory floors will sparkle like diamonds," your audience will find it hard to believe, which may prevent them from believing the rest of your message.

To increase desire, as well as boost your credibility, provide support for your claims. Creative writers find many ways to provide support: testimonials from satisfied users, articles written by industry experts, competitive comparisons, product samples and free demonstrations, independent test results, even movies or computer animations that show a product in action. You can also highlight guarantees that demonstrate your faith in your product and your willingness to back it up.

Motivating Action   After you have raised enough interest and built up the reader's desire for your offering, you're ready to ask your audience to take action. Whether you want people to pick up the phone to place an order or visit your website to download a free demo version of your software, try to persuade them to do it right away. You might offer a discount for the first 1,000 people to order, put a deadline on the offer, or simply remind them that the sooner they order, the sooner they'll be able to enjoy the product's benefits. Even potential buyers who want the product can get distracted or forget to respond, so the sooner you can encourage action, the better.

Take care to maintain the respectful, professional tone you've been using up to this point. Don't resort to gimmicks and desperate-sounding pleas for the customer's business. Make sure your final impression is compelling and positive. For instance, in a sales letter, the postscript (P.S.) below your signature is often one of the first and last parts people read. Use this valuable space to emphasize the key benefit you have to offer and to emphasize the advantages of ordering soon.

Maintaining High Standards of Ethics, Legal Compliance, and Etiquette

The word *persuasion* has negative connotations for some people, especially in a marketing or sales context. However, ethical and effective businesspeople view persuasion as a positive force, aligning their own interests with what is best for their audiences. They influence audience members by providing information and aiding understanding, which allows audiences the freedom to choose.[20] To maintain the highest standards of business ethics, make every attempt to persuade without manipulating. Choose words that won't be misinterpreted, and be sure you don't distort the truth. Adopt the "you" attitude by showing honest concern for your audience's needs and interests. Your consideration of audience needs is more than ethical; it's the proper use of persuasion.

As marketing and selling grow increasingly complex, so do the legal ramifications of marketing and sales messages. In the United States, the Federal Trade Commission (FTC) has the authority to impose penalties against advertisers who violate federal standards for truthful advertising. Other federal agencies have authority over advertising in specific industries, such as transportation and financial services. Individual states have additional laws that apply. Pay close attention to the following legal aspects of marketing and sales communication:[21]

- Marketing and sales messages must be truthful and nondeceptive.
- You must back up your claims with evidence.
- Marketing and sales messages are considered binding contracts in many states.
- In most cases, you can't use a person's name, photograph, or other identity without permission.

In addition, before you launch a marketing or sales campaign, make sure you're up to date on the latest regulations affecting customer privacy and data security.

Meeting your ethical and legal obligations will go a long way toward maintaining good communication etiquette as well. However, you may still face etiquette decisions within ethical and legal boundaries. For instance, you can produce a marketing campaign that complies with all applicable laws and yet is still offensive or insulting to your audience. An audience-centered approach, involving respect for your readers and their values, should help you avoid any such etiquette missteps.

Margin notes:

To keep readers interested, use strong, colorful language without overdoing it.

After you've generated sufficient interest and desire, you're ready to persuade readers to take the preferred action.

Marketing and sales messages are covered by a wide range of laws and regulations.

Maintaining high ethical standards is a key aspect of good communication etiquette.

Common Examples of Marketing and Sales Messages

From simple letters to interactive kiosks, the variety of marketing and sales messages in today's business environment is seemingly endless. From cars to clothes to luxury vacations, the ability to combine words, images, video, and sounds makes it easier to use a variety of logical and emotional appeals. However, no matter how advanced the technology becomes, successful persuasive communication will always be built around the basics: understanding audience needs, out-communicating competitors, and providing clear, compelling information that encourages customers to make a decision in your favor (see Figure 9.4).

Even the most technologically advanced persuasive tools and media follow the basic guidelines of persuasive communication.

FIGURE 9.4   Multimedia Persuasion
Saturn uses multimedia technology to persuasively present the safety features of its Vue sport utility vehicle. By allowing the audience to interact with various graphical presentations, Saturn effectively combines logical and emotional appeals.

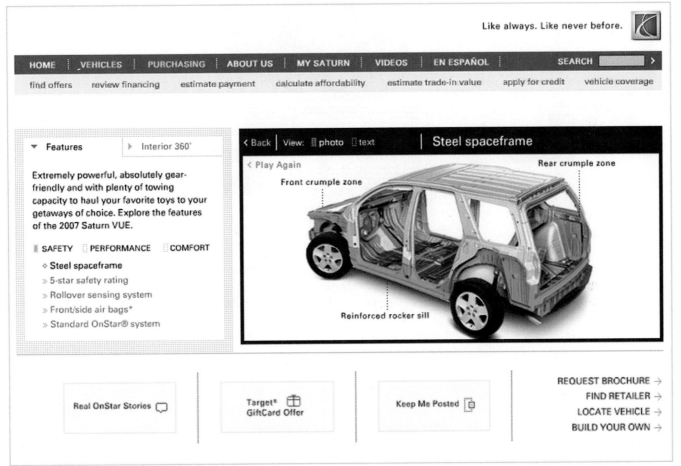

Pointers for Developing Marketing and Sales Messages
- Get attention with an intriguing opening that suggests strong audience benefits.
- Make sure the central selling point is clear and relevant to the audience.
- Don't overload the audience with details or minor benefits; sequence the message in a way that is easy to follow.
- Support all claims with objective evidence.
- Design graphical elements to work in harmony with text.
- Anticipate questions and objections and answer them ahead of time.
- Make sure your logical and emotional appeals align with the audience's wants and needs.
- Reduce the perceived risk of responding (such as by offering a money-back guarantee).
- Be positive and confident without being pushy.
- Emphasize the benefits of responding and make the desired response easy to accomplish.

FIGURE 9.5   Opt-In E-Mail Newsletter

Zazú, a salon chain in Illinois, demonstrates the "you" attitude by sending its e-mail newsletters only to those clients who have specifically requested it.

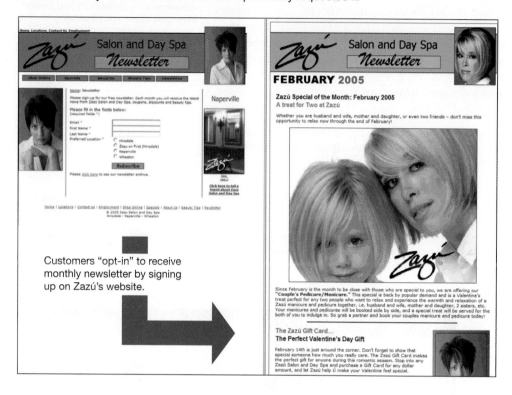

Customers "opt-in" to receive monthly newsletter by signing up on Zazú's website.

Technology also gives communicators new ways to demonstrate sensitivity to user needs. One example is automated updates from blogs and websites, alerting customers to information in which they've expressed an interest. *Opt-in* e-mail newsletters are another technology that shows the "you" attitude at work. Unlike the unwelcome spam messages that litter e-mail inboxes these days, opt-in messages are sent only to those people who have specifically requested information (see Figure 9.5).

Reviewing Key Points

This chapter highlights how to use the three-step writing process for persuasive messages. It encourages you to pay special attention to planning activities such as analyzing your purpose, analyzing your audience, establishing your credibility, and striving for high ethical standards. The chapter discusses strategies for persuasive messages. It helps you learn about balancing emotional and logical appeals and using the AIDA plan to develop your messages. It also examines two types of persuasive requests: action requests and claims.

This chapter addresses the special challenges of creating marketing and sales messages and describes six strategies for writing sales messages: assessing customer needs, analyzing the competition, determining selling points and benefits, anticipating objections, applying the AIDA model, and maintaining high standards of ethics, legal compliance, and etiquette.

The next chapter will discuss business reports and proposals. You'll learn about the common purposes of reports, and you'll see how to apply the three-step writing process to reports and proposals. The chapter will also explain the special analysis and investigation tasks that you'll need to complete when planning business reports and proposals.

Test Your Knowledge

1. What are some questions to ask when gauging the audience's needs during the planning of a persuasive message?

2. What role do demographics and psychographics play in audience analysis during the planning of a persuasive message?

3. How do emotional appeals differ from logical appeals?

4. What three types of reasoning can you use in logical appeals?

5. What is the AIDA model, and how does it apply to persuasive messages?

Apply Your Knowledge

1. When writing persuasive messages, why is it so important to give special attention to the analysis of your purpose and audience?

2. How are persuasive messages different from routine messages?

3. When is it appropriate to use the direct organizational approach in persuasive messages?

4. Imagine yourself working as an engineer, a graphic designer in an advertising agency, or a sales representative for a company that sells building supplies to homebuilders. Now try to imagine as many of your daily tasks as would require persuasion. Who are your audiences, and how do their needs and characteristics affect the way you develop your persuasive messages at work?

5. Ethical Choices   Are emotional appeals ethical? Why or why not?

Practice Your Knowledge

Exercises for Perfecting Your Writing

Analyzing Persuasive Messages: Teamwork   With another student, analyze the persuasive e-mail message at Host Marriott (Figure 9.2 on page 234) by answering the following questions:

1. What techniques are used to capture the reader's attention?

2. Does the writer use the direct or the indirect organizational approach? Why?

3. Is the subject line effective? Why or why not?

4. Does the writer use an emotional or a logical appeal? Why?

5. What reader benefits are included?

6. How does the writer establish credibility?

7. What tools does the writer use to reinforce his position?

Persuasive Messages: Subject Lines   Compose effective subject lines for the following e-mail messages:

8. A recommendation to your branch manager to install wireless networking throughout the facility. Your primary reason is that management has encouraged more teamwork, and those teams often congregate in meeting rooms, the cafeteria, and other places that lack network access—without which they can't do much of the work they are expected to do.

9. A sales brochure to be sent to area residents soliciting customers for your new business, "Meals à la Car," a carryout dining service that delivers from most local area restaurants. Diners place orders online, and individual households can order from up to three restaurants at a time to accommodate different tastes. The price is equal to the standard menu prices plus a 10 percent delivery charge.

10. A special request to the company president to allow managers to carry over their unused vacation days to the following year. Apparently, many managers canceled their fourth-quarter vacation plans to work on the installation of a new company computer system. Under their current contract, vacation days not used by December 31 aren't accruable.

Marketing and sales messages: Features and Benefits   Determine whether the following sentences focus on features or benefits; rewrite them as necessary to focus all the sentences on benefits.

11. All-Cook skillets are coated with a durable, patented nonstick surface.

12. You can call anyone and talk as long you like on Saturdays and Sundays with this new cell phone plan.

Activities

For active links to all websites discussed in this chapter, visit this text's website at www.prenhall.com/bovee. Locate your book and click on its Companion Website link. Then select Chapter 9, and click on "Featured Websites." Locate the name of the page or the URL related to the material in the text. Please note that links to sites that become inactive after publication of the book will be removed from the Featured Websites section.

1. **Analyze This Document**   Read the following document, then (1) analyze the strengths and weaknesses of each sentence, and (2) revise the document so that it follows this chapter's guidelines:

   At Tolson Auto Repair, we have been in business for over 25 years. We stay in business by always taking into account what the customer wants. That's why we are writing. We want to know your opinions to be able to better conduct our business.

   Take a moment right now and fill out the enclosed questionnaire. We know everyone is busy, but this is just one way we have of making sure our people do their job correctly. Use the enclosed envelope to return the questionnaire.

   And again, we're happy you chose Tolson Auto Repair. We want to take care of all your auto needs.

2. **Analyze This Document**   Read the following document, then (1) analyze the strengths and weaknesses of each sentence, and (2) revise the document so that it follows this chapter's guidelines:

   Dear TechStar Computing:

   I'm writing to you because of my disappointment with my new multimedia PC display. The display part works all right, but the audio volume is also set too high and the volume knob doesn't turn it down. It's driving us crazy. The volume knob doesn't seem to be connected to anything but simply spins around. I can't believe you would put out a product like this without testing it first.

   I depend on my computer to run my small business and want to know what you are going to do about it. This reminds me of every time I buy electronic equipment from what seems like any company. Something is always wrong. I thought quality was supposed to be important, but I guess not.

   Anyway, I need this fixed right away. Please tell me what you want me to do.

3. **Analyze This Document**   Read the following document, then (1) analyze the strengths and weaknesses of each sentence and (2) revise the document so that it follows this chapter's guidelines:

We know how awful dining hall food can be, and that's why we've developed the "Mealaweek Club." Once a week, we'll deliver food to your dormitory or apartment. Our meals taste great. We have pizza, buffalo wings, hamburgers and curly fries, veggie roll-ups, and more!

When you sign up for just six months, we will ask what day you want your delivery. We'll ask you to fill out your selection of meals. And the rest is up to us. At "Mealaweek," we deliver! And payment is easy. We accept MasterCard and Visa or a personal check. It will save money, especially when compared with eating out.

Just fill out the enclosed card and indicate your method of payment. As soon as we approve your credit or check, we'll begin delivery. Tell all your friends about Mealaweek. We're the best idea since sliced bread!

4. **Ethical Choices**   Your boss has asked you to post a message on the company's internal blog urging everyone in your department to donate money to the company's favorite charity, an organization that operates a special summer camp for physically challenged children. You wind up writing a lengthy posting packed with facts and heartwarming anecdotes about the camp and the children's experiences. When you must work that hard to persuade your audience to take an action such as donating money to a charity, aren't you being manipulative and unethical? Explain.

5. **Internet**   Visit the Federal Trade Commission website and read the "Catch the Bandit in Your Mailbox" consumer warning at www.ftc.gov/bcp/conline/pubs/tmarkg/bandit.htm. Select one or two marketing or sales letters you've recently received and see whether they contain any of the suspicious content mentioned in the FTC warning. What does the FTC suggest you do with any materials that don't sound legitimate?

6. **Revising a Letter: Request for a Rent Refund from Kukyendahl Joint, Inc.**   The following persuasive request for adjustment contains many flaws. Using what you've learned in the chapter, read the message carefully and analyze its faults. Then use the questions below to outline and write an improved message.

CMSI
CONTRACT
MANAGEMENT
SERVICES
INCORPORATED

March 22, 2007

Mr. Robert Bechtold, Manager
Kukyendahl Joint, Inc.
88 North Park Road
Houston, TX 77005

Re: Last Warning

Dear Mr. Bechtold:

Enclosed is a summary of recent ETS-related court cases in which landlords and owners were held responsible for providing toxin-free air for their tenants. In most of these cases, owners were also required to reimburse rents and pay damages for the harm done before the environmental tobacco smoke problem was remedied.

We've been plagued with this since we moved in on January 2, 2007. You haven't acted on our complaints, or responded to our explanations that secondhand smoke is making us sick, filtering in from nearby offices. You must act now or you will be hearing from our lawyers. We've told you that we were forced to hire contractors to apply weather stripping and seal openings. This cost us $3,000 (bills attached) and we expect reimbursement. But the smoke is still coming in. We also want a refund for the $9,000 we've paid you in rent since January. Call us immediately at (832) 768-3899, or our attorneys will be calling you.

Cigarette smoke from tenants on either side of us, and perhaps above and below as well, has been infiltrating our space and you have done nothing, despite our pleas, to stop it. This is unacceptable. This is a known human carcinogen. Ask the Environmental Protection Agency, which classified it as this Group A toxin. It causes lung, breast, cervical, and endocrine cancer in nonsmokers. You wouldn't want to breathe it, either.

One employee already quit who suffered from asthma. Another is threatening because he's a high risk for heart attack. Migraines, bronchitis, respiratory infections—all caused by the 4,600 chemicals in ETS, including poisons such as cyanide, arsenic, formaldehyde, carbon monoxide, and ammonia. We've had them all—the illnesses, that is.

Secondhand smoke is even more dangerous than what smokers inhale, since the inhalation process burns off some of the toxins. Sick time has already cost CMSI valuable business and lowered productivity. Plus many of us are considering finding other jobs unless our office air becomes safe to breathe again. But as the court cases prove, the responsibility for fixing this problem is yours. We expect you to live up to that responsibility immediately. Frankly, we're fed up with your lack of response.

Kathleen Thomas
Manager

   a. Describe the flaws you discovered in this persuasive request for adjustment.

   b. Develop a plan for rewriting the letter. The following steps will help you organize your thoughts before you begin writing:
     1. Should you use a direct or an indirect approach?
     2. How can you use the "you" attitude to gain attention in the opening?
     3. What can you do to establish your credibility?
     4. How can you improve the order of material presented in the body of the letter?
     5. Create an appropriate closing.

   c. Now rewrite the letter. Don't forget to leave ample time for revision of your own work before you turn it in.

7. Revising a Sales Brochure: From ScrubaDub About Its Car Care Club The following sales brochure falls short of its objectives. Use what you know about sales messages to analyze its flaws. Then follow the steps below to produce a better version.

11 locations in Massachusetts and Rhode Island
Bob and Dan Paisner, Owners

We are pleased to announce that ScrubaDub has added a new service, the Car Care Club.

It costs $5.95 for a lifetime membership (your car's lifetime) and features our computer automation. You'll be given a bar-coded sticker for your windshield so our computers can identify you as a club member when you pull in. If you sign up within the next 30 days, we will grant you a SuperWash for free.

The new club offers the standard ScrubaDub Touch-less systems to protect your finishes, our private formula Superglo detergent to clean your car safely and thoroughly, wheel sensors to prescribe the right treatment for whitewalls, wire, or chrome, soft, heated well water to eliminate spots, soft-cloth drying for final gloss. We also recycle our water and grant you a free wash on your birthday.

In addition, club members only will have access to a 48-hour guarantee (free rewashes) or 4 days if you purchased the premium Super Wash, Luxury Wash, Special or Works Wash. After ten washes, our computer will award you a free wash. Also available only to club members are $5 rebates for foam waxes (Turtle Wax, Simonize, or Blue Coral). Some additional specials will be granted by us to car club members, on an unplanned basis.

We can handle special requests if you inquire of our Satisfaction Supervisors. We honor our customers with refunds if they remain unsatisfied after a rewash. This is our Bumper-to-Bumper Guarantee.

a. Describe the mistakes made by the writers of this brochure.

b. Develop a plan for improving the brochure. The following questions will help you organize your thinking:
   1. What can you assume about the audience, which is made up of regular customers?
   2. How can you use this information to develop a better opening?
   3. Since customers already know ScrubaDub, what can you do to improve the body of the brochure? Can you identify selling points versus benefits? What about the use of language and the tone of the text?
   4. Does this brochure make effective use of the AIDA model?
   5. How would you improve the "call to action," the point in the message in which it asks the reader to make a purchase decision?

c. Now rewrite the sales letter. Don't forget to leave ample time for revision of your work before you turn it in.

8. Revising a Persuasive E-Mail Message: E-Cruiting at Boulder Construction   This "persuasive" e-mail message, from Shelby Howard to Sheila Young, probably won't work effectively. Can you identify the mistakes the writer has made? Follow the steps below to analyze and improve on this persuasive request for action.

To: sryoung@sprenco.com
Subject: Recruiting tactics

Dear Sheila: I think we should try e-cruiting. I want you to use the huge websites of résumés now listed on the Internet. They provide the software for your searches through these thousands of résumés they receive, so it shouldn't be too difficult. But you will have to define the qualifications you want first. Then they'll supply the résumés that fit.

Eventually, you can develop a website for our company that will post job listings. Then you'll get replies from the kinds of people who might not otherwise post their résumés online. Some of them may be good employees we've been looking for.

Costs breakdowns are: About $1,300 apiece per candidate for traditional (newspaper ad) hiring. Plus your time for prescreening. For e-cruiting, approximately $183 per candidate, with prescreening supplied by jobsearch databases such as monster.com, hotjobs.com, or careermosaic.com. They will, however, charge us about $100–300 per month to list our jobs, rather than the $1,000 the local paper charges us for a Sunday ad. Online job posting word length: unlimited.

You might have to wade through the 30,000 to 100,000 Internet sites now devoted to recruiting. Better stick with the names I've already mentioned. You'll be accessing about 150 million Internet users in the United States, 74 percent of them over the age of 18 looking for jobs.

Right now, our competitors aren't using this method and I can't figure out why. I'm thinking it could be a way to reach talent we might otherwise miss. Maybe they just haven't figured this out yet. You know the ones I mean—the talented individuals we compete for with other construction companies, even though we offer good jobs and benefits.

I read that Bank of Montreal relied on e-cruiting this year. They say they saved $1 million, but we'll have to see how accurate that is with our own trial. Only two percent of building industry employers use e-cruiting. Sixty percent of computer companies use it, probably because surfing the Internet is no hassle for them. They insist hiring time per candidate is reduced from six weeks to one hour, but I'll have to see that to believe it! Something about not having to wait for snail mail résumés. But then they also don't get to screen candidates by sight first, so maybe it's a toss-up. On the other hand, they can e-mail questions back and forth.

Well, why don't we give it a go anyway?

    a. Describe the flaws in approach and execution of this persuasive request for action.

    b. Develop a plan for improving the message. The following questions should help to stimulate your ideas:
        1. Starting with the subject line, how can you focus on your audience's needs?
        2. What would be a better opening? Why?
        3. How can you reorganize the body of the message to improve the reader's interest and receptivity to the new idea?
        4. How can you handle facts, statistics, benefits, and appeals more skillfully?
        5. What should be included in the conclusion?

    c. Now rewrite this persuasive request for action.

9. Analyzing a Sales Package: Learning from the Direct-Mail Pros   The daily mail often brings a selection of sales messages to your front door. Find a direct-mail package from your mailbox that includes a sales letter. Then answer the following questions to help you analyze and learn from the approach used by the communication professionals who prepare these glossy sales messages. Your instructor might also ask you to share the package and your observations in a class discussion.

    a. Who is the intended audience?

    b. What are the demographic and psychographic characteristics of the intended audience?

    c. What is the purpose of the direct-mail package? Has it been designed to solicit a phone-call response, make a mail-order sale, obtain a charitable contribution, or do something else?

    d. What, if any, technique was used to encourage you to open the envelope?

    e. What kind of letter is included? Is it fully printed, printed with a computer fill-in of certain specific information, or fully computer typed? Is the letter personalized with your name or your family's name? If so, how many times?

    f. Did the letter writer follow the AIDA model? If not, explain the letter's organization.

    g. What needs does it appeal to?

    h. What emotional appeals and logical arguments does the letter use?

    i. What selling points and consumer benefits does the letter offer?

    j. How many and what kinds of enclosures (such as brochures or CD-ROMs) were included for support?

    k. Does the letter or package have an unusual format? Does it use eye-catching graphics?

    l. Is the message in the letter and on the supporting pieces believable? Would the package sell the product or service to you? Why or why not?

Expand Your Knowledge

Exploring the Best of the Web

Influence an Official and Promote Your Cause   At the Thomas site compiled by the Library of Congress, http://thomas.loc.gov, you'll discover voluminous information about federal legislation, congressional members, and committee reports. You can also access committee homepages and numerous links to government agencies, current issues, and historical documents. You'll find all kinds of regulatory information, including laws and relevant issues that might affect you in the business world. Visit the site and stay informed. Maybe you'll want to convince a government official to support a business-related issue that affects you. Explore the data at the Thomas site, and find an issue you can use to practice your skills at writing a persuasive message.

Exercises

1. What key ideas would you include in an e-mail message to persuade your congressional representative to support an issue important to you?
2. In a letter to a senator or member of Congress, what information would you include to convince the reader to vote for an issue supporting small business?

3. When sending a message to someone who daily receives hundreds of written appeals, what attention-getting techniques can you use? How can you get support for a cause that concerns you as a businessperson?

Exploring the Web on Your Own

Review these chapter-related websites on your own to learn more about writing persuasive messages.

1. Learn the tips and techniques of a professional copywriter at Nick Usborne's blog, http://nickusborne.typepad.com/blog.

2. Explore some classic examples of persuasive messages at the National Archives' Powers of Persuasion online exhibit featuring patriotic posters from World War II, www.archives.gov/exhibits/powers_of_persuasion/powers_of_persuasion_intro.html.

3. See how professional advertising copywriters employ persuasion in their work; take the free tutorial at www.adcopywriting.com.

Learn Interactively

Interactive Study Guide

Visit www.prenhall.com/bovee, then locate your book and click on its Companion Website link. Select Chapter 9 to take advantage of the interactive "Chapter Quiz" to test your knowledge of chapter concepts. Receive instant feedback on whether you need additional studying. Also, visit the "Study Hall," where you'll find an abundance of valuable resources that will help you succeed in this course.

Peak Performance Grammar and Mechanics

If your instructor has required the use of "Peak Performance Grammar and Mechanics," either in your online course, through the access-code protected portion of the Companion

Website, or on CD, you can continue to improve your skill with commas, semicolons, and colons by using the "Peak Performance Grammar and Mechanics" module. Click "Punctuation," and then click "Punctuation I." Take the Pretest to determine whether you have any weak areas. Then review those areas in the Refresher Course. Take the Follow-Up Test to check your grasp of commas, semicolons, and colons. For an extra challenge or advanced practice, take the Advanced Test. Finally, for additional reinforcement in commas, go to the "Improve Your Grammar, Mechanics, and Usage" section that follows the cases, and complete the "Level 1: Self-Assessment" exercises.

CASES

Apply the three-step writing process to the following cases, as assigned by your instructor.

▌E-MAIL SKILLS

1. That's the Point: E-Mail Encouraging Your Boss to Blog

You've been trying for months to convince your boss, Will Florence, to start blogging. You've told him that top executives in numerous industries now use blogging as a way to connect with customers and other stakeholders without going through the filters and barriers of formal corporate communications. He was just about convinced—until he read the blog by Bob Lutz, the co-chair and design chief of General Motors.

"Look at this!" he calls from his office. "Bob Lutz is one of the most respected executives in the world, and all these people are criticizing him on his own blog. Sure, a lot of the responses are positive, but quite a few are openly hostile, disagreeing with GM strategy, criticizing the products, criticizing the subjects he chooses for his blog—you name it. If blogging is all about opening yourself up to criticism from every bystander with a keyboard, no way am I going to start a blog."

Your Task Write Florence an e-mail (w_florence@sprenco.com) persuading him that the freewheeling nature of blog communication is its key advantage, not a disadvantage at all. While they may not always agree with what he has to say, automotive enthusiasts and car buyers respect Lutz for communicating in his own words—and for giving them the opportunity to respond. For background information, read some of the postings from Lutz and other GM executives at http://fastlane.gmblogs.com.[22]

▌PODCASTING SKILLS

2. Listen Up: Promoting a Podcast Station

Podcasting, the technique of recording individual sound files that people download from the Internet to listen to on their computers or music players, is quickly redefining the concept of radio. A growing crowd of musicians, essayists, journalists, and others with compelling content use podcasting to reach audiences they can't get to through traditional broadcast radio. The good news is that anyone with a microphone and a computer can record podcasts. That's also the bad news, at least from your perspective as a new podcaster: With so many podcasts now on the Internet, potential listeners have thousands and thousands of audio files to select from.

Your new podcast, School2Biz, offers advice to business students making the transition from college to career. You provide info on everything from preparing résumés to interviewing to finding one's place in the business world and building a successful career. As you expand your audience, you'd eventually like to turn School2Biz into a profitable operation (perhaps by selling advertising time during your podcasts). For now, you're simply offering free advice.

Your Task You've chosen The Podcast Bunker (www.podcastbunker.com) as the first website on which to promote School2Biz. The site also lets podcasters promote their feeds with brief text listings, such as this description of Pet Talk Radio: "A weekly lifestyle show for people with more than a passing interest in pets. Hosted by Brian Pickering & Kaye Browne with Australia's favourite vet Dr Harry Cooper & animal trainer Steve Austin."

As your instructor indicates, either write a 50-word description of your new podcast that can be posted on Podcast Bunker or record a 30-second podcast describing the new service. Make up any information you need to describe School2Biz. Be sure to mention who you are and why the information you present is worth listening to.[23]

3. Your New Kentucky Home: Letter Promoting the Bluegrass State

Like all states, Kentucky works hard to attract businesses that are considering expanding into the state or relocating entirely from another state. The Kentucky Cabinet for Economic Development is responsible for reaching out to these companies and overseeing the many incentive programs the state offers to both new and established businesses.

Your Task As the communication director of the Kentucky Cabinet for Economic Development, you play the lead role in reaching out to companies that want to expand or relocate to Kentucky. Visit www.thinkkentucky.com <http://www.thinkkentucky.com/> and download the Think

Kentucky brochure (look under the "Why Kentucky" linke). Identify the eight benefits the state uses to promote Kentucky as a great place to locate a business. Summarize these eight reasons in a form letter that will be sent to business executives throughout the country. Be sure to introduce yourself and your purpose in the letter, and close with a compelling call to action (have them reach you by telephone at 800-626-2930 or by e-mail at econdev@ky.gov). As you plan your letter, try to imagine yourself as the CEO of a company and consider what a complex choice it would be to move to another state.

■ WEB WRITING
■ SKILLS

4. Don't Forget Print: Using the Web to Promote Time Inc.'s Magazine Advertising

After a shaky start as the technology matured and advertisers tried to figure out this new medium, online advertising has finally become a significant force in both consumer and business marketing. Companies in a wide variety of industries are shifting some of the ad budgets from traditional media such as TV and magazines to the increasing selection of advertising possibilities online—and more than a few companies now advertise almost exclusively online. That's fine for companies that sell advertising time and space online, but your job involves selling advertising in those print magazines that are worried about losing market share to online publishers.

Online advertising has two major advantages that you can't really compete with: interactivity and the ability to precisely target individual audience members. On the other hand, you have several advantages going for you, including the ability to produce high-color photography, the physical presence of print (such as when a magazine sits on a table in a doctor's waiting room), portability, guaranteed circulation numbers, and close reader relationships that go back years or decades in many cases.

Your Task You work as an advertising sales specialist for the Time Inc. division of Time Warner, which publishes more than 150 magazines around the world. Write a brief persuasive message about the benefits of magazine advertising; the statement will be posted on the individual websites of Time Inc.'s numerous magazines, so you can't narrow in on any single publication. Also, Time Inc. coordinates its print publications with an extensive online presence (including thousands of paid online ads), so you can't bash online advertising, either.[24]

■ E-MAIL
■ SKILLS

5. Give a Little to Get a Lot: Suggesting Free Wireless at Starbucks

Like many students at the University of Wisconsin, Madison, you like to escape from your cramped apartment to work on school projects at local coffee shops. With your wireless-equipped laptop, you hunt for places that offer free wireless so you can access course websites, do research, and occasionally see how Badger athletic teams are doing. But there's a problem: At the Starbucks right around the corner, you have to pay for wireless access through the service offered by T-Mobile. Several of the locally owned coffee houses offer free wireless, but the closest one is a mile from your apartment. That's a long walk in a Wisconsin winter.

Your Task Write a persuasive message to Starbucks suggesting that the company drop its agreement with T-Mobile and offer free wireless instead. Try to convince the firm that free wireless will attract enough additional coffee-buying customers to offset the loss of revenue from wireless—and help Starbucks overcome the "big corporation" image that prompts some coffee drinkers to patronize locally owned establishments instead. Although you don't have the data to prove that the cost of offering free wireless would be more than offset by increased coffee sales, at least make a convincing argument that Starbucks should consider making the change. You'll post your message to the Starbucks website, www.starbucks.com, which has a limit of 2,600 characters for such messages.[25]

6. Outsourcing: Letter from Kelly Services Offering Solutions

Kelly Services is a global Fortune 500 company that offers staffing solutions that include temporary services, staff leasing, outsourcing, and vendor on-site and full-time placement. Kelly provides employees who have a wide range of skills across many disciplines, including office services, accounting, engineering, information technology, law, science, marketing, light industrial, education, health care, and home care.

Companies use Kelly Services to strategically balance workload and workforce during peaks and valleys of demand, to handle special projects, and to evaluate employees prior to making a full-time hiring decision. This dramatic change in business has spurred the rapid growth of the contingent employment industry.

In turn, many individuals are choosing the flexibility of personal career management, increasing options of where, when, and how to work. Therefore, more and more workers are becoming receptive to being a contract, temporary, or consulting employee.

This flexibility offers advantages to both the company and the employee. Both have the opportunity to evaluate one another prior to making a long-term commitment. Kelly Services earns a fee when its employees are hired permanently, but employers find that it's a small price to pay for such valuable preview time, which saves everyone the cost and pain of a bad hiring decision.

With 2,500 offices in 26 countries, Kelly provides its customers nearly 700,000 employees annually. The company provides staffing solutions to more than 90 percent of the Fortune 500 companies. Kelly has received many supplier awards for providing outstanding and cost-efficient staffing services, including DaimlerChrysler's Gold Award, Ford Motor Company's Q1 Preferred Quality Award, Intel Corporation's Supplier Continuous Quality Improvement (SCQI) Award, and DuPont Legal's Challenge Award.

As companies increasingly face new competitive pressures to provide better service and quality at lower prices, many are turning to outsourcing suppliers to deliver complete operational management of specific functions or support departments, allowing the company the necessary time to focus on its core competencies. One solution is to choose a single supplier such as the Kelly Management Services (KMS) division to deliver "full-service" outsourcing.

KMS combines management experience, people process improvements, technology enhancements, and industry expertise to optimize customer operations and reduce cost. KMS understands the unique challenges companies are facing in today's increasingly fast-paced business world and can provide customers with services across multiple functional offerings, including call center operations, warehousing, distribution and light assembly, back office and administrative functions, and mail and reprographic services.

Your Task Write a sales letter to companies similar to DaimlerChrysler, Ford, Intel, and DuPont explaining what Kelly has to offer. For current information, visit the Kelly website at www.kellyservices.com.[26]

7. Always Urgent: Memo Pleading Case for Hosting a Red Cross Blood Drive

This morning as you drove to your job as food services manager at the Pechanga Casino Entertainment Center in Temecula, California, you were concerned to hear on the radio that the local Red Cross chapter put out a call for blood because national supplies have fallen dangerously low. During highly publicized disasters, people are emotional and eager to help out by donating blood. But in calmer times, only 5 percent of eligible donors think of giving blood. You're one of those few.

Not many people realize that donated blood lasts for only 72 hours. Consequently, the mainstay of emergency blood supplies must be replenished in an ongoing effort. No one is more skilled, dedicated, or efficient in handling blood than the American Red Cross, which is responsible for half the nation's supply of blood and blood products.

Donated blood helps victims of accidents and disease, as well as surgery patients. Just yesterday you were reading about a girl named Melissa, who was diagnosed with multiple congenital heart defects and underwent her first open-heart surgery at 1 week old. Now 5, she's used well over 50 units of donated blood, and she wouldn't be alive without them. In a thank-you letter, her mother lauded the many strangers who had "given a piece of themselves" to save her precious daughter—and countless others. You also learned that a donor's pint of blood can benefit up to four other people.

Today, you're going to do more than just roll up your own sleeve. You know the local Red Cross chapter takes its Blood Mobile to corporations, restaurants, beauty salons—anyplace willing to host public blood drives. What if you could convince the board of directors to support a blood drive at the casino? The slot machines and gaming tables are usually full, hundreds of employees are on hand, and people who've never visited before might come down to donate blood. The positive publicity certainly couldn't hurt Pechanga's community image. With materials from the Red Cross, you're confident you can organize Pechanga's hosting effort and handle the promotion. (Last year you headed the casino's successful Toys for Tots drive.)

To give blood, one must be healthy, be at least 17 years old (with no upper age limit), and weigh at least 110 pounds. Donors can give every 56 days. You'll be urging Pechanga donors to eat well, drink water, and be rested before the Blood Mobile arrives.[27]

Your Task Write a memo persuading the Pechanga board of directors to host a public Red Cross blood drive. You can learn more about what's involved in hosting a blood drive at www.givelife.org (click on "Sponsor a Drive"). Ask the board to provide bottled water, orange juice, and snacks for donors. You'll organize food service workers to handle the distribution, but you'll need the board's approval to let your team volunteer during work hours. Use a combination of logical and emotional appeals.

8. Lock Legends: Letter Requesting Refund and Damages from Brookstone

As a professional photographer, you travel the world for business, leaving from your home base in Williamstown, Massachusetts. Last month it was a trip to Australia, and you thought you'd finally found a way around the "no-locks-on-checked baggage" rules.

After the terrorist attacks of September 11, 2001, the United States' Travel Security Administration (TSA) forbid airline passengers to check locked luggage. TSA inspectors want easy access so that they can open and check bags for security purposes. But since you carry so much expensive equipment, including numerous camera bags, you've been nervous about the safety of your belongings—not to mention the loss of privacy.

So you were relieved when you read Joe Sharkey's "On the Road" column in the *New York Times* just before your trip. The columnist extolled a newly announced TSA program allowing airline travelers to lock their luggage *if they use special TSA-approved locks*, certified by a company called Travel Sentry. You immediately went to the Brookstone store in Albany after reading its web advertisement for "The luggage locks security won't cut off. Our Easycheck™ locks are certified by Travel Sentry™ and feature a secure system accepted and recognized by the Transportation Security Administration (TSA). Airport security personnel can now inspect and re-lock your bags quickly and easily." You bought eight locks, at $20 for each set of two.

When you left the Albany airport, TSA inspectors assured you that they had a master key for these locks, just as Sharkey's column had promised they would. But when you got to Melbourne after changing planes in Chicago and Los Angeles, you were stunned to discover the condition of your luggage. One bag was missing the new lock entirely; another was missing the lock and had a rip all along the seam—perhaps from an irritated inspector? Inside a third bag you found its broken Easycheck lock, with a terse TSA inspection notice reminding you that locked baggage is not allowed. On the return trip you tried again, using three of your remaining locks on camera bags. They arrived with no locks and no inspection notices.

You've now called the airports in Chicago and Cleveland, where TSA inspectors told you they'd "never heard of the program." Brookstone will replace the broken lock, but the woman on the phone wasn't sure about the ones that went missing entirely, since you have nothing left to bring into the store except your receipt.

Your Task After 10 minutes listening to music while on hold for the TSA, you've abandoned the idea of a phone complaint to the government agency. You're going to write a letter to Brookstone (120 Washington Ave., Albany, NY 12203) requesting damages for the ripped luggage (a 24-inch Expandable Ballistic Suitor, $320) and a refund for all eight locks ($80). Six of them were ruined or missing and your last two are essentially useless.[28]

9. No More Driving: Message About Telecommuting to Bachman, Trinity, and Smith

Sitting in your Dallas office at the accounting firm of Bachman, Trinity, and Smith, clacking away on your computer, it seems as though you could be doing this work from your home. You haven't spoken to any coworkers in more than two hours. As long as you complete your work on time, does your location matter?

As an entry-level accountant, you've participated in on-location audits at major companies for nearly a year now. If your bosses trust you to work while staying at a hotel, why not let you work from home, where you already have an office with computer, phone, and fax machine? You'd love to regain those two hours you lose commuting to and from work every day.[29]

Your Task To support this idea, visit the website of the Telework Coalition website at www.telecoa.org <http://www.telcoa.org/> (be sure to check out the "Reference" page). You'll find statistics and other support for an e-mail message persuading your boss, senior partner Marjorie Bachman, to grant you a six-month trial as a telecommuter.

10. Tangled Web: E-Mail to Purely Software Regarding an Online Order Duplication

Last week you ordered new design software for your boss, Martin Soderburgh, at ArtAlive, the small art consulting business where you work. As he requested, you used his Visa card to order Adobe InDesign and Adobe Photoshop from an Internet vendor, Purely Software.com.

When you didn't receive the usual e-mail order confirmation, you called the company's toll-free number. The operator said the company's website was having problems, and he took a second order over the phone: $649.00 for Adobe InDesign, $564.00 for Adobe Photoshop, including tax and shipping. Four days later, ArtAlive received two shipments of the software, and your boss's credit card was charged $1,213.00 twice, for a total of $2,426.00.[30]

Your Task Technically, you authorized both orders. But you understood during the phone call that the first order was cancelled, although you have no written proof. Send a persuasive e-mail to customerservice@purelysoftware.com, requesting (1) an immediate credit to your boss's Visa account and (2) a postage-paid return label for the duplicate order.

11. Selling Your Idea: Sales Letter Promoting a Product of Your Own Invention

You never intended to become an inventor, but you saw a way to make something work more easily, so you set to work. You developed a model, found a way to mass-produce it, and set up a small manufacturing studio in your home. You know that other people are going to benefit from your invention. Now all you need is to reach that market.

Your Task Imagine a useful product that you have invented—perhaps something related to a hobby or sporting activity. List the benefits and features of your imaginary product. Then write a sales letter for it, using what you've learned in this chapter and making up details as you need them.

12. Instant Promotion: Text Message from Hilton Hotels to Frequent Guests

Hilton Hotels now uses an SMS (short messaging service) to send text messaging promotions to customers who've signed up as "HHonors" members. But you work in marketing, and that means you're often struggling to condense elaborate travel packages into 65 enticing words (system maximum).

For example, today's promotion offers "A Golfer's Dream Come True: 'I just played a round of golf by the pyramids!'" For $575 per person per day (double room), valid through January 15, 2008, travelers can stay in the Hilton Pyramids Golf Resort in Cairo, Egypt, for 7 nights/8 days, including breakfast, service charge, and tax. They'll be met at the airport, given transportation to the resort, plus two rounds of golf per person at Dreamland Golf course and two rounds of golf per person at Soleimaneia Pyramids Golf & Country Club course. That's 88 words so far.

But you also need to convey that the Dreamland course wraps like a serpent around the Hilton resort. Its lush greens and lakes, designed by Karl Litten, contrast sharply with the golden desert, culminating in a stunning view of the great Pyramids of Giza, one of the seven wonders of the world. The Soleimaneia course features the "biggest floodlit driving course in Egypt." The travel package provides free transportation to this nearby course.

Rates, of course, are subject to availability and other restrictions may apply. But interested travelers should mention code G7 Pyramids Golf Special when they call Hilton Reservations Worldwide. They can also e-mail RM_PYRAMIDS_GOLF@hilton.com, or call the Cairo hotel directly at 20 2 8402402.[31]

Your Task Write the persuasive text message; your space limit is 65 words.

IM SKILLS

13. Helping Children: Instant Message Holiday Fund Drive at IBM

At IBM, you're one of the coordinators for the annual Employee Charitable Contributions Campaign. Since 1978, the company has helped employees contribute to more than 2,000 health and human service agencies. These groups may offer child care, treat substance abuse, provide health services, or fight illiteracy, homelessness, and hunger. Some offer disaster relief or care for the elderly. All deserve support. They're carefully screened by IBM, one of the largest corporate contributors of cash, equipment, and people to nonprofit organizations and educational institutions, both in the United States and around the world. As your literature states, the program "has engaged our employees more fully in the important mission of corporate citizenship."

During the winter holidays, you target agencies that cater to the needs of displaced families, women, and children. It's not difficult to raise enthusiasm. The prospect of helping children enjoy the holidays—children who otherwise might have nothing—usually awakens the spirit of your most distracted workers. But some of them wait until the last minute and then forget.

They have until Friday, December 16, to come forth with cash contributions. To make it in time for holiday deliveries, they can also bring in toys, food, and blankets through Tuesday, December 20. They shouldn't have any trouble finding the collection bins; they're everywhere, marked with bright red banners. But some will want to call you with questions or (you hope) to make credit card contributions: 800-658-3899, ext. 3342.[32]

Your Task It's December 14. Write a 75- to 100-word instant message encouraging last-minute gifts.

E-MAIL SKILLS

14. Helping Out: Message to Whole Foods Market Managers

Whole Foods Market has grown into a nationwide chain by catering to consumer desires for healthier foods and environmentally sensitive household products. For instance, meats come from animals that were never fed antibiotics, and the cheese is from cows said to be raised on small farms and treated humanely.

Along with selling these products, the company makes a commitment "to the neighborhood and larger community that we serve and in which we live." Whole Foods not only donates 5 percent of after-tax profits to not-for-profit organizations but also financially supports employees who volunteer their time for community service projects. Many Whole Foods stores donate goods and supplies to soup kitchens in their local communities. Company executives want to encourage this type of activity, which reflects the "Whole Foods, Whole People, Whole Planet" corporate motto.

You are the manager of the Whole Foods Market on Ponce de Leon Avenue in Atlanta, Georgia. You've been very successful with a program you developed for donating surplus food to local food banks. You've been asked by top executives to help other Whole Foods stores coordinate this effort into a chainwide food donation program, "Whole Foods for Life." Ideally, by streamlining the process chainwide, the company would be able to increase the number of people it helps and to get more of its employees involved.

You don't have a great deal of extra money for the program, so the emphasis has to be on using resources already available to the stores. One idea is to use trucks from suburban stores to make the program "mobile." Another idea is to join forces with a retailing chain to give food and clothing to individuals. You've decided that the key will be to solicit input from the other stores so that they'll feel more involved in the final outcome as the larger food-donation program takes shape.[33]

Your Task Send a persuasive e-mail message to all managers at Whole Foods Market, explaining the new program and requesting that they help by pooling ideas they've gleaned from their local experience. Even if they don't have food-donation programs currently in place, you want to hear ideas from them and their employees for this charitable project. With their help, you'll choose the best ideas to develop the new "Whole Foods for Life" program.[34]

Improve Your Grammar, Mechanics, and Usage

Level 1: Self-Assessment—Commas

Review Section 2.6 in the Handbook of Grammar, Mechanics, and Usage, and then look at the following 15 items.

In items 1–15, insert required commas.

1. Please send us four cases of filters two cases of wing nuts and a bale of rags.

2. Your analysis however does not account for returns.

3. As a matter of fact she has seen the figures.

4. Before May 7 1999 they wouldn't have minded either.

5. After Martha has gone talk to me about promoting her.

6. Stoneridge Inc. will go public on September 9 2005.

7. We want the new copier not the old model.

8. "Talk to me" Sandra said "before you change a thing."

9. Because of a previous engagement Dr. Stoeve will not be able to attend.

10. The company started attracting attention during the long hard recession of the mid-1970s.

11. You can reach me at this address: 717 Darby Place Scottsdale Arizona 85251.

12. Transfer the documents from Fargo North Dakota to Boise Idaho.

13. Sam O'Neill the designated representative is gone today.

14. With your help we will soon begin.

15. She may hire two new representatives or she may postpone filling those territories until spring.

Level 2: Workplace Applications

The following items contain numerous errors in grammar, capitalization, punctuation, abbreviation, number style, word division, and vocabulary. Rewrite each sentence in the space provided, correcting all errors. Write *C* in the space after any sentence that is already correct.

1. A pitfall of internal promotions is, that a person may be given a job beyond their competence.

2. What makes this development possible is the technological advances in todays workplace.

3. We have up to date physical safeguards, such as secure areas in buildings, electronic safeguards, such as passwords and encryption, and we have procedural safeguards, such as customer authentication procedures.

4. When asked why BASF need to bring in a consultant after so many years, process development quality assurance manager Merritt Sink says that experience is extremely important on these type of projects.

5. Looking at just one growth indicator imports to the United States from China "ballooned" to $102 billion in 2005; compared with 15 billion in 1994.

6. Levi Strauss was the first major manufacturer to develop and do publicity about a formal Code of Conduct for it's contract manufacturers.

7. In foreign countries, while the local labor laws may be comparable or even more stringent than in the United States, law enforcement mechanisms are weak or nonexistent often.

8. Hyundai Motor Co., South Koreas' largest-automotive producer are building a $1 billion assembly and manufacturing plant in Montgomery, Alabama.

9. The long term success of some Internet products rest heavily on broadbands wide acceptance.

10. Being creative, flexibility, and dynamic planning are the critical elements of any successful, manufacturing process.

11. "Starbucks expanded the Frappucciono family to satisfy customers by offering a broader array of blended beverages," said Howard Behar, Starbucks president, North American Operations.

12. Internationally-renowned interior designer, Jacques Garcia will be designing the hotel's interiors; the gardens will also be designed by him.

13. Anyone who thinks they know what a CEO does is probably wrong, according to Eric Kriss; a professional Chief Executive.

14. Doctor Ichak Adizes, who founded the Adizes institute, headquartered in Santa Barbara, Calif. has spent decade's studying the life cycle of businesses.

15. The best job-description in the world wont provide you with a trusted executive, finely-honed interviewing skills only will help one do that.

Level 3: Document Critique

The following document may contain errors in grammar, capitalization, punctuation, abbreviation, number style, vocabulary, and spelling. You may also discover problems with wordiness, usage, organization, and tone for a sales message. Correct all errors using standard proofreading marks (see Appendix C).

To: <Promotional Customer List2>

From: Sasha Morgenstern <smorgenstern@insure.com>

Subject: Insurence Service

Dear potential buyers:

You will be able to compare prices from more than three hundredinsurance companies'. Or find the lower rates for any insurance, such as Term life Automobile; Medical. dental. "No-exam" whole life, workers' compensation, Medicare supplements; Fixed annuities

$500 Dollar Guaranttes

We'll find you the lowest U.S. rates for term life insurance, or we'll deliver $500 to you overnight. Plus, every quote will carry a $five hundred dollar guarrantee of uptotheday accurracy.

"Insure.com provides rock-bottom quotes." — Forbes

All quotes are free and accurrate; We offer Lightning-Fast Service

What their saying about us can be found at www.insure.com. Our speedy service is being talked about by everyone, which has received high ratings and postive reviews from every major business publication "Nation's Business" "Kiplinger's Personal Finance" Good Housekeeping, The Los Angeles Times, "Money" "U.S. News & World Report"

Expert AdviSe Will be provided with No Sales Pitch:

You will not be dealing with insurance agents to save you time and money. But if you want advise our saleried insurance experts are available at our toll-free customer service number. We hope you will take a moment to peruse our webstie, www.insure.com today if possible.

Very truly yours,

Sasha Morgenstern

Longer Business Messages

Unit 4

Understanding and Planning Reports and Proposals

Learning Objectives

After studying this chapter, you will be able to

1 Adapt the three-step writing process to reports and proposals

2 Distinguish among informational reports, analytical reports, and proposals

3 Describe an effective process for conducting business research

4 Define primary and secondary research and explain when you use each method

5 Name nine criteria for evaluating the credibility of an information source

6 Explain how to plan and conduct information interviews

7 Explain the differences between writing a summary, drawing a conclusion, and developing a recommendation

8 Discuss three major ways to organize analytical reports

Beth Uyenco's observation (at the left) refers to her specific line of expertise, finding the best advertising media options for her clients, but it applies to every facet of business. Being good at whatever professional specialty you choose is important, of course, but real success comes from being able to communicate your expertise to others. Reports are one of the most common opportunities you'll have to share your expertise, so learning the fundamentals of effective reports—and learning how to write them in a fast, efficient manner—will serve you well at every step of your career.[1]

Applying the Three-Step Writing Process to Reports and Proposals

In previous chapters, you learned to use the three-step writing process when developing shorter business messages; now it's time to apply those skills to longer messages. Reports fall into three basic categories (Figure 10.1):

Reports can be classified as informational reports, analytical reports, and proposals.

- **Informational reports** offer data, facts, feedback, and other types of information, without analysis or recommendations.
- **Analytical reports** offer both information and analysis, and they can also include recommendations.
- **Proposals** offer structured persuasion for internal or external audiences.

FIGURE 10.1   Common Business Reports and Proposals

You will have the opportunity to read and write many types of reports in your career; here are some of the most common.

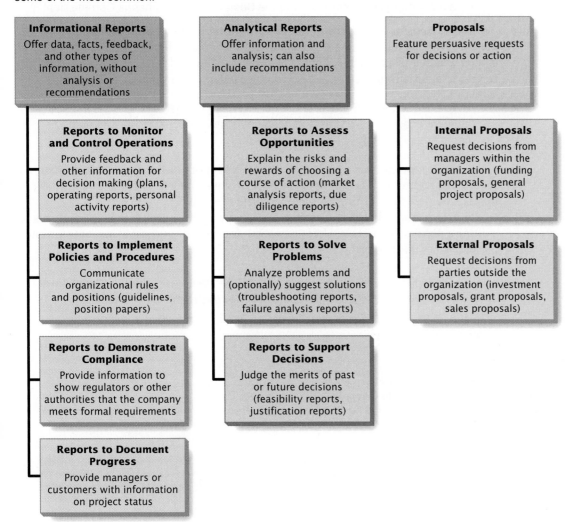

The nature of these reports varies widely, from one-page trip reports that follow a standard format to detailed business plans and proposals that can run hundreds of pages. No matter what the circumstances, try to view every business report as an opportunity to demonstrate your understanding of your audience's challenges and your ability to contribute to your organization's success.

The three-step process (see Figure 10.2) is easily adapted to reports and, in fact, makes these larger projects much easier by ensuring a methodical, efficient approach to planning, writing, and completing.

Analyzing the Situation

The complexity of many reports and the amount of work involved put a premium on carefully analyzing the situation before you begin to write. Pay special attention to your **statement of purpose**, which explains *why* you are preparing the report and what you plan to deliver in the report.

The most useful way to phrase your purpose statement is to begin with an infinitive phrase (*to* plus a verb), which helps pin down your general goal (*to inform, to identify, to analyze,* and so on). For instance, in an informational report, your statement of purpose can be as simple as one of these:

Define your purpose clearly so you don't waste time with unnecessary rework.

- To identify potential markets for our new phone-based videogames
- To update the board of directors on the progress of the research project
- To submit required information to the Securities and Exchange Commission

Your statement of purpose for an analytical report often needs to be more comprehensive. When Linda Moreno, the cost accounting manager for Electrovision, a high-tech company based in Los Gatos, California, was asked to find ways of reducing employee travel and entertainment costs, she phrased her statement of purpose accordingly:

> . . . to analyze the T&E [travel and entertainment] budget, evaluate the impact of recent changes in airfares and hotel costs, and suggest ways to tighten management's control over T&E expenses.

Because Moreno was assigned an analytical report rather than an informational report, she had to go beyond merely collecting data; she had to draw conclusions and make recommendations. You'll see her complete report in Chapter 11.

Proposals must also be guided by a clear statement of purpose to help you focus on crafting a persuasive message. Here are several examples of purpose statements for internal and external proposals:

> To secure funding in next year's budget for new conveyor systems in the warehouse
>
> To get management approval to reorganize the North American salesforce
>
> To secure $2 million from outside investors to start production of the new titanium mountain bike

FIGURE 10.2   Three-Step Writing Process for Reports and Proposals
The three-step writing process becomes even more valuable with reports and proposals. By guiding your work at each step, the process helps you make the most of the time and energy you invest.

Planning

Analyze the Situation
Clarify the problem or opportunity at hand, define your purpose, develop an audience profile, and develop a work plan.

Gather Information
Determine audience needs and obtain the information necessary to satisfy those needs; conduct a research project if necessary.

Select the Right Medium
Choose the best medium for delivering your message; consider delivery through multiple media.

Organize the Information
Define your main idea, limit your scope, select a direct or an indirect approach, and outline your content using an appropriate structure for an informational report, analytical report, or proposal.

Writing

Adapt to Your Audience
Be sensitive to audience needs with a "you" attitude, politeness, positive emphasis, and bias-free language. Build a strong relationship with your audience by establishing your credibility and projecting your company's image. Control your style with a tone and voice appropriate to the situation.

Compose the Message
Choose strong words that will help you create effective sentences and coherent paragraphs throughout the introduction, body, and close of your report or proposal.

Completing

Revise the Report
Evaluate content and review readability; edit and rewrite for conciseness and clarity.

Produce the Report
Use effective design elements and suitable layout for a clean, professional appearance; seamlessly combine textual and graphical elements.

Proofread the Report
Review for errors in layout, spelling, and mechanics.

Distribute the Report
Deliver your report using the chosen medium; make sure all documents and all relevant files are distributed successfully.

1   2   3

Remember, the more specific your purpose statement, the more useful it will be as a guide to planning your report. Furthermore, if you've been assigned the report by someone else, always double-check your statement of purpose with that person to make sure you've interpreted the assignment correctly.

In addition to considering your purpose carefully, you will also want to prepare a *work plan* for most reports and proposals in order to make the best use of your time. For simpler reports, the work plan can be an informal list of tasks and a simple schedule. However, if you're preparing a lengthy report, particularly when you're collaborating with others, you'll want to develop a more detailed work plan (Figure 10.3).

A detailed work plan saves time and often produces more effective reports.

FIGURE 10.3   Work Plan for a Report

A formal work plan such as this is a vital tool for planning and managing complex writing projects. The preliminary outline here helps guide the research; the report writers may well modify the outline when they begin writing the report.

States the problem clearly enough for anyone to understand

STATEMENT OF THE PROBLEM
The rapid growth of our company over the past five years has reduced the sense of community among our staff. People no longer feel like part of an intimate organization that values teamwork.

PURPOSE AND SCOPE OF WORK
The purpose of this study is to determine whether a company newsletter would help rebuild a sense of community within the workforce. The study will evaluate the impact of newsletters in other companies and will attempt to identify features that might be desirable in our own newsletter. Such variables as length, frequency of distribution, types of articles, and graphic design will be considered. Costs will be estimated for several approaches, including print and electronic versions. In addition, the study will analyze the personnel and procedures required to produce a newsletter.

Explains exactly what will be covered by the research and included in the final report

Identifies the tasks to be accomplished and does so in clear, simple terms

SOURCES AND METHODS OF DATA COLLECTION
Sample newsletters will be collected from 10–20 companies similar to ours in size, growth rate, and types of employees. The editors will be asked to comment on the impact of their publications on employee morale. Our own employees will be surveyed to determine their interest in a newsletter and their preferences for specific features. Production procedures and costs will be analyzed through conversations with newsletter editors, printers, and our website development team.

Offers a preliminary outline to help readers understand the issues that will be addressed in the report

PRELIMINARY OUTLINE
The preliminary outline for this study is as follows:
  I. Do newsletters affect morale?
    A. Do people read them?
    B. How do employees benefit?
    C. How does the company benefit?
  II. What are the features of good newsletters?
    A. How long are they?
    B. What do they contain?
    C. How often are they published?
    D. How are they designed?
  III. How should a newsletter be produced?
    A. Should it be written and edited internally or externally?
    B. Should it be printed or produced electronically?
    C. If electronic, should it be formatted as e-mail, a blog, or regular web content?
  IV. What would a newsletter cost?
    A. What would the personnel cost be?
    B. What would the material cost be?
    C. What would outside services cost?
  V. Should we publish a company newsletter?
  VI. If so, what approach should we take?

Identifies who is responsible for each task and when it will be completed

TASK ASSIGNMENTS AND SCHEDULE
Each phase of this study will be completed by the following dates:

Collect/analyze newsletters	Hank Waters	September 15, 2007
Interview editors by phone	Hank Waters	September 22, 2007
Survey employees	Julienne Cho	September 29, 2007
Develop sample	Hank Waters	October 6, 2007
Develop cost estimates	Julienne Cho	October 13, 2007
Prepare report	Hank Waters	October 20, 2007
Submit final report	Hank Waters	October 24, 2007

Gathering Information

Some reports require formal research projects in order to gather all the necessary information.

The sheer volume of information needed for many reports and proposals requires careful planning, and you may even require a separate research project just to acquire the data and information you need. To stay on schedule and on budget, be sure that you review both your statement of purpose and your audience's needs so that you collect all the information you need—and only the information you need. In some cases, you won't be able to collect every piece of information you'd like, so prioritize your needs up front and focus on the most important questions.

Selecting the Right Medium

The best medium for any given report might be anything from a professionally printed and bound document to an online executive dashboard that displays nothing but report highlights.

In addition to the general media selection criteria discussed in Chapter 3, consider several points for reports and proposals. First, for many reports and proposals, audiences have specific media requirements, and you might not have a choice. For instance, executives in many corporations now expect to review many reports via their in-house intranets, sometimes in conjunction with an *executive dashboard*, a customized online presentation of key business information such as revenues and project progress. Second, consider how your audience wants to provide feedback on your report or proposal. Do they prefer to write comments on a printed document or to use commenting and markup features in software? Third, will people need to search through your document frequently or update it in the future? Delivering a report as an electronic file makes both tasks far easier. Fourth, bear in mind that your choice of media also sends a message. For instance, a routine sales report dressed up in expensive multimedia will look like a waste of valuable company resources.

Organizing Your Information

The direct approach is by far the most popular and convenient for business reports; it saves time, makes the rest of the report easier to follow, and produces a more forceful report. However, the confidence implied by the direct report may be misconstrued as arrogance, especially if you're a junior member of a status-conscious organization. On the other hand, the indirect approach gives you a chance to prove your points and gradually overcome your audience's reservations. The longer the message, though, the less effective an indirect approach is likely to be. Therefore, carefully consider report length before deciding on the direct or indirect approach. Both approaches have merit, and business-people often combine them, revealing their conclusions and recommendations as they go along, rather than putting them first or last (see Figure 10.4).

Supporting Your Messages with Reliable Information

Many of your business reports will require some level of research.

As you've probably discovered while doing school projects, research involves a lot more than simply typing a few terms into a search engine. Good research requires a clear process:

1. **Plan your research.** Planning is the most important step of any research project; a solid plan yields better results in less time.

2. **Locate the data and information you need.** The research plan tells you *what* to look for, so your next step is to figure out *where* these data and information are and *how* to access them.

3. **Process the data and information you located.** The data and information you find probably won't be in a form you can use immediately and will require some processing, such as statistical analysis, to resolve the differences between two expert opinions.

FIGURE 10.4   Direct Approach Versus Indirect Approach in a Report Introduction
Compare the introductions of these two reports, based on the same general outline. In the direct version, a series of statements summarizes the conclusion reached about each main topic in the outline. In the indirect version, the same topics are introduced in the same order but without drawing any conclusions about them. Instead, the conclusions appear in the body of the report.

DIRECT APPROACH

Since the company's founding 25 years ago, we have provided regular repair service for all our electric appliances. This service has been an important selling point as well as a source of pride for our employees. However, rising labor costs have made it impossible to maintain profitability while offering competitive service rates. Last year, we lost $500,000 on our repair business.

Because of your concern over these losses, you have asked me to study the pros and cons of discontinuing our repair service. With the help of John Hudson and Susan Lefkowitz, I have studied the issue for the past two weeks and have come to the conclusion that we have been embracing an expensive, impractical tradition.

By withdrawing from the electric appliance repair business, we can substantially improve our financial performance without damaging our reputation with customers. This conclusion is based on three basic points that are covered in the following pages:

- It is highly unlikely that we will ever be able to make a profit in the repair business.
- We can refer customers to a variety of qualified repair firms without significantly reducing customer satisfaction.
- Closing down the service operation will create few internal problems.

INDIRECT APPROACH

Since the company's founding 25 years ago, we have provided regular repair service for all our electric appliances. This service has been an important selling point as well as a source of pride for our employees. However, rising labor costs have made it impossible to maintain profitability while offering competitive service rates.

Because of your concern over these losses, you have asked me to study the pros and cons of discontinuing our repair service. With the help of John Hudson and Susan Lefkowitz, I have studied the issue for the past two weeks. The following pages present my findings for your review. The analysis addressed three basic questions:

- What is the extent of our losses, and what can we do to turn the business around?
- Would withdrawal hurt our sales of electrical appliances?
- What would be the internal repercussions of closing down the repair business?

4. **Apply your findings.** You can apply your research findings in three ways: summarizing information, drawing conclusions, or developing recommendations.

5. **Manage information efficiently.** Many companies today are trying to maximize the return on the time and money they invest in business research by collecting and sharing research results in a variety of computer-based systems, known generally as **knowledge management systems.**

Planning Your Research

To spend your research time and money wisely, start with a clear goal in mind. Start by developing a **problem statement** that will define the purpose of your research—the decision you need to make or the conclusion you need to reach at the end of the process. Next, identify the information you need in order to make that decision or reach that conclusion. You can then begin to generate the questions that will constitute your research. As you list questions you want to ask, you might compile more questions than you have time or money to answer. If so, you will need to prioritize your information needs and concentrate on the most vital questions.

With a prioritized list of questions, you're just about ready to get started with your research. Before taking that step, however, it's important to be aware that research carries some significant ethical responsibilities. Your research tactics affect the people from whom you gather data and information, the people who read your results, and the people

Your problem statement will help direct your research.

who are affected by the way you present those results. To avoid ethical lapses, keep the following points in mind:

Privacy is one of the hottest issues in the research field today.

- Keep an open mind so that you don't skew the research toward answers you want or expect to see.
- Respect the privacy of your research participants; don't observe people without their consent, and don't mislead people about the purposes of your research.[2]
- Document sources and give appropriate credit.
- Respect your sources' *intellectual property rights* (the ownership of unique ideas that have commercial value in the marketplace).[3]

In addition to ethics, research etiquette deserves careful attention, too. For example, respect the time of anyone who agrees to be interviewed or to be a research participant, and maintain courtesy throughout the interview or research process.

Locating Data and Information

A good plan and careful prioritization tell you *what* you need to know and *why* you need to know it; the next step is to identify *where* that information might exist and *how* to locate it. The range of sources available to business researchers today is remarkable, almost overwhelming at times. If you have a question about an industry, a company, a market, a new technology, or a financial topic, chances are somebody else has already researched the subject. Research done previously for another purpose is considered **secondary research**; sources for such research information include magazines, newspapers, public websites, books, and other reports. Don't let the name *secondary* fool you, though. You want to start with secondary research because it can save you considerable time and money for many projects. In contrast, **primary research** is new research done specifically for your current project and includes surveys, interviews, observations, and experiments.

Primary research contains information that you gather specifically for a new research project; secondary research contains information that others have gathered (and published, in many cases).

Evaluating Sources

In every research project, you have the responsibility to verify the quality of the sources you use. The Internet has made this challenge easier in one respect, since it's usually possible to cross-check information by referring to multiple sources. At the same time, online research is more difficult, because so much bad information exists on the Internet, from doctored photos to unverified "facts" to biased sources. To avoid tainting your results and damaging your reputation, ask yourself the following questions about each piece of material:

Evaluate your sources carefully to avoid embarrassing and potentially damaging mistakes.

- **Does the source have a reputation for honesty and reliability?** For example, try to find out how the source accepts articles and whether it has an editorial board, peer review, or fact-checking procedures.
- **Is the source potentially biased?** To interpret an organization's information, you need to know its point of view.
- **What is the purpose of the material?** For instance, was the material designed to inform others of new research, advance a political position, or promote a product?
- **Is the author credible?** Is the author a professional journalist? An informed amateur? Merely someone with an opinion?
- **Where did the source get *its* information?** Try to find out who collected the data, the methods they used, their qualifications, and their professional reputation.
- **Can you verify the material independently?** Verification can uncover biases or mistakes—particularly important when the information goes beyond simple facts to include projections, interpretations, and estimates.
- **Is the material current?** Make sure you are using the most current information available by checking the publication date of a source.
- **Is the material complete?** Have you accessed the entire document or only a selection from it? If it's a selection, which parts were excluded? Do you need more detail?

You probably won't have time to conduct a thorough background check on all your sources, so focus your efforts on the most important or most suspicious pieces of information.

Conducting Secondary Research

Even if you intend to eventually conduct primary research, most projects start with a review of secondary research. Inside your company, you might be able to find a variety of reports, memos, and other documents that could help. Outside the company, business researchers can choose from a wide range of print and online resources both in libraries and online.

You'll want to start most projects by conducting secondary research first.

Finding Information at the Library   Public and university libraries offer an enormous array of business books, electronic databases, newspapers, periodicals, directories, almanacs, and government publications. Many of these may be unavailable through a standard web search or may be available only with a subscription. Libraries are also where you'll find one of your most important resources: librarians. Reference librarians are trained in research techniques and can often help you find obscure information you can't find on your own. They can also direct you to the typical library's many sources of business information:

Even in the Internet age, libraries offer information and resources you can't find anywhere else—including experienced research librarians.

- **Newspapers and periodicals.** Libraries offer access to a wide variety of popular magazines, general business magazines, *trade journals* (which provide information about specific professions and industries), and *academic journals* (which provide research-oriented articles from researchers and educators).
- **Business books.** Although less timely than newspapers and periodicals, business books provide in-depth coverage of a variety of business topics.
- **Directories.** Thousands of directories are published in print and electronic formats in the United States, and many include membership information for all kinds of professions, industries, and special-interest groups.
- **Almanacs and statistical resources.** Almanacs are handy guides to factual and statistical information about countries, politics, the labor force, and so on. One of the most extensive is the *Statistical Abstract of the United States* (available online at www.census.gov).
- **Government publications.** Information on laws, court decisions, tax questions, regulatory issues, and other governmental concerns can often be found in collections of government documents.
- **Electronic databases.** Databases offer vast collections of computer-searchable information, often in specific areas such as business, law, science, technology, and education. Some libraries offer remote online access to some or all databases; for others you'll need to visit in person.

Local, state, and federal government agencies publish a huge array of information that is helpful to business researchers.

Finding Information Online   The Internet can be a tremendous source of business information, provided you know where to look and how to use the tools available. **Search engines** scan millions of websites to identify individual webpages that contain a specific word or phrase you've asked for. For all their ease and power, search engines have three disadvantages: (1) no human editors are involved to evaluate the quality of the results; (2) various engines use different search techniques, so often find different sites; and (3) search engines can't reach the content on restricted-access websites (sometimes called the *hidden Internet*).

Conduct online research with extreme care; much of the information online has not been subjected to the same quality controls common in traditional offline publishing.

Web directories address the first major shortcoming of search engines by using human editors to categorize and evaluate websites. *Metacrawlers* or *metasearch* engines address the second shortcoming by formatting your search request for the specific requirements of multiple search engines. **Online databases** help address the third shortcoming of search engines by offering access to the newspapers, magazines, and journals that you're likely to need for many research projects. Check with a librarian to find the right databases for your projects.

Web directories rely on human editors to evaluate and select websites.

Search engines, web directories, databases, and metacrawlers work in different ways, and you can get unpredictable results if you don't know how each one operates.

Be aware that search engines, metacrawlers, and databases continue to evolve, and no two of them work in exactly the same way. Make sure you understand how to optimize your search and interpret the results. With a *keyword search*, the engine or database attempts to find items that include all of the words you enter. A *Boolean search* lets you define a query with greater precision, using such operators as AND (the search must include two terms linked by AND), OR (it can include either or both words), or NOT (the search ignores items with whatever word comes after NOT). *Natural language searches* let you ask questions in everyday English. *Forms-based searches* help you create powerful queries by simply filling out an online form that lets you specify such parameters as date ranges, language, Internet domain name, and even file and media types.[4]

To make the best use of any search engine or database, keep the following points in mind:

- Read the instructions and pay attention to the details.
- Review the search and display options carefully so you don't misinterpret the results.
- Try variations of your terms, such as *child*, *adolescent*, and *youth* or *management* and *managerial*.
- User fewer search terms to find more results; use more search terms to find fewer results.

If you want to monitor a particular information source over time, see if it offers a newsfeed subscription via RSS or another format. News aggregators such as NewsGator (www.newsgator.com) and NewzCrawler (www.newzcrawler.com) let you subscribe to specific information channels at thousands of websites, blogs, and newsgroups.[5]

Proper documentation of the sources you use is both ethical and an important resource for your readers.

Documenting Your Sources   Documenting your sources serves three important functions: It properly and ethically credits the person who created the original material, it shows your audience that you have sufficient support for your message, and it helps your readers explore your topic in more detail if desired. Be sure to take advantage of the source documentation tools in your word processor; Microsoft Word automatically tracks and numbers endnotes for you, and you can use the "table of authorities" feature to create a bibliography of all the sources you've used. Software such as Microsoft's OneNote makes it easier to collect and organize notes wherever and however you find vital information, from meetings to websites to e-mail messages.[6]

Appendix B discusses the common methods of documenting sources. Whatever method you choose, documentation is necessary for books, articles, tables, charts, diagrams, song lyrics, scripted dialogue, letters, speeches—anything that you take from someone else, including ideas and information that you've re-expressed through paraphrasing or summarizing. However, you do not have to cite a source for knowledge that's generally known among your readers, such as the fact that Microsoft is a large software company and that computers are pervasive in business today.

Conducting Primary Research

Surveys and interviews are the most common primary research techniques.

If secondary research can't provide the information and insights you need, your next choice is to gather the information yourself with primary research. Primary research encompasses a variety of methods, from observations to experiments such as test marketing. However, for most business projects, the two most common primary research methods are surveys and interviews.

For a survey to produce valid results, it must be based on a representative sample of respondents.

Conducting Surveys   A carefully prepared and conducted survey can provide invaluable insights, but only if it is *reliable* (would produce identical results if repeated) and *valid* (measures what it's supposed to measure). For important surveys, consider hiring a research specialist to avoid errors in design and implementation. To develop an effective survey questionnaire, follow these tips:[7]

- **Provide clear instructions.** Respondents need to know exactly how to fill out your questionnaire.

- **Don't ask for information that people can't be expected to remember.** For instance, a question such as "How many times did you go grocery shopping last year" will generate unreliable answers.
- **Keep the questionnaire short and easy to answer.** Don't make any individual questions difficult to answer, and don't expect people to give you more than 10 or 15 minutes of their time.
- **Whenever possible, formulate questions to provide answers that are easy to analyze.** Numbers and facts are easier to summarize than opinions, for instance.
- **Avoid leading questions that could bias your survey.** If you ask, "Do you prefer that we stay open in the evenings for customer convenience?" you'll no doubt get a "yes." Instead, ask, "What time of day do you normally do your shopping?"
- **Avoid ambiguous questions.** If you ask, "Do you shop at the mall often?" some people might interpret *often* to mean "every day," whereas others might think it means "once a week" or "once a month."
- **Ask only one thing at a time.** A compound question such as "Do you read books and magazines?" doesn't allow for the respondent who reads one but not the other.

The Internet is quickly becoming the preferred survey mechanism for many researchers, and dozens of companies now offer online survey services.[8] Compared to traditional mail and in-person techniques, online surveys are usually faster to create, easier to administer, quicker to analyze, and less expensive overall. The interactive capabilities of the web can enhance all kinds of surveys, from simple opinion polls to complex purchase simulations. However, online surveys require the same care as any other type of survey, including being on guard against sampling bias.[9]

Conducting Interviews   Getting in-depth information straight from an expert can be a great method for collecting primary information. Like surveys, interviews require careful planning to get the best results. The answers you receive are influenced by the types of questions you ask, by the way you ask them, and by your subject's cultural and language background. Other potentially significant factors include the person's race, gender, age, educational level, and social status, so know your subject before you start writing questions.[10]

Ask **open-ended questions** to invite the expert to offer opinions, insights, and information, such as "Why do you believe that South America represents a better opportunity than Europe for this product line?" Ask **closed questions** to elicit a specific answer, such as yes or no. However, including too many closed questions in an interview will make the experience feel more like a simple survey and won't take full advantage of the interview setting.

Think carefully about the sequence of your questions and the subject's potential answers so you can arrange them in an order that helps uncover layers of information. Also consider providing the other person with a list of questions at least a day or two before the interview, especially if you'd like to quote your subject in writing or if your questions might require your subject to conduct research or think extensively about the answers. If you want to record the interview, ask the person ahead of time and respect his or her wishes.

Face-to-face interviews give you the opportunity to gauge the reaction to your questions and observe the nonverbal signals that accompany the answers, but interviews don't necessarily have to take place in person. E-mail interviews are becoming more common, partly because they give subjects a chance to think through their responses thoroughly, rather than rushing to fit the time constraints of a face-to-face interview.[11]

Using Your Research Results

Once you've collected your data, the next step is to transform it into the specific content you need. This step can involve quoting, paraphrasing, or summarizing textual material; drawing conclusions; and making recommendations.

Interviews are easy to conduct but require careful planning to produce useful results.

Choose question types that will generate the specific information you need.

Face-to-face interviews give you the opportunity to gauge nonverbal responses as well.

After you collect your data, the next step is converting it into usable information.

Document Makeover

Improve This Report

To practice correcting drafts of actual documents, visit your online course or the access-code-protected portion of the Companion Website. Click "Document Makeovers," then click Chapter 10. You will find a personal activity report that contains problems and errors relating to what you've learned in this chapter about planning business reports and proposals. Use the "Final Draft" decision tool to create an improved version of this personal activity report. Check the report for parallel construction, appropriate headings, suitable content, positive and bias-free language, and use of the "you" attitude.

Quoting, Paraphrasing, and Summarizing Information

Quoting a source means reproducing the content exactly and indicating who created the information originally.

You can use information from secondary sources in three ways. *Quoting* a source means you reproduce it exactly as you found it, and you either set it off with quotation marks (for shorter passages) or extract it in an indented paragraph (for longer passages). Use direct quotations when the original language will enhance your argument or when rewording the passage would lessen its impact. However, too much quoting creates a choppy patchwork of varying styles and gives the impression that all you've done is piece together the work of other people.

Paraphrasing is expressing someone else's ideas in your own words.

You can often maximize the impact of secondary material in your own writing by *paraphrasing* it, restating it in your own words and with your own sentence structures.[12] Paraphrasing helps you maintain consistent tone while using vocabulary familiar to your audience. Of course, you still need to credit the originator of the information, but not with quotation marks or indented paragraphs.

Summarizing is similar to paraphrasing but distills the content into fewer words.

Summarizing is similar to paraphrasing but presents the gist of the material in fewer words than the original. An effective summary identifies the main ideas and major support points from your source material but leaves out most details, examples, and other information that is less critical to your audience. Like quotations and paraphrases, summaries also require complete documentation of your sources. Summarizing is not always a simple task, and your audience will judge your ability to separate significant issues from less significant details. Identify the main idea and the key support points, and separate these from details, examples, and other supporting evidence (see Table 10.1).

Table 10.1	Summarizing Effectively	
Original Material (110 Words)	**45-Word Summary**	**22-Word Summary**
Our facilities costs spiraled out of control last year. The 23 percent jump was far ahead of every other cost category in the company and many times higher than the 4 percent average rise for commercial real estate in the Portland metropolitan area. The rise can be attributed to many factors, but the major factors include repairs (mostly electrical and structural problems at the downtown office), energy (most of our offices are heated by electricity, the price of which has been increasing much faster than for oil or gas), and last but not least, the loss of two sublease tenants whose rent payments made a substantial dent in our cost profile for the past five years.	Our facilities costs jumped 23 percent last year, far ahead of every other cost category in the company and many times higher than the 4 percent local average. The major factors contributing to the increase are repairs, energy, and the loss of two sublease tenants.	Our facilities costs jumped 23 percent last year, due mainly to rising repair and energy costs and the loss of sublease income.

Main idea

Major support points

Details

Of course, all three approaches require careful attention to ethics. When quoting directly, take care not to distort the original intent of the material by quoting selectively or out of context. And never succumb to **plagiarism**, presenting someone else's words as your own.

Never present someone else's words as your own.

Drawing Conclusions

A **conclusion** is a logical interpretation of facts and other information. A sound conclusion not only is logical but flows from the information included in your report, meaning that it should be based on the information included in the report and shouldn't rely on information that isn't in the report.

A conclusion interprets the information presented in the report.

Reaching good conclusions based on the evidence at hand is one of the most important skills you can develop in your business career. In fact, the ability to see patterns and possibilities that others can't see is one of the hallmarks of innovative business leaders. Consequently, take your time with this part of the process.

Making Recommendations

Whereas a conclusion interprets information, a **recommendation** suggests what to do about the information. The difference between a conclusion and a recommendation can be seen in the following example:

A recommendation tells readers what should be done with the information in the report.

Conclusion	Recommendation
On the basis of its track record and current price, I conclude that this company is an attractive buy.	I recommend that we write a letter to the board of directors offering to buy the company at a 10 percent premium over the current market value of its stock.

To be credible, recommendations must be based on logical analysis and sound conclusions. They must also be practical and acceptable to the people who have to make your recommendations work. Finally, when making a recommendation, be certain that you have adequately described the steps that come next. Don't leave your readers wondering what they need to do in order to act on your recommendation.

Planning Informational Reports

Informational reports provide the feedback that employees, managers, and others need in order to make decisions, take action, and respond to changes. As Figure 10.1 on page 267 indicated, information reports can be grouped into four general categories:

Informational reports are used to monitor and control operations, to implement policies and procedures, to demonstrate compliance, and to document progress.

- **Reports to monitor and control operations.** Managers rely on a wide range of reports to see how well their companies are functioning. *Plans* establish expectations and guidelines to direct future action. The most important of these are *business plans*, which summarize a proposed business venture, communicate the company's goals, highlight how management intends to achieve those goals, and explain why customers will be motivated to buy the company's products or services. *Operating reports* provide feedback on a wide variety of an organization's functions, including sales, inventories, expenses, shipments, and so on. *Personal activity reports* provide information regarding an individual's experiences during sales calls, industry conferences, market research trips, and so on.
- **Reports to implement policies and procedures.** *Policy reports* range from brief descriptions of business procedures to manuals that run dozens or hundreds of pages. *Position papers* outline an organization's official position on issues that affect the company's success.

- **Reports to demonstrate compliance.** Businesses are required to submit a variety of *compliance reports*, from tax returns to reports describing the proper handling of hazardous materials.
- **Reports to document progress.** Supervisors, investors, and customers frequently expect to be informed of the progress of projects and other activities. *Progress reports* range from simple updates in memo form to comprehensive status reports.

In most cases, the direct approach is the best choice for informational reports, since you are simply conveying information. However, if the information is disappointing, such as a project that is behind schedule or over budget, you might consider building up to the bad news through an indirect approach. In general, let the nature of whatever you're describing dictate your structure. Most informational reports use a **topical organization**, arranging material in one of the following ways:

- **Comparison:** Showing similarities and differences (or advantages and disadvantages) between two or more entities
- **Importance:** Building up from the least important item to the most important (or from most important to the least if you don't think your audience will read the entire report)
- **Sequence:** Organizing the steps or stages in a process or procedure
- **Chronology:** Organizing a chain of events in order from oldest to newest, such as what happened in January, what happened in February, and so on
- **Geography:** Organizing by region, city, state, country, or other geographic unit
- **Category:** Grouping by topical category, such as sales, profit, cost, or investment

Figure 10.5 offers an example of an effective information report.

Planning Analytical Reports

The purpose of analytical reports is to analyze, to understand, to explain—to think through a problem or an opportunity and figure out how it affects the company and how the company should respond. In many cases, you'll also be expected to make a recommendation based on your analysis. As you also saw in Figure 10.1, analytical reports fall into three basic categories:

- **Reports to assess opportunities.** Every business opportunity carries some degree of risk and also requires a variety of decisions and actions in order to capitalize on the opportunity. You can use analytical reports to assess both risk and required decisions and actions. For instance, *market analysis reports* are used to judge the likelihood of success for new products or sales. *Due diligence reports* examine the financial aspects of a proposed decision, such as acquiring another company.
- **Reports to solve problems.** Managers often assign *troubleshooting reports* when they need to understand why something isn't working properly and what needs to be done to fix it. A variation, the *failure analysis report*, studies events that happened in the past, with the hope of learning how to avoid similar failures in the future.
- **Reports to support decisions.** *Feasibility reports* are called for when managers need to explore the ramifications of a decision they're about to make, such as switching materials used in a manufacturing process. *Justification reports* explain a decision that has already been made.

Writing analytical reports presents a greater challenge than writing informational reports, for three reasons: the quality of your reasoning, the quality of your writing, and the responsibility that comes with persuasion. First, you're doing more than simply delivering information—you're also thinking through a problem or opportunity and presenting your conclusions. The best writing in the world can't compensate for shaky analysis. Second, when your analysis is complete, you need to present your thinking in a

FIGURE 10.5   Effective Informational Report

Roger Watson's personal activity report for July is a good example of efficiently conveying key information points. Note the use of hyperlinks to maps, photos, and a related report, all of which are stored on the same secure intranet site.

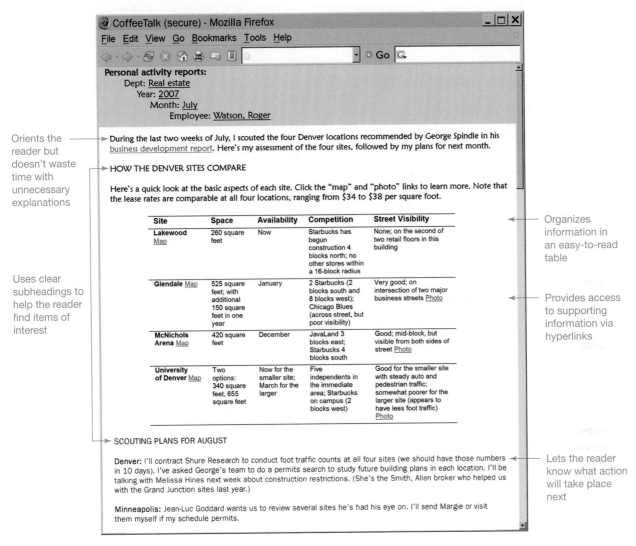

Orients the reader but doesn't waste time with unnecessary explanations

Uses clear subheadings to help the reader find items of interest

Organizes information in an easy-to-read table

Provides access to supporting information via hyperlinks

Lets the reader know what action will take place next

compelling and persuasive manner. Third, analytical reports often convince other people to make significant financial and personnel decisions, so your reports carry the added responsibility of the consequences of these decisions.

Focusing on Conclusions

When writing for audiences that are likely to accept your conclusions—either because they've asked you to perform an analysis or they trust your judgment—consider a direct approach that focuses immediately on your conclusions. This structure communicates the main idea quickly, but it does present some risks. Even if audiences trust your judgment, they may have questions about your data or the methods you used. Moreover, starting with a conclusion may create the impression that you have oversimplified the situation. To give readers the opportunity to explore the thinking behind your conclusion, support that conclusion with solid reasoning and evidence (Figure 10.6).

Focusing on conclusions is often the best approach when you're addressing a receptive audience.

FIGURE 10.6   Preliminary Outline of a Research Report Focusing on Conclusions

Cynthia Zolonka works on the human resources staff of a bank in Houston, Texas. Her company decided to have an outside firm handle its employee training, and a year after the outsourcing arrangement was established, Zolonka was asked to evaluate the results. Her analysis shows that the outsourcing experiment was a success, and she opens with that conclusion but supports it with clear evidence. Readers who accept the conclusion can stop reading, and those who desire more information can continue.

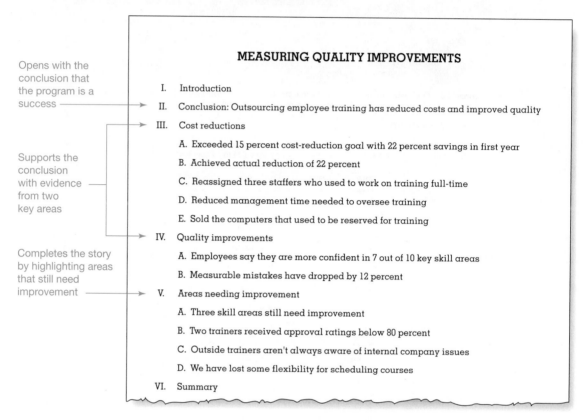

Opens with the conclusion that the program is a success

Supports the conclusion with evidence from two key areas

Completes the story by highlighting areas that still need improvement

MEASURING QUALITY IMPROVEMENTS

I.   Introduction

II.   Conclusion: Outsourcing employee training has reduced costs and improved quality

III. Cost reductions
   A. Exceeded 15 percent cost-reduction goal with 22 percent savings in first year
   B. Achieved actual reduction of 22 percent
   C. Reassigned three staffers who used to work on training full-time
   D. Reduced management time needed to oversee training
   E. Sold the computers that used to be reserved for training

IV.   Quality improvements
   A. Employees say they are more confident in 7 out of 10 key skill areas
   B. Measurable mistakes have dropped by 12 percent

V.   Areas needing improvement
   A. Three skill areas still need improvement
   B. Two trainers received approval ratings below 80 percent
   C. Outside trainers aren't always aware of internal company issues
   D. We have lost some flexibility for scheduling courses

VI.   Summary

Focusing on Recommendations

When readers want to know what you think they should do, organize your report to focus on recommendations.

A slightly different approach is useful when your readers want to know what they ought to do in a given situation (as opposed to what they ought to conclude). You'll often be asked to solve a problem or assess an opportunity, rather than just study it. The actions you want your readers to take become the main subdivisions of your report.

When structuring a report around recommendations, use the direct approach as you would for a report that focuses on conclusions. Then unfold your recommendations using a series of five steps:

1. Establish the need for action in the introduction by briefly describing the problem or opportunity.
2. Introduce the benefit(s) that can be achieved if the recommendation is adopted, along with any potential risks.
3. List the steps (recommendations) required to achieve the benefit, using action verbs for emphasis.
4. Explain each step more fully, giving details on procedures, costs, and benefits; if necessary, also explain how risks can be minimized.
5. Summarize your recommendations.

Focusing on Logical Arguments

When readers are skeptical or hostile to the conclusion or recommendation you plan to make, use an indirect approach that logically builds toward your conclusion or recommendation. If you guide the audience along a rational path toward the answer, they are more likely to accept it when they encounter it. The two most common logical approaches are known as the *2 + 2 = 4 approach*, in which you convince readers by demonstrating that everything adds up to your conclusion, and the *yardstick approach*, in which you use a number of criteria to decide which option to select from two or more possibilities (see Figure 10.7).

Logical arguments can follow two basic approaches: 2 + 2 = 4 (adding everything up) and the yardstick method (comparing ideas against a predetermined set of standards).

FIGURE 10.7   Analytical Report Focusing on Logical Arguments

As national sales manager of a New Hampshire sporting goods company, Binh Phan was concerned about his company's ability to sell to its largest customers. His boss, the vice president of marketing, shared these concerns and asked Phan to analyze the situation and recommend a solution. In this troubleshooting report, his main idea is that the company should establish separate sales teams for these major accounts, rather than continue to service them through the company's four regional divisions. However, Phan knew his plan would be controversial because it required a big change in the company's organization and in the way sales reps are paid. His thinking had to be clear and easy to follow, so he focused on logical argumentation.

MEMO

DATE: September 12, 2007
TO: Robert Mendoza, Vice President of Marketing
FROM: Binh Phan, National Sales Manager   *BP*
SUBJECT: Major accounts sales problems

Clarifies who requested the report, when it was requested, and who wrote it →

As you requested on August 20, this report outlines the results of my investigation into the recent slowdown in sales to major accounts and the accompanying rise in sales- and service-related complaints from some of our largest customers.

Over the last four quarters, major account sales dropped 12%, whereas overall sales were up 7%. During the same time, we've all noticed an increase in both formal and informal complaints from larger customers, regarding how confusing and complicated it has become to do business with us.

← *Highlights the serious nature of the problem*

Explains how the information used in the analysis was collected →

My investigation started with in-depth discussions with the four regional sales managers, first as a group and then individually. The tension I felt in the initial meeting eventually bubbled to the surface during my meetings with each manager. Staff members in each region are convinced that other regions are booking orders they don't deserve, with one region doing all the legwork only to see another region get the sale, the commission, and the quota credit.

I followed up these formal discussions by talking informally and exchanging e-mail with several sales representatives from each region. Virtually everyone who is involved with our major national accounts has a story to share. No one is happy with the situation, and I sense that some reps are walking away from major customers because the process is so frustrating.

The decline in sales to our major national customers and the increase in their complaints stem from two problems: (1) sales force organization and (2) commission policy.

ORGANIZATIONAL PROBLEMS

← *Organizational problems are the first "2" in Phan's 2 + 2 = 4 approach*

Describes the first problem and explains how it occurred, without blaming anyone personally →

When we divided the national sales force into four geographical regions last year, the idea was to focus our sales efforts and clarify responsibilities for each prospective and current customer. The regional managers have gotten to know their market territories very well, and sales have increased beyond even our most optimistic projections.

However, while solving one problem, we have created another. In the past 12 to 18 months, several regional customers have grown to national status, and a few retailers have taken on (or expressed interest in) our products. As a result, a significant portion of both current sales and future opportunities lies with these large national accounts.

I uncovered more than a dozen cases in which sales representatives from two or more regions found themselves competing with each other by pursuing the same customers from different locations. Moreover, the complaints from our major accounts about overlapping or nonexistent account coverage are a direct result of the regional organization. In some cases, customers aren't sure which of our representatives they're supposed to call with problems and orders. In other cases, no one has been in contact with them for several months.

(continued)

FIGURE 10.7   (continued)

2

Brings the first problem to life by complementing the general description with a specific example

For example, having retail outlets across the lower tier of the country, AmeriSport received pitches from reps out of our West, South, and East regions. Because our regional offices have a lot of negotiating freedom, the three were offering different prices. But all AmeriSport buying decisions were made at the Tampa headquarters, so all we did was confuse the customer. The irony of the current organization is that we're often giving our weakest selling and support efforts to the largest customers in the country.

COMMISSION PROBLEMS

Commission problems are the second "2" in Phan's 2 + 2 = 4 approach

The regional organization problems are compounded by the way we assign commissions and quota credit. Salespeople in one region can invest a lot of time in pursuing a sale, only to have the customer place the order in another region. So some sales rep in the second region ends up with the commission on a sale that was partly or even entirely earned by someone in the first region. Therefore, sales reps sometimes don't pursue leads in their regions, thinking that a rep in another region will get the commission.

Simplifies the reader's task by maintaining a parallel structure for the discussion of the second problem: a general description followed by a specific example

For example, Athletic Express, with outlets in 35 states spread across all four regions, finally got so frustrated with us that the company president called our headquarters. Athletic Express has been trying to place a large order for tennis and golf accessories, but none of our local reps seem interested in paying attention. I spoke with the rep responsible for Nashville, where the company is headquartered, and asked her why she wasn't working the account more actively. Her explanation was that last time she got involved with Athletic Express, the order was actually placed from their L.A. regional office, and she didn't get any commission after more than two weeks of selling time.

RECOMMENDATIONS

Phan concludes the 2 + 2 = 4 approach: organizational problems + commission problems = the need for a new sales structure

Our sales organization should reflect the nature of our customer base. To accomplish that goal, we need a group of reps who are free to pursue accounts across regional borders—and who are compensated fairly for their work. The most sensible answer is to establish a national account group. Any customers whose operations place them in more than one region would automatically be assigned to the national group.

Explains how the new organizational structure will solve both problems

Acknowledges that the recommended solution does create a temporary compensation problem, but expresses confidence that a solution to that can be worked out

In addition to solving the problem of competing sales efforts, the new structure will also largely eliminate the commission-splitting problem because regional reps will no longer invest time in prospects assigned to the national accounts team. However, we will need to find a fair way to compensate regional reps who are losing long-term customers to the national team. Some of these reps have invested years in developing customer relationships that will continue to yield sales well into the future, and everyone I talked to agrees that reps in these cases should receive some sort of compensation. Such a "transition commission" would also motivate the regional reps to help ensure a smooth transition from one sales group to the other. The exact nature of this compensation would need to be worked out with the various sales managers.

3

SUMMARY

The regional sales organization is effective at the regional and local levels but not at the national level. We should establish a national accounts group to handle sales that cross regional boundaries. Then we'll have one set of reps who are focused on the local and regional levels and another set who are pursuing national accounts.

Neatly summarizes both the problem and the recommended solution

To compensate regional reps who lose accounts to the national team, we will need to devise some sort of payment to reward them for the years of work invested in such accounts. This can be discussed with the sales managers once the new structure is in place.

Planning Proposals

The specific formats for proposals are innumerable, but they can be grouped into two general categories. *Internal proposals* (see Figure 10.8) request decisions from managers within the organization, such as proposals to buy new equipment or launch new research projects. *External proposals* request decisions from parties outside the organization. Examples include *investment proposals*, which request funding from external investors; *grant proposals*, which request funds from government agencies and other sponsoring

FIGURE 10.8   Shandel Cohen's Internal Proposal

Shandel Cohen's internal proposal seeks management's approval to install an automatic mail-response system. Because the company manufactures computers, she knows that her boss won't object to a computer-based solution. Also, since profits are always a concern, her report emphasizes the financial benefits of her proposal. Her report describes the problem, her proposed solutions, the benefits to the company, and the projected costs.

MEMO

DATE: July 8, 2007
TO: Jamie Engle
FROM: Shandel Cohen   *SC*
SUBJECT: Saving $145k/year with an automated e-mail response system

Catches the reader's attention with a compelling promise in subject line

THE PROBLEM:
Expensive and Slow Response to Customer Information Requests

Our new product line has been very well received, and orders have surpassed our projections. This very success, however, has created a shortage of printed brochures, as well as considerable overtime for people in the customer response center. As we introduce upgrades and new options, our printed materials quickly become outdated. If we continue to rely on printed materials for customer information, we have two choices: Distribute existing materials (even though they are incomplete or inaccurate) or discard existing materials and print new ones.

Describes the current situation and explains why it should be fixed

THE SOLUTION:
Automated E-mail Response System

With minor additions and modifications to our current e-mail system, we can set up an automated system to respond to customer requests for information. This system can save us time and money and can keep our distributed information current.

Explains the proposed solution in enough detail to make it convincing, without burdening the reader with excessive detail

Automated e-mail response systems have been tested and proven effective. Many companies already use this method to respond to customer information requests, so we won't have to worry about relying on untested technology. Using the system is easy, too: Customers simply send a blank e-mail message to a specific address, and the system responds by sending an electronic copy of the requested brochure.

Benefit #1: Always-Current Information

Rather than discard and print new materials, we would only need to keep the electronic files up to date on the server. We would be able to provide customers and our field sales organization with up-to-date, correct information as soon as the upgrades or options are available.

Builds reader interest in the proposed solution by listing a number of compelling benefits

Benefit #2: Instantaneous Delivery

Almost immediately after requesting information, customers would have that information in hand. Electronic delivery would be especially advantageous for our international customers. Regular mail to remote locations sometimes takes weeks to arrive, by which time the information may already be out of date. Both customers and field salespeople will appreciate the automatic mail-response system.

Benefit #3: Minimized Waste

With our current method of printing every marketing piece in large quantities, we discard thousands of pages of obsolete catalogs, data sheets, and other materials every year. By maintaining and distributing the information electronically, we would eliminate this waste. We would also free up a considerable amount of expensive floor space and shelving that is required for storing printed materials.

(continued)

FIGURE 10.8   (continued)

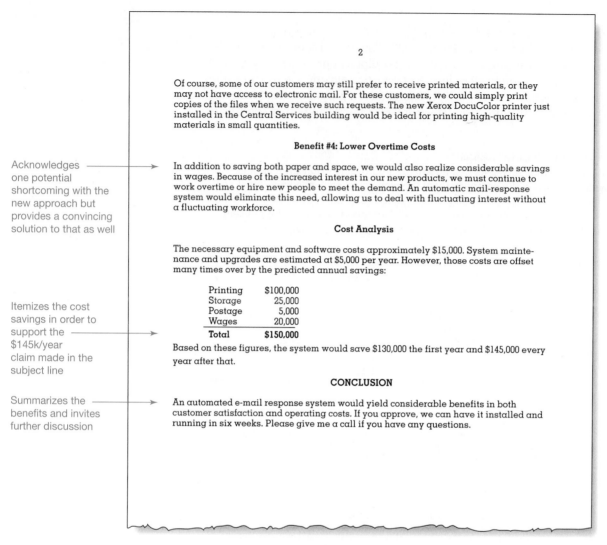

2

Of course, some of our customers may still prefer to receive printed materials, or they may not have access to electronic mail. For these customers, we could simply print copies of the files when we receive such requests. The new Xerox DocuColor printer just installed in the Central Services building would be ideal for printing high-quality materials in small quantities.

Benefit #4: Lower Overtime Costs

In addition to saving both paper and space, we would also realize considerable savings in wages. Because of the increased interest in our new products, we must continue to work overtime or hire new people to meet the demand. An automatic mail-response system would eliminate this need, allowing us to deal with fluctuating interest without a fluctuating workforce.

Cost Analysis

The necessary equipment and software costs approximately $15,000. System maintenance and upgrades are estimated at $5,000 per year. However, those costs are offset many times over by the predicted annual savings:

Printing	$100,000
Storage	25,000
Postage	5,000
Wages	20,000
Total	**$150,000**

Based on these figures, the system would save $130,000 the first year and $145,000 every year after that.

CONCLUSION

An automated e-mail response system would yield considerable benefits in both customer satisfaction and operating costs. If you approve, we can have it installed and running in six weeks. Please give me a call if you have any questions.

Annotations (left margin):

Acknowledges one potential shortcoming with the new approach but provides a convincing solution to that as well

Itemizes the cost savings in order to support the $145k/year claim made in the subject line

Summarizes the benefits and invites further discussion

---

organizations; and *sales proposals*, which suggest individualized solutions for potential customers and request purchase decisions.

The most significant factor in planning a proposal is whether the recipient has asked you to submit a proposal. *Solicited proposals* are generally prepared at the request of external parties that require a product or a service, but they may also be requested by such internal sources as management or the board of directors. Some external parties prepare a formal invitation to bid on their contracts, called a **request for proposals (RFP)**, which includes instructions that specify the exact type of work to be performed or products to be delivered, along with budgets, deadlines, and other requirements. Other companies then respond by preparing proposals that show how they would meet those needs. In most cases, organizations that issue RFPs also provide strict guidelines on what the proposals should include, and you need to follow these guidelines carefully in order to be considered. RFPs can seem surprisingly picky, even to the point of specifying the size of paper to use, but you must follow every detail.

Unsolicited proposals offer more flexibility but a completely different sort of challenge since recipients aren't expecting to receive them. In fact, your audience may not be aware of the problem or opportunity you are addressing, so before you can propose a solution, you might first need to convince your readers that a problem or opportunity exists. Consequently, an indirect approach is often the wise choice for unsolicited proposals.

Regardless of its format and structure, a good proposal explains what a project or course of action will involve, how much it will cost, and how the recipient and his or her organization will benefit.

Caption (left margin): Buyers solicit proposals by publishing a request for proposals (RFP).

Reviewing Key Points

This chapter addresses the planning stage for reports and proposals, explaining that the three-step process applies equally well to long business messages. The chapter describes analyzing the situation, including writing the statement of purpose and preparing the work plan. It also covers the tasks involved in supporting your reports and proposals with reliable information, including conducting secondary and primary research, documenting sources, analyzing your findings, summarizing your research, drawing conclusions, and developing recommendations. The chapter concludes with three sections on planning informational reports, analytical reports, and proposals.

The next chapter discusses the second and third steps of the writing process: writing and completing reports and proposals. In addition to the writing and completing steps, you will learn about the most common visuals used to supplement your messages as well as the various components that go into formal reports and proposals.

Test Your Knowledge

1. How are reports for monitoring and controlling operations used?

2. How does primary research differ from secondary research?

3. What makes a survey reliable and valid?

4. How does a conclusion differ from a recommendation?

5. How do proposal writers use an RFP?

Apply Your Knowledge

1. Why must you be careful when using information from the Internet in a business report?

2. Why do you need to evaluate the sources you uncover in your research?

3. If you were writing a recommendation report for an audience that doesn't know you, would you use a direct approach focusing on the recommendation or an indirect approach focusing on logic? Why?

4. Why are unsolicited proposals more challenging to write than solicited proposals?

5. Ethical Choices   Companies occasionally make mistakes that expose confidential information, such as when employees lose laptop computers containing sensitive data files or webmasters forget to protect confidential webpages from search engine indexes. If you conducted an online search that turned up competitive information on webpages that were clearly intended to be private, what would you do? Explain your answer.

Practice Your Knowledge

Activities

For active links to all websites discussed in this chapter, visit this text's website at www.prenhall.com/bovee. Locate your book and click on its Companion Website link. Then select Chapter 10, and click on "Featured Websites." Locate the name of the page or the URL related to the material in the text. Please note that links to sites that become inactive after publication of the book will be removed from the Featured Websites section.

1. **Analyze This Document**   The Securities and Exchange Commission (SEC) requires all public companies to file a comprehensive annual report (form 10-K) electronically. Many companies post links to these reports on their websites along with links to other company reports. Visit Dell's website at www.dell.com and find the company's most recent annual reports: 10-K and Year in Review (click on "About Dell" on the homepage, then click on the "Investors" link). Compare the style and format of the two reports. For which audience(s) is the Year in Review targeted? Who besides the SEC might be interested in the Annual Report 10-K? Which report do you find easier to read? More interesting? More detailed?

2. **Finding Information: Surveys**   You work for a movie studio that is producing a young director's first motion picture, the story of a group of unknown musicians finding work and making a reputation in a competitive industry. Unfortunately, some of your friends leave the screening, saying that the 182-minute movie is simply too long. Others said they couldn't imagine any sequences to cut out. Your boss wants to test the movie on a regular audience and ask viewers to complete a questionnaire that will help the director decide whether edits are needed and, if so, where. Design a questionnaire that you can use to solicit valid answers for a report to the director about how to handle the audience's reaction to the movie.

3. **Internet**   Read the step-by-step hints and examples for writing a funding proposal at www.learnerassociates.net/proposal. Review the entire sample proposal online. What details did the writer decide to include in the appendixes? Why was this material placed in the appendixes and not the main body of the report? According to the writer's tips, when is the best time to prepare a Project Overview?

4. **Analyzing the Situation: Statement of Purpose**   Sales at The Style Shop, a clothing store for men, have declined for the third month in a row. Your boss is not sure whether this decline is due to a weak economy or if it's due to another, unknown reason. She has asked you to investigate the situation and to submit a report to her highlighting some possible reasons for the decline. Develop a statement of purpose for your report.

5. **Teamwork: Planning an Unsolicited Proposal**   Break into small groups and identify an operational problem occurring at your campus—perhaps involving registration, university housing, food services, parking, or library services. Then develop a workable solution to that problem. Finally, develop a list of pertinent facts that your team will need to gather to convince the reader that the problem exists and that your solution will work.

6. **Preparing the Work Plan**   The lawn surrounding the Town Centre shopping center looks as if it could use better care. You're the assistant to the center's general manager, who must approve any new contracts for lawn service. You want to prepare a formal study of the current state of your lawn's health. Your report will include conclusions and recommendations for your boss's consideration. Draft a work plan, including the problem statement, the statement of purpose and scope, a description of what will result from your investigation, the sources and methods of data collection, and a preliminary outline.

7. **Finding Secondary Information**   Using online, database, or printed sources, find the following information. Be sure to properly cite your source using the formats discussed in Appendix B.

   a. Contact information for the American Management Association

   b. Median weekly earnings of men and women by occupation

   c. Current market share for Perrier water

   d. Performance ratios for office supply retailers

   e. Annual stock performance for Hewlett-Packard (HP)

   f. Number of franchise outlets in the United States

   g. Composition of the U.S. workforce by profession

8. **Finding Information: Company Information**   Select any public company and find the following information:

   a. Names of the company's current officers

   b. List of the company's products or services (if the company has a large number of products, list the product lines or divisions instead)

   c. Some important current issues in the company's industry

   d. Outlook for the company's industry as a whole

9. **Finding Information: Interviews**   You're conducting an information interview with a manager in another division of your company. Partway through the interview, the manager shows clear signs of impatience. How should you respond? What might you do differently to prevent this from happening in the future? Explain your answers.

10. **Processing Information: Documenting Sources**   Select five business articles from sources such as journals, books, newspapers, or websites. Develop a resource list using Appendix B as a guideline.

11. **Organizing Reports: Deciding on Format**   Go to the library or visit www.annualreportservice.com and review the annual reports recently released by two cor-

porations in the same industry. Analyze each report and be prepared to discuss the following questions in class:

a. What organizational differences, if any, do you see in the way each corporation discusses its annual performance? Are the data presented clearly so that shareholders can draw conclusions about how well the company performed?

b. What goals, challenges, and plans do top managers emphasize in their discussion of results?

c. How do the format and organization of each report enhance or detract from the information being presented?

12. **Organizing Reports: Choosing a Direct or Indirect Approach**   Of the organizational approaches introduced in the chapter, which is best suited for writing a report that answers the following questions? Briefly explain why.

a. In which market segment—energy drinks or traditional soft drinks—should Fizz Drinks, Inc., introduce a new drink to take advantage of its enlarged research and development budget?

b. Should Major Manufacturing, Inc., close down operations of its antiquated Bellville, Arkansas, plant despite the adverse economic impact on the town that has grown up around the plant?

c. Should you and your partner adopt a new accounting method to make your financial statements look better to potential investors?

d. Should Grand Canyon Chemicals buy disposable test tubes to reduce labor costs associated with cleaning and sterilizing reusable test tubes?

e. What are some reasons for the recent data loss at the college computer center, and how can we avoid similar problems in the future?

13. **Teamwork: Report Structure**   You and a classmate are helping Linda Moreno prepare her report on Electrovision's travel and entertainment costs (see pages 318–331). This time, however, the report is to be informational rather than analytical, so it will not include recommendations. Review the existing report and determine what changes would be needed to make it an informational report. Be as specific as possible. For example, if your team decides the report needs a new title, what title would you use? Now draft a transmittal memo for Moreno to use in conveying this informational report to Dennis McWilliams, Electrovision's vice president of operations.

14. **Organizing Reports: Structuring Informational Reports**   Assume that your college president has received many student complaints about campus parking problems. You are appointed to chair a student committee organized to investigate the problems and recommend solutions. The president gives you the file labeled "Parking: Complaints from Students," and you jot down the essence of the complaints as you inspect the contents. Your notes look like this:

- Inadequate student spaces at critical hours
- Poor night lighting near the computer center
- Inadequate attempts to keep resident neighbors from occupying spaces
- Dim marking lines
- Motorcycles taking up full spaces
- Discourteous security officers
- Spaces (usually empty) reserved for college officials
- Relatively high parking fees
- Full fees charged to night students even though they use the lots only during low-demand periods
- Vandalism to cars and a sense of personal danger
- Inadequate total space

- Resident harassment of students parking on the street in front of neighboring houses

Now prepare an outline for an informational report to be submitted to committee members. Use a topical organization for your report that categorizes this information.

Expand Your Knowledge

Exploring the Best of the Web

The Library That Never Closes Start your business research by visiting the Internet Public Library at www.ipl.org. Visit the reference center and explore the many online references available. These cover topics such as business, economics, law, government, science, technology, computers, education, and more. You can even submit questions for the IPL staff. Click on the "Business" subject collection, then click on "Business Directories" to perform these tasks.

Exercises

1. Select five companies and use the links provided to find contact information (address, phone, website, officers' names, and so on) for each company. What kinds of contact information did you find at the company websites?
2. Gather information about the U.S. budget by using one of the site's directories: A Business Researcher's Interests. Why is using a directory such as this one an efficient way to obtain information?
3. Go back to the library's main reference center and click on "Reference." Follow some of the reference links. How might these links help you when performing business research?

Exploring the Web on Your Own

Review these chapter-related websites on your own to improve your research skills.

1. What's involved in a business plan? BizPlanIt.Com, www.bizplanit.com, offers tips and advice, a free e-mail newsletter, and a sample virtual business plan (click on "Bizplan Resources," then "The Virtual Business Plan"). You'll find suggestions on what details and how much information to include in each section of a business plan.
2. Learn how to make your website more usable and more useful by following the methods that professional web designers use. Visit Usability First, www.usabilityfirst. com.
3. If you're having trouble tracking down a specific company in your research, try SuperPages at www.bigbook. com, where you'll find more than 16 million listings searchable by keywords, name, and location.

Learn Interactively

Interactive Study Guide

Visit www.prenhall.com/bovee, then locate your book and click on its Companion Website link. Select Chapter 10 to take advantage of the interactive Chapter Quiz to test your knowledge of chapter concepts. Receive instant feedback on whether you need additional studying. Also, visit the Study Hall, where you'll find an abundance of valuable resources that will help you succeed in this course.

Peak Performance Grammar and Mechanics

If your instructor has required the use of "Peak Performance Grammar and Mechanics," either in your online course, through the access-code protected portion of the Companion Website, or on CD, you can improve your skill with periods, question marks, and other punctuation by using the "Peak Performance Grammar and Mechanics" module. Click "Punctuation," then "Punctuation II." Take the Pretest to determine whether you have any weak areas. Then review those areas in the Refresher Course. Take the Follow-Up Test to check your grasp of various punctuation elements. For an extra challenge or advanced practice, take the Advanced Test. Finally, for additional reinforcement in periods, question marks, and exclamation points, go to the "Improve Your Grammar, Mechanics, and Usage" section that follows the cases, and complete the "Level 1: Self-Assessment" exercises.

CASES

Apply the three-step writing process to the following cases, as assigned by your instructor.

Informational Reports

1. My Progress to Date: Interim Progress Report on Your Academic Career

As you may know, the paperwork involved in getting a degree or certificate is nearly as challenging as any course you could take.

Your Task Prepare an interim progress report detailing the steps you've taken toward completing your graduation or certification requirements. After examining the requirements listed in your college catalog, indicate a realistic schedule for completing those that remain. In addition to course requirements, include steps such as completing the residency requirement, filing necessary papers, and paying necessary fees. Use a memo format for your report, and address it to anyone who is helping or encouraging you through school.

2. Who Said What: Personal Activity Report of a Meeting

Meetings, conferences, and conventions abound in the academic world, and you have probably attended your share.

Your Task Prepare a personal activity report on a meeting, convention, or conference that you recently attended. Use a memo format, and direct the report to other students in your field who were not able to attend.

3. Check That Price Tag: Informational Report on Trends in College Costs

Your college's administration has asked you to compare your college's tuition costs with those of a nearby college and determine which has risen more quickly. Research the trend by checking your college's annual tuition costs for each of the most recent four years. Then research the four-year tuition trends for a neighboring college. For both colleges, calculate the percentage change in tuition costs from year to year and between the first and fourth year.

Your Task Prepare an informal report (using the letter format) presenting your findings and conclusions to the president of your college. Include graphics to explain and support your conclusions.

4. Get a Move on It: Lasting Guidelines for Moving into College Dormitories

Moving into a college dormitory is one experience you weren't quite prepared for. In addition to lugging all your earthly belongings up four flights of stairs in 90-degree heat, channeling electrical cords to the one room outlet tucked in the corner of the room, lofting your beds, and negotiating with your roommate over who gets the bigger closet, you had to hug your parents goodbye in the parking lot in front of the entire freshman class—or so it seemed. Now that you are a pro, you've offered to write some lasting guidelines for future freshmen so they know what is expected of them on moving day.

Your Task Prepare an informational report for future freshmen classes outlining the rules and procedures to follow when moving into a college dorm. Lay out the rules such as starting time, handling trash and empty boxes, items permitted and not permitted in dorm rooms, common courtesies, parking, and so on. Be sure to mention what the policy is for removing furniture from the room, lofting beds, and overloading electrical circuits. Of course, any recommendations on how to handle disputes with roommates would be helpful. So would some brief advice on how to cope with anxious parents. Direct your memo report to the college dean.

Analytical Reports

5. My Next Career Move: Feasibility Report Organized Around Recommendations

If you've ever given yourself a really good talking-to, you'll be quite comfortable with this project.

Your Task Write a memo report directed to yourself and signed with a fictitious name. Indicate a possible job that your college education will qualify you for, mention the advantages of the position in terms of your long-range goals, and then outline the actions you must take to get the job.

6. Staying the Course: Unsolicited Proposal

Think of a course you would love to see added to the curriculum at your school. Conversely, if you would like to see a course offered as an elective rather than being required, write your e-mail report accordingly. Construct a sequence of logical reasons to support your choice (this is the 2 + 2 = 4 approach mentioned in the chapter).

Your Task Plan and draft a short e-mail proposal to be submitted to the academic dean by e-mail. Be sure to include all the reasons supporting your idea.

7. Planning My Program: Problem-Solving Report

Assume that you will have time for only one course next term. Identify the criteria you will use to decide which of several courses to take (this is the yardstick approach mentioned in the chapter).

Your Task List the pros and cons of four or five courses that interest you, and use the selection criteria you identified to choose the one course that is best for you to take at this time. Write your report in memo format, addressing it to your academic adviser.

8. Restaurant Review: Troubleshooting Report on a Restaurant's Food and Operations

Visit any restaurant, possibly your school cafeteria. The workers and fellow customers will assume that you are an ordinary customer, but you are really a spy for the owner.

Your Task After your visit, write a short letter to the owner explaining (a) what you did and what you observed, (b) any violations of policy that you observed, and (c) your recommendations for improvement. The first part of your report (what you did and what you observed) will be the longest. Include a description of the premises, inside and out. Tell how long it took for each step of ordering and receiving your meal. Describe the service and food thoroughly. You are interested in both the good and bad aspects of the establishment's décor, service, and food. For the second section (violations of policy), use some common sense. If all the servers but one have their hair covered, you may assume that policy requires hair to be covered; a dirty window or restroom obviously violates policy. The last section (recommendations for improvement) involves professional judgment. What management actions will improve the restaurant?

9. On the Books: Troubleshooting Report on Improving the Campus Bookstore

Imagine that you are a consultant hired to improve the profits of your campus bookstore.

Your Task Visit the bookstore and look critically at its operations. Then draft a letter to the bookstore manager, offering recommendations that would make the store more profitable, perhaps suggesting products it should carry, hours that it should remain open, or added services that it should make available to students. Be sure to support your recommendations.

10. Day and Night: Problem-Solving Report on a 24-hour Convenience Store

When a store is open all day, every day, when's the best time to restock the shelves? That's the challenge at Store 24, a retail chain that never closes. Imagine you're the assistant manager of a Store 24 branch that just opened near your campus. You want to set up a restocking schedule that won't conflict with prime shopping hours. Think about the number of customers you're likely to serve in the morning, afternoon, evening, and overnight hours. Consider, too, how many employees you might have during these four periods.

Your Task Write a problem-solving report in letter form to the store manager (Isabel Chu) and the regional manager (Eric Angstrom), who must agree on a solution to this problem. Discuss the pros and cons of each of the four periods, and include your recommendation for restocking the shelves.

Proposals

11. "Would You Carry It?" Unsolicited Sales Proposal Recommending a Product to a Retail Outlet

Select a product you are familiar with, and imagine that you are the manufacturer trying to get a local retail outlet to carry it. Use the Internet and other resources to gather information about the product.

Your Task Write an unsolicited sales proposal in letter format to the owner (or manager) of the store, proposing that the item be stocked. Use the information you gathered to describe some of the product's features and benefits to the store. Then make up some reasonable figures, highlighting what the item costs, what it can be sold for, and what services your company provides (return of unsold items, free replacement of unsatisfactory items, necessary repairs, and so on).

12. Where Is Everybody? Proposal to Sell GPS Fleet Tracking System

As a sales manager for Air-Trak, one of your responsibilities is writing sales proposals for potential buyers of your company's Cloudberry tracking system. Cloudberry uses the Global Positioning System (GPS) to track the location of vehicles and other assets. For example, the dispatcher for a trucking company can simply click a map display on a computer screen to find out where all the company's trucks are at that instant. Air-Trak lists the following as benefits of the system:

- Making sure vehicles follow prescribed routes with minimal loitering time
- "Geofencing," in which dispatchers are alerted if vehicles leave assigned routes or designated service areas
- Route optimization, in which fleet managers can analyze routes and destinations to find the most time- and fuel-efficient path for each vehicle
- Comparisons between scheduled and actual travel
- Enhanced security, protecting both drivers and cargos

Your Task Write a brief proposal to Doneta Zachs, fleet manager for Midwest Express, 338 S.W. 6th, Des Moines, Iowa, 50321. Introduce your company, explain the benefits of the Cloudberry system, and propose a trial deployment in which you would equip five Midwest Express trucks. For the purposes of this assignment, you don't need to worry about the technical details of the system; focus on promoting the benefits and asking for a decision regarding the test project. (You can learn more about the Air-Trak and the Cloudberry system at www.air-trak.com.)[13]

Improve Your Grammar, Mechanics, and Usage

Level 1: Self-Assessment—Dashes and Hyphens

Review Sections 2.7 and 2.8 in the Handbook of Grammar, Mechanics, and Usage, and then look at the following 15 items.

In items 1–15, insert the required dashes (—) and hyphens (-).

1. Three qualities speed, accuracy, and reliability are desirable in any applicant to the data entry department.

2. A highly placed source explained the top secret negotiations.

3. The file on Marian Gephardt yes, we finally found it reveals a history of late payments.

4. They're selling a well designed machine.

5. A bottle green sports jacket is hard to find.

6. Argentina, Brazil, Mexico these are the countries we hope to concentrate on.

7. Only two sites maybe three offer the things we need.

8. How many owner operators are in the industry?

9. Your ever faithful assistant deserves without a doubt a substantial raise.

10. Myrna Talefiero is this organization's president elect.

11. Stealth, secrecy, and surprise those are the elements that will give us a competitive edge.

12. The charts are well placed on each page unlike the running heads and footers.

13. We got our small business loan an enormous advantage.

14. Ron Franklin do you remember him? will be in town Monday.

15. Your devil may care attitude affects everyone involved in the decision making process.

Level 2: Workplace Applications

The following items contain numerous errors in grammar, capitalization, punctuation, abbreviation, number style, word division, and vocabulary. Rewrite each sentence in the space provided, correcting all errors. Write *C* in the space after any sentence that is already correct.

1. Commerce One helps its customer's to more efficiently lower administrative costs, improve order times, and to manage contract negotiations.

2. The intermodal bus vehicle seats up to 35 passengers, but is equipped with a 20 feet standardized container in the rear. The same container one sees on ships, trains and on planes.

3. "The American Dream of innovation, persistence, and a refusal to except the status quo has just created, in our opinion, Americas newest and most exciting company to watch," said James Gaspard President of Neoplan USA.

4. This new, transportation paradigm may have a global affect and the barriers to entry will be extremely costly too overcome.

5. Autobytel also owns and operates Carsmart.com and Autosite.com as well as AIC Automotive Information Center] a provider of automotive marketing data and technology.

6. Mymarket.com offers a low cost high reward, entry into e-commerce not only for buyers but also suppliers.

7. Eclipse Aviation's main competitor are another start-up Safire Aircraft of west Palm Beach, Fl.

8. After identifying the factors that improve a industrial process, additional refining experiments must be conducted to confirm the results.

9. The fair labor standards Act regulates minimum wages, establishes overtime compensation, and it outlaws labor for children.

10. The Chinese government are supporting use of the Internet as a business tool because it is seen by it as necessary to enhance competitiveness.

11. At a certain point in a company's growth, the entrepreneur, who wants to control everything, can no longer keep up so they look mistakenly for a better manager and call that person a CEO.

12. City Fresh foods is paid by City health agencies to provide Ethnic food to the homebound "elderly" in the Boston Area.

13. Being in business since 1993, Miss Rosen has boiled down her life story into a 2-minute sound bight for sales prospects.

14. Anyone that wants to gain a new perspective on their product or service must cast aside one's own biases.

15. If I was Bill Gates, I'd handle the Federal government's antitrust lawsuit much different.

Level 3: Document Critique

The following document may contain errors in grammar, capitalization, punctuation, abbreviation, number style, vocabulary, and spelling. You may also find problems with organization, format, and word use. Correct all errors using standard proofreading marks (see Appendix C).

Memo

Date   March 14 2007

To   Jeff Black and HR staff

FROM: Carrie andrews

Subject: Recruiting and hiring Seminar

As you all know the process of recruiting screening and hiring new employees might be a legal minefield. Because we don't have an inhouse lawyer to help us make every decision, its important for all of us to be aware of what actions are legally acceptible and what isn't. Last week I attended a American management Association seminar on this subject. I given enough useful information to warrant updating our online personnel handbook and perhaps developing a quick training session for all interviewing teams. First, heres a quick look at the things I learned.

Avoiding Legal Mistakes

- How to write recruiting ads that accurately portray job openings and not discriminate.

- Complying with the Americans with Disabilities Act

- How to use an employment agency effectively and safe (without risk of legal entanglements)

How to Screen and Interview More Effectively

- How to sort through résumés more efficient (including looking for telltale signs of false information)

- We can avoid interview questions that could get us into legal trouble

- When and how to check criminal records

Measuring Applicants

- Which type of preemployment tests have been proven most effective?

- Which drug-testing issues and recommendations effect us

as you can see the seminar addressed alot of important information. We covering the basic guidelines for much of this already; but a number of specific recommendations and legal concepts should be emphisized and underline.

It will take me a couple of weeks to get the personel handbook updated: but we don't have any immediate hiring plans anyway so that shouldn't be too much of a problem unless you think I should ocmplete it sooner and then we can talk about that.

I'll keep the seminar handouts and my notes on my desk in case you want to peruse them.

After the handbook is updated by me, we can get together and decide whether we need to train the interviewing team members.

Although we have a lot of new information, what people need to be aware of can be highlighted and the new sections can be read as schedules allow, although they might be reluctant to do this and we can also talk about that later, at a time of your conveinence that you can select later.

If you have any questions in the mean-time; don't hesitate to e-mail me or drop by for a chat.

11

Writing and Completing Reports and Proposals

Learning Objectives

After studying this chapter, you will be able to

1   Describe the four functions of a report introduction

2   Explain how the introduction and close of a proposal differ from the introduction and close of an informational or analytical report

3   Identify three elements that help readers find their way through long reports and proposals

4   Identify five technological tools that can help you create compelling reports in less time

5   Explain the criteria for deciding which points to illustrate with visuals

6   Identify the most common visuals used in business reports and proposals

7   Identify the nine prefatory parts of a formal report

8   Differentiate between a synopsis and an executive summary

Focusing on the content of your longer business documents is not only natural but necessary, because doing so helps ensure complete, correct information. However, once you have the technical content in place, you need to stand back and view the document from the perspective of your audience—the people you expect to read and act on the information. Is your message clear, compelling, and concise? Is it something a real, living, breathing person could be expected to read and understand? Remember Tania Menegatti's advice (quoted on the left) whenever you're writing and completing reports and proposals: Even with the most complex documents, another human being is at the receiving end of your communication efforts.[1]

Writing Reports and Proposals

This chapter builds on the writing techniques and ideas you learned in Chapter 4 with issues that are particularly important when preparing longer message formats. In addition, you'll get an introduction to creating effective visuals, which are a vital aspect of many reports and proposals. As with shorter messages, take a few moments before you start writing to make sure you're ready to adapt your approach to your audience.

Adapting to Your Audience

Adapting to your audience begins with being sensitive to audience needs: adopting the "you" attitude, maintaining a strong sense of etiquette, emphasizing the positive, and using bias-free language. Reports and proposals can put heavy demands on your readers, so the "you" attitude takes on even greater importance with these long messages (Figure 11.1).

Many companies have specific guidelines for communicating with public audiences, so make sure you're aware of these preferences before you start writing. If you know your readers reasonably well and your report is likely to meet with their approval, you can generally adopt an informal tone. To make your tone less formal, speak to readers in the first person, refer to them as *you*, and refer to yourself as *I* (or *we* if there are multiple report authors). To make your tone more formal, use the impersonal journalism style: Emphasize objectivity, avoid personal opinions, and build your argument on provable facts. Eliminate all references to *you* and *I* (including *we*, *us*, and *our*). Be careful to avoid jokes, similes, and metaphors, and try to minimize the use of colorful adjectives or adverbs. Note that communicating with people in other cultures often calls for more formality in reports, both to respect cultural preferences and to reduce the risk of miscommunication—informal elements such as humor and casual language tend to translate poorly from one culture to another.

Long or complex reports demand a lot from readers, making the "you" attitude even more important.

Reports destined for audiences outside the United States often require a more formal tone to match the expectations of audiences in many other countries.

Composing Reports and Proposals

When you compose reports and proposals, follow the writing advice offered in Chapter 4: Select the best words, create the most effective sentences, and develop coherent paragraphs. As with other written business communications, the text of reports and proposals has three main sections: an introduction (or *opening*), a body, and a close.

FIGURE 11.1 The "You" Attitude in Complex Reports
Websites, which in many instances function like long, complex reports, offer many good examples of the "you" attitude. CancerHelp, the cancer information website of Cancer Research UK, helps visitors find the information they need from a variety of online reports, even if they're new to the web.

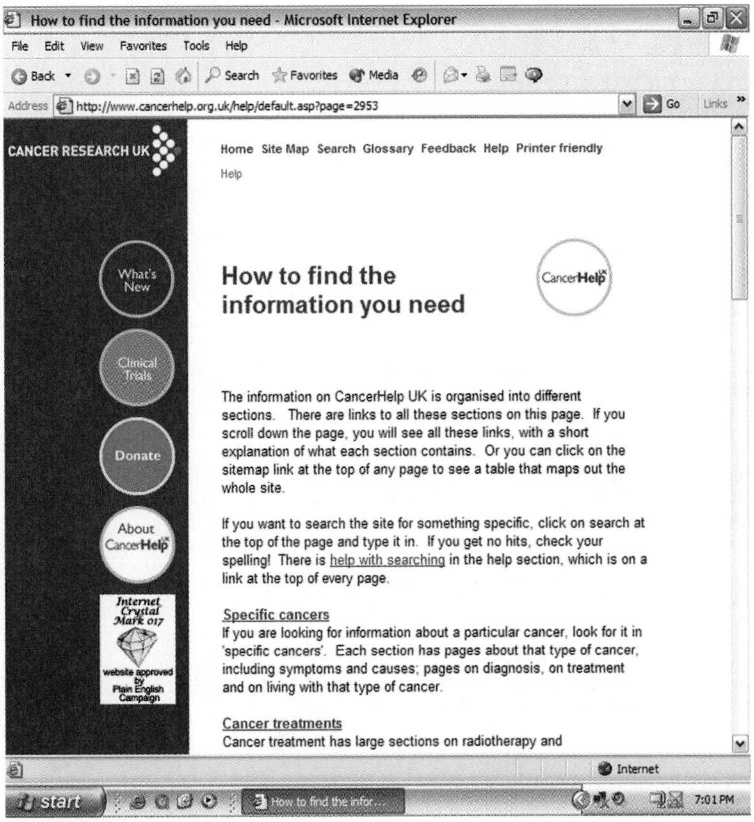

An effective *introduction* accomplishes at least four things:

■ Puts the report or proposal in context by tying it to a problem or an assignment
■ Introduces the subject or purpose of the report or proposal and indicates why the subject is important
■ Previews the main ideas and the order in which they'll be covered
■ Establishes the tone of the document and the writer's relationship with the audience

> Your introduction needs to put the report in context for the reader, introduce the subject, preview main ideas, and establish the tone of the document.

FIGURE 11.2   Analytical Report

In this recommendation to her company's board of directors, Alycia Jenn provides enough information to persuade her high-level audience, without burdening them with lots of technical details. She makes a strong case that her firm must move beyond a website that is simply a static presentation of products to a fully functional e-commerce website that allows shoppers to interact with virtual products on-screen, place orders, check order status, and so on. She also explains how the small company could implement her ideas.

MEMO

DATE: July 6, 2007
TO: Board of Directors, Executive Committee members
FROM: Alycia Jenn, Business Development Manager
SUBJECT: Website expansion

> *Reminds readers of the origin and purpose of the report*

In response to your request, my staff and I investigated the potential for expanding our website from its current "brochureware" status (in which we promote our company and its products but don't provide any way to place orders online) to full e-commerce capability (including placing orders and checking on order delivery status). After analyzing the behavior of our customers and major competitors and studying the overall development of electronic retailing, we have three recommendations:

> *Clarifies the recommendation by listing the necessary actions in clear, direct language*

1. We should expand our online presence from "brochureware" to e-commerce capability within the next six months.

2. We should engage a firm that specializes in online retailing to design and develop the new e-commerce capabilities.

3. We must take care to integrate online retailing with our store-based and mail-order operations.

1. WE SHOULD EXPAND THE WEBSITE TO FULL E-COMMERCE CAPABILITY

> *Presents logical reasons for recommending that the firm expand its website to include e-commerce*

First, does e-commerce capability make sense today for a small company that sells luxury housewares? Even though books and many other products are now commonly sold online, in most cases, this enterprise involves simple, low-cost products that don't require a lot of hands-on inspection before purchasing. As we've observed in our stores, shoppers like to interact with our products before purchasing them. However, a small but growing number of websites do sell specialty products, using such tactics as "virtual product tours" (in which shoppers can interactively view a product in three dimensions, rather than simply looking at a static photograph) and generous return policies (to reduce the perceived risk of buying products online).

Second, do we need to establish a presence now in order to remain competitive in the future? The answer is an overwhelming "yes." The initial steps taken by our competitors are already placing us at a disadvantage among those shoppers who are already comfortable buying online, and every trend indicates our minor competitive weakness today will turn into a major weakness in the next few years:

> *Supports the reasoning with evidence*

• Several of our top competitors are beginning to implement full e-commerce, including virtual product tours. Our research suggests that these companies aren't yet generating significant financial returns from these online investments, but their online sales are growing.

• Younger consumers who grew up with the World Wide Web will soon be reaching their peak earning years (ages 35-54). This demographic segment expects e-commerce in nearly every product category, and we'll lose them to the competition if we don't offer it.

• The web is erasing geographical shopping limits, presenting both a threat and an opportunity. Even though our customers can now shop websites anywhere in the world (so that we have thousands of competitors instead of a dozen), we can now target customers anywhere in the world.

(continued)

FIGURE 11.2 continued

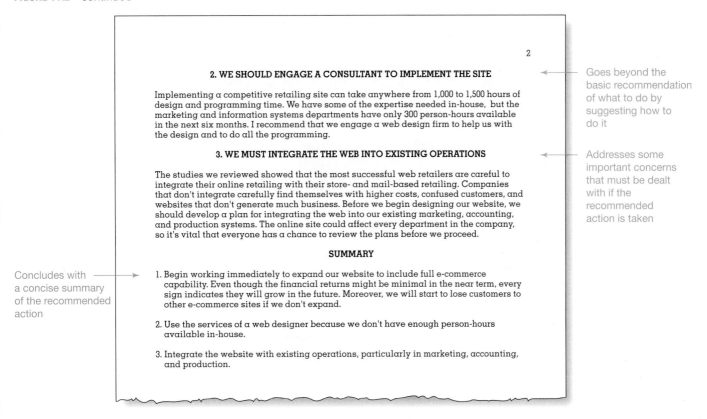

2

2. WE SHOULD ENGAGE A CONSULTANT TO IMPLEMENT THE SITE

Implementing a competitive retailing site can take anywhere from 1,000 to 1,500 hours of design and programming time. We have some of the expertise needed in-house, but the marketing and information systems departments have only 300 person-hours available in the next six months. I recommend that we engage a web design firm to help us with the design and to do all the programming.

3. WE MUST INTEGRATE THE WEB INTO EXISTING OPERATIONS

The studies we reviewed showed that the most successful web retailers are careful to integrate their online retailing with their store- and mail-based retailing. Companies that don't integrate carefully find themselves with higher costs, confused customers, and websites that don't generate much business. Before we begin designing our website, we should develop a plan for integrating the web into our existing marketing, accounting, and production systems. The online site could affect every department in the company, so it's vital that everyone has a chance to review the plans before we proceed.

SUMMARY

1. Begin working immediately to expand our website to include full e-commerce capability. Even though the financial returns might be minimal in the near term, every sign indicates they will grow in the future. Moreover, we will start to lose customers to other e-commerce sites if we don't expand.

2. Use the services of a web designer because we don't have enough person-hours available in-house.

3. Integrate the website with existing operations, particularly in marketing, accounting, and production.

Annotations (right margin):

Goes beyond the basic recommendation of what to do by suggesting how to do it

Addresses some important concerns that must be dealt with if the recommended action is taken

Annotation (left margin):

Concludes with a concise summary of the recommended action

The *body* presents, analyzes, and interprets the information gathered during your investigation and supports your recommendations or conclusions (see Figure 11.2).

The *close* is the final section in the text of your report or proposal. It has four important functions:

- Emphasizes your main points
- Summarizes the benefits to the reader if the document suggests a change or some other course of action
- Refers to all the pieces and reminds readers how those pieces fit together
- Brings all the action items together in one place

Keep in mind that the close gives you one last chance to make sure that your report says what you intended, so make sure it carries a strong, clear message.[2]

The following two sections offer advice on drafting content for reports and proposals.

The body of your report presents, analyzes, and interprets the information you gathered during your investigation.

The close might be the only part of your report some readers have time for, so make sure it conveys the full weight of your message.

Drafting Report Content

Your credibility and career advancement are on the line with every business report you write, so make sure your content is

- **Accurate.** If an audience suspects that your information is shaky, they'll start to view all your work with a skeptical eye.
- **Complete.** Include everything necessary for readers to understand the situation, problem, or proposal. Support all key assertions using an appropriate combination of illustrations, explanations, and facts.[3]
- **Balanced.** Present all sides of the issue fairly and equitably, and include all the essential information, even if some of the information doesn't support your line of reasoning.
- **Clear and logical.** Clear sentence structure and good transitions are essential.[4] Save your readers time by making sure your sentences are uncluttered, contain well-chosen words, and proceed logically. Make your transitions just as clear and logical; identify the ideas that belong together, and organize them in a way that's easy to understand.[5]

FIGURE 11.3   Progress Report

Note how Carlyce Johnson offers her client a complete, but efficient, update of her company's landscaping services. In addition to providing routine information, she also informs the client of progress in two problem areas, one that her firm has been able to resolve and one that they've just discovered. In the case of the problem with the soil, she might have been tempted not to share any information with the client until she'd resolved the problem, but doing so could affect the client's budgets and other plans. Johnson does the right thing by telling the client about the problem early.

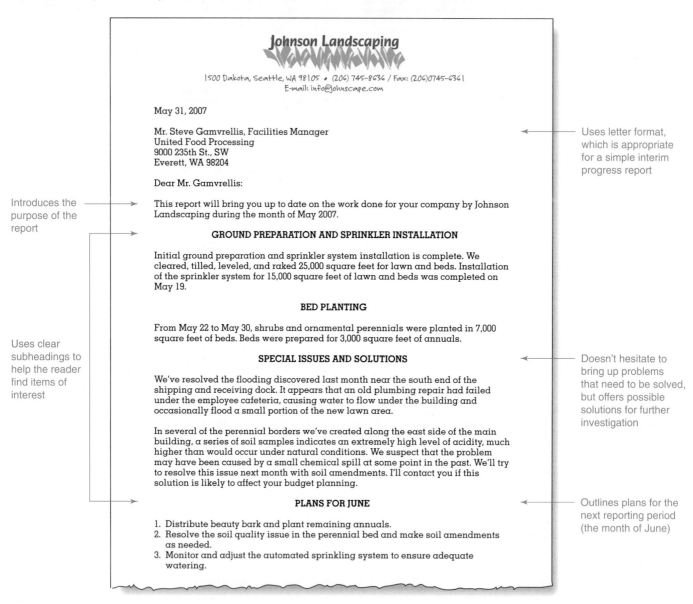

Uses letter format, which is appropriate for a simple interim progress report

Introduces the purpose of the report

Uses clear subheadings to help the reader find items of interest

Doesn't hesitate to bring up problems that need to be solved, but offers possible solutions for further investigation

Outlines plans for the next reporting period (the month of June)

The image above shows a letter on Johnson Landscaping letterhead:

Johnson Landscaping

1500 Dakota, Seattle, WA 98105 • (206) 745-8636 / Fax: (206)0745-6361
E-mail: info@johnscape.com

May 31, 2007

Mr. Steve Gamvrellis, Facilities Manager
United Food Processing
9000 235th St., SW
Everett, WA 98204

Dear Mr. Gamvrellis:

This report will bring you up to date on the work done for your company by Johnson Landscaping during the month of May 2007.

GROUND PREPARATION AND SPRINKLER INSTALLATION

Initial ground preparation and sprinkler system installation is complete. We cleared, tilled, leveled, and raked 25,000 square feet for lawn and beds. Installation of the sprinkler system for 15,000 square feet of lawn and beds was completed on May 19.

BED PLANTING

From May 22 to May 30, shrubs and ornamental perennials were planted in 7,000 square feet of beds. Beds were prepared for 3,000 square feet of annuals.

SPECIAL ISSUES AND SOLUTIONS

We've resolved the flooding discovered last month near the south end of the shipping and receiving dock. It appears that an old plumbing repair had failed under the employee cafeteria, causing water to flow under the building and occasionally flood a small portion of the new lawn area.

In several of the perennial borders we've created along the east side of the main building, a series of soil samples indicates an extremely high level of acidity, much higher than would occur under natural conditions. We suspect that the problem may have been caused by a small chemical spill at some point in the past. We'll try to resolve this issue next month with soil amendments. I'll contact you if this solution is likely to affect your budget planning.

PLANS FOR JUNE

1. Distribute beauty bark and plant remaining annuals.
2. Resolve the soil quality issue in the perennial bed and make soil amendments as needed.
3. Monitor and adjust the automated sprinkling system to ensure adequate watering.

■ **Documented properly.** Properly document and give credit to your sources, as Chapter 10 explains.

Keeping these points in mind will help you draft the most effective introduction, body, and close for your report (see Figure 11.3).

Carefully select the elements to include in your introduction; strive for a balance between necessary, expected information and brevity.

Report Introduction   The specific elements you should include in an introduction depend on the nature and length of the report, the circumstances under which you're writing it, and your relationship with the audience. An introduction could contain all of the following topics, although you'll want to pick and choose the best ones to include for the particular report you are writing:

- **Authorization.** When, how, and by whom the report was authorized; who wrote it; and when it was submitted.
- **Problem/opportunity/purpose.** The reason the report was written and what is to be accomplished as a result of your having written it.
- **Scope.** What is and what isn't going to be covered in the report.
- **Background.** The historical conditions or factors that led up to the report.
- **Sources and methods.** The primary and secondary research that provided information for the report.
- **Definitions.** A list of terms that might be unfamiliar to your audience, along with brief definitions.
- **Limitations.** Factors beyond your control that affect report quality, such as budgets, schedule constraints, or limited access to information or people (however, don't apologize or try to explain away personal shortcomings).
- **Report organization.** The organization of the report (what topics are covered and in what order), possibly with a rationale for following this plan.

In a relatively brief report, these topics may be discussed in only a paragraph or two. In a longer formal report, the discussion of these topics may span several pages and constitute a significant section within the report.

Report Body   As with the introduction, the body of your report can require some tough decisions about which elements to include and how much detail to offer. Your decisions depend on many variables, including the needs of your audience. Provide only enough detail in the body to support your conclusions and recommendations; you can put additional detail in tables, charts, and appendixes. The topics commonly covered in a report body include

> The report body should contain only enough information to convey your message in a convincing fashion.

- Explanations of a problem or opportunity
- Facts, statistical evidence, and trends
- Results of studies or investigations
- Discussion and analyses of potential courses of action
- Advantages, disadvantages, costs, and benefits of a particular course of action
- Procedures or steps in a process
- Methods and approaches
- Criteria for evaluating alternatives and options
- Conclusions and recommendations
- Supporting reasons for conclusions or recommendations

For analytical reports using the direct organizational approach, you'll generally state your conclusions or recommendations in the introduction and use the body of your report to provide your evidence and support. If you're using an indirect approach, you'll likely use the body to discuss your logic and reserve your conclusions or recommendations until the very end.

Report Close   The content and length of your report close depend on your choice of direct or indirect order, among other variables. If you're using a direct approach, you can end with a summary of key points, listed in the order they appear in the report body. If you're using an indirect approach, you can use the close to present your conclusions or recommendations if you didn't end the body with them. However, don't introduce new facts in your close; your audience should have all the information they need by the time they reach this point.

> The nature of your close depends on the type of report (informational or analytical) and the approach (direct or indirect).

If your report is intended to prompt others to action, use the ending to spell out exactly what should happen next. If you'll be taking all the actions yourself, make sure your readers understand this fact so that they'll know what to expect from you.

In a short report, the close may be only a paragraph or two. However, the close of a long report may have separate sections for conclusions, recommendations, and actions. Using separate sections helps your reader locate this material and focus on each element. If you have multiple conclusions, recommendations, or actions, you may want to number and list them.

> For long reports, you may need to divide your close into separate sections for conclusions, recommendations, and actions.

Drafting Proposal Content

With proposals, the content for each section is governed by many variables—the most important being the source of your proposal. If your proposal is unsolicited, you have some latitude in the scope and organization of content. However, if you are responding to a request for proposals, you need to follow the instructions in the RFP in every detail.

Approach proposals the same way you approach persuasive messages.

The general purpose of any proposal is to persuade readers to do something, so your writing approach is similar to that used for persuasive messages, including the use of the AIDA method of gaining attention, building interest, creating desire, and motivating action as an effective structure. Here are some additional strategies to strengthen your argument:[6]

Business proposals need to provide more than just attractive ideas—readers look for evidence of practical, achievable solutions.

- Demonstrate your knowledge.
- Provide concrete information and examples.
- Research the competition so you know what other proposals your audience is likely to read.
- Prove that your proposal is appropriate and feasible for your audience.
- Relate your product, service, or personnel to the reader's exact needs.
- Package your proposal attractively.

Moreover, make sure your proposal is letter perfect, inviting, and readable. Readers will prejudge the quality of your products, services, and capabilities by the quality of the proposal you submit. Errors, omissions, or inconsistencies will work against you—and maybe even cost you important career and business opportunities.

Proposal Introduction   The introduction describes the problem you want to solve or the opportunity you want to exploit, along with your proposed solution. If your proposal is solicited, its introduction should refer to the RFP so that readers know which RFP you're responding to. The following topics are commonly covered in a proposal introduction:

In an unsolicited proposal, your introduction needs to convince readers that a problem or opportunity exists.

- **Background or statement of the problem.** Briefly reviews the reader's situation and establishes a need for action. In unsolicited proposals, you may need to convince readers that a problem or opportunity exists before you can convince them to accept your solution.
- **Solution.** Briefly describes the change you propose and highlights your key selling points and their benefits to your audience.
- **Scope.** States the boundaries of the proposal—what you will and will not do. Sometimes called "Delimitations."
- **Organization.** Orients the reader to the remainder of the proposal and calls attention to the major divisions of information.

In short proposals, your discussion of these topics will be brief—perhaps only a sentence or two for each one. For long, formal proposals, each of these topics may warrant separate subheadings and several paragraphs of discussion.

Readers understand that a proposal is a persuasive message, so they're willing to accommodate a degree of promotional emphasis in your writing—as long as it is professional and focused on their needs.

Proposal Body   The proposal's body has the same purpose as the body of other reports: It gives complete details on the proposed solution and specifies what the anticipated results will be. Because a proposal is by definition a persuasive message, your audience expects you to promote your offering in a confident but professional and objective manner.

In addition to providing facts and evidence to support your conclusions, an effective body covers this information:

The work plan indicates exactly how you will accomplish the solution presented in the proposal.

- **Proposed solution.** Describes what you have to offer: your concept, product, or service. This section may also be titled "Technical Proposal," "Research Design," "Issues for Analysis," or "Work Statement."
- **Work plan.** Explains the steps you'll take, their timing, the methods or resources you'll use, and the person(s) responsible. Specifically includes when the work will begin, how it will be divided into stages, when you will finish, and whether any follow-up is involved. Keep in mind that if your proposal is accepted, the work plan is contractually binding, so don't promise more than you can deliver.

- **Statement of qualifications.** Describes your organization's experience, personnel, and facilities—as they relate to audience needs.
- **Costs.** Covers pricing, reimbursable expenses, discounts, and so on. If you're responding to an RFP, follow the instructions it contains.

In an informal proposal, discussion of some or all of these elements may be grouped together and presented in a letter format, as the proposal in Figure 11.4 does. In a formal proposal, the discussion of these elements might be quite long and thorough.

FIGURE 11.4   Solicited Proposal

This informal, solicited proposal provides the information the customer needs to make a purchase. Note that by signing the proposal and returning it, the customer will enter into a legal contract to pay for the services described.

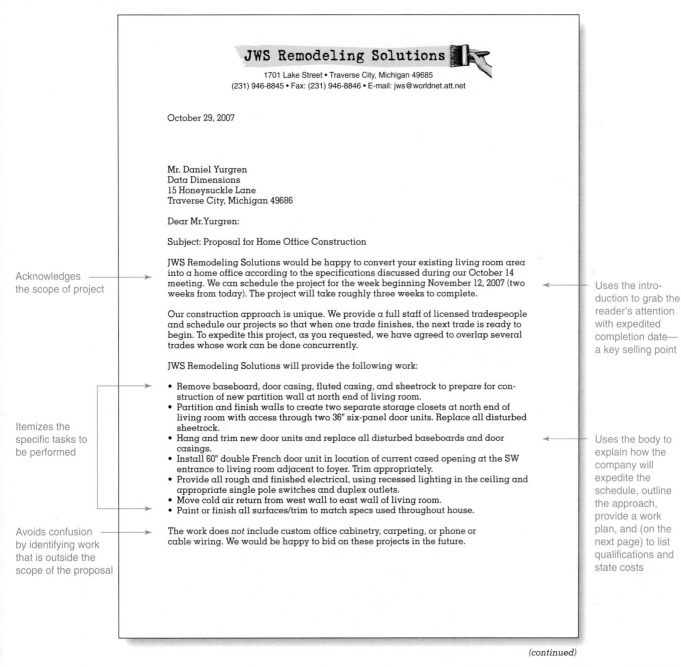

(continued)

FIGURE 11.4 continued

Mr. Daniel Yurgren   October 29, 2007   Page 2

JWS Remodeling Solutions has been in business in the Michigan area for over 17 years. We have a strong reputation for being a quality builder. We take great pride in our work and we treat all projects with the same high-level attention, regardless of their size or scope. Our tradespeople are all licensed, insured professionals with years of experience in their respective crafts. Enclosed is a copy of our company brochure discussing our qualifications in greater detail, along with a current client list. Please contact any of the names on this list for references.

Increases desire by highlighting qualifications

The total cost for this project is $6,800, broken down as follows:

Helps reader accept the cost total by breaking it down into specific categories

Materials and supplies	$3,800
Labor	2,700
Disposal fees	300
Total	$6,800

An initial payment of $3,800 is due upon acceptance of this proposal. The remaining $3,000 is due upon completion of the work.

If you would like to have JWS Remodeling Solutions complete this work, please sign one copy of this letter and return it to us with your deposit in the enclosed envelope. We currently anticipate no construction delays, since the materials needed for your job are in stock and our staff of qualified workers is available during the period mentioned. If you have any questions regarding the terms of this proposal, please call me.

Sincerely,

Jordan W Spurrier

Jordan W. Spurrier
President

Enclosures (3)

Accepted by:

Makes letter a binding contract, if signed

_____   _____
Daniel Yurgren   Date

Pointers for Develping Proposals

- Carefully review and follow all requirements listed in the RFP (if applicable).
- Define the scope of work you intend to complete.
- Determine the methods and procedures to be used.
- Carefully estimate requirements for time, personnel, and costs.
- Write, format, and deliver the proposal exactly as the RFP specifies.
- Open by stating the purpose of the proposal, defining the scope of work, presenting helpful background information, and explaining any relevant restrictions or limitations.
- In the body, provide details and specify anticipated results, including methods, schedule, facilities, quantities, equipment, personnel, and costs.
- Close by summarizing key selling points and benefits, then ask for a decision from the audience.

The close is your last chance to convince the reader of the merits of your proposal, so make doubly sure it's clear, compelling, and audience-oriented.

Proposal Close   The final section of a proposal generally summarizes the key points, emphasizes the benefits that readers will realize from your solution, summarizes the merits of your approach, restates why you and your firm are a good choice, and asks for a decision from the client. In both formal and informal proposals, make this section relatively brief, assertive (but not brash or abrupt), and confident.

Table 11.1 summarizes the items to consider including in the introduction, body, and close of a report or proposal.

Table 11.1 Report and Proposal Contents

Report Contents	Proposal Contents

Report Contents

Introduction

- **Authorization.** Review who authorized the report (when, how), who wrote it, when it was submitted.
- **Problem/purpose.** Explain the reason for the report's existence and what the report will achieve.
- **Scope.** Describe what will and won't be covered in the report—indicating size and complexity.
- **Background.** Review historical conditions or factors that led up to the report.
- **Sources and methods.** Discuss the primary and secondary sources consulted and methods used.
- **Definitions.** List terms and their definitions—including any terms that might be misinterpreted. Terms may also be defined in the body, explanatory notes, or glossary.
- **Limitations.** Discuss factors beyond your control that affect report quality—not an excuse for a poor study or bad report.
- **Report organization.** Tell what topics are covered in what order.

Body

- **Explanations.** Give complete details of the problem, project, or idea.
- **Facts, statistical evidence, and trends.** Lay out the results of studies or investigations.
- **Analysis of action.** Discuss potential courses of action.
- **Pros and cons.** Explain advantages, disadvantages, costs, and benefits of a particular course of action.
- **Procedures.** Outline steps for a process.
- **Methods and approaches.** Discuss how you've studied a problem (or gathered evidence) and arrived at your solution (or collected your data).
- **Criteria.** Describe the benchmarks for evaluating options and alternatives.
- **Conclusions and recommendations.** Discuss what you believe the evidence reveals and what you propose should be done about it.
- **Support.** Give the reasons behind your conclusions or recommendations.

Close

- **For direct order.** Summarize key points (except in short memos), listing them in the order they appear in the body. Briefly restate your conclusions or recommendations, if appropriate.
- **For indirect order.** You may use the close to present your conclusions or recommendations for the first time—just be sure not to present any new facts.
- **For motivating action.** Spell out exactly what should happen next and provide a schedule with specific task assignments.

Proposal Contents

Introduction

- **Background or statement of the problem.** Briefly review the reader's situation, establish a need for action, and explain how things could be better. In unsolicited proposals, convince readers that a problem or opportunity exists.
- **Solution.** Briefly describe the change you propose, highlighting your key selling points and their benefits to show how your proposal will solve the reader's problem.
- **Scope.** State the boundaries of the proposal—what you will and will not do.
- **Report organization.** Orient the reader to the remainder of the proposal and call attention to the major divisions of thought.

Body

- **Facts and evidence to support your conclusions.** Give complete details of the proposed solution and anticipated results.
- **Proposed approach.** Describe your concept, product, or service. Stress reader benefits and emphasize any advantages you have over your competitors.
- **Work plan.** Describe how you'll accomplish what must be done (unless you're providing a standard, off-the-shelf item). Explain the steps you'll take, their timing, the methods or resources you'll use, and the persons(s) responsible. State when work will begin, how it will be divided into stages, when you'll finish, and whether follow-up will be needed.
- **Statement of qualifications.** Describe your organization's experience, personnel, and facilities—relating it all to readers' needs. Include a list of client references.
- **Costs.** Prove that your costs are realistic—break them down so that readers can see the cost of labor, materials, transportation, travel, training, and other categories.

Close

- **Review of argument.** Briefly summarize the key points.
- **Review of reader benefits.** Briefly summarize how your proposal will help the reader.
- **Review of the merits of your approach.** Briefly summarize why your approach will be more effective than that of competitors.
- **Restatement of qualifications.** Briefly reemphasize why you and your firm should do the work.
- **Request.** Ask for a decision from the reader.

Helping Readers Find Their Way

In a short report, readers are in little danger of getting lost; however, as the length of a report increases, so do the opportunities for readers to become confused and lose track of the relationships among ideas. Moreover, readers today often lack the time or the inclination to plow through long reports. They want to browse quickly. To help readers find what they're looking for and stay on track, make good use of these elements:

Help your readers find what they want and stay on track with headings, transitions, previews, and reviews.

- **Headings and links.** Readers should be able to follow the structure of your document and pick up the key points of your message from the headings and subheadings. For online reports, where the difficulty of reading on screen makes clear headings crucial, make generous use of hyperlinks to help your readers navigate the report and access additional information.
- **Transitions.** Chapter 4 defines transitions as words or phrases that tie ideas together and show how one thought is related to another. In a long report, an entire paragraph might be used to highlight transitions from one section to the next.
- **Previews and reviews.** *Preview sections* introduce important topics by helping readers get ready for new information. *Review sections* come after a body of material and summarize the information for your readers, helping them absorb details.

Using Technology to Craft Reports and Proposals

Creating lengthy reports and proposals can be a huge task, so take advantage of technological tools to help throughout the process. You've read about some of these tools in earlier chapters; here are some of the most important ones for developing reports and proposals:

Look for ways to utilize technology to reduce the mechanical work involved in writing long reports.

- **Templates.** Beyond simply formatting documents, report templates can identify the specific sections required for each type of report and even automatically insert headings for each section.
- **Linked and embedded documents.** In many reports and proposals, you'll include graphics, spreadsheets, databases, and other elements produced in other software programs. Just make sure you know how the software handles the files or you may receive some unpleasant surprises. For instance, in Microsoft Office, you can choose to either *link* or *embed* an incoming element, such as a table from a spreadsheet. If you link, the element will get updated whenever you or someone else updates the spreadsheet. In contrast, if you embed it, the files are no longer connected; changes in the spreadsheet will not show up in the report document.
- **Electronic forms.** For recurring forms such as sales reports and compliance reports, consider creating a word processor file that combines boilerplate text for material that doesn't change from report to report. To accommodate information that does change (such as last week's sales results), use *form tools* such as text boxes (in which users can type new text) and check boxes (which can be used to select from a set of predetermined choices).
- **Electronic documents.** Portable Document Format (PDF) files have become a universal replacement for printed reports and proposals. With a copy of Adobe Acrobat (a separate product from the free Acrobat Reader), you can quickly convert reports and proposals to PDF files that are easy and safe to share electronically.
- **Multimedia documents.** When the written word isn't enough, combine your report with video clips, animation, presentation software slides, and other elements.

Today's computer technology also makes it easy to add a wide variety of compelling visuals to your reports, which you'll learn more about in the next section.

Illustrating Your Reports with Effective Visuals

Carefully crafted visuals enhance the power of your words.

Well-designed visuals can bring your messages to life and help you connect to your audiences both intellectually and emotionally. Visuals enhance the communication power of textual messages, and they can often convey some message points (such as spatial

Document Makeover

Improve This Report

To practice correcting drafts of actual documents, visit your online course or the access-code-protected portion of the Companion Website. Click "Document Makeovers," then click Chapter 11. You will find a policy report that contains problems and errors relating to what you've learned in this chapter about composing business reports and proposals. Use the Final Draft decision tool to create an improved version of this report. Check the message for an effective opening, consistent levels of formality or informality, and the use of headings, transitions, previews, and reviews to help orient readers.

relationships and procedures) more effectively and more efficiently than words. Visuals attract and hold attention, helping your audience understand and remember your message. Busy readers often jump to visuals to try to get the gist of a message, and well-done visuals can draw readers deeper into your reports and presentations.

To be effective, however, visuals need to be planned and selected carefully. When you're deciding which points to present visually, think of the five Cs:

- **Clear.** If you're having difficultly conveying an idea in words, see if a visual element can do the job better. Pictures can be particularly helpful when communicating with multilingual audiences.
- **Complete.** Visuals, particularly tables, can be a great way to provide the supporting details for your main idea or recommendation.
- **Concise.** If a particular section of your message seems to require extensive description or explanation, see whether there's a way to convey this information visually.
- **Connected.** Whenever you want readers to see such a connection—similarities or differences, correlations, cause-and-effect relationships, and so on—see whether a chart, diagram, or other illustration can help.
- **Compelling.** Your readers live in a highly visual world. When a point can be expressed equally well via text or visuals, consider adding the visual in order to make your report or presentation more compelling.

Effective visuals are clear, complete, concise, connected, and compelling.

Strong visuals enhance the descriptive and persuasive power of your writing, but it's important not to overdo them. Cramming too many visuals into a report can distract your readers by (a) requiring them to jump back and forth between text and visuals and (b) breaking up the flow of text on the page or screen.

Maintain a balance between text and visuals, and pace your visuals in a way that emphasizes your key textual points.

Choosing the Right Visual for the Job

Once you've identified which points would benefit most from visual presentation, your next decision is choosing the types of visuals to use. As you can see in Figure 11.5, you have many choices for business graphics. For certain types of information, the decision is usually obvious. If you want to present a large set of numerical values or detailed textual information, for example, a table is the obvious choice in most cases. Also, certain visuals are used more commonly for certain applications; for instance, your audience expects pie charts to be used to show the percentages that make up a whole.

You have many types of visuals to choose from, and each is best suited to particular communication tasks.

Tables

When you need to present detailed, specific information, choose a **table**, a systematic arrangement of data in columns and rows. Tables are ideal when your audience needs information that would be either difficult or tedious to handle in the main text. Most

Printed tables can display extensive amounts of data.

FIGURE 11.5   Selecting the Best Visual
Choose your visuals carefully for maximum communication effectiveness.

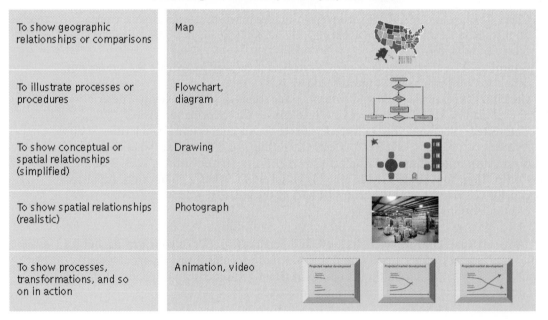

| Communication Challenge | Effective Visual Choice |

Presenting Data

To present individual, exact values	Table
To show trends in one or more variables, or the relationship between those variables, over time	Line chart, bar chart
To compare two or more sets of data	Bar chart, line chart
To show frequency or distribution of parts in a whole	Pie chart

Presenting Information, Concepts, and Ideas

To show geographic relationships or comparisons	Map
To illustrate processes or procedures	Flowchart, diagram
To show conceptual or spatial relationships (simplified)	Drawing
To show spatial relationships (realistic)	Photograph
To show processes, transformations, and so on in action	Animation, video

tables contain the standard parts illustrated in Table 11.2. Follow these guidelines to create clear, effective tables:

- Use common, understandable units, and clearly identify them: dollars, percentages, price per ton, and so on.
- Express all items in a column in the same unit, and round off for simplicity.
- Label column headings clearly, and use a subhead if necessary.
- Separate columns or rows with lines or extra space to make the table easy to follow.
- Don't cram so much information into a table that it becomes difficult to read.
- Document the source of data using the same format as a text footnote (see Appendix B).

Table 11.2	Parts of a Table			
	Multicolumn Heading			
Sub, Heading	**Subheading**	**Subheading**	**Subheading**	**Single-Column Heading**
Row heading	xxx	xxx	xxx	xxx
Row heading	xxx	xxx	xxx	xxx
Subheading	xxx	xxx	xxx	xxx
Subheading	xxx	xxx	xxx	xxx
Total	xxx	xxx	xxx	xxx
Source: (In the same format as a text footnote; see Appendix B)				
*Footnote (For an explanation of elements in the table, a superscript number or small letter may be used instead of an asterisk or other symbol.)				

Line and Surface Charts

A **line chart** (Figure 11.6) illustrates trends over time or plots the relationship of two variables. In line charts showing trends, the vertical, or *y*, axis shows the amount, and the horizontal, or *x*, axis shows the time or other quantity against which the amount is being measured. Moreover, you can plot just a single line or overlay multiple lines to compare different entities.

Line charts are commonly used to show trends over time or the relationship between two variables.

A **surface chart**, also called an **area chart**, is a form of line chart with a cumulative effect; all the lines add up to the top line, which represents the total (see Figure 11.7). This form of chart helps you illustrate changes in the composition of something over time. When preparing a surface chart, put the most important segment against the baseline, and restrict the number of strata to four or five.

Bar Charts and Pie Charts

A **bar chart** (Figure 11.8) portrays numbers by the height or length of its rectangular bars, making a series of numbers easy to read or understand. Bar charts are particularly valuable when you want to

Bar charts can show a variety of relationships among two or more variables.

- Compare the size of several items at one time
- Show changes in one item over time
- Indicate the composition of several items over time
- Show the relative size of components of a whole

FIGURE 11.6   Line Chart
This two-line chart compares the temperatures measured inside two cement kilns from 8:00 A.M. to 5:00 P.M.

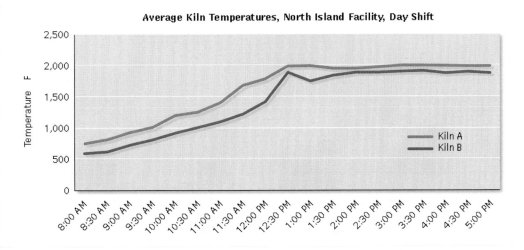

FIGURE 11.7 Surface Chart

Surface or area charts can show a combination of trends over time and the individual contributions of the components of a whole.

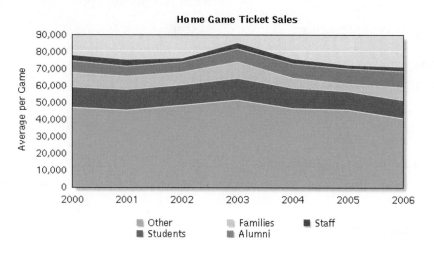

FIGURE 11.8 The Versatile Bar Chart

These charts show just four of the many variations available for bar charts: *singular* (11.8a: "CommuniCo Staff Computer Skills"), *grouped* (11.8b: "Worldwide Market Share"), *segmented* (11.8c: "CommuniCo Preferred Communication Media"), and *combination* (11.8d: "CommuniCo Employee Training Costs").

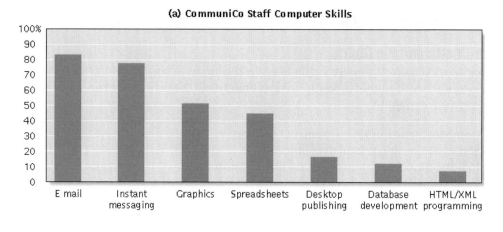

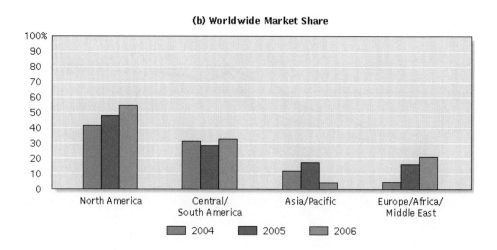

Grouped bar charts compare more than one set of data, using a different color or pattern for each set. Segmented bar charts, also known as stacked bar charts, show how individual components contribute to a total number, using a different color or pattern for each component. Combination bar and line charts compare quantities that require different intervals.

Like segmented bar charts and area charts, a **pie chart** shows how the parts of a whole are distributed (see Figure 11.9). However, pie charts have the advantage of familiarity; most people expect parts of a whole to be displayed via a pie chart. When creating pie charts, limit the number of slices to keep the chart from getting cluttered. If necessary, lump the smallest pieces together in a "miscellaneous" category. Ideally, the largest or most important slice of the pie, the segment you want to emphasize, is placed at the 12 o'clock position; the rest are arranged clockwise either in order of size or in some other logical progression. Remember, the segments must add up to 100 percent if percentages are used or to the total number if numbers are used.

Most readers expect pie charts to show the distribution of parts within a whole.

Flowcharts and Organization Charts

A **flowchart** (see Figure 11.10) illustrates a sequence of events from start to finish; it is indispensable when illustrating processes, procedures, and sequential relationships. For general business purposes, you don't need to be too concerned about the specific shapes, but keep them consistent. However, you should be aware that there is a formal flowchart "language," in which each shape has a specific meaning (diamonds are decision points, rectangles are process steps, and so on). If you're communicating with computer programmers and others who are accustomed to formal flowcharting, make sure you use the correct symbols in each case to avoid confusion.

FIGURE 11.8 continued

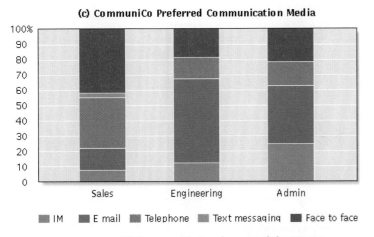

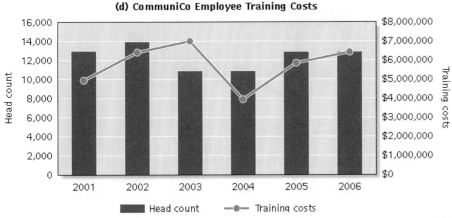

FIGURE 11.9   Pie Chart

When creating pie charts, use different colors or patterns to distinguish the various pieces. Label all the segments and indicate their value in either percentages or units of measure so that your readers will be able to judge the value of the wedges.

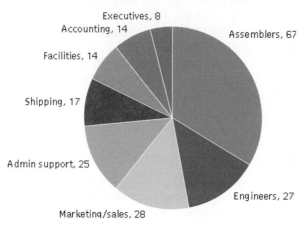

Year End Head Count by Function

FIGURE 11.10   Flowchart

Flowcharts show sequences of events and are most valuable when the process or procedure has a number of decision points and variable paths.

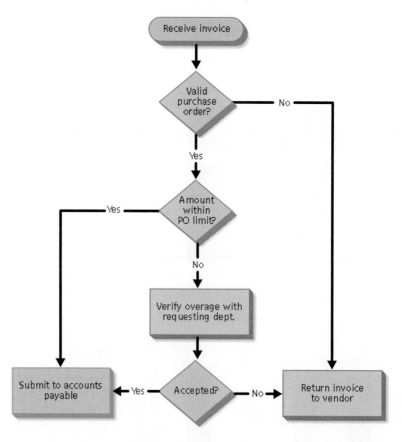

As the name implies, an **organization chart** illustrates the positions, units, or functions of an organization and the way they interrelate. An organization's normal communication channels are almost impossible to describe without the benefit of a chart like the one in Figure 11.11.

FIGURE 11.11 Organization Chart
An organization chart is the expected way to illustrate the hierarchy of positions in an organization.

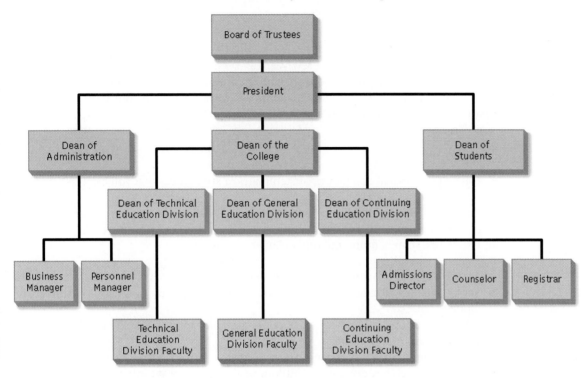

Maps, Drawings, Diagrams, and Photographs

Maps are useful for showing market territories, distribution routes, and facilities locations. Rapid progress is being made in the area of mapping software, such as Google Earth (http://earth.google.com), which combines search engine, mapping, and satellite photo technologies.[7]

You probably won't need to create a large number of drawings, diagrams, or photographs to accompany your business messages. However, when you do have the opportunity, knowing some of the basics can help you make the most of these potentially compelling elements. Drawings and diagrams are most often used to show how something looks or operates. Diagrams can be much clearer than words alone when it comes to giving your audience an idea of how an item looks or can be used.

Photographs offer both functional and decorative value. In the past, their use was limited to specialized documents such as annual reports and product brochures; however, with low-cost digital photography now widely available, virtually all writers can have the ability to add photographs to print documents, presentations, and webpages.

> Use maps to represent statistics by geographic area and to show spatial relationships.

> Use drawings and diagrams to show how something works or how it is made or used; drawings are sometimes better than photographs because they let you focus on the most important details.

> Use photographs for visual appeal and to show exact appearances.

Animation and Video

Computer animation and video are among the most specialized forms of business visuals. When they are appropriate and done well, they offer unparalleled visual impact. At a simple level, you can animate shapes and text within Microsoft PowerPoint, although the possibilities are somewhat limited. At a more sophisticated level, software programs such as Macromedia Flash enables the creation of multimedia files that include computer animation, digital video, and other elements. A wide variety of tools are also available for digital video production. Chances are you won't have to use these tools yourself, but if you do employ a specialist to create animation or video for websites or presentations, make sure the results complement, rather than distract from, your message.

Designing Effective Visuals

Technology has put powerful graphics tools in the hands of virtually every business computer user, so you no longer have to rely on professional designers as much as businesspeople had to do only a few years ago. That's the good news. The bad news is that computers can't provide the specialized training and hands-on experience of a professional designer. Computers make it easy to create visuals, but they also make it easy to create bad visuals. However, by following some basic advice and design principles, you can create all the basic visuals you need—visuals that are both attractive and effective:[8]

- Have a professional designer create templates or style guides that you can use for recurring tasks.
- Be careful with the templates that are included with some commercial software programs; some are cluttered and inappropriate for serious business uses.
- Use colors, shapes, fonts, and other elements consistently.
- To emphasize differences, use contrasting colors.
- To emphasize similarities, use complementary or similar colors.
- Try to balance design elements so that pages or screens don't look cramped or lopsided.
- Select colors and other design elements carefully to emphasize major points and de-emphasize minor points.
- Limit the number of colors and design elements you use; avoid *chartjunk*, decorative elements that clutter documents without adding any relevant information.[9]
- Understand the expectations of your audience; for example, green is associated with money in the United States but not in countries whose currencies are different colors.

In addition to creating effective visuals, make sure your visuals are smoothly integrated with the text. First, try to position your visuals so that your audience won't have to flip back and forth (in printed documents) or scroll (on screen) between the visuals and the text. Second, clearly refer to visuals by number in the text of your report, and help your readers understand the significance of visuals by referring to them before readers encounter them in the document or on the screen. Third, write effective *titles*, *captions*, and *legends* to complete the integration of your text and visuals. A **title** provides a short description that identifies the content and purpose of the visual. A **caption** usually offers additional discussion of the visual's content and can be several sentences long if appropriate. A **legend** helps readers "decode" the visual by explaining what various colors, symbols, or other design choices mean.

Finally, check your visuals carefully for accuracy. Check for mistakes such as typographical errors, inconsistent color treatment, confusing or undocumented symbols, and misaligned elements. Make sure that your computer hasn't done something unexpected, such as arranging pie chart slices in an order you don't want or plotting line charts in unusual colors. Make sure your visuals are properly documented. Most importantly, make sure your visuals are honest, that they don't intentionally or unintentionally distort the truth.

Completing Reports and Proposals

As with shorter messages (Chapter 5), once you have finished your first draft, you need to perform four tasks to complete your document: revise, produce, proofread, and distribute.

Revising Your Reports and Proposals

The revision process is essentially the same for reports as for any business message, although it may take considerably longer, depending on the length of your document. Evaluate your organization, style, and tone, making sure that you've said what you want to say and that you've said it in the most logical order and in a way that responds to your audience's needs. Then work to improve the report's readability by varying sentence length, keeping paragraphs short, using lists and bullets, and adding headings and subheadings. Keep revising the content until it is clear, concise, and compelling. Remember that even minor mistakes can affect your credibility.

The revision process for long reports is the same as for short messages, although it can take considerably longer.

Producing a Formal Report

The parts included in a report depend on the type of report you are writing, the requirements of your audience, the organization you're working for, and the length of your report. The components listed in Figure 11.12 fall into three categories, according to their location in a report: prefatory parts, text, and supplementary parts. The instructions here pertain primarily to printed reports, but you will of course adapt many of these elements to reports delivered electronically.

The number and variety of parts you include in a report depend on the type of report, audience requirements, organizational expectations, and report length.

Most prefatory parts (such as the table of contents) should be placed on their own pages. However, the various parts in the report text are often run together and seldom stand alone. If your introduction is only a paragraph long, don't bother with a page break before moving into the body of your report. If the introduction runs longer than a page, however, a page break can signal the reader that a major shift is about to occur in the flow of the report.

For an illustration of how the various parts fit together in an actual report, see Figure 11.13 beginning on page 318. This 14-page report was prepared by Linda Moreno, manager of the cost accounting department at Electrovision, a high-tech company based

FIGURE 11.12 Parts of a Formal Report
Formal reports can contain a variety of prefatory and supplemental parts in addition to the main text.

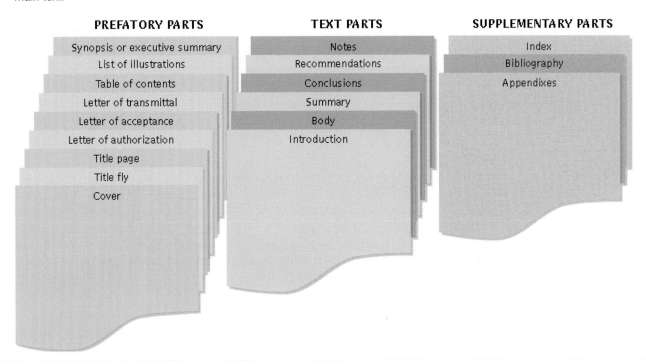

PREFATORY PARTS	TEXT PARTS	SUPPLEMENTARY PARTS
Synopsis or executive summary	Notes	Index
List of illustrations	Recommendations	Bibliography
Table of contents	Conclusions	Appendixes
Letter of transmittal	Summary	
Letter of acceptance	Body	
Letter of authorization	Introduction	
Title page		
Title fly		
Cover		

FIGURE 11.13   Analyzing an Effective Analytical Report

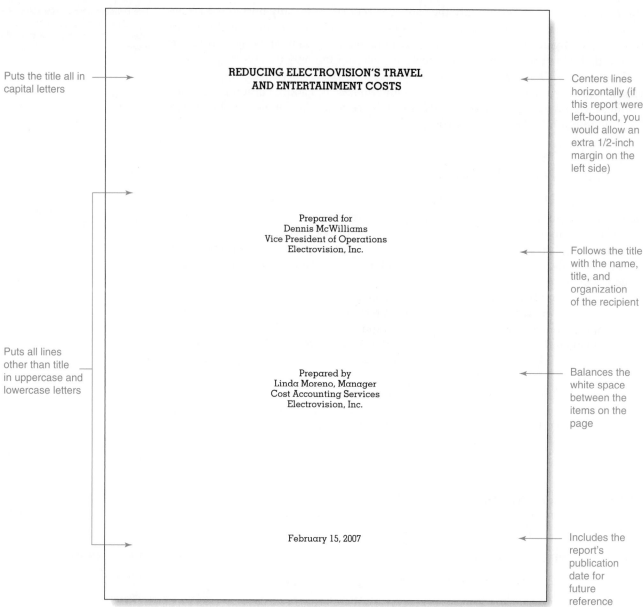

Puts the title all in capital letters

Puts all lines other than title in uppercase and lowercase letters

REDUCING ELECTROVISION'S TRAVEL
AND ENTERTAINMENT COSTS

Prepared for
Dennis McWilliams
Vice President of Operations
Electrovision, Inc.

Prepared by
Linda Moreno, Manager
Cost Accounting Services
Electrovision, Inc.

February 15, 2007

Centers lines horizontally (if this report were left-bound, you would allow an extra 1/2-inch margin on the left side)

Follows the title with the name, title, and organization of the recipient

Balances the white space between the items on the page

Includes the report's publication date for future reference

The "how to" tone of Moreno's title is appropriate for an action-oriented report that emphasizes recommendations. A neutral title, such as "An Analysis of Electrovision's Travel and Entertainment Costs," would be more suitable for an informational report.

in Los Gatos, California. Electrovision's main product is optical character recognition equipment, which is used by the U.S. Postal Service for sorting mail. Moreno's job is to help analyze the company's costs. Moreno used direct order and organized her report based on conclusions and recommendations.

Formal reports can contain a variety of prefatory parts, from a cover page to a synopsis or executive summary.

Prefatory Parts

Prefatory parts come before the main text of your report and help readers decide whether and how to read the report:[10]

FIGURE 11.13 continued

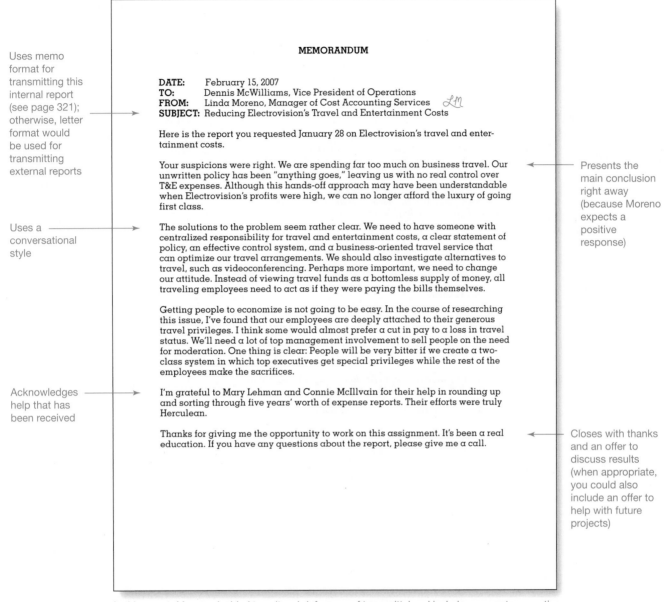

Uses memo format for transmitting this internal report (see page 321); otherwise, letter format would be used for transmitting external reports

Uses a conversational style

Acknowledges help that has been received

MEMORANDUM

DATE: February 15, 2007
TO: Dennis McWilliams, Vice President of Operations
FROM: Linda Moreno, Manager of Cost Accounting Services *LM*
SUBJECT: Reducing Electrovision's Travel and Entertainment Costs

Here is the report you requested January 28 on Electrovision's travel and entertainment costs.

Your suspicions were right. We are spending far too much on business travel. Our unwritten policy has been "anything goes," leaving us with no real control over T&E expenses. Although this hands-off approach may have been understandable when Electrovision's profits were high, we can no longer afford the luxury of going first class.

The solutions to the problem seem rather clear. We need to have someone with centralized responsibility for travel and entertainment costs, a clear statement of policy, an effective control system, and a business-oriented travel service that can optimize our travel arrangements. We should also investigate alternatives to travel, such as videoconferencing. Perhaps more important, we need to change our attitude. Instead of viewing travel funds as a bottomless supply of money, all traveling employees need to act as if they were paying the bills themselves.

Getting people to economize is not going to be easy. In the course of researching this issue, I've found that our employees are deeply attached to their generous travel privileges. I think some would almost prefer a cut in pay to a loss in travel status. We'll need a lot of top management involvement to sell people on the need for moderation. One thing is clear: People will be very bitter if we create a two-class system in which top executives get special privileges while the rest of the employees make the sacrifices.

I'm grateful to Mary Lehman and Connie McIllvain for their help in rounding up and sorting through five years' worth of expense reports. Their efforts were truly Herculean.

Thanks for giving me the opportunity to work on this assignment. It's been a real education. If you have any questions about the report, please give me a call.

Presents the main conclusion right away (because Moreno expects a positive response)

Closes with thanks and an offer to discuss results (when appropriate, you could also include an offer to help with future projects)

In this report, Moreno decided to write a brief memo of transmittal and include a separate executive summary. Short reports (fewer than 10 pages) often combine the synopsis or executive summary with the memo or letter of transmittal.

■ **Cover.** If your company doesn't provide them, you can find something suitable in a good stationery store. Think carefully about the title you put on the cover. Give readers all the information they need (the who, what, when, where, why, and how of the subject), but be concise.

FIGURE 11.13   continued

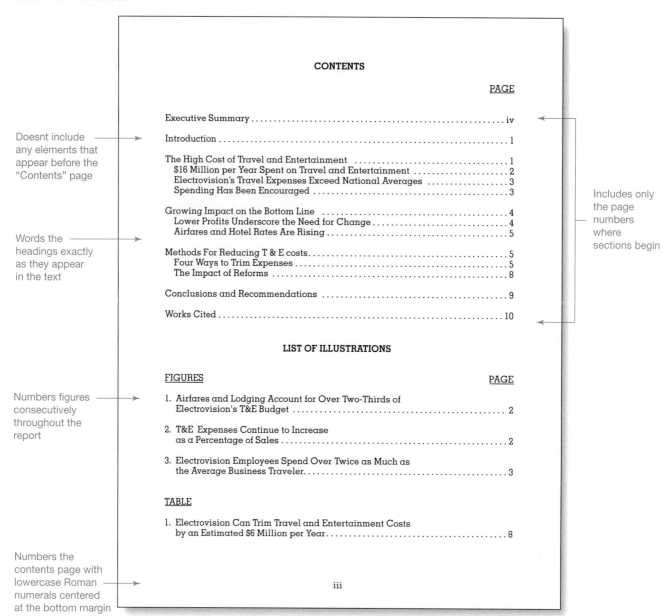

Doesnt include any elements that appear before the "Contents" page

Words the headings exactly as they appear in the text

Numbers figures consecutively throughout the report

Numbers the contents page with lowercase Roman numerals centered at the bottom margin

Includes only the page numbers where sections begin

CONTENTS

LIST OF ILLUSTRATIONS

iii

Moreno included only first- and second-level headings in her table of contents, even though the report contains third-level headings. She prefers a shorter table of contents that focuses attention on the main divisions of thought. She used informative titles, which are appropriate for a report to a receptive audience.

- ■ **Title fly.** Most formal reports begin with a plain sheet of paper that has only the title of the report on it.
- ■ **Title page.** The title page includes four blocks of information: (1) the title of the report; (2) the name, title, and address of the person, group, or organization that authorized the report; (3) the name, title, and address of the person, group, or organization that prepared the report; and (4) the date on which the report was submitted.

FIGURE 11.13 continued

Begins by stating the purpose of the report →

Presents the points in the executive summary (see page 326) in the same order as they appear in the report, using subheadings that summarize the content of the main sections of the report

Continues numbering the executive summary pages with lowercase Roman numerals →

EXECUTIVE SUMMARY

This report analyzes Electrovision's travel and entertainment (T&E) costs and presents recommendations for reducing those costs.

Travel and Entertainment Costs Are Too High

Travel and entertainment is a large and growing expense category for Electrovision. The company spends over $16 million per year on business travel, and these costs have been increasing by 12 percent annually. Company employees make roughly 3,390 trips each year at an average cost per trip of $4,720. Airfares are the biggest expense, followed by hotels, meals, and rental cars.

The nature of Electrovision's business does require extensive travel, but the company's costs are excessive: Our employees spend more than twice the national average on travel and entertainment. Although the location of the company's facilities may partly explain this discrepancy, the main reason for our high costs is a management style that gives employees little incentive to economize.

Cuts Are Essential

Electrovision management now recognizes the need to gain more control over this element of costs. The company is currently entering a period of declining profits, prompting management to look for every opportunity to reduce spending. At the same time, rising airfares and hotel rates are making T&E expenses more significant.

Electrovision Can Save $6 Million per Year

Fortunately, Electrovision has a number of excellent opportunities for reducing T&E costs. Savings of up to $6 million per year should be achievable, judging by the experience of other companies. A sensible travel-management program can save companies as much as 35 percent a year (Gilligan 39–40), and we should be able to save even more, since we purchase many more business-class tickets than the average. Four steps will help us cut costs:

1. Hire a director of travel and entertainment to assume overall responsibility for T&E spending, policies, and technologies, including the hiring and management of a national travel agency.
2. Educate employees on the need for cost containment, both in avoiding unnecessary travel and reducing costs when travel is necessary.
3. Negotiate preferential rates with travel providers.
4. Implement technological alternatives to travel, such as virtual meetings.

As necessary as these changes are, they will likely hurt morale, at least in the short term. Management will need to make a determined effort to explain the rationale for reduced spending. By exercising moderation in their own travel arrangements, Electrovision executives can set a good example and help other employees accept the changes. On the plus side, using travel alternatives such as web conferencing will reduce the travel burden on many employees and help them balance their business and personal lives.

Targets a receptive audience with a hard-hitting tone in the executive summary (a more neutral approach would be better for hostile or skeptical readers)

Executive summary uses the same font and paragraph treatment as the text of the report

iv

Moreno decided to include an executive summary because her report is aimed at a mixed audience, some of whom are interested in the details of her report and others who just want the "big picture." The executive summary is aimed at the second group, giving them enough information to make a decision without burdening them with the task of reading the entire report.

Her writing style matches the serious nature of the content without sounding distant or stiff. Moreno chose the formal approach because several members of her audience are considerably higher up in the organization, and she did not want to sound too familiar. In addition, her company prefers the impersonal style for formal reports.

■ **Letter of authorization.** If you received written authorization to prepare the report, you may want to include that letter or memo in your report.
■ **Letter of transmittal.** This letter or memo introduces the report on your behalf. The opening discusses scope, methods, and limitations. The body can highlight important sections of the report, suggest follow-up studies, offer details to help readers use the

FIGURE 11.13   continued

Centers the title of the report on the first page of the text, 2 inches from the top of the page →

REDUCING ELECTROVISION'S TRAVEL AND ENTERTAINMENT COSTS

INTRODUCTION

Electrovision has always encouraged a significant amount of business travel. To compensate employees for the stress and inconvenience of frequent trips, management has authorized generous travel and entertainment (T&E) allowances. This philosophy has been good for morale, but last year Electrovision spent $16 million on travel and entertainment—$7 million more than it spent on research and development.

← Opens by establishing the need for action

This year's T&E costs will affect profits even more, due to increases in airline fares and hotel rates. Also, the company anticipates that profits will be relatively weak for a variety of other reasons. Therefore, Dennis McWilliams, Vice President of Operations, has asked the accounting department to explore ways to reduce the T&E budget.

The purpose of this report is to analyze T&E expenses, evaluate the effect of recent hotel and airfares increases, and suggest ways to tighten control over T&E costs. The report outlines several steps that could reduce Electrovision's expenses, but the precise financial impact of these measures is difficult to project. The estimates presented here provide a "best guess" view of what Electrovision can expect to save.

In preparing this report, the accounting department analyzed internal expense reports for the past five years to determine how much Electrovision spends on travel and entertainment. These figures were then compared with average statistics compiled by Dow Jones (publisher of the *Wall Street Journal*) and presented as the Dow Jones Travel Index. We also analyzed trends and suggestions published in a variety of business journal articles to see how other companies are coping with the high cost of business travel.

← Mentions sources and methods to increase credibility and to give readers a complete picture of the study's background

THE HIGH COST OF TRAVEL AND ENTERTAINMENT

Although many companies view travel and entertainment as an incidental cost of doing business, the dollars add up. At Electrovision the bill for airfares, hotels, rental cars, meals, and entertainment totaled $16 million last year. Our T&E budget has increased by 12 percent per year for the past five years. Compared to the average U.S. business traveler, Electrovision's expenditures are high, largely because of management's generous policy on travel benefits.

Uses the arabic numeral 1 for the first page, centering the number about 1 inch from the bottom of the page →

1

In her brief introduction, Moreno counts on topic sentences and transitions to indicate that she is discussing the purpose, scope, and limitations of the study.

report, and acknowledge help from others. The close can include a note of thanks for the assignment, an expression of willingness to discuss the report, and an offer to assist with future projects (see Figure 11.13 on page 319).

■ **Table of contents.** The contents page lists report parts and text headings to indicate the location and relative importance of the information in the report. You may show only the top two or three levels of headings or only first-level headings. Word headings

FIGURE 11.13 (continued)

Places the visual as close as possible to the point it illustrates

Gives each visual a title that clearly indicates what it's about; titles are consistently placed to the left of each visual

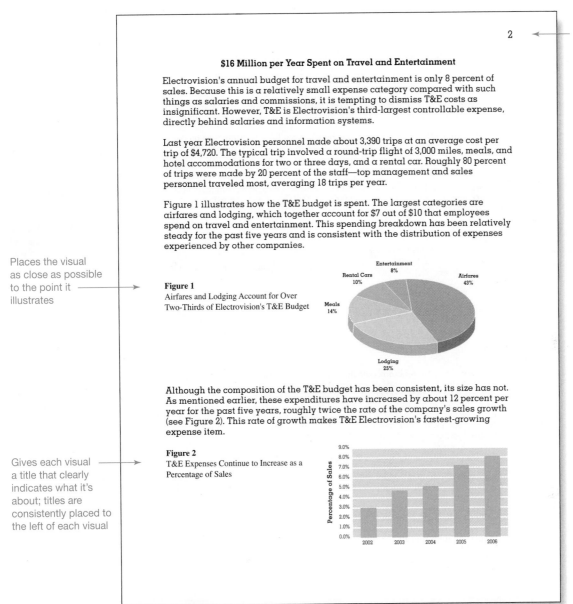

2 — Uses arabic numerals to number the second and succeeding pages of the text in the upper right-hand corner where the top and right-hand margins meet

Moreno opens the first main section of the body with a topic sentence that introduces an important fact about the subject of the section. Then she orients the reader to the three major points developed in the section.

exactly as they are in the report text. List all prefatory parts that come after the contents page and all supplementary parts. If you have fewer than four visuals, you may wish to list them in the contents (see Figure 11.13 page 320).

■ **List of illustrations.** The list of illustrations gives the titles and page numbers of visuals. If you have enough space on a single page, include the list of illustrations directly

FIGURE 11.13   continued

3

Electrovision's Travel Expenses Exceed National Averages

Much of our travel budget is justified. Two major factors contribute to Electrovision's high T&E budget:

* With our headquarters on the West Coast and our major customer on the East Coast, we naturally spend a lot of money on cross-country flights.

* A great deal of travel takes place between our headquarters here on the West Coast and the manufacturing operations in Detroit, Boston, and Dallas. Corporate managers and division personnel make frequent trips to coordinate these disparate operations.

However, even though a good portion of Electrovision's travel budget is justifiable, the company spends considerably more on T&E than the average business traveler (see Figure 3).

Figure 3
Electrovision Employees Spend Over Twice as Much as the Average Business Traveler

Source: *Wall Street Journal* and company records

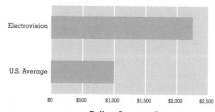

The Dow Jones Travel Index calculates the average cost per day of business travel in the United States, based on average airfare, hotel rates, and rental car rates. The average fluctuates weekly as travel companies change their rates, but it has been running at about $1,000 per day for the last year or so. In contrast, Electrovision's average daily expense over the past year has been $2,250—a hefty 125 percent higher than average. This figure is based on the average trip cost of $4,720 listed earlier and an average trip length of 2.1 days.

Spending Has Been Encouraged

Although a variety of factors may contribute to this differential, Electrovision's relatively high T&E costs are at least partially attributable to the company's philosophy and management style. Since many employees do not enjoy business travel, management has tried to make the trips more pleasant by authorizing business-class airfare, luxury hotel accommodations, and full-size rental cars. The sales staff is encouraged to entertain clients at top restaurants and to invite them to cultural and sporting events.

Numbers the visuals consecutively and refers to them in the text by their numbers

Introduces visuals before they appear and indicates what readers should notice about the data

The chart in Figure 3 is simple but effective; Moreno includes just enough data to make her point. Notice how she is as careful about the appearance of her report as she is about the quality of its content.

beneath the table of contents. Otherwise, put the list on the page after the contents page. When tables and figures are numbered separately, they should also be listed separately. The two lists can appear on the same page if they fit; otherwise, start each list on a separate page.

FIGURE 11.13   continued

Uses a bulleted list to make it easy for readers to identify and distinguish related points

4

The cost of these privileges is easy to overlook, given the weakness of Electrovision's system for keeping track of T&E expenses:

- The monthly financial records do not contain a separate category for travel and entertainment; the information is buried under Cost of Goods Sold and under Selling, General, and Administrative Expenses.

- Each department head is given authority to approve any expense report, regardless of how large it may be.

- Receipts are not required for expenditures of less than $100.

- Individuals are allowed to make their own travel arrangements.

- No one is charged with the responsibility for controlling the company's total spending on travel and entertainment.

Leaves an extra line of white space above headings to help readers associate each heading with the text it describes

GROWING IMPACT ON THE BOTTOM LINE

During the past three years, the company's healthy profits have resulted in relatively little pressure to push for tighter controls over all aspects of the business. However, as we all know, the situation is changing. We're projecting flat to declining profits for the next two years, a situation that has prompted all of us to search for ways to cut costs. At the same time, rising airfares and hotel rates have increased the impact of T&E expenses on the company's financial results.

Lower Profits Underscore the Need for Change

The next two years promise to be difficult for Electrovision. After several years of steady increases in spending, the Postal Service is tightening procurement policies for automated mail-handling equipment. Funding for the A-12 optical character reader has been canceled. As a consequence, the marketing department expects sales to drop by 15 percent. Although Electrovision is negotiating several other promising R&D contracts, the marketing department does not foresee any major procurements for the next two to three years.

At the same time, Electrovision is facing cost increases on several fronts. As we have known for several months, the new production facility now under construction in Salt Lake City, Utah, is behind schedule and over budget. Labor contracts in Boston and Dallas will expire within the next six months, and plant managers there anticipate that significant salary and benefits concessions may be necessary to avoid strikes.

Moreover, marketing and advertising costs are expected to increase as we attempt to strengthen these activities to better cope with competitive pressures. Given the expected decline in revenues and increase in costs, the Executive Committee's prediction that profits will fall by 12 percent in the coming fiscal year does not seem overly pessimistic.

Uses informative headings to focus reader attention on the main points (such headings are appropriate when a report uses direct order and is intended for a receptive audience; however, descriptive headings are more effective when a report is in indirect order and readers are less receptive)

Moreno designed her report to include plenty of white space so even those pages that lack visuals are still attractive and easy to read.

■ **Synopsis.** A **synopsis** is a brief overview (one page or less) of a report's most important points—it can also be called an **abstract**. The phrasing of a synopsis can be either informative (presenting the main points in the order they appear in the text) or descriptive (simply telling what the report is about), depending on whether the report is in direct or indirect order.

FIGURE 11.13 continued

Documents the facts to add weight to Moreno's argument →

Gives recommendations an objective flavor by pointing out both the benefits and the risks of taking action →

5

Airfares and Hotel Rates Are Rising

Business travelers have grown accustomed to frequent fare wars and discounting in the travel industry in recent years. Excess capacity and aggressive price competition, particularly in the airline business, made travel a relative bargain.

However, that situation has changed as weaker competitors have been forced out and the remaining players have grown stronger and smarter. Airlines and hotels are better at managing inventory and keeping occupancy rates high, which translates into higher costs for Electrovision. Last year saw some of the steepest rate hikes in years. Business airfares (tickets most likely to be purchased by business travelers) jumped more than 40 percent in many markets. The trend is expected to continue, with rates increasing another 5 to 10 percent overall (Phillips 331; "Travel Costs Under Pressure" 30; Dahl B6).

Given the fact that air and hotel costs account for 70 percent of our T&E budget, the trend toward higher prices in these two categories will have serious consequences, unless management takes action to control these costs.

METHODS FOR REDUCING T&E COSTS

By implementing a number of reforms, management can expect to reduce Electrovision's T&E budget by as much as 40 percent. This estimate is based on the general assessment made by American Express (Gilligan 39) and on the fact that we have an opportunity to significantly reduce air travel costs by eliminating business-class travel. However, these measures are likely to be unpopular with employees. To gain acceptance for such changes, management will need to sell employees on the need for moderation in T&E allowances.

Four Ways to Trim Expenses

By researching what other companies are doing to curb T&E expenses, the accounting department has identified four prominent opportunities that should enable Electrovision to save about $6 million annually in travel-related costs.

Institute Tighter Spending Controls

A single individual should be appointed director of travel and entertainment to spearhead the effort to gain control of the T&E budget. More than a third of all U.S. companies now employ travel managers ("Businesses Use Savvy Managers" 4). The director should be familiar with the travel industry and should be well versed in both accounting and information technology. The director should also report to the vice president of operations. The director's first priorities should be to establish a written T&E policy and a cost-control system.

Electrovision currently has no written policy on travel and entertainment, a step that is widely recommended by air travel experts (Smith D4). Creating a policy

Moreno creates a forceful tone by using action verbs in the third-level subheadings of this section. This approach is appropriate to the nature of the study and the attitude of the audience. However, in a status-conscious organization, the imperative verbs might sound a bit too presumptuous coming from a junior member of the staff.

■ **Executive summary.** Instead of a synopsis or abstract, many report writers prefer an **executive summary**—a fully developed "mini" version of the report itself, which may contain headings, transitions, and even visual aids. Executive summaries help readers who lack the time or motivation to study the complete text. Keep the length of an executive summary proportionate to the length of the report. Reports of fewer than 10 pages usually don't feature a synopsis or executive summary, unless your organization expects one.

FIGURE 11.13 continued

8

The Impact of Reforms

By implementing tighter controls, reducing unnecessary expenses, negotiating more favorable rates, and exploring alternatives to travel, Electrovision should be able to reduce its T&E budget significantly. As Table 1 illustrates, the combined savings should be in the neighborhood of $6 million, although the precise figures are somewhat difficult to project.

Table 1
Electrovision Can Trim Travel and Entertainment Costs by an Estimated $6 Million per Year

SOURCE OF SAVINGS	ESTIMATED SAVINGS
Switching from business-class to coach airfare	$2,300,000
Negotiating preferred hotel rates	940,000
Negotiating preferred rental car rates	460,000
Systematically searching for lower airfares	375,000
Reducing interdivisional travel	675,000
Reducing seminar and conference attendance	1,250,000
TOTAL POTENTIAL SAVINGS	**$6,000,000**

To achieve the economies outlined in the table, Electrovision will incur expenses for hiring a director of travel and for implementing a T&E cost-control system. These costs are projected at $115,000: $105,000 per year in salary and benefits for the new employee and a one-time expense of $10,000 for the cost-control system. The cost of retaining a full-service travel agency is negligible, even with the service fees that many are now passing along from airlines and other service providers.

The measures required to achieve these savings are likely to be unpopular with employees. Electrovision personnel are accustomed to generous T&E allowances, and they are likely to resent having these privileges curtailed. To alleviate their disappointment

- Management should make a determined effort to explain why the changes are necessary.

- The director of corporate communication should be asked to develop a multifaceted campaign that will communicate the importance of curtailing T&E costs.

- Management should set a positive example by adhering strictly to the new policies.

- The limitations should apply equally to employees at all levels in the organization.

Uses complete sentence to help readers focus immediately on the point of the table

Includes financial estimates to help management envision the impact of the suggestions, even though estimated savings are difficult to project

Uses informative title in the table, which is consistent with the way headings are handled in this report and is appropriate for a report to a receptive audience

Note how Moreno calls attention in the first paragraph to items in the following table, without repeating the information in the table.

In a long report, the closing section may be labeled "Summary" or "Conclusions and Recommendations." Since Moreno organized her report in a direct pattern, her closing is relatively brief. When using the indirect approach, you may use the close to present your recommendations and conclusions for the very first time, in which case this section could be relatively extensive.

FIGURE 11.13   continued

Uses a descriptive heading for the last section of the text (in informational reports, this section is often called "Summary"; in analytical reports, it is called "Conclusions" or "Conclusions and Recommendations")

Emphasizes the recommendations by presenting them in list format

Summarizes conclusions in the first two paragraphs—a good approach because Moreno organized her report around conclusions and recommendations, so readers have already been introduced to them

9

CONCLUSIONS AND RECOMMENDATIONS

Electrovision is currently spending $16 million per year on travel and entertainment. Although much of this spending is justified, the company's costs are high relative to competitors' costs, mainly because Electrovision has been generous with its travel benefits.

Electrovision's liberal approach to travel and entertainment was understandable during years of high profitability; however, the company is facing the prospect of declining profits for the next several years. Management is therefore motivated to cut costs in all areas of the business. Reducing T&E spending is particularly important because the bottom-line impact of these costs will increase as airline fares increase.

Electrovision should be able to reduce T&E costs by as much as 40 percent by taking four important steps:

1. *Institute tighter spending controls.* Management should hire a director of travel and entertainment who will assume overall responsibility for T&E activities. Within the next six months, this director should develop a written travel policy, institute a T&E budget and a cost-control system, and retain a professional, business-oriented travel agency that will optimize arrangements with travel providers.

2. *Reduce unnecessary travel and entertainment.* Electrovision should encourage employees to economize on T&E spending. Management can accomplish this by authorizing fewer trips and by urging employees to be more conservative in their spending.

3. *Obtain lowest rates from travel providers.* Electrovision should also focus on obtaining the best rates on airline tickets, hotel rooms, and rental cars. By channeling all arrangements through a professional travel agency, the company can optimize its choices and gain clout in negotiating preferred rates.

4. *Replace travel with technological alternatives.* With the number of computers already installed in our facilities, it seems likely that we could take advantage of desktop videoconferencing and other distance-meeting tools. Technological alternatives won't be quite as feasible with customer sites, since these systems require compatible equipment at both ends of a connection, but such systems are certainly a possibility for communication with Electrovision's own sites.

Because these measures may be unpopular with employees, management should make a concerted effort to explain the importance of reducing travel costs. The director of corporate communication should be given responsibility for developing a plan to communicate the need for employee cooperation.

Moreno doesn't introduce any new facts in this section. In a longer report she might have divided this section into subsections, labeled "Conclusions" and "Recommendations," to distinguish between the two.

Supplementary Parts

The supplementary parts provide additional detail and reference materials.

Supplementary parts follow the text of the report and provide information for readers who seek more detailed discussion. Supplements are more common in long reports than in short ones. They typically include appendixes, bibliography, and index.

- **Appendixes.** An appendix contains additional information for those readers who want it—information related to the report but not included in the text because it is

FIGURE 11.13 continued

Lists references alphabetically by the author's last name, and when the author is unknown, by the title of the reference (see Appendix B for additional details on preparing reference lists)

10

WORKS CITED

Barker, Julie. "How to Rein in Group Travel Costs." *Successful Meetings* Feb. 2004: 31.

"Businesses Use Savvy Managers to Keep Travel Costs Down." *Christian Science Monitor* 17 July 2004: 4.

Dahl, Jonathan. "2000: The Year Travel Costs Took Off." *Wall Street Journal* 29 Dec. 2004: B6.

Gilligan, Edward P. "Trimming Your T&E Is Easier Than You Think." *Managing Office Technology* Nov. 2004: 39–40.

Miller, Lisa. "Attention, Airline Ticket Shoppers." *Wall Street Journal* 7 July 2004: B6.

"Online Meeting Solutions." *Webex.com.* 2005. WebEx, 14 September 2005, <http://www.webex.com/solutions/online-meetings-solutions.html>.

Phillips, Edward H. "Airlines Post Record Traffic." *Aviation Week & Space Technology* 8 Jan. 2005: 331.

Rowe, Irene Vlitos. "Global Solution for Cutting Travel Costs." *European* 12 Oct. 2004: 30.

Smith, Carol. "Rising, Erratic Airfares Make Company Policy Vital." *Los Angeles Times* 2 Nov. 2004: D4.

Solheim, Shelley. "Web Conferencing Made Easy." *eWeek* 22 Aug. 2005: 26.

"Travel Costs Under Pressure." *Purchasing* 15 Feb. 2004: 30.

Moreno's list of references follows the style recommended in *The MLA Style Manual*. The box below shows how these sources would be cited following APA style.

10

REFERENCES

Barker, J. (2004, February). How to rein in group travel costs. *Successful Meetings*, 31.

Businesses use savvy managers to keep travel costs down. (2004, July 17). *Christian Science Monitor*, 4.

Dahl, J. (2004, December 29). 2000: The year travel costs took off. *Wall Street Journal*, B6.

Gilligan, E. (2004, November). Trimming your T&E is easier than you think. *Managing Office Technology*, 39–40.

Miller, L. (2004, July 7). Attention, airline ticket shoppers. *Wall Street Journal*, B6.

Phillips, E. (2005, January 8). Airlines post record traffic. *Aviation Week & Space Technology*, 331.

Rowe, I. (2004, October 12). Global solution for cutting travel costs. *European*, 30.

Smith, C. (2004, November 2). Rising, erratic airfares make company policy vital. *Los Angeles Times*, D4.

Solheim, S. (2005, August 22). Web conferencing made easy. *eWeek*, 26.

Travel costs under pressure. (2004, February 15). *Purchasing*, 30.

Webex.com. (2005). *Online Meeting Solutions.* Retrieved 14 September 2005, from http://www.webex.com/solutions/online-meetings-solutions.html.

too lengthy, is too bulky, or lacks direct relevance. Appendixes contain sample questionnaires and cover letters, sample forms, computer printouts, spreadsheets, and so on. Be sure to list appendixes in your table of contents and refer to them as appropriate in the text.

■ **Bibliography.** The bibliography lists the secondary sources you consulted. For more on citing sources, see Appendix B, "Documentation of Report Sources."

■ **Index.** An index is an alphabetical list of names, places, and subjects mentioned in the report, along with the pages on which they occur (see the index for this book for an example).

Producing a Formal Proposal

Formal proposals contain many of the same components as other formal reports, but the special nature of proposals does require some unique elements (see Figure 11.14).

Prefatory Parts

The cover, title fly, title page, table of contents, and list of illustrations are handled the same as in other formal reports. However, other prefatory parts are handled quite differently, such as the copy of the RFP, the synopsis or executive summary, and the letter of transmittal.

> If there's likely to be any confusion over which RFP you're responding to, include the RFP in your proposal. If the RFP is long, include just its introductory sections.

■ **Copy of the RFP.** Instead of having a letter of authorization, a solicited proposal should follow whatever instructions are in the request for proposals. In some cases, the issuer of the RFP will tell you to include the entire RFP in your proposal; others may want you to simply identify it by a name and tracking number.

■ **Synopsis or executive summary.** Although you may include a synopsis or an executive summary, these components are often less useful in a formal proposal than in a report. In an unsolicited proposal, your transmittal letter will already have caught the reader's interest. In a solicited proposal, the introduction would provide an adequate preview of the contents.

■ **Letter of transmittal.** If the proposal is solicited, the transmittal letter follows the pattern for good-news messages, highlighting those aspects of your proposal that may give you a competitive advantage. If the proposal is unsolicited, the transmittal letter should follow the advice you learned for persuasive messages (see Chapter 9). The letter must persuade the reader that you have something worthwhile to offer that justifies reading the entire proposal.

FIGURE 11.14   Parts of a Formal Proposal
Like formal reports, formal proposals can contain a wide variety of elements in addition to the main text.

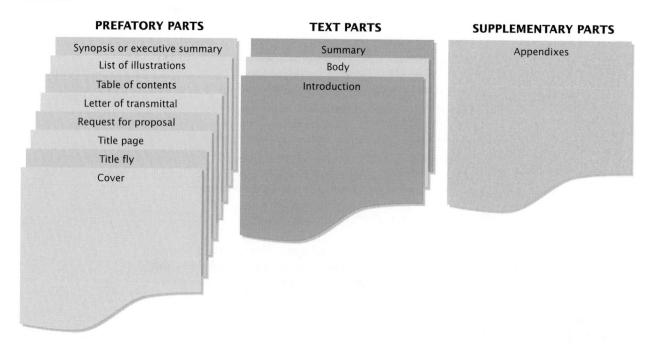

PREFATORY PARTS
- Synopsis or executive summary
- List of illustrations
- Table of contents
- Letter of transmittal
- Request for proposal
- Title page
- Title fly
- Cover

TEXT PARTS
- Summary
- Body
- Introduction

SUPPLEMENTARY PARTS
- Appendixes

FIGURE 11.15   Dixon O'Donnell's Informal Solicited Proposal
This solicited proposal efficiently communicates the scope of the project, the firm's qualifications, and a detailed cost breakdown.

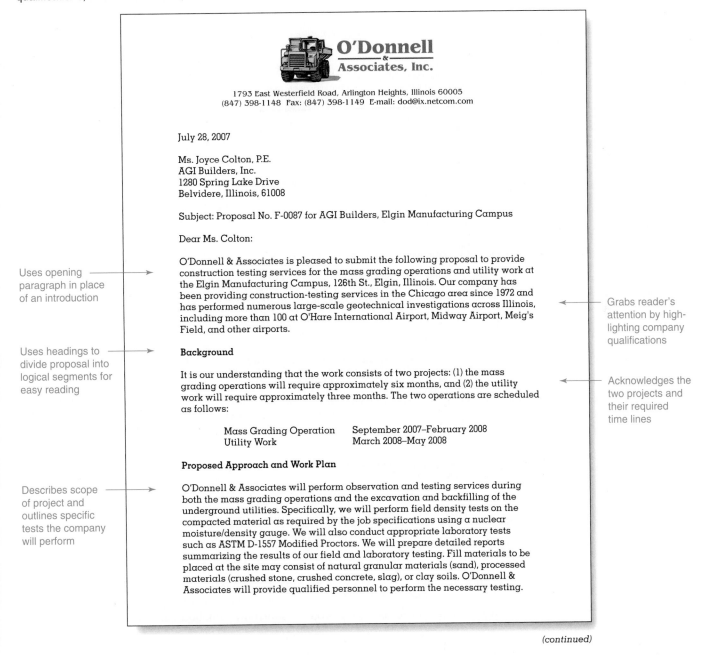

Uses opening paragraph in place of an introduction

Uses headings to divide proposal into logical segments for easy reading

Describes scope of project and outlines specific tests the company will perform

Grabs reader's attention by highlighting company qualifications

Acknowledges the two projects and their required time lines

(continued)

Text of the Proposal

Just as with reports, the text of a proposal is composed of an introduction, body, and close. The introduction presents and summarizes the problem you intend to solve and your solution. It highlights the benefits the reader will receive from the solution. The body explains the complete details of the solution: how the job will be done, how it will be broken into tasks, what method will be used to do it (including the required equipment, material, and personnel), when the work will begin and end, how much the entire job will cost (including a detailed breakdown), and why your company is qualified. The close emphasizes the benefits readers will realize from your solution, and it urges readers to act.

Figure 11.15 is an informal proposal submitted by Dixon O'Donnell, vice president of O'Donnell & Associates, a geotechnical engineering firm that conducts a variety of

The introduction of a proposal needs to summarize the problem or opportunity that your proposal intends to address.

FIGURE 11.15   continued

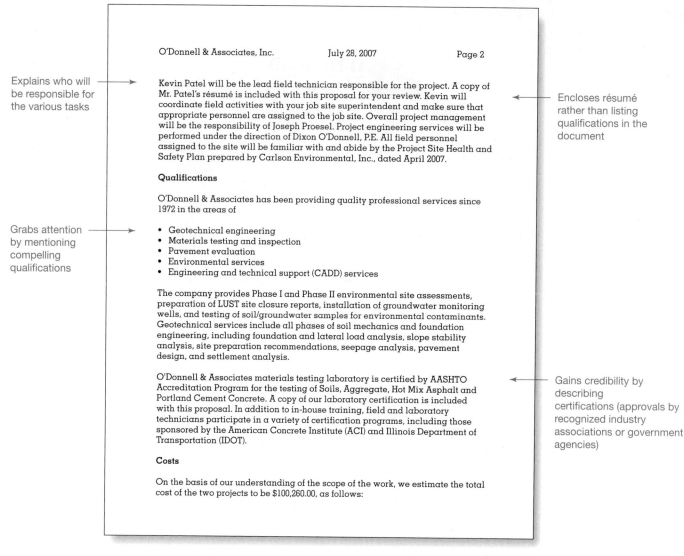

Explains who will be responsible for the various tasks

Grabs attention by mentioning compelling qualifications

Encloses résumé rather than listing qualifications in the document

Gains credibility by describing certifications (approvals by recognized industry associations or government agencies)

(continued)

environmental testing services. The company is bidding on the mass grading and utility work specified by AGI Builders. As you review this document, pay close attention to the specific items addressed in the proposal's introduction, body, and closing.

Proofreading Your Reports and Proposals

After assembling your report or proposal in its final form, review it thoroughly one last time, looking for inconsistencies, errors, and missing components. Proofing can catch minor flaws that might diminish your credibility—and major flaws that might damage your career.

Proofreading the textual part of your report is essentially the same as proofreading any business message—you check for typos, spelling errors, and mistakes in punctuation. However, reports often have elements that may not be included in other messages, so don't forget to proof your visuals thoroughly and make sure they are positioned correctly. If you need specific tips on proofreading documents, look back at Chapter 5.

Whenever possible, arrange for someone with "fresh eyes" to proofread the report, somebody who hasn't been involved with the text so far. At this point in the process, you are so familiar with the content that your mind will fill in missing words, fix misspelled

Whenever possible, have someone who hasn't seen the report before proofread it for you.

FIGURE 11.15 continued

O'Donnell & Associates, Inc.   July 28, 2007   Page 3

Cost Estimates

Cost Estimate: Mass Grading	Units	Rate ($)	Total Cost ($)
Field Inspection			
Labor	1,320 hours	$38.50	$ 50,820.00
Nuclear Moisture Density Meter	132 days	35.00	4,620.00
Vehicle Expense	132 days	45.00	5,940.00
Laboratory Testing			
Proctor Density Tests (ASTM D-1557)	4 tests	130.00	520.00
Engineering/Project Management			
Principal Engineer	16 hours	110.00	1,760.00
Project Manager	20 hours	80.00	1,600.00
Administrative Assistant	12 hours	50.00	600.00
Subtotal			**$ 65,860.00**

Cost Estimate: Utility Work	Units	Rate ($)	Total Cost ($)
Field Inspection			
Labor	660 hours	$38.50	$ 25,410.00
Nuclear Moisture Density Meter	66 days	5.00	2,310.00
Vehicle Expense	66 days	45.00	2,970.00
Laboratory Testing			
Proctor Density Tests (ASTM D-1557)	2 tests	130.00	260.00
Engineering/Project Management			
Principal Engineer	10 hours	110.00	1,100.00
Project Manager	20 hours	80.00	1,600.00
Administrative Assistant	15 hours	50.00	750.00
Subtotal			**$ 34,400.00**

Total Project Costs			**$100,260.00**

This estimate assumes full-time inspection services. However, our services may also be performed on an as-requested basis, and actual charges will reflect time associated with the project. We have attached our standard fee schedule for your review. Overtime rates are for hours in excess of 8.0 hours per day, before 7:00 a.m., after 5:00 p.m., and on holidays and weekends.

Itemizes costs by project and gives supporting detail

Provides alternative option in case full-time service costs exceed client's budget

(continued)

words, and subconsciously compensate for other flaws without you even being aware of it. Someone with fresh eyes might see mistakes that you've passed over a dozen times without noticing. An ideal approach is to have two people review it, one who is an expert in the subject matter and one who isn't. The first person can ensure its technical accuracy, and the second can ensure that a wide range of readers will understand it.[11]

Distributing Your Reports and Proposals

All of the distribution issues you explored in Chapter 5 apply to reports and proposals, but pay particular attention to the length and complexity of your documents. For physical distribution, consider spending the extra money for a professional courier or package delivery service, if that will help your document stand apart from the crowd. The online tracking offered by FedEx, UPS, and other services can verify that your document arrived

FIGURE 11.15   continued

Uses brief closing to emphasize qualifications and ask for client decision

O'Donnell & Associates, Inc.   July 28, 2007   Page 4

Authorization

With a staff of over 30 personnel, including registered professional engineers, resident engineers, geologists, construction inspectors, laboratory technicians, and drillers, we are convinced that O'Donnell & Associates is capable of providing the services required for a project of this magnitude.

If you would like our firm to provide the services as outlined in this proposal, please sign this letter and return it to us along with a certified check in the amount of $10,000 (our retainer) by August 15, 2007. Please call me if you have any questions regarding the terms of this proposal or our approach.

Provides deadline and makes response easy

Sincerely,

Dixon O'Donnell

Dixon O'Donnell
Vice President

Enclosures

Accepted for AGI BUILDERS, INC.

By_____   Date _____

Makes letter a binding contract, if signed

Many businesses use the Adobe Portable Document Format (PDF) to distribute reports electronically.

safely. On the other hand, if you've prepared the document for a single person or small group, delivering it in person can be a nice touch. Not only can you answer any immediate questions about it, but you can also promote the results in person—reminding the recipient of the benefits contained in your report or proposal.

For electronic distribution, unless your audience specifically requests a word processor file, provide documents in PDF format. Most people are reluctant to open word processor files these days, particularly from outsiders, given the vulnerability of such files to macro viruses and other contaminations. Moreover, PDF format lets you control how your document is displayed on your audience's computer, ensuring that your readers see your document as you intended. In addition, making documents available as downloadable PDF files is almost universally expected these days, if only for the sake of convenience.

If your company or client expects you to distribute your reports via a web-based *content management system*, *intranet* (a secure internal website), or *extranet* (a secure external website), be sure to upload the correct file(s) to the correct online location. Verify the on-screen display of your report after you've posted it, too; make sure graphics, charts, links, and other elements are in place and operational.

Reviewing Key Points

This chapter discusses the essential tasks in the second and third steps of the three-step process: writing and completing reports and proposals. Writing includes the familiar tasks of adapting to your audience and composing your content, with additional advice on helping readers find their way and using technology to craft reports and proposals. The chapter continues with an introduction to supporting your reports with visuals, from tables to various charts to animation and video. The chapter concludes with a look at the tasks involved in completing reports and proposals, including assembling the prefatory and supplementary parts that precede and follow the main text. Proofreading and distributing wrap up the discussion.

The next chapter discusses giving oral presentations. You will learn how to plan, write, and complete business speeches and presentations. You will learn about the various types of presentation visuals, and you will find out how to master the art of delivery, including practicing, overcoming anxiety, handling questions, and giving presentations online.

Test Your Knowledge

1. Why must the introduction of an unsolicited proposal include a statement of the problem or opportunity that the proposal addresses?

2. What navigational elements can you use to help readers follow the structure and flow of information in a long report?

3. Both bar charts and pie charts can show the relative size of related variables; when would you use a pie chart rather than a bar chart?

4. How does a flowchart differ from an organization chart?

5. What is the equivalent of a letter of authorization for a proposal?

Apply Your Knowledge

1. Should a report always explain the writer's method of gathering evidence or solving a problem? Why or why not?

2. When you read a graph, how can you be sure that the visual impression you are receiving is an accurate reflection of reality? Please explain.

3. What similarities do you see between visuals and nonverbal communication? Explain your answer.

4. You're writing a report to the director of human resources on implementing teams throughout your company. You want to emphasize that since the new approach was implemented six months ago, absenteeism and turnovers have been sharply reduced in all but two departments. How do you visually present your data in the most favorable light? Explain.

5. **Ethical Choices**   If a company receives a solicited formal proposal outlining the solution to a particular problem, is it ethical for the company to adopt the proposal's recommendations without hiring the firm that submitted the proposal? Why or why not?

Practice Your Knowledge

Activities

For active links to all websites discussed in this chapter, visit this text's website at www.prenhall.com/bovee. Locate your book and click on its Companion Website link. Then select Chapter 11, and click on "Featured Websites." Locate the name of the page or the URL related to the material in the text. Please note that links to sites that become inactive after publication of the book will be removed from the Featured Websites section.

1. **Teamwork**   You and a classmate are helping Linda Moreno prepare her report on Electrovision's travel and entertainment costs (see Figure 11.13). This time, however, the report is to be informational rather than analytical, so it will not include

recommendations. Review the existing report and determine what changes would be needed to make it an informational report. Be as specific as possible. For example, if your team decides the report needs a new title, what title would you use? Now draft a transmittal memo for Moreno to use in conveying this informational report to Dennis McWilliams, Electrovision's vice president of operations.

2. **Internet**   Government reports vary in purpose and structure. Read through the Department of Education's report "Helping Your Child Become a Reader," available online at www.ed.gov. What is the purpose of this document? Does the title communicate this purpose? What type of report is this, and what is the report's structure? Which prefatory and supplementary parts are included? Now analyze the visuals. What types are included in this report. Are they all necessary? Are the titles and legends sufficiently informative? How does this report take advantage of the online medium to enhance readability?

3. **Choosing the Right Visual**   You're preparing the annual report for FretCo Guitar Corporation. For each of the following types of information, select the right chart or visual to illustrate the text. Explain your choices.

   a. Data on annual sales for the past 20 years

   b. Comparison of FretCo sales, product by product (electric guitars, bass guitars, amplifiers, acoustic guitars), for this year and last year

   c. Explanation of how a FretCo acoustic guitar is manufactured

   d. Explanation of how the FretCo Guitar Corporation markets its guitars

   e. Data on sales of FretCo products in each of 12 countries

   f. Comparison of FretCo sales figures with sales figures for three competing guitar makers over the past 10 years

4. **Creating Maps**   You work for C & S Holdings, a company that operates coin-activated, self-service car washes. Research shows that the farther customers live from a car wash, the less likely they are to visit. You know that 50 percent of customers at each of your car washes live within a 4-mile radius of the location, 65 percent live within 6 miles, 80 percent live within 8 miles, and 90 percent live within 10 miles. C & S's owner wants to open two new car washes in your city and has asked you to prepare a report recommending locations. Using a map of your city (try www.mappoint.com or www.mapquest.com), choose two possible locations for car washes and create a visual depicting the customer base surrounding each location (make up whatever population data you need).

5. **Composing Reports: Navigational Clues**   Review a long business article in a journal or newspaper. Highlight examples of how the article uses heading, transitions, and previews and reviews to help the readers find their way.

6. **Ethical Choices**   Your boss has asked you to prepare a feasibility report to determine whether the company should advertise its custom-crafted cabinetry in the weekly neighborhood newspaper. Based on your primary research, you think it should. As you draft the introduction to your report, however, you discover that the survey administered to the neighborhood newspaper subscribers was flawed. Several of the questions were poorly written and misleading. You used the survey results, among other findings, to justify your recommendation. The report is due in three days. What actions might you want to take, if any, before you complete your report?

7. **Producing Reports: Letter of Transmittal**   You are president of the Friends of the Library, a nonprofit group that raises funds and provides volunteers to support your local library. Every February, you send a report of the previous year's activities and accomplishments to the County Arts Council, which provides an annual grant of $1,000 toward your group's summer reading festival. Now it's February 6, and you've completed your formal report. Here are the highlights:

   - Back-to-school book sale raised $2,000.

   - Holiday craft fair raised $1,100.

   - Promotion and prizes for summer reading festival cost $1,450.

   - Materials for children's program featuring local author cost $125.

   - New reference databases for library's career center cost $850.

   - Bookmarks promoting library's website cost $200.

   Write a letter of transmittal to Erica Maki, the council's director. Because she is expecting this report, you can use the direct approach. Be sure to express gratitude for the council's ongoing financial support.

8. **Executive Summaries**   Visit the website of the U.S. Citizenship and Immigration Services (a division of the U.S. Department of Homeland Security) at http://uscis.gov. Find a report entitled "Triennial Comprehensive Report on Immigration" and follow the link to the executive summary. Using the information in this chapter, analyze the executive summary and offer specific suggestions for revising it.

9. Composing Reports: Navigational Clues Review a long business article from a journal, newspaper, or website. Highlight examples of how the article uses headings, transitions, and previews and reviews to help the readers find their way.

Expand Your Knowledge

Exploring the Best of the Web

Brush Up on Your Computer Graphics Skills Need some help using graphics software? Get started at the About.com graphics software website, http://graphicssoft.about.com. Take the tutorials and learn how to manage fonts, images, and a variety of graphics-related tasks. View the illustrated demonstrations. Read the instructional articles. Learn how to use the most common file formats for graphics. Expand your knowledge of the basic principles of graphic design, and master some advanced color tips and theory. Don't leave without following the links to recommended books and magazines. Explore About.com's Graphics Software section and answer these questions.

Exercises

1. What are the most common file formats for online visuals?
2. What does color depth mean in computer visuals?
3. What is dithering, and how can it affect your visuals?

Exploring the Web on Your Own

Review these chapter-related websites to learn more about writing reports and proposals.

1. Plan your way to profit by learning how to write effective business plans. Refer to the Business Planning section on the Small Business Administration website, www.sba.gov (look under "Starting Your Business").

2. Improve the quality of your reports by following an effective proofreading strategy. Visit Purdue University's Online Writing Lab, owl.english.purdue.edu, and search for "Editing and Proofreading Strategies."

3. Deborah Kluge's proposal writing blog offers tips, techniques, and checklists to help you craft more successful proposals; learn more at www.proposalwriter.com/weblog.

Learn Interactively

Interactive Study Guide

Visit www.prenhall.com/bovee, then locate your book and click on its Companion Website link. Select Chapter 11 to take advantage of the interactive "Chapter Quiz" to test your knowledge of chapter concepts. Receive instant feedback on whether you need additional studying. Also, visit the "Study Hall," where you'll find an abundance of valuable resources that will help you succeed in this course.

Peak Performance Grammar and Mechanics

If your instructor has required the use of "Peak Performance Grammar and Mechanics," either in your online course, through the access-code protected portion of the Companion Website, or on CD, you can continue to improve your skill with periods, question marks, and other punctuation by using the "Peak Performance Grammar and Mechanics" module. Click "Punctuation," then "Punctuation II." Take the Pretest to determine whether you have any weak areas. Then review those areas in the Refresher Course. Take the Follow-Up Test to check your grasp of various punctuation elements. For an extra challenge or advanced practice, take the Advanced Test. Finally, for additional reinforcement in periods, question marks, and exclamation points, go to the "Improve Your Grammar, Mechanics, and Usage" section that follows the cases, and complete the "Level 1: Self-Assessment" exercises.

CASES

Apply the three-step writing process to the following cases, as assigned by your instructor.

Short Reports

1. Giving It the Online Try: Report Analyzing the Advantages and Disadvantages of Corporate Online Learning

As the newest member of the corporate training division of Paper Products, Inc., you have been asked to investigate and analyze the merits of creating online courses for the company's employees. The president of your company thinks so-called e-learning might be a good employee benefit as well as a terrific way for employees to learn new skills that they can use on the job. You've already done your research and here's a copy of your notes:

Online courses open up new horizons for working adults, who often find it difficult to juggle conventional classes with jobs and families.

Adults over 25 now represent nearly half of higher-ed students; most are employed and want more education to advance their careers.

Some experts believe that online learning will never be as good as face-to-face instruction.

Online learning requires no commute and is appealing for employees who travel regularly.

Enrollment in courses offered online by postsecondary institutions is expected to increase from 2 million students in 2001 to 5 million students in 2006.

E-learning is a cost-effective way to get better-educated employees.

More than one-third of the $50 billion spent on employee training every year is spent on e-learning.

At IBM, some 200,000 employees received education or training online last year, and 75 percent of the company's Basic Blue course for new managers is online. E-learning cut IBM's training bill by $350 million last year—mostly because online courses don't require travel.

There are no national statistics, but a recent report from the Chronicle of Higher Education found that institutions are seeing dropout rates that range from 20 to 50 percent for online learners. The research does not adequately explain why the dropout rates for e-learners are higher.

A recent study of corporate online learners reported that employees want the following things from their online courses: college credit or a certificate; active correspondence with an online facilitator who has frequent virtual office hours; access to 24-hour, seven-day-a-week technical support; and the ability to start a course anytime.

Corporate e-learners said that their top reason for dropping a course was lack of time. Many had trouble completing courses from their desktops because of frequent distractions caused by coworkers. Some said they could only access courses through the company's intranet, so they couldn't finish their assignments from home.

Besides lack of time, corporate e-learners cited the following as e-learning disadvantages: lack of management oversight; lack of motivation; problems with technology; lack of student support; individual learning preferences; poorly designed courses; substandard/inexperienced instructors.

A recent study by GE Capital found that finishing a corporate online course was dependent on whether managers gave reinforcement on attendance, how important employees were made to feel, and whether employee progress in the course was tracked.

Sun Microsystems found that interactivity can be a critical success factor for online courses. Company studies showed that only 25 percent of employees finish classes that are strictly self-paced. But 75 percent finish when given similar assignments and access to tutors through e-mail, phone, or online discussion groups.

Company managers must supervise e-learning just as they would any other important initiative.

For online learning to work, companies must develop a culture that takes online learning just as seriously as classroom training.

For many e-learners, studying at home is optimal. Whenever possible, companies should offer courses through the Internet or provide intranet access at home. Having employees studying on their own time will more than cover any added costs.

Corporate e-learning has flared into a $2.3 billion market, making it one of the fastest-growing segments of the education industry.

Rather than fly trainers to 7,000 dealerships, General Motors University now uses interactive satellite broadcasts to teach salespeople the best way to highlight features on the new Buick.

Fast and cheap, e-training can shave companies' training costs while it saves employees travel time.

Pharmaceutical companies such as Merck are conducting live, interactive classes over the web, allowing sales reps to learn about the latest product information at home rather than flying them to a conference center.

McDonald's trainers can log into Hamburger University to learn such skills as how to assemble a made-to-order burger or properly place the drink on a tray.

One obstacle to the spread of online corporate training is the mismatch between what employees really need—customized courses that are tailored to a firm's products and its unique corporate culture—and what employers can afford.

80 percent of companies prefer developing their own online training courses in-house. But creating even one customized e-course can take months, involve armies of experts, and cost anywhere from $25,000 to $50,000. Thus, most companies either stick with classroom training or buy generic courses on such topics as how to give performance appraisals, understanding basic business ethics, and so on. Employers can choose from a wide selection of non-customized electronic courses.

For online learning to be effective, content must be broken into short "chunks" with lots of pop quizzes, online discussion groups, and other interactive features that let students demonstrate what they've learned. For instance, Circuit City's tutorial on digital camcorders consists of three 20-minute segments. Each contains audio demonstrations of how to handle customer product queries, tests on terminology, and "try-its" that propel trainees back onto the floor to practice what they've learned.

Dell Computer expects 90 percent of its learning solutions to be totally or partially technology enabled.

The Home Depot has used e-training to cut a full day from the time required to train new cashiers.

Online training has freed up an average of 17 days every year for Black & Decker's sales representatives.

Your Task Write a short (three- to five-page) memo report to the director of human resources, Kerry Simmons, presenting the advantages and disadvantages of e-learning and making a recommendation as to whether Paper Products, Inc., should invest time and money in training its employees this way. Be sure to organize your information so that it is clear, concise, and logically presented. Simmons likes to read the "bottom line" first, so be direct: Present your recommendation up front and support your recommendation with your findings.[12]

2. Selling Overseas: Research Report on the Prospects for Marketing a Product in Another Country

Select a fairly inexpensive product that you currently own and a country that you're not very familiar with. The product could be a moderately priced watch, radio, or other device. Now imagine that you are with the international sales department of the company that manufactures and sells the item and that you are proposing to make it available in the country you have selected.

The first step is to learn as much as possible about the country where you plan to market the product. Check almanacs, encyclopedias, the Internet, and library databases for the most recent information, paying particular attention to descriptions of the social life of the inhabitants, their economic conditions, and cultural traditions that would encourage or discourage use of the product.

Your Task Write a short report that describes the product you plan to market abroad, briefly describes the country you have selected, indicates the types of people in this country who would find the product attractive, explains how the product would be transported into the country (or possibly manufactured there if materials and labor are available), recommends a location for a regional sales center, and suggests how the product should be sold. Your report is to be submitted to the chief operating officer of the company, whose name you can either make up or find in a corporate directory. The report should include your conclusions (how the product will do in this new environment) and your recommendations for marketing (steps the company should take immediately and those it should develop later).

3. A Ready-Made Business: Finding the Right Franchise Opportunity

After 15 years in the corporate world, you're ready to strike out on your own. Rather than building a business from the ground up, however, you think that buying a franchise is a better idea. Unfortunately, some of the most lucrative franchise opportunities, such as the major fast-food chains, require significant start-up costs—some more than a half million dollars. Fortunately, you've met several potential investors who seem willing to help you get started in exchange for a share of ownership. Between your own savings and these investors, you estimate that you can raise from $350,000 to $600,000, depending on how much ownership share you want to concede to the investors.

You've worked in several functional areas already, including sales and manufacturing, so you have a fairly well-rounded business résumé. You're open to just about any type of business, too, as long as it provides the opportunity to grow; you don't want to be so tied down to the first operation that you can't turn it over to a hired manager and expand into another market.

Your Task To convene a formal meeting with the investor group, you need to first draft a report outlining the types of franchise opportunities you'd like to pursue. Write a brief report identifying five franchises that you would like to explore further (choose five based on your own personal interests and the criteria identified above). For each possibility, identify the nature of the business, the financial requirements, the level of support the company provides, and a brief statement of why you could run such a business successfully (make up any details you need). Be sure to carefully review the information you find about each franchise company to make sure you can qualify for it. For instance, McDonald's doesn't allow investment partnerships to buy franchises, so you won't be able to start up a McDonald's outlet until you have enough money to do it on your own.

For a quick introduction to franchising, see How Stuff Works (www.howstuffworks.com/franchising). You can learn more about the business of franchising at Franchising.com (www.franchising.com) and search for specific franchise opportunities at FranCorp Connect (www.francorpconnect.com). In addition, many companies that sell franchises, such as Subway, offer additional information on their websites.

Long Reports

4. Moving the Workforce: Understanding Commute Patterns

Your company is the largest private employer in your metropolitan area, and the 43,500 employees in your workforce have a tremendous impact on local traffic. A group of city and county transportation officials recently approached your CEO with a request to explore ways to reduce this impact. The CEO has assigned you the task of analyzing the workforce's transportation habits and attitudes as a first step toward identifying potential solutions. He's willing to consider anything from subsidized bus passes to company-owned shuttle buses to telecommuting, but the decision requires a thorough understanding of employee transportation needs. Tables 11.3 through 11.7 summarize data you collected in an employee survey.

Your Task Present the results of your survey in an informational report using the data provided in Tables 11.3 through 11.7.

5. Face-off: Informational Report Comparing and Contrasting Two Companies in the Same Industry

Your boss, Dana Hansell, has been searching for some solid companies to personally invest in for the long term. After reviewing security analysts' reports and financial statements for several candidates, Hansell has narrowed the list to these leading industry competitors:

- Boeing; Airbus (aerospace and airline industry)
- HP; Dell (computers and software industry)
- Merrill Lynch; Schwab (finance, banking, and insurance industry)
- Barnes & Noble; Amazon.com (online retailing)
- UPS; FedEx (trucking and freight industry)

According to Hansell, all of these candidates have about the same financial outlook for the future, so she is not interested in obtaining more financial performance detail. Instead,

Table 11.3	Employee Carpool Habits	
Frequency of Use: Carpooling	**Portion of Workforce**	
Every day, every week	10,138 (23%)	
Certain days, every week	4,361 (10%)	
Randomly	983 (2%)	
Never	28,018 (64%)	

Table 11.4	Use of Public Transportation	
Frequency of Use: Public Transportation	**Portion of Workforce**	
Everyday, every week	23,556 (54%)	
Certain days, every week	2,029 (5%)	
Randomly	5,862 (13%)	
Never	12,053 (28%)	

Table 11.5 — Effect of Potential Improvements to Public Transportation

Which of the Following Would Encourage You to Use Public Transportation More Frequently (check all that apply)*	Portion of Respondents
Increased perceptions of safety	4,932 (28%)
Improved cleanliness	852 (5%)
Reduced commute times	7,285 (41%)
Greater convenience: fewer transfers	3,278 (18%)
Greater convenience: more stops	1,155 (6%)
Lower (or subsidized) fares	5,634 (31%)
Nothing could encourage me to take public transportation	8,294 (46%)

*Note: This question was asked of those respondents who use public transportation randomly or never, a subgroup that represents 17,915 employees or 41 percent of the workforce.

Table 11.6 — Distance Traveled to/from Work

Distance You Travel to Work (one way)	Portion of Workforce
Less than 1 mile	531 (1%)
1–3 miles	6,874 (16%)
4–10 miles	22,951 (53%)
11–20 miles	10,605 (24%)
More than 20 miles	2,539 (6%)

Table 11.7 — Is Telecommuting an Option?

Does the Nature of Your Work Make Telecommuting a Realistic Option?	Portion of Workforce
Yes, every day	3,460 (8%)
Yes, several days a week	8,521 (20%)
Yes, random days	12,918 (30%)
No	18,601 (43%)

your boss is looking for more qualitative information, such as

- Fundamental philosophical differences in management styles, launching and handling products and services, marketing products and services, and approach to e-commerce that sets one rival company apart from the other
- Future challenges that each competitor faces
- Important decisions made by the two competitors and how those decisions affected their company
- Fundamental differences in each company's vision of its industry's future (for instance, do they both agree on what consumers want, what products to deliver, and so on?)
- Specific competitive advantages held by each rival

- Past challenges each competitor has faced and how each met those challenges
- Strategic moves made by one rival that might affect the other
- Company success stories
- Brief company background information (Hansell already has some from the brokers' reports)
- Brief comparative statistics such as annual sales, market share, number of employees, number of stores, types of equipment, number of customers, sources of revenue, and so on

Hansell has heard that you are the department's most proficient researcher and an effective writer. You have been assigned the task of preparing a formal, long informational report for her. You need not make a recommendation or come to any conclusions; Hansell will do that based on the informational content of your report.

Your Task Select two industry competitors from the above list (or another list provided by your instructor), and write a long, formal, informational report comparing and contrasting how the two companies are addressing the topics outlined by Hansell. Of course, not every topic will apply to each company, and some will be more important than others—depending on the companies you select. Hansell will invest in only one of the two companies in your report. (*Note*: Because these topics require considerable research, your instructor may choose to make this a team project.)

6. Secondary Sources: Report Based on Library and Online Research

As a college student and active consumer, you may have considered one or more of the following questions at some point in the past few years:

a. What criteria distinguish the top-rated MBA programs in the country? How well do these criteria correspond to the needs and expectations of business? Are the criteria fair for students, employers, and business schools?

b. Which of three companies you might like to work for has the strongest corporate ethics policies?

c. What will the music industry look like in the future? What's next after online stores such as Apple iTunes and digital players such as the iPod?

d. Which industries and job categories are forecast to experience the greatest growth—and therefore the greatest demand for workers—in the next 10 years?

e. What has been the impact of Starbucks' aggressive growth on small, independent coffee shops? On mid-sized chains or franchises? In the United States or in another country?

f. How large is the "industry" of major college sports? How much do the major football or basketball programs contribute—directly or indirectly—to other parts of a typical university?

g. How much have minor league sports—baseball, hockey, arena football—grown in small- and medium-market cities? What is the local economic impact when these municipalities build stadiums and arenas?

Your Task Answer one of the preceding questions using secondary research sources for information. Be sure to document your sources in the correct form. Give conclusions and offer recommendations where appropriate.

Proposals

7. Polishing the Presenters: Offering Your Services as a Presentation Trainer

Presentations can make—or break—both careers and businesses. A good presentation can bring in millions of dollars in new sales or fresh investment capital. A bad presentation might cause any number of troubles, from turning away potential customers to upsetting fellow employees to derailing key projects. To help business professionals plan, create, and deliver more effective presentations, you offer a three-day workshop that covers the essentials of good presentations:

- Understanding your audience's needs and expectations
- Formulating your presentation objectives
- Choosing an organizational approach
- Writing openings that catch your audience's attention
- Creating effective graphics and slides
- Practicing and delivering your presentation
- Leaving a positive impression on your audience
- Avoiding common mistakes with Microsoft PowerPoint
- Making presentations online using webcasting tools
- Handling questions and arguments from the audience
- Overcoming the top 10 worries of public speaking (including *How can I overcome stage fright?* and *I'm not the performing type; can I still give an effective presentation?*)

Workshop benefits: Students will learn how to prepare better presentations in less time and deliver them more effectively.

Who should attend: Top executives, project managers, employment recruiters, sales professionals, and anyone else who gives important presentations to internal or external audiences.

Your qualifications: 18 years of business experience, including 14 years in sales and 12 years in public speaking. Experience speaking to audiences as large as 5,000 people. More than a dozen speech-related articles published in professional journals. Have conducted successful workshops for nearly 100 companies.

Workshop details: Three-day workshop (9 A.M. to 3:30 P.M.) that combines lectures, practice presentations, and both individual and group feedback. Minimum number of students: 6. Maximum number of students per workshop: 12.

Pricing: The cost is $3,500, plus $100 per student; 10 percent discount for additional workshops.

Other information: Each attendee will have the opportunity to give three practice presentations that will last from 3 to 5 minutes. Everyone is encouraged to bring PowerPoint files containing slides from actual business presentations. Each attendee will also receive a workbook and a digital video recording of his or her final class presentation on DVD. You'll also be available for phone or e-mail coaching for six months after the workshop.

Your Task Identify a company in your local area that might be a good candidate for your services. Learn more about the company by visiting its website so you can personalize your proposal. Using the information listed above, prepare a sales proposal that explains the benefits of your training and what students can expect during the workshop.

8. Healthy Alternatives: Proposal to Sell Snacks and Beverages at Local High Schools

For years, a controversy has been brewing over the amount of junk food and soft drinks being sold through vending machines in local schools. Schools benefit from revenue-sharing arrangements, but many parents and health experts are concerned about the negative effects of these snacks and beverages. You and your brother have almost a decade of experience running espresso and juice stands in malls and on street corners, and you'd love to find some way to expand your business into schools. After a quick brainstorming session, the two of you craft a plan that makes good business sense while meeting the financial concerns of school administrators and the nutritional concerns of parents and dieticians. Here are the notes from your brainstorming session:

- Set up portable juice bars on school campuses, offering healthy fruit and vegetable drinks along with simple, healthy snacks
- Offer schools 30 percent of profits in exchange for free space and long-term contracts
- Provide job-training opportunities for students (during athletic events, etc.)
- Provide detailed dietary analysis of all products sold
- Establish a nutritional advisory board composed of parents, students, and at least one certified health professional
- Assure schools and parents that all products are safe (e.g., no stimulant drinks, no dietary supplements, and so on)
- Support local farmers and specialty food preparers by buying locally and giving these vendors the opportunity to test market new products at your stands

Your Task Based on the ideas listed, draft a formal proposal to the local school board, outlining your plan to offer healthier alternatives to soft drinks and prepackaged snack foods. Invent any details you need to complete your proposal.

Improve Your Grammar, Mechanics, and Usage

Level 1: Self-Assessment—Quotation Marks, Parentheses, Ellipses, Underscores, and Italics

Review Sections 2.10, 2.11, 2.12, and 3.2 in the "Handbook of Grammar, Mechanics, and Usage," and then look at the following 15 items.

In items 1–15, insert quotations marks, parentheses, ellipses, and underscores (for italics) wherever necessary:

1. Be sure to read How to Sell by Listening in this month's issue of Fortune.

2. Her response see the attached memo is disturbing.

3. Contact is an overused word.

4. We will operate with a skeleton staff during the holiday break December 21 through January

5. The SBP's next conference, the bulletin noted, will be held in Minneapolis.

6. Sara O'Rourke a reporter from The Wall Street Journal will be here on Thursday.

7. I don't care why you didn't fill my order; I want to know when you'll fill it.

8. The term up in the air means undecided.

9. Her assistant the one who just had the baby won't be back for four weeks.

10. Ask not what your country can do for you is the beginning of a famous quotation from John F. Kennedy.

11. Whom do you think Time magazine will select as its Man of the year?

12. Do you remember who said And away we go?

13. Refinements in robotics may prove profitable. More detail about this technology appears in Appendix A.

14. The resignation letter begins Since I'll never regain your respect and goes on to explain why that's true.

15. You must help her distinguish between i.e. which means that is and e.g. which means for example.

Level 2: Workplace Applications

The following items contain numerous errors in grammar, capitalization, punctuation, abbreviation, number style, word division, and vocabulary. Rewrite each sentence in the space provided, correcting all errors. Write *C* in the space after any sentence that is already correct.

1. For the lst time, thank's to largely deals with the big chains like Stop & Shop, Sheila's Snak Treetz are showing a profit.

2. The premise for broadband, sometimes called simply 'high speed Internet', is that consumers need a more fast pipeline for getting digital information in our homes.

3. After moving into they're own factory, the Anderson's found theirselves in the market for an oven with airflow controls.

4. Cash-strapped entrepreneurs have learned penny-pinching, cost-cutting, credit-stretching techniques.

5. Designs in the Rough send out some 7 million catalogs a year yet until recently the company did'nt need a warehouse and they hadn't hardly any carrying costs.

6. Blockbuster estimates that 70 percent of the US population live within a 10 minute drive of a Blockbuster store.

7. Nestle Waters North America are the exclusive importer of globally-recognized brands such as: Perrier and Vittel from France and, S. Pelligrino from Italy,

8. The U.S. hispanic community; the largest Minority Group in the country; commands a impressive total purchasing power estimated at more than $500 billion dollars.

9. We conducted a six-month pilot in Chicago, to insure the affectiveness of the program.

10. A series of 7-Eleven television spots help make the term brain freeze part of every day American language.

11. The ad agencies accounts include the following consumer-brands; Wal-Mart, Southwest airlines, Kinko's, Land Rover, and Krispy Kreme.

12. PETsMART allows pets and their humans to together stroll the aisles of its stores; the number one Specialty Retailer of pet supplies.

13. Signature Fruit Co. has confirmed its closing it's Gridley, CA peach plant this Fall.

14. To unite the company's 91 franchisees around a common corporate identity WingsToGo have setup a corporate intranet.

15. It would be well for you to contract with an Internet service provider—a ISP - to both run and to maintain your website.

Level 3: Document Critique

The following document may contain errors in grammar, capitalization, punctuation, abbreviation, number style, vocabulary, and spelling. You may also find problems with organization, format, and word use. Correct all errors using standard proofreading marks (see Appendix C).

Memorandum

From: Kris Beiersdorf

Date: 18 April 2007

RE PROJECT: Contract no. 79371 DuPage county

To: Ken Estes, Northern Illinois concrete

Memco Construction is pleased to submit a road construction proposal for the above project. Our company has been providing quality materials and subcontracting services for highway reconstruction projects for over twenty-three years. Our most recent jobs in Illinois have included Illinois State Route 60 resurfacing, and reconstructing Illinois tollway 294.

Should you have any questions about this proposal please contact me at the company 847-672-0344, direct extension #30) or by e-mail at kbeirsdorf@memcocon.com.

Based on the scope of the work outlined: the total cost of this job is projected by us to run ninety-nine thousand, two hundred eighty-three dollars. Because material quantities can vary once a project gets underway a separate page will be attached by us to this memorandum detailing our per-unit fees. Final charges will be based on the exact quantity of materials used for the job, and anything that accedes this estimate will be added of course.

Our proposal assumes that the following items will be furnished by other contractors (at no cost to Memco). All forms, earthwork and clearing; All prep work; Water at project site; Traffic control setup, devices, and maintenance—Location for staging, stockpiling, and storing material and equipment at job sight.

If we win this bid, we are already to begin when the apropriate contracts have been signed by us and by you.

12

Planning, Writing, and Completing Oral Presentations

From the Real World

"Our job is to ensure that every conversation is a win."

—Dan Talbott

Senior client relationship director, HP

www.hp.com

Learning Objectives

After studying this chapter, you will be able to

1 Explain the importance of oral presentations to your career success

2 Explain how to adapt the three-step writing process to oral presentations

3 Discuss the three functions of an effective introduction

4 Identify ways to get and keep your audience's attention during your presentation

5 Explain how visuals enhance oral presentations and list several popular types of visuals

6 Explain the importance of design consistency in electronic slides and other visuals

7 Highlight seven major issues to consider when you're preparing to give a presentation online

8 Identify six ways that effective speakers use to handle questions responsively

Presentations make everyone nervous, but imagine how nervous you might be if you were making a presentation with millions, even billions, of dollars on the line. When Hewlett-Packard (HP) was in the running for a huge computer services contract from Procter & Gamble (P&G), Dan Talbott lead a team of 80 colleagues through a series of pressure-packed presentations to P&G. At the outset, HP was considered a distant third behind Electronic Data Systems and IBM, and its initial presentation was shaky. Talbott and his team regrouped, starting with a thorough critique of every one of the more than 200 PowerPoint slides in their presentation. They made sure every slide had a clear message that was focused on audience needs.

That rigorous review produced a string of successful presentations that ultimately helped HP win a 10-year contract worth $3 billion. You may never be on stage with that much at stake, but you can make every one of your presentations successful through the same careful attention to quality.[1]

Building Your Career with Oral Presentations

Oral presentations, delivered in person or online, offer important opportunities to put all your communication skills on display—research, planning, writing, visual design, and interpersonal and nonverbal communication. Presentations also let you demonstrate your ability to think on your feet, grasp complex issues, and handle challenging situations—all attributes that executives look for when searching for talented employees to promote.

If the thought of giving a speech or presentation makes you nervous, try to keep three points in mind. First, everybody—even professional speakers and entertainers—gets nervous when speaking in front of groups. Second, being nervous is actually a good thing; it means you care about the topic, your audience, and your career success. Third, with practice, you can convert those nervous feelings into positive energy that helps you give more compelling presentations.

Although you don't often write out presentations word for word, nearly every task in the three-step writing process applies to oral presentations, with a few important modifications (see Figure 12.1).

While you don't usually write your oral presentations word for word, the three-step writing process is easily adaptable to oral presentations.

Step 1: Planning Your Presentation

Planning oral presentations is much like planning any other business message: You (1) analyze the situation, (2) gather information, (3) select the right medium, and (4) organize the information. Gathering information for oral presentations is essentially the same as for written communication projects (see Chapter 10). Be sure to provide full credit for any sources you use, too. Work these credits into your talk when appropriate and add citations to your presentation slides, handouts, and other materials. The other three planning tasks have some special applications when it comes to oral presentations; they are covered in the following sections.

Analyzing the Situation

As with written communications, analyzing the situation involves defining your purpose and developing an audience profile. The purpose of most of your presentations will be to inform or to persuade, although you may occasionally need to make a

FIGURE 12.1   The Three-Step Process for Developing Oral Presentations
The three-step process is easy to apply to speeches, in-person presentations, and even online presentations.

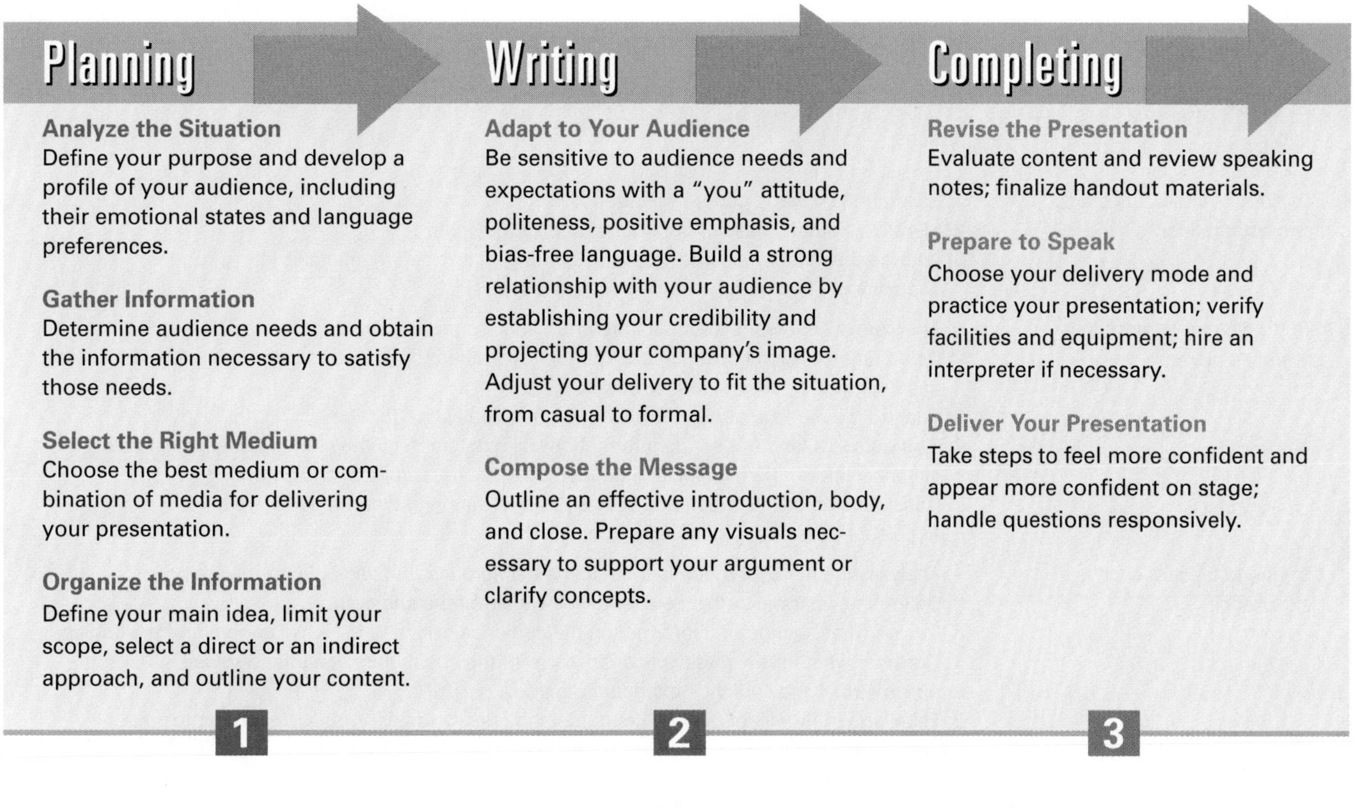

Planning

Analyze the Situation
Define your purpose and develop a profile of your audience, including their emotional states and language preferences.

Gather Information
Determine audience needs and obtain the information necessary to satisfy those needs.

Select the Right Medium
Choose the best medium or combination of media for delivering your presentation.

Organize the Information
Define your main idea, limit your scope, select a direct or an indirect approach, and outline your content.

1

Writing

Adapt to Your Audience
Be sensitive to audience needs and expectations with a "you" attitude, politeness, positive emphasis, and bias-free language. Build a strong relationship with your audience by establishing your credibility and projecting your company's image. Adjust your delivery to fit the situation, from casual to formal.

Compose the Message
Outline an effective introduction, body, and close. Prepare any visuals necessary to support your argument or clarify concepts.

2

Completing

Revise the Presentation
Evaluate content and review speaking notes; finalize handout materials.

Prepare to Speak
Choose your delivery mode and practice your presentation; verify facilities and equipment; hire an interpreter if necessary.

Deliver Your Presentation
Take steps to feel more confident and appear more confident on stage; handle questions responsively.

3

collaborative presentation, such as when you're leading a problem-solving or brainstorming session.

When you develop your audience profile, start with the advice in Chapter 3 and then consider two other important issues. First, try to anticipate what sort of emotional state your audience members are likely to be in. Will they accept your message automatically, or will they fight you every step of the way—even if it's just one or two audience members who feel the need to "perform" in front of their colleagues by putting on a public display of resistance? Second, determine whether your audience is comfortable listening to the language you speak. If not, you might need to provide additional written support materials or modify your presentation accordingly.

As you analyze the situation, also consider the circumstances. Is the audience in the room or online? How many people will be present? Can you control the environment to minimize distractions? What equipment will you need? All these variables can influence not only the style of your presentation but even the content itself.

Table 12.1 offers a summary of the key steps in analyzing an audience for oral presentations. For even more insight into audience evaluation (including emotional and cultural issues), consult a good public speaking textbook.

> Knowing your audience's state of mind will help you adjust both your message and your delivery.

> Try to learn as much as you can about the setting and circumstances of your presentation, from the size of the audience to potential interruptions.

Selecting the Right Medium

> Expect to give many presentations via electronic media in your career.

The task of selecting the right medium might seem obvious—after all, you are speaking, so it's an oral medium. However, technology offers an array of choices these days, ranging from live, in-person presentations to online **webcasts** that people either view live or download later from your website.

Organizing Your Presentation

Organizing a presentation involves the same tasks as organizing a written message: Define your main idea, limit your scope, select a direct or an indirect approach, and outline your content. Keep in mind that audiences for oral presentations are more or less trapped in your time frame and sequence. When reading written reports, audiences can skip back and forth, backing up if they miss a point or become confused and jumping ahead if they

Table 12.1	Analyzing Audiences for Oral Presentations
Task	**Actions**
To determine audience size and composition	1. Estimate how many people will attend. 2. Identify what they have in common and how they differ. 3. Analyze the mix of men and women, age ranges, socioeconomic and ethnic groups, occupations, and geographic regions represented.
To predict the audience's probable reaction	1. Analyze why audience members are attending the presentation. 2. Determine the audience's general attitude toward the topic: interested, moderately interested, unconcerned, open-minded, or hostile. 3. Analyze the mood that people will be in when you speak to them. 4. Find out what kind of backup information will most impress the audience: technical data, historical information, financial data, demonstrations, samples, and so on. 5. Consider whether the audience has any biases that might work against you. 6. Anticipate possible objections or questions.
To gauge the audience's experience	1. Analyze whether everybody has the same background and level of understanding. 2. Determine what the audience already knows about the subject. 3. Decide what background information the audience will need to better understand the subject. 4. Consider whether the audience is familiar with the vocabulary you intend to use. 5. Analyze what the audience expects from you. 6. Think about the mix of general concepts and specific details you will need to present.

aren't interested in a particular part. For some presentations, you should plan to be flexible and respond to audience feedback, such as skipping over sections the audience doesn't need to hear or going into more detail in other sections.

Define Your Main Idea

If you've ever heard a speaker struggle to get his or her main point across ("What I really mean to say is . . ."), you know how frustrating such an experience can be for an audience. To avoid that struggle, figure out the one message you want audience members to walk away with. Then compose a one-sentence summary that links your subject and purpose to your audience's frame of reference. Here are some examples:

If you can't express your main idea in a single sentence, you probably haven't defined it clearly enough.

- Convince management that reorganizing the technical support department will improve customer service and reduce employee turnover.
- Convince the board of directors that we should build a new plant in Texas to eliminate manufacturing bottlenecks and improve production quality.
- Address employee concerns regarding a new health-care plan by showing how the plan will reduce costs and improve the quality of their care.

Each of these statements puts a particular slant on the subject, one that directly relates to the audience's interests. By focusing on your audience's needs and using the "you" attitude, you help keep their attention and convince them that your points are relevant.

Limit Your Scope

For many business presentations, you will be expected to stay within a fixed time frame, so matching the scope of your material to these length expectations is essential. If you overestimate the amount of material you can cover, you're left with only unpleasant alternatives: rushing, skipping some information, or trying to steal a few minutes from the next presenter. Conversely, if you don't have enough material prepared to fill your time slot, you might be left standing in front of the audience trying to ad-lib information you haven't prepared.

Limiting your scope is important for two reasons: to ensure that your presentation fits the allotted time and to make sure your content meets audience needs and expectations.

Even when you don't have a time limit, though, audiences always appreciate shorter presentations. Studies show that audience attention levels and retention rates drop sharply after 20 minutes, and venture capitalists (investors who fund many new companies) expect entrepreneurs to get to the point within 15 minutes.[2] If you have a lot of supporting details that are important, explain the major concepts in your presentation and refer your audience to printed documents or websites for the additional information.

The only sure way to know how much material you can cover in a given time is to practice your presentation after you complete it. However, during the planning stage, you can use two techniques to estimate time requirements. First, if you will be using overhead transparencies or electronic slides, figure on 3 or even 4 minutes per slide.[3] For instance, if you have 20 minutes, plan on roughly six or seven slides. If you're whipping through slides faster than that, your slides are probably too simple or you're not engaging the audience with enough discussion. Second, most people speak between 125 and 150 words per minute, so you can practice a small portion of your presentation while recording it to tape or your computer, then go back and count how many words you used. From that test sample, you can estimate how much material you can cover in a given time frame.

The only sure way to measure the length of your presentation is to complete a practice run.

Of course, always be sure to factor in time for introductions, coffee breaks, demonstrations, question-and-answer sessions, and anything else that takes away from your speaking time.

Choose Your Approach

With a well-defined main idea to guide you and a clear idea about the scope of your presentation, you can begin to arrange your message. If you have 10 minutes or less to deliver your message, organize your presentation much as you would a letter or a brief memo: Use the direct approach if the subject involves routine information or good news, and use

Organize short presentations the same way you would a letter or brief memo.

the indirect approach if the subject involves bad news or persuasion. Plan your introduction to arouse interest and to give a preview of what's to come. For the body of the presentation, be prepared to explain the who, what, when, where, why, and how of your subject. In the final section, review the points you've made, and close with a statement that will help your audience remember the subject of your speech (Figure 12.2).

Longer presentations are organized like reports. If the purpose is to motivate or inform, you'll typically use a direct approach and a structure imposed naturally by the subject: importance, sequence, chronology, spatial orientation, geography, or category (as discussed in Chapter 10). If your purpose is to analyze, persuade, or collaborate, organize your material around conclusions and recommendations or around a logical argument. Use a direct approach if the audience is receptive and indirect if you expect resistance.

Prepare Your Outline

In addition to planning your speech, a presentation outline helps you plan your speaking notes.

A presentation outline performs the same all-important function as an outline for a written report: helping you organize the message in a way that maximizes its impact on your audience. Prepare your outline in several stages:[4]

■ State your purpose and main idea, then use these to guide the rest of your planning.
■ Organize your major points and subpoints in logical order, expressing each major point as a single, complete sentence.
■ Identify major points in the body first, then outline the introduction and close.
■ Identify transitions between major points or sections, then write these transitions in full sentence form.
■ Prepare your bibliography or source notes; highlight those sources you want to identify by name during your talk.

FIGURE 12.2   Effective Outline for a 10-Minute Progress Report
In this outline of a short presentation that updates management on the status of a key project, the presenter has some bad news to deliver. She therefore chose an indirect approach so she could lay out the reasons for the delay before sharing the news of the schedule slip.

Progress Report: August 2007

Purpose: To update the Executive Committee on our product development schedule.

I.   Review goals and progress
   A. Mechanical design:
      1. Goal: 100%
      2. Actual: 80%
      3. Reason for delay: Unanticipated problems with case durability
   B. Software development:
      1. Goal: 50%
      2. Actual: 60%
   C. Material sourcing:
      1. Goal: 100%
      2. Actual: 45% (and materials identified are at 140% of anticipated costs)
      3. Reason for delay: Purchasing is understaffed and hasn't been able to research sources adequately
II. Discuss schedule options
   A. Option 1: Reschedule product launch date
   B. Option 2: Launch on schedule with more expensive materials
III. Suggest goals for next month
IV. Q&A

FIGURE 12.3   Effective Outline for a 30-Minute Presentation
This outline clearly identifies the purpose and the distinct points to be made in the introduction, body, and close. Notice also how the speaker wrote her major transitions in full-sentence form to be sure she can clearly phrase these critical passages when it's time to speak.

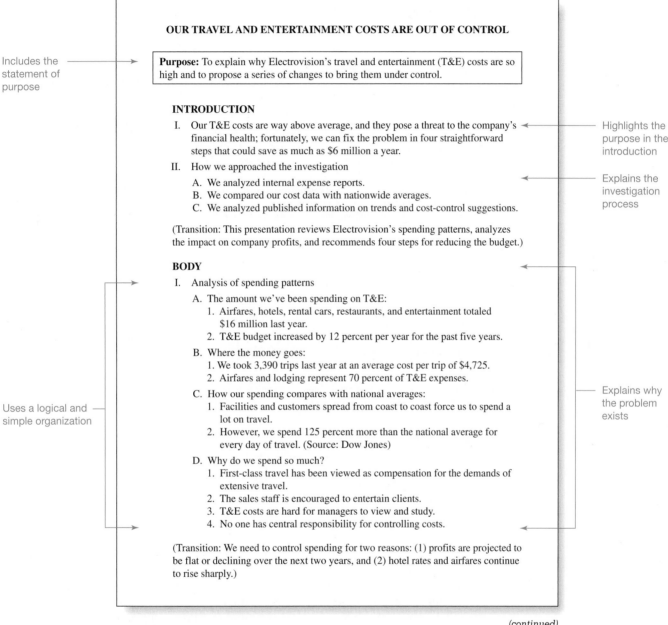

Includes the statement of purpose

Uses a logical and simple organization

Highlights the purpose in the introduction

Explains the investigation process

Explains why the problem exists

OUR TRAVEL AND ENTERTAINMENT COSTS ARE OUT OF CONTROL

Purpose: To explain why Electrovision's travel and entertainment (T&E) costs are so high and to propose a series of changes to bring them under control.

INTRODUCTION

I.   Our T&E costs are way above average, and they pose a threat to the company's financial health; fortunately, we can fix the problem in four straightforward steps that could save as much as $6 million a year.

II. How we approached the investigation
    A. We analyzed internal expense reports.
    B. We compared our cost data with nationwide averages.
    C. We analyzed published information on trends and cost-control suggestions.

(Transition: This presentation reviews Electrovision's spending patterns, analyzes the impact on company profits, and recommends four steps for reducing the budget.)

BODY

I.   Analysis of spending patterns
    A. The amount we've been spending on T&E:
        1. Airfares, hotels, rental cars, restaurants, and entertainment totaled $16 million last year.
        2. T&E budget increased by 12 percent per year for the past five years.
    B. Where the money goes:
        1. We took 3,390 trips last year at an average cost per trip of $4,725.
        2. Airfares and lodging represent 70 percent of T&E expenses.
    C. How our spending compares with national averages:
        1. Facilities and customers spread from coast to coast force us to spend a lot on travel.
        2. However, we spend 125 percent more than the national average for every day of travel. (Source: Dow Jones)
    D. Why do we spend so much?
        1. First-class travel has been viewed as compensation for the demands of extensive travel.
        2. The sales staff is encouraged to entertain clients.
        3. T&E costs are hard for managers to view and study.
        4. No one has central responsibility for controlling costs.

(Transition: We need to control spending for two reasons: (1) profits are projected to be flat or declining over the next two years, and (2) hotel rates and airfares continue to rise sharply.)

(continued)

■ Choose a compelling title; even if the title won't be published, it will help you focus your thoughts around your main idea.

Figure 12.3 is an outline for a 30-minute analytical presentation. It is organized around conclusions and presented in direct order. This outline is based on Chapter 11's Electrovision report, written by Linda Moreno.

Many speakers like to prepare both a detailed *planning outline* and a simpler *speaking outline* that provides all the cues and reminders they need to present their material. To prepare an effective speaking outline, follow these steps:[5]

You may find it helpful to create a simpler speaking outline from your planning outline.

■ Start with the planning outline, then strip away anything you don't plan to say to your audience (statement of general purpose, main idea, bibliography, and so on).

FIGURE 12.3   continued

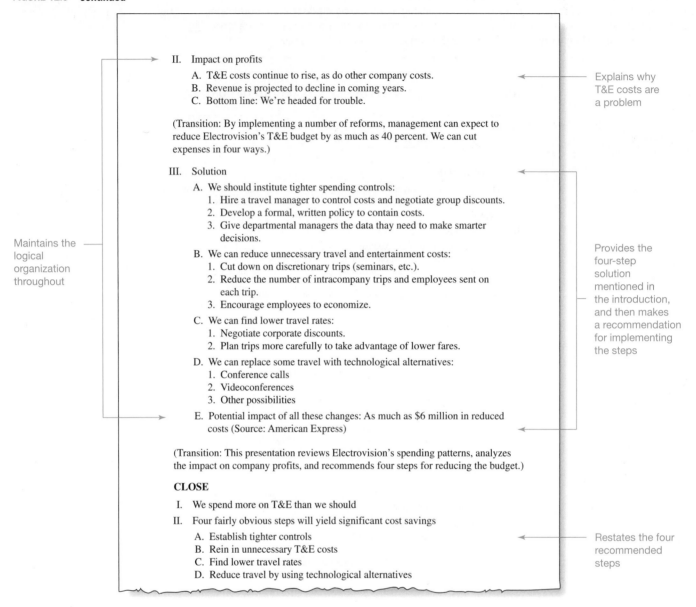

Maintains the logical organization throughout

II. Impact on profits
    A. T&E costs continue to rise, as do other company costs.
    B. Revenue is projected to decline in coming years.
    C. Bottom line: We're headed for trouble.

Explains why T&E costs are a problem

(Transition: By implementing a number of reforms, management can expect to reduce Electrovision's T&E budget by as much as 40 percent. We can cut expenses in four ways.)

III. Solution
    A. We should institute tighter spending controls:
        1. Hire a travel manager to control costs and negotiate group discounts.
        2. Develop a formal, written policy to contain costs.
        3. Give departmental managers the data thay need to make smarter decisions.
    B. We can reduce unnecessary travel and entertainment costs:
        1. Cut down on discretionary trips (seminars, etc.).
        2. Reduce the number of intracompany trips and employees sent on each trip.
        3. Encourage employees to economize.
    C. We can find lower travel rates:
        1. Negotiate corporate discounts.
        2. Plan trips more carefully to take advantage of lower fares.
    D. We can replace some travel with technological alternatives:
        1. Conference calls
        2. Videoconferences
        3. Other possibilities
    E. Potential impact of all these changes: As much as $6 million in reduced costs (Source: American Express)

Provides the four-step solution mentioned in the introduction, and then makes a recommendation for implementing the steps

(Transition: This presentation reviews Electrovision's spending patterns, analyzes the impact on company profits, and recommends four steps for reducing the budget.)

CLOSE

  I. We spend more on T&E than we should
  II. Four fairly obvious steps will yield significant cost savings
    A. Establish tighter controls
    B. Rein in unnecessary T&E costs
    C. Find lower travel rates
    D. Reduce travel by using technological alternatives

Restates the four recommended steps

- ■ Condense points and transitions to key words or phrases, choosing words that will prompt you to remember what each point is about.
- ■ Add delivery cues, such as places in your outline where you plan to pause for emphasis or use a visual.
- ■ Arrange your notes on cards (or sheets of paper, if you prefer); number your cards (or sheets of paper) so that you can keep them in order. (If you plan to use PowerPoint or other presentation software, you can also use the "notes" field on each slide for speaking notes.)

Step 2: Writing Your Presentation

Although you usually don't write out a presentation word for word, you still engage in the writing process—developing your ideas, structuring support points, phrasing your transitions, and so on. Depending on the situation and your personal style, your eventual presentation might follow these initial words closely, or you might express your thoughts in fresh, spontaneous language. Before you get to the actual writing phase, though, consider how you should adapt your style to your audience.

Adapting to Your Audience

Your audience's size, your subject, your purpose, your budget, and the time available for preparation all influence the style of your presentation. If you're speaking to a small group, particularly people you already know, you can use a casual style that encourages audience participation. A small conference room, with your audience seated around a table, may be appropriate. Use simple visuals, and invite your audience to interject comments. Deliver your remarks in a conversational tone, using notes to jog your memory if necessary.

If you're addressing a large audience or the event is important, establish a more formal atmosphere. During formal presentations, speakers are often located on a stage or platform, standing behind a lectern and using a microphone so that their remarks can be heard throughout the room or captured for broadcasting or webcasting.

Whether your presentation is formal or informal, strive for simple, familiar vocabulary and define any special terms you do need to use. And keep things simple. If you repeatedly stumble over a word as you rehearse, use a different one.[6]

> Adapting to your audience involves a number of issues, from speaking style to technology choices.

Composing Your Presentation

Just like written documents, oral presentations are composed of distinct elements: the introduction, the body, and the close.

Introduction

A good introduction arouses the audience's interest in your topic, establishes your credibility, and prepares the audience for what will follow. That's a lot to pack into the first few minutes of your presentation, so give yourself plenty of time to develop the words and visuals you'll use to get your presentation off to a great start.

> An effective introduction arouses interest in your topic, establishes your credibility, and prepares the audience for the body of your presentation.

Arousing Audience Interest   If you will be discussing important matters that directly and immediately affect the members of your audience, they will probably listen regardless of how you begin. However, if the subject matter itself won't grab their attention, you'll need to craft an introduction that will. Find a way to encourage people to take the subject personally. For example, if you wanted to interest younger employees in the company pension plan—which they won't benefit from until many years in the future—you might begin like this:

> If somebody offered to give you $200,000 in exchange for $5 per week, would you be interested? That's the amount you can expect to collect during your retirement years if you choose to contribute to the voluntary pension plan. Although retirement is many years away for most of you, it is an important financial decision that you should consider now. During the next 20 minutes, I'll give you the information you need to make the choice that's best for you and your family.

Table 12.2 suggests several other techniques you can use to arouse audience interest and keep listeners involved. Regardless of which technique you choose, always make sure that the introduction matches the tone of your presentation. Most of all, be natural. Nothing turns off the average audience faster than a trite, staged beginning.

Building Your Credibility   Audiences tend to decide within a few minutes whether you're worth listening to, so establishing your credibility quickly is vital.[7] If you're a well-known expert or have earned your audience's trust in other situations, you're already ahead of the game. If you need to build credibility during your opening remarks, the techniques for doing so depend on whether you will be introducing yourself or having someone else introduce you. In more formal situations, a master of ceremonies, conference chair, or

> If someone else will be introducing you to the audience, you can ask this person to present your credentials as well.

Table 12.2	Six Ways to Get Attention During Your Introduction
Unite the audience around a common goal	Invite them to help solve a problem, capitalize on an opportunity, or otherwise engage in the topic of your presentation.
Tell a story	Slice-of-life stories are naturally interesting and can be compelling. Be sure your story illustrates an important point.
Pass around a sample	Psychologists say that you can get people to remember your points by appealing to their senses. The best way to do so is to pass around a sample. If your company is in the textile business, let the audience handle some of your fabrics. If you sell chocolates, give everybody a taste.
Ask a question	Asking questions will get the audience actively involved in your presentation and, at the same time, will give you information about them and their needs.
State a startling statistic	People love details. If you can interject an interesting statistic, you can often wake up your audience.
Use humor	Even though the subject of most business presentations is serious, including a light comment now and then can perk up the audience. Just be sure the humor is relevant to the presentation and not offensive to the audience. In general, avoid humor when you and the audience don't share the same native language.

other person might be available to introduce you; he or she can present your credentials so that you won't appear boastful.

If you will be introducing yourself, keep your comments simple but don't be afraid to mention your accomplishments. You might say something like this:

> I'm Karen Whitney, a market research analyst with Information Resources Corporation. For the past five years, I've specialized in studying high-technology markets. Your director of engineering, John LaBarre, asked me to talk about recent trends in computer-aided design so that you'll have a better idea of how to direct your research efforts.

This speaker establishes credibility by tying her credentials to the purpose of her presentation. By mentioning her company's name, her specialization and position, and the name of the audience's boss, she lets her listeners know immediately that she is qualified to tell them something they need to know.

Previewing Your Message   A good introduction gives your listeners a preview of what's ahead, just as the introduction in a report helps readers understand what is coming. Summarize the main idea of your presentation, identify major supporting points, and indicate the order in which you'll develop those points. With that framework established, the audience will understand how the individual facts and figures are related to your main idea as you move into the body of your presentation. Of course, if you're building up to a conclusion or recommendation indirectly, you'll need to consider how much to reveal during your introduction.

Use the preview to help your audience understand the importance, the structure, and the content of your message.

Body

The bulk of your speech or presentation is devoted to a discussion of the main points in your outline. No matter what organizational pattern you're using, your goals are to make sure that (1) the organization of your presentation is clear and (2) your presentation holds the audience's attention.

Connecting Your Ideas   In written documents, you can show how ideas are related with a variety of design clues: headings, paragraph indentions, white space, and lists. However, with oral communication—particularly when you aren't using visuals for support—you have to rely primarily on spoken words to link various parts and ideas.

For the small links between sentences and paragraphs, use one or two transitional words: *therefore, because, in addition, in contrast, moreover, for example, consequently,*

Use transitions to repeat key ideas, particularly in longer presentations.

nevertheless, or *finally*. To link major sections of a presentation, use complete sentences or paragraphs, such as "Now that we've reviewed the problem, let's take a look at some solutions." Every time you shift topics, be sure to stress the connection between ideas by summarizing what's been said and previewing what's to come. The longer your presentation, the more important your transitions become. If you will be presenting many ideas, audience members may have trouble absorbing them and seeing the relationships among them.

Holding Your Audience's Attention   A successful introduction will have grabbed your audience's attention; now the body of your presentation needs to hold that attention. In this challenge, you have to compensate for another inescapable fact of oral presentations: Your audience can think and read faster than you can speak. If you don't keep their minds engaged, they'll start doing a thousand other things besides paying attention to you. Here are a few helpful tips for keeping the audience tuned into your message:

- Keep relating your subject to your audience's needs. People are interested in things that affect them personally. As much as possible, present every point in light of your audience's needs and values.
- Anticipate—and answer—your audience's questions as you move along so they don't get confused or distracted.
- Use clear, vivid language and throw in some variety as well; repeating the same words and phrases over and over puts people to sleep.
- Show how your subject is related to ideas that audience members already understand, and give people a way to categorize and remember your points.[8]
- Ask for opinions or pause occasionally for questions or comments; feedback also gives your audience a chance to temporarily switch from listening to participating.
- Illustrate your ideas with visuals, which enliven your message, help you connect with audience members, and help them remember your message more effectively (see "Enhancing Your Presentation with Effective Visuals," pages 364–370).

> The most important way to hold an audience's attention is to show how your message relates to their individual needs and concerns.

Close

The close is critical for two reasons: Audiences tend to focus more carefully as they wait for you to wrap up, and they will leave with your final words ringing in their ears. Before closing your presentation, tell listeners that you're about to finish so that they'll make one final effort to listen intently. Don't be afraid to sound obvious. Consider saying something such as "In conclusion" or "To sum it all up." You want people to know that this is the final segment of your presentation.

> Plan your close carefully so that your audience leaves with your main idea fresh in their minds.

Restating Your Main Points   Repeat your main idea, emphasizing what you want your audience to do or to think, and stress the key motivating factor that will encourage them to respond that way. Reinforce your theme by restating your main supporting points, such as this speaker did in a presentation on the company's executive compensation program:

> We can all be proud of the way our company has grown. However, if we want to continue that growth, we need to take four steps to ensure that our best people don't start looking for opportunities elsewhere.
>
> - One, increase the overall level of compensation
> - Two, install a cash bonus program
> - Three, offer a variety of stock-based incentives
> - Four, improve our health insurance and pension benefits
>
> By taking these steps, we can ensure that our company retains the management talent it needs to face our industry's largest competitors.

Such repetition of key ideas greatly improves the chance that your audience will hear your message in the way you intended.

Describing Next Steps   Some presentations require the audience to reach a decision or agreement. If the audience agrees on an issue covered in the presentation, verify that consensus. If they don't agree, acknowledge the lack of consensus, then be ready to suggest a method of resolving the differences. If you're not sure in advance how your audience will respond, prepare two closes, one that acknowledges the agreement reached and one that accommodates the fact that the audience didn't reach agreement (such as laying out a timetable for reaching a decision).

If you expect any action to occur as a result of your speech, be sure to explain who is responsible for doing what. List the action items with an estimated completion date and the name of the person or team responsible. This public commitment to action is good insurance that something will happen.

> If you need to have the audience make a decision or agree to take action, make sure the responsibilities for doing so are clear.

Ending on a Strong Note   Even if the presentation raised tough questions or the audience is in disagreement about some key issues, make sure your final remarks are upbeat and memorable. Conclude with a call to action or some encouraging words. For instance, you might stress the benefits of action or express confidence in the listeners' ability to accomplish the work ahead. An alternative is to end with a question or a statement that will leave your audience thinking. Be sure to spend plenty of time composing your closing remarks so that you can leave on a strong note. You don't want to wind up on stage with nothing to say but "Well, I guess that's it."

> Plan your final statement carefully so you can end on a strong, positive note.

Enhancing Your Presentations with Effective Visuals

Visuals can improve the quality and impact of your oral presentation by creating interest, illustrating points that are difficult to explain in words alone, adding variety, and increasing the audience's ability to absorb and remember information. Behavioral research has shown that visuals can improve learning by up to 400 percent because humans can process visuals 60,000 times faster than text.[9]

You can select from a variety of visuals to enhance oral presentations, each with unique advantages and disadvantages:

> Thoughtfully designed visuals create interest, illustrate complex points in your message, add variety, and help the audience absorb and remember information.

- **Overhead transparencies.** Overhead transparencies have been the workhorses of business presentations for decades, and some professionals still prefer them to electronic presentations. Transparencies don't require the latest computer or projection equipment, you can write on them during a presentation, and they never crash on you—as computers have been known to do. However, they're limited to static displays and they're impossible to edit once you've printed them.
- **Electronic presentations.** Electronic presentations are the visual aid of choice in most business situations today. An **electronic presentation**, or *slide show*, consists of a series of **electronic slides** composed using popular computer software such as Microsoft PowerPoint or Apple Keynote. To display an electronic presentation, you simply connect your computer to a portable projector (some are now small enough to carry

> In most businesses, electronic presentations are now the presentation technology of choice, although they're certainly not the only option.

Document Makeover

Improve This Speech

To practice correcting drafts of actual documents, visit your online course or the access-code-protected portion of the Companion Website. Click "Document Makeovers," then click Chapter 12. You will find a speech that contains problems and errors relating to what you've learned in this chapter about preparing effective speeches and oral presentations. Use the Final Draft decision tool to create an improved version of this speech. Check the message for effective choices in scope, style, opening, use of transitions, and closing.

around in your pocket) or a built-in unit that's part of a multimedia system in a conference room. Electronic presentations are easy to edit and update; you can add sound, photos, video, and animation; they can be incorporated into online meetings, webcasts, and *webinars* (a common term for web-based seminars); and you can record self-running presentations for trade shows, websites, and other uses. The primary disadvantage is complexity, relying on a computer and a display projector.

- **Chalkboards and whiteboards.** Chalkboards and whiteboards are effective tools for the flexible, spontaneous nature of workshops and brainstorming sessions. New electronic whiteboards let you capture the information written on them.
- **Flip charts.** Flip charts are great for recording comments and questions during your presentation or for keeping track of ideas during a brainstorming session.
- **Other visuals.** Be creative when choosing visuals to support your presentation. A video recording of a group of customers talking about your company can have a lot more impact than a series of slides that summarize what they said. Samples of products and materials let your audience experience your subject directly. Designers and architects use mock-ups and models to help people envision what a final creation will look like.

This chapter focuses on electronic presentations, the mainstay of business presentations today, although most of these design tips apply to overhead transparencies as well.

Once you've decided on the form your visuals will take, think through your presentation plan carefully before you start creating anything. Visuals are powerful devices, and that power can just as easily harm your efforts as help. Above all, remember that visuals support your spoken message; they should never replace it or overshadow it.

> Think through your presentation outline carefully before designing your visuals.

Creating Effective Slides

When creating slides or other visuals, let accuracy and simplicity guide you. First, it takes less time to create simple materials. Second, simple visuals reduce the chances of distraction and misinterpretation. Third, the more "bells and whistles" you have in your presentation, the more likely it is that something will go wrong.

Writing Readable Content   Effective slides start with readable content. Crowded slides are irritating to audiences because they are difficult to read. Remember that slides are not intended to display your entire script or highlight each point you make.[10] Instead, use slides to supplement your words and help the audience follow the flow of ideas. View them as simplified outlines of your presentation and use them to highlight key points, summarize and preview your message, signal major shifts in thought, illustrate concepts, or help create interest.

> Packing slides with too much information is a common beginner's mistake; use slide text to emphasize key points, not to convey your entire message.

Keep the text on your slides short and simple:

- Limit each slide to one thought, concept, or idea.
- Limit the content to about 40 words—with no more than six lines of text containing about six or seven words per line.
- Write short bulleted phrases rather than long sentences or blocks of text.
- Phrase list items in parallel grammatical form to facilitate quick reading.
- Use active voice.
- Include short informative titles.

Figure 12.4 is a good example of text slides that have been revised according to these principles to make their content more readable.

Modifying Graphics for Slides   Like text, graphics also need to be simplified for use on slides. Start by reducing the level of detail, eliminating anything that is not absolutely essential. If necessary, break information into more than one illustration. Look for shorter variations of numerical values. For instance, round off a number such as $12,500.72 to $12 or $12.5, then label the axis to indicate thousands.

FIGURE 12.4   Writing Readable Content for Slides

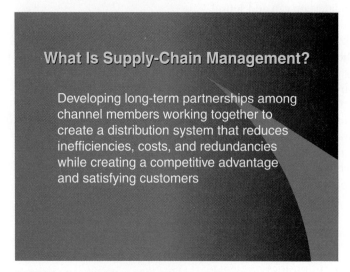

FIGURE 12.4a   **Inappropriate paragraph style**

FIGURE 12.4b   **Appropriate bulleted phrases**

The definition provided in Figure 12.4a was taken from a persuasive report written by the speaker. The paragraph style is inappropriate for slides and difficult to read. Figure 12.4b restates the definition in short phrases that highlight the key points of the definition. The speaker will explain these points while showing the slide.

FIGURE 12.4c   **Inappropriate wordy bullets**

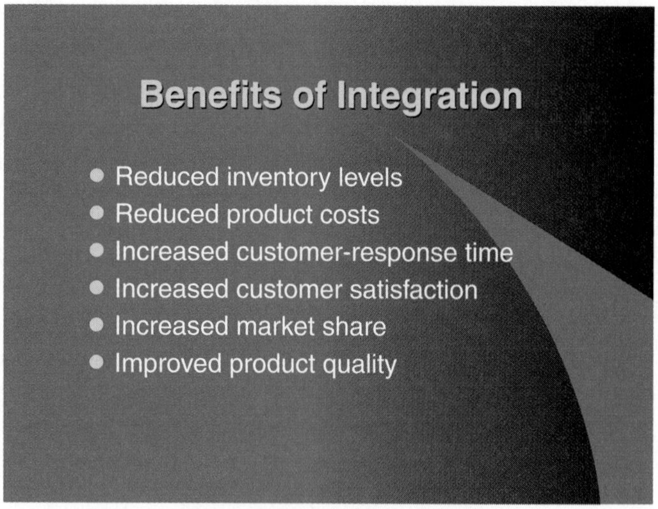

FIGURE 12.4d   **Appropriate concise bullets**

Both the title and the bullet points in Figure 12.4c are longer than they need to be, making the slide difficult to read. In Figure 12.4d, the sentences are converted to short, parallel phrases, and the slide's title is condensed.

With the basic design in place, use graphical elements to highlight key points. Use arrows, boldface type, and color to direct your audience's eyes to the main point of a visual. Summarize the intent of the graphic in one clear phrase, such as "Earnings have increased by 15 percent." Leave plenty of white space, use colors that stand out from the slide's background, and choose a font that's clear and easy to read.

Selecting Design Elements   Once you've composed the text and created the graphic elements of your slides, you're ready to focus on putting them together in an attractive, professional layout. Chapter 11 highlights six principles of effective design: consistency, contrast, balance, emphasis, simplicity, and audience experience and expectations. Pay close attention to these principles as you select the color, background and foreground designs, artwork, fonts, and type styles for your slides:

- **Color.** Color is a critical design element that can grab attention, emphasize important ideas, and create contrast. Research shows that color visuals can account for 60 percent of an audience's acceptance or rejection of an idea. Color can increase willingness to read by up to 80 percent, and it can enhance learning and improve retention by more than 75 percent.[11] Your color choices can also stimulate various emotions, as Table 12.3 suggests. Keep in mind that some colors work better together than others. Contrasting colors increase readability, whereas colors closer in hue, such as brown on green or blue on purple, decrease readability.[12] Finally, remember that colors may have a different meaning in certain cultures. So if you are creating slides for international audiences, be sensitive to cultural differences.

  > Color is more than just decoration; colors have meanings themselves, based on both cultural experience and the relationships that you established between the colors in your designs.

- **Background designs and artwork.** Electronic slides have two layers or levels of graphic design: the background and the foreground. The background is the equivalent of paper in a printed report; generally speaking, the less your background does, the better. Cluttered or flashy backgrounds tend to distract from your message.

- **Foreground designs and artwork.** The foreground contains the unique text and graphic elements that make up each individual slide. In the foreground, artwork can be either functional or decorative. Functional artwork includes photos, technical drawings, charts, and other visual elements containing information that's part of your message. In contrast, decorative artwork is there simply to enhance the look of your slides. Minimize the visual impact of decorative artwork—particularly the cartoony clip art that your software probably offers—so that it doesn't overwhelm your slides.

  > Artwork in the foreground of your slides can be either decorative or functional; use decorative artwork sparingly.

- **Fonts and type styles.** Type is harder to read on screen than on the printed page because projectors have lower *resolution* (the ability to display fine details) than the printers typically available in offices today. Consequently, you need to choose fonts and type styles with care. Sans serif fonts are usually easier to read than serif fonts (see Figure 12.5). Use both uppercase and lowercase letters, with extra white space between lines of text, and limit your fonts to one or two per slide. Choose font sizes that are easy to read from anywhere in the room, usually between 24 and 36 points.

  > Many of the fonts available on your computer are difficult to read on screen, so they aren't good choices for presentation slides.

With so many choices at your fingertips, maintaining consistency in your design is critical. Fortunately, software designed specifically for presentations makes consistency easy to achieve. You simply create a *slide master* using the colors, fonts, and other design elements you've chosen, then these choices automatically show up on every slide in the presentation (see Figure 12.6).

> Design inconsistencies confuse and annoy audiences; don't change colors and other design elements randomly throughout your presentation.

Table 12.3	Color and Emotion	
Color	**Emotional Associations**	**Best Uses**
Blue	Peaceful, soothing, tranquil, cool, trusting	Background for electronic business presentations (usually dark blue); safe and conservative
White	Neutral, innocent, pure, wise	Font color of choice for most electronic business presentations with a dark background
Yellow	Warm, bright, cheerful, enthusiastic	Text bullets and subheadings with a dark background
Red	Passionate, dangerous, active, painful	Promote action or stimulate audience; seldom used as a background ("in the red" specifically refers to financial losses)
Green	Assertive, prosperous, envious, relaxed	Highlight and accent color (green symbolizes money in the United States but not in other countries).

FIGURE 12.5   Selecting Readable Fonts and Type Styles

Times New Roman is a standard font for many print documents, but as you can see in Figure 12.5a, the serifs of this font make it difficult to read on screen. The italicized type is also hard to read on screen. As Figure 12.5b shows, sans serif fonts such as Arial are a better choice for slides; they are cleaner and easier to read from a distance.

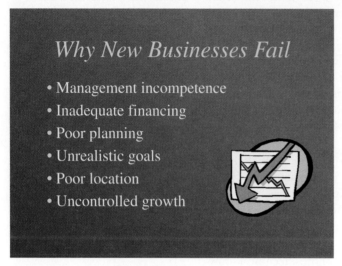

FIGURE 12.5a   Times New Roman font    **FIGURE 12.5b   Arial font**

Adding Animation and Special Effects   Today's presentation software offers many options for livening up your slides, including sound, animation, video clips, transition effects, and hyperlinks. As always, think about the impact that all these effects will have on your audience and use only those special effects that support your message.[13]

Functional animation involves motion that is directly related to your message, such as a highlight arrow that moves around the screen to emphasize specific points in a technical diagram. Such animation is also a great way to demonstrate sequences and procedures. In contrast, *decorative animation*, such as having a block of text cartwheel in from offscreen, needs to be used with great care. These effects don't add any functional value, and they easily distract audiences.

Transitions control how one slide replaces another, such as having the current slide gently fade out before the next slide fades in. Subtle transitions like this can ease your viewers' gaze from one slide to the next, but many of the transition effects now available

> Some of the slide transitions available in presentation software are distracting and can quickly begin to annoy audiences.

FIGURE 12.6   PowerPoint Slide Master

The slide master ensures consistency of the recurring design elements—headings, colors, bullets, and so on—in all your slides. When your slides are consistent, readers have less work to do and can therefore pay more attention to your message.

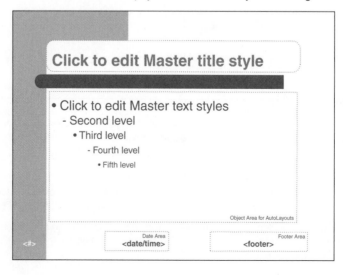

are little more than distractions, so it's best to avoid them. **Builds** control the release of text, graphics, and other elements on individual slides. With builds you can make your bullet points appear one at a time rather than having all of them appear on a slide at once, thereby making it easier for you and the audience to focus on each new message point.

A **hyperlink** instructs your computer to jump to another slide in your presentation, to a website, or to another program entirely. Hyperlinks can be also assigned to **action buttons**, which are a variety of preprogrammed icons available in PowerPoint. Action buttons let you perform such common tasks as jumping forward or backward to a specific slide or opening a document or spreadsheet. Using hyperlinks and action buttons is also a great way to build flexibility into your presentations so that you can instantly change the flow of your presentation in response to audience feedback.

Multimedia elements offer the ultimate in active presentations. Integrating short video clips can be a great way to add interest to your presentation. However, keep these clips short; audiences dislike being forced to sit through long speeches online.[14] For more advanced digital video, you can use such specialized products as Adobe Premiere Pro or Macromedia Director (samples of which can be viewed at the respective companies' websites).

> You can increase the flexibility of your presentation slides with hyperlinks that let you jump to different slides, websites, or other displays at will.

Giving Presentations Online

In some companies, online presentations have already become a routine matter, conducted via internal groupware, virtual meeting systems, or webcast systems designed specifically for online presentations. In most cases, you'll communicate through some combination of audio, video, and data presentations (for instance, your PowerPoint slides). Your audience will view your presentation either on their individual computer screens or via a projector in a conference room.

The benefits of online presentations are considerable, including the opportunity to communicate with a geographically dispersed audience at a fraction of the cost of travel and the ability for a project team or an entire organization to meet at a moment's notice. However, the challenges for a presenter can be significant, thanks to that layer of technology between you and your audience. Many of those "human moments" that guide and encourage you through an in-person presentation won't travel across the digital divide. For instance, it's often harder to tell whether your audience is bored or confused, since your view of them is usually confined to small video images.

To ensure successful online presentations, keep the following advice in mind:

> Online presentations give you a way to reach more people in less time, but they require special preparation and skills.

- **Consider sending preview study materials ahead of time.** Doing so lets your audience familiarize themselves with any important background information.
- **Keep your content—and your presentation of it—as simple as possible.** Break complicated slides down into multiple slides if necessary, and keep the direction of your discussion clear so that no one gets lost.
- **Ask for feedback frequently.** You won't have as much of the visual feedback that alerts you when audience members are confused, and many online viewers will be reluctant to call attention to themselves by interrupting you to ask for clarification.
- **Consider the viewing experience from the audience's side.** Will they be able to see what you think they can see? For instance, webcast video is typically displayed in a small window on-screen, so viewers may miss important details.
- **Make sure your audience can receive the sort of content you intend to use.** For instance, some corporate *firewalls* don't allow streaming media, so your webcast video might not survive the trip.[15]
- **Allow plenty of time for everyone to get connected and familiar with the screen they're viewing.** Build extra time into your schedule to ensure that everyone is connected and ready to start.

Last but not least, don't get lost in the technology. Use these tools whenever they'll help, but remember that the most important aspect of any presentation is getting the audience to receive, understand, and embrace your message.

> Once you master the technology, you can spend less time thinking about it and more time thinking about the most important elements of the presentation: your message and your audience.

Step 3: Completing Your Presentation

With a draft of your presentation in hand, you're ready to complete the development of your presentation. As with written communication, this third step starts with the all-important task of revising your message to ensure appropriate content. Edit your presentation for clarity and conciseness as you would any business message. If you're using electronic slides, make sure they are readable, concise, consistent from slide to slide, and fully operational (including transitions, builds, and animations).

Finalizing Slides and Support Materials

Electronic presentation software can help you throughout the editing and revision process. As Figure 12.7 shows, the *slide sorter view* lets you see some or all of the slides in your presentation on a single screen. Use this view to add and delete slides, reposition slides, check slides for design consistency, and verify the operation of animation and transition effects.

FIGURE 12.7   Slide Sorter View
Examining thumbnails of all your slides on one screen is the best way to check the overall design of your presentation. The slide sorter also makes it easy to review the order and organization of your presentation. To change the position of any slide, simply click and drag it to a new position.

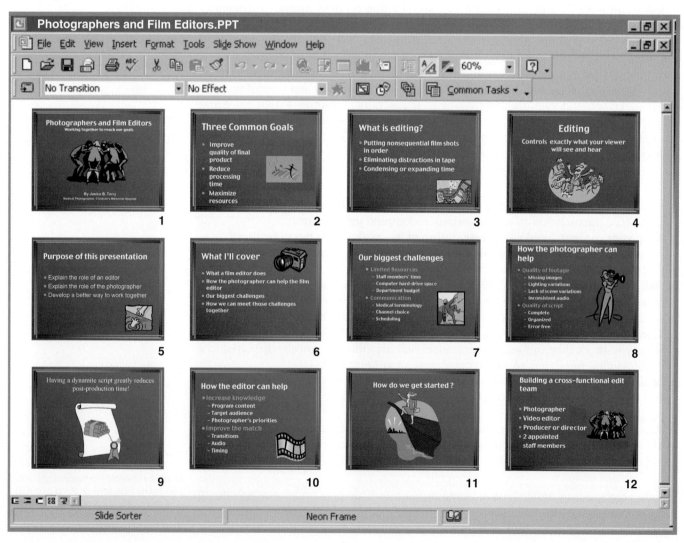

In addition to the content slides that you've already created, you can help your audience follow the flow of your presentation by creating three types of *navigational slides*:

- **Cover slides.** Make a good first impression on your audience with a cover slide, the equivalent of a report's title page.
- **Introduction slides.** Introduction slides define the topic of your presentation, clarify the topic, emphasize why you are speaking on this topic, and establish any expectations you may have of the audience.[16]
- **Blueprint slides.** For longer presentations, consider using *blueprint slides* that show the audience where you are in the presentation (Figure 12.8).

With your slides working properly and in clear, logical order, consider whether some additional material will help your audience either during or after your presentations. *Handouts* are a terrific way to offer your audience additional material without overloading your slides with information. Possibilities for good handout materials include complex charts and diagrams that are too unwieldy for the screen, articles and technical papers, case studies, lists of websites, and printed copies of your slides.[17]

> Navigational slides help your audience keep track of what you've covered already and what you plan to cover next.

> Use handout materials to support the points made in your presentation and to offer the audience additional information on your topic.

Preparing to Speak

With all of your materials ready, your next step is to decide which method of speaking you want to use. You have three options: memorizing your material word for word, reading a printout of your material, or speaking from notes. Memorizing is usually not a good choice. In the best of circumstances, you'll probably sound stilted; in the worst, you might forget your lines. Besides, you'll often need to address audience questions during your speech, so you must be flexible enough to adjust your speech as you go. However, memorizing a quotation, an opening paragraph, or a few concluding remarks can bolster your confidence and strengthen your delivery.

Reading your speech is sometimes necessary, such as when delivering legal information, policy statements, or other messages that must be conveyed in an exact manner. However, for most business presentations, reading is a poor choice because it limits your interaction with the audience and lacks the fresh, dynamic feel of natural talking. (In any event, *never* stand in front of an audience and simply read the text on your slides.) If you do plan to read a prepared speech, practice enough so that you can still maintain eye contact with your audience. Print your speech with triple-spaced lines, wide margins, and

FIGURE 12.8   Blueprint Slides
A blueprint slide near the beginning of a presentation (Figure 12.8a), lets the audience know what to expect. As the speaker finishes each section, the blueprint is then shown again and updated to indicate progress (see the yellow checkmark and text in Figure 12.8b).

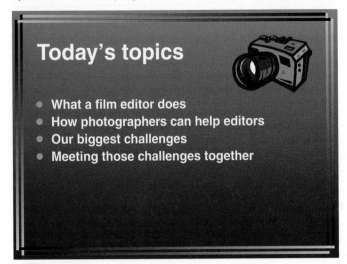

FIGURE 12.8a

FIGURE 12.8b

large type. You might even want to include stage cues, such as *pause, raise hands, lower voice*.

Speaking from notes, with the help of an outline, note cards, or visuals, is usually the most effective and easiest delivery mode. This approach gives you something to refer to and still allows for plenty of eye contact, interaction with the audience, and improvisation in response to audience feedback.

Practicing Your Delivery

You're now just one step away from giving your presentation, and it's a step that too many novice presenters overlook: practicing the delivery of your presentation. So many things can go wrong in a major presentation, including equipment glitches, timing problems, and that sinking feeling that you don't know what to say next. That's why experienced speakers always practice important presentations. If you can arrange an audience of several helpful colleagues, by all means do so. They can tell you if your slides are understandable and whether your delivery is effective. A day or two before you're ready to step on stage for an important talk, make sure you can give a positive response to the following questions:

- Can you present your material naturally, without reading your slides word-for-word?
- Is the equipment working—and do you know how to work it?
- Is your timing on track?
- Can you easily pronounce all the words you plan to use?
- Have you decided how you're going to introduce your slides?
- Have you anticipated likely questions and objections?

With experience, you'll get a feel for how much practice is enough in any given situation. For an important presentation, four or five practice runs is not excessive. Your credibility is dramatically enhanced when you move seamlessly through your presentation, matching effective words with each slide. Practicing helps keep you on track, helps you maintain a conversational tone with your audience, and boosts your confidence and composure.

If you're addressing an audience that doesn't speak your language, consider using an interpreter. Working with an interpreter does constrain your presentation somewhat. For one thing, you must speak slowly enough for the interpreter to keep up with you; however, don't speak so slowly that the rest of your audience loses interest. Send your interpreter a copy of your speech and visuals as far in advance of your presentation as possible. If your audience is likely to include persons with hearing impairments, be sure to team up with a sign-language interpreter as well.

Any time you deliver an oral presentation to people from other cultures, you may need to adapt the content of your presentation. It is also important to take into account any cultural differences in appearance, mannerisms, and other customs. Your interpreter or host will be able to suggest appropriate changes for a specific audience or particular occasion.

Overcoming Anxiety

If you're nervous about facing an audience, remember that nervousness is an indication that you care about your audience, your topic, and the occasion. Such stimulation can give you the extra energy you need to make your presentation sparkle. Here are some ways to harness your nervous energy to become a more confident speaker:[18]

- **Prepare more material than necessary.** Combined with a genuine interest in your topic, extra knowledge will reduce your anxiety.
- **Practice.** The more familiar you are with your material, the less panic you'll feel.
- **Think positively.** See yourself as polished and professional, and your audience will too.

Marginal notes:

Speaking from carefully prepared notes is the easiest and most effective delivery mode for most speakers.

The more you practice, the more confidence you'll have in yourself and your material.

You'll know you've practiced enough when you can present the material at a comfortable pace and in a conversational tone, without the need to read your slides or constantly refer to your notes.

Preparation is the best antidote for anxiety.

- **Visualize your success.** Visualize mental images of yourself in front of the audience, feeling confident, prepared, and able to handle any situation that might arise.[19]
- **Take a few deep breaths.** Before you begin to speak, remember that your audience wants you to succeed, too.
- **Be ready.** Have your first sentence memorized and on the tip of your tongue.
- **Be comfortable.** Dress appropriately for the situation but as comfortably as possible. Drink plenty of water ahead of time to ensure that your voice is well hydrated (bring a bottle of water with you, too). The fewer physical distractions you have, the better you'll perform.
- **Don't panic.** If you sense that you're starting to race, pause and arrange your notes or perform some other small task while taking several deep breaths. Then start again at your normal pace. If you feel that you're losing your audience, try to pull them back by involving them in the action; ask for their opinions or pause for questions.
- **Concentrate on your message and your audience, not on yourself.** When you're busy thinking about your subject and observing your audience's response, you tend to forget your fears.
- **Maintain eye contact with friendly audience members.** Looking directly at your listeners will make you appear sincere, confident, and trustworthy. It also helps you get an idea of the impression you're creating.
- **Keep going.** Things usually get better as you move along, with each successful minute giving you more and more confidence.

Handling Questions Responsively

The question-and-answer period is one of the most important parts of an oral presentation. Questions give you a chance to obtain important information, to emphasize your main idea and supporting points, and to build enthusiasm for your point of view. When you're speaking to high-ranking executives in your company, the question-and-answer period will often consume most of the time allotted for you presentation.[20]

> Don't leave the question-and-answer period to chance: Anticipate potential questions and think through your answers.

Preparation is essential. Even if you can't anticipate every single question, learn enough about your audience to get an idea of their concerns. Think through answers to questions you're likely to get, even those that you don't have a complete answer to. Don't assume you can handle whatever comes up.[21]

Pay attention to the questioner's body language and facial expression to help determine what the person really means (assuming you can see your audience). Repeat the question to confirm your understanding and to ensure that the entire audience has heard it. If the question is vague or confusing, ask for clarification; then give a simple, direct answer. If you're asked to choose between two alternatives, don't feel you must do so. Offer your own choice instead, if it makes more sense.[22]

Be sure to answer the question you're asked. Don't sidestep it, ignore it, laugh it off, or get so caught up in the situation that you forget to respond. If giving an adequate answer would take too long, simply say, "I'm sorry, we don't have time to get into that issue right now, but if you'll see me after the presentation, I'll be happy to discuss it with you." If you don't know the answer, don't pretend that you do. Instead, say something like "I don't have those figures. I'll get them for you as quickly as possible."

You have less control over the proceedings during the question-and-answer session, but establish some ground rules up front. If appropriate—and it wouldn't be appropriate to do so if your audience consists of potential investors or your company's top managers—announce a time limit or a question limit per person. Plus, give as many audience members as possible a chance to participate by calling on people from different parts of the room.

> Maintaining control during the question-and-answer session can be a challenge, particularly if any audience members outrank you in the corporate hierarchy.

If audience members try to turn a question into an opportunity to make their own minipresentations, remember that it's up to you to stay in control. You might admit that you and the questioner have differing opinions and, before calling on someone else, offer to get back to the questioner once you've done more research. Or you might simply respond with a brief answer, avoiding a lengthy debate or additional questions.[23]

If you ever face hostile questions, respond honestly and directly while keeping your cool.

If a question ever puts you on the hot seat, respond honestly, but remember to keep your cool. Look the person in the eye, answer the question as well as you can, and keep your emotions under control. Avoid getting into a heated argument. Defuse hostility by paraphrasing the question and asking the questioner to confirm that you've understood it correctly. Maintain a businesslike tone of voice and a pleasant expression.[24]

When the time allotted for your presentation is up, call a halt to the question-and-answer session. Prepare the audience for the end by saying something like, "Our time is almost up. Let's have one more question." After you've made your reply, summarize the main idea of the presentation and thank people for their attention. Conclude the way you opened: by looking around the room and making eye contact. Then gather your notes and leave the podium, maintaining the same confident demeanor you've had from the beginning.

Reviewing Key Points

This chapter discusses giving oral presentations, both in person and online. You have learned to plan your speeches and presentations by studying your purpose and profiling your audience. The chapter talks about how to organize and compose your presentation, and how to develop the introduction, body, and close.

The chapter discusses creating effective slides by choosing color, background design, fonts, and type styles. This chapter also talks about mastering the art of delivery. You have learned how to get ready to speak, overcome anxiety, present visuals effectively, and handle questions responsively.

The next two chapters discuss some of the most important business communication efforts in which you'll ever engage: applying and interviewing for employment. You will learn how to search for that perfect job in today's changing workplace, how to prepare a résumé that gets attention, and how to perform well in interviews.

Test Your Knowledge

1. What are three most common purposes of an oral business presentation?

2. What three goals should you accomplish during the introduction of an oral presentation?

3. What techniques can you use to get an audience's attention during your introduction?

4. What three tasks should you accomplish in the close of your presentation?

5. What steps can you take to ensure success with online presentations?

Apply Your Knowledge

1. Why is it important to limit the scope of oral presentations?

2. How might the audience's attitude affect the amount of audience interaction during or after a presentation? Explain your answer.

3. If you were giving an oral presentation on the performance of a company product, what three attention-getters might you use to enliven your talk?

4. From the speaker's perspective, what are the advantages and disadvantages of responding to questions from the audience throughout an oral presentation, rather than just afterward? From the listener's perspective, which approach would you prefer? Why?

5. Ethical Choices How can you use design elements and special effects to persuade an audience? Is it ethical to do so?

Practice Your Knowledge

Activities

For active links to all websites discussed in this chapter, visit this text's website at www.prenhall.com/bovee. Locate your book and click on its Companion Website link. Then select Chapter 12, and click on "Featured Websites." Locate the name of the page or the URL related to the material in the text. Please note that links to sites that become inactive after publication of the book will be removed from the Featured Websites section.

1. **Analyze This Document**   Locate the transcript of a speech, either online or through your school library. Good sources include Yahoo's directory of commencement speeches (http://dir.yahoo.com/Education/Graduation/Speeches) and the publication *Vital Speeches of the Day* (recent years are available in the ProQuest database; ask at your library). Many corporate websites also have archives of executives' speeches; look in the "investor relations" section. Examine both the introduction and the close of the speech you've chosen, then analyze how these two sections work together to emphasize the main idea. What action does the speaker want the audience to take? Next, identify the transitional sentences or phrases that clarify the speech's structure for the listener, especially those that help the speaker shift between supporting points. Using these transitions as clues, list the main message and supporting points; then indicate how each transitional phrase links the current supporting point to the succeeding one. Prepare a two- to three-minute oral presentation summarizing your analysis for your class.

2. **Creating Effective Slides: Content**   Look through recent issues (print or online) of *BusinessWeek*, *Fortune*, or other business publications for articles discussing challenges that a specific company or industry is facing. Using the articles and the guidelines discussed in this chapter, create three to five slides summarizing these issues. If you don't have access to computer presentation software or a word processor, you can draw the slides on plain paper.

3. **Mastering Delivery: Analysis**   Attend a presentation at your school or in your town, or watch a speech on television. Categorize the speech as one that motivates or entertains, one that informs or analyzes, or one that persuades or urges collaboration. Then compare the speaker's delivery with the concepts presented in this chapter. Write a two-page report analyzing the speaker's performance and suggesting improvements.

4. **Mastering Delivery: Nonverbal Signals**   Observe and analyze the delivery of a speaker in a school, work, or other setting. What type of delivery did the speaker use? Was this delivery appropriate for the occasion? What nonverbal signals did the speaker use to emphasize key points? Were these signals effective? Which nonverbal signals would you suggest to further enhance the delivery of this oral presentation—and why?

5. **Ethical Choices**   Think again about the oral presentation you observed and analyzed in the previous activity. How could the speaker have used nonverbal signals to unethically manipulate the audience's attitudes or actions?

6. **Teamwork**   You've been asked to give an informative 10-minute talk on vacation opportunities in your home state. Draft your introduction, which should last no more than 2 minutes. Then pair off with a classmate and analyze each other's introductions. How well do these two introductions arouse the audience's interest, build credibility, and preview the presentation? Suggest how these introductions might be improved.

7. Oral Presentations: Self-Assessment   How good are you at planning, writing, and delivering oral presentations? Rate yourself on each of the following elements of the oral presentation process. Then examine your ratings to identify where you are strongest and where you can improve, using the tips in this chapter.

Elements of the Presentation Process	Always	Frequently	Occasionally	Never
1. I start by defining my purpose.	____	____	____	____
2. I analyze my audience before writing an oral presentation.	____	____	____	____
3. I match my presentation length to the allotted time.	____	____	____	____
4. I begin my oral presentations with an attention-getting introduction.	____	____	____	____
5. I look for ways to build credibility as a speaker.	____	____	____	____
6. I cover only a few main points in the body of my presentation.	____	____	____	____
7. I use transitions to help listeners follow my ideas.	____	____	____	____
8. I review main points and describe next steps in the close.	____	____	____	____
9. I practice my presentation beforehand.	____	____	____	____
10. I prepare in advance for questions and objections.	____	____	____	____
11. I conclude oral presentations by summarizing my main idea.	____	____	____	____

8. Delivering Oral Presentations: Possible Topics   Perhaps one of the following topics interests you:

   a. What I expect to learn in this course

   b. Past public speaking experiences: the good, the bad, and the ugly

   c. I would be good at teaching _____.

   d. I am afraid of _____.

   e. It's easy for me to _____.

   f. I get angry when _____.

   g. I am happiest when I _____.

   h. People would be surprised if they knew that I _____.

   i. My favorite older person

   j. My favorite charity

   k. My favorite place

   l. My favorite sport

   m. My favorite store

   n. My favorite television show

   o. The town you live in suffers from a great deal of juvenile vandalism. Explain to a group of community members why juvenile recreational facilities should be built instead of a juvenile detention complex.

p. You are speaking to the Humane Society. Support or oppose the use of animals for medical research purposes.

q. You are talking to civic leaders of your community. Try to convince them to build an art gallery.

r. You are speaking to a first-grade class at an elementary school. Explain why they should brush their teeth after meals.

s. You are speaking to a group of traveling salespeople. Convince them that they should wear their seatbelts while driving.

t. You are speaking to a group of elderly people. Convince them to adopt an exercise program.

u. Energy issues (supply, conservation, alternative sources, national security, global warming, pollution, etc.)

v. Financial issues (banking, investing, family finances, etc.)

w. Government (domestic policy, foreign policy, Social Security taxes, welfare, etc.)

x. Interesting new technologies (virtual reality, geographic information systems, nanotechnology, bioengineering, etc.)

y. Politics (political parties, elections, legislative bodies and legislation, the presidency, etc.)

z. Sports (amateur and professional, baseball, football, golf, hang gliding, hockey, rock climbing, tennis, etc.)

Choose a topic and prepare a brief presentation (5–10 minutes) to be given to your class.

Expand Your Knowledge

Exploring the Best of the Web

Look Smart in Your Electronic Presentations   Visit the presentation center at 3M, www.3m.com/meetingnetwork/presentations, and follow the expert advice on creating and delivering effective oral presentations. Find out why a bad presentation can kill even the best idea. Did you pick the right colors? Is your presentation too long? Too wordy? Find out why a strong template is the key to positive first impressions. Review the tips for better presentation. Download some templates and look smart.

Exercises

Log on and learn the secrets from the pros, then address these questions:

1. What three questions should you answer for a successful presentation?

2. What common PowerPoint pitfalls should you avoid?

3. What are the two common causes of presentation paralysis?

Exploring the Web on Your Own

Review these chapter-related websites on your own to enhance your oral presentation skills and knowledge.

1. Develop better presentations with the helpful advice at Epson's Presenters Online website, www.presentersonline.com.

2. Visit the Advanced Public Speaking Institute, at www.public-speaking.org, and learn how to be the best public speaker you can be.

3. MasterViews International offers comprehensive information on dozens of PowerPoint topics at www.masterviews.com <http://masterviews.com/>.

Learn Interactively

Interactive Study Guide

Visit www.prenhall.com/bovee, then locate your book and click on its Companion Website link. Select Chapter 12 to take advantage of the interactive "Chapter Quiz" to test your knowledge of chapter concepts. Receive instant feedback on whether you need additional studying. Also, visit the "Study Hall," where you'll find an abundance of valuable resources that will help you succeed in this course.

Peak Performance Grammar and Mechanics

If your instructor has required the use of "Peak Performance Grammar and Mechanics," either in your online course, through the access-code protected portion of the Companion Website, or on CD, you can improve your skill with mechanics by using the "Peak Performance Grammar and Mechanics" module. Click "Mechanics of Style." Take the Pretest to determine whether you have any weak areas. Then review those areas in the Refresher Course. Take the Follow-Up Test to check your grasp of mechanics. Finally, for additional reinforcement in capitals, italics, and abbreviations, go to the "Improve Your Grammar, Mechanics, and Usage" section that follows, and complete the "Level 1: Self-Assessment" exercises.

Improve Your Grammar, Mechanics, and Usage

Level 1: Self-Assessment—Capitals and Abbreviations

Review Sections 3.1 and 3.3 in the "Handbook of Grammar, Mechanics, and Usage," and then look at the following 15 items.

In items 1–15, indicate proper capitalization by underlining appropriate letters with three underscores. Circle abbreviations that should be spelled out, and insert abbreviations where appropriate.

1. Dr. paul hansen is joining our staff.

2. New caressa skin cream should be in a position to dominate that market.

3. Send this report to mister h. k. danforth, rural route 1, warrensburg, new york 12885.

4. You are responsible for training my new assistant to operate the xerox machine.

5. She received her master of business administration degree from the university of michigan.

6. The building is located on the corner of madison and center streets.

7. Call me at 8 tomorrow morning, pacific standard time, and I'll have the information you need.

8. When jones becomes ceo next month, we'll need your input asap.

9. Address it to art bowers, chief of production.

10. Please rsvp to sony corp. just as soon as you know your schedule.

11. The data-processing department will begin work on feb. 2, just one wk. from today.

12. You are to meet him on friday at the un building in nyc.

13. Whenever you can come, professor, our employees will greatly enjoy your presentation.

14. At 50 per box, our std. contract forms are $9 a box, and our warranty forms are $7.95 a box.

15. We plan to establish a sales office on the west coast.

Level 2: Workplace Applications

The following items contain numerous errors in grammar, capitalization, punctuation, abbreviation, number style, word division, and vocabulary. Rewrite each sentence in the space provided, correcting all errors. Write *C* in the space after any sentence that is already correct.

1. Mc'Donalds and Sears' have partnered with the television program, "Its Showtime At The Apollo." To offer talented kids the opportunity too appear on national television.

2. Tiffany & Co., the internationally-renowned jeweler and specialty retailer plan to open a 5000 square feet store in Walnut Creek, CA next year.

3. If none of the solutions seem satisfying, pick the more easier one.

4. Ken Baker, the west coast bureau chief for Us magazine, will be responsible for overseeing all of magazine reporting in Hollywood, conducting high profile, celebrity interviews, for identifying news stories, and assist in the generation of cover concepts.

5. With experience managing numerous enthusiast brands, including "Kawasaki" and "Skechers," Juxt Interactive are cementing their role as a leader in strategic, integrated campaigns.

6. You're message, tone, and product positioning has to be right on to be excepted and successful.

7. As I begun to put the team together, it became apparent to myself that my idea was ahead of it's time.

8. Many think that the primary market for newspapers are the readers, however advertisers generate the majority of revenues.

9. REIs second website, www.REI-outlet.com, features items that are not available at REI's physical stores, catalog, or main website.

10. The company's C.E.O., who we had saw at the awards dinner wednesday night, was fired the next day.

11. A designer of high priced purses such as Kate Spade or Louis Vitton generally limit distribution to exclusive boutiques or high end retail stores: such as Neiman-Marcus.

12. There is many indications that an economic recovery is underway, and will continue to stabilize and build however modestly.

13. We bought the equipment at a second hand store which turned out to be shoddy and defective.

14. Experts site 2 principle reasons for Webvan's failure; consumer resistance and over expansion.

15. Implementation of the over time hours guidelines will be carried out by the Human Resources Staff members.

Level 3: Document Critique

The following document may contain errors in grammar, punctuation, capitalization, abbreviation, number style, vocabulary, and spelling. You may also find problems with organization, format, and word use. Correct all errors using standard proofreading marks (see Appendix C).

Date: Thu, 25 April, 2007

From: Steve Pendergrass <spender@manchcc.edu>

To: Gregory Hansford <gregory.hansford@manchcc.edu>

CC:

BCC:

Attached:

Subject: Library Hours

Dear Mr. Hansford,

There is a favorite place in which Manchester students study on our campus: the library because of the quiet atmosphere excellent resources, and helpful staff. With a ajustment in library hours there assets could be taken advantage of by more students.

In an informal survey of the students in my English class, a desire for the library to be open more hours on the weekends became evident. Many students find weekends best for researching term papers: because that's when large blocks of time can be found in their schedules.

I'd like to sight several reasons for the change I am about to propose to encourage your interest and desire for my suggestion. Understandable, librarians need a day off. Perhaps students and librarians could both be accomodated if the library closed at five p.m. on Friday night. Friday night is the time most students like to relax and attend sports events or parties. The libary could then be open on Saturdays from ten a.m. until 4:30 p.m. To make this arrangement fair to librarians; perhaps their schedules could be staggered so that nobody would have to work every Saturday or those scheduled to work on Saturdays could be given Mondays or Fridays off.

Consider implementing this new schedule this Fall. Another much-appreciated service for students will be performed if you do this.

Sincerely: Steve Pendergrass, student

Writing Employment Messages and Interviewing for Jobs

Unit 5

13

Building Careers and Writing Résumés

From the Real World

"At our office, these résumés are rejected without even being read."

—Ed Tazzia
Managing partner, Gundersen Partners
www.gpllc.com

Learning Objectives

After studying this chapter, you will be able to

1 Discuss how employers view today's job market

2 List three things you can do before you graduate and while you're job hunting that will make you more valuable to employers

3 Describe the approach most employers take to finding potential new employees

4 Discuss how to choose the appropriate résumé organization and list the advantages and disadvantages of the three common options

5 List the major sections of a traditional résumé

6 Describe what you should do to adapt your résumé to a scannable format

Follow Ed Tazzia's advice, (see left) and you can avoid the regrettable fate that befalls too many job seekers: failing to even get to the interview stage because of some silly and avoidable error on your résumé. Tazzia's comment refers specifically to résumés with amateurish designs—too many type fonts and sizes, too much color, excessive boldface, and italics all over the place.[1] However, his observation also speaks to a couple of larger truth about résumés and your job search in general. First, perceptions can make or break your job search, and no perception is more important than the first impression you make with your résumé and cover letter. Second, today's employers are frequently overwhelmed by the number of résumés they receive. To narrow the list of potential candidates to a manageable number, many are forced to aggressively filter all those incoming résumés and as Tazzia notes, poor design is enough to get a résumé eliminated from consideration.

Building a Career with Your Communication Skills

Fortunately, avoiding the mistakes that Ed Tazzia describes and creating a compelling package of job search materials is not that difficult. In fact, throughout this course, you've been practicing the skills you'll need. Now it's just a matter of adapting those skills to the challenges of finding and landing the ideal job. The skills you've learned in research, planning, and writing will help you every step of the way.

Understanding Today's Dynamic Workplace

The job market you read about this year might not be the same market you try to enter a year or two from now. However, you can count on a few forces that are likely to affect your entry into the job market and your career success in years to come:[2]

- **Less stability.** Your career will be affected by globalization, mergers and acquisitions, a short-term mentality driven by the demands of stockholders, ethical upheavals, and the relentless quest for lower costs.
- **Loss of lifetime employment.** Boeing, the Chicago-based aerospace giant, speaks of lifetime *employability*, rather than lifetime employment, putting the responsibility on employees to keep their skills up-to-date—even changing careers if necessary.
- **Growth of small business.** Small business continues to be the primary engine of job creation in the United States, so chances are good that you'll work for a small firm at some point.
- **More independent contractors.** As companies try to become more flexible, more employees are going solo and setting up shop as independent contractors.

For many workers, the employment picture is less stable today than it was in years past.

How should you respond to all these forces? First, take charge of your career; don't assume your employer or anybody else is watching out for your future. Second, understand how the job market works, starting with the perspective of today's employers.

Changes in the job market mean you need to take charge of your career, rather than counting on a single employer to look out for you.

How Employers View Today's Job Market

From the employer's perspective, the employment process is always a question of balance. A stable workforce improves business performance, yet many employers feel they need the flexibility to shrink and expand payrolls as business conditions change. Rather than looking for long-term employees for every position, many employers now fill some needs by hiring temporary workers or engaging contractors on a project-by-project basis. The broader and deeper your skills are, the more attractive you will be—as an employee or an independent contractor, if you choose that route at some point.

The nature of the job market fluctuates with the ups and downs of the economy.

Many U.S. employers are now also more willing to move jobs to cheaper labor markets outside the country and to recruit globally to fill positions in the United States. Both trends have stirred controversy, especially in the technology sector, as U.S. firms have recruited top engineers and scientists from other countries while shifting mid- and low-range jobs to India, China, Russia, and other countries with lower wage structures.[3]

Employers also struggle with the ups and downs of the economy. When unemployment is low, the balance of power shifts to employees, who are then better positioned to ask for better wages and benefits. When unemployment is high, the power shifts back to employers, who can afford to be more selective and less accommodating. In other words, pay attention to the economy whenever you're job hunting.

What Employers Look For in Job Applicants

Given the forces in the contemporary workplace, employers are looking for people who are able and willing to adapt to the new dynamics of the business world, can survive and thrive in fluid and uncertain situations, and continue to learn throughout their careers. Companies want team players with strong work records, leaders who are versatile, and employees with diversified skills and varied job experience.[4] In addition, most employers expect college graduates to be sensitive to intercultural differences and to have a sound understanding of international affairs.[5] In fact, in some cases, your chances of being hired are better if you've studied abroad, learned another language, or can otherwise demonstrate an appreciation of other cultures.

Most employers value employees who are flexible, adaptable, and sensitive to the complex dynamics of today's business world.

385

Adapting to Today's Job Market

Adapting to the workplace is a lifelong process of seeking the best fit between what you want to do and what employers are willing to pay you to do. Start your career quest by figuring out what you want to do, what you have to offer, and how to make yourself more attractive to employers.

What Do You Want to Do?

Economic necessities and the vagaries of the marketplace will influence much of what happens in your career, of course; nevertheless, it's wise to start your employment search by examining your own values and interests.

- **What would you like to do every day?** Research occupations that interest you.
- **How would you like to work?** How much variety do you like? Do you prefer to work with products, machines, people, ideas, figures, or some combination?
- **What specific compensation do you expect?** What's your ultimate goal? Are you willing to settle for less money in order to do something you really love?
- **Can you establish some general career goals?** Consider where you'd like to start, where you'd like to go from there, and the ultimate position you'd like to attain.
- **What size company would you prefer?** Do you like the idea of working for a small, entrepreneurial operation or a large corporation?
- **What sort of corporate culture are you most comfortable with?** Casual or formal? Teamwork or individualism? Do you like or loathe competitive environments?
- **What location would you like?** Would you like to work in a city, a suburb, a small town, an industrial area, or an uptown setting?

What Do You Have to Offer?

Knowing what you *want* to do is one thing. Knowing what you *can* do is another. You may already have a good idea of what you can offer employers. If not, some brainstorming can help you identify your skills, interests, and characteristics. Start by jotting down ten achievements you're proud of, then think carefully about what specific skills these achievements demanded of you. As you analyze your achievements, you'll begin to recognize a pattern of skills. Which of them might be valuable to potential employers?

Next, look at your educational preparation, work experience, and extracurricular activities. What do your knowledge and experience qualify you to do? What have you learned from volunteer work or class projects that could benefit you on the job? Have you held any offices, won any awards or scholarships, mastered a second language?

Take stock of your personal characteristics. Are you aggressive, a born leader? Or would you rather follow? Are you outgoing, articulate, great with people? Or do you prefer working alone? Make a list of what you believe are your four or five most important qualities. Ask a relative or friend to rate your traits as well.

If you're having difficulty figuring out your interests, characteristics, or capabilities, consult your college placement office for tests that can help you identify interests, aptitudes, and personality traits.

How Can You Make Yourself More Valuable?

While you're figuring out what you want from a job and what you can offer an employer, you can take positive steps now toward building your career:

- **Keep an employment portfolio.** Your portfolio is a great resource for writing your résumé, and it gives employers tangible evidence of your professionalism. Collect anything that shows your ability to perform, whether it's in school, on the job, or in other venues. Many colleges now offer students the chance to create an *e-portfolio*, a multimedia presentation of your skills and experiences. It's an extensive résumé that links to an electronic collection of your student papers, solutions to tough problems, internship and work projects, and anything else that demonstrates your accomplishments

Have you thought long and hard about what you really want to do in your career? The choices you make now could influence your life for years to come.

No matter what profession you're in, you are a valuable package of skills and capabilities; make sure you have a clear picture of your own strengths.

Your college placement office can point you to a variety of tests to gauge your interest and suitability for a variety of career possibilities.

Take an active approach to making yourself a more attractive job candidate—and it's never too early to start.

and activities.[6] To distribute the portfolio to potential employers, you can burn a CD-ROM or store your portfolio on a website—whether a personal site, your college's site (if student pages are available), or a site such as www.collegegrad.com. (However, you *must* check with an employer before including any items that belong to the company or contain sensitive information.)

- **Take interim assignments.** As you search for a permanent job, consider temporary jobs, freelance work, or internships. These short-term assignments help you gain valuable experience, contacts, important references, and items for your portfolio.[7]
- **Continue to polish and update your skills.** Take courses and pursue other educational or life experiences that would be hard to get while working full-time.

Even after an employer hires you, continue to improve your skills in order to distinguish yourself from your peers. Acquire as much technical knowledge as you can, build broad-based life experience, and develop your social skills. Learn to respond to change in positive, constructive ways; doing so will help you adapt if your "perfect" career path eludes your grasp. Learn to see every job or project as an opportunity to learn and expand. And share what you know with others; helping others excel is a skill, too.[8]

> Keep your eyes and your mind open as you approach every experience in school, part-time jobs, and social engagements.

Securing Employment in Today's Job Market

After you've armed yourself with knowledge of today's workplace and your potential role in it, it's time to launch an efficient, productive process to find that ideal position. Figure 13.1 shows the six most important tasks in the job search process. This chapter discusses the first two, and Chapter 14 explores the final four. The more you know about this process, the more successful you'll be in your job search. Plus, it's important to keep in mind that employers and job candidates approach the process differently.

Understanding Employers' Approach to the Employment Process

You can save considerable time and effort by understanding how employers approach the recruiting process (see Figure 13.2). Generally, employers prefer to look for candidates within their own organization or through referrals from people they know and trust.

FIGURE 13.1   The Employment Search
Finding the ideal job opportunity is a six-step process.

FIGURE 13.2   How Organizations Prefer to Find New Employees

Employers often prefer to look at their existing workforce to find candidates for new jobs and promotions. If no suitable candidates can be found, they'll begin to look outside the firm, starting with people whom company insiders already know.

Most Preferred				Least Preferred
1. Look for someone inside the organization	**2.** Rely on contacts and personal recommendations	**3.** Hire an employment agency or search firm	**4.** Review unsolicited résumés	**5.** Place help-wanted ads

It's important to understand that the easiest way for you to find jobs (through companies' help-wanted advertising) is the least-preferred channel for many companies to find new employees.

Personal contacts are often a prime source of jobs, regardless of whether a candidate has just graduated from college or has been out of school for several years.[9]

Many employers send representatives to college campuses to conduct student interviews, which are usually coordinated by the campus placement office. In addition, many employers accept unsolicited résumés, and most keep unsolicited résumés on file or in a database. Employers recruit candidates through employment agencies, state employment services, temporary staffing services, and the employment bureaus operated by some trade associations. They also post jobs through ads in newspapers, trade magazines, campus publications, their own websites, and job sites such as www.monster.com. A variety of specialty websites are now springing up as well, focusing on narrow parts of the job market or offering technology that promises to do a better job of matching employers and job searchers. For example, www.mkt10.com lets applicants know how their chances compare with those of other people applying for the same jobs and suggests alternative jobs that might be better fits.[10]

Looking at Figure 13.2, you'll notice that the easiest way for you to find out about new opportunities—through the employer's outside advertising—is the employer's least-preferred way of finding new employees. As many as 80 percent of all job openings are never advertised, a phenomenon known as the *hidden job market*.[11] To find the best opportunities, it's up to you to take action to get yourself noticed.

Organizing Your Approach to the Employment Process

The employment process can consume many hours of your time over weeks or months, so organize your efforts in a logical, careful manner to save time. Begin by finding out where the job opportunities are, which industries are strong, which parts of the country are booming, and which specific job categories offer the best prospects for the future. From there you can investigate individual organizations, doing your best to learn as much about them as possible.

Staying Abreast of Business and Financial News

With so many print and electronic resources available today, it's easy to stay in touch with what's happening in the business world.

If you have regular access to the Internet, staying on top of business news is easy today. To help you get started, here is a small selection of the many websites that offer business news (some content may require subscriptions):

- *Wall Street Journal*: http://online.wsj.com/public/us
- *New York Times*: www.nyt.com
- *USA Today*: www.usatoday.com
- *BusinessWeek*: www.businessweek.com
- *Business 2.0*: www.business2.com

- *Fast Company*: www.fastcompany.com
- *Fortune*: www.fortune.com
- *Forbes*: www.forbes.com

Use a news aggregator (see Chapter 10) to select the type of stories you're interested in and have them delivered to your screen automatically. As you collect information, start by examining "big-picture" topics—trends, issues, industrywide challenges, and careers—before delving into specific companies that look attractive.

Researching Specific Companies

Once you've identified a promising industry and career field, consult directories of employers at your college library, at your career center, or on the Internet, and compile a list of specific organizations that appeal to you.

As you probably already know, a staggering amount of company and employment information is available online. On company websites, look for the "About Us" or "Company" page to find a company profile, executive biographies, press releases, financial information, and information on employment opportunities. Other pages will provide information on products, locations, and employee benefits. Look for outside sources as well, including the business sections of local newspapers and trade publications that cover the company's industries and markets.

Go beyond every company's own communication materials; find out what others in their industries and communities think about them.

Table 13.1 lists some of the many websites where you can learn more about companies and find job openings. Start with The Riley Guide, www.rileyguide.com, which offers links to hundreds of specialized websites that post openings in specific industries and professions. Your college's career center placement office probably maintains an up-to-date list as well.

Networking

Networking is the process of making informal connections with mutually beneficial business contacts. According to one recent survey, networking is the most common way that employees find jobs.[12] Networking takes place wherever and whenever people talk: at industry functions, at social gatherings, at sports events and recreational activities, in online newsgroups, at alumni reunions, and so on. Read news sites, blogs, and other online sources. Participate in student business organizations, especially those with ties to professional organizations. Visit trade shows to learn about various industries and rub shoulders with people who work in those industries.[13] Don't overlook volunteering; you not only meet people but also demonstrate your ability to solve problems, plan projects, and so on. You can do some good while creating a network for yourself.

Networking with other professionals who have similar interests can be a great way to build your career.

To become a valued network member, you need to be able to help others in some way. You may not have any influential contacts yet, but because you're actively researching a number of industries and trends in your own job search, you probably have valuable information you can share. Or you might simply be able to connect one person with another person who can help. The more you network, the more valuable you become in your network—and the more valuable your network becomes to you.

Seeking Career Counseling

College placement offices offer individual counseling, credential services, job fairs, on-campus interviews, and job listings. They can give you advice on résumé-writing software and provide workshops in job search techniques, résumé preparation, interview techniques, and more.[14] You can also find job counseling online. You might begin your self-assessment, for example, with the Keirsey Temperament Sorter, an online personality test at www.advisorteam.com. For excellent job-seeking pointers and counseling, visit college- and university-run online career centers. Major online job boards such as Monster.com also offer a variety of career planning resources.

Don't overlook the many resources available through your college's placement office.

Table 13.1	Netting a Job on the Web	
Website*	**URL**	**Highlights**
Riley Guide	www.rileyguide.com	Vast collection of links to both general and specialized job sites for every career imaginable; don't miss this one—it'll save you hours and hours of searching
Monster	www.monster.com	One of the most popular job sites, with hundreds of thousands of openings, many from hard-to-find smaller companies; extensive collection of advice on the job search process
MonsterTrak	www.monstertrak.com	Focused on job searches for new college grads; your school's career-center site probably links here
Yahoo! Hotjobs	http://hotjobs.yahoo.com	Another leading job board, formed by recent merger of Hotjobs and Yahoo! Careers
CareerBuilder	www.careerbuilder.com	Fast-growing site affiliated with more than 100 local newspapers around the country
USA Jobs	www.usajobs.opm.gov	The official job search site for the U.S. government, featuring everything from economists to astronauts to border patrol agents
IMDiversity	www.imdiversity.com	Good resource on diversity in the workplace, with job postings from companies that have made a special commitment to promoting diversity in their workforces
Dice.com	www.dice.com	One of the best sites for high-technology jobs
Net-Temps	www.nettemps.com	Popular site for contractors and freelancers looking for short-term assignments
InternshipPrograms.com	www.internships.wetfeet.com	Posts listings from companies looking for interns in a wide variety of professions
SimplyHired.com Indeed.com	www.simplyhired.com www.indeed.com	Specialized search engines that look for job postings on hundreds of websites worldwide; they find many postings that aren't listed on "job board" sites such as Monster.com

* Note: This list represents only a small fraction of the hundreds of job-posting sites and other resources available online; be sure to check with your college's career center for the latest information.

Preparing Résumés

To distinguish yourself from all the other people looking for work, you need to start with a well-written résumé. Some job searchers are intimidated by the prospect of writing a résumé, but your résumé is really just another specialized business message. Follow the three-step writing process, and it'll be easier than you thought (see Figure 13.3).

Planning Your Résumé

As with other business messages, planning a résumé means analyzing your purpose and your audience, gathering information, choosing the best medium, and organizing your content.

FIGURE 13.3   Three-Step Writing Process for Résumés

Writing your résumé doesn't need to be a long, painful experience if you follow the three-step writing process. Pay particular attention to the "you" attitude and quality throughout; your résumé will probably get tossed aside if it doesn't speak to audience needs or if it has mistakes.

Planning

Analyze the Situation
Recognize that the purpose of your résumé is to get an interview, not to get a job.

Gather Information
Research target industries and companies so that you know what they're looking for in new hires; learn about various jobs and what to expect.

Select the Right Medium
Start with a traditional paper résumé and develop scannable, plain text, or HTML versions as needed.

Organize the Information
Choose an organizational model that highlights your strengths and downplays your shortcomings.

1

Writing

Adapt to Your Audience
Plan your wording carefully so that you can catch a recruiter's eye within seconds; translate your education and experience into attributes that target employers find valuable.

Compose the Message
Write clearly and succinctly, using active, powerful language that is appropriate to the industries and companies you're targeting; use a professional tone in all communications, even when using e-mail.

2

Completing

Revise the Message
Evaluate your content and review readability, clarity, and accuracy.

Produce the Message
Use effective design elements and suitable layout for a clean, professional appearance.

Proofread the Message
Review for errors in layout, spelling, and mechanics; mistakes can cost you interview opportunities.

Distribute the Message
Deliver your résumé following the specific instructions of each employer or job board website.

3

Analyzing Your Purpose and Audience

A **résumé** is a structured, written summary of a person's education, employment background, and job qualifications. (By the way, if employers ask to see your "CV," they're referring to your *curriculum vitae*, the term used instead of *résumé* in some professions and in many countries outside the United States.) Before you begin writing a résumé, make sure you understand its true function—as an advertisement intended to stimulate an employer's interest in meeting you and learning more about you (see Table 13.2).

> Once you view your résumé as a persuasive business message, it's easier to decide what should and shouldn't be in it.

Table 13.2 Fallacies and Facts About Résumés	
Fallacy	**Fact**
• The purpose of a résumé is to list all your skills and abilities.	• The purpose of a résumé is to kindle employer interest and generate an interview.
• A good résumé will get you the job you want.	• All a résumé can do is get you in the door.
• Your résumé will be read carefully and thoroughly by an interested employer.	• Your résumé probably has less than 45 seconds to make an impression.
• The more good information you present about yourself in your résumé, the better.	• Too much information on a résumé may actually kill the reader's appetite to know more.
• If you want a really good résumé, have it prepared by a résumé service.	• Prepare your own résumé—unless the position is especially high-level or specialized. Even then, you should check carefully before using a service.

A successful résumé inspires a prospective employer to invite you to interview with the company. Thus, your purpose in writing your résumé is to create interest—*not* to tell readers every little detail.[15]

Since you've already completed a good deal of research on specific companies, you should know quite a bit about the organizations you'll be applying to. But take some time now to learn what you can about the individuals who may be reading your résumé. If you're applying to a Fortune 500 company, you may have to make some educated guesses about the people in the human resources department and what their needs might be. But in smaller companies, you may be able to learn the name of the recruiter or manager you'll be addressing. Either way, try to put yourself in your audience's position so that you'll be able to tailor your résumé to satisfy your audience's needs. Why would they be interested in learning more about you?

Gathering Pertinent Information

If you haven't been keeping a log or journal of your accomplishments so far, you may need to do some research on yourself. Gather all the pertinent personal history you can think of, including all the specific dates, duties, and accomplishments of any previous jobs you've held. Itemize your educational experience, including degrees, skills certificates, academic awards, and scholarships. Also, gather any relevant information about personal endeavors such as offices held in nonprofit organizations or speeches given. You'll save time by having all this material at your fingertips before you begin composing your résumé.

Selecting the Best Medium

Your job search might involve various media formats, including an uploaded Word document, a plain text document that you paste into an online form, or a multimedia résumé available online or on CD-ROM. Your choice of medium involves the requirements of your target employers (many have specific instructions on their websites; follow these carefully) and the attributes you're trying to promote. For instance, if you're applying for a sales position, a video clip of yourself on CD-ROM can be a strong persuader.

However, as impressive as personal websites and CD-ROM e-portfolios are, it's always a good idea to prepare a basic paper résumé and keep copies on hand. You never know when someone might ask for it, and not all employers want to bother with electronic media when all they want to know is your basic profile.

Organizing Your Résumé Around Your Strengths

The key to organizing a résumé is aligning your personal strengths with both the general and specific qualities that your target employers are looking for.

The most successful résumés convey seven qualities that employers seek: They demonstrate that you (1) think in terms of results, (2) know how to get things done, (3) are well rounded, (4) show signs of career progress and professional development, (5) have personal standards of excellence, (6) are flexible and willing to try new things, and (7) communicate effectively.

Although you may want to include a little information in all categories, you'll naturally want to emphasize the information that does the best job of aligning your career objectives with the needs of your target employers—and that does so without misrepresenting the facts.[16] Do you have something in your history that might trigger an employer's red flag? Here are some common problems and some quick suggestions for overcoming them:[17]

Frequent job changes and gaps in your work history are two of the more common issues that employers may perceive as weaknesses.

- **Frequent job changes.** If you've had a number of short-term jobs of a similar nature, such as independent contracting and temporary assignments, see if you can group them under a single heading. Also, if you were a victim of circumstances in positions that were eliminated as a result of mergers or other factors beyond your control, find a subtle way to convey that information.

- **Gaps in work history.** Mention relevant experience and education you gained during employment gaps, such as volunteer or community work.
- **Inexperience.** Mention related volunteer work. List relevant course work and internships. Also, offer hiring incentives such as "willing to work nights and weekends."
- **Overqualification.** Tone down your résumé, focusing exclusively on the experience and skills that relate to the position.
- **Long-term employment with one company.** Itemize each position held at the firm to show "interior mobility" and increased responsibilities.
- **Job termination for cause.** Be honest with interviewers. Show that you're a hardworking employee and counter their concerns with proof, such as recommendations and examples of completed projects.
- **Criminal record.** Opinions differ on whether to divulge a criminal record on your résumé, although you must do so if you're asked a legal question on the matter during an interview or on an application form.

To focus attention on your strongest points, adopt the appropriate organizational approach—make your résumé chronological, functional, or a combination of the two. The "right" choice depends on your background and your goals.

The Chronological Résumé   In a **chronological résumé**, the work experience section dominates and is placed immediately after the name and address and optional objective. You develop this section by listing your jobs sequentially in reverse order, beginning with the most recent position and working backward toward earlier jobs. Under each listing, describe your responsibilities and accomplishments, giving the most space to the most recent positions (see Figures 13.4 and 13.5 for examples of ineffective and effective approaches). If you're just graduating from college with limited professional experience, you can vary this chronological approach by putting your educational qualifications before your experience.

The chronological approach is the most common way to organize a résumé, and many employers prefer it. This approach has three key advantages: (1) Employers are familiar with it and can easily find information, (2) it highlights growth and career progression, and (3) it highlights employment continuity and stability.[18] Recruiter Robert Nesbit speaks for many employers: "Unless you have a really compelling reason, don't use any but the standard chronological format. Your résumé should not read like a treasure map, full of minute clues to the whereabouts of your jobs and experience. I want to be able to grasp quickly where a candidate has worked, how long, and in what capacities."[19]

> The chronological résumé is the most common approach, but it might not be right for you at a particular stage in your career.

The Functional Résumé   A **functional résumé**, sometimes called a *skills résumé*, emphasizes your skills and capabilities, identifying employers and academic experience in subordinate sections. This pattern stresses individual areas of competence rather than job history. The functional approach also has three advantages: (1) Without having to read through job descriptions, employers can see what you can do for them, (2) you can emphasize earlier job experience, and (3) you can deemphasize any lack of career progress or lengthy unemployment. However, you should be aware that because the functional résumé can obscure your work history, many employment professionals are suspicious of it—and some assume that candidates who use it are trying to hide something. In fact, Monster.com lists the functional résumé as one of employers' "Top 10 Pet Peeves."[20]

> The functional résumé is often considered by people with limited or spotty employment history, but many employers are suspicious of this résumé format.

The Combination Résumé   A **combination résumé** includes the best features of the chronological and functional approaches (see Figure 13.6). Nevertheless, it is not commonly used, and it has two major disadvantages: (1) It tends to be longer, and (2) it can be repetitive if you have to list your accomplishments and skills in both the functional section and the chronological job descriptions.[21]

> If you don't have a lot of work history to show, consider a combination résumé to highlight your skills while still providing a chronological history of your employment.

FIGURE 13.4   Ineffective Chronological Résumé

This chronological résumé exhibits a wide range of problems. The language is self-centered and unprofessional, and the organization forces the reader to dig out essential details—and today's recruiters don't have the time or the patience for that. Compare this with the improved version in Figure 13.5.

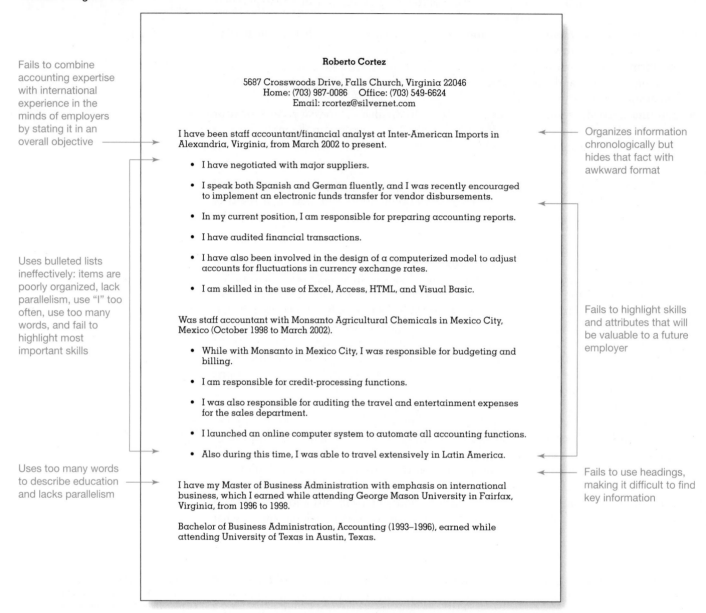

Fails to combine accounting expertise with international experience in the minds of employers by stating it in an overall objective

Uses bulleted lists ineffectively: items are poorly organized, lack parallelism, use "I" too often, use too many words, and fail to highlight most important skills

Uses too many words to describe education and lacks parallelism

Organizes information chronologically but hides that fact with awkward format

Fails to highlight skills and attributes that will be valuable to a future employer

Fails to use headings, making it difficult to find key information

Roberto Cortez

5687 Crosswoods Drive, Falls Church, Virginia 22046
Home: (703) 987-0086   Office: (703) 549-6624
Email: rcortez@silvernet.com

I have been staff accountant/financial analyst at Inter-American Imports in Alexandria, Virginia, from March 2002 to present.

- I have negotiated with major suppliers.

- I speak both Spanish and German fluently, and I was recently encouraged to implement an electronic funds transfer for vendor disbursements.

- In my current position, I am responsible for preparing accounting reports.

- I have audited financial transactions.

- I have also been involved in the design of a computerized model to adjust accounts for fluctuations in currency exchange rates.

- I am skilled in the use of Excel, Access, HTML, and Visual Basic.

Was staff accountant with Monsanto Agricultural Chemicals in Mexico City, Mexico (October 1998 to March 2002).

- While with Monsanto in Mexico City, I was responsible for budgeting and billing.

- I am responsible for credit-processing functions.

- I was also responsible for auditing the travel and entertainment expenses for the sales department.

- I launched an online computer system to automate all accounting functions.

- Also during this time, I was able to travel extensively in Latin America.

I have my Master of Business Administration with emphasis on international business, which I earned while attending George Mason University in Fairfax, Virginia, from 1996 to 1998.

Bachelor of Business Administration, Accounting (1993–1996), earned while attending University of Texas in Austin, Texas.

As you look at a number of sample résumés, you'll probably notice variations on the three basic formats presented here. Study these other options in light of effective communication principles; if you find one that seems like the best fit for your unique situation, by all means use it.

Writing Your Résumé

Until employers meet you in person, your résumé (and perhaps your cover letter) is usually the only information they have about you, so make sure that information is clear and compelling.

As you follow the three-step process to develop your résumé, keep four points in mind. First, treat your résumé with the respect it deserves. Until you're able to meet with employers in person, you *are* your résumé, and a single mistake or oversight can cost you interview opportunities. Second, give yourself plenty of time. Don't put off preparing

FIGURE 13.5 Effective Chronological Résumé

This version does a much better job of presenting the candidate's ability to contribute to a new employer. Notice in particular how easy it is to scan through this résumé to find sections of interest.

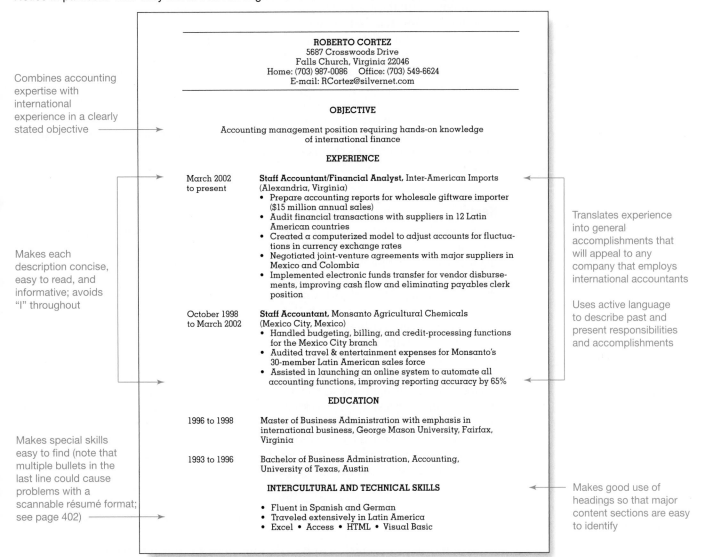

Combines accounting expertise with international experience in a clearly stated objective

Makes each description concise, easy to read, and informative; avoids "I" throughout

Makes special skills easy to find (note that multiple bullets in the last line could cause problems with a scannable résumé format; see page 402)

ROBERTO CORTEZ
5687 Crosswoods Drive
Falls Church, Virginia 22046
Home: (703) 987-0086   Office: (703) 549-6624
E-mail: RCortez@silvernet.com

OBJECTIVE

Accounting management position requiring hands-on knowledge
of international finance

EXPERIENCE

March 2002 to present — **Staff Accountant/Financial Analyst,** Inter-American Imports (Alexandria, Virginia)
- Prepare accounting reports for wholesale giftware importer ($15 million annual sales)
- Audit financial transactions with suppliers in 12 Latin American countries
- Created a computerized model to adjust accounts for fluctuations in currency exchange rates
- Negotiated joint-venture agreements with major suppliers in Mexico and Colombia
- Implemented electronic funds transfer for vendor disbursements, improving cash flow and eliminating payables clerk position

October 1998 to March 2002 — **Staff Accountant,** Monsanto Agricultural Chemicals (Mexico City, Mexico)
- Handled budgeting, billing, and credit-processing functions for the Mexico City branch
- Audited travel & entertainment expenses for Monsanto's 30-member Latin American sales force
- Assisted in launching an online system to automate all accounting functions, improving reporting accuracy by 65%

EDUCATION

1996 to 1998 — Master of Business Administration with emphasis in international business, George Mason University, Fairfax, Virginia

1993 to 1996 — Bachelor of Business Administration, Accounting, University of Texas, Austin

INTERCULTURAL AND TECHNICAL SKILLS

- Fluent in Spanish and German
- Traveled extensively in Latin America
- Excel • Access • HTML • Visual Basic

Translates experience into general accomplishments that will appeal to any company that employs international accountants

Uses active language to describe past and present responsibilities and accomplishments

Makes good use of headings so that major content sections are easy to identify

---

Planning

Analyze the Situation
Decide on the best way to combine finance and international experience.

Gather Information
Research target positions to identify key employer needs.

Select the Right Medium
Start with a traditional paper résumé and develop scannable or plain text versions as needed.

Organize the Information
Choose the chronological format since it fits this strong employment history perfectly.

Writing

Adapt to Your Audience
Translate specific experience into general qualifications that all international companies will find valuable.

Compose the Message
Write clearly and succinctly, using active, powerful language that is appropriate to the financial management profession.

Completing

Revise the Message
Evaluate your content and review readability, clarity, and accuracy.

Produce the Message
Use effective design elements and suitable layout for a clean, professional appearance.

Proofread the Message
Review for errors in layout, spelling, and mechanics.

Distribute the Message
Deliver your résumé and other employment messages following the specific instructions of each employer or job board website.

1   **2**   **3**

your résumé until the last second and then try to write it in one sitting. Third, learn from good models. You can find thousands of sample résumés online at college websites and job sites such as Monster.com. Fourth, don't get frustrated by the conflicting advice you'll read about résumés; they are more art than science. Consider the alternatives and choose the approach that makes the most sense to you, given everything you know about successful business communication.

If you feel uncomfortable writing about yourself, you're not alone. Many people, even accomplished writers, find it difficult to write their own résumés. If you get stuck, find a classmate or friend who is also writing a résumé and swap projects for a while. By working on each other's résumés, you might be able to speed up the process for both of you.

Keeping Your Résumé Honest

Résumé fraud has reached epidemic proportions, but employers are fighting back with more rigorous screening techniques.

Somehow, the idea that "everybody lies on their résumés" has crept into popular consciousness, and dishonesty in the job search process has reached epidemic proportions. As many as half of the résumés now sent to employers contain false information. And it's not just the simple fudging of a fact here and there. Dishonest applicants are getting bolder all the time—buying fake diplomas online, paying a computer hacker to insert their names into prestigious universities' graduation records, and signing up for services that offer phony employment verification.[22]

Applicants with integrity know they don't need to stoop to lying to compete in the job market. If you are tempted to stretch the truth, bear in mind that professional recruiters have seen every trick in the book, and employers who are fed up with the dishonesty are getting more aggressive at uncovering the truth. Nearly all employers do some form of background checking, from contacting references to verifying employment to checking for criminal records. In addition to using their own resources, U.S. companies now spend more than $2 billion a year on outside services that specialize in verifying résumés and application information.[23] In a recent survey in Great Britain, 25 percent of employers reported withdrawing job offers after discovering that applicants lied on their résumés.[24] And even if you were to get past these filters, you'd probably be exposed on the job when you couldn't live up to your own résumé. Résumé fabrications have been known to catch up to people many years into their careers, with embarrassing consequences.

If you're not sure whether to include something in your résumé, ask yourself this: Would you be willing to say the same thing to an interviewer in person? If you wouldn't be comfortable saying it in person, don't say it in your résumé. Keep your résumé honest so that it represents who you really are and leads you toward jobs that are truly right for you.

Adapting Your Résumé to Your Audience

No matter which format you use or what information you include, the single most important concept to keep in mind as you write your résumé is to translate your past accomplishments into perceived future potential. In other words, employers are certainly interested in what you've done in the past, but they're more interested in what you can do for them in the future. If necessary, customize your résumé for individual companies, too.

Keep in mind that you may need to "translate" your skills and experiences into the terminology of the hiring organization. For instance, military experience can develop a number of skills that are valuable in business, but military terminology can sound like a foreign language to people who aren't familiar with it. Isolate the important general concepts and present them in common business language. Similarly, educational achievements in other countries might not align with the standard U.S. definitions of high schools, community colleges, technical and trade schools, and universities. If necessary, include a brief statement explaining how your degree or certificate relates to U.S. expectations—or how your U.S. degree relates to expectations in other countries, if you're applying for work abroad.

FIGURE 13.6 Combination Résumé

With her limited work experience in her field of interest, Erica Vorkamp opted for a combination résumé to highlight her skills. Her employment history is complete and easy to find, but it isn't featured to the same degree as the other elements. Also, because she created an HTML version and posted it on her personal website, she is able to provide instant links to other information, such as samples of her work and testimonials from people who have worked with her in the past.

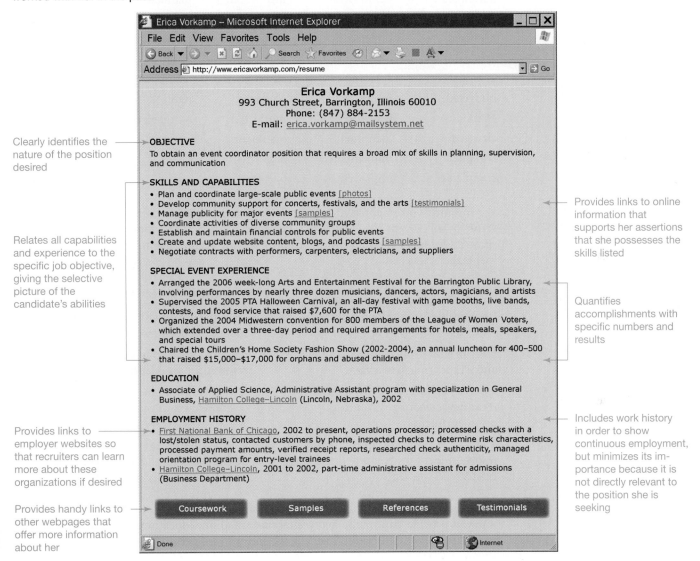

Clearly identifies the nature of the position desired

Relates all capabilities and experience to the specific job objective, giving the selective picture of the candidate's abilities

Provides links to employer websites so that recruiters can learn more about these organizations if desired

Provides handy links to other webpages that offer more information about her

Provides links to online information that supports her assertions that she possesses the skills listed

Quantifies accomplishments with specific numbers and results

Includes work history in order to show continuous employment, but minimizes its importance because it is not directly relevant to the position she is seeking

---

Regardless of your background, it's up to you to combine your experiences into a straightforward message that communicates what you can do for your potential employer.[25] Think in terms of an image or a theme you'd like to project. Are you academically gifted? A campus leader? A well-rounded person? A creative genius? A technical wizard? By knowing yourself and your audience, you'll focus successfully on the strengths needed by potential employers.

Although your résumé is a highly factual document, it should still tell the "story of you," giving readers a clear picture of the sort of employee you are.

Composing Your Résumé

Write your résumé using a simple and direct style. Use short, crisp phrases instead of whole sentences, and focus on what your reader needs to know. Avoid using the word *I*, which can sound both self-involved and repetitious by the time you outline all

Draft your résumé using short, crisp phrases built around strong verbs and nouns.

your skills and accomplishments. Instead, start your phrases with strong action verbs such as these:[26]

accomplished	coordinated	initiated	participated	set up
achieved	created	installed	performed	simplified
administered	demonstrated	introduced	planned	sparked
approved	developed	investigated	presented	streamlined
arranged	directed	joined	proposed	strengthened
assisted	established	launched	raised	succeeded
assumed	explored	maintained	recommended	supervised
budgeted	forecasted	managed	reduced	systematized
chaired	generated	motivated	reorganized	targeted
changed	identified	operated	resolved	trained
compiled	implemented	organized	saved	transformed
completed	improved	oversaw	served	upgraded

For instance, you might say, "Implemented a new patient-tracking system that reduced errors by 80 percent" or "Managed a fast-food restaurant and four employees." Here are some additional examples of how to phrase your accomplishments using active statements that show results:

Instead of This	Write Active Statements That Show Results
Responsible for developing a new filing system	Developed a new filing system that reduced paperwork by 50 percent
I was in charge of customer complaints and all ordering problems	Handled all customer complaints and resolved all product order discrepancies
I won a trip to Europe for opening the most new customer accounts in my department	Generated the highest number of new customer accounts in my department
Member of special campus task force to resolve student problems with existing cafeteria assignments	Assisted in implementing new campus dining program that balances student wishes with cafeteria capacity

In addition to presenting your accomplishments effectively, think carefully about the way you provide your name and contact information, educational credentials, employment history, activities and achievements, and relevant personal data.

Be sure to provide complete and accurate contact information; mistakes in this section of the résumé are surprisingly common.

Name and Contact Information   Employers obviously need to know who you are and where you can be reached. Your name and contact information constitute the heading of your résumé, so include the following:

- Your name
- Physical address (both permanent and temporary if you're likely to move during the job search process)
- E-mail address
- Phone number(s)
- The URL of your personal webpage or e-portfolio (if you have one)

Be sure that everything in your résumé heading is well organized and clearly laid out on the page.

If the only e-mail address you have is through your current employer, get a free personal e-mail address from one of the many services that offer them, such as Hotmail or

Yahoo!. It's not fair to your current employer to use company resources for a job search; moreover, it sends a bad signal to potential employers. Also, if your personal e-mail address is anything like *precious.princess@something.com* or *PsychoDawg@something.com*, get a new e-mail address for your business correspondence.

Career Objective or Summary of Qualifications   Experts disagree about the need to state a career objective on your résumé. Some argue that your objective is obvious from your qualifications, so stating your objective seems redundant. Some also maintain that such a statement labels you as being interested in only one thing and thus limits your possibilities as a candidate (especially if you want to be considered for a variety of openings). Other experts argue that employers will try to categorize you anyway, so you might as well make sure they attach the right label. They maintain that stating your objective up front gives employers an immediate idea of what you're all about.

Remember, your goal is to generate interest immediately. Consider the situation and the qualities the employer is looking for. If a stated objective will help you look like the perfect fit, then you should definitely consider adding it, as these two examples do:

A software sales position in a growing company requiring international experience

Advertising assistant with print media emphasis requiring strong customer-contact skills

Both these objectives have an important aspect: Even though they are stating "your" objective, they are really about the employer's needs. Avoid such self-absorbed statements as "A fulfilling position that provides ample opportunity for career growth and personal satisfaction." Writers who include such statements have completely forgotten about audience focus and the "you" attitude.

A good alternative to a simple statement of career objectives is to highlight your strongest points in a brief *summary of qualifications*. A good summary of qualifications not only identifies the type of job you're interested in but also gives employers a compelling reason to consider you. Use short, direct phrases that highlight what you can bring to a new employer:

Summary of qualifications: Ten years of experience in commission selling, consistently meeting or exceeding sales goals through creative lead generation, effective closing techniques, and solid customer service.

Whether you opt for a career objective or a summary of qualifications, make it strong, concise, and convincing.

Education   If you're still in school or recently graduated, education is probably your strongest selling point. Present your educational background in depth, choosing facts that support your "theme." Starting with the most recent, list the name and location of each school you attended, along with the term of your enrollment (in months and years), your major and minor fields of study, significant skills and abilities you've developed in your course work, and the degrees or certificates you've earned. If you're still working toward a degree, include in parentheses the expected date of completion. Highlight courses that are particularly relevant to the job you are seeking, and indicate any scholarships, awards, or academic honors you've received.

The education section also includes off-campus training sponsored by business or government. Include any relevant seminars or workshops you've attended, as well as the certificates or other documents you've received. Mention high school or military training only if the associated achievements are pertinent to your career goals.

Whether you list your grade point average depends on the job you want and the quality of your grades. If you choose to show a grade point average, be sure to mention the scale, especially if it isn't a four-point scale. If your grades are better within your major than in other courses, you can also list your GPA as "Major GPA" and include only those courses within your major.

Get a professional-sounding e-mail address for business correspondence (such as firstname.lastname@ something.com), if you don't already have one.

Whether you choose to open with a career objective or a summary of qualifications, remember that the important point is to generate interest immediately.

Your education might be one of your strongest selling points, so think carefully about how you will present it.

When you describe past job responsibilities, be sure to relate them to the needs of potential employers—identify the skills and knowledge from these previous jobs that you can apply to a future job.

Work Experience, Skills, and Accomplishments   Like the education section, the work experience section should focus on your overall theme. Align your past with the employer's future. Call attention to the skills you've developed on the job and to your ability to handle increasing responsibility. If you have worked your way through school and contributed significantly to your education expenses, say so.

List your jobs in reverse chronological order and include any part-time, summer, or intern positions, even if unrelated to your current career objective. Include the name and location of the employer. If readers are unlikely to recognize the organization, briefly describe what it does. When you want to keep the name of your current employer confidential, you can identify the firm by industry only ("a large video-game developer"). If an organization's name or location has changed since you worked there, state the current name and location, and then include the old information as "formerly . . . ." Before or after each job listing, state your job title and give the years you worked in the job; use the phrase "to present" to denote current employment. Indicate whether a job was part-time.

Whenever you can, quantify your accomplishments in numerical terms: sales increases, customer satisfaction scores, measured productivity, and so on.

Devote the most space to the jobs that are related to your target position. If you were personally responsible for something significant, be sure to mention it. Facts about your skills and accomplishments are the most important information you can give a prospective employer, so quantify them whenever possible:

Designed a new ad that increased sales by 9 percent

Raised $2,500 in 15 days for cancer research

You may also include information describing other aspects of your background that pertain to your career objective, such as fluency in multiple languages. If samples of your work might increase your chances of getting the job, insert a line at the end of your résumé offering to supply them on request, or indicate they're available in your e-portfolio.

Don't overlook personal accomplishments that indicate special skills or qualities, but make sure they are relevant to the jobs you're seeking.

Activities and Achievements   Your résumé should describe any volunteer activities that demonstrate career-related abilities. List projects that require leadership, organization, teamwork, and cooperation. List skills you learned in these activities, and explain how these skills are related to the job for which you're applying. Include speaking, writing, or tutoring experience; participation in athletics or creative projects; fundraising or community-service activities; and offices held in academic or professional organizations. (However, mention of political or religious organizations may be a red flag to someone with differing views, so use your judgment.) Note any awards you've received and quantify your achievements whenever possible. If your activities have been extensive, you may want to combine them into related groups.

Personal Data   Personal data is another common source of confusion with résumés. Most experts advise you to skip personal interests unless including them enhances the employer's understanding of why you would be the best candidate for the job.[27] For instance, your achievements as an amateur artist could appeal to an advertising agency, even if you're applying for a technical or business position, because its shows an appreciation for the creative process.

Some information is best excluded from your résumé. Civil rights laws prohibit employers from discriminating on the basis of gender, marital or family status, age (although only persons aged 40 to 70 are protected), race, religion, national origin, and physical or mental disability. So be sure to exclude any items that could encourage discrimination, even subconsciously. Also exclude salary information, reasons for leaving jobs, names of previous supervisors, your Social Security number, and student ID number.

If military service is relevant to the position, you may list it in this section (or under "Education" or "Work Experience"). List the date of induction, the branch of service, where you served, the highest rank you achieved, any accomplishments related to your career goals, and the date you were discharged.

Completing Your Résumé

The last step in the three-step writing process is no less important than the other two. As with any other business message, you need to revise your résumé, produce it in an appropriate form, and proofread it for any errors before distributing it to your target employers.

Try to keep your résumé to one page. If you have a great deal of experience and are applying for a higher-level position, you may need to prepare a somewhat longer résumé. The important thing is to have enough space to present a persuasive, accurate, and concise portrait of your skills and accomplishments.

Revising Your Résumé

Ask professional recruiters to list the most common mistakes they see on résumés, and you'll hear the same things over and over again. Keep your résumé out of the recycling bin by avoiding these flaws:

Avoid the common errors that will get your résumé excluded from consideration.

- Too long or too wordy
- Too short or sketchy
- Hard to read
- Poorly written
- Displaying weak understanding of the business world or of a particular industry
- Poor-quality printing or cheap paper
- Full of spelling and grammar errors
- Boastful
- Gimmicky design

Producing Your Résumé

Good design is a must, and it's not hard to achieve. As you can see in Figures 13.4, 13.5, and 13.6, good designs feature simplicity, order, plenty of white space, and easy-to-read typefaces (note that many of the fonts on your computer are *not* appropriate for a résumé). Make your subheadings easy to find and easy to read, placing them either above each section or in the left margin. Use lists to itemize your most important qualifications, and leave plenty of white space, even if doing so forces you to use two pages rather than one. Color is not necessary by any means, but if you add color, make it subtle and sophisticated, such as in a thin horizontal line under your name and address. The most common way to get into trouble with résumé design is going overboard (see Figure 13.7).

Effective résumé designs are simple, clean, and professional—not gaudy, clever, or cute.

Depending on the companies you apply to, you might want to produce your résumé in as many as six forms (all are explained in the following sections):

Start with a traditional printed résumé, but realize that you may need to create several other versions during your job search.

- Printed traditional résumé
- Printed scannable résumé
- Electronic plain text file
- Microsoft Word file
- HTML format
- PDF file

Printing a Traditional Résumé   The traditional paper résumé still has a place in this world of electronic job searches, if only to have a few ready whenever one of your networking contacts asks for a copy. Paper falls into three general categories: basic, low-cost paper used for photocopying and printing (avoid this paper; it makes your résumé look cheap); predesigned papers with borders and backgrounds (avoid these; they make your résumé look gimmicky); and heavier, higher-quality papers designed specifically for résumés and other important documents. Choose a white or slightly off-white paper from this third category; these papers are more expensive, but you don't need much, and it's a worthwhile investment.

Strive for a clean, classy look in your printed résumé, using professional-grade paper and a clean, high-quality printer.

FIGURE 13.7 Ineffective Résumé Design

This truly jarring résumé exhibits numerous flaws: distracting lines, bad font choices, unprofessional colors. The well-written information is completely lost in all the visual "noise."

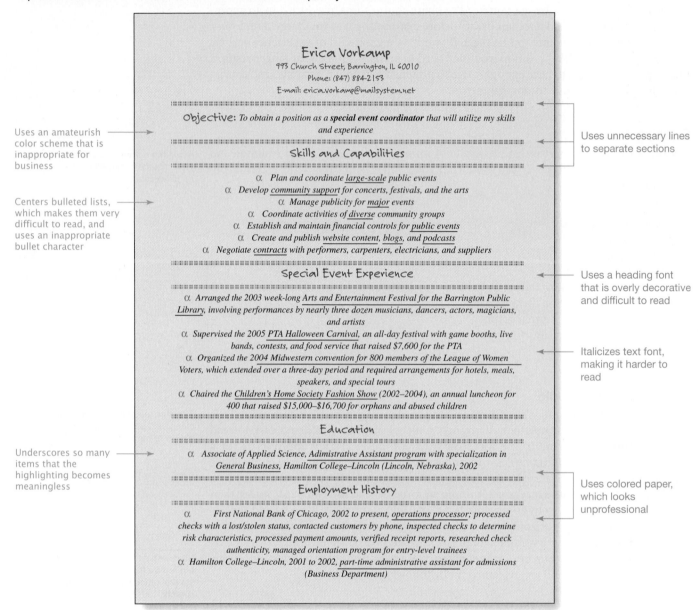

Uses an amateurish color scheme that is inappropriate for business

Centers bulleted lists, which makes them very difficult to read, and uses an inappropriate bullet character

Underscores so many items that the highlighting becomes meaningless

Uses unnecessary lines to separate sections

Uses a heading font that is overly decorative and difficult to read

Italicizes text font, making it harder to read

Uses colored paper, which looks unprofessional

Make sure the printer you use is well-maintained with adequate toner or ink. Don't tolerate any streaks, stray lines, or poor print quality. You wouldn't walk into an interview looking messy, so make sure your résumé doesn't look that way, either.

Printing a Scannable Résumé To cope with the flood of unsolicited paper résumés in recent years, many companies now optically scan incoming paper résumés into a database. When hiring managers want to interview candidates for job openings, they search the database for the most attractive candidates. These systems typically display a list of possible candidates, each with a percentage score indicating how closely the résumé reflects the employer's requirements.[28] Nearly all large companies now use these systems, as do many mid-sized companies and even some smaller firms.[29]

The emergence of such scanning systems has important implications for your résumé. First, the *optical character recognition* (*OCR*) software used in these systems doesn't actually "read" anything; it merely looks for shapes that match stored profiles of

Converting your résumé to scannable format is easy to do—and extremely important.

13: Building Careers and Writing Résumés

FIGURE 13.8   Scannable Résumé

This version of the chronological résumé from Figure 13.5 shows the changes necessary for it to be successfully scanned. Notice that it doesn't have any special characters or design elements that are likely to confuse the scanning software.

Removes all boldfacing, nontext characters such as bullets, and two-column formatting

Includes carefully selected keyword list derived from descriptions of target jobs

Uses a dash instead of bullet point character in bulleted lists

Uses ample white space to help ensure accurate scanning

Roberto Cortez
5687 Crosswoods Drive
Falls Church, Virginia 22046
Home phone: (703) 987-0086
Office phone: (703) 549-6624
E-mail: RCortez@silvernet.com

KEYWORDS

Financial executive, accounting management, international finance, financial analyst, accounting reports, financial audit, computerized accounting model, exchange rates, joint-venture agreements, budgets, billing, credit processing, online systems, MBA, fluent Spanish, fluent German, Excel, Access, Visual Basic, team player, willing to travel

OBJECTIVE

Accounting management position requiring hands-on knowledge of international finance

EXPERIENCE

Staff Accountant/Financial Analyst, Inter-American Imports (Alexandria, Virginia), March 2002 to present
— Prepare accounting reports for wholesale giftware importer ($15 million annual sales)
— Audit financial transactions with suppliers in 12 Latin American countries
— Created a computerized model to adjust for fluctuations in currency exchange rates
— Negotiated joint-venture agreements with major suppliers in Mexico and Colombia
— Implemented electronic funds transfer for vendor disbursements, improving cash flow and eliminating payables clerk position

Staff Accountant, Monsanto Agricultural Chemicals (Mexico City, Mexico), October 1998 to March 2002
— Handled budgeting, billing, and credit-processing functions for the Mexico City branch
— Audited travel & entertainment expenses for Monsanto's 30-member Latin American sales force
— Assisted in launching an online system to automate all accounting functions, improving reporting accuracy by 65%

EDUCATION

Master of Business Administration with emphasis in international business, George Mason University (Fairfax, Virginia), 1996 to 1998

Bachelor of Business Administration, Accounting, University of Texas (Austin, Texas), 1993 to 1996

INTERCULTURAL AND TECHNICAL SKILLS

— Fluent in Spanish and German
— Traveled extensively in Latin America
— Excel, Access, HTML, Visual Basic

characters. If the OCR software can't make sense of your fancy fonts or creative page layout, it will enter gibberish into the database. To create a scannable résumé, follow these guidelines (see Figure 13.8):[30]

- Use a clean, common sans serif font such as Optima or Arial, and size it between 10 and 14 points.
- Make sure that characters do not touch one another, including the slash (/).
- Don't use side-by-side columns (the OCR software reads one line all the way across the page).
- Don't use ampersands (&), percent signs (%), foreign-language characters (such as é and ö), or bullet symbols (use a dash—not a lowercase "o"—in place of a bullet symbol).

- Put each phone number and e-mail address on its own line.
- Print on white, plain paper (speckles and other background coloration can confuse the OCR software).

Your scannable résumé will probably be longer than your traditional résumé because you can't compress text into columns and because you need plenty of white space between headings and sections. If your scannable résumé runs more than one page, make sure your name appears on every subsequent page (in case the pages become separated). Before sending a scannable résumé, check the company's website or call the human resources department to see whether it has any specific requirements other than those discussed here.

Figure 13.8 also shows an important feature of a scannable résumé, the *keyword summary*. This is a list of 20 to 30 words and phrases that define your skills, experience, education, professional affiliations, and so on. Employers generally search for nouns (since verbs tend to be generic rather than specific to a particular position or skill), so make your keywords nouns as well. Use abbreviations sparingly and only when they are well-known and unambiguous, such as *MBA*. Place this list right after your name and address.

One good way to identify which keywords to include in your summary is to underline all the skills listed in ads for the types of jobs you're interested in. (Another advantage of staying current by reading periodicals, networking, and so on is that you'll develop a good ear for current terminology.) Be sure to include only those keywords that correspond with your skills and experience.

> Think carefully about the keywords you include in your scannable résumé; they need to appeal to recruiters and reflect your qualities accurately.

> A plain text version of your résumé is simply a computer file without any of the formatting that you typically apply using a word processor.

Creating a Plain Text File of Your Résumé   An increasingly common way to get your information into an employer's database is by entering a *plain text* version (sometimes referred to as an *ASCII text version*) of your résumé into an online form. This approach has the same goal as a scannable résumé, but it's faster, easier, and less prone to errors than the scanning process. If you have the option of mailing a scannable résumé or submitting plain text online, go with plain text.

In addition, when employers or networking contacts ask you to e-mail your résumé, they'll often want to receive it in plain text format in the body of your e-mail message. Thanks to the prevalence of computer viruses these days, many employers will refuse to open an e-mail attachment.

Plain text is just what it sounds like: no font selections, no bullet symbols, no colors, no lines or boxes, and so on. A plain text version is easy to create with your word processor. Start with the file you used to create your scannable résumé, use the *save as* choice to save it as "plain text" or whichever similarly labeled option your software has, then verify the result using a basic text editor (such as Microsoft's Notepad). If necessary, reformat the page manually, moving text and inserting spaces as needed. For simplicity's sake, left-justify all your headings, rather than trying to center them manually. You can put headings in all caps or underline them with a row of dashes to separate them from blocks of text.

Creating a Word File of Your Traditional Résumé   In some cases, an employer or job-posting website will let you upload a Microsoft Word file directly. (Although there are certainly other word processors on the market, particularly on Apple and Linux systems, Microsoft Word is the de facto standard in business these days.) This method of transferring information preserves the design and layout of your traditional printed résumé and saves you the trouble of creating a plain text version. However, read the instructions carefully. For instance, you can upload a Word résumé to Monster.com, but the site asks you to follow some specific formatting instructions to make sure your file isn't garbled.[31]

Before you submit a Word file to anyone, make sure your system is free from viruses. Infecting a potential employer's PC is not the way to make a good first impression.

Creating an HTML Version of Your Résumé   You can probably find several uses for an HTML version of your résumé, including sending it as a fully formatted e-mail message, posting it on your personal webpage, and including it in your e-portfolio. You don't need to know HTML to create a basic HTML résumé; use the "save as webpage" feature in your word processor.

A major benefit of an HTML résumé is providing links to supporting details and other materials from within your résumé. You can link to papers you've written, recommendations you've received, and sound or video clips that directly support your résumé.

Creating a PDF Version of Your Résumé   A safe and simple electronic alternative for your résumé is PDF format. PDF files are viewable on virtually any computer, and recipients generally aren't reluctant to view them (unlike Word files). However, creating a PDF file does require Adobe Acrobat or one of several other programs capable of converting word processor files to PDF (the free Acrobat Reader is not capable of creating files).

Proofreading Your Résumé

Employers view your résumé as a concrete example of your attention to quality and detail. Your résumé doesn't need to be good or pretty good—it needs to be *perfect*. Job seekers have committed every error, from forgetting to put their own names on their résumés to misspelling "Education."[32] Not only is your résumé one of the most important documents you'll ever write, it's also one of the shortest, so there's every reason to make it perfect. Check all headings and lists for clarity and parallelism, and be sure that your grammar, spelling, and punctuation are correct. Ask at least three or four other people to read it, too. As the creator of the material, you could stare at a mistake for weeks and not see it.

> Your résumé can't be "pretty good" or "almost perfect"—it needs to be *perfect*, so proofread it thoroughly and ask several other people to verify it, too.

Distributing Your Résumé

What you do to distribute your résumé depends on the number of employers you target and their preferences for receiving résumés. Employers usually list their preferences on their websites, so verify this information to make sure that your résumé ends up in the right format and in the right channel. Beyond that, here are some general delivery tips:

> When distributing your résumé, pay close attention to the specific wishes of each and every employer.

- **Mailing your traditional and scannable résumés.** Take some care with the packaging. Spend a few extra cents to mail these documents in a flat 9 × 12 envelope, or better yet, use Priority Mail, which gives you a sturdy cardboard mailer and faster delivery for just a few more dollars. Consider sending both formats to each employer. In your cover letter, explain that for the employer's convenience, you're sending both standard and scannable versions.

- **Faxing your traditional and scannable résumés.** If you know that an employer prefers résumés via fax, be sure to include a standard fax cover sheet, along with your cover letter, followed by your résumé. Set the fax machine to "fine" mode to help ensure a high-quality printout on the receiving end.

- **E-mailing your résumé.** Unless someone specifically asks for a Word document as an attachment, don't send it—it probably won't be opened. Instead, insert plain text into the body of the e-mail message or attach a PDF file. If you know a reference number or a job ad number, include it in your e-mail subject line.

Document Makeover

Improve This Résumé

To practice correcting drafts of actual documents, visit your online course or the access-code-protected portion of the Companion Website. Click "Document Makeovers," then click Chapter 13. You will find a résumé that contains problems and errors relating to what you've learned in this chapter about writing effective résumés and application letters. Use the "Final Draft" decision tool to create an improved version of this document. Check the résumé for spelling and grammatical errors, effective use of verbs and pronouns, inclusion of unnecessary information, or omission of important facts.

- **Submitting your résumé online.** The details of submitting résumés online vary from site to site, so be sure to read the instructions thoroughly. Some sites let you upload files directly from your computer; others instruct you to cut and paste blocks of plain text into specific fields in an online form. Whenever you do this, be sure to cut and paste, rather than retype information; you've already proofed this material, and you don't want to create any new mistakes while rekeying it.

- **Posting a résumé on your website.** If you wish to post your résumé on your website, you'll need to find some way of providing potential employers with your URL; recruiters won't take the time to use search engines to find your site.[33]

- **Posting your résumé with an index service or job site.** Make sure you explore all your online options. Websites such as Monster.com, CareerBuilder.com, and Yahoo! Hotjobs have rapidly become a major force in recruiting. Don't forget to check specialty sites as well, such as those maintained by professional societies in your fields of interest. However, before you upload your résumé to any site, learn about its confidentiality protection. Some sites allow you to specify levels of confidentiality, such as letting employers search your qualifications without seeing your personal contact information or preventing your current employer from seeing your résumé. In any case, carefully limit the amount of personal information you provide online. Never put your Social Security number, student ID number, or driver's license number online.

Reviewing Key Points

This chapter discusses searching for employment and creating an effective résumé. It explains how to build toward a career by understanding and adapting to today's changing workplace, as well as how to stay abreast of business news, research specific companies, engage in networking, and use career counseling.

The chapter discusses how to prepare effective résumés using the three-step writing process. It describes the three most common types of résumé organization: chronological, functional, and combination. And it itemizes the types of sections to include in your résumé. In addition, the chapter explains how to produce up to six versions of your résumé, depending on what potential employers require. It also explains how to proof and distribute your résumé.

The next chapter completes the employment communication package by discussing other employment messages, such as application letters, job-inquiry letters, and application follow-ups, and helping you prepare to interview. You will learn about the sequence and types of interviews, as well as what employers are looking for. You'll learn how to prepare for a job interview by planning ahead for questions and answers. You'll also learn about the various stages of an interview and how to take notes. Finally, you'll learn about following up after the interview with thank-you messages and letters of inquiry.

Test Your Knowledge

1. What steps can you take to make yourself more valuable to an employer?

2. What is a résumé, and why is it important to adopt a "you" attitude when preparing one?

3. Why do most employers prefer the chronological résumé over the functional résumé?

4. What are some of the most common problems with résumés?

5. Why is it important to provide a keyword summary in a scannable or plain text résumé?

Apply Your Knowledge

1. If you're still a year or two away from graduation, should you worry about your job search? Explain your answer.

2. One of the disadvantages of computerized résumé scanning is that some qualified applicants will be missed because the technology isn't perfect. However, more companies are using this approach to deal with the flood of résumés they receive. Do you think that scanning is a good idea? Please explain.

3. Stating your career objective on a résumé or application might limit your opportunities by labeling you too narrowly. Not stating your objective, however, might lead an employer to categorize you incorrectly. Which outcome is riskier? Do summaries of qualifications overcome such drawbacks? If so, how? Explain briefly.

4. Some people don't have a clear career path when they enter the job market. If you're in this situation, how would your uncertainty affect the way your write your résumé?

5. **Ethical Choices**   Between your sophomore and junior year, you quit school for a year to earn the money to finish college. You worked as a loan processing assistant in a finance company, checking references on loan applications, typing, and filing. Your manager made a lot of the fact that he had never attended college. He seemed to resent you for pursuing your education, but he never criticized your work, so you thought you were doing okay. After you'd been working there for six months, he fired you, saying that you failed to be thorough enough in your credit checks. You were actually glad to leave, and you found another job right away at a bank doing similar duties. Now that you've graduated from college, you're writing your résumé. Will you include the finance company job in your work history? Please explain.

Practice Your Knowledge

Activities

For active links to all websites discussed in this chapter, visit this text's website at www.prenhall. com/bovee. Locate your book and click on its Companion Website link. Then select Chapter 13, and click on "Featured Websites." Locate the name of the page or the URL related to the material in the text. Please note that links to sites that become inactive after publication of the book will be removed from the Featured Websites section.

1. **Analyze This Document**   Read the following résumé information, then (1) analyze the strengths or weaknesses of the information, and (2) create a résumé that follows the guidelines presented in this chapter.

Sylvia Manchester
765 Belle Fleur Blvd.
New Orleans, LA 70113
(504) 312-9504
smanchester@rcnmail.com

PERSONAL: Single, excellent health, 5'8", 116 lbs.; hobbies include cooking, dancing, and reading.

JOB OBJECTIVE: To obtain a responsible position in marketing or sales with a good company.

EDUCATIONAL HISTORY AND ACHIEVEMENTS

BA degree in biology, University of Louisiana, 1998. Graduated with a 3.0 average. Member of the varsity cheerleading squad. President of Panhellenic League. Homecoming queen.

WORK EXPERIENCE

Fisher Scientific Instruments, 2004 to now, field sales representative. Responsible for calling on customers and explaining the features of Fisher's line of laboratory instruments. Also responsible for writing sales letters, attending trade shows, and preparing weekly sales reports.

<u>Fisher Scientific Instruments, 2001–2003, customer service representative</u>. Was responsible for handling incoming phone calls from customers who had questions about delivery, quality, or operation of Fisher's line of laboratory instruments. Also handled miscellaneous correspondence with customers.

<u>Medical Electronics, Inc., 1998–2001, administrative assistant to the vice president of marketing</u>. In addition to handling typical secretarial chores for the vice president of marketing, I was in charge of compiling the monthly sales reports, using figures provided by members of the field sales force. I also was given responsibility for doing various market research activities.

<u>New Orleans Convention and Visitors Bureau, 1995–1998, summers, tour guide</u>. During the summers of my college years, I led tours of New Orleans for tourists visiting the city. My duties included greeting conventioneers and their spouses at hotels, explaining the history and features of the city during an all-day sight-seeing tour, and answering questions about New Orleans and its attractions. During my fourth summer with the bureau, I was asked to help train the new tour guides. I prepared a handbook that provided interesting facts about the various tourist attractions, as well as answers to the most commonly asked tourist questions. The Bureau was so impressed with the handbook they had it printed up so that it could be given as a gift to visitors.

<u>University of Louisiana, 1995–1998, part-time clerk in admissions office</u>. While I was a student in college, I worked 15 hours a week in the admissions office. My duties included filing, processing applications, and handling correspondence with high school students and administrators.

2. **Work-Related Preferences: Self-Assessment** What work-related activities and situations do you prefer? Evaluate your preferences in each of the following areas. Use the results as a good start for guiding your job search.

Activity or Situation	Strongly Agree	Agree	Disagree	No Preference
1. I want to work independently.	_____	_____	_____	_____
2. I want variety in my work.	_____	_____	_____	_____
3. I want to work with people.	_____	_____	_____	_____
4. I want to work with technology.	_____	_____	_____	_____
5. I want physical work.	_____	_____	_____	_____
6. I want mental work.	_____	_____	_____	_____
7. I want to work for a large organization.	_____	_____	_____	_____
8. I want to work for a nonprofit organization.	_____	_____	_____	_____
9. I want to work for a small family business.	_____	_____	_____	_____
10. I want to work for a service business.	_____	_____	_____	_____
11. I want regular, predictable work hours.	_____	_____	_____	_____
12. I want to work in a city location.	_____	_____	_____	_____
13. I want to work in a small town or suburb.	_____	_____	_____	_____
14. I want to work in another country.	_____	_____	_____	_____
15. I want to work outdoors.	_____	_____	_____	_____
16. I want to work in a structured environment.	_____	_____	_____	_____

3. **Internet**   Based on the preferences you identified in the self-assessment (Activity 2) and the academic, professional, and personal qualities you have to offer, perform an Internet search for an appropriate career, using any of the websites listed in Table 13.1. Draft a one-page report indicating how the career you select and the job openings you find match your strengths and preferences.

4. **Teamwork**   Working with another student, change the following statements to make them more effective for a résumé by using action verbs.
   a. Have some experience with database design.
   b. Assigned to a project to analyze the cost accounting methods for a large manufacturer.
   c. I was part of a team that developed a new inventory control system.
   d. Am responsible for preparing the quarterly department budget.
   e. Was a manager of a department with seven employees working for me.
   f. Was responsible for developing a spreadsheet to analyze monthly sales by department.
   g. Put in place a new program for ordering supplies.

5. **Résumé Preparation: Work Accomplishments**   Using your team's answers to Activity 4, make the statements stronger by quantifying them (make up any numbers you need).

6. **Ethical Choices**   Assume that you achieved all the tasks shown in Activity 4 not as an individual employee, but as part of a work team. In your résumé, must you mention other team members? Explain your answer.

7. **Résumé Preparation: Scannable or Plain Text Version**   At your instructor's discretion, create either a scannable or plain text version of the résumé you revised in Activity 1. Be sure to create the keyword summary that either version will require.

Expand Your Knowledge

Exploring the Best of the Web

Post an Online Résumé   At CareerBuilder, www. careerbuilder.com, you'll find sample résumés, tips on preparing different types of résumés (including scannable ones), links to additional articles, and expert advice on creating résumés that bring positive results. After you've polished your résumé-writing skills, you can search for jobs online using the site's numerous links to national and international industry-specific websites. You can access the information at CareerBuilder to develop your résumé and then post it with prospective employers—all free of charge. Take advantage of what this site offers, and get ideas for writing or improving a résumé.

Exercises

1. Before writing a new résumé, make a list of action verbs that describe your skills and experience.
2. Describe the advantages and disadvantages of chronological and functional résumé formats. Do you think a combination résumé would be an appropriate format for your new résumé? Explain why or why not.
3. List some of the tips you learned for preparing an electronic résumé.

Exploring the Web on Your Own

Review these chapter-related websites on your own to learn more about writing résumés and cover letters.

1. Get the latest news on hiring trends and other vital career information at the Quintessential Careers blog, www.quintcareers.com/career_blog.

2. To find out what happens when résumés are scanned, log on to Proven Résumés, www.provenresumes.com/reswkshps/electronic/scnres.html.

3. Visit Career One Stop, www.careeronestop.com, to see short videos of real people doing real work in hundreds of different professions.

Learn Interactively

Interactive Study Guide

Visit www.prenhall.com/bovee, then locate your book and click on its Companion Website link. Select Chapter 13 to take advantage of the interactive "Chapter Quiz" to test your knowledge of chapter concepts. Receive instant feedback on whether you need additional studying. Also, visit the "Study Hall," where you'll find an abundance of valuable resources that will help you succeed in this course.

Peak Performance Grammar and Mechanics

If your instructor has required the use of "Peak Performance Grammar and Mechanics," either in your online course, through the access-code protected portion of the Companion Website, or on CD, you can continue to improve your skill with mechanics by using the "Peak Performance Grammar and Mechanics" module. Click "Mechanics of Style." Take the Pretest to determine whether you have any weak areas. Then review those areas in the Refresher Course. Take the Follow-Up Test to check your grasp of mechanics. Finally, for additional reinforcement in numbers, go to the "Improve Your Grammar, Mechanics, and Usage" section that follows the cases, and complete the "Level 1: Self-Assessment" exercises.

CASES

Apply the three-step writing process to the following cases, as assigned by your instructor.

1. Taking Stock and Taking Aim: Résumé Tailored for the Right Job

Think about yourself. What are some things that come easily to you? What do you enjoy doing? In what part of the country would you like to live? Do you like to work indoors? Outdoors? A combination of the two? How much do you like to travel? Would you like to spend considerable time on the road? Do you like to work closely with others or more independently? What conditions make a job unpleasant? Do you delegate responsibility easily, or do you like to do things yourself? Are you better with words or numbers? Better at speaking or writing? Do you like to work under fixed deadlines? How important is job security to you? Do you want your supervisor to state clearly what is expected of you, or do you like the freedom to make many of your own decisions?

Your Task After answering these questions, gather information about possible jobs that suit your profile by consulting reference materials (from your college library or placement center) and by searching the Internet (using some of the search strategies discussed in Chapter 10). Next, choose a location, a company, and a job that interests you. With guidance from your instructor, decide whether to apply for a job you're qualified for now or one you'll be qualified for with additional education. Then, as directed by your instructor, write a résumé.

■WEB ■SKILLS

2. Scanning the Possibilities: Résumé for the Internet

In your search for a position, you discover Career Magazine, a website that lists hundreds of companies advertising on the Internet. Your chances of getting an interview with a leading company will be enhanced if you submit your résumé and cover letter electronically. On the web, explore www.careermag.com.

Your Task Prepare a scannable résumé that could be submitted to one of the companies advertising at the Career Magazine website. Print out the résumé for your instructor.

■WEB ■SKILLS

3. "Help Wanted": Application for a Job Listed in the Classified Section

Among the jobs listed in today's *Chicago Tribune* are the following:

ACCOUNTING ASSISTANT
Established leader in the vacation ownership industry has immediate opening in its Northbrook corp. accounting dept. for an Accounting Assistant. Responsibilities include: bank reconciliation, preparation of deposits, AP, and cash receipt posting. Join our fast-growing company and enjoy our great benefits package. Flex work hours, medical, dental insurance. Fax résumé to Lisa: 847-564-3876.

ADMINISTRATIVE ASSISTANT
Fast-paced Wood Dale office seeks professional with strong computer skills. Proficient in MS Word & Excel, PowerPoint a plus. Must be detail oriented, able to handle multiple tasks, and possess strong communication skills. Excellent benefits, salary, and work environment. Fax résumé to 630-350-8649.

CUSTOMER SERVICE
A nationally known computer software developer has an exciting opportunity in customer service and inside sales support in its fast-paced downtown Chicago office. You'll help resolve customer problems over the phone, provide information, assist in account management, and administer orders. If you're friendly, self-motivated, energetic, and have 2 years of experience, excellent problem-solving skills, organizational, communication, and PC skills, and communicate well over the phone, send résumé to J. Haber, 233 North Lake Shore Drive, Chicago, IL 60641.

SALES-ACCOUNT MANAGER

MidCity Baking Company is seeking an Account Manager to sell and coordinate our programs to major accounts in the Chicago market. The candidate should possess strong analytical and selling skills and demonstrate computer proficiency. Previous sales experience with major account level assignment desired. A degree in business or equivalent experience preferred. For confidential consideration please mail résumé to Steven Crane, Director of Sales, MidCity Baking Company, 133 N. Railroad Avenue, Northlake, IL 60614.

Your Task Write a résumé for one of these potential employers (make up any information you need or adapt your own résumé).

Improve Your Grammar, Mechanics, and Usage

Level 1: Self-Assessment—Numbers

Review Section 3.4 in the Handbook of Grammar, Mechanics, and Usage, and then look at the following 15 items.

For items 1–15, correct number style wherever necessary:

1. We need to hire one office manager, four bookkeepers, and twelve clerk-typists.

2. The market for this product is nearly six million people in our region alone.

3. Make sure that all 1835 pages are on my desk no later than nine o'clock a.m.

4. 2004 was the year that José Guiterez sold more than $50 thousand dollars worth of stock.

5. Our deadline is 4/7, but we won't be ready before 4/11.

6. 95 percent of our customers are men.

7. More than ½ the U.S. population is female.

8. Cecile Simmons, thirty-eight, is the first woman in this company to be promoted to management.

9. Last year, I wrote 20 15-page reports, and Michelle wrote 24 three-page reports.

10. Of the 15 applicants, seven are qualified.

11. Our blinds should measure 38 inches wide by 64 and one-half inches long by 7/16 inches deep.

12. Deliver the couch to seven eighty-three Fountain Rd., Suite three, Procter Valley, CA 92074.

13. Here are the corrected figures: 42.7% agree, 23.25% disagree, 34% are undecided, and the error is .05%

14. You have to agree that 50,000,000 U.S. citizens cannot be wrong.

15. We need a set of shelves 10 feet, eight inches long.

Level 2: Workplace Applications

The following items contain numerous errors in grammar, capitalization, punctuation, abbreviation, number style, word division, and vocabulary. Rewrite each sentence in the space provided, correcting all errors. Write C in the space after any sentence that is already correct.

1. Speaking at a recent software conference Alan Nichols; ceo of Tekco Systems; said the companys' goal is to reduce response time to 2 to 4 hrs., using software as an enabler.

2. Selling stocks short are the latest rage on wall street, where lately things have just gone from bad to worst.

3. As Electronic Commerce grows people are trying to find new ways to make money off of it.

4. We give a notification not only to the customer but also our salespeople that the product has been shipped because they will want to follow up.

5. When deciding between these various suppliers, we found that each of them offer both advantages and also disadvantages.

6. I found the book, "Marketing is Easy, Selling is Hard," for three different prices on the Internet: $14, $13.25, and $12.00.

7. United Agra Products, a distributor of fertilizers and seeds, in transmission of customer orders over it's private network faced the possibility of serious bottlenecks.

8. The answers you receive on your questionnaire, are influenced by the types of question you ask, the way they are asked, and your subjects cultural and language background.

9. The creation of hazardous by products, like silver in film processing, require us to collect our used chemicals for disposal at a hazardous-waste-facility.

10. As a source of ingredients for our products, we try to establish relationships with small cooperative or farming communities - often in developing countries – because, we believe that the best way to improve peoples' lives is to give them a chance at self reliance.

11. A entrepreneur really should never be in any organization that get's so big that it looses intimacy.

12. Racecar Driver Eddie Cheever, is founder of Aleanza Marketing Group, a seven-person company that handles $10 million dollars in sponsorship campaigns for Cheevers' team Red Bull Cheever Racing.

13. Over the last six years, Business Cluster Development have started 13 technology related incubators, that they call 'business clusters.'

14. In an interview, Gary Hoover said "When I dreamed up Bookstop, we asked people, "If there was a bookstore that carried a huge selection of books and had them all at discount prices, would you go there"? and we got a lot of yawns".

15. The chief attraction of vending machines are their convenience, they are open 24 hours a day, on the other hand, vending machine prices are no bargain.

Level 3: Document Critique

The following document may contain errors in grammar, capitalization, punctuation, abbreviation, number style, vocabulary, and spelling. You may also find problems with word use and format. Correct all errors using standard proofreading marks (see Appendix C).

THE EXECUTVE SUMMARY
(EXCERPT)

Purpose of the Proposal

This document will acquaint the reader with 3 principle topics by

- Showing what the San Diego State University (SDSU) *Suntrakker* project is

- Showing that the team-oriented, inerdepartmental diciplines at SDSU possesses the tenacity and knowhow to build and race a solar-powered vehical in the World solar Challenge Race in Austrailia next year;

- Define and articulate how this business team expect to promote and generate the neccesary support; funds, and materials from the student body, alumni, community and local businesses to sieze and executive this opportunity;

Project Profile

The *Suntrakker* Solar Car project was conceived by a small group of San Diego State university engineering students motivated by the successof of the General motors "Sunrayce," committed itself to designing and building a superior solar-powered vehicle to compete in the world Solar Challenge. From modest Beginnings, the *Suntrakker* project quickly revolved into a cross-disciplinary educational effort encompassing students from many colleges of San Diego State University. The project has provides students participants and volunteers with valuable real life experiences and has brought them together in an effort that benefits not only the students and the university but also the environment.

Sponsors of this project are not only contributing to the successful achievment of the overall *Suntrakker* project but will also enhance their goodwill, advertising, and name promotion by association with the project. In addition, the *Suntrakker* offers a unique opportunity for the companies who can donate parts and accessories to showcase their name and test field their products in public in this highly publicized international contest.

14

Applying and Interviewing for Employment

From the Real World

"Avoid becoming so focused on saying the 'right thing' that you don't give an accurate portrayal of your skills and interests. . . . The hiring manager is trying to get to know you, so do your best to provide a glimpse into what type of employee you'll be."[1]

—Max Messmer
Chairman and CEO,
Robert Half International
www.rhi.com

Learning Objectives

After studying this chapter, you will be able to

1 Define the purpose of application letters and explain how to apply the AIDA organizational approach to them

2 Describe the typical sequence of job interviews

3 Describe briefly what employers look for during an employment interview and preemployment testing

4 List six tasks you need to complete to prepare for a successful job interview

5 Explain the three stages of a successful employment interview

6 Identify the most common employment messages that follow an interview and explain when you would use each one

Max Messmer's observation (at left) about employment interviewing highlights an important point that is too easy to forget during the often-stressful process of looking for a job: An interview should be approached as a business conversation in which both parties get to know each other better. Don't view it as a test in which you try to guess the "right" answers—or as an interrogation in which you have to defend your background and skills. Treat your interviews as opportunities to share information. After all, you need to determine which company is the right employer for you, just as those companies need to determine whether you are the right employee for them. You'll learn more this way, and you'll lower the stress level, too.

This chapter will give you a foundation for successful interviewing, along with tips on writing effective application letters and other important employment-related messages.

Writing Application Letters and Other Employment Messages

Your résumé (see Chapter 13) is the centerpiece of your job-search package, but it needs support from several other employment messages, including application letters, job-inquiry letters, application forms, and follow-up notes.

Application Letters

Whenever you submit your résumé, accompany it with an **application letter**, also known as a *cover letter*, to let readers know what you're sending, why you're sending it, and how they can benefit from reading it. The three-step process of planning, writing, and completing an application letter involves the same tasks you've used throughout this course. Start by researching the organization, then focus on your audience so that you can show you've done your homework. During your research, try to find out the name, title, and department of the person you're writing to. If you can't find a specific name, use something like "Dear Hiring Manager."[2] If you're applying for work in another country, be sure to research the hiring practices prevalent in that culture and adjust your letter format as needed.

Remember that your reader's in-box is probably overflowing with résumés and cover letters, so respect his or her time. Avoid gimmicks and don't repeat information that already appears in your résumé. Keep your letter straightforward, fact-based, short, upbeat, and professional. Here are some quick tips to help you write effective cover letters:[3]

- Be as clear as possible about the kind of opportunity you seek.
- Show that you understand the company and the position.
- Never volunteer salary information unless an employer asks for it.
- Keep it short—and keep e-mail cover letters even shorter; in just two or three paragraphs, convey how your strengths and character would fit the position.
- Show some personality; this will help balance the choppy, shorthand style of your résumé.
- Meticulously check your spelling, mechanics, and grammar; errors will send your message directly to the recycling bin. And be aware that potential employers will treat your e-mail messages every bit as seriously as formal, printed letters.[4]

If you're sending a **solicited application letter** in response to an announced job opening, you'll usually know what qualifications the organization is seeking (see Figure 14.1). In contrast, if you're sending an **unsolicited application letter** to an organization that has not announced an opening, you'll need to do some research to identify the requirements the position is likely to have (see Figure 14.2). (Note that even though these documents are referred to as letters, they can be e-mail messages as well.)

Both solicited and unsolicited application letters present your qualifications similarly. The main difference is in the opening paragraph. In a solicited letter, you need no special attention-getter because you have been invited to apply. In an unsolicited letter, you need to start by capturing the reader's attention and interest.

Getting Attention

Like your résumé, your application letter is a form of advertising, so organize it as you would a sales letter: Use the AIDA approach, focus on your audience, and emphasize reader benefits (as discussed in Chapter 9). Make sure your style projects confidence, without being arrogant. To sell a potential employer on your merits, you must believe in yourself and sound as though you do.

The opening paragraph of your application letter has two important tasks to accomplish: (1) clearly stating your reason for writing and (2) giving the recipient a reason to keep reading by demonstrating that you have some immediate potential for meeting the company's needs. Consider this opening:

> With the recent slowdown in corporate purchasing, I can certainly appreciate the challenge of new fleet sales in this business environment. With my high energy level and 16 months of new-car sales experience, I believe I can produce the results you listed as vital in your September 23 ad in the *Baltimore Sun*.

This applicant does a smooth job of mirroring the company's stated needs while highlighting his personal qualifications along with evidence that he understands the

FIGURE 14.1   Effective Solicited Application Letter

This letter was written in response to a help-wanted ad. Notice how Kenneth Sawyer highlights his qualifications and mirrors the requirements specified in the ad. He grabs attention by focusing on the phrase "proven skills," which was used in the ad: He not only elaborates on his own proven skills throughout the letter but even mentions the term in his closing paragraph.

Here is the help wanted ad to which Sawyer is responding

> **Administrative Assistant**
> **Cummings and Welbane**
>
> Put your business and computer skills to work in a challenging and rewarding career at Cummings and Welbane. The successful candidate for this position will have proven skills in the entire Microsoft Office suite, including PowerPoint and Access, and will be expected to become a productive member of the team immediately. This office produces a wide range of printed and electronic documents, electronic presentations, and databases. A flexible work style is a plus, too, as you'll be assisting executives in a variety of locations around our Chapel Hill facility. Please mail your résumé to Angela Clair, Director of Administration, 770 Campus Point Dr., Chapel Hill, NC 27514.

2893 Jack Pine Road
Chapel Hill, NC 27514
February 3, 2007

Ms. Angela Clair
Director of Administration
Cummings and Welbane, Inc.
770 Campus Point Drive
Chapel Hill, NC 27514

Dear Ms. Clair:

States the reason for writing and links the writer's experience to qualifications identified in the ad →

In the January 31 issue of the *Chapel Hill Post*, your ad mentioned "proven skills." I believe I have what you are looking for in an administrative assistant. In addition to experience in a variety of office settings, I am familiar with the computer software used in your office.

I recently completed a three-course sequence at Hamilton College on Microsoft Office applications, including Word, Excel, PowerPoint, and Access, and I've created files using all four of these applications. In addition, a workshop on "Designing and Producing Professional Documents with Microsoft Publisher" gave me experience designing, formatting, and printing the wide variety of reports and sales materials used in your office.

← Discusses how specific skills apply to the job sought, showing that Sawyer understands the job's responsibilities

Describes an achievement mentioned in the résumé and refers the reader to the enclosure →

These skills have been invaluable to me as assistant to the chief nutritionist at our campus cafeteria (please refer to my résumé). I'm particularly proud of the order-confirmation system I designed, which has sharply reduced the problems of late shipments and depleted inventories.

Because "proven skills" are best explained in person, I would appreciate an interview with you. Please phone me any afternoon between 3 and 5 p.m. at (919) 220-6139 to let me know the day and time most convenient for you.

← Asks for an interview while continuing the "proven skills" theme; facilitates the reader's response by providing specific information about telephoning

Sincerely,

Kenneth Sawyer

Kenneth Sawyer

broader market. The letter balances his relative lack of experience with enthusiasm and knowledge of the industry. Table 14.1 highlights some other ways that you can spark interest and grab attention in your opening paragraph.

Building Interest and Increasing Desire

Use the middle section of your letter to expand on your opening, presenting a more complete picture of your strengths.

The middle section of your letter presents your strongest selling points in terms of their potential benefit to the organization, thereby building interest in you and creating a desire to interview you. Be specific, and back up your assertions with convincing evidence:

> **Poor:** I completed three college courses in business communication, earning an A in each course, and have worked for the past year at Imperial Construction.

FIGURE 14.2 Effective Unsolicited Application Letter

Glenda Johns's experience as a clerk and an assistant manager gives her a good idea of the qualities that Wal-Mart is likely to be looking for in future managers. She uses these insights to craft the opening of her letter.

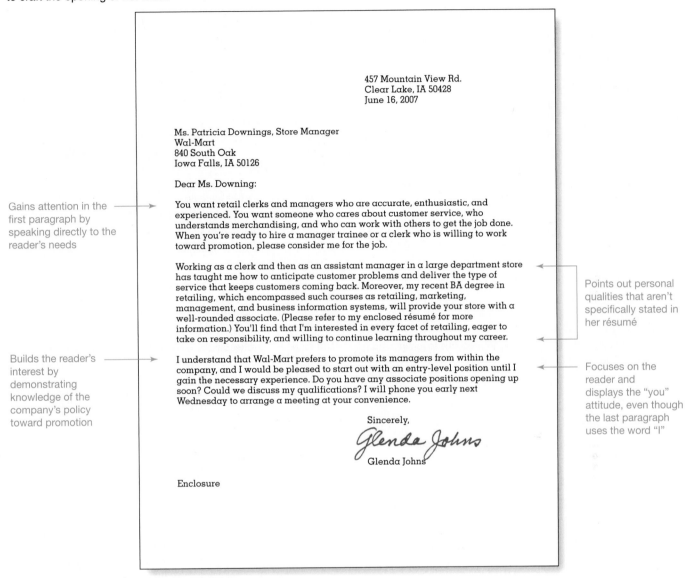

Gains attention in the first paragraph by speaking directly to the reader's needs

Builds the reader's interest by demonstrating knowledge of the company's policy toward promotion

Points out personal qualities that aren't specifically stated in her résumé

Focuses on the reader and displays the "you" attitude, even though the last paragraph uses the word "I"

Improved: Using the skills gained from three semesters of college training in business communication, I developed a collection system for Imperial Construction that reduced annual bad-debt losses by 25 percent. By emphasizing a win-win scenario for the company and its clients with incentives for on-time payment, the system was also credited with improving customer satisfaction.

When writing a solicited letter in response to an advertisement, be sure to discuss each requirement specified in the ad. If you are deficient in any of these requirements, stress other solid selling points to help strengthen your overall presentation.

Don't restrict your message to just core job duties, either. Also highlight personal characteristics, as long as they apply to the targeted position, such as your diligence or your ability to work hard, learn quickly, handle responsibility, or get along with people:

While attending college full-time, I trained three hours a day with the varsity track team. In addition, I worked part-time during the school year and up to

Table 14.1	Tips for Getting Attention in Application Letters
Tip	**Example**
Unsolicited Application Letters	
• Show how your strongest skills will benefit the organization	If you need a regional sales specialist who consistently meets sales targets while fostering strong customer relationships, please consider my qualifications.
• Describe your understanding of the job's requirements and then show how well your qualifications fit them	Your annual report stated that improving manufacturing efficiency is one of the company's top priorities for next year. Through my postgraduate research in systems engineering and consulting work for several companies in the industry, I've developed reliable methods for quickly identifying ways to cut production time while reducing resource usage.
• Mention the name of a person known to and highly regarded by the reader	When Janice McHugh of your franchise sales division spoke to our business communication class last week, she said you often need promising new marketing graduates at this time of year.
• Refer to publicized company activities, achievements, changes, or new procedures	Today's issue of the *Detroit News* reports that you may need the expertise of computer programmers versed in robotics when your Lansing tire plant automates this spring.
• Use a question to demonstrate your understanding of the organization's needs	Can your fast-growing market research division use an interviewer with two years of field survey experience, a B.A. in public relations, and a real desire to succeed? If so, please consider me for the position.
• Use a catchphrase opening if the job requires ingenuity and imagination	*Haut monde*—whether said in French, Italian, or Arabic, it still means "high society." As an interior designer for your Beverly Hills showroom, not only could I serve and sell to your distinguished clientele, but I could do it in all these languages. I speak, read, and write them fluently.
Solicited Application Letters	
• Identify where you discovered the job opening; describe what you have to offer	Your ad in the April issue of *Travel & Leisure* for a cruise-line social director caught my eye. My eight years of experience as a social director in the travel industry would allow me to serve your new Caribbean cruise division well.

60 hours a week each summer in order to be totally self-supporting while in college. I can offer your organization the same level of effort and perseverance.

Don't bring up salary in your application letter unless the recipient has previously asked you to include your salary requirements.

Mention your salary requirements *only* if the organization has asked you to state them. If you don't know the salary that's appropriate for the position and someone with your qualifications, you can find typical salary ranges at the Bureau of Labor Statistics website, www.bls.gov or a number of commercial sites, including Monster.com. If you do state a target salary, tie it to the benefits you would provide:

For the past two years, I have been helping a company similar to yours organize its database marketing efforts. I would therefore like to receive a salary in the same range (the mid-40s) for helping your company set up a more efficient customer database.

Toward the end of this section, refer the reader to your résumé by citing a specific fact or general point covered there:

As you can see in the attached résumé, I've been working part-time with a local publisher since my sophomore year. During that time, I've used client interactions as an opportunity to build strong customer service skills.

Motivating Action

The final paragraph of your application letter has two important functions: to ask the reader for a specific action and to facilitate a reply. In almost all cases, the action you request is an interview. Offer to come to the employer's office at a convenient time or, if the firm is some distance away, to meet with its nearest representative or arrange a telephone interview. Include your phone number and the best time to reach you—or, if you wish to be in control, by mentioning that you will follow up with a phone call in a few days. Refer again to your strongest selling point and, if desired, your date of availability:

> After you have reviewed my qualifications, could we discuss the possibility of putting my marketing skills to work for your company? Because I will be on spring break the week of March 8, I would like to arrange a time to talk then. I will call in late February to schedule a convenient time when we could discuss employment opportunities at your company.

In the final paragraph of your application letter, respectfully ask for specific action and make it easy for the reader to respond.

Application Follow-Ups

If your application letter and résumé fail to bring a response within a month or so, follow up with a second letter or e-mail message to let the company know you are still interested. This follow-up also gives you a chance to update your original application with any recent job-related information:

> Since applying to you on May 3 for an executive assistant position, I have completed a course in office management at South River Community College and received straight A's. I am now a proficient user of MS Word, including macros and other complex functions.
>
> Please keep my application in your active file, and let me know when you need a skilled executive assistant.

Even if you've received a letter acknowledging your application and saying that it will be kept on file, don't hesitate to send a follow-up letter three months later to show that you are still interested:

> Three months have elapsed since I applied to you for an underwriting position, but I want to let you know that I am still very interested in joining your company.
>
> I recently completed a four-week temporary work assignment at a large local insurance agency. I learned several new verification techniques that could increase my value to your underwriting department.
>
> Please keep my application in your active file, and let me know when a position opens for a capable underwriter.

Whatever the circumstances, a follow-up message can demonstrate that you're sincerely interested in working for the organization, persistent in pursuing your goals, and committed to upgrading your skills.

Think creatively about a follow-up letter; show that you've continued to add to your skills or that you've learned more about the company or the industry.

Understanding the Interviewing Process

An **employment interview** is a formal meeting during which both you and the prospective employer ask questions and exchange information. These meetings have a dual purpose: (1) The organization's main objective is to find the best person available for the job by determining whether you and the organization are a good match, and (2) your main objective is to find the job best suited to your goals and capabilities.

Adjust your job search to the company's size and hiring practices. Large organizations that hire hundreds of new employees every year typically take a more systematic approach to the recruiting and interviewing process than small local businesses do. In general, the easiest way to connect with a big company is through your campus placement office; the most efficient way to approach a smaller business is often contacting the company directly.

Regardless of which path you choose, interviewing takes time, so start seeking jobs well in advance of the date you want to start work. During downturns in the economy, early planning is even more crucial. Many employers become more selective and many corporations reduce their campus visits and campus hiring programs, so more of the job-search burden falls on you. Whatever shape the economy is in, try to secure as many interviews as you can, both to improve the chances of receiving a job offer and to give yourself more options when you do get offers.

The Typical Sequence of Interviews

Most employers interview an applicant two or three times before deciding to make a job offer. Applicants often face a sequence of interviews, each with a different purpose.

First is the preliminary *screening stage*, which helps employers screen out unqualified applicants. Screening can take place on campus, at company offices, or via telephone or computer. Many companies use standardized evaluation sheets to "grade" the applicants so that all the candidates will be measured against the same criteria. Time is limited, so keep your answers short while providing a few key points that differentiate you from other candidates.

The next stage of interviews helps the organization narrow the field even further. Typically, if you're invited to visit a company, you will talk with a variety of people, including a member of the human resources department, one or two potential colleagues, and your potential supervisor. Your best approach during this *selection stage* of interviews is to show interest in the job, relate your skills and experience to the organization's needs, listen attentively, ask insightful questions, and display enthusiasm.

If the interviewers agree that you're a good candidate, you may receive a job offer, either on the spot or a few days later by phone, mail, or e-mail. In other cases, you may be invited back for a final evaluation by a higher-ranking executive who has the authority to make the hiring decision and to decide on your compensation. An underlying objective of the *final stage* is often to sell you on the advantages of joining the organization.

Common Types of Interviews

Organizations use various types of interviews to discover as much as possible about you and other applicants. A **structured interview** is generally used in the screening stage. Working from a checklist, the interviewer asks you a series of prepared questions in a set order. Although useful for gathering facts, the structured interview is generally regarded as a poor measure of an applicant's personal qualities. Nevertheless, some companies use structured interviews to create uniformity in their hiring process.[5]

By contrast, the **open-ended interview** is less formal and unstructured, more like a conversation between peers. The interviewer poses broad, open-ended questions and encourages you to talk freely. This type of interview is good for bringing out your personality and for testing professional judgment, but remember you're in a business situation so keep your answers focused.

Some organizations perform **group interviews**, meeting with several candidates simultaneously to see how they interact. This type of interview is useful for judging interpersonal skills.

The most unnerving type of interview is the **stress interview**, during which you might be asked pointed questions designed to unsettle you, or you might be subjected to long periods of silence, criticism, interruptions, and or even hostile reactions by the interviewer. The theory behind this approach is that you'll reveal how well you handle stressful situations, although some experts find the technique of dubious value.[6] If you find yourself in a stress interview, pause for a few seconds to collect your thoughts before continuing, knowing what the interviewer is up to.

Allow plenty of time for your job search, particularly in a slow economy.

During the screening stage of interviews, try to differentiate yourself from other candidates.

During the selection stage of interviews, you may interview with several people, perhaps at the same time.

During the final stage, the interviewer may try to sell you on working for the firm.

A structured interview is controlled by the interviewer to gather facts.

In an open-ended interview, the recruiter encourages you to speak freely.

Group interviews help recruiters see how candidates interact with one another.

Stress interviews help recruiters see how you handle yourself under pressure.

As employers try to cut travel costs, the **video interview** is becoming more popular. Many large companies use videoconferencing systems to screen middle-management candidates or to interview new recruits at universities. Experts recommend that candidates prepare a bit differently for a video interview than for an in-person meeting:[7]

- Ask for a preliminary phone conversation to establish rapport with the interviewer.
- Arrive early enough to get used to the equipment and setting.
- During the interview, speak clearly but not more slowly than normal.
- Sit straight and look up.
- Keep your mannerisms lively without looking forced or fake.

Many companies now use video interviews at some point during the recruiting process.

Many companies have learned that no strong correlation exists between how well people answer interview questions in a traditional interview and how well they perform real tasks on the job. In response, these firms have begun using the **situational interview**, or *behavioral interview*. During such interviews, you may be asked to explain how you would solve a particular business problem, or you might be asked to lead a brainstorming session, engage in role playing, or even make a presentation. Although situational interviewers may strike some candidates as unusual, proponents claim they are much more accurate at predicting success on the job.[8]

In situational interviews, you're asked to explain how you would handle a specific set of circumstances.

What Employers Look For in an Interview

Interviews give employers the chance to go beyond the basic data of your résumé to get to know you and to answer two essential questions. The first is whether you will be a good fit with the organization. For instance, TechTarget, an interactive media company, gives employees an unusual amount of freedom, including the freedom to set their own hours and take as many days off as they want or need—provided they meet their work objectives. To succeed in this environment, employees must be able to handle the responsibility that comes with such independence. As a result, TechTarget's hiring process is focused on filtering out candidates who need a more structured environment.[9]

Compatibility with the organization is judged on the basis of personal background, attitudes, and style.

Some interviewers believe that personal background indicates how well the candidate will fit in, so they might ask about your interests, hobbies, awareness of world events, and so forth. You can expand your potential along these lines by reading widely, making an effort to meet new people, and participating in discussion groups, seminars, and workshops. Interviewers are likely to consider your personal style as well. You can impress them by being open, enthusiastic, and interested. Some interviewers also look for courtesy, sincerity, willingness to learn, and a style that is positive and self-confident.

The second question is whether you can handle the responsibilities of the position. The interviewer should already have some idea of whether you have the right qualifications, based on a review of your résumé. During the interview, you'll probably be asked to describe your education and previous jobs in more depth so that the interviewer can determine how well your skills match the requirements. You may also be asked how you would apply those skills to hypothetical situations on the job.

Suitability for the specific job is judged on the basis of
- *Academic preparation*
- *Work experience*
- *Job-related personality traits*

Preemployment Testing

In an effort to improve the predictability of the selection process and reduce the reliance on the brief interaction that an interview allows, many employers now conduct a variety of preemployment tests.[10] Here is an overview of the most common types of tests:

Preemployment tests attempt to provide objective, quantitative information about a candidate's skills, attitudes, and habits.

- **Integrity tests.** You might not think that a test could identify job candidates who are more likely to steal from their employers or commit other ethical or legal infractions, but employers have had some success in using integrity tests.[11]
- **Personality tests.** Personality tests are used to assess either general character or suitability for the demands of a specific profession. General tests attempt to profile overall

intellectual ability, attitudes toward work, interests, and managerial potential as well as such characteristics as dependability, commitment, honesty, and motivation. The specific tests evaluate whether a candidate is suited to the emotional rigors of demanding positions, such as flight crews, air marshals, police and fire personnel, and nuclear power plant operators.[12]

- **Job skills tests.** The most common type of preemployment tests are those designed to assess the competency or specific abilities needed to perform a job. The most commonly assessed abilities are basic computer skills, clerical skills, basic business and financial acumen, and knowledge of legal and medical terminology.[13]

- **Substance tests.** Drug and alcohol testing is one of the most controversial issues in business today. Some employers believe such testing is absolutely necessary to maintain workplace safety, whereas others view it as an invasion of employee privacy and a sign of disrespect. Some companies test only applicants, but not employees.[14] Nationwide, nearly half of all companies now require applicants to undergo drug and alcohol testing, and this percentage is expected to rise for two reasons: (1) to cut the costs (approximately $100 billion a year) and the reduced productivity associated with drug abuse, and (2) to reduce the number of accidents (substance abusers have two to four times as many accidents as other employees, and drug use is linked to 40 percent of industrial fatalities).[15]

- **Background checks.** In one recent survey of more than 2 million job applicants, 44 percent lied about their employment history, 41 percent lied about their education, and 23 percent claimed to have professional credentials or licenses they didn't have.[16] To uncover such discrepancies, most employers do some sort of background check, including reviewing your credit record, checking to see whether you have a criminal history, and verifying your education. In fact, with so many employers performing background checks these days, you might want to check up on yourself before applying. Make sure your college transcript and credit record are correct and up-to-date so that any errors don't cause problems.[17] And if you have anything posted online at MySpace.com or anywhere else that might be potentially embarrassing, take it down now. Recruiters routinely search for information about candidates online, and you don't want to let some youthful indiscretion hurt your career.[18]

Preparing for a Job Interview

Just as written messages need planning, employment interviews need preparation.

Preparation will help you perform better under pressure; moreover, the more prepared you are, the less nervous you'll be about the interviewing process. To prepare for a successful interview, learn about the organization, think ahead about questions, bolster your confidence, polish your interview style, plan to look good, and be ready when you arrive.

Learn About the Organization

Today's companies expect serious candidates to demonstrate an understanding of the company's operations, its markets, and its strategic and tactical challenges.[19] When you were planning your employment search, you probably already researched the companies you sent your résumé to. But now that you've been invited for an interview, you'll want to fine-tune your research and brush up on the facts you've collected. Table 14.2 lists some of the basic points you will want to know about a company and a specific position.

Think Ahead About Questions

Planning ahead for the interviewer's questions will help you handle them more confidently and successfully. In addition, you will want to prepare insightful questions of your own.

Table 14.2	Finding Out About an Organization and a Job Opportunity

Where to Look and What You Can Learn

- **Company website:** Overall information about the company, including key executives, products and services, locations and divisions, employee benefits, job descriptions
- **Competitors' websites:** Similar information from competitors, including the strengths these companies claim to have
- **Industry-related websites:** Objective analysis and criticism of the company, its products, its reputation, and its management
- **Marketing materials (brochures, catalogs, etc.):** The company's marketing strategy and customer communication style
- **Company publications (both print and electronic):** Key events, stories about employees, new products
- **Blogs:** Analysis and criticism (not always fair or unbiased) of the company, its products and services, its reputation, and its management
- **Periodicals (newspapers and trade journals, both print and online):** In-depth stories about the company and its strategies, products, successes, and failures; you may find profiles of top executives
- **Career center at your college:** Often provide wide array of information about companies that hire graduates
- **Current and former employees:** Insights into the work environment

Points to Learn About the Organization

- Full name
- Location (headquarters and divisions, branches, subsidiaries, or other units)
- Age and brief history
- Products and services
- Industry position (is the company a leader or a minor player; is it an innovator or more of a follower)
- Key financial points (such as stock price and trend, if a public company)
- Growth prospects (is the company investing in its future through research and development; is it in a thriving industry)

Points to Learn About the Position

- Title
- Functions and responsibilities
- Qualifications and expectations
- Career path
- Salary range
- Travel expectations and opportunities
- Relocation expectations and opportunities

Planning for the Employer's Questions

Employers usually gear their interview questions to specific organizational needs. You can expect to be asked about your skills, achievements, and goals, as well as about your attitude toward work and school, your relationships with others, and occasionally your hobbies and interests. You'll also need to anticipate a few particularly tough questions, such as these:

Be prepared to relate your qualifications to the organization's needs.

- **What was the hardest decision you ever had to make?** Be prepared with a good example, explaining why the decision was difficult and how you finally made it.
- **What are your greatest weaknesses?** This question seems to be a stock favorite of some interviewers, although it probably rarely yields useful information. The standard way to reply is to describe a weakness so that it sounds like a virtue, such as working too hard. Of course, interviewers who have asked this question many times have heard similar responses many times as well. An alternative is to describe a relatively minor shortcoming and explain how you're working to improve.
- **What didn't you like about previous jobs you've held?** State what you didn't like and discuss what the experience taught you. Avoid making negative references to former

employers or colleagues. Be aware that when employers ask this question, they're trying to predict if you'll be an unhappy or difficult employee in the event they hire you, so plan your answer with care.[20]

■ **Where do you want to be five years from now?** This questions tests (1) whether you're merely using this job as a stopover until something better comes along and (2) whether you've given thought to your long-term goals. Saying that you'd like to be company president is unrealistic, and yet few employers want people who are content to sit still. Your answer should reflect your desire to contribute to the employer's long-term goals, not just your own goals.

■ **Tell me something about yourself.** Answer that you'll be happy to talk about yourself, and ask what the interviewer wants to know. If this point is clarified, respond. If it isn't, explain how your skills can contribute to the job and the organization.

Practice answering typical interview questions.

To further prepare, jot down a brief answer to each question in Table 14.3. You might also give a list of interview questions to a friend or relative and have that person ask you

Table 14.3   Twenty-Five Common Interview Questions

Questions About College

1. What courses in college did you like most? Least? Why?

2. Do you think your extracurricular activities in college were worth the time you spent on them? Why or why not?

3. When did you choose your college major? Did you ever change your major? If so, why?

4. Do you feel you did the best scholastic work you are capable of?

5. Which of your college years was the toughest? Why?

Questions About Employers and Jobs

6. What jobs have you held? Why did you leave?

7. What percentage of your college expenses did you earn? How?

8. Why did you choose your particular field of work?

9. What are the disadvantages of your chosen field?

10. Have you served in the military? What rank did you achieve? What jobs did you perform?

11. What do you think about how this industry operates today?

12. Why do you think you would like this particular type of job?

Questions About Personal Attitudes and Preferences

13. Do you prefer to work in any specific geographic location? If so, why?

14. How much money do you hope to be earning in 5 years? In 10 years?

15. What do you think determines a person's progress in a good organization?

16. What personal characteristics do you feel are necessary for success in your chosen field?

17. Tell me a story.

18. Do you like to travel?

19. Do you think grades should be considered by employers? Why or why not?

Questions About Work Habits

20. Do you prefer working with others or by yourself?

21. What type of boss do you prefer?

22. Have you ever had any difficulty getting along with colleagues or supervisors? With instructors? With other students?

23. Would you prefer to work in a large or a small organization? Why?

24. How do you feel about overtime work?

25. What have you done that shows initiative and willingness to work?

Source: Adapted from *The Northwestern Endicott Report* (Evanston, Ill.: Northwestern University Placement Center).

various questions at random. This method helps you learn to articulate answers and to look at the person as you answer.

Planning Questions of Your Own

Remember that the interview is a two-way street: The questions you ask are just as important as the answers you provide. By asking insightful questions, you can demonstrate your understanding of the organization, you can steer the discussion into those areas that allow you to present your qualifications to best advantage, and you can verify for yourself whether this is the right opportunity for you. Before the interview, prepare a list of about a dozen questions you need answered in order to evaluate the organization and the job. Here's a list of some things you might want to find out:

> You are responsible for deciding whether the work and the organization are compatible with your goals and values.

- **Are these my kind of people?** Observe the interviewers, and if you can, arrange to talk with other employees.
- **Can I do this work?** Compare your qualifications with the requirements described by the interviewer.
- **Will I enjoy the work?** Will the work give you real feelings of accomplishment and satisfaction?
- **Is the job what I want?** Will it make use of your best capabilities? Does it offer a career path to the long-term goals you've set?
- **Does the job pay what I'm worth?** By comparing jobs and salaries before you're interviewed, you'll know what's reasonable for someone with your skills in your industry.
- **What kind of person would I be working for?** If the interviewer is your prospective boss, watch how others interact with that person, tactfully query other employees, or pose a careful question or two during the interview. If your prospective boss is someone else, discretely ask about that person's name, job title, and responsibilities as a way to learn more.
- **What sort of future can I expect with this organization?** Is this organization in healthy financial shape? Will it grow enough to offer you opportunities to advance?

For a list of good questions that you might use as a starting point, see Table 14.4.

Write your questions on a notepad and bring it to the interview. Work the questions into the conversation naturally, without trying to take control of the interview. Feel free to jot down brief notes during the interview, then fill in the answers from memory afterward.

> Impress the interviewer with your ability to organize and be thorough by bringing a list of questions to the job interview.

Table 14.4	Ten Questions to Ask the Interviewer

1. What are the job's major responsibilities?
2. What qualities do you want in the person who fills this position?
3. How do you measure success for someone in this position?
4. What is the first problem that needs the attention of the person you hire?
5. Would relocation be required now or in the future?
6. Why is this job now vacant?
7. What makes your organization different from others in the industry?
8. How would you define your organization's managerial philosophy?
9. What additional training does your organization provide?
10. Do employees have an opportunity to continue their education with help from the organization?

Bolster Your Confidence

By building your confidence, you'll make a better impression and make the whole process less stressful. The best way to counteract any apprehension is to remove its source. You may feel shy or self-conscious because you think you have some flaw that will prompt others to reject you. Bear in mind, however, that you're often much more conscious of your limitations than other people are.

If some aspect of your appearance or background makes you uneasy, correct it or offset it by emphasizing positive traits such as warmth, wit, intelligence, or charm. Instead of dwelling on your weaknesses, focus on your strengths. Instead of worrying about how you will perform in the interview, focus on how you can help the organization succeed. Remember that all the other candidates for the job are just as nervous as you are. The interviewers may be nervous, too; after all, they're judged on how well they assess candidates, so help them see your positive qualities clearly.

Polish Your Interview Style

Staging mock interviews with a friend is a good way to hone your style.

Competence and confidence are the foundation of your interviewing style, and you can enhance those by giving the interviewer an impression of poise, good manners, and good judgment. You can develop an adept style by staging mock interviews with a friend or using an interview simulator. Tape-record or videotape these mock interviews and then evaluate them yourself. The taping process can be intimidating, but it helps you work out any problems before you begin actual job interviews. Your career center may have computer-based systems for practicing interviews as well (see Figure 14.3).

Nonverbal behavior has a significant effect on the interviewer's opinion of you.

After each practice session, look for opportunities to improve. Have your mock interview partner critique your performance, or critique yourself if you're able to record your practice interviews, using the list of warning signs shown in Table 14.5. Pay particular attention to your nonverbal behavior. In the United States, you are more likely to have a successful interview if you maintain eye contact, smile frequently, sit in an attentive position,

FIGURE 14.3   Interview Simulators
Experts advise you to practice your interview skills as much as possible. You can use a friend or classmate as a practice partner, or you might be able to use one of the interview simulators now available, such as this system from Perfect Interview. Ask at your career center, or search online for "practice interviews" or "interview simulators."

Table 14.5	Warning Signs: 25 Attributes That Interviewers Don't Like to See

- Poor personal appearance
- Overbearing, overaggressive, conceited demeanor; a "superiority complex"; know-it-all attitude
- Inability to express ideas clearly; poor voice, diction, grammar
- Lack of knowledge or experience
- Poor preparation for the interview
- Lack of interest in the job
- Lack of planning for career; lack of purpose, goals
- Lack of enthusiasm; passive and indifferent demeanor
- Lack of confidence and poise; appearance of being nervous and ill at ease
- Insufficient evidence of achievement
- Failure to participate in extracurricular activities
- Overemphasis on money; interest only in the best dollar offer

- Poor scholastic record; just got by
- Unwillingness to start at the bottom; expecting too much too soon
- Tendency to make excuses
- Evasive answers; hedges on unfavorable factors in record
- Lack of fact
- Lack of maturity
- Lack of courtesy; ill-mannered
- Condemnation of past employers
- Lack of social skills
- Marked dislike for schoolwork
- Lack of vitality
- Failure to look interviewer in the eye
- Limp, weak handshake

and use frequent hand gestures. These nonverbal signals convince the interviewer that you're alert, assertive, dependable, confident, responsible, and energetic.[21]

The sound of your voice can also have a major impact on your success in a job interview.[22] You can work with a tape recorder to overcome voice problems. If you tend to speak too rapidly, practice speaking more slowly. If your voice sounds too loud or too soft, practice adjusting it. Work on eliminating speech mannerisms such as *you know*, *like*, and *um*, which might make you sound inarticulate.

> The way you speak is almost as important as what you say.

Plan to Look Good

Clothing and grooming are important elements of preparation because they reveal something about a candidate's personality, professionalism, and ability to sense the unspoken "rules" of a situation. If you're not sure what to wear, dress on the conservative side, in dark, solid colors. Some candidates ask interviewers ahead of time what they should wear. One human resources executive tells job seekers to dress business casual because dressing in a suit, for example, looks awkward at his company.[23] However, in other companies, business casual would be completely out of place in a job interview. Your research into various industries and professions should give you insight into expectations for business attire. Wear the best-quality clothing you can, but remember that clean and appropriate are far more important than expensive and flashy.

> Dress conservatively and be well groomed for every interview.

Good grooming makes any style of clothing look better. Make sure your clothes are clean and unwrinkled, your shoes unscuffed and well shined, your hair neatly styled and combed, your fingernails clean, and your breath fresh. If possible, check your appearance in a mirror before entering the room for the interview. Finally, remember that one of the best ways to look good is to smile at appropriate moments.

Make professional appearance and habits a routine part of your day after you land that first job, too. Some students fail to recognize the need to adjust their dress and personal habits when they make the transition to professional life. Behaviors you may not think about, such as showing up five minutes late to every meeting or wearing a T-shirt to a client's office, could limit your career potential. Again, these may seem like minor issues, but many people are sensitive to these points of business etiquette and consider them a sign of mutual respect. Also, refrain from smoking before the interview (nonsmokers can smell smoke on the clothing of interviewees).

Be Ready When You Arrive

Be ready to go the minute you arrive at the interviewing site; don't fumble around for your résumé or your list of questions.

When you go to your interview, take a small notebook, a pen, a list of the questions you want to ask, several copies of your résumé (protected in a folder), an outline of what you have learned about the organization, and any past correspondence about the position. You may also want to take a small calendar, a transcript of your college grades, a list of references, and a portfolio containing samples of your work, performance reviews, and certificates of achievement.[24]

Be sure you know when and where the interview will be held. The worst way to start any interview is to be late. Verify the route and time required to get there, even if that means traveling there ahead of time. Plan to arrive early.

Once you arrive, you may have to wait for a while. Use this time to review the key messages about yourself you wish to get across in the interview. Conduct yourself professionally while waiting. Avoid chewing gum, eating, or drinking, and show respect for everyone you encounter. Anything you do or say at this stage may get back to the interviewer, so make sure your best qualities show from the moment you enter the premises.

Interviewing for Success

At the screening stage, try to leave the interviewer with one key thought that differentiates you from other candidates.

Your approach to interviews evolves as you move through each stage of the process. At the screening stage, your main objective is to differentiate yourself from the many other candidates who are also being screened. Without resorting to gimmicks, call attention to one key aspect of your personal or professional background that is relevant to the job in question. In addition, you'll want to be prepared in case an employer expects you to demonstrate a particular skill (perhaps problem solving) during the screening interview.

Cover all your strengths during an interview at the selection stage.

If you progress to the initial selection interview, broaden your promotional message. Instead of telegraphing the "headline," give the interviewer the whole story. Touch briefly on all your strengths, but explain three or four of your best qualifications in depth. At the same time, probe for information that will help you evaluate the position objectively.

Emphasize your personality during a final interview.

If you're asked back for a final visit, your chances of being offered a position have improved considerably. At this point, you'll probably talk to a person who has the authority to make an offer and negotiate terms. This individual may have already concluded that your background is right for the job and may be more concerned with sizing up your personality. Both you and the employer need to find out whether there is a good psychological fit. Be honest about your motivations and values. If the interview goes well, your objective should be to clinch the deal on the best possible terms.

Regardless of where you are in the interview process, every interview will proceed through three stages: the warm-up, the question-and-answer session, and the close.

The Warm-Up

The first minute of the interview is crucial.

Of the three stages, the warm-up is the most important, even though it may account for only a small fraction of the time you spend in the interview. Studies suggest that many interviewers, particularly those who are poorly trained in interviewing techniques, make up their minds within the first 20 seconds of contact with a candidate.[25] Don't let your guard down if it appears the interviewer wants to engage in what feels like small talk; these exchanges are every bit as important as structured questions.

Body language is important at this point. Because you won't have time to say much in the first minute or two, you must sell yourself nonverbally. If the interviewer extends a hand, respond with a firm but not overpowering handshake. Repeat the interviewer's name when you're introduced ("It's a pleasure to meet you, Ms. Litton"). Wait until you're asked to be seated. Let the interviewer start the discussion, and listen for cues that tell you what he or she is interested in knowing about you as a potential employee.

The Question-and-Answer Stage

Questions and answers will consume the greatest part of the interview. The interviewer will ask you about your qualifications and discuss many of the points mentioned in your résumé. You'll also be asking questions of your own.

Dealing with Questions

Let the interviewer lead the conversation, and never answer a question before he or she has finished asking it—the last few words of the question might alter how you respond. As questions are asked, tailor your answers to make a favorable impression. Don't limit yourself to yes-or-no answers. If you're asked a difficult question, pause before responding. Think through the implications of the question; for instance, the recruiter may know that you can't answer a question and only wants to know how you'll respond.

> Tailor your answers to emphasize your strengths.

If you periodically ask a question or two from the list you've prepared, when doing so fits the flow of the conversation, you'll not only learn something but also demonstrate your interest. Probe for what the company is looking for in its new employees so that you can show how you meet the firm's needs. Also try to zero in on any reservations the interviewer might have about you so that you can dispel them.

Listening to the Interviewer

Paying attention when the interviewer speaks can be as important as giving good answers or asking good questions. Review the tips on listening offered in Chapter 2.

The interviewer's facial expressions, eye movements, gestures, and posture may tell you the real meaning of what is being said. Be especially aware of how your comments are received. Does the interviewer nod in agreement or smile to show approval? If so, you're making progress. If not, you might want to introduce another topic or modify your approach.

> Paying attention to both verbal and nonverbal messages can help you turn the question-and-answer stage to your advantage.

Fielding Discriminatory Questions

Employers cannot legally discriminate against a job candidate on the basis of race, color, gender, age (at least if you're between 40 and 70), marital status, religion, national origin, or disability, and questions designed to elicit information on these topics are potentially illegal. Individual states and cities have enacted a variety of laws concerning interview questions, so you may have additional protections beyond the federal standards.[26] Table 14.6 compares specific questions that may and may not be asked during an employment interview.

> Well-trained interviewers are aware of questions they shouldn't ask.

If your interviewer asks these personal questions, how you respond depends on how badly you want the job, how you feel about revealing the information asked for, what you think the interviewer will do with the information, and whether you want to work for a company that asks such questions. Remember that you always have the option of simply refusing to answer or of telling the interviewer that you think a particular question is unethical—although either of these responses is likely to leave an unfavorable impression.[27] If you do want the job, you might (1) ask how the question is related to your qualifications, (2) explain that the information is personal, (3) respond to what you think is the interviewer's real concern, or (4) answer both the question and the concern.

> Think about how you might respond if you are asked to answer a potentially unlawful question.

If you do answer an unethical or unlawful question, you run the risk that your answer may hurt your chances, so think carefully before answering.[28] In any event, don't forget the two-way nature of the interview process: The organization is learning about you and you're learning about the organization. Would you want to work for an organization that condones illegal or discriminatory questions or that doesn't train its employees enough to avoid them?

If you believe an interviewer's questions are unreasonable, unrelated to the job, or an attempt to discriminate, you may complain to the nearest field office of the EEOC (find offices online at www.eeoc.gov) or to the state agency that regulates fair employment practices. To report discrimination on the basis of age or physical disability, contact the employer's equal opportunity officer or the U.S. Department of Labor. If you file a

Table 14.6	Interview Questions That May and May Not Be Asked

Interviewers may ask this . . .	But not this
What is your name?	What was your maiden name?
Are you over 18?	When were you born?
Did you graduate from high school?	When did you graduate from high school?
[No questions about race are allowed.]	What is your race?
Can you perform [specific tasks]?	Do you have physical or mental disabilities?
	Do you have a drug or alcohol problem?
	Are you taking any prescription drugs?
Would you be able to meet the job's requirement to frequently work weekends?	Would working on weekends conflict with your religion?
Do you have the legal right to work in the United States?	What country are you a citizen of?
Have you ever been convicted of a felony?	Have you ever been arrested?
This job requires that you speak Spanish. Do you?	What language did you speak in your home when you were growing up?

complaint, be prepared to spend a lot of time and effort on it—and keep in mind that you may not win.[29]

The Close

Like the warm up, the end of the interview is more important than its brief duration would indicate. In the last few minutes, you need to evaluate how well you've done. You also need to correct any misconceptions the interviewer might have.

Concluding Gracefully

Conclude the interview with courtesy and enthusiasm.

You can generally tell when the interviewer is trying to conclude the session. He or she may ask whether you have any more questions, sum up the discussion, change position, or indicate with a gesture that the interview is over. When you get the signal, respond promptly, but don't rush. Be sure to thank the interviewer for the opportunity and express an interest in the organization. If you can do so comfortably, try to pin down what will happen next, but don't press for an immediate decision.

If this is your second or third visit to the organization, the interview may culminate with an offer of employment. You have two options: Accept it or request time to think it over. The best course is usually to wait. If no job offer is made, the interviewer may not have reached a decision yet, but you may tactfully ask when you can expect to know the decision.

Discussing Salary

Research salary ranges in your job, industry, and geographic region before you try to negotiate salary.

If you do receive an offer during the interview, you'll naturally want to discuss salary. However, let the interviewer raise the subject. If asked your salary requirements during the interview or on a job application, you can say that your requirements are open or negotiable or that you would expect a competitive compensation package.[30] If you have added qualifications, point them out: "With my three years of experience in the field, I would expect to start in the middle of the normal salary range."

If you don't like the offer, you might try to negotiate. You'll be in a fairly strong position if your skills are in short supply and you have several other offers. It also helps if you're the favorite candidate and the organization is booming. However, many organizations are relatively rigid in their salary practices, particularly at the entry level. In the United States and some European countries, it is perfectly acceptable to ask, "Is there any room for negotiation?"

Salary will probably be the most important component of your compensation and benefits package, but it's not the only factor by any means. And even if salary isn't negotiable, you may find flexibility in a signing bonus, profit sharing, pension and other retirement benefits, health coverage, vacation time, and other valuable elements in the overall compensation and benefits package.[31]

Negotiating benefits may be one way to get more value from an employment package.

Interview Notes

If yours is a typical job search, you'll have many interviews before you accept an offer. For that reason, keeping a notebook or binder of interview notes can help you refresh your memory of each conversation. As soon as you leave the interview facility, jot down the names and titles of the people you met. Briefly summarize the interviewer's answers to your questions. Then quickly evaluate your performance during the interview, listing what you handled well and what you didn't. Going over these notes can help you improve your performance in the future.[32] In addition to improving your performance during interviews, interview notes will help you keep track of any follow-up messages you'll need to send.

Keep a written record of your job interviews.

Following Up After the Interview

Touching base with the prospective employer after the interview, either by phone or in writing, shows that you really want the job and are determined to get it. Doing so also gives you another chance to demonstrate your communication skills and sense of business etiquette. Following up brings your name to the interviewer's attention once again and reminds him or her that you're actively looking and waiting for the decision.

Thank-You Message

Express your thanks within two days after the interview, even if you feel you have little chance for the job. Not only is this good etiquette, but it leaves a positive impression. Acknowledge the interviewer's time and courtesy, and convey your continued interest, then ask politely for a decision (see Figure 14.4).

A note or phone call thanking the interviewer should be organized like a routine message and close with a request for a decision or future consideration.

Depending on the company and the relationship you've established with the interviewer, the thank-you message can be handled via letter, e-mail, or telephone. Keep your thank-you message brief, and organize it like a routine message. Demonstrate the "you" attitude, and sound positive without sounding overconfident. Even if the interviewer has said that you are unqualified for the job, a thank-you message may keep the door open to future opportunities.

Message of Inquiry

If you're not advised of the interviewer's decision by the promised date or within two weeks, you might make an inquiry. A letter of inquiry (which can be handled by e-mail if the interviewer has given you his or her e-mail address) is particularly appropriate if you've received a job offer from a second firm and don't want to accept it before you have an answer from the first. The following letter illustrates the general plan for a direct request; the writer assumes that a simple oversight, and not outright rejection, is the reason for the delay:

An inquiry about a hiring decision follows the model for a direct request.

> When we talked on April 7 about the fashion coordinator position in your Park Avenue showroom, you indicated that a decision would be made by May 1. I am still enthusiastic about the position and eager to know what conclusion you've reached.

Identifies the position and introduces the main idea

Places the reason for the request second

Makes a courteous request for specific action last, while clearly stating a preference for this organization

To complicate matters, another firm has now offered me a position and has asked that I reply within the next two weeks.

Because your company seems to offer a greater challenge, I would appreciate knowing about your decision by Thursday, May 12. If you need more information before then, please let me know.

Request for a Time Extension

If you receive a job offer while other interviews are still pending, you'll probably want more time to decide, so write to the offering organization and ask for a time extension. Employers understand that candidates often interview with several companies. They want you to be sure you're making the right decision, so most are happy to accommodate you with a reasonable extension.

Preface your request with a friendly opening. Ask for more time, stressing your enthusiasm for the organization. Conclude by allowing for a quick decision if your request for additional time is denied. Ask for a prompt reply confirming the time extension if the organization grants it. This type of letter is, in essence, a direct request. However, because the recipient may be disappointed, be sure to temper your request for an extension with statements indicating your continued interest (see Figure 14.5).

Letter of Acceptance

Use the model for positive messages when you write a letter of acceptance.

When you receive a job offer that you want to accept, reply within five days. Begin by accepting the position and expressing thanks. Identify the job that you're accepting. In the next paragraph, cover any necessary details. Conclude by saying that you look forward to

FIGURE 14.4   E-Mail Thank-You Message

In three brief paragraphs, Michael Espinosa acknowledges the interviewer's time and consideration, expresses his continued interest in the position, explains a crucial discussion point that he has reconsidered, and asks for a decision.

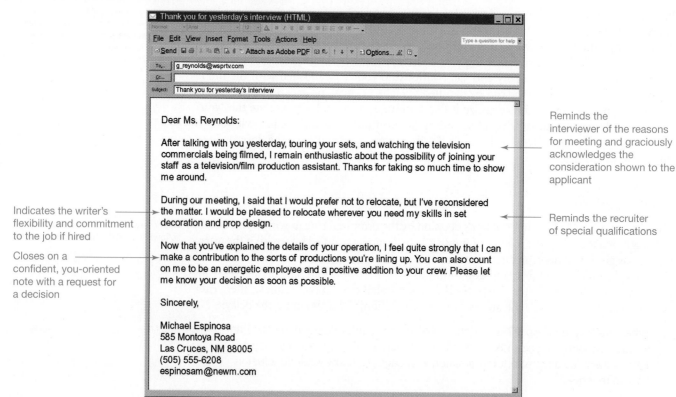

Reminds the interviewer of the reasons for meeting and graciously acknowledges the consideration shown to the applicant

Reminds the recruiter of special qualifications

Indicates the writer's flexibility and commitment to the job if hired

Closes on a confident, you-oriented note with a request for a decision

Document Makeover

Improve This Letter

To practice correcting drafts of actual documents, visit your online course or the access-code-protected portion of the Companion Website. Click "Document Makeovers," then click Chapter 14. You will find a letter that contains problems and errors relating to what you've learned in this chapter about applying and interviewing for employment. Use the "Final Draft" decision tool to create an improved version of this request for a time extension. Check the letter for all the elements necessary to reassure the potential employer, ask for the extension, explain the reasons for the request, offer to compromise, and facilitate a quick reply.

FIGURE 14.5   Effective Request for a Time Extension
If you need to request more time to make a decision about a job offer, make sure to reaffirm that you are still interested in the job.

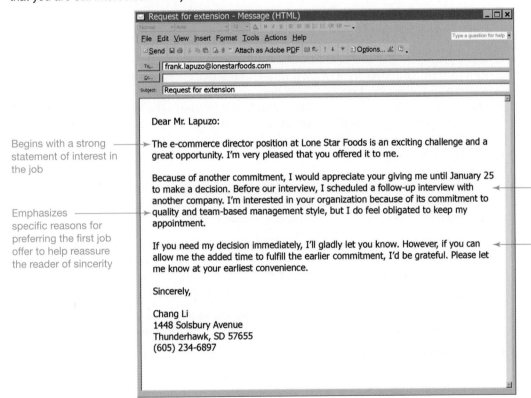

Begins with a strong statement of interest in the job

Emphasizes specific reasons for preferring the first job offer to help reassure the reader of sincerity

Stresses a professional obligation as the reason for the request, rather than the desire to learn what the other company may offer

Closes with an expression of willingness to yield or compromise, while conveying continued interest in the position

reporting for work. As always, a positive letter should convey your enthusiasm and eagerness to cooperate:

> I'm delighted to accept the graphic design position in your advertising department at the salary of $2,875 a month.

Confirms the specific terms the offer with a good news statement at the beginning

> Enclosed are the health insurance forms you asked me to complete and sign. I've already given notice to my current employer and will be able to start work on Monday, January 18.

Covers miscellaneous details in the middle

> The prospect of joining your firm is exciting. Thank you for giving me this opportunity for what I'm sure will be a challenging future.

Closes with another reference to the good news and a look toward the future

Be aware that a job offer and a written acceptance of that offer can constitute a legally binding contract, for both you and the employer. Before you write an acceptance letter, be sure you want the job.

Letter Declining a Job Offer

A letter declining a job offer follows the model for negative messages.

After all your interviews, you may find that you need to write a letter declining a job offer. Use the techniques for negative messages (see Chapter 8): Open warmly, state the reasons for refusing the offer, decline the offer explicitly, and close on a pleasant note, expressing gratitude. By taking the time to write a sincere, tactful letter, you leave the door open for future contact:

Uses a buffer in the opening paragraph —●

One of the most interesting interviews I have ever had was the one last month at your Durham textile plant. I'm flattered that you would offer me the computer analyst position that we talked about.

Precedes the bad news with tactfully phrased reasons for the applicant's unfavorable decision, and leaves the door open —●

During my job search, I applied to five highly rated firms like your own, each one a leader in its field. Both your company and another offered me a position. Because my desire to work abroad can more readily be satisfied by the other company, I have accepted that job offer.

Lets the reader down gently with a sincere and cordial ending —●

I deeply appreciate the time you spent talking with me. Thank you again for your consideration and kindness.

Letter of Resignation

Letters of resignation should always be written in a gracious and professional style that avoids criticism of your employer or your colleagues.

If you get a job offer and are currently employed, you can maintain good relations with your current employer by writing a thoughtful letter of resignation to your immediate supervisor. Follow the advice for negative messages, and make the letter sound positive, regardless of how you feel. Say something favorable about the organization, the people you work with, or what you've learned on the job. Then state your intention to leave and give the date of your last day on the job. Be sure you give your current employer at least two weeks' notice.

Uses an appreciative opening to serve as a buffer —●

My sincere thanks to you and to all the other Emblem Corporation employees for helping me learn so much about serving the public these past two years. You have given me untold help and encouragement.

States reasons before the bad news itself, using tactful phrasing to help keep the relationship friendly, should the writer later want letters of recommendation —●

You may recall that when you first interviewed me, my goal was to become a customer relations supervisor. Because that opportunity has been offered to me by another organization, I am submitting my resignation. I will miss all of you, but I want to take advantage of this opportunity.

I would like to terminate my work here two weeks from today but can arrange to work an additional week if you want me to train a replacement.

My sincere thanks and best wishes to all of you.

Reviewing Key Points

This chapter discusses applying and interviewing for employment. It outlines the steps needed to create effective application letters, then discusses a typical sequence of interviews: screening, selection, and final. It also introduces the various types of interviews, from structured to open-ended to behavioral or situational. The chapter explains how to prepare for a job interview by researching the company and the position, thinking ahead about questions, bolstering your confidence, polishing your interview style, planning to look good, and being ready when you arrive.

This chapter also discusses the three parts of any interview: the important warm-up stage, the question-and-answer stage, and the equally important close. It discusses how to follow up after an interview with a thank-you message and perhaps with a letter of inquiry or a request for a time extension.

You have worked hard to complete this course, and the reward is the ability to accelerate your career with effective business communication skills. Just remember that successful businesspeople never stop learning. As you pursue your career, continue your education and keep polishing the skills you've gained in this course. This textbook can continue to support your efforts, too. Periodically review the sample documents and messages to refresh your memory of the strategies and techniques for effective communication.

Test Your Knowledge

1. What is the primary reason for sending an application letter?

2. What should your objective be during a selection interview?

3. How does a structured interview differ from an open-ended interview and a situational interview?

4. Why are the questions you ask during an interview as important as the answers you give to the interviewer's questions?

5. What are the three stages of every interview, and which is the most important?

Apply Your Knowledge

1. How can you distinguish yourself from other candidates in a screening interview and still keep your responses short and to the point? Explain.

2. What can you do to make a favorable impression when you discover that an open-ended interview has turned into a stress interview? Briefly explain your answer.

3. If you want to switch jobs because you can't work with your supervisor, how can you explain this situation to a prospective employer? Give an example.

4. During a group interview you notice that one of the other candidates is trying to monopolize the conversation. He's always the first to answer, his answer is the longest, and he even interrupts the other candidates while they are talking. The interviewer doesn't seem to be concerned about his behavior, but you are. You would like to have more time to speak so that the interviewer could get to know you better. What should you do?

5. Ethical Choices   Why is it important to distinguish unethical or illegal interview questions from acceptable questions? Explain.

Practice Your Knowledge

Activities

For active links to all websites discussed in this chapter, visit this text's website at www.prenhall.com/bovee. Locate your book and click on its Companion Website link. Then select Chapter 14, and click on "Featured Websites." Locate the name of the page or the URL related to the material in the text. Please note that links to sites that become inactive after publication of the book will be removed from the Featured Websites section.

1. Analyze This Document   Read the following letter, then (1) analyze its strengths or weaknesses and (2) revise it so that it follows this chapter's guidelines.

I'm writing to let you know about my availability for the brand manager job you advertised. As you can see from my enclosed résumé, my background is perfect for the position. Even though I don't have any real job experience, my grades have been outstanding considering that I went to a top-ranked business school.

I did many things during my undergraduate years to prepare me for this job:

- Earned a 3.4 out of a 4.0 with a 3.8 in my business courses
- Elected representative to the student governing association
- Selected to receive the Lamar Franklin Award
- Worked to earn a portion of my tuition

I am sending my résumé to all the top firms, but I like yours better than any of the rest. Your reputation is tops in the industry, and I want to be associated with a business that can pridefully say it's the best.

If you wish for me to come in for an interview, I can come on a Friday afternoon or anytime on weekends when I don't have classes. Again, thanks for considering me for your brand manager position.

2. **Analyze This Document**   Read the following letter, then (1) analyze its strengths or weaknesses and (2) revise it so that it follows this chapter's guidelines.

Did you receive my résumé? I sent it to you at least two months ago and haven't heard anything. I know you keep résumés on file, but I just want to be sure that you keep me in mind. I heard you are hiring health-care managers and certainly would like to be considered for one of those positions.

Since I last wrote you, I've worked in a variety of positions that have helped prepare me for management. To wit, I've become lunch manager at the restaurant where I work, which involved a raise in pay. I now manage a waitstaff of 12 girls and take the lunch receipts to the bank every day.

Of course, I'd much rather be working at a real job, and that's why I'm writing again. Is there anything else you would like to know about me or my background? I would really like to know more about your company. Is there any literature you could send me? If so, I would really appreciate it.

I think one reason I haven't been hired yet is that I don't want to leave Atlanta. So I hope when you think of me, it's for a position that wouldn't require moving. Thanks again for considering my application.

3. **Analyze This Document**   Read the following letter, then (1) analyze its strengths or weaknesses and (2) revise it so that it follows this chapter's guidelines.

Thank you for the really marvelous opportunity to meet you and your colleagues at Starret Engine Company. I really enjoyed touring your facilities and talking with all the people there. You have quite a crew! Some of the other companies I have visited have been so rigid and uptight that I can't imagine how I would fit in. It's a relief to run into a group of people who seem to enjoy their work as much as all of you do.

I know that you must be looking at many other candidates for this job, and I know that some of them will probably be more experienced than I am. But I do want to emphasize that my two-year hitch in the Navy involved a good deal of engineering work. I don't think I mentioned all my shipboard responsibilities during the interview.

Please give me a call within the next week to let me know your decision. You can usually find me at my dormitory in the evening after dinner (phone: 877-9080).

4. **Analyze This Document**   Read the following letter, then (1) analyze its strengths or weaknesses and (2) revise it so that it follows this chapter's guidelines.

I have recently received a very attractive job offer from the Warrington Company. But before I let them know one way or another, I would like to consider any offer that your firm may extend. I was quite impressed with your company during my recent interview, and I am still very interested in a career there.

I don't mean to pressure you, but Warrington has asked for my decision within 10 days. Could you let me know by Tuesday whether you plan to offer me a position? That would give me enough time to compare the two offers.

5. **Analyze This Document**   Read the following letter, then (1) analyze its strengths or weaknesses and (2) revise it so that it follows this chapter's guidelines.

I'm writing to say that I must decline your job offer. Another company has made me a more generous offer, and I have decided to accept. However, if things don't work out for me there, I will let you know. I sincerely appreciate your interest in me.

6. **Teamwork**   Divide the class into two groups. Half the class will be recruiters for a large chain of national department stores looking to fill manager-trainee positions (there are 15 openings). The other half of the class will be candidates for the job. The company is specifically looking for candidates who demonstrate these three qualities: initiative, dependability, and willingness to assume responsibility.

   a. Have each recruiter select and interview an applicant for 10 minutes.

    b. Have all the recruiters discuss how they assessed the applicant in each of the three desired qualities. What questions did they ask or what did they use as an indicator to determine whether the candidate possessed the quality?

    c. Have all the applicants discuss what they said to convince the recruiters that they possessed each of these qualities.

7. **Internet**   Select a large company (one that you can easily find information on) where you might like to work. Use Internet sources to gather some preliminary research on the company; don't limit your search to the company's own website.

    a. What did you learn about this organization that would help you during an interview there?

    b. What Internet sources did you use to obtain this information?

    c. Armed with this information, what aspects of your background do you think might appeal to this company's recruiters?

    d. If you choose to apply for a job with this company, what keywords would you include on your résumé, and why?

8. **Interviews: Being Prepared**   Prepare written answers to 10 of the questions listed in Table 14.3, "Twenty-Five Common Interview Questions."

9. **Interviews: Understanding Qualifications**   Write a short e-mail to your instructor, discussing what you believe are your greatest strengths and weaknesses from an employment perspective. Next, explain how these strengths and weaknesses would be viewed by interviewers evaluating your qualifications.

10. **Ethical Choices**   You have decided to accept a new position with a competitor of your company. Write a letter of resignation to your supervisor, announcing your decision.

    a. Will you notify your employer that you are joining a competing firm? Please explain.

    b. Will you use the direct or the indirect approach? Please explain.

    c. Will you send your letter by e-mail, send it by regular mail, or place it on your supervisor's desk?

Expand Your Knowledge

Exploring the Best of the Web

Prepare and Practice Before That First Interview   How can you practice for a job interview? What are some questions that you might be asked, and how should you respond? What questions are you not obligated to answer? Job-interview.net, www.job-interview.net, provides mock interviews based on actual job openings. It provides job descriptions, questions and answers for specific careers and jobs, and links to company guides and annual reports. You'll find a step-by-step plan that outlines key job requirements, lists practice interview questions, and helps you put together practice interviews. The site offers tips on the keywords to look for in

a job description, which will help you narrow your search and anticipate the questions you might be asked on your first or next job interview.

Exercises

1. What are some problem questions you might be asked during a job interview? How would you handle these questions?
2. Choose a job title from the list, and read more about it. What did you learn that could help during an actual interview for the job you selected?
3. Developing an "interview game plan" ahead of time helps you make a strong, positive impression during an

interview. What are some of the things you can practice to help make everything you do during an interview seem to come naturally?

Exploring the Web on Your Own

Review these chapter-related websites on your own to learn more about interviewing for jobs.

1. Get over 2,000 pages of career advice at Monster.com, www.monster.com, and communicate with career experts in your choice of industry or profession.

2. For a humorous—but effective—take on job searching, visit www.soyouwanna.com, click on Work, then read the articles on interviewing and cover letters.

3. The *Wall Street Journal's* Career Journal website, www.careerjournal.com, offers a wealth of resources on interviewing, salary negotiations, and other vital topics.

Learn Interactively

Interactive Study Guide

Visit www.prenhall.com/bovee, then locate your book and click on its Companion Website link. Select Chapter 14 to take advantage of the interactive "Chapter Quiz" to test your knowledge of chapter concepts. Receive instant feedback on whether you need additional studying. Also, visit the "Study Hall," where you'll find an abundance of valuable resources that will help you succeed in this course.

Peak Performance Grammar and Mechanics

If your instructor has required the use of "Peak Performance Grammar and Mechanics," either in your online course, through the access-code protected portion of the Companion Website, or on CD, you can improve your skill with vocabulary by using the "Peak Performance Grammar and Mechanics" module. Click first on "Vocabulary I," then on "Vocabulary II." In both sections, take the Pretest to determine whether you have any weak areas. Then review those areas in the Refresher Course. Take the Follow-Up Test to check your grasp of using numbers in documents. For an extra challenge or advanced practice, take the Advanced Test. Finally, for additional reinforcement in vocabulary and spelling, go to the "Improve Your Grammar, Mechanics, and Usage" section that follows the cases, and complete the Level 1: Self-Assessment exercises.

CASES

Apply the three-step writing process to the following cases, as assigned by your instructor.

Preparing Other Types of Employment Messages

1. Online Application: Electronic Cover Letter Introducing a Résumé

While researching a digital camera purchase, you stumble on the webzine *Megapixel* (www.megapixel.net), which offers product reviews on a wide array of camera models. The quality of the reviews and the stunning examples of photography on the site inspire you to a new part-time business idea—you'd like to write a regular column for *Megapixel*. The webzine does a great job addressing the information needs of experienced camera users, but you see an opportunity to write for "newbies," people who are new to digital photography and need a more basic level of information.

Your Task Write an e-mail message that will serve as your cover letter and address your message to Denys Bouton, who edits the English edition of *Megapixel* (it is also published in French). Try to limit your message to one screen (generally 20–25 lines). You'll need a creative "hook" and a reassuring approach that identifies you as the right person to launch this new feature in the webzine (make up any details about your background that you may need to complete the message).

2. All Over the Map: Application Letter to Google Earth

You've applied yourself with vigor and resolve for four years, and you're just about to graduate with your business degree. While cruising the web to relax one night, you stumble on something called Google Earth. You're hooked instantly by the ability to zoom all around the globe and look at detailed satellite photos of places you've been to or dreamed of visiting. You can even type in the address of your apartment and get an aerial view of your neighborhood. You're amazed at the three-dimensional renderings of major U.S. cities. Plus, the photographs and maps are linked to Google's other search technologies, allowing you to locate everything from ATMs to coffees shops in your neighborhood.

You've loved maps since you were a kid, and discovering Google Earth is making you wish you had majored in geography instead. Knowing how important it is to follow your heart, you decide to apply to Google anyway, even though

you don't have a strong background in geographic information systems. What you do have is a ton of passion for maps and a good head for business.

Your Task Visit http://earth.google.com/ and explore the system's capabilities (you can download a free copy of the software). In particular, look at the business and government applications of the technology, such as customized aerial photos and maps for real estate sales, land use and environmental impact analysis, and emergency planning for homeland security agencies. Be sure to visit the Community pages as well, where you can learn more about the many interesting applications of this technology. Now draft an application e-mail to Google (address it to jobs@google.com), asking to be considered for the Google Earth team. Think about how you could help the company develop the commercial potential of this product line, and make sure your enthusiasm shines through in the message.

Interviewing with Potential Employers

3. Interviewers and Interviewees: Classroom Exercise in Interviewing

Interviewing is clearly an interactive process involving at least two people. The best way to practice for interviews is to work with others.

Your Task You and all other members of your class are to write letters of application for an entry-level or management-trainee position requiring a pleasant personality and intelligence but a minimum of specialized education or experience. Sign your letter with a fictitious name that conceals your identity. Next, polish (or create) a résumé that accurately identifies you and your educational and professional accomplishments.

Now, three members of the class who volunteer as interviewers divide up all the anonymously written application letters. Then each interviewer selects a candidate who seems the most pleasant and convincing in his or her letter. At this time the selected candidates identify themselves and give the interviewers their résumés.

Each interviewer then interviews his or her chosen candidate in front of the class, seeking to understand how the items on the résumé qualify the candidate for the job. At the end of the interviews, the class may decide who gets the job and discuss why this candidate was successful. Afterward, retrieve your letter, sign it with the right name, and submit it to the instructor for credit.

4. Internet Interview: Exercise in Interviewing

Locate the website of a company in an industry in which you might like to work, then identify an interesting position within the company. Study the company, using the research process described in Chapter 10, and prepare for an interview with that company.

Your Task Working with a classmate, take turns interviewing each other for your chosen positions. Interviewers should take notes during the interview. Once the interview is complete, critique each other's performance (interviewers should critique how well candidates prepared for the interview and answered the questions; interviewees should critique the quality of the questions asked). Write a follow-up letter thanking your interviewer and submit the letter to your instructor.

Following up After the Interview

5. A Slight Error in Timing: Letter Asking for Delay of an Employment Decision

Thanks to a mix-up in your job application scheduling, you accidentally applied for your third-choice job before going after what you really wanted. What you want to do is work in retail marketing with the upscale department store Neiman Marcus in Dallas; what you have been offered is a similar job with Longhorn Leather and Lumber, 55 dry and dusty miles away in Commerce, just south of the Oklahoma panhandle.

You review your notes. Your Longhorn interview was three weeks ago with the human resources manager, R. P. Bronson, a congenial person who has just written to offer you the position. The store's address is 27 Sam Rayburn Drive, Commerce, TX 75428. Mr. Bronson notes that he can hold the position open for 10 days. You have an interview scheduled with Neiman Marcus next week, but it is unlikely that you will know the store's decision within this 10-day period.

Your Task Write to R. P. Bronson, requesting a reasonable delay in your consideration of his job offer.

6. Job Hunt: Set of Employment-Related Letters to a Single Company

Where would you like to work? Choose one of your favorite products, find out which company either manufactures it or sells it in the United States (if it's manufactured in another country). Assume that a month ago you sent your résumé and application letter. Not long afterward, you were invited to come for an interview, which seemed to go very well.

Your Task Use your imagination to write the following: (a) a thank-you letter for the interview, (b) a note of inquiry, (c) a request for more time to decide, (d) a letter of acceptance, and (e) a letter declining the job offer.

Improve Your Grammar, Mechanics, and Usage

Level 1: Self-Assessment—Vocabulary

Review Sections 4.1, 4.2, and 4.3 in the Handbook of Grammar, Mechanics, and Usage, and then look at the following 15 items.

In items 1–7, write the correct word in the space provided:

1. Everyone (*accept/except*) _____ Barbara King has registered for the company competition.

2. We need to find a new security (*device/devise*) _____.

3. The Jennings are (*loath/loathe*) _____ to admit that they are wrong.

4. The judge has ruled that this town cannot enforce such a local (*ordinance/ordnance*) _____.

5. To stay on schedule, we must give (*precedence/precedents*) _____ to the Marley project.

6. This month's balance is greater (*than/then*) _____ last month's.

7. That decision lies with the director, (*who's/whose*) _____ in charge of this department.

In items 8–15, underline errors and write corrections in the space provided:

8. _____ In this department, we see alot of mistakes like that.

9. _____ In my judgement, you'll need to redo the cover.

10. _____ He decided to reveal the information, irregardless of the consequences.

11. _____ Why not go along when it is so easy to accomodate his demands?

12. _____ When you say that, do you mean to infer that I'm being unfair?

13. _____ She says that she finds this sort of ceremony embarassing.

14. _____ All we have to do is try and get along with him for a few more days.

15. _____ A friendly handshake should always preceed negotiations.

Level 2: Workplace Applications

The following items contain numerous errors in grammar, capitalization, punctuation, abbreviation, number style, word division, and vocabulary. Rewrite each sentence in the space provided, correcting all errors. Write *C* in the space after any sentence that is already correct.

1. An entrepreneur and their business, are so closely tied together that a bank will want to see how they handle their personal affairs, before granting a small business line of credit.

2. The companys' annual meeting will be held from 2–4 PM on May 3d in the Santa Fe room at the Marriott hotel..

3. Well over four hundred outstanding students from coast-to-coast, have realized their dreams of a college education thanks to the NASE Scholarship program.

4. If you're home is you're principle place of business you can deduct generally the cost of traveling from you're home, to any business destination.

5. Companies like McLeod USA sprung into being in the 1990's to provide cut rate phone services to small- and medium-size businesses in competition with the established baby bells.

6. Some question whether a 'new economy' exists and if so how it differs from the old economy?

7. When the music industry claimed by stealing intellectual property Napster were committing piracy - Napster argued that it was'nt doing anything illegal or un-ethical.

8. The World Bank plays an important roll in todays fast changing closely-meshed global economy.

9. When it comes to consumer rights the F.D.A., F.T.C., and Agriculture department are concerned not only with safety but also accurate information.

10. Fujitsu, a $50 billion company with 190,000 employees, dominates the Japanese computer industry.

11. The fortune 500 ranks not only corporations by size but also offers brief company descriptions; along with industry statistics, and additional measures of corporate performance.

12. Having bought 55 companies over the past decade, plans to make ten to 15 new acquisitions each year are being made by Cisco Systems.

13. In 1984 Michael Dell decided to sell P.C.'s direct and built to order, now everybody in the industry are trying to imitate Dells' strategy.

14. Resulting in large cost savings for the company, American Express have reduced the number of field office's from 85 to 7 by using virtual teams.

15. In Europe and Asia, people are using mobile phones to send text messages to other users; exchange e-mail; read the morning news; surfing certain websites; and to make purchases such as movie tickets and charge it to they're monthly phone bill.

Level 3: Document Critique

The following document may contain errors in grammar, capitalization, punctuation, abbreviation, number style, vocabulary, and spelling. Based on what you've learned in this chapter, you may also find problems with organization, usage, and word choice. Correct all errors using standard proofreading marks (see Appendix C).

Morgan Mitras

2397 Glencrest ridge, Fort Worth, TEX 76119

(817/ 226-1804

February 2 2007:

Norton Acctg. Group

Ms Nancy Remington, Human Resources

3778 Parkway North

Indianapolis, Indiana 46205

Dear Ms. Remington--

With your companys' reputation for quality, customer service, employee empowerment,

you'll will want to hire someone who is not only accurrate and efficient but also self

motivated and results-oriented—someone who is able to make decisions as well as

coperate with team members and clients. The ad you placed in the February 1st issue of

The Wall Street Journal for someone to fill a financial management position really has me

very excited and eager.

During my 3 years at Tandy corporation -see attached résumé- I've conducted internal

auditing for accounts valued at $450 million dollars. Some of my many, countless

accomplishments include

- Increasing both internal and client support for the auditing process
- I save the company over 2.5 million dollars when I discovered billing errors
- Suggest ways accounts receivable processes could be streamlined

In addition it might be that Norton Accounting may appreciate my ability to complete projects

on time as well as keeping them under budget. One of my priorities is a position in which my

expereince will be broaden: so any opportunity to travel would be welcomed by me!

I'll be in your area during the weak of February 20; I'll call your office on Feb. 8 to see

whether we can arrange to meet. I hope you'll give me a chance, please.

Sincerely,

Morgan Mitras,

Applicant

Format and Layout of Business Documents

The format and layout of business documents vary from country to country; they even vary within regions of the United States. In addition, many organizations develop their own variations of standard styles, adapting documents to the types of messages they send and the kinds of audiences they communicate with. The formats described here are more common than others.

First Impressions

Your documents tell readers a lot about you and about your company's professionalism. So all your documents must look neat, present a professional image, and be easy to read. Your audience's first impression of a document comes from the quality of its paper, the way it is customized, and its general appearance.

Paper

To give a quality impression, businesspeople consider carefully the paper they use. Several aspects of paper contribute to the overall impression:

- **Weight.** Paper quality is judged by the weight of four reams (each a 500-sheet package) of letter-size paper. The weight most commonly used by U.S. business organizations is 20-pound paper, but 16- and 24-pound versions are also used.
- **Cotton content.** Paper quality is also judged by the percentage of cotton in the paper. Cotton doesn't yellow over time the way wood pulp does, plus it's both strong and soft. For letters and outside reports, use paper with a 25 percent cotton content. For memos and other internal documents, you can use a lighter-weight paper with lower cotton content. Airmail-weight paper may save money for international correspondence, but make sure it isn't too flimsy.[1]
- **Size.** In the United States, the standard paper size for business documents is 8½ by 11 inches. Standard legal documents are 8½ by 14 inches. Executives sometimes have heavier 7-by-10-inch paper on hand (with matching envelopes) for personal messages such as congratulations and recommendations.[2] They may also have a box of note cards imprinted with their initials and a box of plain folded notes for condolences or for acknowledging formal invitations.

- **Color.** White is the standard color for business purposes, although neutral colors such as gray and ivory are sometimes used. Memos can be produced on pastel-colored paper to distinguish them from external correspondence. In addition, memos are sometimes produced on various colors of paper for routing to separate departments. Light-colored papers are appropriate, but bright or dark colors make reading difficult and may appear too frivolous.

Customization

For letters to outsiders, U.S. businesses commonly use letterhead stationery, which may be either professionally printed or designed in-house using word-processing templates and graphics. The letterhead includes the company's name and address, usually at the top of the page but sometimes along the left side or even at the bottom. Other information may be included in the letterhead as well: the company's telephone number, fax number, cable address, website address, product lines, date of establishment, officers and directors, slogan, and symbol (logo). Well-designed letterhead gives readers[3]

- Pertinent reference data
- A favorable image of the company
- A good idea of what the company does

For as much as it's meant to accomplish, the letterhead should be as simple as possible. Too much information makes the page look cluttered, occupies space needed for the message, and might become outdated before all the stationery can be used. If you correspond frequently with people abroad, your letterhead must be intelligible to foreigners. It must include the name of your country in addition to your cable, telex, e-mail, or fax information.

In the United States, businesses always use letterhead for the first page of a letter. Successive pages are usually plain sheets of paper that match the letterhead in color and quality. Some companies use a specially printed second-page letterhead that bears only the company's name. Other countries have other conventions.

Many companies also design and print standardized forms for memos and frequently written reports that always require the same sort of information (such as sales reports and expense reports). These forms may be printed in sets for use with carbon paper or in carbonless-copy sets that produce multiple copies automatically. More and more organizations use computers to generate their standardized forms, which can save them both money and time.[4]

Appearance

Produce almost all of your business documents using either a printer (letter-quality, not a dot matrix) or a typewriter. Certain documents, however, should be handwritten (such as a short informal memo or a note of condolence). Be sure to handwrite, print, or type the envelope to match the document. However, even a letter on the best-quality paper with the best-designed letterhead may look unprofessional if it's poorly produced. So pay close attention to all the factors affecting appearance, including the following:

- **Margins.** Companies in the United States make sure that documents (especially external ones) are centered on the page, with margins of at least an inch all around. Using word-processing software, you can achieve this balance simply by defining the format parameters.
- **Line length.** Lines are rarely justified, because the resulting text looks too much like a form letter and can be hard to read (even with proportional spacing). Varying line length makes the document look more personal and interesting.
- **Line spacing.** You can adjust the number of blank lines between elements (such as between the date and the inside address) to ensure that a short document fills the page vertically or that a longer document extends at least two lines of the body onto the last page.
- **Character spacing.** Use proper spacing between characters and after punctuation. For example, U.S. conventions include leaving one space after commas, semicolons, colons, and sentence-ending periods. Each letter in a person's initials is followed by a period and a single space. However, abbreviations such as U.S.A. or MBA may or may not have periods, but they never have internal spaces.
- **Special symbols.** Take advantage of the many special symbols available with your computer's selection of fonts. (In Microsoft Word, click on the Insert menu, then select Symbol.) Table A.1 shows some of the more common symbols used in business documents. In addition, see if your company has a style guide for documents, which may include other symbols you are expected to use.
- **Corrections.** Messy corrections are unacceptable in business documents. If you notice an error after printing a document with your word processor, correct the mistake and reprint. (With informal memos to members of your own team or department, the occasional small correction in pen or pencil is acceptable, but never in formal documents.)

Letters

All business letters have certain elements in common. Several of these elements appear in every letter; others appear only when desirable or appropriate. In addition, these letter parts are usually arranged in one of three basic formats.

Table A.1	Special Symbols on Computer
	Computer symbol
Case fractions	½
Copyright	©
Registered trademark	®
Cents	¢
British pound	£
Paragraph	¶
Bullets	●, ◆, ■, □, ✓, ☑, ⊗
Em dash	—
En dash	–

Standard Letter Parts

The letter in Figure A.1 shows the placement of standard letter parts. The writer of this business letter had no letterhead available but correctly included a heading. All business letters typically include these seven elements.

Heading

Letterhead (the usual heading) shows the organization's name, full address, telephone number (almost always), and e-mail address (often). Executive letterhead also bears the name of an individual within the organization. Computers allow you to design your own letterhead (either one to use for all correspondence or a new one for each piece of correspondence). If letterhead stationery is not available, the heading includes a return address (but no name) and starts 13 lines from the top of the page, which leaves a two-inch top margin.

Date

If you're using letterhead, place the date at least one blank line beneath the lowest part of the letterhead. Without letterhead, place the date immediately below the return address. The standard method of writing the date in the United States uses the full name of the month (no abbreviations), followed by the day (in numerals, without *st, nd, rd,* or *th*), a comma, and then the year: July 14, 2007 (7/14/07). Some organizations follow other conventions (see Table A.2). To maintain the utmost clarity in international correspondence, always spell out the name of the month in dates.[5]

When communicating internationally, you may also experience some confusion over time. Some companies in the United States refer to morning (A.M.) and afternoon (P.M.), dividing a 24-hour day into 12-hour blocks so that they refer to four o'clock in the morning (4:00 A.M.) or four o'clock in the afternoon (4:00 P.M.). The U.S. military and European companies refer to one 24-hour period so that 0400 hours (4:00 A.M.) is always in the morning and 1600 hours (4:00 P.M.) is always in the afternoon.[6] Make sure your references to time are as clear as possible, and be sure you clearly understand your audience's time references.

FIGURE A.1   Standard Letter Parts

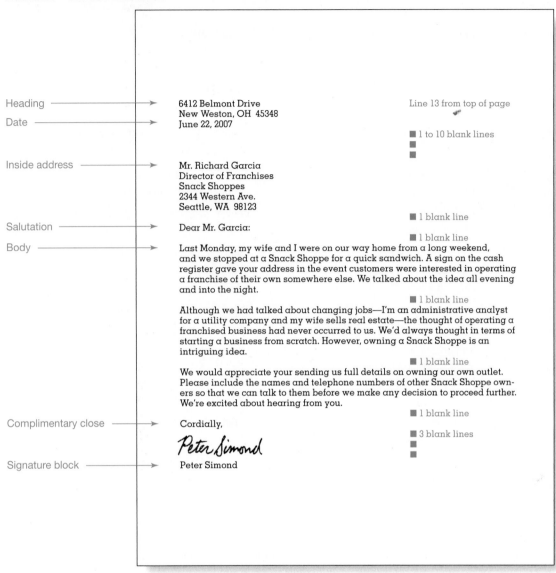

Heading

Date

Inside address

Salutation

Body

Complimentary close

Signature block

6412 Belmont Drive
New Weston, OH 45348
June 22, 2007

Line 13 from top of page

■ 1 to 10 blank lines
■
■

Mr. Richard Garcia
Director of Franchises
Snack Shoppes
2344 Western Ave.
Seattle, WA 98123

■ 1 blank line

Dear Mr. Garcia:

■ 1 blank line

Last Monday, my wife and I were on our way home from a long weekend, and we stopped at a Snack Shoppe for a quick sandwich. A sign on the cash register gave your address in the event customers were interested in operating a franchise of their own somewhere else. We talked about the idea all evening and into the night.

■ 1 blank line

Although we had talked about changing jobs—I'm an administrative analyst for a utility company and my wife sells real estate—the thought of operating a franchised business had never occurred to us. We'd always thought in terms of starting a business from scratch. However, owning a Snack Shoppe is an intriguing idea.

■ 1 blank line

We would appreciate your sending us full details on owning our own outlet. Please include the names and telephone numbers of other Snack Shoppe owners so that we can talk to them before we make any decision to proceed further. We're excited about hearing from you.

■ 1 blank line

Cordially,

■ 3 blank lines
■
■

Peter Simond

Peter Simond

Inside Address

The inside address identifies the recipient of the letter. For U.S. correspondence, begin the inside address at least one line below the date. Precede the addressee's name with a courtesy title, such as *Dr.*, *Mr.*, or *Ms.* The accepted courtesy title for women in business is *Ms.*, although a woman known to prefer the title *Miss* or *Mrs.* is always accommodated. If you don't know whether a person is a man or a woman (and you have no way of finding out), omit the courtesy title. For example, *Terry Smith* could be either a man or a woman. The first line of the inside

Table A.2	Common Date Forms		
Convention	**Description**	**Date—Mixed**	**Date—All Numerals**
U.S. standard	Month (spelled out) day, year	July 14, 2007	7/14/07
U.S. government and some U.S. industries	Day (in numerals) month (spelled out) year	14 July 2007	14/7/07
European	Replace U.S. solidus (diagonal line) with periods	14 July 2007	14.7.2007
International standard	Year month day	2007 July 14	2007,7,14

Table A.3   Forms of Address

Person	In Address	In Salutation
Personal Titles		
Man	Mr. [first & last name]	Dear Mr. [last name]:
Woman[1]	Ms. [first & last name]	Dear Ms. [last name]:
Two men (or more)	Mr. [first & last name] and Mr. [first & last name]	Dear Mr. [last name] and Mr. [last name] *or* Messrs. [last name] and [last name]:
Two women (or more)	Ms. [first & last name] and Ms. [first & last name]	Dear Ms. [last name] and Ms. [last name] *or* Mses. [last name] and [last name]:
One woman and one man	Ms. [first & last name] and Mr. [first & last name]	Dear Ms. [last name] and Mr. [last name]:
Couple (married)	Mr. [husband's first name] and Ms. [wife's first name] [couple's last name]	Dear Mr. and Ms. [last name]:
Couple (married with different last names)	Mr. [first & last name of husband] Ms. [first & last name of wife]	Dear Mr. [husband's last name] and Ms. [wife's last name]:
Couple (married professionals with same title and same last name)	[title in plural form] [husband's first name] and [wife's first name] [couple's last name]	Dear [title in plural form] [last name]:
Couple (married professionals with different titles and same last name)	[title] [first & last name of husband] and [title] [first & last name of wife]	Dear [title] and [title] [last name]:

address would be just *Terry Smith,* and the salutation would be *Dear Terry Smith.* The same is true if you know only a person's initials, as in *S. J. Adams.*

Spell out and capitalize titles that precede a person's name, such as *Professor* or *General* (see Table A.3 for the proper forms of address). The person's organizational title, such as *Director,* may be included on this first line (if it is short) or on the line below; the name of a department may follow. In addresses and signature lines, don't forget to capitalize any professional title that follows a person's name:

Mr. Ray Johnson, Dean

Ms. Patricia T. Higgins
Assistant Vice President

However, professional titles not appearing in an address or signature line are capitalized only when they directly precede the name.

President Kenneth Johanson will deliver the speech.

Maria Morales, president of ABC Enterprises, will deliver the speech.

The Honorable Helen Masters, senator from Arizona, will deliver the speech.

If the name of a specific person is unavailable, you may address the letter to the department or to a specific position within the department. Also, be sure to spell out company names in full, unless the company itself uses abbreviations in its official name.

Other address information includes the treatment of buildings, house numbers, and compass directions (see Table A.4 on page A-6). The following example shows all the information that may be included in the inside address and its proper order for U.S. correspondence:

Ms. Linda Coolidge, Vice President
Corporate Planning Department
Midwest Airlines
Kowalski Building, Suite 21-A

Table A.3	Continued	
Person	**In Address**	**In Salutation**
Professional Titles		
President of a college or university	[title]. [first & last name], President	Dear [title][last name]:
Dean of a school of college	Dean [first & last name] *or*	Dear Dean [last name]:
	Dr., Mr., *or* Ms. [first & last name] Dean of [title]	Dear Dr., Mr., Ms. [last name]:
Professor	Professor Dr. [first & last name]	Dear Professor Dr. [last name]:
Physician	[first & last name], M.D.	Dear Dr. [last name]:
Lawyer	Mr. or Ms. [first & last name] Attorney at Law	Dear Mr. or Ms. Miss [last name]:
Service personnel	[full rank, first & last name, abbreviation of service designation] (add *Retired* if applicable)	Dear [rank][last name]:
Company or corporation	[name of organization]	Ladies and Gentlemen *or* Gentlemen and Ladies:
Governmental Titles		
President of the United States	The President	Dear Mr. *or* Madam President:
Senator of the United States	Honorable [first & last name]	Dear Senator [last name]:
Cabinet member Postmaster General Attorney General	Honorable [first & last name]	Dear Mr. *or* Madam Secretary: Dear Mr. *or* Madam Postmaster General: Dear Mr. *or* Madam Attorney General:
Mayor	Honorable [first & last name] Mayor of [name of city]	Dear Mayor [last name]:
Judge	The Honorable	Dear Judge [last name]:

¹Use Mrs. or Miss only if the recipient has specifically requested that you use one of these titles, otherwise always use Ms. in business correspondence. Also, never refer to a woman by her husband's name (e.g., Mrs. Robert Washington) unless ssdhe specifically requests you do so.

7279 Bristol Ave.
Toledo, OH 43617

Canadian addresses are similar, except that the name of the province is usually spelled out:

Dr. H. C. Armstrong
Research and Development
Commonwealth Mining Consortium
The Chelton Building, Suite 301
585 Second St. SW

Calgary, Alberta T2P 2P5

The order and layout of address information vary from country to country. So when addressing correspondence for other countries, carefully follow the format and information that appear in the company's letterhead. However, when you're sending mail from the United States, be sure that the name of the destination country appears on the last line of the address in capital letters. Use the English version of the country name so that your mail is routed from the United States to the right country. Then, to be sure your mail is routed correctly within

Table A.4	Inside Address Information
Description	**Example**
Capitalize building names	Empire State Building
Capitalize locations within buildings (apartments, suites, rooms)	Suite 1073
Use numerals for all house or building numbers, except the number *one*	One Trinity Lane 637 Adams Avenue, Apt. 7
Spell out compass directions that fall within a street address	1074 West Connover Street
Abbreviate compass directions that follow the street address	783 Main St, N.E., Apt. 27

the destination country, use the foreign spelling of the city name (using the characters and diacritical marks that would be commonly used in the region). For example, the following address uses *Köln* instead of *Cologne*:

H. R. Veith, Director	Addressee
Eisfieren Glaswerk	Company name
Blaubachstrasse 13	Street address
Postfach 10 80 07	Post office box
D-5000 Köln I	District, city
GERMANY	Country

For additional examples of international addresses, see Table A.5.

Be sure to use organizational titles correctly when addressing international correspondence. Job designations vary around the world. In England, for example, a managing director is often what a U.S. company would call its chief executive officer or president, and a British deputy is the equivalent of a vice president. In France, responsibilities are assigned to individuals without regard to title or organizational structure, and in China the title *project manager* has meaning, but the title *sales manager* may not.

To make matters worse, businesspeople in some countries sign correspondence without their names typed below. In Germany, for example, the belief is that employees represent the company, so it's inappropriate to emphasize personal names.[7] Use the examples in Table A.5 as guidelines when addressing correspondence to countries outside the United States.

Salutation

In the salutation of your letter, follow the style of the first line of the inside address. If the first line is a person's name, the salutation is *Dear Mr.* or *Ms. Name.* The formality of the salutation depends on your relationship with the addressee. If in conversation you would say "Mary," your letter's salutation should be *Dear Mary,* followed by a colon. Otherwise, include the courtesy title and last name, followed by a colon. Presuming to write *Dear Lewis* instead of *Dear Professor Chang* demonstrates a disrespectful familiarity that the recipient will probably resent.

If the first line of the inside address is a position title such as *Director of Personnel,* then use *Dear Director.* If the addressee

is unknown, use a polite description, such as *Dear Alumnus, Dear SPCA Supporter,* or *Dear Voter.* If the first line is plural (a department or company), then use *Ladies and Gentlemen* (look again at Table A.3). When you do not know whether you're writing to an individual or a group (for example, when writing a reference or a letter of recommendation), use *To whom it may concern.*

In the United States some letter writers use a "salutopening" on the salutation line. A salutopening omits *Dear* but includes the first few words of the opening paragraph along with the recipient's name. After this line, the sentence continues a double space below as part of the body of the letter, as in these examples:

Thank you, Mr. Brown,	Salutopening
for your prompt payment of your bill.	Body
Congratulations, Ms. Lake!	Salutopening
Your promotion is well deserved.	Body

Whether your salutation is informal or formal, be especially careful that names are spelled right. A misspelled name is glaring evidence of carelessness, and it belies the personal interest you're trying to express.

Body

The body of the letter is your message. Almost all letters are single-spaced, with one blank line before and after the salutation or salutopening, between paragraphs, and before the complimentary close. The body may include indented lists, entire paragraphs indented for emphasis, and even subheadings. If it does, all similar elements should be treated in the same way. Your department or company may select a format to use for all letters.

Complimentary Close

The complimentary close begins on the second line below the body of the letter. Alternatives for wording are available, but currently the trend seems to be toward using one-word closes, such as *Sincerely* and *Cordially.* In any case, the complimentary close reflects the relationship between you and the person you're writing to. Avoid cute closes, such as *Yours for bigger profits.* If your audience doesn't know you well, your sense of humor may be misunderstood.

Table A.5	International Addresses and Salutations		
Country	**Postal Address**	**Address Elements**	**Salutations**
Argentina	Sr. Juan Pérez Editorial Internacional S.A. Av. Sarmiento 1337, 8° P. C C1035AAB BUENOS AIRES - CF ARGENTINA	S.A. = Sociedad Anónima (corporation) Av. Sarmiento (name of street) 1337 (building number) 8° = 8th. P = Piso (floor) C (room or suite) C1035AAB (postcode + city) CF = Capital Federal (federal capital)	Sr. = Señor (Mr.) Sra. = Señora (Mrs.) Srta. = Señorita (Miss) Don't use given names except with people you know well.
Australia	Mr. Roger Lewis International Publishing Pty.Ltd. 166 Kent Street, Level 9 GPO Box 3542 SYDNEY NSW 2001 AUSTRALIA	Pty.Ltd. = Proprietory Limited (corp.) 166 (building number) Kent Street (name of street) Level (floor) GPO Box (post office box) city + state (abbrev.) + postcode	Mr. and Mrs. used on first contact. Ms. not common (avoid use). Business is informal—use given name freely.

Austria	Herrn
	Dipl.-Ing.J.Gerdenitsch
	International Verlag Ges.m.b.H.
	Glockengasse 159
	1010 WIEN
	AUSTRIA
		Herrn = To Mr. (separate line)
		Dipl.-Ing. (engineering degree)
		Ges.m.b.H. (a corporation)
		Glockengasse (street name)
		159 (building number)
		1010 (postcode + city)
		WIEN (Vienna)
			Herr (Mr.)
			Frau (Mrs.)
			Fräulein (Miss) obsolete in business,
			  so do not use.
			Given names are almost never used in
			  business.

Brazil	Ilmo. Sr.
	Gilberto Rabello Ribeiro
	Editores Internacionais S.A.
	Rua da Ajuda, 228-6° Andar
	Caixa Postal 2574
	20040-000
	RIO DE JANEIRO - RJ
	BRAZIL
		Ilmo. = Ilustrissimo (honorific)
		Ilma. = Ilustrissima (hon.female)
		S.A. = Sociedade Anônima (corporation)
		Rua = street, da Ajuda (street name)
		228 (building number)
		6° = 6th. Andar (floor)
		Caixa Postal (P.O. box)
		20040–000 (postcode + city)
		- RJ (state abbrev.)
			Sr. = Senhor (Mr.)
			Sra. = Senhora (Mrs.)
			Srta. = Senhorita (Miss)
			Family name at end,
			  e.g., Senhor Ribeiro (Rabello is
			  mother's family—as in Portugal)
			Given names readily used in business.

China	Xia Zhiyi International Publishing Ltd. 14 Jianguolu Chaoyangqu BEIJING 100025 CHINA	Ltd. (limited liability corporation) 14 (building number) Jianguolu (street name), lu (street) Chaoyangqu (district name) (city + postcode)	Family name (single syllable) first. Given name (2 syllables) second, sometimes reversed. Use Mr. or Ms. at all times (Mr. Xia).
France	Monsieur LEFÈVRE Alain Éditions Internationales S.A. Siège Social Immeuble Le Bonaparte 64–68, av. Galliéni B.P. 154 75942 PARIS CEDEX 19 FRANCE	S.A. = Société Anonyme Siège Social (head office) Immeuble (building + name) 64–68 (building occupies 64, 66, 68) av. = avenue (no initial capital) B.P. = Boîte Postale (P.O. box) 75942 (postcode) CEDEX (postcode for P.O. box)	Monsieur (Mr.) Madame (Mrs.) Mademoiselle (Miss) Best not to abbreviate. Family name is sometimes in all caps with given name following.

Germany	Herrn
	Gerhardt Schneider
	International Verlag GmbH
	Schillerstraβe 159
	44147 DORTMUND
	GERMANY
		Herrn = To Herr (on a separate line)
		GmbH (inc.—incorporated)
		-straβe (street—'β' often written 'ss')
		159 (building number)
		44147 (postcode + city)
			Herr (Mr.)
			Frau (Mrs.)
			Fräulein (Miss) obsolete in business.
			Business is formal: (1) do not use given
			  names unless invited, and (2) use
			  academic titles precisely.

Table A.5   Continued

Country	Postal Address	Address Elements	Salutations
India	Sr. Shyam Lal Gupta International Publishing (Pvt.) Ltd. 1820 Rehaja Centre 214, Darussalam Road Andheri East BOMBAY - 400049 INDIA	(Pvt.) (privately owned) Ltd. (limited liability corporation) 1820 (possibly office #20 on 18th floor) Rehaja Centre (building name) 214 (building number) Andheri East (suburb name) (city + hyphen + postcode)	Shri (Mr.), Shrimati (Mrs.) but English is common business language, so use Mr., Mrs., Miss. Given names are used only by family and close friends.
Italy	Egr. Sig. Giacomo Mariotti Edizioni Internazionali S.p.A. Via Terenzio, 21 20138 MILANO ITALY	Egr. = Egregio (honorific) Sig. = Signor (not nec. a separate line) S.p.A. = Società per Azioni (corp.) Via (street) 21 (building number) 20138 (postcode + city)	Sig. = Signore (Mr.) Sig.ra = Signora (Mrs.) Sig.a (Ms.) Women in business are addressed as Signora. Use given name only when invited.
Japan	Mr. Taro Tanaka Kokusai Shuppan K.K. 10–23, 5-chome, Minamiazabu Minato-ku TOKYO 106 JAPAN	K.K. = Kabushiki Kaisha (corporation) 10 (lot number) 23 (building number) 5-chome (area #5) Minamiazabu (neighborhood name) Minato-ku (city district) (city + postcode)	Given names not used in business. Use family name + job title. Or use family name + "-san" (Tanaka-san) or more respectfully, add "-sama" or "-dono."
Korea	Mr. Kim Chang-ik International Publishers Ltd. Room 206, Korea Building 33-4 Nonhyon-dong Kangnam-ku SEOUL 135-010 KOREA	English company names common Ltd. (a corporation) 206 (office number inside the building) 33-4 (area 4 of subdivision 33) -dong (city neighborhood name) -ku (subdivision of city) (city + postcode)	Family name is normally first but sometimes placed after given name. A two-part name is the given name. Use Mr. or Mrs. in letters, but use job title in speech.
Mexico	Sr. Francisco Pérez Martínez Editores Internacionales S.A. Independencia No.322 Col. Juárez 06050 MEXICO D.F.	S.A. = Sociedad Anónima (corporation) Independencia (street name) No. = Número (number) 322 (building number) Col. = Colonia (city district) Juárez (locality name) 06050 (postcode + city) D.F. = Distrito Federal (federal capital)	Sr. = Señor (Mr.) Sra. = Señora (Mrs.) Srta. = Señorita (Miss) Family name in middle: e.g., Sr. Pérez (Martínez is mother's family). Given names are used in business.
South Africa	Mr. Mandla Ntuli International Publishing (Pty.) Ltd. Private Bag X2581 JOHANNESBURG 2000 SOUTH AFRICA	Pty. = Proprietory (privately owned) Ltd. (a corporation) Private Bag (P.O. Box) (city + postcode) or (postcode + city)	Mnr = Meneer (Mr.) Mev. = Mevrou (Mrs.) Mejuffrou (Miss) is not used in business. Business is becoming less formal, so the use of given names is possible.
United Kingdom	Mr. N. J. Lancaster International Publishing Ltd. Kingsbury House 12 Kingsbury Road EDGEWARE Middlesex HA8 9XG ENGLAND	N. J. (initials of given names) Ltd. (limited liability corporation) Kingsbury House (building name) 12 (building number) Kingsbury Road (name of street/road) EDGEWARE (city—all caps) Middlesex (county—not all caps) HA8 9XG (postcode)	Mr. and Ms. used mostly. Mrs. and Miss sometimes used in North and by older women. Given names—called Christian names—are used in business after some time. Wait to be invited.

Signature Block

Leave three blank lines for a written signature below the complimentary close, and then include the sender's name (unless it appears in the letterhead). The person's title may appear on the same line as the name or on the line below:

Cordially,

Raymond Dunnigan
Director of Personnel

Your letterhead indicates that you're representing your company. However, if your letter is on plain paper or runs to a second page, you may want to emphasize that you're speaking legally for the company. The accepted way of doing that is to place the company's name in capital letters a double space below the complimentary close and then include the sender's name and title four lines below that:

Sincerely,
WENTWORTH INDUSTRIES

(Mrs.) Helen B. Taylor
President

If your name could be taken for either a man's or a woman's, a courtesy title indicating gender should be included, with or without parentheses. Also, women who prefer a particular courtesy title should include it:

Mrs. Nancy Winters
(Miss) Juana Flores
Ms. Pat Li
(Mr.) Jamie Saunders

Additional Letter Parts

Letters vary greatly in subject matter and thus in the identifying information they need and the format they adopt. The letter in Figure A.2 shows how these additional parts should be arranged. The following elements may be used in any combination, depending on the requirements of the particular letter:

- **Addressee notation.** Letters that have a restricted readership or that must be handled in a special way should include such addressee notations as *Personal, Confidential,* or *Please Forward.* This sort of notation appears a double space above the inside address, in all-capital letters.
- **Attention line.** Although not commonly used today, an attention line can be used if you know only the last name of the person you're writing to. It can also direct a letter to a position title or department. Place the attention line on the first line of the inside address and put the company name on the second.[8] Match the address on the envelope with the style of the inside address. An attention line may take any of the following forms or variants of them:

Attention Dr. McHenry
Attention Director of Marketing
Attention Marketing Department

- **Subject line.** The subject line tells recipients at a glance what the letter is about (and indicates where to file the letter for future reference). It usually appears below the salutation, either against the left margin, indented (as a paragraph in the body), or centered. It can be placed above the salutation or at the very top of the page, and it can be underscored. Some businesses omit the word *Subject,* and some organizations replace it with *Re:* or *In re:* (meaning "concerning" or "in the matter of"). The subject line may take a variety of forms, including the following:

Subject: RainMaster Sprinklers
About your February 2, 2007, order
FALL 2007 SALES MEETING
Reference Order No. 27920

- **Second-page heading.** Use a second-page heading whenever an additional page is required. Some companies have second-page letterhead (with the company name and address on one line and in a smaller typeface). The heading bears the name (person or organization) from the first line of the inside address, the page number, the date, and perhaps a reference number. Leave two blank lines before the body. Make sure that at least two lines of a continued paragraph appear on the first and second pages. Never allow the closing lines to appear alone on a continued page. Precede the complimentary close or signature lines with at least two lines of the body. Also, don't hyphenate the last word on a page. All the following are acceptable forms for second-page headings:

Ms. Melissa Baker
May 10, 2007
Page 2

Ms. Melissa Baker, May 10, 2007, Page 2

Ms. Melissa Baker   -2-   May 10, 2007

- **Company name.** If you include the company's name in the signature block, put it all in capital letters a double space below the complimentary close. You usually include the company's name in the signature block only when the writer is serving as the company's official spokesperson or when letterhead has not been used.
- **Reference initials.** When businesspeople keyboard their own letters, reference initials are unnecessary, so they are becoming rare. When one person dictates a letter and another person produces it, reference initials show who

FIGURE A.2 Additional Letter Parts

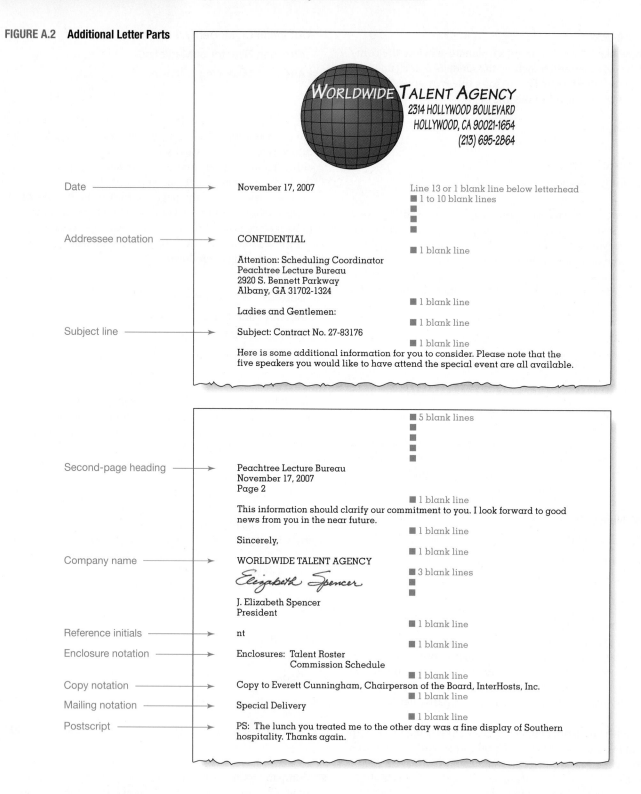

helped prepare it. Place initials at the left margin, a double space below the signature block. When the signature block includes the writer's name, use only the preparer's initials. If the signature block includes only the department, use both sets of initials, usually in one of the following forms: *RSR/sm, RSR:sm,* or *RSR:SM* (writer/preparer). When the writer and the signer are different people, at least the file copy should bear both their initials as well as the typist's: *JFS/RSR/sm* (signer/writer/preparer).

■ **Enclosure notation.** Enclosure notations appear at the bottom of a letter, one or two lines below the reference initials. Some common forms include the following:

Enclosure

Enclosures (2)

Enclosures: Résumé

              Photograph

              Attachment

■ **Copy notation.** Copy notations may follow reference initials or enclosure notations. They indicate who's receiving a *courtesy copy* (*cc*). Some companies indicate copies made on a photocopier (*pc*), or they simply use *copy* (*c*). Recipients are listed in order of rank or (rank being equal) in alphabetical order. Among the forms used are the following:

cc: David Wentworth, Vice President

pc: Dr. Martha Littlefield

Copy to   Hans Vogel
              748 Chesterton Road
              Snowhomish, WA 98290

              c: Joseph Martinez with brochure and technical sheet

When sending copies to readers without other recipients knowing, place *bc, bcc,* or *bpc* ("blind copy," "blind courtesy copy," or "blind photocopy") along with the name and any other information only on the copy, not on the original.

■ **Mailing notation.** You may place a mailing notation (such as *Special Delivery* or *Registered Mail*) at the bottom of the letter, after reference initials or enclosure notations (whichever one is last) and before copy notations. Or you may place it at the top of the letter, either above the inside address on the left side or just below the date on the right side. For greater visibility, mailing notations may appear in capital letters.

■ **Postscript.** A postscript is an afterthought to the letter, a message that requires emphasis, or a personal note. It is usually the last thing on any letter and may be preceded by *P.S., PS., PS:,* or nothing at all. A second afterthought would be designated *P.P.S.* (post postscript). Since postscripts usually indicate poor planning, generally avoid them. However, they're common in sales letters as a punch line to remind readers of a benefit for taking advantage of the offer.

Letter Formats

A letter format is the way of arranging all the basic letter parts. Sometimes a company adopts a certain format as its policy; sometimes the individual letter writer or preparer is allowed to choose the most appropriate format. In the United States, three major letter formats are commonly used:

■ **Block format.** Each letter part begins at the left margin. The main advantage is quick and efficient preparation (see Figure A.3).

■ **Modified block format.** Same as block format, except that the date, complimentary close, and signature block start near the center of the page (see Figure A.4). The modified block format does permit indentions as an option. This format mixes preparation speed with traditional placement of some letter parts. It also looks more balanced on the page than the block format does.

■ **Simplified format.** Instead of using a salutation, this format often weaves the reader's name into the first line or two of the body and often includes a subject line in capital letters (see Figure A.5). With no complimentary close, your signature appears after the body, followed by your printed (or typewritten) name (usually in all capital letters). This format is convenient when you don't know the reader's name; however, some people object to it as mechanical and impersonal (a drawback you can overcome with a warm writing style). Because certain letter parts are eliminated, some line spacing is changed.

These three formats differ in the way paragraphs are indented, in the way letter parts are placed, and in some punctuation. However, the elements are always separated by at least one blank line, and the printed (or typewritten) name is always separated from the line above by at least three blank lines to allow space for a signature. If paragraphs are indented, the indention is normally five spaces. The most common formats for intercultural business letters are the block style and the modified block style.

In addition to these three letter formats, letters may also be classified according to their style of punctuation. *Standard,* or *mixed, punctuation* uses a colon after the salutation (a comma if the letter is social or personal) and a comma after the complimentary close. *Open punctuation* uses no colon or comma after the salutation or the complimentary close. Although the most popular style in business communication is mixed punctuation, either style of punctuation may be used with block or modified block letter formats. Because the simplified letter format has no salutation or complimentary close, the style of punctuation is irrelevant.

Envelopes

For a first impression, the quality of the envelope is just as important as the quality of the stationery. Letterhead and envelopes should be of the same paper stock, have the same color ink, and be imprinted with the same address and logo. Most envelopes used by U.S. businesses are No. 10 envelopes ($9\frac{1}{2}$ inches long), which are sized for an $8\frac{1}{2}$-by-11-inch piece of paper folded in thirds. Some occasions call for a smaller, No. $6\frac{3}{4}$, envelope or for envelopes proportioned to fit special stationery. Figure A.6 shows the two most common sizes.

Addressing the Envelope

No matter what size the envelope, the address is always single-spaced with all lines aligned on the left. The address on the envelope is in the same style as the inside address and presents the same information. The order to follow is from the smallest division to the largest:

1. Name and title of recipient
2. Name of department or subgroup
3. Name of organization
4. Name of building
5. Street address and suite number, or post office box number
6. City, state, or province, and ZIP code or postal code
7. Name of country (if the letter is being sent abroad)

Because the U.S. Postal Service uses optical scanners to sort mail, envelopes for quantity mailings, in particular, should be addressed in the prescribed format. Everything is in capital letters,

FIGURE A.3   Block Letter Format

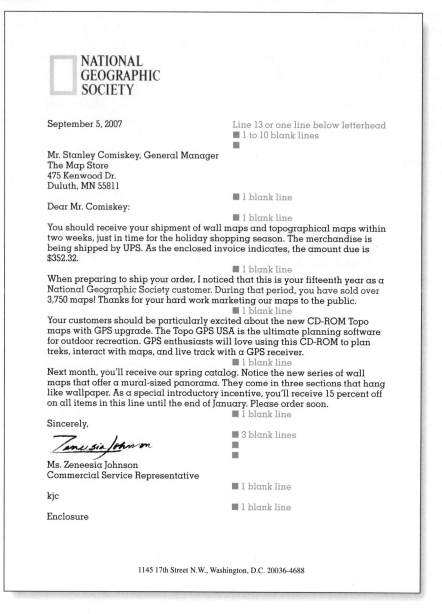

no punctuation is included, and all mailing instructions of interest to the post office are placed above the address area (see Figure A.6). Canada Post requires a similar format, except that only the city is all in capitals, and the postal code is placed on the line below the name of the city. The post office scanners read addresses from the bottom up, so if a letter is to be sent to a post office box rather than to a street address, the street address should appear on the line above the box number. Figure A.6 also shows the proper spacing for addresses and return addresses.

The U.S. Postal Service and the Canada Post Corporation have published lists of two-letter mailing abbreviations for states, provinces, and territories (see Table A.6). Postal authorities prefer no punctuation with these abbreviations, but some executives prefer to have state and province names spelled out in full and set off from city names by a comma. The issue is unresolved, although the comma is most often included. Quantity mailings follow post office requirements. For other letters, a rea-

sonable compromise is to use traditional punctuation, uppercase and lowercase letters for names and street addresses, but two-letter state or province abbreviations, as shown here:

> Mr. Kevin Kennedy
> 2107 E. Packer Drive
> Amarillo, TX 79108

For all out-of-office correspondence, use ZIP and postal codes that have been assigned to speed mail delivery. The U.S. Postal Service has divided the United States and its territories into ten zones (0 to 9); this digit comes first in the ZIP code. The second and third digits represent smaller geographical areas within a state, and the last two digits identify a "local delivery area." Canadian postal codes are alphanumeric, with a three-character "area code" and a three-character "local code"

FIGURE A.4   Modified Block Letter Format

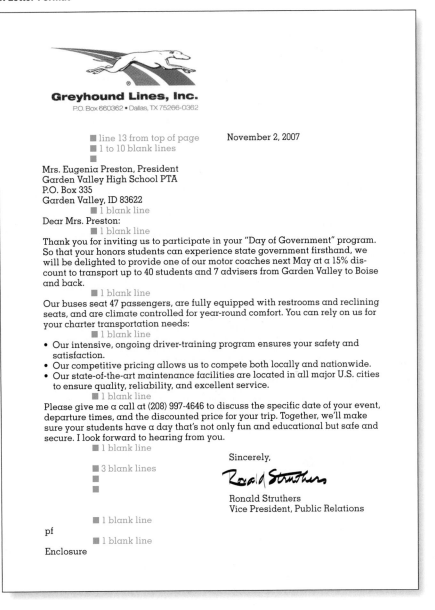

separated by a single space (K2P 5A5). ZIP codes should be separated from state and province names by one space. The Canadian postal code may be treated the same or may be put in the bottom line of the address all by itself.

The U.S. Postal Service has added ZIP + 4 codes, which add a hyphen and four more numbers to the standard ZIP codes. The first two of the new numbers may identify an area as small as a single large building, and the last two digits may identify one floor in a large building or even a specific department of an organization. The ZIP + 4 codes are especially useful for business correspondence. The Canada Post Corporation achieves the same result with special postal codes assigned to buildings and organizations that receive a large volume of mail.

Folding to Fit

The way a letter is folded also contributes to the recipient's overall impression of your organization's professionalism.

When sending a standard-size piece of paper in a No. 10 envelope, fold it in thirds, with the bottom folded up first and the top folded down over it (see Figure A.7 on page A-17); the open end should be at the top of the envelope and facing out. Fit smaller stationery neatly into the appropriate envelope simply by folding it in half or in thirds. When sending a standard-size letterhead in a No. 6¾ envelope, fold it in half from top to bottom and then in thirds from side to side.

International Mail

Postal service differs from country to country. For example, street addresses are uncommon in India, and the mail there is unreliable.[9] It's usually a good idea to send international correspondence by airmail and to ask that responses be sent that way as well. Also, remember to check the postage; rates for sending mail to most other countries differ from the rates for sending mail within your own country.

FIGURE A.5   Simplified Letter Format

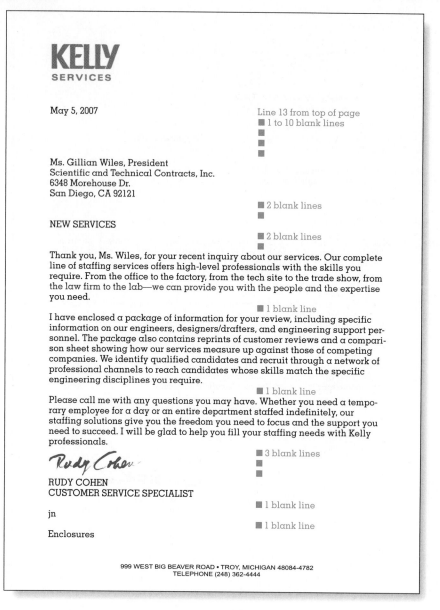

International mail falls into three main categories:

- **LC mail.** An abbreviation of the French *Lettres et Cartes* ("letters and cards"), this category consists of letters, letter packages, aerograms, and postcards.
- **AO mail.** An abbreviation of the French *Autres Objets* ("other articles"), this category includes regular printed matter, books and sheet music, matter for the blind, small packets, and publishers' periodicals (second class).
- **CP mail.** An abbreviation of the French *Colis Postaux* ("parcel post"), this category resembles fourth-class mail, including packages of merchandise or any other articles not required to be mailed at letter rates.

Along with several optional special services, the U.S. Postal Service also offers the following:

- **Express Mail International Service (EMS).** A high-speed mail service to many countries
- **International Priority Airmail (IPA).** An international service that's as fast as or faster than regular airmail service
- **International Surface Air Lift (ISAL).** A service providing quicker delivery and lower cost for all kinds of printed matter
- **Bulk Letter Service to Canada.** An economical airmail service for letters weighing 1 ounce or less
- **Valuepost/Canada.** A reduced postage rate for bulk mailings
- **International Electronic Post (INTELPOST).** A service offering same- or next-day delivery of fax documents
- **International Postal Money Orders.** A service for transferring funds to other countries

FIGURE A.6 Prescribed Envelope Format

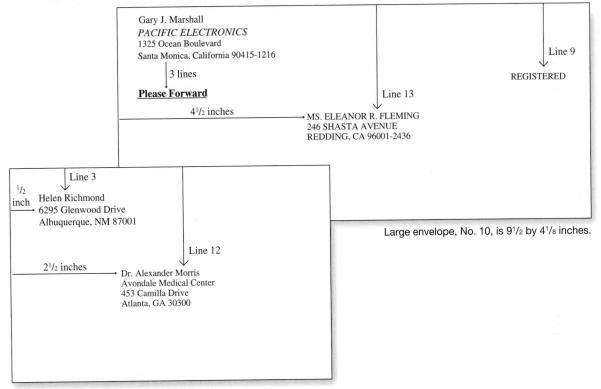

Large envelope, No. 10, is 9¹/₂ by 4¹/₈ inches.

Small envelope, No. 6³/₄, is 6¹/₂ by 3⁵/₈ inches.

To prepare your mail for international delivery, follow the instructions in the U.S. Postal Service Publication 51, *International Postal Rates and Fees.* Be sure to note instructions for the address, return address, and size limits. Envelopes and wrappers must be clearly marked to show their classification (letter, small packet, printed matter, airmail). All registered letters, letter packages, and parcel post packages must be securely sealed. Printed matter may be sealed only if postage is paid by permit imprint, postage meter, precanceled stamps, or second-class imprint. Otherwise, prepare contents so that they're protected without hindering inspection. Finally, because international mail is subject to customs examination in the country of destination, the contents and value must be declared on special forms.

Memos

Many organizations have memo forms preprinted, with labeled spaces for the recipient's name (or sometimes a checklist of all departments in an organization or all persons in a department), the sender's name, the date, and the subject (see Figure A.8). If such forms don't exist, you can use a memo template (which comes with word-processing software and provides margin settings, headings, and special formats), or you can use plain paper. On your document, include a title such as *MEMO* or *INTEROFFICE CORRESPONDENCE* (all in capitals) centered at the top of the page or aligned with the left margin. Also at the top, include the words *To, From, Date,* and *Subject*—followed by the appropriate information—with a blank line between, as shown here:

MEMO

TO:

FROM:

DATE:

SUBJECT:

Sometimes the heading is organized like this:

MEMO

TO: DATE:

FROM: SUBJECT:

You can arrange these four pieces of information in almost any order. The date sometimes appears without the heading *Date.* The subject may be presented with the letters *Re:* (in place of *SUBJECT:*) or may even be presented without any heading (but in capital letters so that it stands out clearly). You may want to include a file or reference number, introduced by the word *File.*

The following guidelines will help you effectively format specific memo elements:

- **Addressees.** When sending a memo to a long list of people, include the notation *See distribution list* or *See below* in the *To* position at the top; then list the names at the end of the memo. Arrange this list alphabetically, except when high-ranking officials deserve more prominent placement. You can also address memos to groups of people—*All Sales Representatives, Production Group, New Product Team.*

| Table A.6 | Two-Letter Mailing Abbreviations for the United States and Canada | | | | | |

State/Territory/Province	Abbreviation	State/Territory/Province	Abbreviation	State/Territory/Province	Abbreviation
United States		Massachusetts	MA	Texas	TX
Alabama	AL	Michigan	MI	Utah	UT
Alaska	AK	Minnesota	MN	Vermont	VT
American Samoa	AS	Mississippi	MS	Virginia	VA
Arizona	AZ	Missouri	MO	Virgin Islands	VI
Arkansas	AR	Montana	MT	Washington	WA
California	CA	Nebraska	NE	West Virginia	WV
Canal Zone	CZ	Nevada	NV	Wisconsin	WI
Colorado	CO	New Hampshire	NH	Wyoming	WY
Connecticut	CT	New Jersey	NJ	**Canada**	
Delaware	DE	New Mexico	NM	Alberta	AB
District of Columbia	DC	New York	NY	British Columbia	BC
Florida	FL	North Carolina	NC	Labrador	NL
Georgia	GA	North Dakota	ND	Manitoba	MB
Guam	GU	Northern Mariana	MP	New Brunswick	NB
Hawaii	HI	Ohio	OH	Newfoundland	NL
Idaho	ID	Oklahoma	OK	Northwest Territories	NT
Illinois	IL	Oregon	OR	Nova Scotia	NS
Indiana	IN	Pennsylvania	PA	Nunavur	NU
Iowa	IA	Puerto Rico	PR	Ontario	ON
Kansas	KS	Rhode Island	RI	Prince Edward Island	PE
Kentucky	KY	South Carolina	SC	Quebec	PQ
Louisiana	LA	South Dakota	SD	Saskatchewan	SK
Maine	ME	Tennessee	TN	Yukon Territory	YT
Maryland	MD	Trust Territories	TT		

- **Courtesy titles.** You need not use courtesy titles anywhere in a memo; first initials and last names, first names, or even initials alone are often sufficient. However, use a courtesy title if you would use one in a face-to-face encounter with the person.
- **Subject line.** The subject line of a memo helps busy colleagues quickly find out what your memo is about. Although the subject "line" may overflow onto a second line, it's most helpful when it's short (but still informative).
- **Body.** Start the body of the memo on the second or third line below the heading. Like the body of a letter, it's usually single-spaced with blank lines between paragraphs. Indenting paragraphs is optional. Handle lists, important passages, and subheadings as you do in letters. If the memo is very short, you may double-space it.
- **Second page.** If the memo carries over to a second page, head the second page just as you head the second page of a letter.

- **Writer's initials.** Unlike a letter, a memo doesn't require a complimentary close or a signature, because your name is already prominent at the top. However, you may initial the memo—either beside the name appearing at the top of the memo or at the bottom of the memo—or you may even sign your name at the bottom, particularly if the memo deals with money or confidential matters.
- **Other elements.** Treat elements such as reference initials, enclosure notations, and copy notations just as you would in a letter.

Memos may be delivered by hand, by the post office (when the recipient works at a different location), or through interoffice mail. Interoffice mail may require the use of special reusable envelopes that have spaces for the recipient's name and department or room number; the name of the previous recipient is simply crossed out. If a regular envelope is used, the words

FIGURE A.7 Folding Standard-Size Letterhead

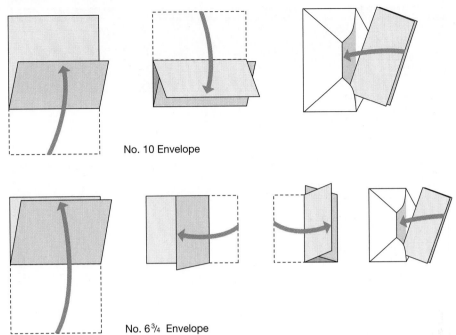

No. 10 Envelope

No. 6¾ Envelope

Interoffice Mail appear where the stamp normally goes, so that it won't accidentally be stamped and mailed with the rest of the office correspondence.

Informal, routine, or brief reports for distribution within a company are often presented in memo form (see Chapter 10). Don't include report parts such as a table of contents and appendixes, but write the body of the memo report just as carefully as you'd write a formal report.

E-Mail

Because e-mail messages can act both as memos (carrying information within your company) and as letters (carrying information outside your company and around the world), their format depends on your audience and purpose. You may choose to have your e-mail resemble a formal letter or a detailed report, or you may decide to keep things as simple as an interoffice memo. A modified memo format is appropriate for most e-mail messages.[10] All e-mail programs include two major elements: the header and the body (see Figure A.9 on the following page).

Header

The e-mail header depends on the particular program you use. Some programs even allow you to choose between a shorter and a longer version. However, most headers contain similar information.

■ **To:** Contains the audience's e-mail address (see Figure A.10 on page A-19). Most e-mail programs also allow you to send mail to an entire group of people all at once. First, you create a distribution list. Then you type the name of the list in the *To:* line instead of typing the addresses of every person in the group.[11] The most common e-mail addresses are addresses such as

nmaa.betsy@c.si.edu (Smithsonian Institute's National Museum of American Art)

webwsj@dowjones.com (*Wall Street Journal*'s home page)

relpubli@mairie-toulouse.mipnet.fr (Municipal Services, Toulouse, France)

FIGURE A.8 Preprinted Memo Form

MEMO

TO: _____

DEPT: _____   FROM: _____

DATE: _____   TELEPHONE: _____

SUBJECT: _____   *For your*
☐ APPROVAL ☐ INFORMATION ☐ COMMENT

FIGURE A.9　A Typical E-Mail Message

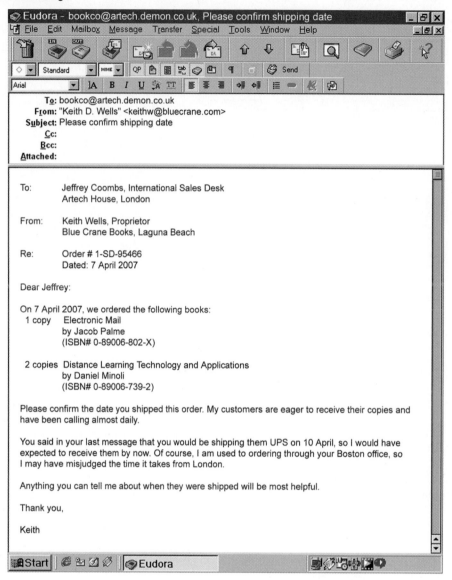

■ **From:** Contains your e-mail address.

■ **Date:** Contains the day of the week, date (day, month, year), time, and time zone.

■ **Subject:** Describes the content of the message and presents an opportunity for you to build interest in your message.

■ **Cc:** Allows you to send copies of a message to more than one person at a time. It also allows everyone on the list to see who else received the same message.

■ **Bcc:** Lets you send copies to people without the other recipients knowing—a practice considered unethical by some.[12]

■ **Attachments:** Contains the name(s) of the file(s) you attach to your e-mail message. The file can be a word-processing document, a digital image, an audio or video message, a spreadsheet, or a software program.[13]

Most e-mail programs now allow you the choice of hiding or revealing other lines that contain more detailed information, including

■ **Message-Id:** The exact location of this e-mail message on the sender's system

■ **X-mailer:** The version of the e-mail program being used

■ **Content type:** A description of the text and character set that is contained in the message

■ **Received:** Information about each of the systems your e-mail passed through en route to your mailbox[14]

Body

The rest of the space below the header is for the body of your message. In the *To:* and *From:* lines, some headers actually print out the names of the sender and receiver (in addition to their e-mail addresses). Other headers do not. If your mail program includes only the e-mail addresses, you might consider including your own memo-type header in the body of your message, as in Figure A.9. The writer even included a second, more specific subject line in his memo-type header. Some recipients may

FIGURE A.10   Anatomy of an E-Mail Address

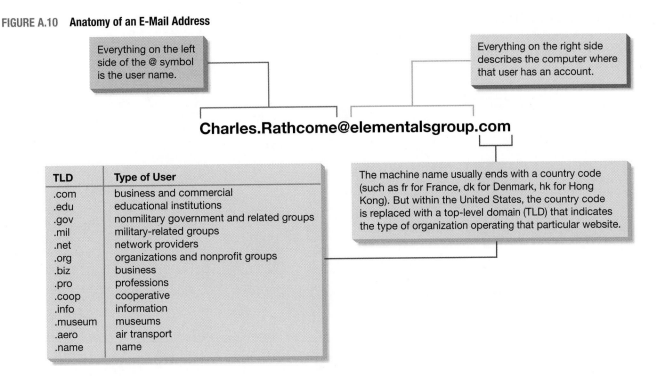

Everything on the left side of the @ symbol is the user name.

Everything on the right side describes the computer where that user has an account.

Charles.Rathcome@elementalsgroup.com

TLD	Type of User
.com	business and commercial
.edu	educational institutions
.gov	nonmilitary government and related groups
.mil	military-related groups
.net	network providers
.org	organizations and nonprofit groups
.biz	business
.pro	professions
.coop	cooperative
.info	information
.museum	museums
.aero	air transport
.name	name

The machine name usually ends with a country code (such as fr for France, dk for Denmark, hk for Hong Kong). But within the United States, the country code is replaced with a top-level domain (TLD) that indicates the type of organization operating that particular website.

applaud the clarity of such second headers; however, others will criticize the space it takes. Your decision depends on how formal you want to be.

Do include a greeting in your e-mail. As pointed out in Chapter 6, greetings personalize your message. Leave one line space above and below your greeting to set it off from the rest of your message. You may end your greeting with a colon (formal), a comma (conversational), or even two hyphens (informal)—depending on the level of formality you want.

Your message begins one blank line space below your greeting. Just as in memos and letters, skip one line space between paragraphs and include headings, numbered lists, bulleted lists, and embedded lists when appropriate. Limit your line lengths to a maximum of 80 characters by inserting a hard return at the end of each line.

One blank line space below your message, include a simple closing, often just one word. A blank line space below that, include your signature. Whether you type your name or use a signature file, including your signature personalizes your message.

Reports

Enhance your report's effectiveness by paying careful attention to its appearance and layout. Follow whatever guidelines your organization prefers, always being neat and consistent throughout. If it's up to you to decide formatting questions, the following conventions may help you decide how to handle margins, headings, spacing and indention, and page numbers.

Margins

All margins on a report page are at least 1 inch wide. For double-spaced pages, use 1-inch margins; for single-spaced pages, set margins between 1¼ and 1½ inches. The top, left, and right margins are usually the same, but the bottom margins can be 1½ times deeper. Some special pages also have deeper top margins. Set top margins as deep as 2 inches for pages that contain major titles: prefatory parts (such as the table of contents or the executive summary), supplementary parts (such as the reference notes or bibliography), and textual parts (such as the first page of the text or the first page of each chapter).

If you're going to bind your report at the left or at the top, add half an inch to the margin on the bound edge (see Figure A.11): The space taken by the binding on left-bound reports makes the center point of the text a quarter inch to the right of the center of the paper. Be sure to center headings between the margins, not between the edges of the paper. Computers can do this for you automatically. Other guidelines for report formats are in the Chapter 12 sample.

Headings

Headings of various levels provide visual clues to a report's organization. Figure 11.13, starting on page 318, shows one good system for showing these levels, but many variations exist. No matter which system you use, be sure to be consistent.

Spacing and Indentions

If your report is double-spaced (perhaps to ease comprehension of technical material), indent all paragraphs five character spaces (or about ½ inch). In single-spaced reports, block the paragraphs (no indentions) and leave one blank line between them.

Make sure the material on the title page is centered and well balanced, as on the title page of the sample report in Chapter 12. When using a typewriter, proper spacing takes some calculation. To center text in left-bound reports, start a quarter inch to the right of the paper's center. From that point,

FIGURE A.11   **Margins for Formal Reports**

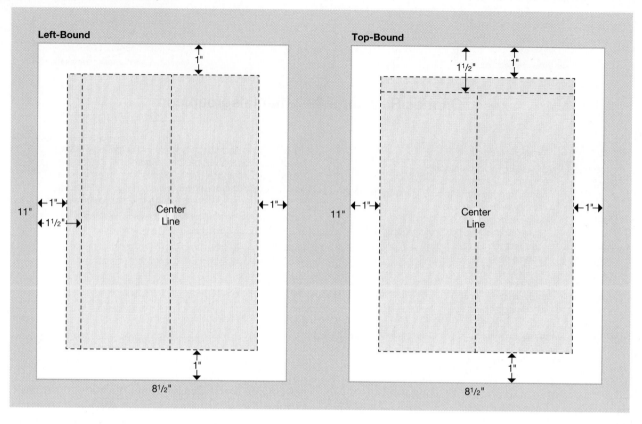

backspace once for each two letters in the line. The line will appear centered once the report is bound.

To place lines of type vertically on the title page, follow these steps:

1. Count the number of lines in each block of copy, including blank lines.
2. Subtract that total from 66 (the number of lines on an 11-inch page); the result is the number of unused lines.
3. Divide the number of unused lines by the number of blank areas (always one more than the number of blocks of copy). The result is the number of blank lines to allocate above, between, and below the blocks of copy.

A computer with a good word-processing program will do these calculations for you at the click of a mouse.

Page Numbers

Remember that every page in the report is counted; however, not all pages show numbers. The first page of the report, normally the title page, is unnumbered. All other pages in the prefatory section are numbered with a lowercase roman numeral, beginning with ii and continuing with iii, iv, v, and so on. The unadorned (no dashes, no period) page number is centered at the bottom margin.

Number the first page of the text of the report with the unadorned arabic numeral 1, centered at the bottom margin (double- or triple-spaced below the text). In left-bound reports, number the following pages (including the supplementary parts) consecutively with unadorned arabic numerals (2, 3, and so on), placed at the top right-hand margin (double- or triple-spaced above the text). For top-bound reports and for special pages having 2-inch top margins, center the page numbers at the bottom margin.

Appendix B

Documentation of Report Sources

Documenting a report is too important a task to undertake haphazardly. By providing information about your sources, you improve your own credibility as well as the credibility of the facts and opinions you present. Documentation gives readers the means for checking your findings and pursuing the subject further. Also, documenting your report is the accepted way to give credit to the people whose work you have drawn from.

What style should you use to document your report? Experts recommend various forms, depending on your field or discipline. Moreover, your employer or client may use a form different from those the experts suggest. Don't let this discrepancy confuse you. If your employer specifies a form, use it; the standardized form is easier for colleagues to understand. However, if the choice of form is left to you, adopt one of the styles described here. Whatever style you choose, be consistent within any given report, using the same order, punctuation, and format from one reference citation or bibliography entry to the next.

A wide variety of style manuals provide detailed information on documentation. Here is a brief annotated list:

- American Psychological Association, *Publication Manual of the American Psychological Association,* 5th ed. (Washington, DC: American Psychological Association, 2001). Details the author-date system, which is preferred in the social sciences and often in the natural sciences as well.
- *The Chicago Manual of Style,* 15th ed. (Chicago: University of Chicago Press, 2003). Often referred to only as "*Chicago*" and widely used in the publishing industry; provides detailed treatment of source documentation and many other aspects of document preparation.
- Joseph Gibaldi, *MLA Style Manual and Guide to Scholarly Publishing,* 2d ed. (New York: Modern Language Association, 1998). Serves as the basis for the note and bibliography style used in much academic writing and is recommended in many college textbooks on writing term papers; provides a lot of examples in the humanities.
- Andrew Harnack and Eugene Kleppinger, *Online! A Reference Guide to Using Internet Sources with 2003 Update* (New York: St. Martin's Press, 2003). Offers an approach to style for citing online references.

Although many schemes have been proposed for organizing the information in source notes, all of them break the information into parts: (1) information about the author (name), (2) information about the work (title, edition, volume number), (3) information about the publication (place, publisher), (4) information about the date, and (5) information on relevant page ranges.

In the following sections, we summarize the major conventions for documenting sources in three styles: *The Chicago Manual of Style* (Chicago), the *Publication Manual of the American Psychological Association* (APA), and the *MLA Style Manual* (MLA).

Chicago Humanities Style

The Chicago Manual of Style recommends two types of documentation systems. The *documentary-note,* or *humanities,* style gives bibliographic citations in notes—either footnotes (when printed at the bottom of a page) or endnotes (when printed at the end of the report). The humanities system is often used in literature, history, and the arts. The other system strongly recommended by *Chicago* is the *author-date* system, which cites the author's last name and the date of publication in the text, usually in parentheses, reserving full documentation for the reference list (or bibliography). For the purpose of comparing styles, we will concentrate on the humanities system, which is described in detail in *Chicago*.

In-Text Citation—Chicago Humanities Style

To document report sources in text, the humanities system relies on superscripts—arabic numerals placed just above the line of type at the end of the reference:

> Toward the end of his speech, Myers sounded a note of caution, saying that even though the economy is expected to grow, it could easily slow a bit.[10]

The superscript lets the reader know how to look for source information in either a footnote or an endnote (see Figure B.1 on the following page). Some readers prefer footnotes so that they can simply glance at the bottom of the page for information. Others prefer endnotes so that they can read the text without a clutter of notes on the page. Also, endnotes relieve the writer from worrying about how long each note will be and

FIGURE B.1   Sample Endnotes—Chicago Humanities Style

Journal article with volume and issue numbers	**NOTES**
	1. James Assira, "Are They Speaking English in Japan?" *Journal of Business Communication* 36, no. 4 (Fall 2002): 72.
Brochure	2. BestTemp Staffing Services, *An Employer's Guide to Staffing Services,* 2d ed. (Denver: BestTemp Information Center, 2000), 31.
Newspaper article, no author	3. "Buying Asian Supplies on the Net," *Los Angeles Times,* 12 February 2000, sec. D, p. 3.
Annual report	4. Eurotec, *2001 Annual Report* (New York: Eurotec, Inc., 2001), 48.
Magazine article	5. Holly Graves, "Prospecting Online," *Business Week,* 17 November 2002, 43–5.
Television broadcast	6. Daniel Han, "Trade Wars Heating Up Around the Globe," *CNN Headline News* (Atlanta: CNN, 5 March 2002).
Internet, World Wide Web	7. "Intel—Company Capsule," Hoover's Online [cited 8 March 2003], 3 screens; available from www.hoovers.com/capsules/13787.html.
Book, component parts	8. Sonja Kuntz, "Moving Beyond Benefits," in *Our Changing Workforce,* ed. Randolf Jacobson (New York: Citadel Press, 2001), 213–27.
Unpublished dissertation or thesis	9. George H. Morales, "The Economic Pressures on Industrialized Nations in a Global Economy" (Ph.D. diss., University of San Diego, 2001), 32–47.
Paper presented at a meeting	10. Charles Myers, "HMOs in Today's Environment" (paper presented at the Conference on Medical Insurance Solution, Chicago, Ill., August 2001), 16–17.
Online magazine article	11. Preston Norwalk, "Training Managers to Help Employees Accept Change," in *Business Line* [online] (San Francisco, 2002 [updated 17 September 2002; cited 3 October 2002]); available from www.busline.com/news.
CD-ROM encyclopedia article, one author	12. Robert Parkings, "George Eastman," *The Concise Columbia Encyclopedia* (New York: Columbia University Press, 1998) [CD-ROM].
Interview	13. Georgia Stainer, general manager, Day Cable and Communications, interview by author, Topeka, Kan., 2 March 2000.
Newspaper article, one author	14. Evelyn Standish, "Global Market Crushes OPEC's Delicate Balance of Interests," *Wall Street Journal,* 19 January 2002, sec. A, p. 1.
Book, two authors	15. Miriam Toller and Jay Fielding, *Global Business for Smaller Companies* (Rocklin, Calif.: Prima Publishing, 2001), 102–3.
Government publication	16. U.S. Department of Defense, *Stretching Research Dollars: Survival Advice for Universities and Government Labs* (Washington, D.C.: GPO, 2002), 126.

how much space it will take away from the page. Both footnotes and endnotes are handled automatically by today's word-processing software.

For the reader's convenience, you can use footnotes for **content notes** (which may supplement your main text with asides about a particular issue or event, provide a cross-reference to another section of your report, or direct the reader to a related source). Then you can use endnotes for **source notes** (which document direct quotations, paraphrased passages, and visual aids). Consider which type of note is most common in your report, and then choose whether to present these notes all as endnotes or all as footnotes. Regardless of the method you choose for referencing textual information in your report, notes for visual aids (both content notes and source notes) are placed on the same page as the visual.

Bibliography—Chicago Humanities Style

The humanities system may or may not be accompanied by a bibliography (because the notes give all the necessary bibliographic information). However, endnotes are arranged in order of appearance in the text, so an alphabetical bibliography can be valuable to your readers. The bibliography may be titled *Bibliography, Reference List, Sources, Works Cited* (if you include only those sources you actually cited in your report), or *Works Consulted* (if you include uncited sources as well). This list of sources may also serve as a reading list for those who want to pursue the subject of your report further, so you may want to annotate each entry—that is, comment on the subject matter and viewpoint of the source, as well as on its usefulness to readers. Annotations may be written in either complete or incomplete sentences. (See the annotated list of style manuals early in

FIGURE B.2   Sample Bibliography—Chicago Humanities Style

BIBLIOGRAPHY

Journal article with volume and issue numbers	Assira, James. "Are They Speaking English in Japan?" *Journal of Business Communication* 36, no. 4 (Fall 2002): 72.
Brochure	BestTemp Staffing Services. *An Employer's Guide to Staffing Services.* 2d ed. Denver: BestTemp Information Center, 2000.
Newspaper article, no author	"Buying Asian Supplies on the Net." *Los Angeles Times,* 12 February 2000, sec. D, p. 3.
Annual report	Eurotec. 2001 *Annual Report.* New York: Eurotec, Inc., 2001.
Magazine article	Graves, Holly. "Prospecting Online." *Business Week,* 17 November 2002, 43–5.
Television broadcast	Han, Daniel. "Trade Wars Heating Up Around the Globe." *CNN Headline News.* Atlanta: CNN, 5 March 2002.
Internet, World Wide Web	"Intel—Company Capsule." *Hoover's Online* [cited 8 March 2003]. 3 screens; Available from www.hoovers.com/capsules/13787.html.
Book, component parts	Kuntz, Sonja. "Moving Beyond Benefits." In *Our Changing Workforce*, edited by Randolf Jacobson. New York: Citadel Press, 2001.
Unpublished dissertation or thesis	Morales, George H. "The Economic Pressures on Industrialized Nations in a Global Economy." Ph.D. diss., University of San Diego, 2001.
Paper presented at a meeting	Myers, Charles. "HMOs in Today's Environment." Paper presented at the Conference on Medical Insurance Solutions, Chicago, Ill., August 2001.
Online magazine article	Norwalk, Preston. "Training Managers to Help Employees Accept Change." In *Business Line* [online]. San Francisco, 2002 [updated 17 September 2002; cited 3 October 2002]. Available from www.busline.com/news.
CD-ROM encyclopedia article, one author	Parkings, Robert. "George Eastman." *The Concise Columbia Encyclopedia.* New York: Columbia University Press, 1998. [CD-ROM].
Interview	Stainer, Georgia, general manager, Day Cable and Communications. Interview by author. Topeka, Kan., 2 March 2000.
Newspaper article, one author	Standish, Evelyn. "Global Market Crushes OPEC's Delicate Balance of Interests." *Wall Street Journal,* 19 January 2002, sec. A, p. 1.
Book, two authors	Toller, Miriam, and Jay Fielding. *Global Business for Smaller Companies.* Rocklin, Calif.: Prima Publishing, 2001.
Government publication	U.S. Department of Defense. *Stretching Research Dollars: Survival Advice for Universities and Government Labs.* Washington, D.C.: GPO, 2002.

this appendix.) A bibliography may also be more manageable if you subdivide it into categories (a classified bibliography), either by type of reference (such as books, articles, and unpublished material) or by subject matter (such as government regulation, market forces, and so on). Following are the major conventions for developing a bibliography according to Chicago style (see Figure B.2):

■ Exclude any page numbers that may be cited in source notes, except for journals, periodicals, and newspapers.

■ Alphabetize entries by the last name of the lead author (listing last name first). The names of second and succeeding authors are listed in normal order. Entries without an author name are alphabetized by the first important word in the title.

■ Format entries as hanging indents (indent second and succeeding lines three to five spaces).

■ Arrange entries in the following general order: (1) author name, (2) title information, (3) publication information, (4) date, (5) periodical page range.

■ Use quotation marks around the titles of articles from magazines, newspapers, and journals—capitalizing the first and last words, as well as all other important words (except prepositions, articles, and coordinating conjunctions).

■ Use italics to set off the names of books, newspapers, journals, and other complete publications—capitalizing the first and last words, as well as all other important words.

■ For journal articles, include the volume number and the issue number (if necessary). Include the year of publication inside parentheses and follow with a colon and the page range of the article: *Journal of Business Communication* 36, no. 4 (2001): 72. (In this source, the volume is 36, the number is 4, and the page is 72.)

■ Use brackets to identify all electronic references: [Online database] or [CD-ROM].

■ Explain how electronic references can be reached: Available from www.spaceless.com/WWWVL.

■ Give the citation date for online references: Cited 23 August 2007.

APA Style

The American Psychological Association (APA) recommends the author-date system of documentation, which is popular in the physical, natural, and social sciences. When using this system, you simply insert the author's last name and the year of publication within parentheses following the text discussion of the material cited. Include a page number if you use a direct quote. This approach briefly identifies the source so that readers can locate complete information in the alphabetical reference list at the end of the report. The author-date system is both brief and clear, saving readers time and effort.

In-Text Citation—APA Style

To document report sources in text using APA style, insert the author's surname and the date of publication at the end of a statement. Enclose this information in parentheses. If the author's name is referred to in the text itself, then the number can be omitted from parenthetical material.

> Some experts recommend both translation and back-translation when dealing with any non-English-speaking culture (Assira, 2001).

> Toller and Fielding (2000) make a strong case for small companies succeeding in global business.

Personal communications and interviews conducted by the author would not be listed in the reference list at all. Such citations would appear in the text only.

> Increasing the role of cable companies is high on the list of Georgia Stainer, general manager at Day Cable and Communications (personal communication, March 2, 2007).

List of References—APA Style

For APA style, list only those works actually cited in the text (so you would not include works for background or for further reading). Report writers must choose their references judiciously. Following are the major conventions for developing a reference list according to APA style (see Figure B.3):

■ Format entries as hanging indents.

■ List all author names in reversed order (last name first), and use only initials for the first and middle names.

■ Arrange entries in the following general order: (1) author name, (2) date, (3) title information, (4) publication information, (5) periodical page range.

■ Follow the author name with the date of publication in parentheses.

■ List titles of articles from magazines, newspapers, and journals without underlines or quotation marks. Capitalize only the first word of the title, any proper nouns, and the first word to follow an internal colon.

■ Italicize titles of books, capitalizing only the first word, any proper nouns, and the first word to follow a colon.

■ Italicize names of magazines, newspapers, journals, and other complete publications—capitalizing all the important words.

■ For journal articles, include the volume number (in italics) and, if necessary, the issue number (in parentheses). Finally, include the page range of the article: *Journal of Business Communication,* 36(4), 72. (In this example, the volume is 36, the number is 4, and the page number is 72.)

■ Include personal communications (such as letters, memos, e-mail, and conversations) only in text, not in reference lists.

■ Electronic references include author, date of publication, title of article, name of publication (if one), volume, date of retrieval (month, day, year), and the source.

■ For electronic references, indicate the actual year of publication and the exact date of retrieval.

■ For electronic references, specify the URL; leave periods off the ends of URLs.

MLA Style

The style recommended by the Modern Language Association of America is used widely in the humanities, especially in the study of language and literature. Like APA style, MLA style uses brief parenthetical citations in the text. However, instead of including author name and year, MLA citations include author name and page reference.

In-Text Citation—MLA Style

To document report sources in text using MLA style, insert the author's last name and a page reference inside parentheses following the cited material: (Matthews 63). If the author's name is mentioned in the text reference, the name can be omitted from the parenthetical citation: (63). The citation indicates that the reference came from page 63 of a work by Matthews. With the author's name, readers can find complete publication information in the alphabetically arranged list of works cited that comes at the end of the report.

> Some experts recommend both translation and back-translation when dealing with any non-English-speaking culture (Assira 72).

> Toller and Fielding make a strong case for small companies succeeding in global business (102–03).

FIGURE B.3   Sample References—APA Style

Journal article with volume and issue numbers	REFERENCES
	Assira, J. (2002). Are they speaking English in Japan? *Journal of Business Communication, 36*(4), 72.
Brochure	BestTemp Staffing Services. (2000). *An employer's guide to staffing services* (2d ed.) [Brochure]. Denver: BestTemp Information Center.
Newspaper article, no author	Buying Asian supplies on the net. (2000, February 12). *Los Angeles Times*, p. D3.
Annual report	Eurotec. (2001). 2001 *annual report*. New York: Eurotec.
Magazine article	Graves, H. (2002, November 17). Prospecting online. *Business Week*, 43–45.
Television broadcast	Han, D. (2002, March 5). Trade wars heating up around the globe. *CNN Headline News*. [Television broadcast]. Atlanta, GA: CNN.
Internet, World Wide Web	Hoover's Online. (2003). *Intel—Company Capsule*. Retrieved March 8, 2002, from http://www.hoovers.com/capsules/13787.html
Book, component parts	Kuntz, S. (2001). Moving beyond benefits. In Randolph Jacobson (Ed.), *Our changing workforce* (pp. 213–227). New York: Citadel Press.
Unpublished dissertation or thesis	Morales, G. H. (2001). *The economic pressures on industrialized nations in a global economy*. Unpublished doctoral dissertation, University of San Diego.
Paper presented at a meeting	Myers, C. (2001, August). *HMOs in today's environment*. Paper presented at the Conference on Medical Insurance Solutions, Chicago, IL.
Online magazine article	Norwalk, P. (2002, July 17). Training managers to help employees accept change. *Business Line*. Retrieved March 8, 2002, from http://www.busline.com/news
CD-ROM encyclopedia article, one author	Parkings, R. (1998). George Eastman. On *The concise Columbia encyclopedia*. [CD-ROM]. New York: Columbia University Press.
Interview	*Cited in text only, not in the list of references.*
Newspaper article, one author	Standish, E. (2002, January 19). Global market crushes OPEC's delicate balance of interests. *Wall Street Journal*, p. A1.
Book, two authors	Toller, M., & Fielding, J. (2001). *Global business for smaller companies*. Rocklin, CA: Prima Publishing.
Government publication	U.S. Department of Defense. (2002). *Stretching research dollars: Survival advice for universities and government labs*. Washington, DC: U.S. Government Printing Office.

List of Works Cited—MLA Style

The *MLA Style Manual* recommends preparing the list of works cited first so that you will know what information to give in the parenthetical citation (for example, whether to add a short title if you're citing more than one work by the same author, or whether to give an initial or first name if you're citing two authors who have the same last name). The list of works cited appears at the end of your report, contains all the works that you cite in your text, and lists them in alphabetical order. Following are the major conventions for developing a reference list according to MLA style (see Figure B.4):

- Format entries as hanging indents.
- Arrange entries in the following general order: (1) author name, (2) title information, (3) publication information, (4) date, (5) periodical page range.
- List the lead author's name in reverse order (last name first), using either full first names or initials. List second and succeeding author names in normal order.
- Use quotation marks around the titles of articles from magazines, newspapers, and journals—capitalize all important words.
- Italicize the names of books, newspapers, journals and other complete publications, capitalizing all main words in the title.

FIGURE B.4   Sample Works Cited—MLA Style

WORKS CITED

Journal article with volume and issue numbers

Assira, James. "Are They Speaking English in Japan?" *Journal of Business Communication* 36.4 (2002): 72.

Brochure

BestTemp Staffing Services. *An Employer's Guide to Staffing Services.* 2d ed. Denver: BestTemp Information Center, 2000.

Newspaper article, no author

"Buying Asian Supplies on the Net." *Los Angeles Times* 12 Feb. 2000: D3.

Annual report

Eurotec. *2000 Annual Report.* New York: Eurotec, Inc., 2001.

Magazine article

Graves, Holly. "Prospecting Online." *Business Week* 17 Nov. 2002: 43–45.

Television broadcast

Han, Daniel. "Trade Wars Heating Up Around the Globe." *CNN Headline News.* CNN, Atlanta. 5 Mar. 2002.

Internet, World Wide Web

"Intel—Company Capsule." *Hoover's Online.* 2003. Hoover's Company Information. 8 Mar. 2002 <http://www.hoovers.com/capsules/13787.html>.

Book, component parts

Kuntz, Sonja. "Moving Beyond Benefits." *Our Changing Workforce.* Ed. Randolf Jacobson. New York: Citadel Press, 2001. 213–27.

Unpublished dissertation or thesis

Morales, George H. "The Economic Pressures on Industrialized Nations in a Global Economy." Diss. U of San Diego, 2001.

Paper presented at a meeting

Myers, Charles. "HMOs in Today's Environment." Conference on Medical Insurance Solutions. Chicago. 13 Aug. 2001.

Online magazine article

Norwalk, Preston. "Training Managers to Help Employees Accept Change." *Business Line* 17 July 2002. 8 Mar. 2002 <http://www.busline.com/news/>.

CD-ROM encyclopedia article, one author

Parkings, Robert. "George Eastman." *The Concise Columbia Encyclopedia.* CD-ROM. New York: Columbia UP, 1998.

Interview

Stainer, Georgia, general manager, Day Cable and Communications. Telephone interview. 2 Mar. 2000.

Newspaper article, one author

Standish, Evelyn. "Global Market Crushes OPEC's Delicate Balance of Interests." *Wall Street Journal* 19 Jan. 2002: A1.

Book, two authors

Toller, Miriam, and Jay Fielding. *Global Business for Smaller Companies.* Rocklin, CA: Prima Publishing, 2001.

Government publication

United States. Department of Defense. *Stretching Research Dollars: Survival Advice for Universities and Government Labs.* Washington: GPO, 2002.

- For journal articles, include the volume number and the issue number (if necessary). Include the year of publication inside parentheses and follow with a colon and the page range of the article: *Journal of Business Communication* 36, 4 (2001): 72. (In this source, the volume is 36, the number is 4, and the page is 72.)
- Electronic sources are less fixed than print sources, and they may not be readily accessible to readers. So citations for electronic sources must provide more information. Always try to be as comprehensive as possible, citing whatever information is available.
- The date for electronic sources should contain both the date assigned in the source and the date accessed by the researcher.
- The URL for electronic sources must be as accurate and complete as possible, from access-mode identifier (http, ftp, gopher, telnet) to all relevant directory and file names. Be sure to enclose this path inside angle brackets: <http://www.hoovers.com/capsules/13787.html>.

Correction Symbols

Instructors often use these short, easy-to-remember correction symbols and abbreviations when evaluating students' writing. You can use them too, to understand your instructor's suggestions and to revise and proofread your own letters, memos, and reports. Refer to the Handbook of Grammar, Mechanics, and Usage (pp. H-1–H-29) for further information.

Content and Style

Acc	Accuracy. Check to be sure information is correct.
ACE	Avoid copying examples.
ACP	Avoid copying problems.
Adp	Adapt. Tailor message to reader.
App	Follow proper organization approach. (Refer to Chapter 4.)
Assign	Assignment. Review instructions for assignment.
AV	Active verb. Substitute active for passive.
Awk	Awkward phrasing. Rewrite.
BC	Be consistent.
BMS	Be more sincere.
Chop	Choppy sentences. Use longer sentences and more transitional phrases.
Con	Condense. Use fewer words.
CT	Conversational tone. Avoid using overly formal language.
Depers	Depersonalize. Avoid attributing credit or blame to any individual or group.
Dev	Develop. Provide greater detail.
Dir	Direct. Use direct approach; get to the point.
Emph	Emphasize. Develop this point more fully.
EW	Explanation weak. Check logic; provide more proof.
Fl	Flattery. Avoid compliments that are insincere.
FS	Figure of speech. Find a more accurate expression.

GNF	Good news first. Use direct order.
GRF	Give reasons first. Use indirect order.
GW	Goodwill. Put more emphasis on expressions of goodwill.
H/E	Honesty/ethics. Revise statement to reflect good business practices.
Imp	Imply. Avoid being direct.
Inc	Incomplete. Develop further.
Jar	Jargon. Use less specialized language.
Log	Logic. Check development of argument.
Neg	Negative. Use more positive approach or expression.
Obv	Obvious. Do not state point in such detail.
OC	Overconfident. Adopt humbler language.
OM	Omission.
Org	Organization. Strengthen outline.
OS	Off the subject. Close with point on main subject.
Par	Parallel. Use same structure.
Pom	Pompous. Rephrase in down-to-earth terms.
PV	Point of view. Make statement from reader's perspective rather than your own.
RB	Reader benefit. Explain what reader stands to gain.
Red	Redundant. Reduce number of times this point is made.
Ref	Reference. Cite source of information.
Rep	Repetitive. Provide different expression.
RS	Resale. Reassure reader that he or she has made a good choice.
SA	Service attitude. Put more emphasis on helping reader.
Sin	Sincerity. Avoid sounding glib or uncaring.
SL	Stereotyped language. Focus on individual's characteristics instead of on false generalizations.
Spec	Specific. Provide more specific statement.

SPM	Sales promotion material. Tell reader about related goods or services.
Stet	Let stand in original form.
Sub	Subordinate. Make this point less important.
SX	Sexist. Avoid language that contributes to gender stereotypes.
Tone	Tone needs improvement.
Trans	Transition. Show connection between points.
UAE	Use action ending. Close by stating what reader should do next.
UAS	Use appropriate salutation.
UAV	Use active voice.
Unc	Unclear. Rewrite to clarify meaning.
UPV	Use passive voice.
USS	Use shorter sentences.
V	Variety. Use different expression or sentence pattern.
W	Wordy. Eliminate unnecessary words.
WC	Word choice. Find a more appropriate word.
YA	"You" attitude. Rewrite to emphasize reader's needs.

Grammar, Mechanics, and Usage

Ab	Abbreviation. Avoid abbreviations in most cases; use correct abbreviation.
Adj	Adjective. Use adjective instead.
Adv	Adverb. Use adverb instead.
Agr	Agreement. Make subject and verb or noun and pronoun agree.
Ap	Appearance. Improve appearance.
Apos	Apostrophe. Check use of apostrophe.
Art	Article. Use correct article.
BC	Be consistent.
Cap	Capitalize.
Case	Use cases correctly.
CoAdj	Coordinate adjective. Insert comma between coordinate adjectives; delete comma between adjective and compound noun.

CS	Comma splice. Use period or semicolon to separate clauses.
DM	Dangling modifier. Rewrite so that modifier clearly relates to subject of sentence.
Exp	Expletive. Avoid expletive beginnings, such as it is, there are, there is, this is, and these are.
F	Format. Improve layout of document.
Frag	Fragment. Rewrite as complete sentence.
Gram	Grammar. Correct grammatical error.
HCA	Hyphenate compound adjective.
lc	Lowercase. Do not use capital letter.
M	Margins. Improve frame around document.
MM	Misplaced modifier. Place modifier close to word it modifies.
NRC	Nonrestrictive clause (or phrase). Separate from rest of sentence with commas.
P	Punctuation. Use correct punctuation.
Par	Parallel. Use same structure.
PH	Place higher. Move document up on page.
PL	Place lower. Move document down on page.
Prep	Preposition. Use correct preposition.
RC	Restrictive clause (or phrase). Remove commas that separate clause from rest of sentence.
RO	Run-on sentence. Separate two sentences with comma and coordinating conjunction or with semicolon.
SC	Series comma. Add comma before *and*.
SI	Split infinitive. Do not separate *to* from rest of verb.
Sp	Spelling error. Consult dictionary.
S-V	Subject-verb pair. Do not separate with comma.
Syl	Syllabification. Divide word between syllables.
WD	Word division. Check dictionary for proper end-of-line hyphenation.
WW	Wrong word. Replace with another word.

Proofreading Marks

Symbol	Meaning	Symbol Used in Context	Corrected Copy
═══	Align horizontally	meaningful result	meaningful result
‖	Align vertically	1. Power cable 2. Keyboard	1. Power cable 2. Keyboard
(bf)	Boldface	Recommendations (bf)	**Recommendations**
≡	Capitalize	Pepsico, Inc.	PepsiCo, Inc.
⊐⊏	Center	Awards Banquet	Awards Banquet
⌣	Close up space	self- confidence	self-confidence
ℓ	Delete	harrassment and abuse	harassment
(ds)	Double-space	text in first line text in second line (ds)	text in first line text in second line
∧	Insert	tirquoise shirts	turquoise and white shirts
∨	Insert apostrophe	our teams goals	our team's goals
∧	Insert comma	a, b and c	a, b, and c
⯑	Insert hyphen	third quarter sales	third-quarter sales
⊙	Insert period	Harrigan et al	Harrigan et al.
∀ ∀	Insert quotation marks	This team isn't cooperating.	This "team" isn't cooperating.
#	Insert space	real estate testcase	real estate test case
(ital)	Italics	Quarterly Report (ital)	*Quarterly Report*
/	Lowercase	TULSA, South of here	Tulsa, south of here
⌣	Move down	Sincerely,	Sincerely,
⊏	Move left	Attention: Security	Attention: Security
⊐	Move right	February 2, 2003	February 2, 2003
⌐¬	Move up	THIRD-QUARTER SALES	THIRD-QUARTER SALES
(STET)	Restore	staff talked openly and frankly (STET)	staff talked openly
⌒	Run lines together	Manager, Distribution	Manager, Distribution
(ss)	Single space	text in first line text in second line	text in first line text in second line
⬭	Spell out	COD	cash on delivery
(sp)	Spell out	Assn. of Biochem. Engrs.	Association of Biochemical Engineers
⌐	Start new line	Marla Fenton, Manager, Distribution	Marla Fenton, Manager, Distribution
¶	Start new paragraph	¶The solution is easy to determine but difficult to implement in a competitive environment like the one we now face.	The solution is easy to determine but difficult to implement in a competitive environment like the one we now face.
∿	Transpose	airy, light, casual tone	light, airy, casual tone

Your instructor may elect to show you one or more of the videos described on the following pages. These programs supplement course concepts with real-life examples of business people meeting important communication challenges. This video guide includes several review and analysis questions as well as exercises for each video. Be sure to review the appropriate page ahead of time so that you'll know what to look for when you watch the video.

Ethical Communication

Learning Objectives

After viewing this video, you will be able to

1. Describe a process for deciding what is ethical or unethical
2. Explain the importance of meeting your personal and professional responsibilities in an ethical manner
3. Discuss the possible consequences of ethical and unethical choices an talk about the impact of these choices on direct and related audiences

Background Information

Communication is ethical when it includes all relevant information, when it's true in every sense, and when it isn't deceptive in any way. In contrast, communication is unethical when it includes false information, fails to include important information, or otherwise misleads an audience. To avoid unethical choices in your communication efforts, you must consider not only legal issues but also the needs of your audience and the expectations of society and your employer. In turn, companies that demonstrate high standards of ethics maintain credibility with employees, customers, and other stakeholders.

The Video

This video identifies two important tools in a communicator's toolbox: honesty and objectivity. These tools help businesspeople resolve ethical dilemmas and avoid ethical lapses, both within the company and during interactions with outside audiences. Poor ethical choices can damage a company's credibility and put employees, customers, and the surrounding community at risk. Unfortunately, some ethical choices are neither clear nor simple, and you may face situations in which the needs of one group or individual must be weighed against the needs of another.

Discussion Questions

1. Would you ever consider compromising your ethics for self-gain? If so, under what circumstance? If not, why?

2. The video mentions the role of misrepresentations in the collapse of Enron. If you were the head of communications at Enron and had some knowledge of the true nature of the company's financial condition, what would you have done?
3. Identify risks involved when you choose to act in an unethical manner.
4. How can you be an effective business communicator without credibility?
5. Is it ethical to call in sick to work, even though you are not ill? What happens to your credibility if someone finds out you were not sick?

Follow-Up Assignment

Many businesses, from small companies to large corporations, formulate codes of ethics that outline ethical standards for employees. Review IBM's guidelines, which are posted on its website at www.ibm.com/investor/corpgovernance/cgbeg.phtml. Now answer the following questions:

1. What does IBM want employees to do if they are aware of unethical situations within the organization?
2. How does IBM view misleading statements or innuendos about competitors?
3. What advice does IBM give employees on the subject of receiving gifts from people outside the company?

For Further Research

Advertising communications, particularly advertising aimed at children, can present a variety of ethical concerns. The article provided at www.mediascope.org/pubs/ibriefs/cha.htm reports statistics on the advertising of alcohol and tobacco products and discusses the negative effect these advertisements can have on children. To what extent was it ethical for Anheuser Busch to use the Budweiser frog or for Philip Morris to use Joe Camel in their advertisements, given that many children were able to identify with both characters?

Learning to Listen: Second City Communications

Learning Objectives

After viewing this video, you will be able to

1. Understand the functions of interpersonal communication in the workplace
2. Identify the ways to overcome barriers to effective communication
3. Discuss the importance of active listening both socially and professionally

Background Information

Chicago's Second City Improv is more than the world's best-known comedy theater. Second City now brings its famous brand of humor to corporate giants such as Coca-Cola, Motorola, and Microsoft. With over 40 years of experience in corporate services, Second City's teachers help business professionals develop communication skills through lessons in improvisational theater. Business Communications Training is Second City's fastest growing practice, fueled by the demands of more than 200 Fortune 500 companies. Workshops are tailored to clients' needs in such areas as listening and giving presentations, collaborative leadership and team skills, interviewing, breaking down barriers to successful communication, and using humor to convey important messages. The next time you watch improvisational sketch comedy, ask yourself how a lesson in the art of "Improv" might give your career a boost.

The Video

In these two video segments, you'll see Second City's training techniques in action. The first segment addresses the need to listen actively, and the second explores techniques for encouraging innovation. The second clip is less focused on communication, but you can see how the techniques for stimulating innovation work equally well for fostering meaningful, two-way conversation that encourages people to open up rather than shut down.

Discussion Questions

1. How do the exercises featured in this video address the contrasting needs of the trial lawyer, the divorce lawyer, and the media buyer?
2. Since you would never be expected in real-life conditions to speak without using the word *I*, what is the value of the exercise in which the workshop attendees were required to carry on a conversation without using *I*?
3. What other workshops might Tom Yorton want to offer companies in response to the current economic and political climate?
4. How might the "Yes and" rule of improvisation be used to train customer service representatives at an L.L. Bean or a Dell computer call center? Without physical cues, such as facial expression and body languages, is the "Yes and" rule still effective?
5. As president and managing director of Second City Communications, Tom Yorton says the following: "You have to be willing to fail to be able to get the results you want . . . to connect with an audience." Do you agree that this statement is as true in business as it is in comedy? Support your chosen position.

Follow-Up Assignment

Enjoy Second City Communication's website at www.secondcity.com. If you are a loyal fan, you might want to check out the book titles offered and read more about the group's history. Now explore Second City's Corporate Services: Scan the client roster, read the testimonials, and then select a case study that you find compelling. If you are currently employed, which workshop would be most beneficial to you and to your work team? Explain your choice. If you are not currently employed, how might you and your fellow business students benefit from a Second City workshop? Which workshop would you most like to participate in? Explain how you think it might help you in terms of your social life, your career planning, and your interviewing skills.

For Further Research

The importance of active listening is at the core of *consultative selling*, an approach that emphasizes posing questions to the potential buyer in order to identify needs and expectations—rather than rattling off a prepared sales speech. Public SpeakingSkills.com (www.publicspeakingskills.com) is one of many companies that offer training in consultative selling. Review the description of the company's Consultative Selling and Negotiating Skills course. Do the principles espoused match the concept of the "you" attitude and the elements of ethical communication that you've learned so far?

Communicating in the Global Workplace

Learning Objectives

After viewing this video, you will be able to

1. Discuss the challenges of communicating in the global workplace
2. Identify barriers to effective communication across borders
3. Explain the critical role of time in global communication efforts

Background Information

Many businesses are crossing national boundaries to engage in international business. However, operating in a global environment presents a variety of challenges related to culture and communication. Understanding and respecting these challenges can mean the difference between success and failure, so executives must make sure that employees are educated on cultural issues before attempting to do business in other countries.

The Video

This video identifies the challenges to effective communication in the global marketplace, including the barriers posed by language, culture, time, and technology. You will see that a significant amount of research needs to be conducted before a company can engage in successful global business ventures. For instance, if communicators are unaware of differences in gestures, expressions, and dialect, they can inadvertently offend or confuse their audiences. In addition, time zone differences require organizations to plan carefully in advance so that they can develop, translate, and deliver information in a timely manner.

Discussion Questions

1. Language can be a barrier to effective communication. What steps can a company take to minimize language barriers across borders?

2. What characteristics of a country's culture need to be researched to ensure business success across borders?

3. How does a company ensure that a message is properly translated into the local language and dialect of the people it conducts business with?

4. What challenges does a company face when trying to hold a conference call or video meeting with affiliates and employees around the world?

5. The video mentions that some companies have trusted contacts in a country they wish to do business with, whereas other companies rely on a significant amount of research to learn more about culture and other local characteristics. What method do you feel is most effective for gathering useful, accurate, and up-to-date information regarding cultural issues?

Follow-Up Assignment

The Coca-Cola Company has local operations in more than 200 countries throughout the world. Visit www.coca-cola.com to learn more about the company's business activities in a variety of countries. What steps does Coke take to communicate through its website with customers around the world? Does the company strive to develop products that meet local tastes and needs? If so, how and why?

For Further Research

Choose a country other than the United States, and research your selection using both online and library resources to identify important cultural characteristics specific to that country. For example, you may want to gather information about gestures and other nonverbal communication that would be considered offensive, about work habits, or about laws related to conducting business in that country. The characteristics you identify should be useful and accurate.

Based on what you've learned about this country and your personal beliefs, values, and life experiences, is there any risk that you might have a prejudiced or ethnocentric viewpoint regarding people from this country? Why or why not?

Impact of Culture on Business: Spotlight on Latin America

Learning Objectives

After viewing this video, you will be able to

1. List key aspects of Latin American cultures and indicate the influences on their development
2. Identify factors that might lead to cultural change in Latin America
3. Explain some of the major cultural contrasts within Latin America and their impact on international business operations

Background Information

To a large degree, culture defines the way all human beings interpret and respond to life's changing circumstances. When you interact with people from your own culture, your shared experiences and expectations usually enhance the communication process by providing a common language and frame of reference.

However, when you communicate across cultural boundaries, a lack of awareness of your audience's culture—and the subconscious ways that your own culture shapes your perceptions—can result in partial or even total failure of the communication process. Moreover, culture is rarely static, so impressions you may have gathered at one point in your life may need to be revisited and revised over time.

The Video

This video takes a broad look at Latin America's various countries and cultures and explores the business implications of cultural similarities and differences. You'll learn how cultural groups that may appear identical on the surface can in fact have subtle but profound differences. Although communication is just one of many topics discussed in the video, you will get a sense of just how important—and challenging—communication can be when conducting business across cultural boundaries.

Discussion Questions

1. Explain what the video means when it says that your own culture can "sneak up on you."
2. How is business influencing the economic gulf between urban and rural populations in Latin America?
3. How have imperial conquests and slavery affected the populations and cultures of Latin America?
4. How do many outsiders view the issue of business and government corruption in Latin America?
5. Is business etiquette in most of Latin America considered relatively formal or relatively informal?

Follow-Up Assignment

The World Bank plays an important role in today's fast-changing, closely meshed global economy. Visit the bank's website at www.worldbank.org and explore the initiatives programs under way in the Latin American region. How is the bank using this website to foster better communication between Latin America and the rest of the world?

For Further Research

In today's global marketplace, knowing as much as possible about your international customers' business practices and customs could give you a strategic advantage. To help you successfully conduct business around the globe, navigate the resources at the U.S. Government Export Portal. Start at www.export.gov, then click on "Market Research" and then on "Country Information—Quick Reference (TIC)." Click anywhere on the world map to learn more about each country.

How can resources such as this website help U.S. businesses communicate more successfully with customers, employees, and other groups in Latin America?

Technology and the Tools of Communication

Learning Objectives

After viewing this video, you will be able to

1. Identify technology-related issues to consider when developing communication strategies

2. Identify advantages of using technology as a tool for effective communication
3. Differentiate between "push" and "pull" communication

Background Information

From instant messaging to online meetings, technology has become an integral element of business communication. When used with care, technological tools can help you reach more people in less time with more effective messages. However, when technology is misused or misunderstood, it can cause more problems than it solves. Knowing which technologies to use in every situation—and knowing how to use each one—are vital to your success.

The Video

This video discusses how the Internet, e-mail, voicemail, and other devices have revolutionized the way people communicate. These technological tools increase the speed, frequency, and range of business communication. The video also discusses factors to consider when choosing the most appropriate vehicle for your communication, including the all important challenge of getting and keeping your audience's attention. The advantages of using technological communication tools are presented throughout the video.

Discussion Questions

1. Identify six questions you need to consider when choosing a technology vehicle for your messages.
2. List the advantages of communicating via e-mail within an organization.
3. What role does technology play in ensuring effective communication within an organization?
4. What are some of the more common challenges that business communicators can encounter when they use technology for communication purposes?
5. Identify the difference between "push" and "pull" communications, and provide an example of each method.

Follow-Up Assignment

VolResource (at www.volresource.org.uk/samples/olcomms. htm) provides practical and informative resources for volunteer organizations that are trying to develop online communication strategies. The VolResource website further details questions that need to be addressed in the process of developing an effective communication strategy for any organization. What issues do you think are the most important to consider? Why?

For Further Exploration

Visit the Yellow Freight website at www.yellowfreight.com and explore the various e-commerce tools this company utilizes to communicate effectively with its customers. Examine these tools and consider their effectiveness. What are some of the advantages of these online communication tools? How do they benefit the client? How do they benefit Yellow Freight?

Effective Oral Presentations

Learning Objectives

After viewing this video, you will be able to

1. Reiterate the importance of knowing your audience before creating and delivering oral presentations
2. Discuss the role of teamwork in preparing and delivering complex presentations
3. Explain the importance of anticipating objections likely to be raised during a presentation

Background Information

Oral presentations are a vital communication medium in most companies. In particular, important decisions often involve one or more presentations, either in person or online, in which people advocating a specific choice present their case to the people responsible for making the decision. Such presentations usually combine informational and analytical reporting, along with the persuasive aspects of a proposal. Beyond the mere delivery of information, however, presentations also involve an element of performance. Audiences search for both verbal and nonverbal clues to help them assess presenters' knowledge, confidence, and credibility.

The Video

This video follows three colleagues as they create and deliver a presentation that seeks to convince the audience to approve the purchase of a particular software system that will be used to manage the company's sales force. The presenters explain the importance of understanding the expectations of their audience, from the types of visuals they prefer to the objections they are likely to raise. The team also explains how they took advantage of each member's individual strengths to create a more effective presentation.

Discussion Questions

1. How did the presenters demonstrate their knowledge of the audience?
2. Why did one presenter use a $100 bill as a prop?
3. What are the risks of using props such as the $100 bill?
4. How did the presenters prepare for objections raised by the audience?
5. How would the team need to modify its presentation for an online webcast instead of an in-person oral presentation?

Follow-Up Assignment

Podcasts (audio only) and vidcasts (podcasts with video) are quickly catching on as a medium for business presentations. Visit http://podcasts.yahoo.com/ and click on the Business category. Select any three podcasts. Listen to them while taking careful notes so that you can compare the three selections in terms of grabbing your attention, keeping your attention, and effectively communicating the podcast's information. Which of the three podcasts is the most effective? Why?

For Further Research

Musicians, actors, jugglers—virtually everyone who performs in public experiences *performance anxiety* or *stage fright*, as it is commonly known. This anxiety is simply the natural outcome of caring about how well you do. After all, if you didn't care, you wouldn't feel anxious. Seasoned performers not only recognize that anxiety is natural but they also have learned how to use this emotion to their advantage by giving them extra energy. Visit www.petethomas.co.uk/performance-nerves.html and www.jugglingdb.com (search for "stage fright," then click on the "Collective wisdom on stage fright") and read how these accomplished performers handle the anxiety of performing in public. How can you adapt their techniques to business presentations?

Interviewing Skills

Learning Objectives

After viewing this video, you will be able to

1. Explain how the AIDA approach helps create effective application letters
2. Identify mistakes that can cause an otherwise qualified candidate to lose out on a job opportunity
3. Explain why planning for tough questions is such an important part of your interviewing strategy

Background Information

Most companies would admit that the employment interview is an imperfect test of a candidate's skills and personality fit with the organization. In response, some are beginning to add testing, job simulations, and other evaluation tools to the selection process. However, the classic face-to-face interview remains the dominant decision-making tool in the hiring process, so developing your interviewing skills will be vital to your success at every stage in your career.

The Video

This video follows the progress of two candidates applying and interviewing for a technical writing position. One candidate has more experience in this area, but his approach to the interview process ends up costing him the job opportunity. In contrast, a candidate with less experience takes a confident and creative approach that nets her the job.

Discussion Questions

1. Why are multiple StayCom managers involved in this interviewing process? Couldn't one manager handle it?
2. Why does one of the managers compare an application letter to a news story?
3. What steps did Cheryl Yung take to overcome a potential shortcoming in her qualifications?
4. What mistakes did candidate Buddy McCoy make in his interview?
5. Why would the interviewers care about the interpersonal skills of someone who will be writing for a living?

Follow-Up Assignment

Nonverbal cues are important in every communication scenario, but perhaps never more important than in job interviews. Not only are interviewers looking for any clues they can find that will guide their decisions but they tend to make up their minds quickly—perhaps even before the candidate has said anything at all. Read the advice on nonverbal communication in interviews at www.careerjournal.com/jobhunting/interviewing/20021205-raudsepp.html. Distill this information down to a half dozen or so key points that you can write on a note card to study before you step into your next job interview.

For Further Research

You look great in your new interview outfit, your hair is perfect but not too perfect, your smile radiates positive energy, and you're ready to dazzle the interviewer. Then, oops—you discover that your first interview will be held over the telephone, so none of your visual cues will help you at this stage. Don't fret; read the telephone interviewing advice at http://interview.monster.com/articles/phone, and you'll be ready to dazzle the interviewer long-distance.

Handbook of Grammar, Mechanics, and Usage

Grammar and mechanics are nothing more than the way words are combined into sentences. Usage is the way words are used by a network of people—in this case, the community of business-people who use English. You'll find it easier to get along in this community if you know the accepted standards of grammar, mechanics, and usage. This handbook offers you valuable opportunities in three sections:

- **Diagnostic Test of English Skills.** Testing your current knowledge of grammar, mechanics, and usage helps you find out where your strengths and weaknesses lie. This test offers 60 items taken from the topics included in this Handbook.
- **Assessment of English Skills.** After completing the diagnostic test, use the assessment form to highlight those areas you most need to review.
- **Essentials of Grammar, Mechanics, and Usage with Practice Sessions.** This section helps you quickly review the basics. You can study the things you've probably already learned but may have forgotten about grammar, punctuation, capitalization, mechanics (including capitalization, abbreviation, number style, and word division), and vocabulary (including frequently confused words, frequently misused words, frequently misspelled words, and transitional words and phrases). Practice sessions throughout this section help you test yourself and reinforce what you learn. Use this essential review not only to study and improve your English skills but also as a reference for any questions you may have during this course.

Without a firm grasp of the basics of grammar, punctuation, mechanics, and vocabulary, you risk being misunderstood, damaging your company's image, losing money for your company, and possibly even losing your job. However, once you develop strong English skills, you will create clear and concise messages, you will enhance your company's image as well as your own, and you will not only increase your company's profits but expand your own chances of success.

Diagnostic Test of English Skills

Use this test to help you determine whether you need more practice with grammar, punctuation, mechanics, or vocabulary. When you've answered all the questions, ask your instructor for an answer sheet so that you can score the test. On the Assessment of English Skills form (page H-2), record the number of questions you answered correctly in each section.

The following choices apply to items 1–10. In each blank, write the letter of the choice that best describes the problem with each sentence.

A. Sentence incomplete
B. Too many phrases/clauses strung together
C. Modifying elements misplaced (dangling)
D. Structure not parallel
E. Nothing wrong

____ 1. Stop here.
____ 2. Your duties are interviewing, hiring, and also to fire employees.
____ 3. After their presentation, I was still undecided.
____ 4. Speaking freely, the stock was considered a bargain.
____ 5. Margaret, pressed for time, turned in unusually sloppy work.
____ 6. Typing and filing, routine office chores.
____ 7. With care, edit the report.
____ 8. When Paul came to work here, he brought some outmoded ideas, now he has accepted our modern methods.
____ 9. To plan is better than improvising.
____ 10. Hoping to improve performance, practice is advisable.

The following choices apply to items 11–20. In each blank, write the letter of the choice that identifies the underlined word(s) in each sentence.

A. Subject
B. Predicate (verb)
C. Object
D. Modifier
E. Conjunction/preposition

____ 11. Take his <u>memo</u> upstairs.
____ 12. Before leaving, he <u>repaired</u> the photocopier.
____ 13. <u>Velnor, Inc.,</u> will soon introduce a new product line.
____ 14. We must hire only <u>qualified</u>, ambitious graduates.
____ 15. They <u>are having</u> trouble with their quality-control systems.
____ 16. <u>After</u> she wrote the report, Jill waited eagerly for a response.
____ 17. The route to the plant isn't paved <u>yet</u>.
____ 18. See <u>me</u> after the meeting.
____ 19. Your new <u>home</u> is ready and waiting.
____ 20. BFL is large <u>but</u> caring.

In the blanks for items 21–30, write the letter of the word that best completes each sentence.

_____ 21. Starbucks (A. is, B. are) opening five new stores in San Diego in the next year.

_____ 22. There (A. is, B. are) 50 applicants for the job opening.

_____ 23. Anyone who wants to be (A. their, B. his or her) own boss should think about owning a franchise.

_____ 24. Neither of us (A. was, B. were) prepared for the meeting.

_____ 25. Another characteristic of a small business is that (A. they tend, B. it tends) to be more innovative than larger firms.

_____ 26. After he had (A. saw, B. seen) the revised budget, Raymond knew he wouldn't be getting a new desk.

_____ 27. The number of women-owned small businesses (A. has, B. have) increased sharply in the past two decades.

_____ 28. If I (A. was, B. were) you, I'd stop sending personal e-mails at work.

_____ 29. Eugene (A. lay, B. laid) the files on the desk.

_____ 30. Either FedEx or UPS (A. has, B. have) been chosen as our preferred shipping service.

The following choices apply to items 31–40. In each blank, write the letter of the choice that best describes each sentence.

A. All punctuation used correctly
B. Some punctuation used incorrectly or incorrectly omitted

_____ 31. The president who rarely gave interviews, agreed to write an article for the company newsletter.

_____ 32. Give the assignment to Karen Schiff, the new technical writer.

_____ 33. Could you please send a replacement for Item No. 3-303.

_____ 34. Debbie said that, "technicians must have technical degrees."

_____ 35. We'll have branches in Bakersfield, California, Reno, Nevada, and Medford, Oregon.

_____ 36. Before leaving her secretary finished typing the memo.

_____ 37. How many of you consider yourselves "computer literate?"

_____ 38. This, then, is our goal: to increase market share by 50 percent.

_____ 39. They plan to move soon, however, they still should be invited.

_____ 40. Health, wealth, and happiness—those are my personal goals.

The following choices apply to items 41–50. In each blank, write the letter of the choice that best describes the problem with each sentence.

A. Error in punctuation
B. Error in use of abbreviations or symbols
C. Error in use of numbers
D. Error in capitalization
E. No errors

_____ 41. Most of last year's sales came from the midwest.

_____ 42. We can provide the items you are looking for @ $2 each.

_____ 43. Alex noted: "few of our competitors have tried this approach."

_____ 44. Address the letter to professor Elliott Barker, Psychology Department, North Dakota State University.

_____ 45. They've recorded 22 complaints since yesterday, all of them from long-time employees.

_____ 46. Leslie's presentation—"New Markets for the Nineties"—was well organized.

_____ 47. We're having a sale in the childrens' department, beginning Wednesday, August 15.

_____ 48. About 50 of the newly inducted members will be present.

_____ 49. Mister Spencer has asked me to find ten volunteers.

_____ 50. Let's meet in Beth and Larry's office at one o'clock.

In the blanks for items 51–60, write the letter of the word that best completes each sentence.

_____ 51. Will having a degree (A. affect, B. effect) my chances for promotion?

_____ 52. Place the latest drawings (A. beside, B. besides) the others.

_____ 53. Try not to (A. loose, B. lose) this key; we will charge you a fee to replace it.

_____ 54. Let us help you choose the right tie to (A. complement, B. compliment) your look.

_____ 55. The five interviewers should discuss the candidates' qualifications (A. among, B. between) themselves.

_____ 56. New employees spend their time looking for (A. perspective, B. prospective) clients.

_____ 57. Are the goods you received different (A. from, B. than) the goods you ordered?

_____ 58. He took those courses to (A. farther, B. further) his career.

_____ 59. We are (A. anxious, B. eager) to see you next Thursday.

_____ 60. All commissions will be (A. disbursed, B. dispensed, C. dispersed) on the second Friday of every month.

Assessment of English Skills

In the space provided below, record the number of questions you answered correctly.

Questions	Number You Got Correct	Skill Area
1–10	_____	Sentence structure
11–20	_____	Grammar: Parts of speech
21–30	_____	Grammar: Verbs and agreement
31–40	_____	Punctuation
41–50	_____	Punctuation and mechanics
51–60	_____	Vocabulary

If you scored 8 or lower in any of the skills areas, focus on those areas in the appropriate sections of this Handbook.

Essentials of Grammar, Mechanics, and Usage

The sentence below looks innocent, but is it really?

> We sell tuxedos as well as rent.

You might sell rent, but it's highly unlikely. Whatever you're selling, some people will ignore your message because of a blunder like this. The following sentence has a similar problem:

> Vice President Eldon Neale told his chief engineer that he would no longer be with Avix, Inc., as of June 30.

Is Eldon or the engineer leaving? No matter which side the facts are on, the sentence can be read the other way. Now look at this sentence:

> The year before we budgeted more for advertising sales were up.

Confused? Perhaps this is what you meant:

> The year before, we budgeted more for advertising. Sales were up.

Maybe you meant this:

> The year before we budgeted more for advertising, sales were up.

The meaning of language falls into bundles called sentences. A listener or reader can take only so much meaning before filing a sentence away and getting ready for the next one. So, as a business writer, you have to know what a sentence is. You need to know where one ends and the next one begins.

If you want to know what a sentence is, you have to find out what goes into it, what its ingredients are. Luckily, the basic ingredients of an English sentence are simple: The parts of speech combine with punctuation, mechanics, and vocabulary to convey meaning.

1.0 Grammar

Grammar is the study of how words come together to form sentences. Categorized by meaning, form, and function, English words fall into various parts of speech: nouns, pronouns, verbs, adjectives, adverbs, prepositions, conjunctions, articles, and interjections. You will communicate more clearly if you understand how each of these parts of speech operates in a sentence.

1.1 Nouns

A noun names a person, place, or thing. Anything you can see or detect with one of your other senses has a noun to name it. Some things you can't see or sense are also nouns—ions, for example, or space. So are things that exist as ideas, such as accuracy and height. (You can see that something is accurate or that a building is tall, but you can't see the idea of accuracy or the

idea of height.) These names for ideas are known as abstract nouns. The simplest nouns are the names of things you can see or touch: car, building, cloud, brick.

1.1.1 Proper Nouns and Common Nouns

So far, all the examples of nouns have been common nouns, referring to general classes of things. The word *building* refers to a whole class of structures. Common nouns such as *building* are not capitalized.

If you want to talk about one particular building, however, you might refer to the Glazier Building. The name is capitalized, indicating that *Glazier Building* is a proper noun.

Here are three sets of common and proper nouns for comparison:

Common	Proper
city	Kansas City
company	Blaisden Company
store	Books Galore

1.1.2 Nouns as Subject and Object

Nouns may be used in sentences as subjects or objects. That is, the person, place, idea, or thing that is being or doing (subject) is represented by a noun. So is the person, place, idea, or thing that is being acted on (object). In the following sentence, the nouns are underlined.

> The <u>secretary</u> keyboarded the <u>report</u>.

The secretary (subject) is acting in a way that affects the report (object). The following sentence is more complicated:

> The <u>installer</u> delivered the <u>carpeting</u> to the <u>customer</u>.

Installer is the subject. *Carpeting* is the object of the main part of the sentence (acted on by the installer), whereas *customer* is the object of the phrase *to the customer*. Nevertheless, both *carpeting* and *customer* are objects.

1.1.3 Plural Nouns

Nouns can be either singular or plural. The usual way to make a plural noun is to add *s* to the singular form of the word:

Singular	Plural
rock	rocks
picture	pictures
song	songs

Many nouns have other ways of forming the plural. (Letters, numbers, and words used as words are sometimes made plural by adding an apostrophe and an *s*.) Very often, *'s* is used with abbreviations that have periods, lowercase letters that stand alone, and capital letters that might be confused with words when made into plurals:

> Spell out all *St.*'s and *Ave.*'s.
>
> He divided the page with a row of *x*'s.
>
> Sarah will register the *A*'s through the *G*'s at the convention.

In other cases, however, the apostrophe may be left out:

> They'll review their ABCs.
>
> The stock market climbed through most of the 1980s.
>
> Circle all *the*s in the paragraph.

In some of these examples, the letters used as letters and words used as words are *italicized* (a mechanics issue that is discussed later).

Other nouns, such as those below, are so-called irregular nouns; they form the plural in some way other than by simply adding *s*:

Singular	Plural
tax	taxes
specialty	specialties
cargo	cargoes
shelf	shelves
child	children
woman	women
tooth	teeth
mouse	mice
parenthesis	parentheses
son-in-law	sons-in-law
editor-in-chief	editors-in-chief

Rather than memorize a lot of rules about forming plurals, use a dictionary. If the dictionary says nothing about the plural of a word, it's formed the usual way: by adding *s*. If the plural is formed in some irregular way, the dictionary often shows the plural spelling.

1.1.4 Possessive Nouns

A noun becomes possessive when it's used to show the ownership of something. Then you add *'s* to the word:

> the man's car   the woman's apartment

However, ownership does not need to be legal:

> the secretary's desk   the company's assets

Also, ownership may be nothing more than an automatic association:

> a day's work   the job's prestige

An exception to the rule about adding *'s* to make a noun possessive occurs when the word is singular and already has two "s" sounds at the end. In cases like the following, an apostrophe is all that's needed:

> crisis' dimensions   Mr. Moses' application

When the noun has only one "s" sound at the end, however, retain the *'s*:

> Chris's book   Carolyn Nuss's office

With hyphenated nouns (compound nouns), add *'s* to the last word:

Hyphenated Noun	Possessive Noun
mother-in-law	mother-in-law's
mayor-elect	mayor-elect's

To form the possessive of plural nouns, just begin by following the same rule as with singular nouns: add *'s*. However, if the plural noun already ends in an *s* (as most do), drop the one you've added, leaving only the apostrophe:

> the clients' complaints   employees' benefits

Practice Session: Nouns

Underline the preferred choice within each set of parentheses in the following sentences.

1. We are moving company headquarters to New York (*City, city*).
2. The historic Bradbury (*Building, building*) is the site of the press conference; the (*Building, building*) is located in downtown Los Angeles.
3. During the conference, our staff will be staying at the Hyatt, Hilton, and Marriott (*Hotels, hotels*).
4. Accuracy requires that you cross your (*ts, t's*) and dot your (*is, i's*).
5. The industry has been on a downward spiral since the early (*1990's, 1990s*).
6. The new (*shelfs, shelves*) will be installed on Friday.
7. Our (*specialtys, specialties*) are unparalleled service and premium brands.
8. As a result of several Internet-related (*cases, case's*), the copyright laws are under scrutiny.
9. Before a job interview, you should learn about the (*company's, companies'*) mission statement.
10. Sending the newsletter to the printer is the (*editor's-in-chief, editor-in-chief's*) responsibility.
11. All the downtown (*business', businesses', businesses's*) signs must be repainted.
12. Because the (*passenger's, passengers'*) luggage had been damaged, they had to file claims with the airline.
13. Dealing with angry customers is all in a (*days, day's, days'*) work for Mr. Jemas.
14. Its large airport is one of (*Dallases, Dallas', Dallas's*) main appeals for industrial firms.
15. We were skeptical of (*Jone's, Jones', Jones's*) plan.

1.2 Pronouns

A pronoun is a word that stands for a noun; it saves repeating the noun:

> Drivers have some choice of weeks for vacation, but *they* must notify this office of *their* preference by March 1.

The pronouns *they* and *their* stand in for the noun *drivers*. The noun that a pronoun stands for is called the antecedent of the pronoun; *drivers* is the antecedent of *they* and *their*.

When the antecedent is plural, the pronoun that stands in for it has to be plural; *they* and *their* are plural pronouns because *drivers* is plural. Likewise, when the antecedent is singular, the pronoun has to be singular:

> We thought the *contract* had expired, but we soon learned that *it* had not.

1.2.1 Multiple Antecedents

Sometimes a pronoun has a double (or even a triple) antecedent:

> *Kathryn Boettcher* and *Luis Gutierrez* went beyond *their* sales quotas for January.

If taken alone, *Kathryn Boettcher* is a singular antecedent. So is *Luis Gutierrez*. However, when together they are the plural antecedent of a pronoun, so the pronoun has to be plural. Thus the pronoun is *their* instead of *her* or *his*.

1.2.2 Unclear Antecedents

In some sentences the pronoun's antecedent is unclear:

> Sandy Wright sent Jane Brougham *her* production figures for the previous year. *She* thought they were too low.

To which person does the pronoun *her* refer? Someone who knew Sandy and Jane and knew their business relationship might be able to figure out the antecedent for *her*. Even with such an advantage, however, a reader might receive the wrong meaning. Also, it would be nearly impossible for any reader to know which name is the antecedent of *she*.

The best way to clarify an ambiguous pronoun is usually to rewrite the sentence, repeating nouns when needed for clarity:

> Sandy Wright sent her production figures for the previous year to Jane Brougham. *Jane* thought they were too low.

The noun needs to be repeated only when the antecedent is unclear.

1.2.3 Gender-Neutral Pronouns

The pronouns that stand for males are *he, his,* and *him*. The pronouns that stand for females are *she, hers,* and *her*. However, you'll often be faced with the problem of choosing a pronoun for a noun that refers to both females and males:

> Each manager must make up (his, her, his or her, its, their) own mind about stocking this item and about the quantity that (he, she, he or she, it, they) can sell.

This sentence calls for a pronoun that's neither masculine nor feminine. The issue of gender-neutral pronouns responds to efforts to treat females and males evenhandedly. Here are some possible ways to deal with this issue:

> Each manager must make up *his* . . .
> (Not all managers are men.)

> Each manager must make up *her* . . .
> (Not all managers are women.)

> Each manager must make up *his* or *her* . . .
> (This solution is acceptable but becomes awkward when repeated more than once or twice in a document.)

> Each manager must make up *her* . . . Every manager will receive *his* . . . A manager may send *her* . . .
> (A manager's gender does not alternate like a windshield wiper!)

> Each manager must make up *their* . . .
> (The pronoun can't be plural when the antecedent is singular.)

> Each manager must make up *its* . . .
> (*It* never refers to people.)

The best solution is to make the noun plural or to revise the passage altogether:

> Managers must make up *their* minds . . .
> Each manager must decide whether . . .

Be careful not to change the original meaning.

1.2.4 Case of Pronouns

The case of a pronoun tells whether it's acting or acted upon:

> *She sells* an average of five packages each week.

In this sentence, *she* is doing the selling. Because *she* is acting, *she* is said to be in the nominative case. Now consider what happens when the pronoun is acted upon:

> After six months, Ms. Browning promoted *her*.

In this sentence, the pronoun *her* is acted upon. The pronoun *her* is thus said to be in the objective case.

Contrast the nominative and objective pronouns in this list:

Nominative	Objective
I	me
we	us
he	him
she	her
they	them
who	whom
whoever	whomever

Objective pronouns may be used as either the object of a verb (such as *promoted*) or the object of a preposition (such as *with*):

> Rob worked with *them* until the order was filled.

In this example, *them* is the object of the preposition *with* because Rob acted upon—worked with—them. Here's a sentence with three pronouns, the first one nominative, the second the object of a verb, and the third the object of a preposition:

> *He* paid *us* as soon as the check came from *them*.

He is nominative; *us* is objective because it's the object of the verb *paid*; *them* is objective because it's the object of the preposition *from*.

Every writer sometimes wonders whether to use *who* or *whom*:

> (Who, Whom) will you hire?

Because this sentence is a question, it's difficult to see that *whom* is the object of the verb *hire*. You can figure out which pronoun to use if you rearrange the question and temporarily try *she* and *her* in place of *who* and *whom*: "Will you hire *she*?" or "Will you hire *her*?" *Her* and *whom* are both objective, so the correct choice is "*Whom* will you hire?" Here's a different example:

> (Who, Whom) logged so much travel time?

Turning the question into a statement, you get:

> *He* logged so much travel time.

Therefore, the correct statement is:

> *Who* logged so much travel time?

1.2.5 Possessive Pronouns

Possessive pronouns work like possessive nouns: They show ownership or automatic association.

her job	their preferences
his account	its equipment

However, possessive pronouns are different from possessive nouns in the way they are written. That is, possessive pronouns never have an apostrophe.

Possessive Noun	Possessive Pronoun
the woman's estate	her estate
Roger Franklin's plans	his plans
the shareholders' feelings	their feelings
the vacuum cleaner's attachments	its attachments

The word *its* is the possessive of *it*. Like all other possessive pronouns, its has no apostrophe. Some people confuse *its* with *it's*, the contraction of *it is*. Contractions are discussed later.

Practice Session: Pronouns

Underline the preferred choice within each set of parentheses in the following sentences.

1. Just between you and (*I, me*), I don't think we will make the deadline.
2. The final speaker at the luncheon was (*she, her*).
3. When you are finished, give the report to (*he, him*).
4. (*We, Us*) telemarketers have a tarnished reputation.
5. The company is sending the marketing communications staff—Mary-Ann, Alan, and (*I, me, myself*)—to the conference.
6. The company will issue (*their, its*) annual report next month.
7. Anyone who hasn't yet turned in (*their, his or her*) questionnaire should do so by tomorrow.
8. (*Who, Whom*) shall I say called?
9. To (*who, whom*) should I address the letter?
10. (*Who, Whom*) will they hire?
11. We need more people in our department like (*she, her*).
12. When dealing with an angry customer, try to calm (*him, him or her, them*) down.
13. It was either Sarah or Charlene who left (*her, their*) briefcase on the train.
14. The company needs to update (*its, it's*) website.
15. (*Who, Whom*) do you think will be given the promotion?
16. Be sure to include (*your, you're*) e-mail address on the form.
17. Each brand should have (*its, their*) own trademark.
18. The "dynamic duo"—Bruce and (*I, me*)—are in charge of next week's office party.
19. The supervisor thanked the team members for (*their, they're*) support.
20. The pharmaceutical giant agreed to take (*their, its*) diet drug off the market.

1.3 Verbs

A verb describes an action:

> They all *quit* in disgust.

It may also describe a state of being:

> Working conditions *were* substandard.

The English language is full of action verbs. Here are a few you'll often run across in the business world:

verify	perform	fulfill
hire	succeed	send
leave	improve	receive
accept	develop	pay

You could undoubtedly list many more.

The most common verb describing a state of being instead of an action is *to be* and all its forms:

> I *am, was*, or *will be*; you *are, were*, or *will be*

Other verbs also describe a state of being:

> It *seemed* a good plan at the time.
>
> She *sounds* impressive at a meeting.

These verbs link what comes before them in the sentence with what comes after; no action is involved. (See Section 1.7.5 for a fuller discussion of linking verbs.)

1.3.1 Verb Tenses
English has three simple verb tenses: present, past, and future.

Present: Our branches in Hawaii *stock* other items.

Past: We *stocked* Purquil pens for a short time.

Future: Rotex Tire Stores *will stock* your line of tires when you begin a program of effective national advertising.

With most verbs (the regular ones), the past tense ends in *ed*, and the future tense always has *will* or *shall* in front of it. But the present tense is more complex, depending on the subject:

	First Person	**Second Person**	**Third Person**
Singular	I stock	you stock	he/she/it stocks
Plural	we stock	you stock	they stock

The basic form, *stock*, takes an additional *s* when *he, she,* or *it* precedes it. (See Section 1.3.4 for more on subject-verb agreement.)

In addition to the three simple tenses, there are three perfect tenses using forms of the helping verb *have*. The present perfect tense uses the past participle (regularly the past tense) of the main verb, *stocked*, and adds the present-tense *have* or *has* to the front of it:

(I, we, you, they) *have stocked*.

(He, she, it) *has stocked*.

The past perfect tense uses the past participle of the main verb, *stocked*, and adds the past-tense *had* to the front of it:

(I, you, he, she, it, we, they) *had stocked*.

The future perfect tense also uses the past participle of the main verb, *stocked*, but adds the future-tense *will have*:

(I, you, he, she, it, we, they) *will have stocked*.

Keep verbs in the same tense when the actions occur at the same time:

When the payroll checks *came* in, everyone *showed* up for work.

We *have found* that everyone *has pitched* in to help.

When the actions occur at different times, you may change tense accordingly:

The shipment *came* last Wednesday, so if another one *comes* in today, please *return* it.

The new employee *had been* ill at ease, but now she *has become* a full-fledged member of the team.

1.3.2 Irregular Verbs
Many verbs don't follow in every detail the patterns already described. The most irregular of these verbs is *to be*:

Tense	Singular	Plural
Present:	I *am*	we *are*
	you *are*	you *are*
	he, she, it *is*	they *are*
Past:	I *was*	we *were*
	you *were*	you *were*
	he, she, it *was*	they *were*

The future tense of *to be* is formed in the same way that the future tense of a regular verb is formed.

The perfect tenses of *to be* are also formed as they would be for a regular verb, except that the past participle is a special form, *been*, instead of just the past tense:

Present perfect: you have been

Past perfect: you had been

Future perfect: you will have been

Here's a sampling of other irregular verbs:

Present	Past	Past Participle
begin	began	begun
shrink	shrank	shrunk
know	knew	known
rise	rose	risen
become	became	become
go	went	gone
do	did	done

Dictionaries list the various forms of other irregular verbs.

1.3.3 Transitive and Intransitive Verbs
Many people are confused by three particular sets of verbs:

lie/lay   sit/set   rise/raise

Using these verbs correctly is much easier when you learn the difference between transitive and intransitive verbs.

Transitive verbs convey their action to an object; they "transfer" their action to an object. Intransitive verbs do not.

Here are some sample uses of intransitive and transitive verbs:

Intransitive	Transitive
We should include in our new offices a place to *lie* down for a nap.	The workers will be here on Monday to *lay* new carpeting.
Even the way an interviewee *sits* is important.	That crate is full of stemware, so *set* it down carefully.
Salaries at Compu-Link, Inc., *rise* swiftly.	They *raise* their level of production every year.

The workers *lay* carpeting, you *set* down the crate, they *raise* production; each action is transferred to something. In the intransitive sentences, one *lies* down, an interviewee *sits*, and salaries *rise* without (at least grammatically) affecting anything else. Intransitive sentences are complete with only a subject and a verb; transitive sentences are not complete unless they also include an object, or something to transfer the action to.

Tenses are a confusing element of the *lie/lay* problem:

Present	Past	Past Participle
I lie	I lay	I have lain
I lay (something down)	I laid (something down)	I have laid (something down)

The past tense of *lie* and the present tense of *lay* look and sound alike, even though they're different verbs.

1.3.4 Subject-Verb Agreement

Whether regular or irregular, every verb must agree with its subject, both in person (first, second, or third) and in number (single or plural).

	First Person	Second Person	Third Person
Singular	I *am;* I *write*	you *are;* you *write*	he/she/it *is;* he/she/it *writes*
Plural	we *are;* we *write*	you *are;* you *write*	they *are;* they *write*

In a simple sentence, making a verb agree with its subject is a straightforward task:

Hector Ruiz *is* a strong competitor. (third-person singular)

We *write* to you every month. (first-person plural)

Confusion sometimes arises when sentences are a bit more complicated. For example, be sure to avoid agreement problems when words come between the subject and verb. In the following examples, the verb appears in italics, and its subject is underlined:

The <u>analysis</u> of existing documents *takes* a full week.

Even though *documents* is a plural, the verb is in the singular form. That's because the subject of the sentence is *analysis*, a singular noun. The phrase *of existing documents* can be disregarded. Here is another example:

The <u>answers</u> for this exercise *are* in the study guide.

Take away the phrase *for this exercise* and you are left with the plural subject *answers*. Therefore, the verb takes the plural form.

Verb agreement is also complicated when the subject is not a specific noun or pronoun and when the subject may be considered either singular or plural. In such cases, you have to analyze the surrounding sentence to determine which verb form to use.

The <u>staff</u> *is* quartered in the warehouse.

The <u>staff</u> *are* at their desks in the warehouse.

The <u>computers</u> and the <u>staff</u> *are* in the warehouse.

Neither the staff nor the <u>computers</u> *are* in the warehouse.

<u>Every</u> computer *is* in the warehouse.

Many a <u>computer</u> *is* in the warehouse.

Did you notice that words such as *every* use the singular verb form? In addition, when an *either/or* or a *neither/nor* phrase combines singular and plural nouns, the verb takes the form that matches the noun closest to it.

In the business world, some subjects require extra attention. Company names, for example, are considered singular and therefore take a singular verb in most cases—even if they contain plural words:

<u>Stater Brothers</u> *offers* convenient grocery shopping.

In addition, quantities are sometimes considered singular and sometimes plural. If a quantity refers to a total amount, it takes a singular verb; if a quantity refers to individual, countable units, it takes a plural verb:

Three <u>hours</u> *is* a long time.

The eight <u>dollars</u> we collected for the fund *are* tacked on the bulletin board.

Fractions may also be singular or plural, depending on the noun that accompanies them:

One-third of the <u>warehouse</u> *is* devoted to this product line.

One-third of the <u>products</u> *are* defective.

For a related discussion, see Section 1.7.2, "Longer Sentences," later in this Handbook.

1.3.5 Voice of Verbs

Verbs have two voices, active and passive. When the subject comes first, the voice is active. When the object comes first, the voice is passive:

Active: The buyer paid a large amount.

Passive: A large amount was paid by the buyer.

The passive voice uses a form of the verb *to be*, which adds words to a sentence. In the example, the passive-voice sentence uses eight words, whereas the active-voice sentence uses only six to say the same thing. The words *was* and *by* are unnecessary to convey the meaning of the sentence. In fact, extra words usually clog meaning. So be sure to opt for the active voice when you have a choice.

At times, however, you have no choice:

Several items *have been taken*, but so far we don't know who took them.

The passive voice becomes necessary when you don't know (or don't want to say) who performed the action; the active voice is bolder and more direct.

1.3.6 Mood of Verbs

You have three moods to choose from, depending on your intentions. Most of the time you use the indicative mood to make a statement or to ask a question:

The secretary *mailed* a letter to each supplier.

Did the secretary *mail* a letter to each supplier?

When you wish to command or request, use the imperative mood:

Please *mail* a letter to each supplier.

Sometimes, especially in business, a courteous request is stated like a question; in that case, however, no question mark is required:

Would you *mail* a letter to each supplier.

The subjunctive mood, most often used in formal writing or in presenting bad news, expresses a possibility or a recommendation. The subjunctive is usually signaled by a word such as *if* or *that*. In these examples, the subjunctive mood uses special verb forms:

If the secretary *were to mail* a letter to each supplier, we might save some money.

I suggested that the secretary *mail* a letter to each supplier.

Although the subjunctive mood is not used as often as it once was, it's still found in such expressions as *Come what may* and *If I were you*. In general, it is used to convey an idea that is contrary to fact: If iron *were* lighter than air.

Practice Session: Verbs

Underline the preferred choice within each set of parentheses in the following sentences.

1. When Hastings (*come, comes, came*) in, tell him I (*want, wanted*) to see him.
2. Even though Sheila (*knowed, knew*) the right password, she typed it incorrectly.
3. The presentation had not yet (*began, begun*) when Charles arrived.
4. What I always say is, let sleeping dogs (*lay, lie*).
5. The workers (*lay, laid*) the tile in the executive bathroom yesterday.
6. This is where the president of the board (*sits, sets*) during meetings.
7. Just (*sit, set*) the boxes down over there.
8. Do you think management will (*raise, rise*) prices across the board next week?
9. A list of promotions (*was, were*) posted on the company intranet.
10. The supervisor of the assembly-line workers (*is, are*) being replaced.
11. The committee (*is, are*) considering the proposal today.
12. The board and the committee (*is, are*) having a joint meeting on June 25.
13. Neither the board nor the committee (*is, are*) expected to approve the proposal.
14. Every member of the board (*is, are*) going to make a statement.
15. Katten and Associates (*represent, represents*) clients in the entertainment industry.
16. Five hours (*is, are*) all I can give you to get the project done.
17. Half of the vacant lots (*is, are*) already sold.
18. Half of the hall (*is, are*) reserved for the luncheon.
19. Mario suggested that the public relations department (*send, sends*) out a news release about the merger.
20. If I (*was, were*) CEO, I'd fire the whole accounting staff.

1.4 Adjectives

An adjective modifies (tells something about) a noun or pronoun. Each of the following phrases says more about the noun or pronoun than the noun or pronoun would say alone.

an *efficient* staff	a *heavy* price
brisk trade	*poor* you

Adjectives always tell us something that we wouldn't know without them. So you don't need to use adjectives when the noun alone, or a different noun, will give the meaning:

a *company* employee

(An employee ordinarily works for a company.)

a *crate-type* container

(*Crate* gives the entire meaning.)

Verbs in the *ing* (present participle) form can be used as adjectives:

A *boring* job can sometimes turn into a *fascinating* career.

So can the past participle of verbs:

A freshly *painted* house is a *sold* house.

Adjectives modify nouns more often than they modify pronouns. When adjectives do modify pronouns, however, the sentence usually has a linking verb:

They were *attentive*.   It looked *appropriate*.
He seems *interested*.   You are *skillful*.

At times, a series of adjectives precedes a noun:

It was a *long* and *active* workday.

Such strings of adjectives are acceptable as long as they all convey a different part of the phrase's meaning. However, adjectives often pile up in front of a noun, like this:

The *superficial, obvious* answer was the one she gave.
The most valuable animal on the ranch is a *small black* horse.

The question is whether a comma should be used to separate the adjectives. The answer is to use a comma when the two adjectives independently modify the noun; do not use a comma when one of the adjectives is closely identified with the noun. In the first example above, the answer was both superficial and obvious. But in the second example, the black horse is small.

Another way to think about this is to use the word *and* as a replacement for the comma. Study the following example:

We recommend a diet of leafy green vegetables.
We recommend a diet of green, leafy vegetables.

Because some green vegetables are not leafy (cucumbers and zucchini, for example), it is correct to leave out the comma in the first example so that you know which kind of green vegetables are being discussed. But because all leafy vegetables are also green (green and leafy), the comma must be included in the second example.

You might also try switching the adjectives. If the order of the adjectives can be reversed without changing the meaning of the phrase, you should use a comma. If the order cannot be reversed, you should not use a comma. Consider these examples:

Here's our *simplified credit* application.
Here's our *simplified, easy-to-complete* application.
Here's our *easy-to-complete, simplified* application.

A credit application may be simple or complex; however, you cannot talk about a credit, simplified application; therefore, leave the comma out of the first example. The application in the second and third examples is both simplified and easy to complete, no matter how you arrange the words, so include the comma in these examples.

1.4.1 Comparative Degree
Most adjectives can take three forms: simple, comparative, and superlative. The simple form modifies a single noun or pronoun. Use the comparative form when comparing two items.

When comparing three or more items, use the superlative form.

Simple	Comparative	Superlative
hard	harder	hardest
safe	safer	safest
dry	drier	driest

The comparative form adds *er* to the simple form, and the superlative form adds *est*. (The *y* at the end of a word changes to *i* before the *er* or *est* is added.)

A small number of adjectives are irregular, including these:

Simple	Comparative	Superlative
good	better	best
bad	worse	worst
little	less	least

When the simple form of an adjective is two or more syllables, you usually add *more* to form the comparative and *most* to form the superlative:

Simple	Comparative	Superlative
useful	more useful	most useful
exhausting	more exhausting	most exhausting
expensive	more expensive	most expensive

The most common exceptions are two-syllable adjectives that end in *y*:

Simple	Comparative	Superlative
happy	happier	happiest
costly	costlier	costliest

If you choose this option, change the *y* to *i* and tack *er* or *est* onto the end.

Some adjectives cannot be used to make comparisons because they themselves indicate the extreme. For example, if something is perfect, nothing can be more perfect. If something is unique or ultimate, nothing can be more unique or more ultimate.

1.4.2 Hyphenated Adjectives
Many adjectives used in the business world are actually combinations of words: *up-to-date* report, *last-minute* effort, *fifth-floor* suite, *well-built* engine. As you can see, they are hyphenated when they come before the noun they modify. However, when they come after the noun they modify, they are not hyphenated. In the following example, the adjectives appear in italics and the nouns they modify are underlined:

The <u>report</u> is *up to date* because of our team's *last-minute* <u>efforts</u>.

Hyphens are not used when part of the combination is a word ending in *ly* (because that word is usually not an adjective).

Hyphens are also omitted from word combinations that are used frequently.

We live in a *rapidly shrinking* world.

Our *highly motivated* employees will be well paid.

Please consider renewing your *credit card* account.

Send those figures to our *data processing* department.

Our new intern is a *high school* student.

1.5 Adverbs

An adverb modifies a verb, an adjective, or another adverb:

Modifying a verb:	Our marketing department works *efficiently*.
Modifying an adjective:	She was not dependable, although she was *highly* intelligent.
Modifying another adverb:	His territory was *too* broadly diversified, so he moved *extremely* cautiously.

Most of the adverbs mentioned are adjectives turned into adverbs by adding *ly*, which is how many adverbs are formed:

Adjective	Adverb
efficient	efficiently
extreme	extremely
high	highly
official	officially
separate	separately
special	specially

Some adverbs are made by dropping or changing the final letter of the adjective and then adding *ly:*

Adjective	Adverb
due	duly
busy	busily

Other adverbs don't end in *ly* at all. Here are a few examples of this type:

often	fast	too
soon	very	so

Some adverbs are difficult to distinguish from adjectives. For example, in the following sentences, is the underlined word an adverb or an adjective?

They worked <u>well</u>.

The baby is <u>well</u>.

In the first sentence, *well* is an adverb modifying the verb worked. In the second sentence, *well* is an adjective modifying the noun *baby*. To choose correctly between adverbs and

adjectives, remember that verbs of being link a noun to an adjective describing the noun. In contrast, you would use an adverb to describe an action verb.

Adjective	Adverb
He is a *good* worker. (What kind of worker is he?)	He works *well*. (How does he work?)
It is a *real* computer. (What kind of computer is it?)	It *really* is a computer. (To what extent is it a computer?)
The traffic is *slow*. (What quality does the traffic have?)	The traffic moves *slowly*. (How does the traffic move?)

1.5.1 Negative Adverbs

Negative adverbs (such as *neither, no, not, scarcely,* and *seldom*) are powerful words and therefore do not need any help in conveying a negative thought. In fact, using double negatives gives a strong impression of illiteracy, so avoid sentences like these:

I don't want no mistakes.
(Correct: "I don't want any mistakes," or "I want no mistakes.")

They couldn't hardly read the report.
(Correct: "They could hardly read the report," or "They couldn't read the report.")

They scarcely noticed neither one.
(Correct: "They scarcely noticed either one," or "They noticed neither one.")

1.5.2 Comparative Degree

Like adjectives, adverbs can be used to compare items. Generally, the basic adverb is combined with *more* or *most,* just as long adjectives are. However, some adverbs have one-word comparative forms:

One Item	Two Items	Three Items
quickly	more quickly	most quickly
sincerely	less sincerely	least sincerely
fast	faster	fastest
well	better	best

Practice Session: Adjectives and Adverbs

Underline the preferred choice within each set of parentheses in the following sentences.

1. I always choose the (*less, least*) expensive brand.
2. Which would be (*better, best*), the store brand or the generic brand?
3. This audit couldn't have come at a (*worse, worst*) time.
4. When it comes to data analysis, Claire is (*more competent, competenter*) than Alexander.
5. The ad agency's campaign for our new vitamin supplement is (*unique, very unique, most unique*), to say the least.
6. A corporation can benefit from a (*well written, well-written*) annual report.

7. The chairman's introductory message to the annual report was (*well written, well-written*).
8. Even a (*beautifully written, beautifully-written*) report can be hampered by poor design and production.
9. According to Bank of America, the number of (*credit-card, credit card*) applications has tripled in the past year.
10. Angela wasn't feeling (*good, well*), so she went home early.
11. Harrison and Martinez work (*good, well*) together.
12. We are (*real, really*) excited about next week's product launch.
13. Could this project be moving any more (*slow, slowly*) through the bureaucratic system?
14. We (*could hardly, couldn't hardly*) wait to see how the brochure had turned out.
15. Today TeKTech is (*more heavy, more heavily, most heavily*) involved in nanotechnology, compared to five years ago.

1.6 Other Parts of Speech

Nouns, pronouns, verbs, adjectives, and adverbs carry most of the meaning in a sentence. Four other parts of speech link them together in sentences: prepositions, conjunctions, articles, and interjections.

1.6.1 Prepositions

Prepositions are words like these:

of	to	for	with
at	by	from	about

Some prepositions consist of more than one word—like these:

because of	in addition to	out of	except for

And some prepositions are closely linked with a verb. When using phrases such as *look up* and *wipe out*, keep the phrase intact and do not insert anything between the verb and the preposition.

Prepositions most often begin prepositional phrases, which function like adjectives and adverbs by telling more about a pronoun, noun, or verb:

of a type	*by* Friday
to the point	*with* characteristic flair

To prevent misreading, prepositional phrases should be placed near the element they modify:

Of all our technicians, <u>she</u> is the best trained.

They couldn't see the <u>merit</u> *in my proposal.*

Someone left a <u>folder</u> *on my desk.*

It was once considered totally unacceptable to put a preposition at the end of a sentence. Now you may:

I couldn't tell what they were interested in.

What did she attribute it to?

However, be careful not to place prepositions at the end of sentences when doing so is unnecessary. In fact, avoid using any

unnecessary preposition. In the following examples, the prepositions in parentheses should be omitted:

All (of) the staff members were present.

I almost fell off (of) my chair with surprise.

Where was Mr. Steuben going (to)?

They couldn't help (from) wondering.

The opposite problem is failing to include a preposition when you should. Consider the two sentences that follow:

Sales were over $100,000 for Linda and Bill.

Sales were over $100,000 for Linda and for Bill.

The first sentence indicates that Linda and Bill had combined sales over $100,000; the second, that Linda and Bill each had sales over $100,000, for a combined total in excess of $200,000. The preposition *for* is critical here.

Prepositions are also required in sentences like this one:

Which type of personal computer do you prefer?

Certain prepositions are used with certain words. When the same preposition can be used for two or more words in a sentence without affecting the meaning, only the last preposition is required:

We are familiar (*with*) and satisfied *with* your company's products.

But when different prepositions are normally used with the words, all the prepositions must be included:

We are familiar *with* and interested *in* your company's products.

Here is an incomplete list of prepositions that are used in a particular way with particular words:

among/between: *Among* is used to refer to three or more (*Circulate the memo among the staff*); *between* is used to refer to two (*Put the copy machine between Judy and Dan*).

as if/like: *As if* is used before a clause (*It seems as if we should be doing something*); *like* is used before a noun or pronoun (*He seems like a nice guy*).

have/of: *Have* is a verb used in verb phrases (*They should have checked first*); *of* is a preposition and is never used in such cases.

in/into: *In* is used to refer to a static position (*The file is in the cabinet*); *into* is used to refer to movement toward a position (*Put the file into the cabinet*).

And here is an incomplete list of some prepositions that have come to be used with certain words:

according to

agree to (a proposal)

agree with (a person)

buy from

capable of

comply with

conform to

differ from (things)

differ with (person)

different from

get from (receive)

get off (dismount)

in accordance with

in search of

independent of

interior to

plan to

prefer to

prior to

reason with

responsible for

similar to

talk to (without interaction)

talk with (with interaction)

wait for (person or thing)

wait on (like a waiter)

1.6.2 Conjunctions

Conjunctions connect the parts of a sentence: words, phrases, and clauses. You are probably most familiar with coordinating conjunctions such as the following:

and	for	or	yet
but	nor	so	

Conjunctions may be used to connect clauses (which have both a subject and a predicate) with other clauses, to connect clauses with phrases (which do not have both a subject and a predicate), and to connect words with words:

We sell designer clothing *and* linens.

(Words with words)

Their products are expensive *but* still appeal to value-conscious consumers.

(Clauses with phrases)

I will call her on the phone today, *or* I will visit her office tomorrow.

(Clauses with clauses)

Some conjunctions are used in pairs:

both . . . and	neither . . . nor	whether . . . or
either . . . or	not only . . . but also	

With paired conjunctions, you must be careful to construct each phrase in the same way.

They *not only* <u>are out of</u> racquets *but also* <u>are out of</u> balls.

They are *not only* <u>out of</u> racquets *but also* <u>out of</u> balls.

They <u>are out of</u> *not only* racquets *but also* balls.

In other words, the construction that follows each part of the pair must be parallel, containing the same verbs, prepositions, and so on. The same need for parallelism exists when using conjunctions to join the other parts of speech:

He is listed in *either* <u>your</u> roster *or* <u>my</u> roster.

He is listed *neither* <u>in</u> your roster *nor* <u>on</u> the master list.

They *both* <u>gave</u> *and* <u>received</u> notice.

A certain type of conjunction is used to join clauses that are unequal—that is, to join a main clause to one that is subordinate or dependent. Here is a partial list of conjunctions used to introduce dependent clauses:

although	before	once	unless
as soon as	even though	so that	until
because	if	that	when

Using conjunctions is also discussed in Sections 1.7.3 and 1.7.4.

1.6.3 Articles and Interjections

Only three articles exist in English: *the, a,* and *an.* These words are used, like adjectives, to specify which item you are talking about.

Interjections are words that express no solid information, only emotion:

Wow!	Well, well!
Oh, no!	Good!

Such purely emotional language has its place in private life and advertising copy, but it only weakens the effect of most business writing.

Practice Session: Prepositions, Conjunctions, and Articles

Circle the letter of the preferred choice in each pair of sentences.

1. **a.** If we want to have the project done next week, we'll need those balance sheets by Wednesday.
   b. If we want to have the project done next week, by Wednesday we'll need those balance sheets.

2. **a.** From where did that information come?
   b. Where did that information come from?

3. **a.** Please look up the shipping rates for packages to France.
   b. Please look the shipping rates up for packages to France.

4. **a.** You need to indicate the type job you're seeking.
   b. You need to indicate the type of job you're seeking.

5. **a.** Michael got the actuarial data off of the Internet.
   b. Michael got the actuarial data off the Internet.

6. **a.** When the meeting is over, Michelle will prepare the minutes.
   b. When the meeting is over with, Michelle will prepare the minutes.

7. **a.** Sharon is familiar and knowledgeable about HTML coding.
   b. Sharon is familiar with and knowledgeable about HTML coding.

8. **a.** We'll be deciding among the four applicants this afternoon.
   b. We'll be deciding between the four applicants this afternoon.

9. a. Since Marshall isn't here, it looks like the conference call will have to be canceled.
   b. Since Marshall isn't here, it looks as if the conference call will have to be canceled.

10. a. I would have had the memo done sooner, but my computer crashed.
   b. I would of had the memo done sooner, but my computer crashed.

11. a. Once we have the survey results, we can put them in the report.
   b. Once we have the survey results, we can put them into the report.

12. a. If you agree with the settlement, I can prepare the final papers.
   b. If you agree to the settlement, I can prepare the final papers.

13. a. It is important that you provide not only your name but also your address and telephone number.
   b. It is important that you provide not only your name but also address and telephone number.

14. a. The conference will be held in either March or July.
   b. The conference will be held either in March or July.

15. a. Please prepare an RFP for the construction job.
   b. Please prepare a RFP for the construction job.

1.7 Sentences

Sentences are constructed with the major building blocks, the parts of speech.

> Money talks.

This two-word sentence consists of a noun (*money*) and a verb (*talks*). When used in this way, the noun works as the first requirement for a sentence, the subject, and the verb works as the second requirement, the predicate. Now look at this sentence:

> They merged.

The subject in this case is a pronoun (*they*), and the predicate is a verb (*merged*). This is a sentence because it has a subject and a predicate. Here is yet another kind of sentence:

> The plans are ready.

This sentence has a more complicated subject, the noun *plans* and the article *the*; the complete predicate is a state-of-being verb (*are*) and an adjective (*ready*).

Without a subject (who or what does something) and a predicate (the doing of it), you have merely a collection of words, not a sentence.

1.7.1 Commands

In commands, the subject (always *you*) is only understood, not stated:

> (You) Move your desk to the better office.

> (You) Please try to finish by six o'clock.

1.7.2 Longer Sentences

More complicated sentences have more complicated subjects and predicates, but they still have a simple subject and a predicate verb. In the following examples, the subject is underlined once, the predicate verb twice:

> <u>Marex</u> and <u>Contron</u> <u><u>enjoy</u></u> higher earnings each quarter.
> (*Marex* [and] *Contron* do something; *enjoy* is what they do.)

> My <u>interview</u>, coming minutes after my freeway accident, <u><u>did</u></u> not <u><u>impress</u></u> or <u><u>move</u></u> anyone.
> (*Interview* is what did something. What did it do? It *did* [not] *impress* [or] *move*.)

> In terms of usable space, a steel <u>warehouse</u>, with its extremely long span of roof unsupported by pillars, <u><u>makes</u></u> more sense.
> (*Warehouse* is what *makes*.)

These three sentences demonstrate several things. First, in all three sentences, the simple subject and predicate verb are the "bare bones" of the sentence, the parts that carry the core idea of the sentence. When trying to find the subject and predicate verb, disregard all prepositional phrases, modifiers, conjunctions, and articles.

Second, in the third sentence the verb is singular (*makes*) because the subject is singular (*warehouse*). Even though the plural noun *pillars* is closer to the verb, *warehouse* is the subject. So *warehouse* determines whether the verb is singular or plural. Subject and predicate must agree.

Third, the subject in the first sentence is compound (*Marex* [and] *Contron*). A compound subject, when connected by *and*, requires a plural verb (*enjoy*). Also in the second sentence, compound predicates are possible (*did* [not] *impress* [or] *move*).

Fourth, the second sentence incorporates a group of words—*coming minutes after my freeway accident*—containing a form of a verb (*coming*) and a noun (*accident*). Yet this group of words is not a complete sentence for two reasons:

- Not all nouns are subjects: *Accident* is not the subject of *coming*.
- Not all verbs are predicates: A verb that ends in *ing* can never be the predicate of a sentence (unless preceded by a form of *to be*, as in *was coming*).

Because they don't contain a subject and a predicate, the words *coming minutes after my freeway accident* (called a phrase) can't be written as a sentence. That is, the phrase cannot stand alone; it cannot begin with a capital letter and end with a period. So a phrase must always be just one part of a sentence.

Sometimes a sentence incorporates two or more groups of words that do contain a subject and a predicate; these word groups are called clauses:

> My *interview*, because it <u><u>came</u></u> minutes after my freeway accident, <u><u>did</u></u> not <u><u>impress</u></u> or <u><u>move</u></u> anyone.

The independent clause is the portion of the sentence that could stand alone without revision:

> My <u>interview</u> <u><u>did</u></u> not <u><u>impress</u></u> or <u><u>move</u></u> anyone.

The other part of the sentence could stand alone only by removing *because:*

(because) It <u>came</u> minutes after my freeway accident.

This part of the sentence is known as a dependent clause; although it has a subject and a predicate (just as an independent clause does), it's linked to the main part of the sentence by a word (*because*) showing its dependence.

In summary, the two types of clauses—dependent and independent—both have a subject and a predicate. Dependent clauses, however, do not bear the main meaning of the sentence and are therefore linked to an independent clause. Nor can phrases stand alone, because they lack both a subject and a predicate. Only independent clauses can be written as sentences without revision.

1.7.3 Sentence Fragments

An incomplete sentence (a phrase or a dependent clause) that is written as though it were a complete sentence is called a fragment. Consider the following sentence fragments:

Marilyn Sanders, having had pilferage problems in her store for the past year. Refuses to accept the results of our investigation.

This serious error can easily be corrected by putting the two fragments together:

Marilyn Sanders, having had pilferage problems in her store for the past year, refuses to accept the results of our investigation.

Not all fragments can be corrected so easily. Here's more information on Sanders's pilferage problem.

Employees a part of it. No authority or discipline.

Only the writer knows the intended meaning of those two phrases. Perhaps the employees are taking part in the pilferage. If so, the sentence should read:

Some employees are part of the pilferage problem.

On the other hand, it's possible that some employees are helping with the investigation. Then the sentence would read:

Some employees are taking part in our investigation.

It's just as likely, however, that the employees not only are taking part in the pilferage but are also being analyzed:

Those employees who are part of the pilferage problem will accept no authority or discipline.

Even more meanings could be read into these fragments. Because fragments can mean so many things, they mean nothing. No well-written memo, letter, or report ever demands the reader to be an imaginative genius.

One more type of fragment exists, the kind represented by a dependent clause. Note what *because* does to change what was once a unified sentence:

Our stock of sprinklers is depleted.

Because our stock of sprinklers is depleted.

Although the second version contains a subject and a predicate, adding *because* makes it a fragment. Words such as *because* form a special group of words called subordinating conjunctions. Here's a partial list:

after	if	unless
although	since	whenever
even if	though	while

When a word of this type begins a clause, the clause is dependent and cannot stand as a sentence. However, if a dependent clause is combined with an independent clause, it can convey a complete meaning. The independent clause may come before or after the dependent clause:

We are unable to fill your order because our stock of sprinklers is depleted.

Because our stock of sprinklers is depleted, we are unable to fill your order.

Also, to fix a fragment that is a dependent clause, remove the subordinating conjunction. Doing so leaves a simple but complete sentence:

Our stock of sprinklers is depleted.

The actual details of a situation will determine the best way for you to remedy a fragment problem.

The ban on fragments has one exception. Some advertising copy contains sentence fragments, written knowingly to convey a certain rhythm. However, advertising is the only area of business in which fragments are acceptable.

1.7.4 Fused Sentences and Comma Splices

Just as there can be too little in a group of words to make it a sentence, there can also be too much:

All our mail is run through a postage meter every afternoon someone picks it up.

This example contains two sentences, not one, but the two have been blended so that it's hard to tell where one ends and the next begins. Is the mail run through a meter every afternoon? If so, the sentences should read:

All our mail is run through a postage meter every afternoon. Someone picks it up.

Perhaps the mail is run through a meter at some other time (morning, for example) and is picked up every afternoon:

All our mail is run through a postage meter. Every afternoon someone picks it up.

The order of words is the same in all three cases; sentence division makes all the difference. Either of the last two cases is grammatically correct. The choice depends on the facts of the situation.

Sometimes these so-called fused sentences have a more obvious point of separation:

> Several large orders arrived within a few days of one another, too many came in for us to process by the end of the month.

Here the comma has been put between two independent clauses in an attempt to link them. When a lowly comma separates two complete sentences, the result is called a comma splice. A comma splice can be remedied in one of three ways:

- Replace the comma with a period and capitalize the next word: ". . . one another. Too many . . . ".
- Replace the comma with a semicolon and do not capitalize the next word: ". . . one another; too many . . . ". This remedy works only when the two sentences have closely related meanings.
- Change one of the sentences so that it becomes a phrase or a dependent clause. This remedy often produces the best writing, but it takes more work.

The third alternative can be carried out in several ways. One is to begin the blended sentence with a subordinating conjunction:

> Whenever several large orders arrived within a few days of one another, too many came in for us to process by the end of the month.

Another way is to remove part of the subject or the predicate verb from one of the independent clauses, thereby creating a phrase:

> Several large orders arrived within a few days of one another, too many for us to process by the end of the month.

Finally, you can change one of the predicate verbs to its *ing* form:

> Several large orders arrived within a few days of one another, too many coming in for us to process by the end of the month.

At other times a simple coordinating conjunction (such as *or*, *and*, or *but*) can separate fused sentences:

> You can fire them, or you can make better use of their abilities.
> Margaret drew up the designs, and Matt carried them out.
> We will have three strong months, but after that sales will taper off.

Be careful using coordinating conjunctions: Use them only to join simple sentences that express similar ideas.

Also, because they say relatively little about the relationship between the two clauses they join, avoid using coordinating conjunctions too often: *and* is merely an addition sign; *but* is just a

turn signal; *or* only points to an alternative. Subordinating conjunctions such as *because* and *whenever* tell the reader a lot more.

1.7.5 Sentences with Linking Verbs

Linking verbs were discussed briefly in the section on verbs (Section 1.3). Here you can see more fully the way they function in a sentence. The following is a model of any sentence with a linking verb:

> A (*verb*) B.

Although words such as *seems* and *feels* can also be linking verbs, let's assume that the verb is a form of *to be:*

> A *is* B.

In such a sentence, A and B are always nouns, pronouns, or adjectives. When one is a noun and the other is a pronoun, or when both are nouns, the sentence says that one is the same as the other:

> She is president.
> Rachel is president.

When one is an adjective, it modifies or describes the other:

> She is forceful.

Remember that when one is an adjective, it modifies the other as any adjective modifies a noun or pronoun, except that a linking verb stands between the adjective and the word it modifies.

1.7.6 Misplaced Modifiers

The position of a modifier in a sentence is important. The movement of *only* changes the meaning in the following sentences:

> Only we are obliged to supply those items specified in your contract.
> We are obliged only to supply those items specified in your contract.
> We are obliged to supply only those items specified in your contract.
> We are obliged to supply those items specified only in your contract.

In any particular set of circumstances, only one of those sentences would be accurate. The others would very likely cause problems. To prevent misunderstanding, place such modifiers as close as possible to the noun or verb they modify.

For similar reasons, whole phrases that are modifiers must be placed near the right noun or verb. Mistakes in placement create ludicrous meanings.

> Antia Information Systems has bought new computer chairs for the programmers *with more comfortable seats.*

The anatomy of programmers is not normally a concern of business writers. Obviously, the comfort of the chairs was the issue:

Antia Information Systems has bought new computer chairs *with more comfortable seats* for the programmers.

Here is another example:

I asked him to file all the letters in the cabinet that had been answered.

In this ridiculous sentence the cabinet has been answered, even though no cabinet in history is known to have asked a question. *That had been answered* is too far from *letters* and too close to *cabinet*. Here's an improvement:

I asked him to file in the cabinet all the letters that had been answered.

In some cases, instead of moving the modifying phrase closer to the word it modifies, the best solution is to move the word closer to the modifying phrase.

Practice Session: Sentences

Circle the letter of the preferred choice in each group of sentences.

1. **a.** Cyberterrorism—orchestrated attacks on a company's information systems for political or economic purposes—is a very real threat.
   b. Cyberterrorism—orchestrated attacks on a company's information systems for political or economic purposes—are a very real threat.

2. **a.** E-mail, phone calls, and faxes, each one a distraction, interrupts employees when they work.
   b. E-mail, phone calls, and faxes, each one a distraction, interrupt employees when they work.

3. **a.** About 35 percent of major U.S. companies keep tabs on workers. Because they want to protect valuable company information.
   b. About 35 percent of major U.S. companies keep tabs on workers, because they want to protect valuable company information.
   c. About 35 percent of major U.S. companies keep tabs on workers; because they want to protect valuable company information.

4. **a.** Despite its small size and relative isolation in the Arctic Circle. Finland leads the pack in mobile phone technology and its applications.
   b. Despite its small size and relative isolation in the Arctic Circle; Finland leads the pack in mobile phone technology and its applications.
   c. Despite its small size and relative isolation in the Arctic Circle, Finland leads the pack in mobile phone technology and its applications.

5. **a.** Many employees erroneously believe that their e-mail and voice mail messages are private they're surprised when e-mail ends up in places where they did not intend it to go.
   b. Many employees erroneously believe that their e-mail and voice mail messages are private, they're surprised when e-mail ends up in places where they did not intend it to go.

   c. Many employees erroneously believe that their e-mail and voice mail messages are private, so they're surprised when e-mail ends up in places where they did not intend it to go.

6. **a.** Each day people in the United States treat themselves to more than 3 million Krispy Kreme doughnuts, they buy more than 11,000 dozen of those doughnuts every hour.
   b. Each day people in the United States treat themselves to more than 3 million Krispy Kreme doughnuts, buying more than 11,000 dozen of those doughnuts every hour.

7. **a.** The procedure for making Krispy Kreme doughnuts takes about an hour, the manufacturing process begins long before local stores crank up their production lines.
   b. The procedure for making Krispy Kreme doughnuts takes about an hour; the manufacturing process begins long before local stores crank up their production lines.
   c. The procedure for making Krispy Kreme doughnuts takes about an hour. But the manufacturing process begins long before local stores crank up their production lines.

8. **a.** After blending the ingredients, the doughnut mix is stored in Krispy Kreme's warehouse for a week.
   b. After blending the ingredients, Krispy Kreme's warehouse is used to store the doughnut mix for a week.
   c. After the ingredients have been blended, the doughnut mix is stored in Krispy Kreme's warehouse for a week.

9. **a.** All the company's bikes are custom-made by Green Gear Cycling to meet the rider's size and component preferences.
   b. All the company's bikes are custom-made to meet the rider's size and component preferences by Green Gear Cycling.

10. **a.** Catering to its customers, about 2,000 bikes are built annually by Green Gear Cycling.
    b. Catering to its customers, about 2,000 bikes are built by Green Gear Cycling annually.
    c. Catering to its customers, Green Gear Cycling builds about 2,000 bikes annually.

2.0 Punctuation

On the highway, signs tell you when to slow down or stop, where to turn, when to merge. In similar fashion, punctuation helps readers negotiate your prose. The proper use of punctuation keeps readers from losing track of your meaning.

2.1 Periods

Use a period (1) to end any sentence that is not a question, (2) with certain abbreviations, and (3) between dollars and cents in an amount of money.

2.2 Question Marks

Use a question mark after any direct question that requests an answer:

Are you planning to enclose a check, or shall we bill you?

Don't use a question mark with commands phrased as questions for the sake of politeness:

> Will you send us a check today.

2.3 Exclamation Points

Use exclamation points after highly emotional language. Because business writing almost never calls for emotional language, you will seldom use exclamation points.

2.4 Semicolons

Semicolons have three main uses. One is to separate two closely related independent clauses:

> The outline for the report is due within a week; the report itself is due at the end of the month.

A semicolon should also be used instead of a comma when the items in a series have commas within them:

> Our previous meetings were on November 11, 2004; February 20, 2005; and April 28, 2006.

Finally, a semicolon should be used to separate independent clauses when the second one begins with a word such as *however, therefore,* or *nevertheless* or a phrase such as *for example* or *in that case:*

> Our supplier has been out of part D712 for 10 weeks; however, we have found another source that can ship the part right away.
>
> His test scores were quite low; on the other hand, he has a lot of relevant experience.

Section 4.4 has more information on using transitional words and phrases.

2.5 Colons

Use a colon after the salutation in a business letter. You also use a colon at the end of a sentence or phrase introducing a list or (sometimes) a quotation:

> Our study included the three most critical problems: insufficient capital, incompetent management, and inappropriate location.

In some introductory sentences, phrases such as *the following* or *that is* are implied by using a colon.

A colon should not be used when the list, quotation, or idea is a direct object or part of the introductory sentence:

> We are able to supply
>
> staples
>
> wood screws
>
> nails
>
> toggle bolts
>
> This shipment includes 9 DVDs, 12 CDs, and 14 USB flash drives.

Another way you can use a colon is to separate the main clause and another sentence element when the second explains, illustrates, or amplifies the first:

> Management was unprepared for the union representatives' demands: this fact alone accounts for their arguing well into the night.

However, in contemporary usage, such clauses are frequently separated by a semicolon.

Practice Session: Punctuation 1

Circle the letter of the preferred choice in the following groups of sentences.

1. a. She asked me whether we should increase our insurance coverage?
   b. She asked me whether we should increase our insurance coverage.

2. a. Would you please let me know when the copier is free.
   b. Would you please let me know when the copier is free?

3. a. You won't want to miss this exciting seminar!
   b. You won't want to miss this exciting seminar.

4. a. The officers of the board of directors are John Rogers, president, Robin Doug Donlan, vice president for programming, Bill Pittman, vice president for operations, and Mary Sturhann, secretary.
   b. The officers of the board of directors are John Rogers, president; Robin Doug Donlan, vice president for programming; Bill Pittman, vice president for operations; and Mary Sturhann, secretary.
   c. The officers of the board of directors are John Rogers, president; Robin Doug Donlan, vice president for programming; Bill Pittman, vice president for operations, and Mary Sturhann, secretary.

5. a. Edward Jones is the best brokerage house in America; it's got more offices than any other brokerage house.
   b. Edward Jones is the best brokerage house in America, it's got more offices than any other brokerage house.

6. a. One of the SEC's top priorities is to crack down on insider trading, however it readily admits that it has not been very successful to date.
   b. One of the SEC's top priorities is to crack down on insider trading; however, it readily admits that it has not been very successful to date.

7. a. To keep on top of financial news, you should consult newspapers aimed specifically at investors, such as *Investor's Business Daily* and *Barron's.*
   b. To keep on top of financial news, you should consult newspapers aimed specifically at investors; such as, *Investor's Business Daily* and *Barron's.*
   c. To keep on top of financial news, you should consult newspapers aimed specifically at investors; such as *Investor's Business Daily* and *Barron's.*

8. **a.** Dear Dr. Schatzman,
    b. Dear Dr. Schatzman:

9. **a.** The three basic concepts that guide accountants are: the fundamental accounting equation, double-entry book-keeping, and the matching principle.
    b. The three basic concepts that guide accountants are the fundamental accounting equation, double-entry book-keeping, and the matching principle.
    c. The three basic concepts that guide accountants are the fundamental accounting equation; double-entry book-keeping; and the matching principle.

10. **a.** Accountants are guided by three basic concepts, the fundamental accounting equation, double-entry book-keeping, and the matching principle.
    b. Accountants are guided by three basic concepts: the fundamental accounting equation; double-entry book-keeping; and the matching principle.
    c. Accountants are guided by three basic concepts: the fundamental accounting equation, double-entry book-keeping, and the matching principle.

2.6 Commas

Commas have many uses; the most common is to separate items in a series:

> He took the job, learned it well, worked hard, and succeeded.
> Put paper, pencils, and paper clips on the requisition list.

Company style often dictates omitting the final comma in a series. However, if you have a choice, use the final comma; it's often necessary to prevent misunderstanding.

A second place to use a comma is between independent clauses that are joined by a coordinating conjunction (*and, but, or or*) unless one or both are very short:

> She spoke to the sales staff, and he spoke to the production staff.
> I was advised to proceed and I did.

A third use for the comma is to separate a dependent clause at the beginning of a sentence from an independent clause:

> Because of our lead in the market, we may be able to risk introducing a new product.

However, a dependent clause at the end of a sentence is separated from the independent clause by a comma only when the dependent clause is unnecessary to the main meaning of the sentence:

> We may be able to introduce a new product, although it may involve some risk.

A fourth use for the comma is after an introductory phrase or word:

> Starting with this amount of capital, we can survive in the red for one year.

> Through more careful planning, we may be able to serve more people.
> Yes, you may proceed as originally planned.

However, with short introductory prepositional phrases and some one-syllable words (such as *hence* and *thus*), the comma is often omitted:

> Before January 1 we must complete the inventory.
> Thus we may not need to hire anyone.
> In short the move to Tulsa was a good idea.

Fifth, commas are used to surround nonrestrictive phrases or words (expressions that can be removed from the sentence without changing the meaning):

> The new owners, the Kowacks, are pleased with their purchase.

Sixth, commas are used between adjectives modifying the same noun (coordinate adjectives):

> She left Monday for a long, difficult recruiting trip.

To test the appropriateness of such a comma, try reversing the order of the adjectives: *a difficult, long recruiting trip*. If the order cannot be reversed, leave out the comma (*a good old friend* isn't the same as *an old good friend*). A comma is also not used when one of the adjectives is part of the noun. Compare these two phrases:

> a distinguished, well-known figure
> a distinguished public figure

The adjective-noun combination of *public* and *figure* has been used together so often that it has come to be considered a single thing: *public figure*. So no comma is required.

Seventh, commas are used both before and after the year in sentences that include month, day, and year:

> It will be sent by December 15, 2007, from our Cincinnati plant.

Some companies write dates in another form: 15 December 2007. No commas should be used in that case. Nor is a comma needed when only the month and year are present (December 2007).

Eighth, commas are used to set off a variety of parenthetical words and phrases within sentences, including state names, dates, abbreviations, transitional expressions, and contrasted elements:

> They were, in fact, prepared to submit a bid.
> Our best programmer is Ken, who joined the company just a month ago.
> Habermacher, Inc., went public in 1999.
> Our goal was increased profits, not increased market share.
> Service, then, is our main concern.
> The factory was completed in Chattanooga, Tennessee, just three weeks ago.
> Joanne Dubiik, M.D., has applied for a loan from First Savings.

I started work here on March 1, 2001, and soon received my first promotion.

Ninth, a comma is used to separate a quotation from the rest of the sentence:

> Your warranty reads, "These conditions remain in effect for one year from date of purchase."

However, the comma is left out when the quotation as a whole is built into the structure of the sentence:

> He hurried off with an angry "Look where you're going."

Finally, a comma should be used whenever it's needed to avoid confusion or an unintended meaning. Compare the following:

> Ever since they have planned new ventures more carefully.
> Ever since, they have planned new ventures more carefully.

2.7 Dashes

Use a dash to surround a comment that is a sudden turn in thought:

> Membership in the IBSA—it's expensive but worth it—may be obtained by applying to our New York office.

A dash can also be used to emphasize a parenthetical word or phrase:

> Third-quarter profits—in excess of $2 million—are up sharply.

Finally, use dashes to set off a phrase that contains commas:

> All our offices—Milwaukee, New Orleans, and Phoenix—have sent representatives.

Don't confuse a dash with a hyphen. A dash separates and emphasizes words, phrases, and clauses more strongly than a comma or parentheses can; a hyphen ties two words so tightly that they almost become one word.

On computer, use the em dash symbol. When typing a dash in e-mail or on a typewriter, type two hyphens with no space before, between, or after.

2.8 Hyphens

Hyphens are mainly used in three ways. The first is to separate the parts of compound words beginning with such prefixes as *self-, ex-, quasi-,* and *all-:*

self-assured	quasi-official
ex-wife	all-important

However, omit hyphens from and close up those words that have prefixes such as *pro, anti, non, re, pre, un, inter,* and *extra:*

prolabor	nonunion
antifascist	interdepartmental

Exceptions occur when (1) the prefix occurs before a proper noun, or (2) the vowel at the end of the prefix is the same as the first letter of the root word:

pro-Republican	anti-American
anti-inflammatory	extra-atmospheric

When in doubt, consult your dictionary.

Hyphens are also used in some compound adjectives, which are adjectives made up of two or more words. Specifically, you should use hyphens in compound adjectives that come before the noun:

> an interest-bearing account   well-informed executives

However, you need not hyphenate when the adjective follows a linking verb:

> This account is interest bearing.
> Their executives are well informed.

You can shorten sentences that list similar hyphenated words by dropping the common part from all but the last word:

> Check the costs of first-, second-, and third-class postage.

Finally, hyphens may be used to divide words at the end of a typed line. Such hyphenation is best avoided, but when you have to divide words at the end of a line, do so correctly (see Section 3.5). A dictionary will show how words are divided into syllables.

2.9 Apostrophes

Use an apostrophe in the possessive form of a noun (but not in a pronoun):

> On *his* desk was a reply to Bette *Ainsley's* application for the *manager's* position.

Apostrophes are also used in place of the missing letter(s) of a contraction:

Whole Words	Contraction
we will	we'll
do not	don't
they are	they're

2.10 Quotation Marks

Use quotation marks to surround words that are repeated exactly as they were said or written:

> The collection letter ended by saying, "This is your third and final notice."

Remember: (1) When the quoted material is a complete sentence, the first word is capitalized. (2) The final comma or period goes inside the closing quotation marks.

Quotation marks are also used to set off the title of a newspaper story, magazine article, or book chapter:

> You should read "Legal Aspects of the Collection Letter" in *Today's Credit*.

The book title is shown here in italics. When typewritten, the title is underlined. The same treatment is proper for newspaper and magazine titles. (Appendix B explains documentation style in more detail.)

Quotation marks may also be used to indicate special treatment for words or phrases, such as terms that you're using in an unusual or ironic way:

> Our management "team" spends more time squabbling than working to solve company problems.

When you are defining a word, put the definition in quotation marks:

> The abbreviation *etc.* means "and so forth."

When using quotation marks, take care to insert the closing marks as well as the opening ones.

Although periods and commas go inside any quotation marks, colons and semicolons go outside them. A question mark goes inside the quotation marks only if the quotation is a question:

> All that day we wondered, "Is he with us?"

If the quotation is not a question but the entire sentence is, the question mark goes outside:

> What did she mean by "You will hear from me"?

2.11 Parentheses

Use parentheses to surround comments that are entirely incidental:

> Our figures do not match yours, although (if my calculations are correct) they are closer than we thought.

Parentheses are also used in legal documents to surround figures in arabic numerals that follow the same amount in words:

> Remittance will be One Thousand Two Hundred Dollars ($1,200).

Be careful to put punctuation (period, comma, and so on) outside the parentheses unless it is part of the statement in parentheses.

2.12 Ellipses

Use ellipsis points, or dots, to indicate that material has been left out of a direct quotation. Use them only in direct quotations and only at the point where material was left out. In the following example, the first sentence is quoted in the second:

> The Dow Jones Industrial Average fell 276.39 points, or 2.6%, during the week to 10292.31.

> According to *The Wall Street Journal*, "The Dow Jones Industrial Average . . . fell 276.39" during the week.

The number of dots in ellipses is not optional; always use three. Occasionally, the points of ellipsis come at the end of a sentence, where they seem to grow a fourth dot. Don't be fooled: One of the dots is a period.

Practice Session: Punctuation 2

Circle the letter of the preferred choice in each group of sentences.

1. **a.** Capital One uses data mining to predict what customers might buy, and how the company can sell those products to them.
    b. Capital One uses data mining to predict what customers might buy and how the company can sell those products to them.

2. **a.** During the three-year lawsuit, pressure built to settle out of court.
    b. During the three-year lawsuit pressure built to settle out of court.

3. **a.** The music store, which had been in the Harper family for three generations, was finally sold to a conglomerate.
    b. The music store which had been in the Harper family for three generations was finally sold to a conglomerate.

4. **a.** After the fire, Hanson resolved to build a bigger better bottling plant.
    b. After the fire, Hanson resolved to build a bigger, better bottling plant.

5. **a.** Wild Oats, a chain of natural food grocery stores, uses kiosks to deliver nutrition information to customers.
    b. Wild Oats; a chain of natural food grocery stores; uses kiosks to deliver nutrition information to customers.

6. **a.** Management consultant Peter Drucker said "The aim of marketing is to know the customer so well that the product or service sells itself.
    b. Management consultant Peter Drucker said, "The aim of marketing is to know the customer so well that the product or service sells itself."

7. **a.** Companies use a wide variety of techniques-contests, displays, and giveaways, to name a few-to sell you things.
    b. Companies use a wide variety of techniques—contests, displays, and giveaways, to name a few—to sell you things.
    c. Companies use a wide variety of techniques—contests, displays, and giveaways to name a few—to sell you things.

8. **a.** Self-insurance plans are not subject to state regulation or premium taxes.
    b. Self insurance plans are not subject to state regulation or premium taxes.
    c. Selfinsurance plans are not subject to state regulation or premium taxes.

9. **a.** Because ours is a non-profit corporation, we don't pay federal taxes.
   b. Because ours is a nonprofit corporation, we don't pay federal taxes.

10. **a.** The decision-making process depends on a buyer's culture, social class, and self-image.
    b. The decision-making process depends on a buyer's culture, social class, and self image.
    c. The decision making process depends on a buyer's culture, social class, and self-image.

11. **a.** Situation factors also play a role in consumer decision-making.
    b. Situation factors also play a role in consumer decision making.

12. **a.** Joel told me, "I can't stop humming this song in my head, "There's a Moon Out Tonight."
    b. Joel told me, "I can't stop humming this song in my head, 'There's a Moon Out Tonight'."
    c. Joel told me, "I can't stop humming this song in my head, 'There's a Moon Out Tonight.'"

13. **a.** An insider at Arthur Andersen said that "the fall of the accounting giant stemmed from a series of poor management decisions made over decades."
    b. An insider at Arthur Andersen said that, "The fall of the accounting giant stemmed from a series of poor management decisions made over decades."

14. **a.** Have you read Jason Zein's article "Measuring the Internet?"
    b. Have you read Jason Zein's article "Measuring the Internet"?

15. **a.** According to Jamba Juice founder Kirk Peron, "jamba" is a West African word meaning *to celebrate.*
    b. According to Jamba Juice founder Kirk Peron, *jamba* is a West African word meaning "to celebrate."
    c. According to Jamba Juice founder Kirk Peron, "jamba" is a West African word meaning to celebrate.

3.0 Mechanics

The most obvious and least tolerable mistakes that a business writer makes are probably those related to grammar and punctuation. However, a number of small details, known as writing mechanics, demonstrate the writer's polish and reflect on the company's professionalism.

3.1 Capitals

Capitals are used at the beginning of certain word groups:

- **Complete sentence:** *Before* hanging up, he said, "*We'll* meet here on Wednesday at noon."
- **Formal statement following a colon:** She has a favorite motto: Where there's a will, there's a way. (Otherwise, the first word after a colon should not be capitalized—see Section 2.5.)
- **Phrase used as sentence:** Absolutely not!
- **Quoted sentence embedded in another sentence:** Scot said, "Nobody was here during lunch hour except me."
- **List of items set off from text:** Three preliminary steps are involved:
  Design review
  Budgeting
  Scheduling

Capitalize proper adjectives and proper nouns (the names of particular persons, places, and things):

Darrell Greene lived in a Victorian mansion.

We sent Ms. Larson an application form, informing her that not all applicants are interviewed.

Let's consider opening a branch in the West, perhaps at the west end of Tucson, Arizona.

As office buildings go, the Kinney Building is a pleasant setting for TDG Office Equipment.

Ms. Larson's name is capitalized because she is a particular applicant, whereas the general term *applicant* is left uncapitalized. Likewise, *West* is capitalized when it refers to a particular place but not when it means a direction. In the same way, *office* and *building* are not capitalized when they are general terms (common nouns), but they are capitalized when they are part of the title of a particular office or building (proper nouns).

Titles within families, governments, or companies may also be capitalized:

I turned down Uncle David when he offered me a job, since I wouldn't be comfortable working for one of my relatives.

We've never had a president quite like President Sweeney.

People's titles are capitalized when they are used in addressing a person, especially in a formal context. They are not usually capitalized, however, when they are used merely to identify the person:

Address the letter to Chairperson Anna Palmer.

I wish to thank Chairperson Anna Palmer for her assistance.

Please deliver these documents to board chairperson Anna Palmer.

Anna Palmer, chairperson of the board, took the podium.

Also capitalize titles if they are used by themselves in addressing a person:

Thank you, Doctor, for your donation.

Always capitalize the first word of the salutation and complimentary close of a letter:

Dear Mr. Andrews: *Yours* very truly,

The names of organizations are capitalized, of course; so are the official names of their departments and divisions. However, do not use capitals when referring in general terms to a department or division, especially one in another organization:

> Route this memo to Personnel.
>
> Larry Tien was transferred to the Microchip Division.
>
> Will you be enrolled in the Psychology Department?
>
> Someone from the engineering department at EnerTech stopped by the booth.
>
> Our production department has reorganized for efficiency.
>
> Send a copy to their school of business administration.

Capitalization is unnecessary when using a word like *company, corporation,* or *university* alone:

> The corporation plans to issue 50,000 shares of common stock.

Likewise, the names of specific products are capitalized, although the names of general product types are not:

> Apple computer   Tide laundry detergent

One problem that often arises in writing about places is the treatment of two or more proper nouns of the same type. When the common word comes before the specific names, it is capitalized; when it comes after the specific names, it is not:

> Lakes Ontario and Huron
>
> Allegheny and Monongahela rivers

The names of languages, races, and ethnic groups are capitalized: *Japanese, Caucasian, Hispanic.* But racial terms that denote only skin color are not capitalized: *black, white.*

When referring to the titles of books, articles, magazines, newspapers, reports, movies, and so on, you should capitalize the first and last words and all nouns, pronouns, adjectives, verbs, adverbs, and prepositions and conjunctions with five letters or more. Except for the first and last words, do not capitalize articles:

> *Economics During the Great War*
>
> "An Investigation into the Market for Long-Distance Services"
>
> "What Successes Are Made Of"

When *the* is part of the official name of a newspaper or magazine, it should be treated this way too: *The Wall Street Journal.*

References to specific pages, paragraphs, lines, and the like are not capitalized: *page 73, line 3.* However, in most other numbered or lettered references, the identifying term is capitalized: *Chapter 4, Serial No. 382-2203, Item B-11.*

Finally, the names of academic degrees are capitalized when they follow a person's name but are not capitalized when used in a general sense:

> I received a bachelor of science degree.
>
> Thomas Whitelaw, Doctor of Philosophy, will attend.

Similarly, general courses of study are not capitalized, but the names of specific classes are:

> She studied accounting as an undergraduate.
>
> She is enrolled in Accounting 201.

3.2 Underscores and Italics

Usually a line typed underneath a word or phrase either provides emphasis or indicates the title of a book, magazine, or newspaper. If possible, use italics instead of an underscore. Italics (or underlining) should also be used for defining terms and for discussing words as words:

> In this report *net sales* refers to after-tax sales dollars.
>
> The word *building* is a common noun and should not be capitalized.

3.3 Abbreviations

Abbreviations are used heavily in tables, charts, lists, and forms. They're used sparingly in prose paragraphs, however. Here are some abbreviations often used in business writing:

Abbreviation	Full Term
b/l	bill of lading
ca.	circa (about)
dol., dols.	dollar, dollars
etc.	et cetera (and so on)
FDIC	Federal Deposit Insurance Corporation
Inc.	Incorporated
L.f.	Ledger folio
Ltd.	Limited
mgr.	manager
NSF or N/S	not sufficient funds
P&L or P/L	profit and loss
reg.	regular
whsle.	wholesale

One way to handle an abbreviation that you want to use throughout a document is to spell it out the first time you use it, follow it with the abbreviation in parentheses, and then use the abbreviation in the remainder of the document.

Because *etc.* contains a word meaning "and," never write *and etc.* In fact, try to limit your use of such abbreviations to tables and parenthetical material.

3.4 Numbers

Numbers may be correctly handled many ways in business writing, so follow company style. In the absence of a set style, however, generally spell out all numbers from one to nine and use arabic numerals for the rest.

There are some exceptions to this general rule. For example, never begin a sentence with a numeral:

> *Twenty* of us produced *641* units per week in the first *12* weeks of the year.

Use numerals for the numbers one through ten if they're in the same list as larger numbers:

> Our weekly quota rose from *9* to *15* to *27*.

Use numerals for percentages, time of day (except with *o'clock*), dates, and (in general) dollar amounts.

> Our division is responsible for *7* percent of total sales.
>
> The meeting is scheduled for *8:30* A.M. on August *2*.
>
> Add *$3* for postage and handling.

Use a comma in numbers expressing thousands (*1,257*), unless your company specifies another style. When dealing with numbers in the millions and billions, combine words and figures: *7.3 million, 2 billion*.

When writing dollar amounts, use a decimal point only if cents are included. In lists of two or more dollar amounts, use the decimal point either for all or for none:

> He sent two checks, one for *$67.92* and one for *$90.00*.

When two numbers fall next to each other in a sentence, use figures for the number that is largest, most difficult to spell, or part of a physical measurement; use words for the other:

> I have learned to manage a classroom of 30 twelve-year-olds.
>
> She's won a bonus for selling 24 thirty-volume sets.
>
> You'll need twenty 3-inch bolts.

In addresses, all street numbers except *One* are in figures. So are suite and room numbers and ZIP codes. For street names that are numbered, practice varies so widely that you should use the form specified on an organization's letterhead or in a reliable directory. All of the following examples are correct:

One Fifth Avenue	297 Ninth Street
1839 44th Street	11026 West 78 Place

Telephone numbers are always expressed in figures. Parentheses may separate the area code from the rest of the number, but a slash or a dash may be used instead, especially if the entire phone number is enclosed in parentheses:

(602) 382-8329	(602/382-8329)	602-382-8329

Percentages are always expressed in figures. The word *percent* is used in most cases, but % may be used in tables, forms, and statistical writing.

Physical measurements such as distance, weight, and volume are also often expressed in figures: *9 kilometers, 5 feet 3 inches, 7 pounds 10 ounces*.

Ages are usually expressed in words—except when a parenthetical reference to age follows someone's name:

> Mrs. Margaret Sanderson is seventy-two.
>
> Mrs. Margaret Sanderson, 72, swims daily.

Also, ages expressed in years and months are treated like physical measurements that combine two units of measure: *5 years 6 months*.

Decimal numbers are always written in figures. In most cases, add a zero to the left of the decimal point if the number is less than one and does not already start with a zero:

1.38	.07	0.2

In a series of related decimal numbers with at least one number greater than one, make sure that all numbers smaller than one have a zero to the left of the decimal point: *1.20, 0.21, 0.09*. Also, express all decimal numbers in a series to the same number of places by adding zeroes at the end:

> The responses were Yes, 37.2 percent; No, 51.0; Not Sure, 11.8.

Simple fractions are written in words, but more complicated fractions are expressed in figures or, if easier to read, in figures and words:

two-thirds	9/32	2 hundredths

A combination of whole numbers and a fraction should always be written in figures. Note that a hyphen is used to separate the fraction from the whole number when a slash is used for the fraction: *2-11/16*.

3.5 Word Division

In general, avoid dividing words at the ends of lines. When you must do so, follow these rules:

- Don't divide one-syllable words (such as *since, walked,* and *thought*); abbreviations (*mgr.*); contractions (*isn't*); or numbers expressed in numerals (*117,500*).
- Divide words between syllables, as specified in a dictionary or word-division manual.
- Make sure that at least three letters of the divided word are moved to the second line: *sin-cerely* instead of *sincere-ly*.
- Do not end a page or more than three consecutive lines with hyphens.
- Leave syllables consisting of a single vowel at the end of the first line (*impedi-ment* instead of *imped-iment*), except when the single vowel is part of a suffix such as *-able, -ible, -ical,* or *-ity* (*re-spons-ible* instead of *re-sponsi-ble*).
- Divide between double letters (*tomor-row*), except when the root word ends in double letters (*call-ing* instead of *cal-ling*).
- Wherever possible, divide hyphenated words at the hyphen only: instead of *anti-inde-pendence*, use *anti-independence*.

Practice Session: Mechanics

Circle the letter of the preferred choice in each of the following groups of sentences.

1. a. When you are in New York City for the sales meeting, be sure to visit the art deco Chrysler Building.
    b. When you are in New York city for the sales meeting, be sure to visit the Art Deco Chrysler building.
    c. When you are in New York City for the sales meeting, be sure to visit the Art Deco Chrysler Building.

2. a. We plan to expand our national operations to the west, as well as the south.
   b. We plan to expand our national operations to the West, as well as the South.
   c. We plan to expand our national operations to the west, as well as the South.

3. a. Lee Marrs, who is President of Lee Marrs Designs, has been chosen to revamp our website.
   b. Lee Marrs, who is president of Lee Marrs Designs, has been chosen to revamp our website.
   c. Lee Marrs, who is President of Lee Marrs Designs, has been chosen to revamp our Website.

4. a. There's one thing we know for sure: Having a good idea doesn't guarantee success.
   b. There's one thing we know for sure: having a good idea doesn't guarantee success.

5. a. Be sure to order manila envelopes in all sizes: 9″ × 12″, 11″, 14″, etc.
   b. Be sure to order manila envelopes in all sizes: 9″ × 12″, 11″, 14″ and etc.

6. a. The traditional trading period for U.S. stock exchanges is 9:30 A.M. to 4 o'clock P.M.
   b. The traditional trading period for U.S. stock exchanges is 9:30 A.M. to 4 P.M.
   c. The traditional trading period for U.S. stock exchanges is 9:30 A.M. to 4:00 P.M.

7. a. The number of members on the board of directors has been reduced from 13 to nine.
   b. The number of members on the board of directors has been reduced from 13 to 9.

8. a. The CDs are priced at $15, $12.95, and $11.00.
   b. The CDs are priced at $15.00, $12.95, and $11.00.
   c. The CDs are priced at $15, $12.95, and $11.

9. a. Twenty people have signed up for the spreadsheet software class, but there is room for 25.
   b. 20 people have signed up for the spreadsheet software class, but there is room for 25.

10. a. The best way to divide the word *sincerely* is "sin-cerely."
    b. The best way to divide the word *sincerely* is "sincere-ly."

4.0 Vocabulary

Using the right word in the right place is a crucial skill in business communication. However, many pitfalls await the unwary.

4.1 Frequently Confused Words

Because the following sets of words sound similar, be careful not to use one when you mean to use the other:

Word	Meaning
accede	to comply with
exceed	to go beyond
accept	to take
except	to exclude
access	admittance
excess	too much
advice	suggestion
advise	to suggest
affect	to influence
effect	the result
allot	to distribute
a lot	much or many
all ready	completely prepared
already	completed earlier
born	given birth to
borne	carried
capital	money; chief city
capitol	a government building
cite	to quote
sight	a view
site	a location
complement	complete amount; to go well with
compliment	expression of esteem; to flatter
corespondent	party in a divorce suit
correspondent	letter writer
council	a panel of people
counsel	advice; a lawyer
defer	to put off until later
differ	to be different
device	a mechanism
devise	to plan
die	to stop living; a tool
dye	to color
discreet	careful
discrete	separate
envelop	to surround
envelope	a covering for a letter
forth	forward
fourth	number four
holey	full of holes
holy	sacred
wholly	completely
human	of people
humane	kindly
incidence	frequency
incidents	events
instance	example
instants	moments

interstate	between states
intrastate	within a state
later	afterward
latter	the second of two
lead	a metal; to guide
led	guided
lean	to rest at an angle
lien	a claim
levee	embankment
levy	tax
loath	reluctant
loathe	to hate
loose	free; not tight
lose	to mislay
material	substance
materiel	equipment
miner	mineworker
minor	underage person
moral	virtuous; a lesson
morale	sense of well-being
ordinance	law
ordnance	weapons
overdo	to do in excess
overdue	past due
peace	lack of conflict
piece	a fragment
pedal	a foot lever
peddle	to sell
persecute	to torment
prosecute	to sue
personal	private
personnel	employees
precedence	priority
precedents	previous events
principal	sum of money; chief; main
principle	general rule
rap	to knock
wrap	to cover
residence	home
residents	inhabitants
right	correct
rite	ceremony
write	to form words on a surface
role	a part to play
roll	to tumble; a list
root	part of a plant
rout	to defeat
route	a traveler's way

shear	to cut
sheer	thin, steep
stationary	immovable
stationery	paper
than	as compared with
then	at that time
their	belonging to them
there	in that place
they're	they are
to	a preposition
too	excessively; also
two	the number
waive	to set aside
wave	a swell of water; a gesture
weather	atmospheric conditions
whether	if
who's	contraction of "who is" or "who has"
whose	possessive form of who

In the preceding list, only enough of each word's meaning is given to help you distinguish between the words in each group. Several meanings are left out entirely. For more complete definitions, consult a dictionary.

Practice Session: Confused Words

In the following sentences, underline the preferred choice within each set of parentheses.

1. If our bid is (*accepted, excepted*), we will begin the project in November.
2. This website offers some great (*advice, advise*) on setting up a new business.
3. How will the accounting scandal (*affect, effect*) Arthur Andersen's future?
4. Most of the costs of the project will be (*born, borne*) by the contractor.
5. In preparing the budget, we have to decide where best to invest our (*capital, capitol*).
6. Be sure to (*cite, site*) the sources for your data when you prepare your report.
7. The acquisition of LPC Group should (*compliment/ complement*) our other holdings.
8. Leo sought the (*council, counsel*) of his attorney before signing the contract.
9. I didn't have to be told to be (*discrete, discreet*) about the sexual harassment case.
10. When Jennings Hardware got behind in its debts, one of the creditors placed a (*lean, lien*) on its building.
11. Mr. Hathaway was (*loath, loathe*) to fire Elizabeth, but he had no choice.
12. To comply with local zoning (*ordinances, ordnances*), we had to replace our sign.
13. As a teenager, Gary Sassaman used to (*pedal, peddle*) newspapers in downtown Pittsburgh.
14. Business owners along El Cajon Boulevard have vowed to (*persecute, prosecute*) anyone caught painting graffiti on their buildings.

15. We don't know of any (*precedence, precedents*) for the exponential growth of sales for this kind of product.
16. The (*principle, principal*) reason for closing down operations was obsolete production equipment that was too expensive to replace.
17. It's hard to say what (*role, roll*) the downturn in the economy played in the failure of Seven Hills Distribution.
18. Sunbeam employees were shocked by new CEO Al Dunlap's (*shear, sheer*) ruthlessness in axing jobs and slashing costs.
19. Now that our area code has changed, we will need to order new (*stationary, stationery*).
20. The Rodriguez brothers couldn't decide (*weather, whether*) to form a partnership or establish a corporation.

4.2 Frequently Misused Words

The following words tend to be misused for reasons other than their sound. Reference books (including the *Random House College Dictionary*, revised edition; Follett's *Modern American Usage*; and Fowler's *Modern English Usage*) can help you with similar questions of usage.

a lot: When the writer means "many," *a lot* is always two separate words, never one.

correspond with: Use this phrase when you are talking about exchanging letters. Use *correspond to* when you mean "similar to." Use either *correspond with* or *correspond to* when you mean "relate to."

disinterested: This word means "fair, unbiased, having no favorites, impartial." If you mean "bored" or "not interested," use *uninterested*.

etc.: This abbreviated form of the Latin phrase *et cetera* means "and so on" or "and so forth." The current tendency among business writers is to use English rather than Latin.

imply/infer: Both refer to hints. Their great difference lies in who is acting. The writer implies; the reader infers, sees between the lines.

lay: This word is a transitive verb. Never use it for the intransitive *lie*. (See Section 1.3.3.)

less: Use *less* for uncountable quantities (such as amounts of water, air, sugar, and oil). Use *fewer* for countable quantities (such as numbers of jars, saws, words, pages, and humans). The same distinction applies to *much* and *little* (uncountable) versus *many* and *few* (countable).

like: Use *like* only when the word that follows is just a noun or a pronoun. Use *as* or *as if* when a phrase or clause follows:

> She looks like him.
>
> She did just as he had expected.
>
> It seems as if she had plenty of time.

many/much: See *less*.

regardless: The *less* ending is the negative part. No word needs two negative parts, so don't add *ir* (a negative prefix) to the beginning. There is no such word as *irregardless*.

to me/personally: Use these phrases only when personal reactions, apart from company policy, are being stated (not often the case in business writing).

try: Always follow with *to*, never *and*.

verbal: People in the business community who are careful with language frown on those who use *verbal* to mean "spoken" or "oral." Many others do say "verbal agreement." Strictly speaking, *verbal* means "of words" and therefore includes both spoken and written words. Follow company usage in this matter.

Practice Session: Misused Words

In the following sentences, underline the preferred choice within each set of parentheses.

1. My boss told me that I still have (*a lot, alot*) to learn.
2. The U.S. Congress corresponds (*to, with*) the British Parliament.
3. I tried to convince my co-workers to sign up for the stress-reduction program, but they all seemed (*uninterested, disinterested*).
4. When you say that the books have some discrepancies, are you (*inferring, implying*) that our accountant is embezzling from us?
5. From the auditor's silent stare, Margaret (*implied, inferred*) that the man was not amused by her jokes.
6. The report came out to (*less, fewer*) pages than we had originally anticipated.
7. Mr. Martens was treating Heather (*like, as if*) she had done something wrong.
8. You have to finish the job, (*irregardless, regardless*) of your loathing for it.
9. When talking to customers on the phone, try (*and, to*) be as pleasant as possible.
10. When making (*an oral, a verbal*) presentation, it's a good idea to make eye contact with your audience.

4.3 Frequently Misspelled Words

All of us, even the world's best spellers, sometimes have to check a dictionary for the spelling of some words. People who have never memorized the spelling of commonly used words must look up so many that they grow exasperated and give up on spelling words correctly.

Don't expect perfection, and don't surrender. If you can memorize the spelling of just the words listed here, you'll need the dictionary far less often, and you'll write with more confidence.

absence	comparative	fluctuation	necessary	rhythmical
absorption	competitor	forty	negligence	ridiculous
accessible	concede		negotiable	
accommodate	congratulations	gesture	newsstand	salable
accumulate	connoisseur	grievous	noticeable	secretary
achieve	consensus			seize
advantageous	convenient	haphazard	occurrence	separate
affiliated	convertible	harassment	omission	sincerely
aggressive	corroborate	holiday		succeed
alignment	criticism		parallel	suddenness
aluminum		illegible	pastime	superintendent
ambience	definitely	immigrant	peaceable	supersede
analyze	description	incidentally	permanent	surprise
apparent	desirable	indelible	perseverance	
appropriate	dilemma	independent	persistent	tangible
argument	disappear	indispensable	personnel	tariff
asphalt	disappoint	insistent	persuade	technique
assistant	disbursement	intermediary	possesses	tenant
asterisk	discrepancy	irresistible	precede	truly
auditor	dissatisfied		predictable	
	dissipate	jewelry	preferred	unanimous
bankruptcy		judgment	privilege	until
believable	eligible	judicial	procedure	
brilliant	embarrassing		proceed	vacillate
bulletin	endorsement	labeling	pronunciation	vacuum
	exaggerate	legitimate	psychology	vicious
calendar	exceed	leisure	pursue	
campaign	exhaust	license		
category	existence	litigation	questionnaire	
ceiling	extraordinary			
changeable		maintenance	receive	
clientele	fallacy	mathematics	recommend	
collateral	familiar	mediocre	repetition	
committee	flexible	minimum	rescind	

Practice Session: Misspelled Words

In the following sentences, underline the preferred choice within each set of parentheses.

1. We try to (*accomodate, accommodate*) any reasonable request from our customers.
2. You will need to (*analyse, analyze*) the sales data to determine which products to phase out.
3. Because the weather in Chicago is so (*changable, changeable*), the conference reception has a backup indoor venue.
4. The board reached a (*concensus, consensus*) on the new CEO.
5. It will be (*embarassing, embarrassing*) for the company if this information leaks out.
6. The auditors discovered the (*existance, existence*) of hidden accounts in foreign banks.
7. Every company should have a written sexual (*harassment, harrassment*) policy.
8. In today's book business, (*independant, independent*) publishers are having a tough time finding distribution.

9. Use your best (*judgment, judgement*) when choosing the paper for our new stationery.
10. The cost of a business (*licence, license, liscence*) varies from city to city.
11. With all the turmoil (*occuring, occurring*) in the stock market, we've decided to shift our investments toward real estate.
12. The marketing survey found that consumers (*prefered, preferred*) brand-name dog food over generic brands.
13. Because her cost-cutting measures saved the company millions of dollars, Carolyn Kelly (*received, recieved*) a raise and a promotion.
14. Please send (*separate, seperate*) invoices for the two projects.
15. My supervisor didn't need to be so (*vicious, viscious*) in his critique of my performance.

4.4 Transitional Words and Phrases

The following sentences don't communicate as well as they might because they lack a transitional word or phrase:

Production delays are inevitable. Our current lag time in filling orders is one month.

A semicolon between the two sentences would signal a close relationship between their meanings, but it wouldn't even hint at what that relationship is. Here are the sentences again, now linked by means of a semicolon, with a space for a transitional word or phrase:

> Production delays are inevitable; _____, our current lag time in filling orders is one month.

Now read the sentence with *nevertheless* in the blank space. Now try *therefore, incidentally, in fact*, and *at any rate* in the blank. Each substitution changes the meaning of the sentence.

Here are some transitional words (called conjunctive adverbs) that will help you write more clearly:

accordingly	furthermore	moreover
anyway	however	otherwise
besides	incidentally	still
consequently	likewise	therefore
finally	meanwhile	

The following transitional phrases are used in the same way:

as a result	in other words
at any rate	in the second place
for example	on the other hand
in fact	to the contrary

When one of these words or phrases joins two independent clauses, it should be preceded by a semicolon and followed by a comma, as shown here:

> The consultant recommended a complete reorganization; moreover, she suggested that we drop several products.

Practice Session Answers

Answers for Nouns: 1. City   2. Building / building   3. hotels   4. *t*'s / *i*'s   5. 1990s   6. shelves   7. specialties   8. cases   9. company's   10. editor-in-chief's   11. businesses'   12. passengers'   13. day's   14. Dallas's   15. Jones's

Answers for Pronouns: 1. me   2. she   3. him   4. We   5. me   6. its   7. his or her   8. Who   9. whom   10. Whom   11. her   12. him or her   13. her   14. its   15. Who   16. your   17. its   18. I   19. their   20. its

Answers for Verbs: 1. comes, want   2. knew   3. begun   4. lie   5. laid   6. sits   7. set   8. raise   9. was   10. is   11. is   12. are   13. is   14. is   15. represents   16. is   17. are   18. is   19. send   20. were

Answers for Adjectives and Adverbs: 1. least   2. better   3. worse   4. more competent   5. unique   6. well-written   7. well written   8. beautifully written   9. credit card   10. well   11. well   12. really   13. slowly   14. could hardly   15. more heavily

Answers for Prepositions, Conjunctions, and Articles: 1. a   2. b   3. a   4. b   5. b   6. a   7. b   8. a   9. b   10. a   11. b   12. b   13. a   14. a   15. a

Answers for Sentences: 1. a   2. b   3. b   4. c   5. c   6. b   7. c   8. c   9. a   10. c

Answers for Punctuation 1: 1. b   2. a   3. b   4. b   5. a   6. b   7. a   8. b   9. b   10. c

Answers for Punctuation 2: 1. b   2. a   3. a   4. b   5. a   6. b   7. b   8. a   9. b   10. a   11. b   12. c   13. a   14. b   15. b

Answers for Mechanics: 1. c   2. b   3. b   4. a   5. a   6. c   7. b   8. b   9. a   10. a

Answers for Confused Words: 1. accepted   2. advice   3. affect   4. borne   5. capital   6. cite   7. complement   8. counsel   9. discreet   10. lien   11. loath   12. ordinances   13. peddle   14. prosecute   15. precedents   16. principal   17. role   18. sheer   19. stationery   20. whether

Answers for Misused Words: 1. a lot   2. to   3. uninterested   4. implying   5. inferred   6. fewer   7. as if   8. regardless   9. to   10. an oral

Answers for Misspelled Words: 1. accommodate   2. analyze   3. changeable   4. consensus   5. embarrassing   6. existence   7. harassment   8. independent   9. judgment   10. license   11. occurring   12. preferred   13. received   14. separate   15. vicious

Answer Key

Answer Key to the Level 1 Self-Assessment Exercises

Chapter 1: Self-Assessment—Nouns

1. Give the balance sheet to Melissa. (1.1.1)
2. We'd like to order 50 more satchels for Craigmont Stores, and three each for the other stores on our list. (1.1.1)
3. Tarnower Corporation donates a portion of its profits to charity every year. (1.1.1)
4. Which aluminum bolts are packaged? (1.1.1)
5. Please send the Joneses a dozen of the following: stopwatches, canteens, headbands, and wristbands. (1.1.1)
6. The technician has already repaired the machine for the client. (1.1.2)
7. An attorney will talk to the group about incorporation. (1.1.2)
8. After her vacation, the buyer prepared a third-quarter budget. (1.1.2)
9. The new flat monitors are serving our department very well. (1.1.2)
10. Accuracy overrides speed in importance. (1.1.2)
11. copies _____ Make sure that all copys include the new addresses. (1.1.2)
12. employees' _____ Ask Jennings to collect all employee's donations for the Red Cross drive. (1.1.4)
13. sons-in-law / businesses Charlie now has two son-in-laws to help him with his two online business's. (1.1.3, 1.1.4)
14. parentheses Avoid using too many parenthesises when writing your reports. (1.1.3)
15. Ness's / week's Follow President Nesses rules about what constitutes a weeks work. (1.1.4)

Chapter 2: Self-Assessment—Pronouns

1. whom _____ To which retailer will you send your merchandise? (1.2)
2. them _____ Have you given John and Nancy a list of parts? (1.2)
3. it/them _____ The main office sent the invoice to Mr. and Mrs. Litvak on December 5. (1.2)
4. its _____ The company settled the company's accounts before the end of the year (1.2)
5. whose _____ Which person's umbrella is this? (1.2)
6. The sales staff is preparing guidelines for __its__ (their, its) clients. (1.2.5)

7. Few of the sales representatives turn in __their__ (their, its) reports on time. (1.2.5)
8. The board of directors has chosen __its__ (their, its) officers. (1.2.5)
9. Gomez and Archer have told __their__ (his, their) clients about the new program. (1.2.1)
10. Each manager plans to expand __his or her__ (his, their, his or her) sphere of control next year. (1.2.3)
11. Has everyone supplied __his or her__ (his, their, his or her) Social Security number? (1.2.3)
12. After giving every employee __a__ (his, their, a) raise, George told __them__ (them, they, all) about the increased work load. (1.2.3, 1.2.4)
13. Bob and Tim have opposite ideas about how to achieve company goals. __Who__ (Who, Whom) do you think will win the debate? (1.2.4)
14. City Securities has just announced __whom__ (who, whom) it will hire as CEO. (1.2.4)
15. Either of the new products would readily find __its__ (their, its) niche in the marketplace. (1.2.5)

Chapter 3: Self-Assessment—Verbs

1. have become (1.3.1)
2. knew (1.3.1)
3. has moved (1.3.1)
4. will do (1.3.1)
5. will have taken (1.3.1)
6. Leslie Cartwright will write the report. (1.3.5)
7. No one ever recorded the transaction. (1.3.5)
8. Has the claims department notified you of your rights? (1.3.5)
9. We depend on their services for our operation. (1.3.5)
10. The customer returned the damaged equipment before we even located a repair facility. (1.3.5)
11. Everyone upstairs (receive/receives) mail before we do. (1.3.4)
12. Neither the main office nor the branches (is/are) blameless. (1.3.4)
13. C&B Sales (is/are) listed in the directory. (1.3.4)
14. When measuring shelves, 7 inches (is/are) significant. (1.3.4)
15. About 90 percent of the employees (plan/plans) to come to the company picnic. (1.3.4)

Chapter 4: Self-Assessment—Adjectives

1. greater (1.4.1)
2. most perfect (1.4.1)
3. most interesting (1.4.1)
4. better (1.4.1)
5. hardest (1.4.1)
6. A highly placed source revealed Dotson's last-ditch efforts to cover up the mistake. (1.4.2)
7. Please send an extra-large dust cover for my photocopier. (1.4.2)
8. A top-secret document was taken from the president's office last night. (1.4.2)
9. A 30-year-old person should know better. (1.4.2)
10. If I write a large-scale report, I want to know that it will be read by upper-level management. (1.4.2)
11. The two companies are engaged in an all-out, no-holds-barred struggle for dominance. (1.4)
12. A tiny metal shaving is responsible for the problem. (1.4)
13. She came to the office with a bruised, swollen knee. (1.4)
14. A chipped, cracked sheet of glass is useless to us. (1.4)
15. You'll receive our usual cheerful, prompt service. (1.4)

Chapter 5: Self-Assessment—Adverbs

1. good (1.5)
2. surely (1.5)
3. sick (1.5)
4. well (1.5)
5. good (1.5)
6. faster (1.5.2)
7. most recently (1.5.2)
8. more happily (1.5.2)
9. better (1.5.2)
10. most logically (1.5.2)
11. He doesn't seem to have any. *OR* He seems to have none. (1.5.1)
12. That machine is scarcely ever used. *OR* That machine is never used. (1.5.1)
13. They can't get any replacement parts until Thursday. *OR* They can get no replacement parts until Thursday. (1.5.1)
14. It wasn't any different from the first event we promoted. *OR* It was no different from . . . (1.5.1)
15. We've looked for it, and it doesn't seem to be anywhere. *OR* it seems to be nowhere (1.5.1)

Chapter 6: Self-Assessment—Prepositions and Conjunctions

1. Where was your argument leading ~~to~~? (1.6.1)
2. I wish he would get off ~~of~~ the phone. (1.6.1)
3. This is a project ~~into which~~ you can sink your teeth into. (1.6.1)
4. U.S. Mercantile must become aware of and sensitive to its customers' concerns. (1.6.1)
5. We are responsible for aircraft safety in the air, in the hangars, and on the runways. (1.6.1)
6. to (1.6.1)
7. among (1.6.1)
8. for (1.6.1)
9. to (1.6.1)
10. from (1.6.1)
11. She is active ~~in~~ not only in a civic group but also in an athletic organization. *OR* She is active in not only a civic group but ~~in~~ also an athletic organization. (1.6.2)
12. That is either a mistake or ~~was~~ an intentional omission. (1.6.2)
13. The question is whether to set up a booth at the convention or ~~be~~ to host a hospitality suite. (1.6.2)
14. We are doing better ~~in~~ both in overall sales and in profits. *OR* in both overall sales and ~~in~~ profits. (1.6.2)
15. She had neither the preferred educational background, nor ~~did she have~~ the suitable experience. (1.6.2)

Chapter 7: Self-Assessment—Periods, Question Marks, and Exclamation Points

1. Dr. Eleanor H. Hutton has requested information on TaskMasters, Inc. (2.1)
2. That qualifies us as a rapidly growing new company, don't you think? (2.2)
3. Our president, Daniel Gruber, is a CPA. On your behalf, I asked him why he started the company. (2.1)
4. In the past three years, we have experienced phenomenal growth of 800 percent. *OR* ! (2.1, 2.3)
5. Contact me at 1358 N. Parsons Avenue, Tulsa, OK 74204. (2.1)
6. Jack asked, "Why does he want to know? Maybe he plans to become a competitor." *OR* ! (2.1, 2.2, 2.3)
7. The debt load fluctuates with the movement of the U.S. prime rate. (2.1)
8. I can't believe we could have missed such a promising opportunity! (2.3)
9. Is consumer loyalty extinct? Yes and no. (2.2, 2.1)
10. Johnson and Kane, Inc., has gone out of business. What a surprise. *OR* ! (2.1, 2.3)
11. Will you please send us a check today so that we can settle your account. (2.1)
12. Mr. James R. Capp will be our new CEO, beginning January 20, 2008. (2.1)
13. The rag doll originally sold for $1,098, but we have lowered the price to a mere $599. (2.1)
14. Will you be able to make the presentation at the conference, or should we find someone else? (2.2)
15. So I ask you, "When will we admit defeat?" Never! (2.2, 2.3)

Chapter 8: Self-Assessment—Semicolons and Colons

1. This letter looks good; that one doesn't. (2.4)
2. I want to make one thing perfectly clear: neither of you will be promoted if sales figures don't improve. (2.5)
3. The Zurich airport has been snowed in; therefore, I won't be able to meet with you before January 4. (2.4)
4. His motivation was obvious: to get Meg fired. (2.5)
5. Only two firms have responded to our survey: J. J. Perkins and Tucker & Tucker. (2.5)
6. Send a copy to Mary Kent, Marketing Director; Robert Bache, Comptroller; and Dennis Mann, Sales Director. (2.4)
7. Please be sure to interview these employees next week: Henry Gold, Doris Hatch, and George Iosupovich. (2.5)

8. We have observed your hard work; because of it, we are promoting you to manager of your department. (2.4)
9. You shipped three items on June 7; however, we received only one of them. (2.4)
10. The convention kit includes the following response cards: giveaways, brochures, and a display rack. (2.5)
11. The workers wanted an immediate wage increase; they had not had a raise in nearly two years. (2.4)
12. This, then, is our goal for 2007: to increase sales 35 percent. (2.5)
13. His writing skills are excellent; however, he still needs to polish his management style. (2.4)
14. We would like to address three issues: efficiency, profitability, and market penetration. (2.5)
15. Remember this rule: When in doubt, leave it out. (2.5)

Chapter 9: Self-Assessment—Commas

1. Please send us four cases of filters, two cases of wing nuts, and a bale of rags. (2.6)
2. Your analysis, however, does not account for returns. (2.6)
3. As a matter of fact, she has seen the figures. (2.6)
4. Before May 7, 1999, they wouldn't have minded either. (2.6)
5. After Martha has gone, talk to me about promoting her. (2.6)
6. Stoneridge, Inc., went public on September 9, 2003. (2.6)
7. We want the new copier, not the old model. (2.6)
8. "Talk to me," Sandra said, "before you change a thing." (2.6)
9. Because of a previous engagement, Dr. Stoeve will not be able to attend. (2.6)
10. The company started attracting attention during the long, hard recession of the mid-1970s. (2.6)
11. You can reach me at this address: 717 Darby Place, Scottsdale, Arizona 85251. (2.6)
12. Transfer the documents from Fargo, North Dakota, to Boise, Idaho. (2.6)
13. Sam O'Neill, the designated representative, is gone today. (2.6)
14. With your help, we will soon begin. (2.6)
15. She may hire two new representatives, or she may postpone filling those territories until spring. (2.6)

Chapter 10: Self-Assessment—Dashes and Hyphens

1. Three qualities—speed, accuracy, and reliability—are desirable in any applicant to the data entry department. (2.7)
2. A highly placed source explained the top-secret negotiations. (2.8)
3. The file on Marian Gephardt—yes, we finally found it—reveals a history of late payments. (2.7)
4. They're selling a well-designed machine. (2.8)
5. A bottle-green sports jacket is hard to find. (2.8)
6. Argentina, Brazil, Mexico—these are the countries we hope to concentrate on. (2.7)
7. Only two sites—maybe three—offer the things we need. (2.7)
8. How many owner-operators are in the industry? (2.8)
9. Your ever-faithful assistant deserves—without a doubt—a substantial raise. (2.8, 2.7)
10. Myrna Talefiero is this organization's president-elect. (2.8)

11. Stealth, secrecy, and surprise—those are the elements that will give us a competitive edge. (2.7)
12. The charts are well-placed on each page—unlike the running heads and footers. (2.8, 2.7)
13. We got our small-business loan—an enormous advantage. (2.8, 2.7)
14. Ron Franklin—do you remember him?—will be in town Monday. (2.7)
15. Your devil-may-care attitude affects everyone involved in the decision-making process (2.8)

Chapter 11: Self-Assessment—Quotation Marks, Parentheses, Ellipses, Underscores, and Italics

1. Be sure to read "How to Sell by Listening" in this month's issue of _Fortune._ (2.10, 3.2)
2. Her response (see the attached memo) is disturbing. (2.11)
3. _Contact_ is an overused word. (3.2)
4. We will operate with a skeleton staff during the holiday break (December 21 through January 2). (2.11)
5. "The SBP's next conference," the bulletin noted, "will be held in Minneapolis." (2.10)
6. Sara O'Rourke (a reporter from _The Wall Street Journal_) will be here on Thursday. (2.11, 3.2)
7. I don't care _why_ you didn't fill my order; I want to know _when_ you'll fill it. (3.2)
8. The term _up in the air_ means "undecided" (2.10, 3.2)
9. Her assistant (the one who just had the baby) won't be back for four weeks. (2.11)
10. "Ask not what your country can do for you . . ." is the beginning of a famous quotation from John F. Kennedy. (2.10, 2.12)
11. Whom do you think _Time_ magazine will select as its Man of the Year? (3.2)
12. Do you remember who said "And away we go"? (2.10)
13. Refinements in robotics may prove profitable. (More detail about this technology appears in Appendix A.) (2.11)
14. The resignation letter begins, "Since I'll never regain your respect . . ." and goes on to explain why that's true. (2.10, 2.12)
15. You must help her distinguish between _i.e._ (which means "that is") and _e.g._ (which means "for example"). (2.10, 3.2)

Chapter 12: Self-Assessment—Capitals and Abbreviations

1. Dr. Paul Hansen is joining our staff. (3.1)
2. New Caressa skin cream should be in a position to dominate that market. (3.1)
3. Send this report to ~~mister~~Mr. H. K. Danforth, ~~rural route~~RR 1, Warrensburg, ~~new york~~NY 12885. (3.1, 3.3)
4. You are responsible for training my new assistant to operate the Xerox machine. (3.1)
5. She received her ~~master of business administration~~MBA degree from the University of Michigan. (3.1, 3.3)
6. The building is located on the corner of Madison and Center streets. (3.1)
7. Call me tomorrow at 8 a.m. ~~morning~~, ~~pacific standard time~~PST, and I'll have the information you need. (3.3)
8. When Jones becomes CEO next month, we'll need your input ASAP. (3.1, 3.3)

9. Address it to A̲rt B̲owers, C̲hief of P̲roduction. (3.1)

10. Please R̲S̲V̲P̲ to Sony ~~corp.~~Corporation just as soon as you know your schedule. (3.1, 3.3)

11. The data processing department will begin work on ~~feb.~~February 2, just one ~~wk.~~week from today. (3.3)

12. You are to meet him on F̲riday at the U̲N̲ building in N̲Y̲C̲. (3.3)

13. Whenever you can come, P̲rofessor, our employees will greatly enjoy your presentation. (3.1)

14. At 50 per box, our ~~std.~~standard contract forms are $9 a box, and our warranty forms are $7.95 a box. (3.3)

15. We plan to establish a sales office on the W̲est C̲oast. (3.1)

Chapter 13: Self-Assessment—Numbers

1. We need to hire ~~one~~1 office manager, ~~four~~4 bookkeepers, and ~~twelve~~12 clerk-typists. (3.4)

2. The market for this product is nearly ~~six~~6 million people in our region alone. (3.4)

3. Make sure that all 1,835 pages are on my desk no later than ~~nine o'clock~~9:00 a.m. (OR nine o'clock in the morning) (3.4)

4. I̲n̲ 2002, ~~was the year that~~José Guiterez sold more than $50,000 ~~thousand dollars~~ worth of stock. (3.4)

5. Our deadline is ~~4/7~~April 7, but we won't be ready before ~~4/11~~April 11. (3.4)

6. ~~95~~Ninety-five percent of our customers are men. (*OR* Of our customers, 95 percent are men.) (3.4)

7. More than ½ h̲alf the U.S. population is female. (3.4)

8. Cecile Simmons, thirty-eight, is the first woman in this company to be promoted to management. (3.4)

9. Last year, I wrote 20 ~~15~~-fifteen-page reports, and Michelle wrote 24 three-page reports. (3.4)

10. Of the 15 applicants, ~~seven~~7 are qualified. (3.4)

11. Our blinds should measure 38 inches wide by 64-8/16 ~~and one half~~ inches long by 7/16 inches deep. (3.4)

12. Deliver the couch to ~~seven eighty-three~~783 Fountain Road, Suite ~~three~~3, Procter Valley, CA 92074. (3.4)

13. Here are the corrected figures: 42.70% agree, 23.25% disagree, 34.0̲0̲% are undecided, and the error is 0.05%. (3.4)

14. You have to agree that 50,̲0̲0̲0̲,̲0̲0̲0̲ million U.S. citizens cannot be wrong. (3.4)

15. We need a set of shelves 10 feet, ~~eight~~8 inches long. (3.4)

Chapter 14: Self-Assessment—Vocabulary

1. except (4.1)

2. device (4.1)

3. loath (4.1)

4. ordinance (4.1)

5. precedence (4.1)

6. than (4.1)

7. who's (4.1)

8. a lot_____ In this department, we see a̲l̲o̲t̲ of mistakes like that. (4.2)

9. judgment_____ In my j̲u̲d̲g̲e̲m̲e̲n̲t̲, you'll need to redo the cover. (4.3)

10. r̲e̲g̲a̲r̲d̲l̲e̲s̲s̲_____ He decided to reveal the information i̲r̲r̲e̲g̲a̲r̲d̲l̲e̲s̲s̲ of the consequences. (4.2)

11. a̲c̲c̲o̲m̲m̲o̲d̲a̲t̲e̲_____ Why not go along when it is so easy to a̲c̲c̲o̲m̲o̲d̲a̲t̲e̲ his demands? (4.3)

12. i̲m̲p̲l̲y̲_____ When you say that, do you mean to i̲n̲f̲e̲r̲ that I'm being unfair? (4.2)

13. e̲m̲b̲a̲r̲r̲a̲s̲s̲i̲n̲g̲_____ She says that she finds this sort of ceremony e̲m̲b̲a̲r̲a̲s̲s̲i̲n̲g̲. (4.3)

14. t̲o̲_____ All we have to do is try a̲n̲d̲ get along with him for a few more days. (4.2)

15. p̲r̲e̲c̲e̲d̲e̲_____ A friendly handshake should always p̲r̲e̲c̲e̲e̲d̲ negotiations. (4.3)

References

Chapter 1

1. Scobleizer blog [accessed 23 December 2005] http://scobleizer.wordpress.com; David Kirkpatrick, "It's Hard to Manage If You Don't Blog," *Fortune*, 4 October 2004, 46.

2. "Top 50 Partners in Total U.S. Trade in 2003," International Trade Administration website [accessed 13 December 2005] www.ita.doc.gov.

3. Richard L. Daft, *Management*, 6th ed. (Cincinnati: Thomson South-Western, 2003), 107.

4. A. Thomas Young, "Ethics in Business: Business of Ethics," *Vital Speeches*, 15 September 1992, 725–730.

5. "Undercover Marketing Uncovered," CBSnews.com, 25 July 2004 [accessed 11 April 2005] www.cbsnews.com; Stephanie Dunnewind, "Teen Recruits Create Word-of-Mouth 'Buzz' to Hook Peers on Products," *Seattle Times*, 20 November 2004 [accessed 11 April 2005] www.seattletimes.com.

6. Philip C. Kolin, *Successful Writing at Work*, 6th ed. (Boston: Houghton Mifflin, 2001), 24–30.

7. Kelli Esters, "Insurance Company to Repay $1.1 Million to Georgia Soldiers," *Ledger-Enquirer* (Columbus, Ga.), 26 May 2005 [accessed 28 June 2005] www.ebsco.com; Diana B. Henriques, "Insurer to Refund Money to Soldiers Who Bought High-Cost Life Policies," *New York Times*, 23 September 2004, C1, C4; Diana B. Henriques, "Going Off to War, and Vulnerable to the Pitches of Salesmen," *New York Times*, 20 July 2004, C1, C6.

8. Daft, *Management*, 155.

9. Joanne Sammer, "United Technologies Offers a Model for Reporting Ethical Issues," *Workforce Management*, August 2004, 64–66.

10. Based in part on Robert Kreitner, *Management*, 9th ed. (Boston: Houghton Mifflin, 2004), 163.

11. Tracy Novinger, *Intercultural Communication, A Practical Guide* (Austin, Tex: University of Texas Press, 2001), 15.

12. Linda Beamer, "Teaching English Business Writing to Chinese-Speaking Business Students," *Bulletin of the Association for Business Communication* 57, no. 1 (1994): 12–18.

13. Edward T. Hall, "Context and Meaning," in *Intercultural Communication: A Reader*, 6th ed., edited by Larry A. Samovar and Richard E. Porter (Belmont, Calif: Wadsworth, 1991), 34–42.

14. Daft, *Management*, 459.

15. Beamer, "Teaching English Business Writing to Chinese-Speaking Business Students."

16. Charley H. Dodd, *Dynamics of Intercultural Communication*, 3rd ed. (Dubuque, Iowa: Brown, 1991), 69–70.

17. Daft, *Management*, 459.

18. James Wilfong and Toni Seger, *Taking Your Business Global* (Franklin Lakes, N.J.: Career Press, 1997), 277–278.

19. Philip R. Harris and Robert T. Moran, *Managing Cultural Differences*, 3rd ed. (Houston: Gulf, 1991), 260.

20. Guo-Ming Chen and William J. Starosta, *Foundations of Intercultural Communication* (Boston: Allyn & Bacon, 1998), 288–289.

21. Novinger, *Intercultural Communication: A Practical Guide*, 54.

22. Lillian H. Chaney and Jeanette S. Martin, *Intercultural Business Communication*, 4th ed. (Upper Saddle River, N.J.: Pearson Prentice Hall, 2007), 9.

23. Daft, *Management*, 455.

24. Project Implicit website [accessed 17 December 2005] https:/implicit.harvard.edu/implicit.

25. Mona Casady and Lynn Wasson, "Written Communication Skills of International Business Persons," *Bulletin of the Association for Business Communication* 57, no. 4 (1994): 36–40.

26. Jensen J. Zhao and Calvin Parks, "Self-Assessment of Communication Behavior: An Experiential Learning Exercise for Intercultural Business Success," *Business Communication Quarterly* 58, no. 1 (1995): 20–26; Dodd, *Dynamics of Intercultural Communication*, 142–143, 297–299; Stephen P. Robbins, *Organizational Behavior*, 6th ed. (Paramus, N.J.: Prentice Hall, 1993), 345.

27. Makezine website [accessed 22 January 2006] www.makezine.com; Jane Spencer, "The Annoying New Face of Customer Service—Virtual Phone Reps Replace the Old Touch-Tone Menus; Making Claire Less Irritating," *Wall Street Journal*, 21 January 2003, D1; Allison Fass, "Speak Easy," *Forbes*, 6 January 2003, 135.

28. Six Apart website [accessed 17 December 2005] www.sixapart.com.

Chapter 2

1. The Container Store website [accessed 19 January 2006] www.containerstore.com; "2005: Best Companies to Work For," *Fortune*, 24 January 2005 [accessed 11 March 2005]

www.fortune.com; Bob Nelson, "Can't Contain Excitement at The Container Store," BizJournals.com [accessed 11 March 2005] www.bizjournals.com; Mike Duff, "Top-Shelf Employees Keep Container Store on Track," *DSN Retailing Today*, 8 March 2004, 7, no. 49; Bob Nelson, "The Buzz at The Container Store," *Corporate Meetings & Incentives*, June 2003, 32; Jennifer Saba, "Balancing Act," *Potentials*, 1 October 2003 [accessed 15 April 2004] www.highbeam.com; Peter S. Cohan, "Corporate Heroes," *Financial Executive*, 1 March 2003 [accessed 15 April 2004] www.highbeam.com; David Lipke, "Container Store's CEO: People Are Most Valued Asset," 13 January 2003, *HFN* [accessed 9 March 2003] www.highbeam.com; Lorrie Grant, "Container Store's Workers Huddle Up to Help You Out," 30 April 2002, *USA Today*, B1.

2. Courtland L. Bovée and John V. Thill, *Business in Action*, 3d ed. (Upper Saddle River, N.J.: Pearson Prentice Hall, 2005), 175.

3. "Five Case Studies on Successful Teams," *HR Focus*, April 2002, 18+.

4. Lynda McDermott, Bill Waite, and Nolan Brawley, "Executive Teamwork," *Executive Excellence*, May 1999, 15.

5. Larry Cole and Michael Cole, "Why Is the Teamwork Buzz Word Not Working?" *Communication World*, February–March 1999, 29; Patricia Buhler, "Managing in the 90s: Creating Flexibility in Today's Workplace," *Supervision*, January 1997, 24+; Allison W. Amason, Allen C. Hochwarter, Wayne A. Thompson, and Kenneth R. Harrison, "Conflict: An Important Dimension in Successful Management Teams," *Organizational Dynamics*, Autumn 1995, 20+.

6. Richard L. Daft, *Management*, 6th ed. (Cincinnati: Thomson South-Western, 2003), 614.

7. Stephen R. Robbins, *Essentials of Organizational Behavior*, 6th ed. (Upper Saddle River, N.J.: Prentice Hall, 2000), 98.

8. Vijay Govindarajan and Anil K. Gupta, "Building an Effective Global Business Team," *MIT Sloan Management Review*, Summer 2001, 63+.

9. Dana May Casperson, *Power Etiquette: What You Don't Know Can Kill Your Career* (New York: AMACOM, 1999), 9.

10. Marilyn Pincus, *Everyday Business Etiquette* (Hauppauge, N.Y.: Barron's Educational Series, 1996), 7, 133.

11. Pincus, *Everyday Business Etiquette*, 136.

12. Casperson, *Power Etiquette: What You Don't Know Can Kill Your Career*, 23.

13. Gerald H. Graham, Jeanne Unrue, and Paul Jennings, "The Impact of Nonverbal Communication in Organizations: A Survey of Perceptions," *Journal of Business Communication* 28, no. 1 (Winter 1991): 45–62.

14. Pincus, *Everyday Business Etiquette*, 100–101.

15. Maggie Jackson, "Turn Off That Cellphone. It's Meeting Time," *New York Times*, 2 March 2003, sec. 3, 12.

16. Casperson, *Power Etiquette: What You Don't Know Can Kill Your Career*, 10–14; Ellyn Spragins, "Introducing Politeness," *Fortune Small Business*, November 2001, 30.

17. Tanya Mohn, "The Social Graces As a Business Tool," *New York Times*, 10 November 2002, sec. 3, 12.

18. Casperson, *Power Etiquette: What You Don't Know Can Kill Your Career*, 19; Pincus, *Everyday Business Etiquette*, 7–8.

19. Casperson, *Power Etiquette: What You Don't Know Can Kill Your Career*, 44–46.

20. Casperson, *Power Etiquette: What You Don't Know Can Kill Your Career*, 109–110.

21. "Better Meetings Benefit Everyone: How to Make Yours More Productive," *Working Communicator Bonus Report*, July 1998, 1.

22. Ken Blanchard, "Meetings Can Be Effective," *Supervisory Management*, October 1992, 5.

23. "Better Meetings Benefit Everyone: How to Make Yours More Productive," 1.

24. Anne Fisher, "Get Employees to Brainstorm Online," *Fortune*, 29 November 2004, 72.

25. Tony Kontzer, "Learning To Share," *Information Week*, 5 May 2003, 28; Jon Udell, "Uniting Under Groove," *InfoWorld*, 17 February 2003 [accessed 9 September 2003] www.elibrary.com; Alison Overholt, "Virtually There?" *Fast Company*, 14 February 2002, 108.

26. Nicole Ridgway, "A Safer Place to Meet," *Forbes*, 28 April 2003, 97.

27. Judi Brownell, *Listening*, 2d edition (Boston: Allyn and Bacon, 2002), 9, 10.

28. Augusta M. Simon, "Effective Listening: Barriers to Listening in a Diverse Business Environment," *Bulletin of the Association for Business Communication* 54, no. 3 (September 1991): 73–74.

29. Robyn D. Clarke, "Do You Hear What I Hear?" *Black Enterprise*, May 1998, 129.

30. Terri Somers, "Gen-Probe's Nordhoff Listens Well, Then Acts," *San Diego Union-Tribune*, 2 November 2004, C1, C6.

31. Dennis M. Kratz and Abby Robinson Kratz, *Effective Listening Skills*, (New York: McGraw-Hill, 1995), 45–53; J. Michael Sproule, *Communication Today* (Glenview, Ill.: Scott, Foresman, 1981), 69.

32. Brownell, *Listening*, 230–231.

33. Kratz and Kratz, *Effective Listening Skills*, 78–79; Sproule, *Communication Today*, 69.

34. Bob Lamons, "Good Listeners Are Better Communicators," *Marketing News*, 11 September 1995, 13+; Phillip Morgan and H. Kent Baker, "Building a Professional Image: Improving Listening Behavior," *Supervisory Management*, November 1985, 35–36.

35. Clarke, "Do You Hear What I Hear?" 29; Dot Yandle, "Listening to Understand," *Pryor Report Management Newsletter Supplement* 15, no. 8 (August 1998): 13.

36. Brownell, *Listening*, 14; Kratz and Kratz, *Effective Listening Skills*, 8–9; Sherwyn P. Morreale and Courtland L. Bovée, *Excellence in Public Speaking* (Orlando, Fla.: Harcourt Brace, 1998), 72–76; Lyman K. Steil, Larry L. Barker, and Kittie W. Watson, *Effective Listening: Key to Your Success* (Reading, Mass.: Addison-Wesley, 1983), 21–22.

37. Patrick J. Collins, *Say It with Power and Confidence* (Upper Saddle River, N.J.: Prentice Hall, 1997), 40–45.

38. Morreale and Bovée, *Excellence in Public Speaking*, 296.

39. Judee K. Burgoon, David B. Butler, and W. Gill Woodall, *Nonverbal Communication: The Unspoken Dialog* (New York: McGraw-Hill, 1996), 137.

40. "Study: Human Lie Detectors Rarely Wrong," *CNN.com*, 14 October 2004 [accessed 14 October 2004] www.cnn.com.

41. Dale G. Leathers, *Successful Nonverbal Communication: Principles and Applications* (New York: Macmillan, 1986), 19.

42. Gerald H. Graham, Jeanne Unrue, and Paul Jennings, "The Impact of Nonverbal Communication in Organizations: A Survey of Perceptions," *Journal of Business Communication* 28, no. 1 (Winter 1991): 45–62.

43. Bremer Communications website [accessed 21 January 2006] www.bremercommunications.com.

44. Virginia P. Richmond and James C. McCroskey, *Nonverbal Behavior in Interpersonal Relations*, (Boston: Allyn and Bacon, 2000), 2–3.

Chapter 3

1. Toby Ward, "Podcasting the Intranet at IBM," *Intranet Blog*, 11 December 2005 [accessed 9 April 2006] http://intranetblog.blogware.com; Stacy Cowley, "IBM Employees Play with Podcasting," *InfoWorld*, 23 November 2005 [accessed 9 April 2006] www.infoworld.com.

2. Sanford Kaye, "Writing Under Pressure," *Soundview Executive Book Summaries* 10, no. 12, part 2 (December 1988): 1–8.

3. Laurey Berk and Phillip G. Clampitt, "Finding the Right Path in the Communication Maze," *IABC Communication World*, October 1991, 28–32.

4. Berk and Clampitt, "Finding the Right Path in the Communication Maze."

5. Skype website [accessed 9 April 2006] www.skype.com; Jon Van, "Technology Notebook Column," *Chicago Tribune*, 13 March 2004 [accessed 19 March 2004] www.ebsco.com.

6. Kris Maher, "The Jungle," *Wall Street Journal*, 5 October 2004, B10.

7. Kevin Maney, "Surge in Text Messaging Makes Cell Operators :-)," *USA Today*, 28 July 2005, B1–B2.

8. David Kirkpatrick, "It's Hard to Manage If You Don't Blog," *Fortune*, 4 October 2004, 46; Lee Gomes, "How the Next Big Thing in Technology Morphed into a Really Big Thing," *Wall Street Journal*, 4 October 2004, B1; Jeff Meisner, "Cutting Through the Blah, Blah, Blah," *Puget Sound Business Journal*, 19–25 November 2004, 27–28; Lauren Gard, "The Business of Blogging," *BusinessWeek*, 13 December 2004, 117–119; Heather Green, "Online Video: The Sequel," *BusinessWeek*, 10 January 2005, 40; Michelle Conlin and Andrew Park, "Blogging with the Boss's Blessing," *BusinessWeek*, 28 June 2004, 100–102.

9. Jonathan A. Segal, "Beware Bashing Bloggers: A Heavy-Handed Approach to Off-Duty Blogging Invites Legal and Employee Relations Problems," *HR Magazine*, June 2005 [accessed 19 January 2006] www.highbeam.com; Julie Badel, "Digital Graffiti: What Every Employer Should Know About Employee Blogging," *ABA Banking Journal*, November 2005 [accessed 19 January 2006] www.highbeam.com.

10. Berk and Clampitt, "Finding the Right Path in the Communication Maze."

11. Berk and Clampitt, "Finding the Right Path in the Communication Maze."

12. Berk and Clampitt, "Finding the Right Path in the Communication Maze."

13. Raymond M. Olderman, *10 Minute Guide to Business Communication* (New York: Alpha Books, 1997), 19–20.

14. Mohan R. Limaye and David A. Victor, "Cross-Cultural Business Communication Research: State of the Art and Hypotheses for the 1990s," *Journal of Business Communication* 28, no. 3 (Summer 1991): 277–299.

15. Susan Hall and Theresa Tiggeman, "Getting the Big Picture: Writing to Learn in a Finance Class," *Business Communication Quarterly* 58, no. 1 (1995): 12–15.

16. Carol S. Mull, "Orchestrate Your Ideas," *Toastmaster*, February 1987, 19.

Chapter 4

1. Plain English Campaign website [accessed 15 April 2006] www.plainenglish.co.uk.

2. Elizabeth Blackburn and Kelly Belanger, "You-Attitude and Positive Emphasis: Testing Received Wisdom in Business Communication," *Bulletin of the Association for Business Communication* 56, no. 2 (June 1993): 1–9.

3. Placard at Alaska Airlines ticket counters, Seattle-Tacoma International Airport, 3 October 2003.

4. Annette N. Shelby and N. Lamar Reinsch, Jr., "Positive Emphasis and You Attitude: An Empirical Study," *Journal of Business Communication* 32, no. 4 (1995): 303–322.

5. Sherryl Kleinman, "Why Sexist Language Matters," *Qualitative Sociology* 25, no. 2 (Summer 2002): 299–304.

6. Judy E. Pickens, "Terms of Equality: A Guide to Bias-Free Language," *Personnel Journal*, August 1985, 24.

7. Lisa Taylor, "Communicating About People with Disabilities: Does the Language We Use Make a Difference?" *Bulletin of the Association for Business Communication* 53, no. 3 (September 1990): 65–67.

8. Susan Benjamin, *Words at Work* (Reading, Mass.: Addison-Wesley, 1997), 136–137.

9. Stuart Crainer and Des Dearlove, "Making Yourself Understood," *Across the Board*, May/June 2004, 23–27.

10. Plain English Campaign website [accessed 3 October 2003] www.plainenglish.co.uk.

11. Susan Jaderstrom and Joanne Miller, "Active Writing," *Office Pro*, November/December 2003, 29.

12. Portions of this section are adapted from Courtland L. Bovée, *Techniques of Writing Business Letters, Memos, and Reports* (Sherman Oaks, Calif.: Banner Books International, 1978), 13–90.

13. Talk Energy website [accessed 29 January 2006] www.talkenergy.com.

14. Robert Hartwell Fiske, *The Dimwit's Dictionary* (Oak Park, Ill.: Marion Street Press, 2002), 16–20.

15. David A. Fryxell, "Lost in Transition?" *Writers Digest,* January 2005, 24–26.

Chapter 5

1. Robert Hartwell Fiske, *The Dictionary of Concise Writing: 10,000 Alternatives to Wordy Phrases* (Oak Park, Ill.: Marion Street Press, 2002), 17.
2. Natalie Canavor and Claire Meirowitz, "Good Corporate Writing: Why It Matters, and What to Do," *Communication World,* July–August 2005, 30–33.
3. Holly Weeks, "The Best Memo You'll Ever Write," *Harvard Management Communication Letter,* Spring 2005, 3–5.
4. William Zinsser, *On Writing Well,* 5th ed. (New York: HarperCollins, 1994), 7, 17.
5. Mary A. DeVries, *Internationally Yours* (Boston: Houghton Mifflin, 1994), 160.
6. Zinsser, *On Writing Well,* 126.
7. Deborah Gunn, "Looking Good on Paper," *Office Pro,* March 2004, 10–11.
8. Jacci Howard Bear, "Desktop Publishing Rules of Page Layout," About.com [accessed 22 August 2005] www.about.com.
9. Robin Williams, *The Non-Designer's Type Book* (Berkeley, Calif.: Peachpit Press, 2006), 123.
10. Jacci Howard Bear, "Desktop Publishing Rules for How Many Fonts to Use," About.com [accessed 22 August 2005] www.about.com.

Chapter 6

1. Robert Scoble and Shel Israel, *Naked Conversations* (Hoboken, N.J.: John Wiley & Sons, 2006), 94–95.
2. Reid Goldsborough, "'Creeping Informality' Can Be Big Mistake in Business E-Mails," *New Orleans City Business,* 14 March 2005, 18; Jack E. Appleman, "Bad Writing Can Cost Insurers Time & Money," *National Underwriter,* 27 September 2004, 34; Adina Genn, "RE: This Is an Important Message, Really," *Long Island Business News,* 5–11 December 2003, 21A; Lynn Lofton, "Regardless of What You Thought, Grammer Rules *Do* Apply to E-Mail," *Mississippi Business Journal,* 23–29 May 2005, 1.
3. Hilary Potkewitz and Rachel Brown "Spread of E-Mail Has Altered Communication Habits at Work," *Los Angeles Business Journal,* 18 April 2005 [accessed 30 April 2006] www.findarticles.com; Nancy Flynn, *Instant Messaging Rules* (New York: AMACOM, 2004), 47–54.
4. Greg Burns, "For Some, Benefits of E-Mail Not Worth Risk," *San Diego Union-Tribune,* 16 August 2005, A1, A8; Pui-Wing Tam, Erin White, Nick Wingfield, and Kris Maher, "Snooping E-Mail by Software Is Now a Workplace Norm," *Wall Street Journal,* 9 March 2005, B1+.
5. Matt Cain, "Managing E-Mail Hygiene," *ZD Net Tech Update,* 5 February 2004 [accessed 19 March 2004] www.techupdate.zdnet.com.
6. Mary Munter, Priscilla S. Rogers, and Jone Rymer, "Business E-Mail: Guidelines for Users," *Business Communication Quarterly,* March 2003, 26+; Renee B.

Horowitz and Marian G. Barchilon, "Stylistic Guidelines for E-Mail," *IEEE Transactions on Professional Communication* 37, no. 4 (December 1994): 207–212.
7. Lizette Alvarez, "Got 2 Extra Hours for Your E-Mail?" *New York Times,* 10 November 2005 [accessed 10 November 2005] www.nytimes.com.
8. "E-Mail Is So Five Minutes Ago," *BusinessWeek Online,* 28 November 2005 [accessed 3 May 2006] www.businessweek.com.
9. Vayusphere website [accessed 22 January 2006] www.vayusphere.com; Christa C. Ayer, "Presence Awareness: Instant Messaging's Killer App," *Mobile Business Advisor,* 1 July 2004 [accessed 22 January 2006] www.highbeam.com; Jefferson Graham, "Instant Messaging Programs Are No Longer Just for Messages," *USA Today,* 20 October 2003, 5D; Todd R. Weiss, "Microsoft Targets Corporate Instant Messaging Customers," *Computerworld,* 18 November 2002, 12; "Banks Adopt Instant Messaging To Create a Global Business Network," *Computer Weekly,* 25 April 2002, 40; Michael D. Osterman, "Instant Messaging in the Enterprise," *Business Communications Review,* January 2003, 59–62; John Pallato, "Instant Messaging Unites Work Groups and Inspires Collaboration," *Internet World,* December 2002, 14+.
10. Mark Gibbs, "Racing to Instant Messaging," *NetworkWorld,* 17 February 2003, 74.
11. "E-Mail Is So Five Minutes Ago."
12. Clint Boulton, "IDC: IM Use Is Booming in Business," *InstantMessagingPlanet.com,* 5 October 2005 [accessed 22 January 2006] www.instantmessagingplanet.com; Jenny Goodbody, "Critical Success Factors for Global Virtual Teams," *Strategic Communication Management,* February/March 2005, 18–21; Ann Majchrzak, Arvind Malhotra, Jeffrey Stamps, and Jessica Lipnack, "Can Absence Make a Team Grow Stronger?" *Harvard Business Review,* May 2004, 131–137; Christine Y. Chen, "The IM Invasion," *Fortune,* 26 May 2003, 135–138; Yudhijit Bhattacharjee, "A Swarm of Little Notes," *Time,* September 2002, A3–A8; Mark Bruno, "Taming the Wild Frontiers of Instant Messaging," *Bank Technology News,* December 2002, 30–31; Richard Grigonis, "Enterprise-Strength Instant Messaging," Convergence.com, 10–15 [accessed March 2003] www.convergence.com.
13. Pallato, "Instant Messaging Unites Work Groups and Inspires Collaboration," 14+.
14. Anita Hamilton, "You've Got Spim!" *Time,* 2 February 2004, [accessed 1 March 2004], www.time.com.
15. Scoble and Israel, *Naked Conversations,* 15–18.
16. GM FastLane blog [accessed 4 May 2006] http://fastlane.gmblogs.com.
17. Paul Chaney, "Thinking Out Loud About a New Branding Strategy and Blog," 31 March 2006 [accessed 4 May 2006] http://radiantmarketinggroup.com.
18. Stephen Baker, "The Inside Story on Company Blogs," *BusinessWeek Online* 14 February 2006 [accessed 15 February 2006] www.businessweek.com; Jeremy Wright,

Blog Marketing (New York: McGraw-Hill, 2006), 45–56; Paul Chaney, "Blogs: Beyond the Hype!" 26 May 2005 [accessed 4 May 2006] http://radiantmarketinggroup.com.

19. Stephen Baker and Heather Green, "Blogs Will Change Your Business," *BusinessWeek*, 2 May 2005, 57–67.

20. Julie Moran Alterio, "Podcasts a Hit Inside and Outside IBM," *The Journal News* (White Plains, N.Y.), 9 January 2006 [accessed 5 May 2006] www.thejournalnews.com.

21. "Turn Your Feed into a Podcast," Lifehacker blog, 12 January 2006 [accessed 6 May 2006] www.lifehacker.com.

22. Michael W. Goeghegan and Dan Klass, *Podcast Solutions: The Complete Guide to Podcasting* (Berkeley, Calif.: Friends of Ed, 2005), 57–86; Todd Cochrane, *Podcasting: The Do-It-Yourself Guide* (Indianapolis, Ind.: Wiley, 2005), 87–136.

23. Adapted from job description for Global Marketing Manager–Apparel, New Balance website [accessed 24 August 2005] www.newbalance.com.

24. Adapted from "How Microsoft Reviews Suppliers," *Fast Company*, Issue 17 [accessed 3 September 2003] http://fastcompany.com.

25. Adapted from Davide Dukcevich, "Instant Business: Retailer Lands' End Profits from Online Chat," Forbes.com, Special to ABCNEWS.com, 29 July 2002 [accessed 21 July 2003] abcnews.go.com; Lands' End website [accessed 5 December 2003] www.landsend.com; Forbes.com staff, "Instant Messaging at Work," Forbes.com, 26 July 2002 [accessed 21 July 2003] www.forbes.com; Tischelle George and Sandra Swanson with Christopher T. Heun, "Not Just Kid Stuff," *InformationWeek*, 3 September 2001 [accessed 21 July 2003] www.informationweek.com.

26. Adapted from Liz Moyer, "California Dreaming," *Forbes*, 8 May 2006 [accessed 8 May 2006] www.forbes.com; "Wachovia to Acquire Golden West Financial, Nation's Most Admired and 2nd Largest Savings Institution," 7 May 2006, Wachovia website [accessed 8 May 2006] www.wachovia.com.

Chapter 7

1. Warren E. Buffett, *Preface* to *A Plain English Handbook*, Plain English website [accessed 12 May 2006] www.plainenglish.gov.

2. Mary Mitchell, "The Circle of Life—Condolence Letters," ULiveandLearn.com [accessed 18 July 2005] www.liveandlearn.com; Donna Larcen, "Authors Share the Words of Condolence," *Los Angeles Times,* 20 December 1991, E11.

3. Adapted from Bruce Frankel and Alex Tresniowski, "Stormy Skies," *People Weekly*, 31 July 2000, 112–115.

4. Adapted from Keith H. Hammonds, "Difference Is Power," *Fast Company,* 36, 258 [accessed 11 July 2000] www.fastcompany.com; Terri Morrison, Wayne Conaway, and George A. Borden, *Kiss, Bow, or Shake Hands* (Avon, Mass.: Adams Media Corp., 1994), 1–5.

5. Adapted from Tom Abate, "Need to Preserve Cash Generates Wave of Layoffs in Biotech Industry," *San Francisco Chronicle*, 10 February 2003 [accessed 18 July 2005] www.sfgate.com.

6. Adapted from Lisa DiCarlo, "IBM Gets the Message—Instantly," Forbes.com, 7 July 2002 [accessed 22 July 2003] www.forbes.com/home/2002/07/0723ibm.html; "IBM Introduces Breakthrough Messaging Technology for Customers and Business Partners," *M2 Presswire*, 19 February 2003 [accessed 24 July 2003] www.proquest.com; "IBM and America Online Team for Instant Messaging Pilot," *M2 Presswire*, 4 February 2003 [accessed 24 July 2003] www.proquest.com.

7. Adapted from CES website [accessed 18 July 2005] www.cesweb.org.

8. Adapted from Michael Mescon, Courtland Bovée, and John Thill, *Business Today*, 10th ed. (Upper Saddle River, N.J.: Prentice Hall, 2002), 220.

9. Adapted from SitePoint website [accessed 12 May 2006] www.sitepoint.com; Dylan Tweney, "The Defogger: Slim Down that Homepage," *Business 2.0*, 13 July 2001 [accessed 1 August 2001] www.business2.com.

10. Public Relations Society of America website [accessed 18 June 2005] www.prsa.org.

11. Adapted from Mitchell, "The Circle of Life—Condolence Letters"; Larcen, "Authors Share the Words of Condolence."

Chapter 8

1. "Inside the KPMG Mess," *BusinessWeek*, 1 September 2005 [accessed 1 September 2005] www.businessweek.com; KPMG Careers website [accessed 19 August 2005] www.kpmgcareers.com; "KPMG LLP Statement Regarding Department of Justice Matter," press release, 16 June 2005 [accessed 19 August 2005] www.us.kpmg.com; "KPMG May Avoid Indictment as U.S. Pushes Settlement, People Say," Bloomberg.com, 4 August 2005 [accessed 19 August 2005] www.bloomberg.com; "KPMG Offers Apology Over Illegal Tax Shelters," *Boston Globe*, 17 June 2005 [accessed 19 August 2005] www.boston.com; Jeff Bailey and Lynnley Browning, "KPMG May Dodge One Bullet, Only to Face Another," *New York Times*, 21 June 2005 [accessed 19 August 2005] www.nytimes.com.

2. Katie Grasso, "Deliver Bad News to Worker Face-to-Face, with Empathy," *Courier-Post* (Camden, New Jersey), 8 February 2006 [accessed 14 May 2006] www.courierpostonline.com.

3. Ian McDonald, "Marsh Can Do $600 Million, But Apologize?" *Wall Street Journal*, 14 January 2005, C1, C3; Adrienne Carter and Amy Borrus, "What If Companies Fessed Up?" *BusinessWeek*, 24 January 2005, 59–60; Patrick J. Kiger, "The Art of the Apology," *Workforce Management*, October 2004, 57–62.

4. "The Power of Apology: Removing the Legal Barriers," A Special Report by the Ombudsman of the Province of British Columbia, February 2006 [accessed 14 May 2006] www.ombud.gov.bc.ca; Ameeta Patel and Lamar Reinsch, "Companies Can Apologize: Corporate Apologies and

Legal Liability," *Business Communication Quarterly*, March 2003 [accessed 1 December 2003] www.elibrary.com.

5. Maura Dolan and Stuart Silverstein, "Court Broadens Liability for Job References," *Los Angeles Times*, 28 January 1997, A1, A11; Frances A. McMorris, "Ex-Bosses Face Less Peril Giving Honest Job References," *Wall Street Journal*, 8 July 1996, B1, B8.

6. "HR Manners," *Workforce Week Management*, January 29–February 4, 2006.

7. Thomas S. Brice and Marie Waung, "Applicant Rejection Letters: Are Businesses Sending the Wrong Message?" *Business Horizons*, March–April 1995, 59–62.

8. Gwendolyn N. Smith, Rebecca F. Nolan, and Yong Dai, "Job-Refusal Letters: Readers' Affective Responses to Direct and Indirect Organizational Plans," *Business Communication Quarterly* 59, no. 1 (1996): 67–73; Brice and Waung, "Applicant Rejection Letters."

9. Judi Brownell, "The Performance Appraisal Interviews: A Multipurpose Communication Assignment," *Bulletin of the Association for Business Communication* 57, no. 2 (1994): 11–21.

10. Brownell, "The Performance Appraisal Interviews."

11. Howard M. Bloom, "Performance Evaluations," *New England Business*, December 1991, 14.

12. David I. Rosen, "Appraisals Can Make—or Break—Your Court Case," *Personnel Journal*, November 1992, 113.

13. Patricia A. McLagan, "Advice for Bad-News Bearers: How to Tell Employees They're Not Hacking It and Get Results," *Industry Week*, 15 February 1993, 42; Michael Lee Smith, "Give Feedback, Not Criticism," *Supervisory Management*, 1993, 4; "A Checklist for Conducting Problem Performer Appraisals," *Supervisory Management*, December 1993, 7–9.

14. Carrie Brodzinski, "Avoiding Wrongful Termination Suits," *National Underwriter Property & Casualty—Risk & Benefits Management*, 13 October 2003 [accessed 2 December 2003] www.elibrary.com.

15. Jane R. Goodson, Gail W. McGee, and Anson Seers, "Giving Appropriate Performance Feedback to Managers: An Empirical Test of Content and Outcomes," *Journal of Business Communication* 29, no. 4 (1992): 329–342.

16. Craig Cox, "On the Firing Line," *Business Ethics*, May–June 1992, 33–34.

17. Cox, "On the Firing Line."

18. Adapted from Sylvia Ann Hewlett and Carolyn Buck Luce, "Off-Ramps and On-Ramps," *Harvard Business Review*, March 2005, 43–54.

19. Adapted from Stanton website [accessed 18 August 2005] www.stanton.com.

20. Adapted from "Bathtub Curve," *Engineering Statistics Handbook*, National Institute of Standards and Technology website [accessed 16 April 2005] www.nist.gov; Robert Berner, "The Warranty Windfall," *BusinessWeek*, 20 December 2004, 84–86; Larry Armstrong, "When Service Contracts Make Sense," *BusinessWeek*, 20 December 2004, 86.

21. Adapted from "FDA Notifies Public That Vail Products, Inc., Issues Nationwide Recall of Enclosed Bed Systems," FDA press release, 30 June 2005 [accessed 18 August 2005] www.fda.gov.

22. Adapted from Pui-Wing Tam, Erin White, Nick Wingfield, and Kris Maher, "Snooping E-Mail by Software Is Now a Workplace Norm," *Wall Street Journal*, 9 March 2005, B1+.

23. Adapted from Alion website [accessed 19 August 2005] www.alionscience.com.

24. Adapted from United Airlines website, [accessed 31 December 2003] www.united.com; "United Airlines First to Offer Inflight Email on Domestic Flights: Verizon Airfone Outfits UAL's Fleet with JetConnectsm," United Airlines press release, [accessed 21 July 2003] www.ual.com; "Laptops Sprout Wings with Verizon Airfone JetConnect Service," *PR Newswire*, 24 September 2002, [accessed 21 July 2003] www.proquest.com; "Verizon Hopes Data Flies with Airfone JetConnect," *Wireless Data News*, 7 May 2003 [accessed 24 July 2003] www.proquest.com.

25. Adapted from Associated Press, "Employers Restricting Use of Cell Phones in Cars," CNN.com/Sci-Tech, 27 August 2001 [accessed 27 August 2001] www.cnn.com; Julie Vallese, "Study: All Cell Phones Distract Drivers," *CNN.com/U.S.*, 16 August 2001 [accessed 7 September 2001] www.cnn.com/2001/US/08/16/cell.phone.driving/index.html.

26. Adapted from Julie Vallese, "Motorized Scooter Injuries on the Rise," CNN.com/U.S., 22 August 2001 [accessed 22 August 2001] www.cnn.com; The Sports Authority website [accessed 28 August 2001] www.thesportauthority.com.

27. Adapted from Sean Doherty, "Dynamic Communications," *Network Computing*, 3 April 2003, 26 [accessed 24 July 2003] http://search.epnet.com; Todd Wasserman, "Post-Merger HP Invents New Image to Challenge Tech Foes IBM and Dell," *Brandweek*, 18 November 2002, [accessed 24 July 2003] http://search.epnet.com, 9; R. P. Srikanth, "IM Tools Are Latest Tech Toys for Corporate Users," *Express Computer*, 1 July 2002 [accessed 21 July 2003] www.expresscomputeronline.com.

Chapter 9

1. Brian Clark, "The Two Most Important Words in Blogging," *Copyblogger* blog [accessed 18 May 2006] www.copyblogger.com.

2. Jay A. Conger, "The Necessary Art of Persuasion," *Harvard Business Review*, May–June 1998, 84–95; Jeanette W. Gilsdorf, "Write Me Your Best Case for…" *Bulletin of the Association for Business Communication* 54, no. 1 (March 1991): 7–12.

3. "Vital Skill for Today's Managers: Persuading, Not Ordering Others," *Soundview Executive Book Summaries*, September 1998, 1.

4. Mary Cross, "Aristotle and Business Writing: Why We Need to Teach Persuasion," *Bulletin of the Association for Business Communication* 54, no. 1 (March 1991): 3–6.

5. Robert T. Moran, "Tips on Making Speeches to International Audiences," *International Management,* April 1980, 58–59.

6. Conger, "The Necessary Art of Persuasion."

7. Raymond M. Olderman, *10-Minute Guide to Business Communication* (New York: Macmillan Spectrum/Alpha Books, 1997), 57–61.

8. Gilsdorf, "Write Me Your Best Case for…".

9. John D. Ramage and John C. Bean, *Writing Arguments: A Rhetoric with Readings,* 3d ed. (Boston: Allyn & Bacon, 1995), 430–442.

10. Philip Vassallo, "Persuading Powerfully: Tips for Writing Persuasive Documents," *et Cetera,* Spring 2002, 65–71.

11. Dianna Booher, *Communicate with Confidence* (New York: McGraw-Hill, 1994), 102.

12. Conger, "The Necessary Art of Persuasion."

13. iPod nano product page, Apple Computer website [accessed 9 November 2005] www.apple.com/ipod.

14. Verizon Wireless website [accessed 23 August 2005] www.verizonwireless.com.

15. Saturn VUE product page, Saturn website [accessed 14 May 2006] www.saturn.com.

16. *Working and Living in France: The Ins and Outs* product page, Insider Paris Guides website [accessed 8 December 2003] www.insiderparisguides.com.

17. Verizon Wireless sales letter, received 1 December 2003.

18. Fast Break Backpack product page, Lands End website, [accessed 8 December 2003], www.landsend.com.

19. iPod nano product page.

20. Gilsdorf, "Write Me Your Best Case for…"

21. *Frequently Asked Advertising Questions: A Guide for Small Business,* U.S. Federal Trade Commission website, [accessed 9 December 2003] www.ftc.gov.

22. Adapted from GM Fastlane Blog [accessed 23 August 2005] http://fastlane.gmblogs.com.

23. Adapted from The Podcast Bunker website [accessed 25 August 2005] www.podcastbunker.com.

24. Adapted from Time Inc. website [accessed 25 August 2005] www.timewarner.com.

25. Adapted from Starbucks website [accessed 23 August 2005] www.starbucks.com.

26. Adapted from Kelly Services website [accessed 9 January 2004] www.kellyservices.com.

27. Adapted from Give Life website [accessed 23 August 2005] www.givelife.org; American Red Cross website [accessed 3 October 2001] www.redcross.org; American Red Cross San Diego Chapter website [accessed 3 October 2001] www.sdarc.org/blood.htm.

28. Adapted from Joe Sharkey, "Luggage Lock Plan Revisited, Again," *New York Times,* 6 January 2004 [accessed 6 January 2004] www.nytimes.com; Brookstone website [accessed 13 January 2004] www.brookstone.com.

29. Adapted from Courtland L. Bovée, and John V. Thill, *Business In Action,* 3d ed. (Upper Saddle River, N.J.: Pearson Prentice Hall, 2005), International Telework Association & Council website [accessed 24 August 2005] www.telecommute.org, 236–237; Jason Roberson,

"Rush-hour Rebellion," *Dallas Business Journal,* 22 June 2001, 31; Carole Hawkins, "Ready, Set, Go Home," *Black Enterprise,* August 2001, 118–124; Wayne Tompkins, "Telecommuting in Transition," *Courier-Journal,* Louisville, Ky., 9 July 2001, 01C.

30. Adapted from CNET Shopper.com [accessed 1 October 2001] http://shopper.cnet.com.

31. Adapted from Sarah Plaskitt, "Case Study: Hilton Uses SMS With Success," *B&T Marketing & Media,* 27 June 2002 [accessed 22 July 2003] www.bandt.com.au; "Wireless Messaging Briefs," *Instant Messaging Planet,* 4 October 2002 [accessed 22 July 2003] www.instantmessagingplanet.com; Hilton Hotels Corporation, *Hoover's Company Capsules,* 1 July 2003 [accessed 24 July 2003] www.proquest.com; Matthew G. Nelson, "Hilton Takes Reservations Wireless," *InformationWeek,* 25 June 2001, 99 [accessed 24 July 2003] www.web22.epnet.com; Hilton Hotels website [accessed 15 January 2004] www.hilton.com.

32. Adapted from "Community Relations," IBM website [accessed 15 January 2004] www.ibm.com; "DAS Faces an Assured Future with IBM," IBM website [accessed 16 January 2004] www-306.ibm.com; IBM website, "Sametime," [accessed 16 January 2004] www.lotus.com.

33. Adapted from Andrew Ferguson, "Supermarket of the Vanities," *Fortune,* 10 June 1996, 30.

34. Adapted from Whole Foods Market website [accessed 9 January 2004] www.wholefoodsmarket.com.

Chapter 10

1. Adapted from Mike Drexler, "Media Midlife Crisis: The Changes are Monumental," *Adweek,* 9 February 2004 [accessed 6 May 2004] www.highbeam.com; Kevin J. Delaney and Robert A. Guth, "Beep. Foosh. Buy Me. Pow." *Wall Street Journal,* 8 April 2004, B1, B7; Stuart Elliot, "Advertising," *New York Times,* 14 April 2004, C8; Ronald Grover, "Can Mad Ave. Make Zap-Proof Ads?" *Business Week,* 2 February 2004, 36; Richard Linnett and Wayne Friedman, "OMD Plans Strategy to Challenge Upfront," *Advertising Age,* 23 June 2003, 1; Katy Bachman, "Research: Beth Uyenco," *Brandweek,* 9 December 2003, SR24; Kate Fitzgerald, "Communication Architects," *Advertising Age,* 5 August 2002, S6; Katy Bachman, "Research: Tony Jarvis," *Mediaweek,* 3 December 2001, SR20.

2. Courtland L. Bovée, Michael J. Houston, and John V. Thill, *Marketing,* 2d ed. (New York: McGraw-Hill, 1995), 194–196.

3. Legal-Definitions.com [accessed 17 December 2003] www.legal-definitions.com.

4. AllTheWeb.com advanced search page [accessed 27 August 2005] www.alltheweb.com; Google advanced search page [accessed 27 August 2005] www.google.com; Yahoo! advanced search page [accessed 27 August 2005] www.yahoo.com.

5. NewsGator website [accessed 24 August 2005] www.newsgator.com; NewzCrawler website [accessed 24 August 2005] www.newzcrawler.com.

6. "Top 10 Benefits of OneNote 2003," Microsoft website [accessed 21 June 2004] www.microsoft.com.

7. Naresh K. Malhotra, *Basic Marketing Research*, (Upper Saddle River, N.J.: Prentice-Hall, 2002), 314–317; "How to Design and Conduct a Study," *Credit Union Magazine*, October 1983, 36–46.

8. American Marketing Association [accessed 14 December 2003] www.marketingpower.com.

9. Karen J. Bannan, "Companies Save Time, Money with Online Surveys," *B to B*, 9 June 2003, 1+; Allen Hogg, "Online Research Overview," American Marketing Association website [accessed 15 December 2003] www.marketingpower.com.

10. Sherwyn P. Morreale and Courtland L. Bovée, *Excellence in Public Speaking* (Fort Worth: Harcourt Brace College Publishers, 1998), 177.

11. Morreale and Bovée, *Excellence in Public Speaking*, 182.

12. Lynn Quitman Troyka, *Simon & Schuster Handbook for Writers*, 6th ed. (Upper Saddle River, N.J.: Simon & Schuster, 2002), 481.

13. Adapted from Air-Trak website [accessed 12 September 2005] www.air-trak.com.

Chapter 11

1. Martin Couzins, "Expert's View: Tania Menegatti on How to Improve Your Communication Skills," *Personnel Today*, 30 August 2005 [accessed 22 May 2006] www.epnet.com.

2. A. S. C. Ehrenberg, "Report Writing—Six Simple Rules for Better Business Documents," *Admap*, June 1992, 39–42.

3. Michael Netzley and Craig Snow, *Guide to Report Writing* (Upper Saddle River, N.J.: Prentice Hall, 2001), 15.

4. Claudia Mon Pere McIsaac, "Improving Student Summaries Through Sequencing," *Bulletin of the Association for Business Communication* (September 1987): 17–20.

5. David A. Hayes, "Helping Students GRASP the Knack of Writing Summaries," *Journal of Reading* (November 1989): 96–101.

6. Philip C. Kolin, *Successful Writing at Work*, 6th ed. (Boston: Houghton Mifflin, 2001), 552–555.

7. Google Earth website [accessed 2 September 2005] http://earth.google.com.

8. Jacci Howard Bear, "Defining the Principles of Design Through Metaphor or Allegory," About.com [accessed 2 September 2005] www.about.com; William Wells, John Burnett, and Sandra Moriarty, *Advertising Principles & Practice*, 6th ed. (Upper Saddle River, N.J.: Prentice Hall, 2003), 373–375.

9. Edward R. Tufte, *The Visual Display of Quantitative Information* (Cheshire, Conn.: Graphic Press, 1983), 113.

10. Michael Netzley and Craig Snow, *Guide to Report Writing* (Upper Saddle River, N.J.: Prentice Hall, 2001), 57.

11. Toby B. Gooley, "Ocean Shipping: RFPs that Get Results," *Logistics Management*, July 2003, 47–52.

12. Adapted from "Home Depot Says E-Learning Is Paying for Itself," *Workforce Management*, 25 February 2004 [accessed 28 February 2004] www.workforce.com; Robert Celaschi, "The Insider: Training," *Workforce Management*, August 2004, 67–69; Joe Mullich, "A Second Act for E-Learning," *Workforce Management*, February 2004, 51–55; Gail Johnson, "Brewing the Perfect Blend," *Training*, December 2003, 30+; Tammy Galvin, "2003 Industry Report," *Training*, October 2003, 21+; William C. Symonds, "Giving It the Old Online Try," *BusinessWeek*, 3 December 2001, 76–80; Karen Frankola, "Why Online Learners Drop Out," *Workforce*, October 2001, 52–60; Mary Lord, "They're Online and on the Job; Managers and Hamburger Flippers Are Being E-Trained at Work," *U.S. News & World Report*, 15 October 2001, 72–77.

Chapter 12

1. "Culture and Philosophy" and "Procter & Gamble Case Study," HP website [accessed 20 September 2005] www.hp.com; Paul McDougall, "Procter & Gamble's Deal with HP Grows," *InformationWeek*, 16 August 2004 [accessed 20 September 2005] www.outsourcingpipeline.com; Bill Breen, "The Big Score," September 2003, *Fast Company*, 64; "HP Finalizes $3 Billion Outsourcing Agreement to Manage Procter & Gamble's IT Infrastructure," press release, HP website, 6 May 2003 [accessed 10 October 2003] www.hp.com; "HP Selected by P&G for $3 Billion, 10-Year Services Contract," press release, HP website, 11 April 2003 [accessed 10 October 2003] www.hp.com.

2. Carmine Gallo, "Loaded for Bore," *BusinessWeek Online*, 5 August 2005 [accessed 19 September 2005] www.businessweek.com.

3. Sarah Lary and Karen Pruente, "Powerless Point: Common PowerPoint Mistakes to Avoid," *Public Relations Tactics*, February 2004, 28.

4. Sherwyn P. Morreale and Courtland L. Bovée, *Excellence in Public Speaking* (Fort Worth, Tex.: Harcourt Brace, 1998), 234–237.

5. Morreale and Bovée, *Excellence in Public Speaking*, 241–243.

6. "Choose and Use Your Words Deliberately," *Soundview Executive Book Summaries* 20, no. 6, pt. 2 (June 1998): 3.

7. Walter Kiechel III, "How to Give a Speech," *Fortune*, 8 June 1987, 180.

8. *Communication and Leadership Program* (Santa Ana, Calif.: Toastmasters International, 1980), 44, 45.

9. "Polishing Your Presentation," 3M Meeting Network [accessed 8 June 2001] www.mmm.com/meetingnetwork/readingroom/meetingguide_pres.html.

10. Claudyne Wilder and David Fine, *Point, Click & Wow* (San Francisco: Jossey-Bass Pfeiffer, 1996), 50.

11. Margo Halverson, "Choosing the Right Colors for Your Next Presentation," 3M Meeting Network [accessed 8 June 2001] www.mmm.com/meetingnetwork/readingroom/meetingguide_right_color.html.

12. Jon Hanke, "Five Tips for Better Visuals," 3M Meeting Network [accessed 8 June 2001] www.mmm.com/meetingnetwork.

13. Lary and Pruente, "Powerless Point: Common PowerPoint Mistakes to Avoid."

14. Jeff Yocom, " TechRepublic Survey Yields Advice on Streaming Video," TechRepublic website [accessed 16 February 2004] www.techrepublic.com.

15. "Webcasting Tips & Advice," Spider Eye Solutions [accessed 13 February 2004] www.spidereye.com.

16. Edward P. Bailey, *Writing and Speaking at Work* (Upper Saddle River, N.J.: Prentice Hall, 1999), 138–145.

17. Ted Simons, "Handouts That Won't Get Trashed," *Presentations,* February 1999, 47–50.

18. Morreale and Bovée, *Excellence in Public Speaking,* 24–25.

19. Jennifer Rotondo and Mike Rotondo, Jr., *Presentation Skills for Managers,* (New York: McGraw-Hill, 2002), 9.

20. Rick Gilbert, "Presentation Advice for Boardroom Success," *Financial Executive,* September 2005, 12.

21. Rotondo and Rotondo, Jr., *Presentation Skills for Managers,* 151.

22. "Control the Question-and-Answer Session," *Soundview Executive Book Summaries* 20, no. 6, pt. 2 (June 1998): 4.

23. Teresa Brady, "Fielding Abrasive Questions During Presentations," *Supervisory Management,* February 1993, 6.

24. Robert L. Montgomery, "Listening on Your Feet," *The Toastmaster,* July 1987, 14–15.

Chapter 13

1. Ed Tazzia, "Wanted: A Résumé That Really Works," *Brandweek,* 15 May 2006, 26.

2. Maureen Jenkins, "Yours for the Taking," *Boeing Frontiers Online,* June 2004 [accessed 25 September 2005] www.boeing.com; "Firm Predicts Top 10 Workforce/ Workplace Trends for 2004, *Enterprise,* 8–14 December 2003, 1–2; Scott Hudson, "Keeping Employees Happy," *Community Banker,* September 2003, 34+; Marvin J. Cetron and Owen Davies, "Trends Now Changing the World: Technology, the Workplace, Management, and Institutions," *Futurist* 35, no. 2 (March/April 2001): 27–42.

3. Jim Puzzanghera, "Coalition of High-Tech Firms to Urge Officials to Help Keep U.S. Competitive," *San Jose Mercury News,* 8 January 2004 [accessed 14 February 2004] www.ebscohost.com.

4. Amanda Bennett, "GE Redesigns Rungs of Career Ladder," *Wall Street Journal,* 15 March 1993, B1, B3.

5. Robin White Goode, "International and Foreign Language Skills Have an Edge," *Black Enterprise,* May 1995, 53.

6. Jeffrey R. Young, "'E-Portfolios' Could Give Students a New Sense of Their Accomplishments," *The Chronicle of Higher Education,* 8 March 2002, A31.

7. Nancy M. Somerick, "Managing a Communication Internship Program," *Bulletin of the Association for Business Communication* 56, no. 3 (1993): 10–20.

8. Joan Lloyd, "Changing Workplace Requires You to Alter Your Career Outlook," *Milwaukee Journal Sentinel,* 4 July 1999, 1; Camille DeBell, "Ninety Years in the World of Work in America," *Career Development Quarterly* 50, no. 1 (September 2001): 77–88.

9. Robert J. Gerberg, *Robert Gerberg's Job Changing System,* summarized by Macmillan Book Clubs, Inc., in the "Macmillan Executive Summary Program," April 1987, 4.

10. Mkt10.com website [accessed 25 September 2005] www.mkt10.com; Olga Kharif, "The Job of Challenging Monster," *BusinessWeek Online,* 6 September 2005 [accessed 25 September 2005] www.businessweek.com; "Job Sites: The 'Second Generation,'" *BusinessWeek Online,* 7 September 2005 [accessed 25 September 2005] www.businessweek.com.

11. Caroline A. Drakeley, "Viral Networking: Tactics in Today's Job Market," *Intercom,* September–October 2003, 4–7.

12. Drakeley, "Viral Networking: Tactics in Today's Job Market," 5.

13. Anne Fisher, "Greener Pastures in a New Field," *Fortune,* 26 January 2004, 48.

14. Cheryl L. Noll, "Collaborating with the Career Planning and Placement Center in the Job-Search Project," *Business Communication Quarterly* 58, no. 3 (1995): 53–55.

15. Rockport Institute, "How to Write a Masterpiece of a Résumé" [accessed 25 September 2005] www.rockportinstitute.com.

16. Pam Stanley-Weigand, "Organizing the Writing of Your Resume," *Bulletin of the Association for Business Communication* 54, no. 3 (September 1991): 11–12.

17. Kim Isaacs, "Resume Dilemma: Criminal Record," Monster.com [accessed 23 May 2006] www.monster.com; Kim Isaacs, "Resume Dilemma: Employment Gaps and Job-Hopping," Monster.com [accessed 23 May 2006] www.monster.com; Susan Vaughn, "Answer the Hard Questions Before Asked," *Los Angeles Times,* 29 July 2001, W1–W2.

18. Richard H. Beatty and Nicholas C. Burkholder, *The Executive Career Guide for MBAs* (New York: Wiley, 1996), 133.

19. Adapted from Burdette E. Bostwick, *How to Find the Job You've Always Wanted* (New York: Wiley, 1982), 69–70.

20. Norma Mushkat Gaffin, "Recruiters' Top 10 Resume Pet Peeves," Monster.com [accessed 19 February 2004] www.monster.com; Beatty and Burkholder, *The Executive Career Guide for MBAs,* 151.

21. Rockport Institute, "How to Write a Masterpiece of a Résumé."

22. "Resume Fraud Gets Slicker and Easier," CNN.com [accessed 11 March 2004] www.cnn.com.

23. Lisa Takeuchi Cullen, "Getting Wise to Lies," *Time,* 1 May 2006, 59; "Resume Fraud Gets Slicker and Easier"; Employment Screening Resources website [accessed 18 March 2004] www.erscheck.com.

24. "Employers Turn Their Fire on Untruthful CVs," *Supply Management,* 23 June 2005, 13.

25. Sal Divita, "If You're Thinking Résumé, Think Creatively," *Marketing News,* 14 September 1992, 29.

26. Rockport Institute, "How to Write a Masterpiece of a Résumé."

27. Rockport Institute, "How to Write a Masterpiece of a Résumé."

28. Ellen Joe Pollock, "Sir: Your Application for a Job Is Rejected; Sincerely, Hal 9000," *Wall Street Journal,* 30 July 1998, A1, A12.

29. "Scannable Resume Design," ResumeEdge.com [accessed 19 February 2004] www.resumeedge.com.

30. Kim Isaacs, "Tips for Creating a Scannable Resume," Monster.com [accessed 19 February 2004] www.monster.com.

31. Kim Isaacs, "Enhance Your Resume for Monster Upload," Monster.com [accessed 19 February 2004] www.monster.com.

32. "The Rogue's Gallery of 25 Awful Résumé Mistakes," CareerExplorer.net [accessed 19 February 2004] www.careerexplorer.net.

33. Regina Pontow, "Electronic Résumé Writing Tips," ProvenRésumés.com [accessed 18 October 1998] www.provenresumes.com/reswkshps/electronic/scnres.html.

Chapter 14

1. Max Messmer, "Five Common Interview Mistakes and How to Avoid Them," *Strategic Finance,* April 2005, 12–14.

2. "The Writer Approach," *Los Angeles Times,* 17 November 2002, W1.

3. Toni Logan, "The Perfect Cover Story," *Kinko's Impress* 2 (2000): 32, 34.

4. James Gonyea, "Money Talks: Salary History Versus Salary Requirements," Monster.com [accessed 19 October 2004] www.monster.com; Marguerite Higgins, "Tech-Savvy Job Hunters Not So Suave in Writing; E-Mail Résumés Appall Employers," *Washington Times,* 17 December 2002 [accessed 22 February 2004] www.highbeam.com; "Keep Goal in Mind When Crafting a Résumé," *Register-Guard* (Eugene, Ore.), 3 August 2003 [accessed 22 February 2004] www.highbeam.com; Anis F. McClin, "Effects of Spelling Errors on the Perception of Writers," *Journal of General Psychology,* January 2002 [accessed 22 February 2004] www.highbeam.com.

5. Samuel Greengard, "Are You Well Armed to Screen Applicants?" *Personnel Journal,* December 1995, 84–95.

6. William Poundstone, "Beware the Interview Inquisition," *Harvard Business Review,* May 2003, 18+.

7. Marcia Vickers, "Don't Touch That Dial: Why Should I Hire You?" *New York Times,* 13 April 1997, F11.

8. Chris Pentilla, "Testing the Waters," *Entrepreneur,* January 2004 [accessed 27 May 2006] www.entrepreneur.com; Terry McKenna, "Behavior-Based Interviewing," *National Petroleum News,* January 2004, 16; Nancy K. Austin, "Goodbye Gimmicks," *Incentive,* May 1996, 241.

9. Patrick J. Sauer, "Open-Door Management," *Inc.,* June 2003, 44.

10. Dino di Mattia, "Testing Methods and Effectiveness of Tests," *Supervision,* August 2005, 4–5.

11. David W. Arnold and John W. Jones, "Who the Devil's Applying Now?" *Security Management,* March 2002, 85–88.

12. Arnold and Jones, "Who the Devil's Applying Now?" 86.

13. Adam Agard, "Preemployment Skills Testing: An Important Step in the Hiring Process," *Supervision,* June 2003, 7+.

14. Andy Meisler, "Negative Results," *Workforce Management,* October 2003, 35+.

15. Tyler D. Hartwell, Paul D. Steele, and Nathaniel F. Rodman, "Workplace Alcohol-Testing Programs: Prevalence and Trends," *Monthly Labor Review,* June 1998, 27–34; "Substance Abuse in the Workplace," *HR Focus,* February 1997, 1, 4+.

16. Thomas A. Buckhoff, "Preventing Fraud by Conducting Background Checks," *CPA Journal,* November 2003, 52.

17. "Check Yourself Before Employer Does," *CA Magazine,* June/July 2005, 12.

18. Scott Medintz, "Talkin' 'Bout MySpace Generation," *Money,* February 2006, 27.

19. Austin, "Goodbye Gimmicks."

20. Katherine Spencer Lee, "Tackling Tough Interview Questions," *Certification Magazine,* May 2005, 35.

21. Robert Gifford, Cheuk Fan Ng, and Margaret Wilkinson, "Nonverbal Cues in the Employment Interview: Links Between Applicant Qualities and Interviewer Judgments," *Journal of Applied Psychology* 70, no. 4 (1985): 729.

22. Dale G. Leathers, *Successful Nonverbal Communication* (New York: Macmillan, 1986), 225.

23. Stephanie Armour, "The New Interview Etiquette," *USA Today,* 23 November 1999, B1, B2.

24. William S. Frank, "Job Interview: Pre-Flight Checklist," *The Career Advisor* [accessed 28 September 2005] http://careerplanning.about.com.

25. T. Shawn Taylor, "Most Managers Have No Idea How to Hire the Right Person for the Job," *Chicago Tribune,* 23 July 2002 [accessed 29 September 2005] www.ebsco.com.

26. Steven Mitchell Sack, "The Working Woman's Legal Survival Guide: Testing," FindLaw.com [accessed 22 February 2004] www.findlaw.com.

27. Gerald L. Wilson, "Preparing Students for Responding to Illegal Selection Interview Questions," *Bulletin of the Association for Business Communication* 54, no. 2 (1991): 44–49.

28. Jeff Springston and Joann Keyton, "Interview Response Training," *Bulletin of the Association for Business Communication* 54, no. 3 (1991): 28–30; Gerald L. Wilson, "An Analysis of Instructional Strategies for Responding to Illegal Selection Interview Questions," *Bulletin of the Association for Business Communication* 54, no. 3 (1991): 31–35.

29. Stephen J. Pullum, "Illegal Questions in the Selection Process: Going Beyond Contemporary Business and Professional Communication Textbooks," *Bulletin of the Association for Business Communication* 54, no. 3 (1991): 36–43; Alicia Kitsuse, "Have You Ever Been Arrested?" *Across the Board,* November 1992, 46–49; Christina L. Greathouse, "Ten Common Hiring Mistakes," *Industry Week,* 20 January 1992, 22–23, 26.

30. "Negotiating Salary: An Introduction," *InformationWeek* online [accessed 22 February 2004] www.infoweek.com.

31. "Negotiating Salary: An Introduction."
32. Harold H. Hellwig, "Job Interviewing: Process and Practice," *Bulletin of the Association for Business Communication* 55, no. 2 (1992): 8–14.

Appendix A

1. Mary A. De Vries, *Internationally Yours* (Boston: Houghton Mifflin, 1994), 9.
2. Patricia A. Dreyfus, "Paper That's Perfect," *Money*, May 1985, 184.
3. "When Image Counts, Letterhead Says It All," *Stamford (Conn.) Advocate and Greenwich Times*, 10 January 1993, F4.
4. Mel Mandell, "Electronic Forms Are Cheap and Speedy," *D&B Reports*, July—August 1993, 44–45.
5. Linda Driskill, *Business and Managerial Communication: New Perspectives* (Orlando, Fla.: Harcourt Brace Jovanovich, 1992), 470.
6. Driskill, *Business and Managerial Communication*, 470.
7. Lennie Copeland and Lewis Griggs, *Going International: How to Make Friends and Deal Effectively in the Global Marketplace*, 2d ed. (New York: Random House, 1985), 24–27.
8. U.S. Postal Service, *Postal Addressing Standards* (Washington, D.C.: GPO, 1992).
9. Copeland and Griggs, *Going International*, 24–27.
10. Renne B. Horowitz and Marian G. Barchilon, "Stylistic Guidelines for E-Mail," *IEEE Transactions on Professional Communications*, 37, no. 4 (1994): 207–212.
11. William Eager, *Using the Internet* (Indianapolis: Que Corporation, 1994), 11.
12. Eager, *Using the Internet*, 10.
13. William Eager, Larry Donahue, David Forsyth, Kenneth Mitton, and Martin Waterhouse, *Net.Search* (Indianapolis: Que Corporation, 1995), 221.
14. Rosalind Resnick and Dave Taylor, Internet Business Guide (Indianapolis: Sams.net Publishing, 1995), 117.
15. James L. Clark and Lyn R. Clark, *How 7: A Handbook for Office Workers*, 7th ed. (Cincinnati: South-Western, 1995), 431–432.

(Photo essay, pp. 16–19) Getty Images—Digital Vision, PhotoEdit, Ethan Hill, Dell, Inc., Belkin Corporation, AGE Fotostock America, Inc., 3M, Ethan Hill, Corbis/SABA Press Photos, Inc., FEDEX Corporation, Masterfile Corporation, AGE Fotostock America, Inc., United Parcel Service, Ezonics Corporation, Getty Images, Inc.—Taxi, Photolibrary.Com, Masterfile Corporation, Staples, Inc., Courtesy of UserLand Frontier News. Figure 1.4: Courtesy of Six Apart. (Figure 2.3) Copyright 2005 WebEx Communications, Inc. www.webex.com. (Figure 2.4) Roger Axtell, *Gestures: The Do's and Taboos of Body Language Around the World,* (New York: Wiley, 1991), 117–119. (Table 2.1) Alf Nucifora, "Voice Mail Demands Good Etiquette from Both Sides," *Puget Sound Business Journal,* 5–11 September 2003, 24; Ruth Davidhizar and Ruth Shearer, "The Effective Voice Mail Message," *Hospital Material Management Quarterly,* 45–49; "How to Get the Most Out of Voice Mail," *The CPA Journal,* February 2000, 11; Jo Ind, "Hanging on the Telephone," *Birmingham Post,* 28 July 1999, PS10; Larry Barker and Kittie Watson, *Listen Up* (New York: St. Martin's Press, 2000), 64–65; Lin Walker, *Telephone Techniques,* (New York: Amacom, 1998), 46–47; Dorothy Neal, *Telephone Techniques,* 2d ed. (New York: Glencoe McGraw-Hill, 1998), 31; Jeannie Davis, *Beyond "Hello"* (Aurora, Col.: Now Hear This, Inc., 2000), 2–3; "Ten Steps to Caller-Friendly Voice Mail," *Managing Office Technology,* January 1995, 25; Rhonda Finniss, "Voice Mail: Tips for a Positive Impression," *Administrative Assistant's Update,* August 2001, 5; "How to Get the Most Out of Voice Mail," *The CPA Journal,* February 2000, 11; Ruth Davidhizar and Ruth Shearer, "The Effective Voice Mail Message," *Hospital Material Management Quarterly,* 45–49; "How to Get the Most Out of Voice Mail," *The CPA Journal,* February 2000, 11. (Table 2.2) Madelyn Burley-Allen, *Listening: The Forgotten Skill,* (New York: Wiley, 1995), 70–71, 119–120; Judi Brownell, *Listening: Attitudes, Principles, and Skills,* (Boston: Allyn and Bacon, 2002); 3, 9, 83, 89, 125; Larry Barker and Kittie Watson, *Listen Up,* (New York: St. Martin's, 2000), 8, 9, 64, **77.** (Table 6.2) Robert Scoble and Shel Israel, *Naked Conversations* (Hoboken, New Jersey: John Wiley & Sons, 2006), 78–81, 190–194; Paul McFedries, *The Complete Idiot's Guide to Creating a Web Page & Blog,* 6th ed. (New York: Alpha, 2004), 206–208, 272–276; Shel Holtz and Ted Demopoulos, *Blogging for Business* (Chicago: Kaplan, 2006), 54–59, 113–114; Denise Wakeman, "Top 10 Blog Writing Tips," Blogarooni.com [accessed 1 February 2006] www.blogarooni.com; Dennis A. Mahoney, "How to Write a Better Weblog," 22 February 2002, A List Apart [accessed 1 February 2006] www.alistapart.com. (Figure 7.1) Courtesy Ace Hardware. (Figure 7.5) Courtesy Herman Miller. (Figure 7.7) Courtesy Discover Communication. (Figure 11.1) Courtesy CancerHelp UK (www.cancerhelp.org.uk). (Figure 12.6) Microsoft PowerPoint 2002 software. (Table 12.2) Adapted from Carmen Matthews, "Speaker's Notes," *Presentations,* April 2005, 42; Eric J. Adams, "Management Focus: User-Friendly Presentation Software," *World Trade,* March 1995, 92. (Table 12.3) Adapted from Claudyne Wilder and David Fine, *Point, Click & Wow* (San Francisco: Jossey-Bass Pfeiffer, 1996), 63, 527. (Figure 13.2) Adapted from Richard Nelson Bolles, *What Color Is Your Parachute?* (Berkeley, Calif.: Ten Speed Press, 1997), 67. (Table 13.1) The Riley Guide [accessed 22 September 2005] www.rileyguide.com; Bethany McLean, "A Scary Monster," *Fortune,* 22 December 2003, 19+; Alan Cohen, "Best Job Hunting Sites," *Yahoo! Internet Life,* May 2002, 90–92; Richard N. Bolles, "Career Strategizing or, What Color Is Your Web Parachute?" *Yahoo! Internet Life,* May 1998, 116, 121; Tara Weingarten, "The All-Day, All-Night, Global, No-Trouble Job Search," *Newsweek,* 6 April 1998, 14; Michele Himmelberg, "Internet an Important Tool in Employment Search," *San Diego Union-Tribune,* 7 September 1998, D2; Gina Imperato, "35 Ways to Land a Job Online," *Fast Company,* August 1998, 192–197; Roberta Maynard, "Casting the Net for Job Seekers," *Nation's Business,* March 1997, 28–29. (Figure 14.3) Courtesy of PerfectInterview.com/Contexxa Corporation. (Table 14.3) Adapted from *The Northwestern Endicott Report* (Evanston, Ill.: Northwestern University Placement Center). (Table 14.4) Marilyn Sherman, "Questions R Us: What to Ask at a Job Interview," *Career World,* January 2004, 20; H. Lee Rust, *Job Search: The Completion Manual for Jobseekers* (New York: American Management Association, 1979), 56. (Table 14.5) Adapted from *The Northwestern Endicott Report* (Evanston: Ill.: Northwestern University Placement Center). (Table 14.6) Deanna G. Kucler, "Interview Questions: Legal or Illegal?" *Workforce Management* [accessed 28 September 2005] www.workforce.com; "Illegal Interview Questions," *USA Today,* 29 January 2001 [accessed 28 September 2005] www.usatoday.com; "Dangerous Questions," *Nation's Business,* May 1999, 22.

SINGLE PC LICENSE AGREEMENT AND LIMITED WARRANTY

READ THIS LICENSE CAREFULLY BEFORE USING THIS PACKAGE. BY USING THIS PACKAGE, YOU ARE AGREEING TO THE TERMS AND CONDITIONS OF THIS LICENSE. IF YOU DO NOT AGREE, DO NOT USE THE PACKAGE. PROMPTLY RETURN THE UNUSED PACKAGE AND ALL ACCOMPANYING ITEMS TO THE PLACE YOU OBTAINED THEM. *THESE TERMS APPLY TO ALL LICENSED SOFTWARE ON THE DISK:*

1. **GRANT OF LICENSE and OWNERSHIP:** The enclosed computer programs and data ("Software") are licensed, not sold, to you by Prentice Education, Inc. publishing as Prentice Hall ("We" or the "Company") and in consideration of your payment of the license fee, which is part of the price you paid of your purchase or adoption of the accompanying Company textbooks and/or other materials, and your agreement to these terms. We reserve any rights not granted to you. You own only the disk(s) but we and/or our licensors own the Software itself. This license allows you to use and display your copy of the Software on a single computer (i.e., with a single CPU) at a single location for <u>academic</u> use only, so long as you comply with the terms of this Agreement. You may make one copy for back up, or transfer your copy to another CPU, provided that the Software is usable on only one computer.

2. **RESTRICTIONS:** You may <u>not</u> transfer or distribute the Software or documentation to anyone else. Except for backup, you may not copy the documentation or the Software. You may <u>not</u> network the Software or otherwise use it on more than one computer or computer terminal at the same time. You may <u>not</u> reverse engineer, disassemble, decompile, modify, adapt, translate, or create derivative works based on the Software or the Documentation. You may be held legally responsible for any copying or copyright infringement that is caused by your failure to abide by the terms of these restrictions.

3. **TERMINATION:** This license is effective until terminated. This license will terminate automatically without notice from the Company if you fail to comply with any provisions or limitations of this license. Upon termination, you shall destroy the Documentation and all copies of the Software. All provisions of this Agreement as to limitation and disclaimer of warranties, limitation of liability, remedies or damages, and our ownership rights shall survive termination.

4. **LIMITED WARRANTY AND DISCLAIMER OF WARRANTY:** Company warrants that for a period of 60 days from the date you purchase this SOFTWARE (or purchase or adopt the accompanying textbook), the Software, when properly installed and used in accordance with the Documentation, will operate in substantial conformity with the description of the Software set forth in the Documentation, and that for a period of 30 days the disk(s) on which the Software is delivered shall be free from defects in materials and workmanship under normal use. The Company does <u>not</u> warrant that the Software will meet your requirements or that the operation of the Software will be uninterrupted or error-free. Your only remedy and the Company's only obligation under these limited warranties is, at the Company's option, return of the disk for a refund of any amounts paid for it by you or replacement of the disk. THIS LIMITED WARRANTY IS THE ONLY WARRANTY PROVIDED BY THE COMPANY AND ITS LICENSORS, AND THE COMPANY AND ITS LICENSORS DISCLAIM ALL OTHER WARRANTIES, EXPRESS OR IMPLIED, INCLUDING WITHOUT LIMITATION, THE IMPLIED WARRANTIES OF MERCHANTABILITY AND FITNESS FOR A PARTICULAR PURPOSE. THE COMPANY DOES NOT WARRANT, GUARANTEE OR MAKE ANY REPRESENTATION REGARDING THE ACCURACY, RELIABILITY, CURRENTNESS, USE, OR RESULTS OF USE, OF THE SOFTWARE.

5. **LIMITATION OF REMEDIES AND DAMAGES:** IN NO EVENT, SHALL THE COMPANY OR ITS EMPLOYEES, AGENTS, LICENSORS, OR CONTRACTORS BE LIABLE FOR ANY INCIDENTAL, INDIRECT, SPECIAL, OR CONSEQUENTIAL DAMAGES ARISING OUT OF OR IN CONNECTION WITH THIS LICENSE OR THE SOFTWARE, INCLUDING FOR LOSS OF USE, LOSS OF DATA, LOSS OF INCOME OR PROFIT, OR OTHER LOSSES, SUSTAINED AS A RESULT OF INJURY TO ANY PERSON, OR LOSS OF OR DAMAGE TO PROPERTY, OR CLAIMS OF THIRD PARTIES, EVEN IF THE COMPANY OR AN AUTHORIZED REPRESENTATIVE OF THE COMPANY HAS BEEN ADVISED OF THE POSSIBILITY OF SUCH DAMAGES. IN NO EVENT SHALL THE LIABILITY OF THE COMPANY FOR DAMAGES WITH RESPECT TO THE SOFTWARE EXCEED THE AMOUNTS ACTUALLY PAID BY YOU, IF ANY, FOR THE SOFTWARE OR THE ACCOMPANYING TEXTBOOK. BECAUSE SOME JURISDICTIONS DO NOT ALLOW THE LIMITATION OF LIABILITY IN CERTAIN CIRCUMSTANCES, THE ABOVE LIMITATIONS MAY NOT ALWAYS APPLY TO YOU.

6. **GENERAL:** THIS AGREEMENT SHALL BE CONSTRUED IN ACCORDANCE WITH THE LAWS OF THE UNITED STATES OF AMERICA AND THE STATE OF NEW YORK, APPLICABLE TO CONTRACTS MADE IN NEW YORK, AND SHALL BENEFIT THE COMPANY, ITS AFFILIATES AND ASSIGNEES. HIS AGREEMENT IS THE COMPLETE AND EXCLUSIVE STATEMENT OF THE AGREEMENT BETWEEN YOU AND THE COMPANY AND SUPERSEDES ALL PROPOSALS OR PRIOR AGREEMENTS, ORAL, OR WRITTEN, AND ANY OTHER COMMUNICATIONS BETWEEN YOU AND THE COMPANY OR ANY REPRESENTATIVE OF THE COMPANY RELATING TO THE SUBJECT MATTER OF THIS AGREEMENT. If you are a U.S. Government user, this Software is licensed with "restricted rights" as set forth in subparagraphs (a)-(d) of the Commercial Computer-Restricted Rights clause at FAR 52.227-19 or in subparagraphs (c)(1)(ii) of the Rights in Technical Data and Computer Software clause at DFARS 252.227-7013, and similar clauses, as applicable.

Should you have any questions concerning this agreement or if you wish to contact the Company for any reason, please contact by email: <u>http://247.prenhall.com</u>, or in writing: Prentice Hall, Director of Media Production, One Lake Street, Upper Saddle River, NJ 07458